Parts 500 to 699
Revised as of April 1, 2009

Housing and Urban Development

Containing a codification of documents of general applicability and future effect

As of April 1, 2009

With Ancillaries

Published by
Office of the Federal Register
National Archives and Records Administration

A Special Edition of the Federal Register

U.S. GOVERNMENT OFFICIAL EDITION NOTICE

Legal Status and Use of Seals and Logos

The seal of the National Archives and Records Administration (NARA) authenticates the Code of Federal Regulations (CFR) as the official codification of Federal regulations established under the Federal Register Act. Under the provisions of 44 U.S.C. 1507, the contents of the CFR, a special edition of the Federal Register, shall be judicially noticed. The CFR is prima facie evidence of the original documents published in the Federal Register (44 U.S.C. 1510).

It is prohibited to use NARA's official seal and the stylized Code of Federal Regulations logo on any republication of this material without the express, written permission of the Archivist of the United States or the Archivist's designee. Any person using NARA's official seals and logos in a manner inconsistent with the provisions of 36 CFR part 1200 is subject to the penalties specified in 18 U.S.C. 506, 701, and 1017.

Use of ISBN Prefix

This is the Official U.S. Government edition of this publication and is herein identified to certify its authenticity. Use of the 0–16 ISBN prefix is for U.S. Government Printing Office Official Editions only. The Superintendent of Documents of the U.S. Government Printing Office requests that any reprinted edition clearly be labeled as a copy of the authentic work with a new ISBN.

 U.S. GOVERNMENT PRINTING OFFICE

U.S. Superintendent of Documents • Washington, DC 20402–0001

http://bookstore.gpo.gov

Phone: toll-free (866) 512-1800; DC area (202) 512-1800

Table of Contents

	Page
Explanation	v

Title 24:

    Subtitle B—REGULATIONS RELATING TO HOUSING AND URBAN DEVELOPMENT (CONTINUED)

        Chapter V—Office of Assistant Secretary for Community Planning and Development, Department of Housing and Urban Development 5

        Chapter VI—Office of Assistant Secretary for Community Planning and Development, Department of Housing and Urban Development [Reserved]

Finding Aids:

    Table of CFR Titles and Chapters 335

    Alphabetical List of Agencies Appearing in the CFR 355

    List of CFR Sections Affected 365

Cite this Code: **CFR**

To cite the regulations in this volume use title, part and section number. Thus, 24 CFR 510.1 refers to title 24, part 510, section 1.

Explanation

The Code of Federal Regulations is a codification of the general and permanent rules published in the Federal Register by the Executive departments and agencies of the Federal Government. The Code is divided into 50 titles which represent broad areas subject to Federal regulation. Each title is divided into chapters which usually bear the name of the issuing agency. Each chapter is further subdivided into parts covering specific regulatory areas.

Each volume of the Code is revised at least once each calendar year and issued on a quarterly basis approximately as follows:

Title 1 through Title 16...as of January 1
Title 17 through Title 27...as of April 1
Title 28 through Title 41...as of July 1
Title 42 through Title 50...as of October 1

The appropriate revision date is printed on the cover of each volume.

LEGAL STATUS

The contents of the Federal Register are required to be judicially noticed (44 U.S.C. 1507). The Code of Federal Regulations is prima facie evidence of the text of the original documents (44 U.S.C. 1510).

HOW TO USE THE CODE OF FEDERAL REGULATIONS

The Code of Federal Regulations is kept up to date by the individual issues of the Federal Register. These two publications must be used together to determine the latest version of any given rule.

To determine whether a Code volume has been amended since its revision date (in this case, April 1, 2009), consult the "List of CFR Sections Affected (LSA)," which is issued monthly, and the "Cumulative List of Parts Affected," which appears in the Reader Aids section of the daily Federal Register. These two lists will identify the Federal Register page number of the latest amendment of any given rule.

EFFECTIVE AND EXPIRATION DATES

Each volume of the Code contains amendments published in the Federal Register since the last revision of that volume of the Code. Source citations for the regulations are referred to by volume number and page number of the Federal Register and date of publication. Publication dates and effective dates are usually not the same and care must be exercised by the user in determining the actual effective date. In instances where the effective date is beyond the cut-off date for the Code a note has been inserted to reflect the future effective date. In those instances where a regulation published in the Federal Register states a date certain for expiration, an appropriate note will be inserted following the text.

OMB CONTROL NUMBERS

The Paperwork Reduction Act of 1980 (Pub. L. 96–511) requires Federal agencies to display an OMB control number with their information collection request.

Many agencies have begun publishing numerous OMB control numbers as amendments to existing regulations in the CFR. These OMB numbers are placed as close as possible to the applicable recordkeeping or reporting requirements.

OBSOLETE PROVISIONS

Provisions that become obsolete before the revision date stated on the cover of each volume are not carried. Code users may find the text of provisions in effect on a given date in the past by using the appropriate numerical list of sections affected. For the period before January 1, 2001, consult either the List of CFR Sections Affected, 1949–1963, 1964–1972, 1973–1985, or 1986–2000, published in eleven separate volumes. For the period beginning January 1, 2001, a "List of CFR Sections Affected" is published at the end of each CFR volume.

INCORPORATION BY REFERENCE

What is incorporation by reference? Incorporation by reference was established by statute and allows Federal agencies to meet the requirement to publish regulations in the Federal Register by referring to materials already published elsewhere. For an incorporation to be valid, the Director of the Federal Register must approve it. The legal effect of incorporation by reference is that the material is treated as if it were published in full in the Federal Register (5 U.S.C. 552(a)). This material, like any other properly issued regulation, has the force of law.

What is a proper incorporation by reference? The Director of the Federal Register will approve an incorporation by reference only when the requirements of 1 CFR part 51 are met. Some of the elements on which approval is based are:

(a) The incorporation will substantially reduce the volume of material published in the Federal Register.

(b) The matter incorporated is in fact available to the extent necessary to afford fairness and uniformity in the administrative process.

(c) The incorporating document is drafted and submitted for publication in accordance with 1 CFR part 51.

What if the material incorporated by reference cannot be found? If you have any problem locating or obtaining a copy of material listed as an approved incorporation by reference, please contact the agency that issued the regulation containing that incorporation. If, after contacting the agency, you find the material is not available, please notify the Director of the Federal Register, National Archives and Records Administration, Washington DC 20408, or call 202-741-6010.

CFR INDEXES AND TABULAR GUIDES

A subject index to the Code of Federal Regulations is contained in a separate volume, revised annually as of January 1, entitled CFR INDEX AND FINDING AIDS. This volume contains the Parallel Table of Statutory Authorities and Agency Rules (Table I). A list of CFR titles, chapters, and parts and an alphabetical list of agencies publishing in the CFR are also included in this volume.

An index to the text of "Title 3—The President" is carried within that volume.

The Federal Register Index is issued monthly in cumulative form. This index is based on a consolidation of the "Contents" entries in the daily Federal Register.

A List of CFR Sections Affected (LSA) is published monthly, keyed to the revision dates of the 50 CFR titles.

REPUBLICATION OF MATERIAL

There are no restrictions on the republication of material appearing in the Code of Federal Regulations.

INQUIRIES

For a legal interpretation or explanation of any regulation in this volume, contact the issuing agency. The issuing agency's name appears at the top of odd-numbered pages.

For inquiries concerning CFR reference assistance, call 202–741–6000 or write to the Director, Office of the Federal Register, National Archives and Records Administration, Washington, DC 20408 or e-mail fedreg.info@nara.gov.

SALES

The Government Printing Office (GPO) processes all sales and distribution of the CFR. For payment by credit card, call toll-free, 866-512-1800, or DC area, 202-512-1800, M-F 8 a.m. to 4 p.m. e.s.t. or fax your order to 202-512-2250, 24 hours a day. For payment by check, write to: US Government Printing Office – New Orders, P.O. Box 979050, St. Louis, MO 63197-9000. For GPO Customer Service call 202-512-1803.

ELECTRONIC SERVICES

The full text of the Code of Federal Regulations, the LSA (List of CFR Sections Affected), The United States Government Manual, the Federal Register, Public Laws, Public Papers, Daily Compilation of Presidential Documents and the Privacy Act Compilation are available in electronic format via *Federalregister.gov*. For more information, contact Electronic Information Dissemination Services, U.S. Government Printing Office. Phone 202-512-1530, or 888-293-6498 (toll-free). E-mail, *gpoaccess@gpo.gov*.

The Office of the Federal Register also offers a free service on the National Archives and Records Administration's (NARA) World Wide Web site for public law numbers, Federal Register finding aids, and related information. Connect to NARA's web site at *www.archives.gov/federal-register*. The NARA site also contains links to GPO Access.

RAYMOND A. MOSLEY,
Director,
Office of the Federal Register.
April 1, 2009.

THIS TITLE

Title 24—HOUSING AND URBAN DEVELOPMENT is composed of five volumes. The first four volumes containing parts 0–199, parts 200–499, parts 500–699, parts 700–1699, represent the regulations of the Department of Housing and Urban Development. The fifth volume, containing part 1700 to end, continues with regulations of the Department of Housing and Urban Development and also includes regulations of the Board of Directors of the Hope for Homeowners Program, and the Neighborhood Reinvestment Corporation. The contents of these volumes represent all current regulations codified under this title of the CFR as of April 1, 2009.

For this volume, Michele Bugenhagen was Chief Editor. The Code of Federal Regulations publication program is under the direction of Michael L. White, assisted by Ann Worley.

Title 24—Housing and Urban Development

(This book contains parts 500 to 699)

	Part
SUBTITLE B—REGULATIONS RELATING TO HOUSING AND URBAN DEVELOPMENT (CONTINUED)	
CHAPTER V—Office of Assistant Secretary for Community Planning and Development, Department of Housing and Urban Development	510
CHAPTER VI—Office of Assistant Secretary for Community Planning and Development, Department of Housing and Urban Development [Reserved]	

Subtitle B—Regulations Relating to Housing and Urban Development (Continued)

CHAPTER V—OFFICE OF ASSISTANT SECRETARY FOR COMMUNITY PLANNING AND DEVELOPMENT, DEPARTMENT OF HOUSING AND URBAN DEVELOPMENT

SUBCHAPTER A—SLUM CLEARANCE AND URBAN RENEWAL

Part		Page
500–509	[Reserved]	
510	Section 312 Rehabilitation Loan Program	7
511	Rental Rehabilitation Grant Program	7

SUBCHAPTER B [RESERVED]

SUBCHAPTER C—COMMUNITY FACILITIES

570	Community development block grants	31
572	Hope for homeownership of single family homes program (HOPE 3)	175
573	Loan guarantee recovery fund	197
574	Housing opportunities for persons with AIDS	202
576	Emergency Shelter Grants Program: Stewart B. McKinney Homeless Assistance Act	216
581	Use of Federal real property to assist the homeless	229
582	Shelter Plus Care	238
583	Supportive Housing Program	251
585	Youthbuild Program	266
586	Revitalizing base closure communities and community assistance—community redevelopment and homeless assistance	282
590	Urban homesteading	291
594	John Heinz Neighborhood Development Program	295
597	Urban empowerment zones and enterprise communities: Round one designations	298
598	Urban Empowerment Zones: Round two and three designations	310
599	Renewal communities	322

SUBCHAPTER A—SLUM CLEARANCE AND URBAN RENEWAL

PARTS 500–509 [RESERVED]

PART 510—SECTION 312 REHABILITATION LOAN PROGRAM

AUTHORITY: 42 U.S.C. 1452b and 3535(d).

§ 510.1 Multi-family property loans.

(a) In cases in which a corporation is a borrower on a section 312 loan, the Assistant Secretary for CPD or his designee may require an officer of the corporation or a principal stockholder to personally guarantee the section 312 loan or to cosign the loan note as a borrower, where necessary to make the finding of acceptable risk required for assumption of the loan.

(b) All partners of any partnership which is a borrower on a section 312 loan shall be personally liable for repayment of the section 312 loan. Limited partners shall assume personal liability by co-signing the loan note as a borrower or by personally guaranteeing the loan.

(c) Any personal guarantee or endorsement shall not relieve the partnership or corporate borrower from securing the section 312 loan by a mortgage or deed of trust on the property to be rehabilitated.

[44 FR 21751, Apr. 11, 1979, as amended at 44 FR 47513, Aug. 13, 1979; 44 FR 55562, Sept. 27, 1979. Redesignated and amended at 61 FR 7061, Feb. 23, 1996]

PART 511—RENTAL REHABILITATON GRANT PROGRAM

Subpart A—General

Sec.
511.1 Applicability and purpose.
511.2 Definitions.
511.3–511.5 [Reserved]

Subpart B—Program Requirements

511.10 Grant requirements.
511.11 Project requirements.
511.12 Conflicts of interest.
511.13 Nondiscrimination, equal opportunity, and affirmative marketing requirements.
511.14 Tenant assistance, displacement, relocation, and acquisition.
511.15 Lead-based paint.
511.16 Other Federal requirements.

Subpart C [Reserved]

Subpart D—Allocation Formula and Reallocations

511.30–511.31 [Reserved]
511.33 Deobligation of rental rehabilitation grant amounts.
511.34 [Reserved]

Subpart E [Reserved]

Subpart F—State Program

511.50 State election to administer a rental rehabilitation program.
511.51 State-administered program.
511.52 [Reserved]

Subpart G [Reserved]

Subpart H—Grant Administration

511.70 Responsibility for grant administration.
511.71 Administrative costs.
511.72 Applicability of uniform Federal administrative requirements.
511.73 Grantee records.
511.74 Audit.
511.75 Disbursement of rental rehabilitation grant amounts: Cash and Management Information System.
511.76 Program income.
511.77 Grant closeout.

Subpart I—Grantee Performance: Review, Reporting and Corrective or Remedial Actions

511.80 Performance review.
511.81 Grantee reports to HUD.
511.82 Corrective and remedial actions.

AUTHORITY: 42 U.S.C. 1437o and 3535(d).

SOURCE: 55 FR 20050, May 14, 1990, unless otherwise noted.

Subpart A—General

§ 511.1 Applicability and purpose.

(a) This part implements the Rental Rehabilitation Program (RRP) contained in section 17 of the United States Housing Act of 1937, as amended (the "Act"). As more fully described in this part, the Act authorizes the Secretary of Housing and Urban Development to make rental rehabilitation grants to help support the rehabilitation of eligible real property to be used for primarily residential rental purposes, and to pay for eligible administrative costs of grantees (not to exceed 10 percent of a grantee's initial grant obligation for Fiscal Year 1988 and later years). Grants are made on a formula basis to cities having populations of 50,000 or more, urban counties, States, and qualifying consortia of geographically proximate units of general local government. States may use all or part of their grants to carry out their own rental rehabilitation programs or to distribute them to eligible units of general local government. HUD will administer a State's grant if the State chooses not to do so.

(b) The purpose of the Program is to help provide affordable, standard permanent housing for low-income families and to increase the availability of housing units for use by housing voucher and certificate holders under section 8 of the United States Housing Act of 1937. Subject to rules for the tenant-based Certificate Program (24 CFR part 882) and for the Housing Voucher Program (24 CFR part 887), certificates and housing vouchers must be allocated to ensure that sufficient resources are available for families in Rental Rehabilitation projects who are required to move out of their units because of the physical rehabilitation activities or because of overcrowding; and at the PHA's discretion, to assist eligible families whose post-rehabilitation rents would be greater than 30 percent of their adjusted incomes.

§ 511.2 Definitions.

The terms *HUD* and *Public Housing Agency (PHA)* are defined in 24 CFR part 5.

Administrative costs means eligible administrative costs as described in § 511.71.

C/MI System means the Cash and Management Information System for drawdown of Rental Rehabilitation grant amounts and collection of program information described in § 511.75.

Certificate means the document issued by a PHA to a family eligible for participation in the tenant-based Section 8 Certificate Program under 24 CFR part 882.

Chief executive officer of a governmental entity means the elected official, or the legally designated official, who has the primary responsibility for the conduct of that entity's governmental affairs. Examples of the "chief executive officer" are: The elected mayor of a municipality; the elected county executive of a county; the chairperson of a county commission or board in a county that has no elected county executive; the official designated under law by the governing body of the unit of general local government; and the Governor of a State.

City means a unit of general local government that was classified as a city under section 102(a)(5) of the Housing and Community Development Act of 1974 for purposes of the Community Development Block Grant (CDBG) Entitlement Program for the fiscal year immediately preceding the fiscal year for which rental rehabilitation grant amounts are made available.

Commit to a specific local project or *commitment* means:

(a) For a project which is privately owned when the commitment is made, a written legally binding agreement between a grantee (or in the case of a State distributing rental rehabilitation grant amounts to units of general local government, a State recipient) and the project owner under which the grantee or State recipient agrees to provide rental rehabilitation grant amounts to the owner for an identifiable rehabilitation project that can reasonably be expected to start construction within 90 days of the agreement and in which the owner agrees to start construction within that period; or

(b) For a project that is publicly owned when the commitment is made, the Pre-Rehabilitation Report submitted under the C/MI System which identifies a specific rehabilitation project that will start rehabilitation within 90 days of receipt of the Pre-Rehabilitation Report. Under both paragraphs (a) and (b) of this definition, the date HUD enters into the C/MI System an acceptable Pre-Rehabilitation Report for a project is deemed to be the date of project commitment.

Completion of rehabilitation means all necessary rehabilitation work has been performed and the project in HUD's judgment complies with the requirements of this part (including the rehabilitation standards adopted under §511.10(e)); the final drawdown has been disbursed for the project; for projects that were publicly owned when commitment occurred, the project has been legally transferred to a private owner; and a Project Completion Report has been submitted and processed in the C/MI System as prescribed by HUD.

Family means a "family" as defined at 24 CFR 812.2.

Grantee means—

(a) Any city, urban county, or approved consortium receiving a grant on the basis of the formula contained in subpart D of this part;

(b) Any State administering a rental rehabilitation program, as provided in §511.51; and

(c) Any unit of general local government receiving a rental rehabilitation grant from HUD, as provided in §511.52.

Housing voucher means the document issued by a PHA to a family eligible for participation in the Section 8 Housing Voucher Program under 24 CFR part 887.

Low-income family means a low-income family, as defined in 24 CFR 813.102.

Manufactured housing means a dwelling unit which meets the requirements of §511.11(c)(4).

Owner means one or more individuals, corporations, partnerships, or other privately-controlled legal entities that hold valid legal title to the project to be rehabilitated.

Project means an entire building (including a manufactured housing unit), or two or more contiguous buildings under common ownership and management, to be rehabilitated with a rental rehabilitation grant, under a commitment by the owner, as a single undertaking under this part.

Rents affordable to low-income families means that the sum of the utility allowance and the rent payable monthly to the owner with respect to a unit is at or below the applicable fair market rent published under 24 CFR part 888 for the Section 8 Certificate Program (24 CFR part 882) or at or below such higher maximum Gross Rent as approved by HUD for units of a given size or type under 24 CFR 882.106(a)(3). In the case of cooperative or mutual housing, rent means the occupancy charges under the occupancy agreement between the members and the cooperative.

State includes any of the 50 States and the Commonwealth of Puerto Rico.

State recipient means any unit of general local government to which a State distributes rental rehabilitation grant amounts, as provided in §511.51 (a)(2) and (a)(3).

Unit or *dwelling unit* means a residential space that qualifies under the laws of the State and locality and under this part as a place of permanent habitation or abode for a family, including an apartment or house that contains a living room, kitchen area, sleeping area, and bathroom(s), or such other definition as may be proposed by a grantee and approved by HUD under this part. The HUD Field Office may approve congregate housing units meeting the requirements of 24 CFR 882.109(m) or single room occupancy units meeting the requirements of 24 CFR 882.109(p) as zero bedroom units for purposes of this part.

Unit of general local government means any city, county, town, township, parish, village, or other general purpose political subdivision of a State.

Urban county means a county that was classified as an urban county under section 102(a)(6) of the Housing and Community Development Act of 1974, as amended, for the fiscal year immediately preceding the fiscal year for which rental rehabilitation grant amounts are made available.

Utility allowance means the amount determined by a PHA under 24 CFR part 882 for the cost of utilities (except telephones) and other housing services that is not included in the rent payable to the owner, but is the responsibility of the family occupying the unit.

Very low income family means a very low income family, as defined in 24 CFR 813.102.

[55 FR 20050, May 14, 1990, as amended at 61 FR 5208, Feb. 9, 1996]

§§ 511.3–511.5 [Reserved]

Subpart B—Program Requirements

§ 511.10 Grant requirements.

A rental rehabilitation program shall comply with the following requirements:

(a) *Lower income benefit*—(1) *100 percent benefit standard.* Except as provided in paragraphs (a)(2) and (a)(3) of this section, all rental rehabilitation grant amounts must be used for the benefit of low-income families.

(2) *Reduction to 70 percent benefit standard.* The 100 percent benefit standard will be reduced to 70 percent if the grantee certifies in its Program Description under § 511.20 (or thereafter in a written amendment to its grant agreement) that:

(i) The reduction is necessary to meet one or both of the following objectives:

(A) To minimize the displacement of tenants in projects to be rehabilitated; or

(B) To provide a reasonable margin for error due to unforeseen, sudden changes in neighborhood rent or for other reasonable contingencies;

(ii) A rental rehabilitation program that meets the 100 percent benefit standard cannot be developed; and

(iii) The public has been consulted regarding this inability.

(3) *Reduction to 50 percent benefit standard.* The benefit standard will be reduced to not less than 50 percent only in extraordinary circumstances approved by HUD. Approval may be granted at the request of the grantee before undertaking any project that will have the effect of reducing the benefit for low-income families for the grantee's program below 70 percent, only where HUD determines that a reduction is necessary to meet an important community need and that the net program impact will strongly favor low-income families. Approval may be granted thereafter only where HUD determines that the grantee made reasonable efforts to meet the higher benefit standard, but was unable to do so because of circumstances beyond its control.

(4) *Definition of benefit.* For purposes of this paragraph (a), benefit for low-income families will be considered to occur only where dwelling units in projects rehabilitated with rental rehabilitation grants are initially occupied by such families after rehabilitation.

(b) *Use of rental rehabilitation grants for housing for families.* (1) Each grantee shall ensure that an equitable share of rental rehabilitation grant amounts will be used to assist in the provision of housing designed for occupancy by families with children, particularly families requiring three or more bedrooms. HUD will assure that on a national basis at least 15 percent of each year's rental rehabilitation grant amounts (excluding those grant amounts expended for administrative costs under § 511.71) are used to rehabilitate units containing three or more bedrooms. HUD reserves the right prospectively to establish three or more bedroom unit targets for individual grantees if the national goal is in danger of not being met, or if HUD finds that a grantee's production of three or more bedroom units is significantly below that of grantees in similar circumstances. In addition, at least 70 percent of each grantee's annual rental rehabilitation grant must be used to rehabilitate units containing two or more bedrooms. HUD may approve a lower percentage standard submitted by the grantee in its Program Description under § 511.20, or thereafter, based on HUD's determination that the lower standard is justified by factors such as a short waiting list of large families requiring assistance or the nature of the housing stock available for rehabilitation.

(2) If a unit of general local government has an ordinance which requires rehabilitation to meet seismic standards, the grantee may use up to the full amount of its annual rental rehabilitation grant for Federal Fiscal Year 1988 and later years (including reallocations under § 511.33(b)) of funds for the same fiscal year) without regard to the requirements of paragraph (b)(1) of this section, but only to the extent it uses such grant amounts to rehabilitate projects to meet the seismic standards required by the local ordinance and to the extent these units in the rehabilitated project are initially occupied after rehabilitation by very low income

families. The grantee or State recipient shall identify as prescribed by HUD in reports required under the C/MI System projects which have been rehabilitated to meet the requirements of a local seismic standards ordinance and contain units which are initially occupied by very low income families after rehabilitation. In determining compliance with paragraph (b)(1) of this section for annual grants under which one or more projects have been rehabilitated to meet the requirements of a local seismic standards ordinance, based on the grantee's or State recipient's reports, HUD will:

(i) Calculate the maximum rental rehabilitation grant amount permissible under §511.11(e)(2)(i) for the project(s) rehabilitated to meet seismic standards;

(ii) Calculate the maximum permissible rental rehabilitation grant amount for the 0 to 1 bedroom units in such project(s) initially occupied by very low income families after rehabilitation;

(iii) Divide the amount calculated in §511.10(b)(2)(ii) by the amount calculated in §511.10(b)(2)(i);

(iv) Multiply the quotient in §511.10(b)(2)(iii) by the actual rental rehabilitation grant amount expended for the project; and

(v) Deduct the product in §511.10(b)(iv) from the amount of the grantee's annual rental rehabilitation grant. The grantee will be required to meet the 70 percent, or other approved level, under this §511.10(b) only as to the amount of its annual grant remaining after making the foregoing deduction.

(c) *Selection of neighborhoods*—(1) *Neighborhood median income and area.* Rental rehabilitation grants shall only be used to assist the rehabilitation of projects located in neighborhoods where the median family income does not exceed 80 percent of the median family income for the area. For purposes of paragraph (c) of this section, *neighborhood* means an area (as determined by the grantee or, as appropriate, the State recipient) that surrounds a project and tends to determine, along with the condition and quality of the project and the dwelling units therein, the rents that are charged for such units. A neighborhood must have a median family income that does not exceed 80 percent of the median family income for the Metropolitan Statistical Area (MSA) in which it is located, or, in the case of a neighborhood not within an MSA, a median family income that does not exceed 80 percent of the median family income for the State's non-metropolitan areas, or at the grantee's option, the non-metropolitan county in which the neighborhood is located.

(2) *Neighborhood rent affordability.* Rental rehabilitation grant amounts shall only be used to assist the rehabilitation of projects located in neighborhoods in which—

(i) The rents for standard units are generally affordable to low-income families at the time of the selection of the neighborhood; and

(ii) The character of the neighborhood indicates that the rents are not likely to increase at a rate significantly greater than the rate for rent increases that can reasonably be anticipated to occur in the market area for the 5-year period following the selection of the neighborhood.

(d) [Reserved]

(e) *Rehabilitation standards.* Each grantee or State recipient shall adopt written rehabilitation standards with which each assisted project must comply after rehabilitation. At a minimum, such standards shall require that after rehabilitation each unit in the entire project must meet the Section 8 Housing Quality Standards for Existing Housing contained at 24 CFR 882.109.

(f) *Eligible project costs.* Eligible project costs include only:

(1) The actual rehabilitation costs necessary to:

(i) Correct substandard conditions, as reasonably defined by the grantee in its rehabilitation standards adopted under §511.10(e);

(ii) Make essential improvements, as reasonably defined by the grantee or State recipient in its rehabilitation standards adopted under §511.10(e), including energy-related repairs, improvements necessary to permit the use of rehabilitated projects by handicapped persons, and activities of lead

§ 511.10

based paint hazards, as required by part 35 of this title;

(iii) Repair major housing systems in danger of failure, as reasonably defined by the grantee or State recipient in its rehabilitation standards under § 511.10(e); and

(2) Other costs (soft costs) that are associated with the rehabilitation or rehabilitation financing; are not for services provided or costs incurred by the grantee, State recipient, or the PHA; and are not paid for as administrative costs under § 511.71. Such costs may include (but are not limited to):

(i) Architectural, engineering or related professional services required in the preparation of rehabilitation plans and drawings or writeups;

(ii) Costs of processing and settling the financing for a project, such as private lender origination fees, credit reports, fees for title evidence, fees for recordation and filing of legal documents, building permits, attorneys' fees, private appraisal fees and fees for an independent rehabilitation cost estimate;

(iii) Relocation payments made to tenants who are displaced by the rehabilitation activities; and

(iv) Costs for the owner to provide information services to tenants as required by §§ 511.13(b), 511.14 (a)(3) and (a)(4), and 511.15(b).

(3)(i) Rehabilitation eligible under § 511.10(f)(1) is limited to work done after the commitment to the project (as defined in § 511.2) is made, except to the extent that such costs also meet all of the following conditions:

(A) Prior to undertaking any rehabilitation before the project is committed in the C/MI System (hereafter called "precommitment rehabilitation"), the owner and grantee or State recipient agree in writing to include such rehabilitation costs in the project cost, if and when the payment is approved for assistance under this part;

(B) The precommitment rehabilitation costs meet all other requirements of this part, including compliance with the other Federal requirements cited in § 511.16, where applicable. In particular, HUD approval of the grantee's certification of completion of environmental responsibilities, when required under 24 CFR part 58, must occur prior to execution of the written agreements to include the costs; and

(C) The precommitment rehabilitation costs were incurred by the owner after the date of the Appropriation Act which made available the grant amounts for the project in question.

(ii) Other project-related costs eligible under § 511.10(f)(2) are also limited to those costs incurred after the commitment to the project is made by the grantee or State recipient and the project is set up in the C/MI System, except to the extent such costs also meet all of the following conditions:

(A) The grantee or State recipient and the owner agreed in writing before the costs were incurred that such costs could be included in the project cost, if and when the project was approved for assistance under this part, or the grantee specifically agrees in writing to include such costs in the project cost on or before the date the project is set up in the C/MI System;

(B) The costs also meet the conditions stated in § 511.10(f)(3)(i)(B) and § 511.10(f)(3)(i)(C).

(4) For projects where the owner or other individuals are performing some or all of the rehabilitation work without compensation (to the extent permitted by § 511.16(a)):

(i) If the owner is not a practicing, licensed contractor, rehabilitation costs eligible under § 511.10(f)(1) are limited to the cost of materials purchased by the owner and used on the project and the cost of other eligible work performed by practicing, licensed contractors, subcontractors or tradesmen on the project.

(ii) If the owner is a practicing, licensed contractor, then eligible project costs may include an amount, in addition to that permitted under paragraph (f)(4)(i) of this section, for the contractor's paid labor, overhead and profit, similar in amount to what these items would be if the work were being performed on a project that was not owned by the contractor.

(iii) Under either paragraph (f)(4)(i) or (f)(4)(ii) of this section, donated labor or work is not part of eligible project cost.

(g) *Project selection priorities*—(1) *Projects with units occupied by very low income families.* While the program can be used for rehabilitating both occupied and vacant units, the grantee shall assure that priority is given to the selection of projects containing units that do not meet the rehabilitation standards adopted under §511.10(e) and which are occupied by very low income families before rehabilitation.

(2) *Units that are accessible to the handicapped.* As stated in 24 CFR 8.30, the grantee shall, subject to the priority in §511.10(g)(1) and in accordance with other requirements in this part, give priority to the selection of projects that will result in dwelling units being made readily accessible to and usable by individuals with handicaps.

(Approved by the Office of Management and Budget under control numbers 2506–0110, 2506–0078, 2506–0080)

[55 FR 20050, May 14, 1990, as amended at 55 FR 36612, Sept. 6, 1990; 61 FR 7061, Feb. 23, 1996; 64 FR 50225, Sept. 15, 1999]

§ 511.11 Project requirements.

(a) *Rehabilitation.* To receive assistance under this part, a project must require rehabilitation, measured by whether the project before the assisted rehabilitation does not meet the rehabilitation standards under §511.10(e). If a project is terminated before completion of rehabilitation (as defined in §511.2), whether voluntarily by the grantee or otherwise, amounts equal to the rental rehabilitation grant amounts already dispersed for the project under the C/MI System are not eligible project costs, whether or not the grantee has already expended such grant amounts to pay for project costs. If such amount is not repaid, the grantee may be subject to corrective and remedial actions under §511.82.

(b) *Primarily residential rental use.* Rental rehabilitation grants shall only be used to rehabilitate projects to be used for "primarily residential rental" use. For purposes of this part, a project is used for primarily residential rental purposes if at least 51 percent of the rentable floor space of the project is used for residential rental purposes after rehabilitation, except that in the case of a two-unit building, at least 50 percent of the rentable floor space after rehabilitation must be used for residential rental purposes after rehabilitation. "Primarily residential rental" use also includes cooperative or mutual housing that has a resale structure that enables the cooperative to maintain rents affordable to low-income families.

(c) *Privately owned real property*—(1) *General.* Rental rehabilitation grant amounts shall only be used for eligible costs of projects that are in private ownership at the time the commitment is made to a specific local project, as defined in §511.2, or projects that are publicly owned at commitment which meet the requirements in §511.11(c)(2).

(2) *Publicly owned project at the time of commitment.* Rental rehabilitation grant amounts may be used to assist publicly owned projects under the following conditions:

(i)(A) For a publicly owned project where the commitment to a specific local project occurs on or after December 22, 1989, the grantee or State recipient—taking into consideration: the size of the project; the complexity of the rehabilitation; the anticipated time necessary to identify, and transfer to, an eligible private owner; and other relevant factors—must determine that it will commence rehabilitation within 90 days of commitment under the C/MI System, and that rehabilitation will be completed and the project transferred to an eligible private owner within the two years and 90 days from the date of commitment in the C/MI system or the time remaining under §511.33(c) for expenditure of the rental rehabilitation grant amounts committed to the project, whichever is shorter. The Project Completion Report under the C/MI system identifying the private entity to which ownership has been transferred shall be submitted within 90 days of the final draw, but not later than two years and 90 days after the date of commitment.

(B) For a publicly owned project where the commitment to a specific local project occurred before December 22, 1989, the grantee or State recipient—taking into consideration: the size of the project; the complexity of the rehabilitation; the anticipated time necessary to identify, and transfer to, an eligible private owner; and other relevant factors—must determine that the rehabilitation will be completed and the project transferred to an eligible private owner within the time remaining for expenditure of the rental rehabilitation fiscal year grant amounts proposed to be used for the project in accordance with § 511.33(c) before drawing down rental rehabilitation grant amounts for the project. The Project Completion Report identifying the private entity to which ownership has been transferred shall be submitted within 90 days of the final draw.

(ii) If the grants or State recipient fails to complete the rehabilitation, transfer the property to an eligible private owner (which includes obtaining the agreements from the new owner required by this part, including § 511.11(d)), and submit the Project Completion Report within the allowable period, then HUD will suspend the grantee's and/or the State recipient's authority to set up any new projects in the C/MI System and may require the grantee to repay to its grant account in the C/MI System all rental rehabilitation grant amounts drawn down with respect to the project. If payment is not received, HUD may proceed to deobligate up to the full amount of the grantee's remaining uncommitted rental rehabilitation grant amounts, whether or not such grant amounts otherwise are available for deobligation under § 511.33(c). A suspension of set-up authority shall terminate when the grantee or State recipient has transferred the project to private ownership, as required by this part, and has submitted a Project Completion Report under the C/MI System identifying the private owner, or repays its grant account as required by this paragraph, or HUD lifts the suspension at its discretion.

(iii) After the grantee has repaid the grant amounts to its grant account as provided in § 511.11(c)(2)(ii), the grant amounts may be committed and expended by the grantee for new projects within the periods originally allowed for these grant amounts, or deobligated by HUD under § 511.33 or § 511.82 to the same extent as any other grant amounts subject to this part.

(3) *Private, non-profit organizations.* Non-profit organizations that are privately controlled are eligible to receive rental rehabilitation grant amounts under the same terms and conditions as any other private project owner under this part. For purposes of this requirement, non-profit organizations must have governing bodies which are controlled 51 percent or more by private individuals who are acting in a private capacity. For purposes of this provision, an individual is deemed to be acting in a private capacity if he or she is not legally bound to act on behalf of a public body (including the grantee), and is not being paid by a public body (including the grantee) while performing functions in connection with the non-profit organization.

(4) *Manufactured housing units.* Notwithstanding whether they are classified as real or personal property under applicable State law, manufactured housing units may be assisted under this part under the following conditions:

(i) The unit is on a permanent foundation;

(ii) The utility hook-ups are permanent;

(iii) The unit is designed for use as a permanent residence;

(iv) The unit also meets the Section 8 Housing Quality Standards for Manufactured Homes set forth in 24 CFR 882.109(o).

(5) *Religious organizations.* Rental Rehabilitation grant amounts may be used to assist the rehabilitation of properties formerly owned by religious organizations, such as churches, provided that both of the following conditions are met:

(i) Title to the property to be rehabilitated must be transferred to a wholly secular entity prior to commitment, and this entity shall comply with all obligations of a project owner under this part. The entity may be an existing or newly established entity (which may be an entity established, but not controlled, by the religious organization); and

(ii) The completed project must be used exclusively by the owner entity for secular purposes, available to all persons regardless of religion, for the period and subject to the obligations described in § 511.11(d). In particular, there must be no religious or membership criteria for tenants of the property.

(d) *Long-term owner obligations.* (1) Each project assisted under this part is subject to the following specific obligations for a period of at least ten years after completion of the rehabilitation:

(i) The project shall remain in private ownership and in primarily residential rental use for the required period, unless the project is sold to another private owner who agrees to continue to manage the property in accordance with Rental Rehabilitation Program requirements for the remainder of the required period, or a hardship exception is approved by the grantee for reasons that occur after completion of the rehabilitation.

(ii) The owner shall not convert the units in the project to condominium ownership or any form of cooperative ownership not eligible for assistance under this part for the required period.

(iii) The owner shall not discriminate against prospective tenants on the basis of their receipt of, or eligibility for, housing assistance under any Federal, State or local housing assistance program or, except for a housing project for elderly persons, on the basis that the tenants have a minor child or children who will be residing with them, for the required period.

(iv) The owner shall comply with the nondiscrimination and equal opportunity requirements and with the affirmative marketing requirements and procedures adopted under §511.13, for the required period.

(2)(i) With respect to projects which are privately owned when the commitment to a specific local project is made, the obligations required under §511.10 (d)(1) and (d)(3) shall be included in the written, legally binding commitment or project agreement between the owner and the grantee or State recipient which is executed on or before the date the project is committed.

(ii) With respect to projects which are publicly owned when the commitment is made, these obligations shall be included in a written agreement between the grantee or State recipient and the private owner, executed on or before completion of rehabilitation.

(iii) By drawing down rental rehabilitation grant amounts for a project which is publicly owned when the commitment is made, the public owner itself accepts the obligations of this part, including §511.11(d)(1)(i) (except for private ownership before completion of rehabilitation), (d)(1)(ii), (d)(1)(iii) and (d)(1)((iv) and agrees to include these obligations in the agreement with the private owner required by §511.11(d)(2)(ii).

(3) The grantee or State recipient shall ensure that the written agreements with private owners required by §511.11 (d)(1) and (d)(2) are legally enforceable, are recorded against the project in the local land records (or in the case of a manufactured housing unit, against the unit in the manner appropriate for such real or personal property under State and local law), and that the agreements contain remedies adequate to enforce their provisions. A remedy will be deemed adequate for purposes of this paragraph if it requires the entire amount of the rental rehabilitation grant assistance for the project to be a secondary lien secured by the property, repayable by the owner, or any subsequent transferee, upon a prohibited conversion, sale or use in an amount equal to the entire amount of such assistance, less 10 percent for each full year after completion of the project up to the time the prohibited conversion, sale or use occurs, except in the case of projects of 25 units or more. For projects of 25 units or more the entire amount of such assistance shall be repaid if the project is converted, sold or used in violation of this section during the 10-year period. Such lien may not be subordinate to a lien in favor of the grantee, State recipient or any person with whom the owner has business or family ties, except as may be necessary to secure federally tax exempt financing for the project.

(e) *Maximum rental rehabilitation grant amounts for projects.* (1) Rental rehabilitation grant amounts used for any project shall not exceed 50 percent of the total eligible project costs, as defined in §511.10(f). However, where refinancing of existing indebtedness is involved, the grantee may approve a higher amount for a project where it determines, and documents in its records, that:

(i)(A) Rehabilitation of the project is important to the overall stability of the neighborhood (as defined at §511.10(c)(2)) and for the provision of housing at rents affordable to low-income families, or

(B) The project has special costs to facilitate use by the elderly or handicapped; and

(ii) The refinancing and the higher grant amount are necessary to make the project feasible.

This higher grant amount may not exceed the lesser of 75 percent of the eligible project costs or 50 percent of the sum of the eligible project costs and the amount necessary to refinance the existing indebtedness.

(2) *Per unit.* (i) Except as provided in paragraph (e)(2)(ii) of this section, the rental rehabilitation grant amounts used for any project may not exceed the sum of the following dollar amounts for dwelling units in the project:

(A) $5,000 per unit for units with no bedrooms;

(B) $6,500 per unit for units with one bedroom;

(C) $7,500 per unit for units with two bedrooms; and

(D) $8,500 per unit for units with three or more bedrooms.

(ii) HUD may approve higher rental rehabilitation grant amounts for projects in areas of high material and labor costs where the grantee demonstrates to HUD's satisfaction that a higher amount is necessary to conduct a rental rehabilitation program in the area and that it has taken every appropriate step to contain the amount of the rental rehabilitation grant within the dollar limits specified in paragraph (e)(2)(i) of this section. These higher amounts will be determined as follows:

(A) HUD may approve higher per unit amounts for a unit of general local government's entire rental rehabilitation program up to, but not to exceed, an amount derived by applying the HUD-approved High Cost Percentage for Base Cities for the area to the applicable per unit dollar limits;

(B) HUD may, on a project-by-project basis, increase the level permitted under §511.11(e)(2)(i) by multiplying the original limits by up to a maximum of 140 percent and then adding the product to the original limits. Therefore, the maximum high cost grant amount per project that may be approved is 240 percent of the original per unit limits.

(f) *Rent or occupancy restrictions.* (1) A project rehabilitated with rental rehabilitation grant amounts under this part is not subject to State or local rent control unless the rent control requirements or agreements:

(i) Were entered into under a State law or local ordinance of general applicability that was enacted and in effect in the jurisdiction before November 30, 1983 and

(ii) Apply generally to projects not assisted under the Rental Rehabilitation Program.

(2) State and local rent controls expressly preempted by paragraph (f) of this section include, but are not limited to, rent laws or ordinances, rent regulating agreements, rent regulations, low income occupancy agreements extending beyond one year from the date of completion of rehabilitation of a project, financial penalties for failure to achieve certain low income occupancy or rent projections, or restrictions on return on investment or other similar policies that prevent an owner, whether for-profit or non-profit, from maximizing return or setting rent levels as the owner chooses. Grantees or State recipients shall not include any preempted rent or occupancy restrictions in any commitments or project agreements with the owners of Rental Rehabilitation projects.

(g) [Reserved]

(Information collection requirements contained in this section have been approved by the Office of Management and Budget under control numbers 2506–0080 and 2506–0110)

[55 FR 20050, May 14, 1990, as amended at 61 FR 7061, Feb. 23, 1996]

§ 511.12 Conflicts of interest.

(a) No person who is an employee, agent, consultant, officer, or elected or appointed official of the grantee or State recipient (or of any public agency that performs administrative functions in the RRP) that receives rental rehabilitation grant amounts and who exercises or has exercised any functions or responsibilities with respect to assisted rehabilitation activities, or who is in a position to participate in a decision-making process or gain inside information with regard to such activities, may obtain a personal or financial interest or benefit from the activity, or have an interest in any contract, subcontract or agreement with respect thereto, or the proceeds thereunder, either for themselves or those with whom they have family or business ties, during their tenure or for one year thereafter.

(b) The appropriate HUD Field Office may grant an exception to the exclusion in paragraph (a) of the section on a case-by-case basis when it determines that such an exception will serve to further the purposes of the Rental Rehabilitation Program and the effective and efficient administration of the local rental rehabilitation program or the project. An exception may be considered only after the grantee or State recipient has provided a disclosure of the nature of the conflict, accompanied by an assurance that there has been public disclosure of the conflict and a description of how the public disclosure was made and an opinion of the grantee's or State recipient's attorney that the interest for which the exception is sought would not violate State or local laws. In determining whether to grant a requested exception, HUD shall consider the cumulative effect of the following factors, where applicable:

(1) Whether the exception would provide a significant cost benefit or an essential degree of expertise to the local rental rehabilitation program or the project that would otherwise not be available;

(2) Whether an opportunity was provided for open competitive bidding or negotiation;

(3) Whether the person affected is a member of a group or class intended to be the beneficiaries of the rehabilitation activity, and the exception will permit such person to receive generally the same interests or benefits as are being made available or provided to the group or class;

(4) Whether the affected person has withdrawn from his or her functions or responsibilities, or the decisionmaking process, with respect to the specific rehabilitation activity in question;

(5) Whether the interest or benefit was present before the affected person was in a position as described in this paragraph;

(6) Whether undue hardship will result either to the grantee, State recipient or the person affected when weighed against the public interest served by avoiding the prohibited conflict; and

(7) Any other relevant considerations.

§ 511.13 Nondiscrimination, equal opportunity, and affirmative marketing requirements.

In addition to the nondiscrimination and equal opportunity requirements set forth in 24 CFR part 5, the following requirements apply:

(a) *Affirmative marketing.* The grantee shall adopt appropriate procedures and requirements for affirmatively marketing units in rehabilitated rental rehabilitation projects through the provision of information regarding the availability of units that are vacant after rehabilitation or that later become vacant. Affirmative marketing steps consist of good faith efforts to provide information and otherwise to attract eligible persons from all racial, ethnic and gender groups in the housing market area to the available housing. (These affirmative marketing procedures will not apply to units rented to families with housing assistance provided by a PHA.) The grantee shall establish procedures, requirements and assessment criteria for marketing units in the Rental Rehabilitation Program that are appropriate to accomplish affirmative marketing objectives. The grantee shall annually assess the affirmative marketing program to determine: Good faith efforts that have been made to carry out such procedures and requirements; objectives that have been met; and corrective actions that are required.

(1) For each grantee, the affirmative marketing requirements and procedures adopted must include:

(i) Methods for how the grantee will inform the public, owners and potential tenants about Federal fair housing laws and the grantee's affirmative marketing policy (such as the use of the Equal Housing Opportunity logotype or slogan in press releases and solicitations for owners, and written communications to fair housing and other groups);

(ii) Requirements and practices each owner (including the grantee or any other public owner) must adhere to in order to carry out the grantee's affirmative marketing procedures and requirements (*e.g.*, use of commercial media, use of community contacts, use of the Equal Housing Opportunity logotype or slogan, display of fair housing poster);

(iii) Procedures to be used by owners (including the grantee or any other public owner) to inform and solicit applications from persons in the housing market area who are not likely to apply for the housing without special outreach (*e.g.*, use of community organizations, churches, employment centers, fair housing groups or housing counseling agencies);

(iv) Records that will be kept describing efforts taken by the grantee and by the owners (including the grantee or any other public owner) to affirmatively market units and records to assess the results of these actions;

(v) A description of how the grantee will assess the affirmative marketing efforts of owners (including the grantee or any other public owner), and the results of those efforts, and what corrective actions will be taken where an owner fails to follow these affirmative marketing requirements.

(2) For States distributing rental rehabilitation grant amounts to units of general local government, the affirmative marketing procedures and requirements shall also set out the actions that State recipients must take to meet the objectives set out in §511.13(b), the record keeping and reporting requirements such State will require of State recipients, and the procedures that such State will follow to determine what action has been taken by State recipients to assess the results of these affirmative marketing efforts.

(3) The grantee or State recipient shall require compliance with the conditions of its affirmative marketing requirements and procedures adopted under paragraph (b) of this section by means of an agreement with the owner that shall be applicable for a period of ten years beginning on the date of completion of rehabilitation, as defined in §511.2.

(b) [Reserved]

(Approved by the Office of Management and Budget under control number 2506-0080)

[55 FR 20050, May 14, 1990, as amended at 61 FR 5208, Feb. 9, 1996]

§511.14 Tenant assistance, displacement, relocation, and acquisition.

(a) *General policies.* The grantee and any State recipient shall:

(1) Ensure that the rehabilitation will not cause the displacement of any very low income family by a family that is not a very low income family.

(2) Consistent with the other goals and objectives of this part, minimize displacement. To the extent feasible, residential occupants shall be provided a reasonable opportunity to lease and occupy a suitable, decent, safe, sanitary and affordable dwelling unit in the project (see paragraph (g)(1)(iii) of this section).

(3) Administer all phases of the RRP, including the selection of units to be rehabilitated and the provision of notices, counseling, referrals, other advisory services and relocation payments, in a manner that does not result in discrimination because of race, color, religion, sex, age, handicap, familial status or national origin.

(4) Adopt and make public a written tenant assistance policy (TAP) that describes the assistance that will be provided to tenants who reside in the project and which includes a statement of nondiscrimination policy consistent with paragraph (a)(3) of this section. The TAP shall comply with the provisions of this section. Each tenant in the project shall be provided a copy of the TAP and advised of the impact of the project on him or her. For privately owned projects, such notice shall be given immediately after submission of the application by the owner of a property, or earlier. For publicly owned projects, such notice shall be given immediately after the commitment (defined in §511.2), or earlier.

(b) *Relocation assistance for displaced persons.* A displaced person (defined in paragraph (g) of this section) must be provided relocation assistance at the

Ofc. of Asst. Secy., Comm. Planning, Develop., HUD §511.14

levels described in, and in accordance with the requirements of, 49 CFR part 24, which contains the government-wide regulations implementing the Uniform Relocation Assistance and Real Property Acquisition Policies Act of 1970 (URA) (42 U.S.C. 4601–4655). Tenants shall be advised of their rights under the Fair Housing Act (42 U.S.C. 3601-19) and of replacement housing opportunities in such a manner that, to the extent possible, tenants are provided a choice between relocating within their own neighborhoods and other neighborhoods consistent with the grantee's or State recipient's responsibility to affirmatively further fair housing. As permitted under 49 CFR 24.2(k), for purposes of making replacement housing payments, the term *initiation of negotiations* means:

(1) For a privately owned project, execution of the legally binding agreement between the grantee or State recipient and the project owner under which the grantee or State recipient agrees to provide rental rehabilitation grant amounts for the project.

(2) For a publicly owned project, the commitment as defined in §511.2 or such earlier notice as the grantee or State recipient determines to be appropriate.

(c) *Real property acquisition requirements.* The acquisition of real property for a project is subject to the URA and the requirements described in 49 CFR part 24, subpart B.

(d) *Application of Community Development Block Grant (CDBG) requirements.* If CDBG funds are used to pay any part of the cost of the rehabilitation activities, as described in 24 CFR 570.202(b) or similar eligible activities, the project is subject to the requirements of section 104(d) of the Housing and Community Development Act of 1974, as amended, and implementing regulations at 24 CFR 570.606(b) (Entitlement Program and HUD-administered Small Cities Program) and 24 CFR 570.496a(b) (State CDBG Program).

(e) *Appeals.* If a person disagrees with the grantee's or State recipient's determination concerning the person's eligibility for, or the amount of, relocation assistance, the person may file a written appeal (request for reconsideration) of that determination with the grantee or State recipient. The appeal procedures to be followed are described in 49 CFR 24.10. A low-income person that has been displaced from a dwelling may submit a further written request for review of the grantee's decision to the appropriate HUD Field Office. However, a low-income person's request for review of a State recipient's decision shall be submitted to the State grantee.

(f) *Compliance responsibility.* (1) The grantee and any State recipient are responsible for ensuring compliance with the URA, the regulations at 49 CFR part 24, and the requirements of this section, notwithstanding any third party's contractual obligation to the grantee or State recipient to comply with these provisions.

(2) The cost of required assistance may be paid from local public funds, funds available under the rules of this part, or funds available from other sources.

(3) The grantee or State recipient must maintain records in sufficient detail to demonstrate compliance with the provisions of this section.

(g) *Definition of a displaced person.* (1) For purposes of this section, the term *displaced person* means any person (family, individual, business, nonprofit organization or farm) that moves from real property, or moves personal property from real property, permanently and involuntarily as a direct result of rehabilitation, demolition or acquisition for a project assisted under this part. Permanent, involuntary moves for an assisted project include a permanent move from the project that is made:

(i) After notice by the property owner, grantee, or State recipient to move permanently from the property, if the move occurs on or after the following date:

(A) If the notice is provided by the property owner, the date that the owner (or person in control of the site) submits a request for assistance under this part that is later approved and funded.

(B) If the notice is provided by the grantee or State recipient, the date of the commitment to a specific local project.

§ 511.15

(ii) Before the date described in paragraph (g)(1)(i) of this section, if either the grantee or HUD determines that the displacement resulted directly from rehabilitation, acquisition or demolition for the project;

(iii) By a tenant-occupant of a dwelling unit after the initiation of negotiations, if:

(A) The tenant has not been provided a reasonable opportunity to lease and occupy a suitable, decent, safe and sanitary dwelling in the project following the completion of the project at a rent, including estimated average utility costs, that does not exceed the greater of:

(*1*) The tenant's rent and estimated average utility costs before the commitment; or

(*2*) The total tenant payment, as determined under 24 CFR 813.107, if the tenant is low-income, or 30 percent of gross household income if the tenant is not low-income; or

(B) The tenant has been required to relocate temporarily, but:

(*1*) The tenant is not offered payment for all reasonable out-of-pocket expenses incurred in connection with the temporary relocation, including the cost of moving to and from the temporarily occupied housing and any increase in rent and utility costs, or other conditions of the temporary relocation are not reasonable, and

(*2*) The tenant does not return to the project; or

(C) The tenant is required to move to another unit within the project but is not offered reimbursement for all reasonable out-of-pocket expenses incurred in connection with the move or other conditions of the move are not reasonable.

(2) A person does not qualify as a displaced person, if:

(i) The person has been evicted for cause based upon a serious or repeated violation of material terms of the lease or occupancy agreement, and the grantee or State recipient determines that the eviction was not undertaken for the purpose of evading the obligation to provide relocation assistance; or

(ii) The person moved into the property after the owner's submission of the request for assistance but, before commencing occupancy, received written notice of the owner's intent to terminate the person's occupancy for the project; or

(iii) The person is ineligible under 49 CFR 24.2(g)(2); or

(iv) The grantee or State recipient determines that the person was not displaced as a direct result of rehabilitation, acquisition or demolition of the project, and the HUD Field Office concurs in that determination.

(3) The grantee may, at any time, ask HUD to determine whether a specific displacement is or would be covered by these rules.

§ 511.15 Lead-based paint.

The Lead-Based Paint Poisoning Prevention Act (42 U.S.C. 4821–4846), the Residential Lead-Based Paint Hazard Reduction Act of 1992 (42 U.S.C. 4851–4856), and implementing regulations at part 35, subparts A, B, J, K, and R of this title apply to activities under these programs.

[64 FR 50225, Sept. 15, 1999]

§ 511.16 Other Federal requirements.

In addition to the Federal requirements set forth in 24 CFR part 5, Grantees and, where applicable, State recipients shall comply with the following requirements:

(a) *Labor standards.* All laborers and mechanics (except laborers and mechanics employed by a State or local government acting as the principal contractor on the project) employed in the rehabilitation of a project assisted under the Rental Rehabilitation Program that contains 12 or more dwelling units after rehabilitation shall be paid wages at rates not less than those prevailing on similar rehabilitation in the locality, if such a rate category exists, or other appropriate rate as determined by the Secretary of Labor in accordance with the Davis-Bacon Act (40 U.S.C. 276a—276a-5), and contracts involving their employment shall be subject to the provisions, as applicable, of the Contract Work Hours and Safety Standards Act (40 U.S.C. 327–333. (If CDBG funds are used to finance certain costs for projects of 8 or more units, these labor standards may apply (see 24 CFR 570.603).) If a project is subject to Federal labor standards requirements, individuals are not permitted to perform work thereon which is covered by such requirements without compensation in accordance with such requirements, except that persons who own a project in their own name may personally perform uncompensated work on their own projects. Grantees, State recipients, owners, contractors and subcontractors shall comply with applicable implementing regulations in 29 CFR parts 1, 3, and 5.

(b) *Environment and historic preservation.* Section 104(g) of the Housing and Community Development Act of 1974 and 24 CFR part 58, which prescribe procedures for compliance with the National Environmental Policy Act of 1969 (42 U.S.C. 4321–4361), and the additional laws and authorities listed at 24 CFR 58.5.

(c) *Pet ownership in housing for the elderly or handicapped.* The provisions of 24 CFR part 243 apply to any project assisted under this part for which preference in tenant selection is given for all units in the project to elderly or handicapped persons or elderly or handicapped families, as defined in 24 CFR 812.2.

(d) *Flood insurance.* (1) Under the Flood Disaster Protection Act of 1973 (42 U.S.C. 4001–4128), a grantee may not approve the commitment of rental rehabilitation grant amounts to a project located in an area identified by the Federal Emergency Management Agency (FEMA) as having special flood hazards, unless:

(i) The community in which the area is situated is participating in the National Flood Insurance Program (see 44 CFR parts 59 through 79), or less than a year has passed since FEMA notification regarding such hazards; and

(ii) Flood insurance is obtained as a condition of approval of the commitment.

(2) Grantees with projects located in an area identified by FEMA as having special flood hazards are responsible for assuring that flood insurance under the National Flood Insurance Program is obtained and maintained.

(3) This paragraph §511.16(g) does not apply in the case of allocations administered by a State under §511.51(a).

(Approved by the Office of Management and Budget under control number 2506–0080)

[55 FR 20050, May 14, 1990, as amended at 61 FR 5208, Feb. 9, 1996]

Subpart C [Reserved]

Subpart D—Allocation Formula and Reallocations

§§ 511.30–511.31 [Reserved]

§ 511.33 Deobligation of rental rehabilitation grant amounts.

(a) Before deobligating grant amounts, HUD will consult with the affected grantee and take into account factors such as timing of the grantee's program year; the timing of State distributions to State recipients, if applicable; the timing of expected project approvals for projects in the grantee's pipeline; climatic or other considerations affecting rehabilitation work schedules; and other relevant considerations. In addition to any remedial deobligation under §511.82, HUD may deobligate any rental rehabilitation grant amounts that are not:

(1) Committed to specific local projects within 3 years of the date of obligation of the grant under §511.21(d) (4 years in the case of a State that distributes rental rehabilitation grant amounts to State recipients); or

(2) Expended for eligible costs within 5 years of such date of obligation (6 years in the case of a State that distributes rental rehabilitation grant amounts to State recipients).

(b) After such consultation, the HUD field office may direct the grantee to proceed with program closeout and may deobligate remaining unexpended grant amounts if the field office determines that any uncommitted funds will not be committed within a reasonable time, only small amounts of funds remain unexpended, or completion of uncompleted projects appears infeasible within a reasonable time. None of the time periods referred to in this section are extended by any suspensions of

§ 511.34

project set-ups or other remedial action imposed by HUD under this part.

[61 FR 7062, Feb. 23, 1996]

§ 511.34 [Reserved]

Subpart E [Reserved]

Subpart F—State Program

§ 511.50 **State election to administer a rental rehabilitation program.**

(a) State allocations may be used to carry out eligible rehabilitation activities in accordance with the requirements of this part in units of general local government that do not receive allocations under subpart D and in cities and urban counties whose allocations are below the minimum amount specified in § 511.31, but may not be used in areas that are eligible for assistance under title V of the Housing Act of 1949, except as specified in paragraph (b) of this section.

(b) For Fiscal Years 1988 through 1991, uncommitted prior year funds may be used by State grantees, by units of general local government receiving funds from State grantees and by units of general local government participating in a HUD-administered State Program in areas eligible for assistance under title V of the Housing Act of 1949. This authority to enter into commitments with owners for projects in title V-eligible areas expires on September 30, 1991.

(Approved by the Office of Management and Budget under control number 2506–0080)

[55 FR 20050, May 14, 1990, as amended at 55 FR 36612, Sept. 6, 1990; 61 FR 7062, Feb. 23, 1996]

§ 511.51 **State-administered program.**

(a) *Type of program.* A State may, in its discretion, use all or part of its rental rehabilitation grant amounts either:

(1) To carry out its own Rental Rehabilitation Program without the active participation of units of general local government;

(2) To distribute grant amounts to State recipients which independently select, enter into commitments with owners for, and manage projects; or

(3) To carry out mixed programs in which both the State and all or some units of general local government each perform specified program functions.

(b) *Sharing grant amounts for administration.* In programs under paragraphs (a)(2) and (a)(3) of this section, a State must share its grant amounts which are available for administrative costs with units of general local government administering the program with the State, under a written agreement as required by § 511.71.

(c) *State Program requirements.* State grantees shall be responsible for administering their rental rehabilitation grant amounts in accordance with all requirements of this part and other applicable laws, notwithstanding their use of units of general local governments to perform program functions under paragraph (a)(2) or (a)(3) of this section. In addition, States that use units of general local government to perform program functions shall:

(1) Ensure that units of general local government carry out their Rental Rehabilitation Program in accordance with requirements of this part and other applicable laws. States shall include in their agreements with their units of general local government such additional provisions as may be appropriate to ensure such compliance and to enable the State to carry out its responsibilities under this part, including the withdrawal and reallocation of rental rehabilitation grant amounts based on unit of general local government noncompliance (including State recipient failure to meet the schedule submitted by the State under § 511.20(b)(8)); and

(2) Conduct such reviews and audits of their units of general local government as may be appropriate to determine whether units of general local government, including State recipients, have carried out their programs in accordance with the requirements of this part, whether they have done so in a timely manner, and whether they have a continuing capacity to do so in a timely manner.

(Approved by the Office of Management and Budget under control number 2506–0080)

[55 FR 20050, May 14, 1990, as amended at 61 FR 7062, Feb. 23, 1996]

§ 511.52 [Reserved]

Subpart G [Reserved]

Subpart H—Grant Administration

§ 511.70 Responsibility for grant administration.

Grantees are responsible for ensuring that rental rehabilitation grants are administered in accordance with the requirements of this part and other applicable laws. A grantee may enter into a written agreement with another unit of State or local government or with a non-governmental entity to administer specified functions under its Rental Rehabilitation Program to the extent not prohibited by HUD. If the grantee is contracting with a non-governmental entity to administer its program or to provide other services, such as cash management responsibilities, the grantee shall follow the procurement standards of 24 CFR 85.36. The use of other governmental units or private contractors does not relieve the grantee of its responsibility for ensuring compliance with this part and other applicable laws.

§ 511.71 Administrative costs.

(a) *Maximum amount.* Any grantee may use not to exceed 10 percent of the grant amount initially obligated to the grantee for Federal Fiscal Year 1988 and later fiscal years for administrative costs eligible under paragraphs (b) and (c) of this section. Eligible grantees may draw down funds to pay for eligible administrative costs through HUD's C/MI System.

(b) *Eligibility.* Eligible administrative costs are reasonable and necessary costs, as described in OMB Circular A-87, incurred by the grantee itself, or by a unit of general local government pursuant to a written cost-sharing agreement with a State grantee (see § 511.51(b)), in carrying out the Rental Rehabilitation Program in accordance with this part. Administrative costs do not include costs of rehabilitation which are incurred by and charged to project owners as eligible project costs under § 511.10(f)(2).

(c) *Written cost-sharing agreement.* A State grantee shall determine the amount of its rental rehabilitation grant that it will permit to be used for administrative expenses, not to exceed the maximum permitted by this section. The State grantee shall share the amount of its rental rehabilitation grant designated for administrative expenses with units of general local government that incur eligible administrative costs in carrying out the Rental Rehabilitation Program, whether the unit of general local government receives a distribution of funds from the State or selects and manages projects independently as a State recipient or whether it performs less comprehensive functions by agreement with the State. Before any eligible administrative expenses are incurred by a unit of general local government under a State's grant, the cost-sharing arrangement shall be specified in a written agreement between the State grantee and each unit of general local government that receives payment from the State for administrative expenses under this part. This agreement shall describe (whether very generally or more specifically) the functions that the unit of general local government shall perform and the terms and conditions under which the unit of general local government participates in the program, including the procedures by which the unit of general local government's compensation for its administrative expenses incurred in performing the authorized functions is to be calculated and paid. HUD will not review the relative sharing of administrative expenses between the State and affected units of general local government, but pursuant to §§ 511.74 and 511.80, it will review and audit the State's program on the eligibility of administrative expenses paid with program funds.

(d) *Allocation of benefit.* Rental rehabilitation grant amounts used for program administration will be deemed to meet program requirements imposed on a percentage of the annual grant basis, such as lower income benefit and use of rental rehabilitation grants for housing for families with children, in the same proportion as the grant amounts for a grant year which are used for eligible project costs meet the grant requirements. For example, if 70 percent of the grant amounts used for

§ 511.72

project costs for Fiscal Year 1989 benefit low-income families, then 70 percent of the Fiscal Year 1989 grant amounts spent for administrative costs will be deemed to benefit low-income persons.

§ 511.72 Applicability of uniform Federal administrative requirements.

Grantees, State recipients and their contractors shall comply with the requirements and standards of OMB Circular No. A-87, "Principles for Determining Costs Applicable to Grants and Contracts with State, Local and Federally recognized Indian Tribal Governments,"[1] OMB Circular A-128, "Audits of State and Local Governments" (implemented at 24 CFR part 44), and with 24 CFR part 85, "Uniform Administrative Requirements for Grants and Cooperative Agreements to State and Local Governments," except for: §§ 85.10, 85.11, 85.25, 85.31, 85.40(b), 85.41, and 85.50. In lieu of §§ 85.25 and 85.50, HUD has adopted § 511.76 and § 511.77, respectively, of this part.

§ 511.73 Grantee records.

(a) *Records to be maintained.* Each grantee shall maintain records as specified by HUD that clearly document its performance under each requirement of this part. States distributing rental rehabilitation grant amounts to State recipients shall also ensure that their recipients maintain such records to document each recipient's performance. The records required by this section shall, at a minimum, include the following:

(1) Records required to comply with § 511.75;

(2) Data on the racial, ethnic, gender, and income level characteristics of

(i) Tenants occupying units before rehabilitation;

(ii) Tenants moving from and (initially after rehabilitation) into projects assisted under this part;

(iii) Applicants for tenancy within 90 days following completion of rehabilitation assisted under this part; and

(iv) Owners of the projects rehabilitated; and

---

[1] OMB Circular No. A-87 is available from HUD Field Offices.

(3) Data indicating the race and ethnicity of households displaced as a result of program activities, and, if available, the address and census tract of the housing units to which each displaced household relocated.

(b) *Retention of records.* Records required to be maintained under paragraph (a) of this section shall be retained for a period of three years from the date of final closeout of the rental rehabilitation grant.

(c) *Public disclosure.* Documents relevant to a grantee's Program Description shall be made available for public review upon request at the grantee's office during normal working hours.

(d) *Federal access to records.* The Secretary, the Inspector General of HUD, the Comptroller General of the United States, or any of their duly authorized representatives, shall have access to all books, accounts, reports, files, and other papers or property of grantees, State recipients, and their contractors pertaining to rental rehabilitation grant amounts for the purpose of making surveys, audits, examinations, excerpts, and transcripts. Grantees or, where applicable, State recipients shall ensure that their agreements with owners require the owners to provide similar access to their records pertaining to the use of rental rehabilitation grant amounts.

(Approved by the Office of Management and Budget under control number 2506–0080)

§ 511.74 Audit.

The financial management systems used by grantees and, where applicable, State recipients shall provide for audits in accordance with 24 CFR part 44.

§ 511.75 Disbursement of rental rehabilitation grant amounts: Cash and Management Information System.

(a) *General.* Rental Rehabilitation grants are managed through HUD's C/MI System for the Rental Rehabilitation Program. The C/MI System is a computerized system which manages program funds, disburses grant amounts, and collects and reports data on properties and tenants assisted under the Program.

(b) *Project set-up.* (1) After the grantee executes the Grant Agreement, complies with the requirements under part

Ofc. of Asst. Secy., Comm. Planning, Develop., HUD § 511.75

58 of this title for release of funds, and submits the appropriate security documents, the grantee may identify (set-up) specific local projects in the C/MI System. State recipients are also granted access to the C/MI System for projects upon designation by the State and submission of the appropriate security documents. Within 12 calendar days of project set-up, grantees and State recipients are required to submit a Pre-Rehabilitation Report to HUD for each project set-up in the C/MI System. Until an acceptable Pre-Rehabilitation Report is received and entered in the C/MI System, grant amounts for the project are not considered "committed," as defined in §511.2, and, therefore, are subject to deobligation to the extent authorized by 24 CFR 511.33(c).

(2) Beginning in Fiscal Year 1991, if Pre-Rehabilitation Reports are not received within 20 days of the project set-up call, the project will be cancelled automatically by the C/MI System. In addition, projects which have been committed in the C/MI System for 6 months without an initial disbursement of funds will be automatically cancelled by the C/MI System.

(c) *Disbursement of rental rehabilitation grant amounts.* After an acceptable Pre-Rehabilitation Report is entered into the C/MI System, obligated grant amounts may be drawn down for the project by the grantee or State recipient by electronic funds transfer to the designated depository institution of the grantee or State recipient within 48 to 72 hours of the disbursement request. Grant amounts for eligible administrative costs may be similarly drawn down by grantees by electronic funds transfer to their designated depository institutions, but State recipients are not permitted to draw down State grant amounts for administrative expenses. Any drawdown is conditioned upon the submission of satisfactory information by the grantee or State recipient about the project or the administrative expenses and compliance with other procedures specified by HUD in HUD's forms and issuances concerning the Rental Rehabilitation Program Cash and Management Information System. Copies of these forms and issuances may be obtained from HUD Field Offices. Drawdowns shall be requested by the grantee or State recipient as closely as possible to the time they are needed by a grantee or State recipient and the owner to pay eligible project costs or by a grantee to pay eligible administrative costs. Drawdowns for project costs shall be requested only for work or services that have been satisfactorily performed, or materials that are acceptable. After receipt in the grantee or State recipient's depository account, grant amounts for project costs shall immediately be disbursed by the grantee or State recipient and the owner in payment for eligible project costs and shall not be disbursed at any time, relative to a project's matching funds, in any greater proportion than the proportion of rental rehabilitation grant amounts to matching funds for the project.

(d) *Payment vouchers.* As post-documentation of each drawdown, a grantee or State recipient must submit to HUD a payment voucher, for each drawdown made by HUD, in the form required for the C/MI System. If the drawdown was for eligible project costs and the payment voucher is not received within ten calendar days of the drawdown, the grantee or State recipient will be suspended from setting up new projects until the required payment voucher is received by HUD. If the drawdown was for administrative costs and the payment voucher is not received within ten calendar days of the drawdown, the grantee will not be allowed to make another drawdown for administrative costs until the payment voucher is received.

(e) *Submission of project completion reports.* After the final draw for a project, a Project Completion Report must be submitted to HUD within 90 days of the drawdown request. However, for projects rehabilitated pursuant to §511.11(c)(2) (publicly owned project at the time of commitment), the Project Completion Report must be submitted within 90 days of the final draw, but not later than 2 years and 90 days after the date of commitment. If a satisfactory Project Completion Report is not submitted by the due date, HUD will suspend further project set-ups for the grantee or State recipient. Project set-ups will remain suspended until a satisfactory Project Completion Report is received and entered into the C/MI System.

(Approved by the Office of Management and Budget under control number 2506–0080)

§ 511.76 Program income.

(a) *General.* Grantees and State recipients are neither encouraged to earn nor discouraged from earning program income in using rental rehabilitation grant amounts under this part.

(b) *Definition of program income.* Program income means gross income received by the grantee or State recipient (or by another party at the direction of the grantee or State recipient) which is directly generated from the use of rental rehabilitation grant amounts. Primarily, it includes but is not limited to, the following:

(1) Repayments of principal (whether in installments or a lump-sum) and any interest or penalty assessment, under the terms of the loan commitment or other project assistance agreement between the owner and the grantee or State recipient, including repayments, pursuant to § 511.11(d)(3), of the rental rehabilitation grant assistance by the owner after completion of rehabilitation; and

(2) Interest earned on program income pending its disposition. Grantees or State recipients are not authorized to deduct costs incident to the generation or management of income from gross income for purposes of determining program income. Governmental fees and taxes, including income taxes, property taxes, special assessments, transfer taxes, recording fees and other normal governmental revenues, do not constitute program income if they are imposed by generally applicable law, regulation, or ordinance and are not imposed in consideration of the project's receipt of assistance under this part. Program income also does not include grant amounts required to be returned to HUD as a result of cancellation of a project before completion, or interest on those grant amounts, or any interest earned by the grantee or State recipient or grant funds after drawdown and before disbursement for eligible costs. (For disposition of such interest, see 24 CFR 85.21(i).)

(c) *Eligible uses.* Program income may be used only as prescribed in paragraphs (c)(1) and (c)(2) of this section.

(1) Program income may be used for any activity which is eligible under this part, except that program income may not be used to pay for administrative costs, as described at § 511.71. In particular, the total of rental rehabilitation grant amounts and Rental Rehabilitation Program income used for any project (except under § 511.76(c)(2)) may not exceed the amount per unit allowed under § 511.11(e)(2) or 50 percent of the total eligible project costs (except as noted in § 511.11(e)(1)).

(2) Program income may also be used to provide rental assistance to lower income tenants in properties rehabilitated through the RRP. This includes the use of program income to pay for administrative costs associated with the provision of rental assistance but not to exceed the amount allowed for administrative fees in the Housing Voucher Program authorized under section 8(o) of the United States Housing Act of 1937, 42 U.S.C. 1437f. In order to use program income for rental assistance, the grantee or State recipient must—

(i) Use the funds to assist low-income tenants who initially occupy properties rehabilitated with rental rehabilitation grant amounts or rental rehabilitation program income;

(ii) Have a written policy which is available to the public stating that program income will be so used and specifying who is eligible to receive such assistance; and

(iii) Have an agreement with the PHA stating that the PHA will utilize the program income to provide rental assistance in accordance with the written policy.

(d) *Timing the use of program income.* Grantees and State recipients shall not commit available rental rehabilitation grant amounts to specific local projects if sufficient program income is on hand and available to fund the project, or a substantial portion of the project. In order to avoid possible overcommitment of funds, grantees and State recipients shall not anticipate the receipt of program income and enter into binding commitments with owners cumulatively exceeding the total amount of program income on hand plus uncommitted rental rehabilitation grant amounts.

(e) *Accounting for and reporting program income.* Program income shall be accounted for and reported in the grantee's Annual Performance Report under § 511.81(b) and in the Cash and Management Information System under § 511.75, in the manner prescribed by HUD.

(f) *Authority of State grantees.* States administering rental rehabilitation grants have discretion to choose whether program income is to be earned at all or is to be paid to or retained by the State or paid to or retained by the State recipient. The State's determination should be contained in a written agreement between the State and its State recipients. However, once earned, program income must be used and accounted for in accordance with this section by the State or by the State recipient, as applicable.

(g) *Authority of urban counties.* Because the configuration of an urban county may change from time to time, particularly at the time of requalification of an urban county in the Community Development Block Grant program, special provisions must be made for urban county program income. The urban county may determine whether program income generated by a project located in a unit of general local government which, for whatever reason, no longer participates in the urban county shall be retained by the urban county for its RRP or by the unit of general local government. However, urban county program income must otherwise be used and accounted for by the urban county and the unit of general local government in accordance with this section.

(h) *Program closeout and disposition of program income.* Program income must be accounted for by the grantee when a Rental Rehabilitation Program is completely closed out for all years. Program "closeout" will occur when the following conditions have been met: All grant funds from all program years (excluding program income) have been expended; the grantee and, if applicable, its State recipients do not expect (or have elected not) to receive any additional rental rehabilitation grant amounts, and the annual performance report covering the last program year has been submitted to HUD. Program income shall be treated in the following manner before and after program closeout:

(1) Before program closeout, program income shall be used for activities eligible under § 511.76(c); and

(2) Program income on hand at the time of program closeout or earned after program closeout may be contributed to HOME or HOPE program grantees as a cash matching contribution in accordance with applicable HOME or HOPE program rules, or may be used for activities that would be eligible under other affordable housing activities, as determined by the recipient.

[55 FR 20050, May 14, 1990, as amended at 58 FR 52567, Oct. 8, 1993; 61 FR 7062, Feb. 23, 1996]

§ 511.77 Grant closeout.

(a) Each individual fiscal year rental rehabilitation grant will be closed out when all grant amounts for the grant to be closed out have been drawn down and expended for completed projects and/or administrative costs, or grant amounts not drawn down and expended have been deobligated by HUD.

(b) Project Completion Reports for all projects utilizing grant amounts from the fiscal year grant(s) to be closed out have been submitted and entered into the C/MI System.

(c) The required reviews and audits to determine whether grantees have satisfied the terms of their grant agreement have been made. Closeout is contingent upon the receipt of the grantee's most recent audit report and audit reports of State recipients, where applicable. For closeout of the grant to proceed, the most recent audit report(s) must be free of any outstanding findings related to the RRP grant to be closed. The audit(s) of the grantee and State recipients, where applicable, should cover all grant amounts from all fiscal years which are to be closed out except as noted in paragraph (c)(2) of this section.

(1) The Single Audit Act prohibits requiring a grantee or State recipient to obtain an audit at its expense covering

only the Rental Rehabilitation Program. (HUD still has the authority to conduct an audit or to contract with an independent public accountant to conduct an audit of the grant. However, HUD must pay for the audit.)

(2) When the previous audit(s) fail to cover all grant amounts under the Grant Agreement, the program may still be closed out, provided the grantee agrees in writing to remit to HUD any costs questioned by a subsequent audit that are disallowed by HUD. This procedure is expected to be used in those cases when both the grantee and HUD want to proceed with the closeout before the next periodic single audit is conducted covering the remaining grant amounts not already audited.

(d) With respect to monitoring the grantee, either:

(1) The HUD Field Office has conducted an on-site monitoring of the grantee and has determined that the grantee's performance, with respect to any grant to be closed out, is satisfactory and is in compliance with Rental Rehabilitation program statutory and regulatory requirements, including §511.10(a) and §511.10(b); or

(2) A grant may be closed before on-site monitoring has been conducted, provided:

(i) The Cash and Management Information reports indicate the grantee's performance is satisfactory and is in compliance with Rental Rehabilitation program statutory and regulatory requirements;

(ii) There are no outstanding monitoring findings; and

(iii) The grantee agrees in writing to pay back the amount of any costs that are later found by HUD to be ineligible based on a subsequent on-site monitoring review or audit.

(Approved by the Office of Management and Budget under control number 2506–0080)

[55 FR 20050, May 14, 1990, as amended at 58 FR 52567, Oct. 8, 1993; 61 FR 7062, Feb. 23, 1996]

Subpart I—Grantee Performance: Review, Reporting and Corrective or Remedial Actions

§511.80 Performance review.

(a) *General.* HUD will review the performance of grantees in carrying out their responsibilities under this part whenever determined necessary by HUD, but at least annually. In conducting performance reviews, HUD will rely primarily on information obtained from the grantee's and, as appropriate, the State recipient's records and reports, findings from on-site monitoring, audit reports, and information generated from the C/MI System. Where applicable, HUD may also consider relevant information pertaining to a grantee's or State recipient's performance gained from other sources, including citizen comments, complaint determinations and litigation. Reviews to determine compliance with specific requirements of this part will be conducted as necessary, with or without prior notice to the grantee or State recipient. Comprehensive performance reviews under the standards in §511.80(b) will be conducted after prior notice to the grantee.

(b) *Standards for comprehensive performance review.* Grantee performance shall be comprehensively reviewed periodically, as prescribed by HUD, to determine:

(1) For grantees that are units of general local government or States administering their own rental rehabilitation grant programs, whether the grantee:

(i) Has carried out its activities in a timely manner, including the commitment of rental rehabilitation grant amounts to specific local projects in accordance with the schedule contained in its Program Description, as provided in §511.20(b)(8), and the completion of projects in accordance with §511.11(a);

(ii) Has carried out its activities in accordance with the requirements of this part; and

(iii) Has a continuing capacity to carry out its activities in accordance with this part and in a timely and cost-effective manner; or

(2) For grantees that are States distributing rental rehabilitation grant

amounts to State recipients, whether the State:

(i) Has distributed these grant amounts in a timely manner and in accordance with the requirements of this part; and

(ii) Has made such reviews and audits of its recipients as may be appropriate to determine whether they have satisfied the requirements of paragraph (b)(1)(i) through (b)(1)(iii) of this section.

[55 FR 20050, May 14, 1990, as amended at 61 FR 7062, Feb. 23, 1996]

§ 511.81 Grantee reports to HUD.

(a) *Management reports.* Grantees shall submit management reports on their Rental Rehabilitation Program in such format and at such time as HUD may prescribe.

(b) [Reserved]

(Approved by the Office of Management and Budget under control number 2506–0080)

[55 FR 20050, May 14, 1990, as amended at 61 FR 7062, Feb. 23, 1996]

§ 511.82 Corrective and remedial actions.

(a) *General.* HUD will use the procedures in this section in conducting the performance review as provided in § 511.80(a) and in taking corrective and remedial actions.

(b) *Performance review.* (1) If HUD determines preliminarily that the grantee has not met the performance review standards in § 511.80, the grantee will be given notice of this determination and an opportunity to demonstrate, within the time prescribed by HUD and on the basis of substantial facts and data, that it has done so.

(2) If the grantee fails to demonstrate to HUD's satisfaction that it has met the performance review standards in § 511.80, HUD will take appropriate corrective or remedial action in accordance with this section.

(c) *Corrective and remedial actions.* In formulating appropriate corrective or remedial actions for performance deficiencies, HUD will take one or more of the actions specified in paragraphs (c)(1), (c)(2), and (c)(3) of this section. The action chosen will be designed to prevent a continuation of the deficiency; mitigate, to the extent possible, its adverse effects or consequences; and prevent its recurrence. In addition to these actions, HUD will take the action specified in paragraph (c)(4) of this section, when paragraph (c)(4) of this section is applicable.

(1) HUD may request the grantee to submit and comply with proposals for action to correct, mitigate and prevent performance deficiencies, including:

(i) Preparing and following a schedule of actions for carrying out the affected rental rehabilitation activities, consisting of schedules, timetables and milestones necessary to implement the affected activities;

(ii) Establishing and following a management plan that assigns responsibilities for carrying out the remedial actions;

(iii) Cancelling or revising activities likely to be affected by a performance deficiency, before expending grant amounts for the activities;

(iv) Reprogramming rental rehabilitation grant amounts that have not yet been expended from affected activities to other eligible activities; and

(v) Suspending disbursement of grant amounts for affected activities for a period of not more than 60 days.

(2) [Reserved]

(3) When HUD determines that a grantee has failed to meet one or more of the requirements of this part, HUD may reduce or withdraw rental rehabilitation grant amounts, or take other action as appropriate, except that rental rehabilitation grant amounts already expended on eligible activities will not be recaptured from existing grant allocations or obligations or deducted from future grants made available to the grantee. For purposes of paragraph (c)(3) of this section—

(i) *Grant amounts already expended on eligible activities* includes all grant amounts that have been disbursed under this part for eligible activities, and

(ii) *Other action as appropriate* means any remedial action legally available, including, without limitation, affirmative litigation, such as suits for declaratory judgment, specific performance, temporary or permanent injunctions, and any other available remedies other than those for recovery of money.

§ 511.82

(4) Where HUD makes a final determination that it has a judicially enforceable claim for money against the grantee in a situation where rental rehabilitation grant amounts have been disbursed to the grantee or State recipient for ineligible costs under this part, HUD will follow the procedures described in the Federal Claims Collection Standards (4 CFR parts 101–105) in order to:

(i) Demand in writing that the grantee or State recipient reimburse HUD in the amount of the ineligible costs, using funds from non-federally derived sources; and

(ii) Initiate affirmative litigation to recover the amount of the ineligible costs, if necessary for collection. HUD's final determination to seek recovery of grant amounts expended on ineligible costs under paragraph (c)(4) of this section shall constitute a claim within the meaning of 31 U.S.C. 3711, *et seq.*, and interest shall be charged on delinquent claims as required by the Federal Claims Collection Standards.

(d) Amounts recovered under paragraph (c)(4) of this section are not rental rehabilitation grant amounts and shall be deposited in the U.S. Treasury's miscellaneous receipts account.

[55 FR 20050, May 14, 1990, as amended at 61 FR 7062, Feb. 23, 1996]

SUBCHAPTER B [RESERVED]

SUBCHAPTER C—COMMUNITY FACILITIES

PART 570—COMMUNITY DEVELOPMENT BLOCK GRANTS

Subpart A—General Provisions

Sec.
570.1 Purpose and primary objective.
570.3 Definitions.
570.4 Allocation of funds.
570.5 Waivers.

Subpart B [Reserved]

Subpart C—Eligible Activities

570.200 General policies.
570.201 Basic eligible activities.
570.202 Eligible rehabilitation and preservation activities.
570.203 Special economic development activities.
570.204 Special activities by Community-Based Development Organizations (CBDOs).
570.205 Eligible planning, urban environmental design and policy-planning-management-capacity building activities.
570.206 Program administrative costs.
570.207 Ineligible activities.
570.208 Criteria for national objectives.
570.209 Guidelines for evaluating and selecting economic development projects.
570.210 Prohibition on use of assistance for employment relocation activities.

Subpart D—Entitlement Grants

570.300 General.
570.301 Activity locations and float-funding.
570.302 Submission requirements.
570.303 Certifications.
570.304 Making of grants.
570.307 Urban counties.
570.308 Joint requests.
570.309 Restriction on location of activities.

Subpart E—Special Purpose Grants

570.400 General.
570.401 Community adjustment and economic diversification planning assistance.
570.402 Technical assistance awards.
570.403 New Communities.
570.404 Historically Black colleges and universities program.
570.405 The insular areas.
570.406 Formula miscalculation grants.
570.410 Special Projects Program.
570.411 Joint Community Development Program.
570.415 Community Development Work Study Program.
570.416 Hispanic-serving institutions work study program.

Subpart F—Small Cities, Non-Entitlement CDBG Grants in Hawaii and Insular Areas Programs

570.420 General.
570.421 New York Small Cities Program design.
570.422-4.25 [Reserved]
570.426 Program income.
570.427 Program amendments.
570.428 [Reserved]
570.429 Hawaii general and grant requirements.
570.431 Citizen participation.
570.440 Application requirements for insular area grants funded under section 106.
570.441 Citizen participation—insular areas.
570.442 Reallocations-Insular Areas.

Subpart G—Urban Development Action Grants

570.450 Purpose.
570.456 Ineligible activities and limitations on eligible activities.
570.457 Displacement, relocation, acquisition, and replacement of housing.
570.461 Post-preliminary approval requirements; lead-based paint.
570.463 Project amendments and revisions.
570.464 Project closeout.
570.465 Applicability of rules and regulations.
570.466 Additional application submission requirements for Pockets of Poverty—employment opportunities.

Subpart H [Reserved]

Subpart I—State Community Development Block Grant Program

570.480 General.
570.481 Definitions.
570.482 Eligible activities.
570.483 Criteria for national objectives.
570.484 Overall benefit to low and moderate income persons.
570.485 Making of grants.
570.486 Local government requirements.
570.487 Other applicable laws and related program requirements.
570.488 Displacement, relocation, acquisition, and replacement of housing.
570.489 Program administrative requirements.
570.490 Recordkeeping requirements.
570.491 Performance and evaluation report.
570.492 State's reviews and audits.
570.493 HUD's reviews and audits.

§ 570.1

570.494 Timely distribution of funds by states.
570.495 Reviews and audits response.
570.496 Remedies for noncompliance; opportunity for hearing.
570.497 Condition of State election to administer State CDBG Program.

Subpart J—Grant Administration

570.500 Definitions.
570.501 Responsibility for grant administration.
570.502 Applicability of uniform administrative requirements.
570.503 Agreements with subrecipients.
570.504 Program income.
570.505 Use of real property.
570.506 Records to be maintained.
570.507 Reports.
570.508 Public access to program records.
570.509 Grant closeout procedures.
570.510 Transferring projects from urban counties to metropolitan cities.
570.511 Use of escrow accounts for rehabilitation of privately owned residential property.
570.512 [Reserved]
570.513 Lump sum drawdown for financing of property rehabilitation activities.

Subpart K—Other Program Requirements

570.600 General.
570.601 Public Law 88-352 and Public Law 90-284; affirmatively furthering fair housing; Executive Order 11063.
570.602 Section 109 of the Act.
570.603 Labor standards.
570.604 Environmental standards.
570.605 National Flood Insurance Program.
570.606 Displacement, relocation, acquisition, and replacement of housing.
570.607 Employment and contracting opportunities.
570.608 Lead-based paint.
570.609 Use of debarred, suspended or ineligible contractors or subrecipients.
570.610 Uniform administrative requirements and cost principles.
570.611 Conflict of interest.
570.612 Executive Order 12372.
570.613 Eligibility restrictions for certain resident aliens.
570.614 Architectural Barriers Act and the Americans with Disabilities Act.

Subpart L [Reserved]

Subpart M—Loan Guarantees

570.700 Purpose.
570.701 Definitions.
570.702 Eligible applicants.
570.703 Eligible activities.
570.704 Application requirements.
570.705 Loan requirements.
570.706 Federal guarantee; subrogation.

570.707 Applicability of rules and regulations.
570.708 Sanctions.
570.709 Allocation of loan guarantee assistance.
570.710 State responsibilities.

Subpart N—Urban Renewal Provisions

570.800 Urban renewal regulations.

Subpart O—Performance Reviews

570.900 General.
570.901 Review for compliance with the primary and national objectives and other program requirements.
570.902 Review to determine if CDBG funded activities are being carried out in a timely manner.
570.903 Review to determine if the recipient is meeting its consolidated plan responsibilities.
570.904 Equal opportunity and fair housing review criteria.
570.905 Review of continuing capacity to carry out CDBG funded activities in a timely manner.
570.906 Review of urban counties.
570.907-570.909 [Reserved]
570.910 Corrective and remedial actions.
570.911 Reduction, withdrawal, or adjustment of a grant or other appropriate action.
570.912 Nondiscrimination compliance.
570.913 Other remedies for noncompliance.

APPENDIX A TO PART 570—GUIDELINES AND OBJECTIVES FOR EVALUATING PROJECT COSTS AND FINANCIAL REQUIREMENTS

AUTHORITY: 42 U.S.C. 3535(d) and 5301-5320.

SOURCE: 40 FR 24693, June 9, 1975, unless otherwise noted.

Subpart A—General Provisions

SOURCE: 53 FR 34437, Sept. 6, 1988, unless otherwise noted.

§ 570.1 **Purpose and primary objective.**

(a) This part describes policies and procedures applicable to the following programs authorized under title I of the Housing and Community Development Act of 1974, as amended:

(1) Entitlement grants program (subpart D);

(2) Nonentitlement Funds: HUD-administered Small Cities and Insular Area programs (subpart F);

(3) State program: State-administered CDBG nonentitlement funds (subpart I);

(4) Special Purpose Grants (subpart E);
(5) Urban Development Action Grant program (subpart G); and
(6) Loan Guarantees (subpart M).

(b) Subparts A, C, J, K, and O apply to all programs in paragraph (a) except as modified or limited under the provisions of these subparts or the applicable program regulations. In the application of the subparts to Special Purpose Grants or the Urban Development Action Grant program, the reference to funds in the form of grants in the term *"CDBG funds"*, as defined in §570.3, shall mean the grant funds under those programs. The subparts do not apply to the State program (subpart I) except to the extent expressly referred to.

(c) The primary objective of the programs authorized under title I of the Housing and Community Development Act of 1974, as amended, is described in section 101(c) of the Act (42 U.S.C. 5301(c)).

[53 FR 34437, Sept. 6, 1988, as amended at 56 FR 56126, Oct. 31, 1991; 61 FR 11475, Mar. 20, 1996; 69 FR 32778, June 10, 2004]

§570.3 Definitions.

The terms *HUD* and *Secretary* are defined in 24 CFR part 5. All of the following definitions in this section that rely on data from the United States Bureau of the Census shall rely upon the data available from the latest decennial census.

Act means title I of the Housing and Community Development Act of 1974 as amended (42 U.S.C. 5301 et seq.).

Age of housing means the number of year-round housing units, as further defined in section 102(a)(11) of the Act.

Applicant means a State or unit of general local government that makes application pursuant to the provisions of subpart E, F, G or M.

Buildings for the general conduct of government shall have the meaning provided in section 102(a)(21) of the Act.

CDBG funds means Community Development Block Grant funds, including funds received in the form of grants under subpart D, F, or §570.405 of this part, funds awarded under section 108(q) of the Housing and Community Development Act of 1974, loans guaranteed under subpart M of this part, urban renewal surplus grant funds, and program income as defined in §570.500(a).

Chief executive officer of a State or unit of general local government means the elected official or the legally designated official, who has the primary responsibility for the conduct of that entity's governmental affairs. Examples of the "chief executive officer" of a unit of general local government are: the elected mayor of a municipality; the elected county executive of a county; the chairperson of a county commission or board in a county that has no elected county executive; and the official designated pursuant to law by the governing body of a unit of general local government.

City means the following:
(1) For purposes of Entitlement Community Development Block Grant and Urban Development Action Grant eligibility:
(i) Any unit of general local government that is classified as a municipality by the United States Bureau of the Census, or
(ii) Any other unit of general local government that is a town or township and that, in the determination of the Secretary:
(A) Possesses powers and performs functions comparable to those associated with municipalities;
(B) Is closely settled (except that the Secretary may reduce or waive this requirement on a case by case basis for the purposes of the Action Grant program); and
(C) Contains within its boundaries no incorporated places as defined by the United States Bureau of the Census that have not entered into cooperation agreements with the town or township for a period covering at least 3 years to undertake or assist in the undertaking of essential community development and housing assistance activities. The determination of eligibility of a town or township to qualify as a city will be based on information available from the United States Bureau of the Census and information provided by the town or township and its included units of general local government.
(2) For purposes of Urban Development Action Grant eligibility only, Guam, the Virgin Islands, American Samoa, the Commonwealth of the

Northern Mariana Islands, the counties of Kauai, Maui, and Hawaii in the State of Hawaii, and Indian tribes that are eligible recipients under the State and Local Government Fiscal Assistance Act of 1972 and located on reservations in Oklahoma as determined by the Secretary of the Interior or in Alaskan Native Villages.

Community Development Financial Institution has the same meaning as used in the Community Development Banking and Financial Institutions Act of 1994 (12 U.S.C. 4701 note).

Consolidated plan. The plan prepared in accordance with 24 CFR part 91, which describes needs, resources, priorities and proposed activities to be undertaken with respect to HUD programs, including the CDBG program. An approved consolidated plan means a consolidated plan that has been approved by HUD in accordance with 24 CFR part 91.

Discretionary grant means a grant made from the various Special Purpose Grants in accordance with subpart E of this part.

Entitlement amount means the amount of funds which a metropolitan city is entitled to receive under the Entitlement grant program, as determined by formula set forth in section 106 of the Act.

Extent of growth lag shall have the meaning provided in section 102(a)(12) of the Act.

Extent of housing overcrowding shall have the meaning provided in section 102(a)(10) of the Act.

Extent of poverty means the number of persons whose incomes are below the poverty level based on data compiled and published by the United States Bureau of the Census available from the latest census referable to the same point or period in time and the latest reports from the Office of Management and Budget. For purposes of this part, the Secretary has determined that it is neither feasible nor appropriate to make adjustments at this time in the computations of "extent of poverty" for regional or area variations in income and cost of living.

Family means all persons living in the same household who are related by birth, marriage or adoption.

Household means all the persons who occupy a housing unit. The occupants may be a single family, one person living alone, two or more families living together, or any other group of related or unrelated persons who share living arrangements.

Income. For the purpose of determining whether a family or household is low- and moderate-income under subpart C of this part, grantees may select any of the three definitions listed below for each activity, except that integrally related activities of the same type and qualifying under the same paragraph of §570.208(a) shall use the same definition of income. The option to choose a definition does not apply to activities that qualify under §570.208(a)(1) (Area benefit activities), except when the recipient carries out a survey under §570.208(a)(1)(vi). Activities qualifying under §570.208(a)(1) generally must use the area income data supplied to recipients by HUD. The three definitions are as follows:

(1)(i) "Annual income" as defined under the Section 8 Housing Assistance Payments program at 24 CFR 813.106 (except that if the CDBG assistance being provided is homeowner rehabilitation under §570.202, the value of the homeowner's primary residence may be excluded from any calculation of Net Family Assets); or

(ii) Annual income as reported under the Census long-form for the most recent available decennial Census. This definition includes:

(A) Wages, salaries, tips, commissions, etc.;

(B) Self-employment income from own nonfarm business, including proprietorships and partnerships;

(C) Farm self-employment income;

(D) Interest, dividends, net rental income, or income from estates or trusts;

(E) Social Security or railroad retirement;

(F) Supplemental Security Income, Aid to Families with Dependent Children, or other public assistance or public welfare programs;

(G) Retirement, survivor, or disability pensions; and

(H) Any other sources of income received regularly, including Veterans' (VA) payments, unemployment compensation, and alimony; or

(iii) Adjusted gross income as defined for purposes of reporting under Internal Revenue Service (IRS) Form 1040 for individual Federal annual income tax purposes.

(2) Estimate the annual income of a family or household by projecting the prevailing rate of income of each person at the time assistance is provided for the individual, family, or household (as applicable). Estimated annual income shall include income from all family or household members, as applicable. Income or asset enhancement derived from the CDBG-assisted activity shall not be considered in calculating estimated annual income.

Insular area shall have the meaning provided in section 102(a)(24) of the Act.

Low- and moderate-income household means a household having an income equal to or less than the Section 8 low-income limit established by HUD.

Low- and moderate-income person means a member of a family having an income equal to or less than the Section 8 low-income limit established by HUD. Unrelated individuals will be considered as one-person families for this purpose.

Low-income household means a household having an income equal to or less than the Section 8 very low-income limit established by HUD.

Low-income person means a member of a family that has an income equal to or less than the Section 8 very low-income limit established by HUD. Unrelated individuals shall be considered as one-person families for this purpose.

Metropolitan area shall have the meaning provided in section 102(a)(3) of the Act.

Metropolitan city shall have the meaning provided in section 102(a)(4) of the Act except that the term "central city" is replaced by "principal city."

Microenterprise shall have the meaning provided in section 102(a)(22) of the Act.

Moderate-income household means a household having an income equal to or less than the Section 8 low-income limit and greater than the Section 8 very low-income limit, established by HUD.

Moderate-income person means a member of a family that has an income equal to or less than the Section 8 low-income limit and greater than the Section 8 very low-income limit, established by HUD. Unrelated individuals shall be considered as one-person families for this purpose.

Nonentitlement amount means the amount of funds which is allocated for use in a State's nonentitlement areas as determined by formula set forth in section 106 of the Act.

Nonentitlement area shall have the meaning provided in section 102(a)(7) of the Act.

Population means the total resident population based on data compiled and published by the United States Bureau of the Census available from the latest census or which has been upgraded by the Bureau to reflect the changes resulting from the Boundary and Annexation Survey, new incorporations and consolidations of governments pursuant to §570.4, and which reflects, where applicable, changes resulting from the Bureau's latest population determination through its estimating technique using natural changes (birth and death) and net migration, and is referable to the same point or period in time.

Small business means a business that meets the criteria set forth in section 3(a) of the Small Business Act (15 U.S.C. 631, 636, 637).

State shall have the meaning provided in section 102(a)(2) of the Act.

Unit of general local government shall have the meaning provided in section 102(a)(1) of the Act.

Urban county shall have the meaning provided in section 102(a)(6) of the Act. For the purposes of this definition, HUD will determine whether the county's combined population contains the required percentage of low- and moderate-income persons by identifying the number of persons that resided in applicable areas and units of general local government based on data from the most recent decennial census, and using income limits that would have applied for the year in which that census was taken.

Urban Development Action Grant (UDAG) means a grant made by the

§ 570.4

Secretary pursuant to section 119 of the Act and subpart G of this part.

[53 FR 34437, Sept. 6, 1988; 53 FR 41330, Oct. 21, 1988, as amended at 56 FR 56126, Oct. 31, 1991; 60 FR 1915, 1943, Jan. 5, 1995; 60 FR 56909, Nov. 9, 1995; 61 FR 5209, Feb. 9, 1996; 61 FR 11475, Mar. 20, 1996; 61 FR 18674, Apr. 29, 1996; 68 FR 69582, Dec. 12, 2003; 69 FR 32778, June 10, 2004]

§ 570.4 Allocation of funds.

(a) The determination of eligibility of units of general local government to receive entitlement grants, the entitlement amounts, the allocation of appropriated funds to States for use in nonentitlement areas, the reallocation of funds, the allocation of appropriated funds to insular areas, and the allocation of appropriated funds for discretionary grants under the Secretary's Fund shall be governed by the policies and procedures described in sections 106 and 107 of the Act, as appropriate.

(b) The definitions in § 570.3 shall govern in applying the policies and procedures described in sections 106 and 107 of the Act.

(c) In determining eligibility for entitlement and in allocating funds under section 106 of the Act for any federal fiscal year, HUD will recognize corporate status and geographical boundaries and the status of metropolitan areas and principal cities effective as of July 1 preceding such federal fiscal year, subject to the following limitations:

(1) With respect to corporate status as certified by the applicable State and available for processing by the Census Bureau as of such date;

(2) With respect to boundary changes or annexations, as are used by the Census Bureau in preparing population estimates for all general purpose governmental units and are available for processing by the Census Bureau as of such date, except that any such boundary changes or annexations which result in the population of a unit of general local government reaching or exceeding 50,000 shall be recognized for this purpose whether or not such changes are used by the Census Bureau in preparing such population estimates; and

(3) With respect to the status of Metropolitan Statistical Areas and principal cities, as officially designated by the Office of Management and Budget as of such date.

(d) In determining whether a county qualifies as an urban county, and in computing entitlement amounts for urban counties, the demographic values of population, poverty, housing overcrowding, and age of housing of any Indian tribes located within the county shall be excluded. In allocating amounts to States for use in nonentitlement areas, the demographic values of population, poverty, housing overcrowding and age of housing of all Indian tribes located in all nonentitled areas shall be excluded. It is recognized that all such data on Indian tribes are not generally available from the United States Bureau of the Census and that missing portions of data will have to be estimated. In accomplishing any such estimates the Secretary may use such other related information available from reputable sources as may seem appropriate, regardless of the data's point or period of time and shall use the best judgement possible in adjusting such data to reflect the same point or period of time as the overall data from which the Indian tribes are being deducted, so that such deduction shall not create an imbalance with those overall data.

(e) Amounts remaining after closeout of a grant which are required to be returned to HUD under the provisions of § 570.509, Grant closeout procedures, shall be considered as funds available for reallocation unless the appropriation under which the funds were provided to the Department has lapsed.

[53 FR 34437, Sept. 6, 1988, as amended at 68 FR 69582, Dec. 12, 2003; 69 FR 32778, June 10, 2004]

§ 570.5 Waivers.

HUD's authority for the waiver of regulations and for the suspension of requirements to address damage in a Presidentially declared disaster area is described in 24 CFR part 5 and in section 122 of the Act, respectively.

[61 FR 11476, Mar. 20, 1996]

Subpart B [Reserved]

Ofc. of Asst. Secy., Comm. Planning, Develop., HUD §570.200

Subpart C—Eligible Activities

SOURCE: 53 FR 34439, Sept. 6, 1988, unless otherwise noted.

§570.200 General policies.

(a) *Determination of eligibility.* An activity may be assisted in whole or in part with CDBG funds only if all of the following requirements are met:

(1) *Compliance with section 105 of the Act.* Each activity must meet the eligibility requirements of section 105 of the Act as further defined in this subpart.

(2) *Compliance with national objectives.* Grant recipients under the Entitlement and HUD-administered Small Cities programs and recipients of insular area funds under section 106 of the Act must certify that their projected use of funds has been developed so as to give maximum feasible priority to activities which will carry out one of the national objectives of benefit to low- and moderate-income families or aid in the prevention or elimination of slums or blight. The projected use of funds may also include activities that the recipient certifies are designed to meet other community development needs having a particular urgency because existing conditions pose a serious and immediate threat to the health or welfare of the community where other financial resources are not available to meet such needs. Consistent with the foregoing, each recipient under the Entitlement or HUD-administered Small Cities programs, and each recipient of insular area funds under section 106 of the Act must ensure and maintain evidence that each of its activities assisted with CDBG funds meets one of the three national objectives as contained in its certification. Criteria for determining whether an activity addresses one or more of these objectives are found in §570.208.

(3) *Compliance with the primary objective.* The primary objective of the Act is described in section 101(c) of the Act. Consistent with this objective, entitlement recipients, non-entitlement CDBG grantees in Hawaii, and recipients of insular area funds under section 106 of the Act must ensure that, over a period of time specified in their certification not to exceed three years, not less than 70 percent of the aggregate of CDBG fund expenditures shall be for activities meeting the criteria under §570.208(a) or under §570.208(d)(5) or (6) for benefiting low- and moderate-income persons. For grants under section 107 of the Act, insular area recipients must meet this requirement for each separate grant. See §570.420(d)(3) for additional discussion of the primary objective requirement for insular areas funded under section 106 of the Act. The requirements for the HUD-administered Small Cities program in New York are at §570.420(d)(2). In determining the percentage of funds expended for such activities:

(i) Cost of administration and planning eligible under §570.205 and §570.206 will be assumed to benefit low and moderate income persons in the same proportion as the remainder of the CDBG funds and, accordingly shall be excluded from the calculation;

(ii) Funds deducted by HUD for repayment of urban renewal temporary loans pursuant to §570.802(b) shall be excluded;

(iii) Funds expended for the repayment of loans guaranteed under the provisions of subpart M shall also be excluded;

(iv) Funds expended for the acquisition, new construction or rehabilitation of property for housing that qualifies under §570.208(a)(3) shall be counted for this purpose but shall be limited to an amount determined by multiplying the total cost (including CDBG and non-CDBG costs) of the acquisition, construction or rehabilitation by the percent of units in such housing to be occupied by low and moderate income persons.

(v) Funds expended for any other activities qualifying under §570.208(a) shall be counted for this purpose in their entirety.

(4) *Compliance with environmental review procedures.* The environmental review procedures set forth at 24 CFR part 58 must be completed for each activity (or project as defined in 24 CFR part 58), as applicable.

(5) *Cost principles.* Costs incurred, whether charged on a direct or an indirect basis, must be in conformance

with OMB Circulars A–87, "Cost Principles for State, Local and Indian Tribal Governments"; A–122, "Cost Principles for Non-profit Organizations"; or A–21, "Cost Principles for Educational Institutions," as applicable.[1] All items of cost listed in Attachment B of these Circulars that require prior Federal agency approval are allowable without prior approval of HUD to the extent they comply with the general policies and principles stated in Attachment A of such circulars and are otherwise eligible under this subpart C, except for the following:

(i) Depreciation methods for fixed assets shall not be changed without HUD's specific approval or, if charged through a cost allocation plan, the Federal cognizant agency.

(ii) Fines and penalties (including punitive damages) are unallowable costs to the CDBG program.

(iii) Pre-award costs are limited to those authorized under paragraph (h) of this section.

(b) *Special policies governing facilities.* The following special policies apply to:

(1) *Facilities containing both eligible and ineligible uses.* A public facility otherwise eligible for assistance under the CDBG program may be provided with CDBG funds even if it is part of a multiple use building containing ineligible uses, if:

(i) The facility which is otherwise eligible and proposed for assistance will occupy a designated and discrete area within the larger facility; and

(ii) The recipient can determine the costs attributable to the facility proposed for assistance as separate and distinct from the overall costs of the multiple-use building and/or facility.

Allowable costs are limited to those attributable to the eligible portion of the building or facility.

(2) *Fees for use of facilities.* Reasonable fees may be charged for the use of the facilities assisted with CDBG funds, but charges such as excessive membership fees, which will have the effect of precluding low and moderate income persons from using the facilities, are not permitted.

(c) *Special assessments under the CDBG program.* The following policies relate to special assessments under the CDBG program:

(1) *Definition of special assessment.* The term "special assessment" means the recovery of the capital costs of a public improvement, such as streets, water or sewer lines, curbs, and gutters, through a fee or charge levied or filed as a lien against a parcel of real estate as a direct result of benefit derived from the installation of a public improvement, or a one-time charge made as a condition of access to a public improvement. This term does not relate to taxes, or the establishment of the value of real estate for the purpose of levying real estate, property, or ad valorem taxes, and does not include periodic charges based on the use of a public improvement, such as water or sewer user charges, even if such charges include the recovery of all or some portion of the capital costs of the public improvement.

(2) *Special assessments to recover capital costs.* Where CDBG funds are used to pay all or part of the cost of a public improvement, special assessments may be imposed as follows:

(i) Special assessments to recover the CDBG funds may be made only against properties owned and occupied by persons not of low and moderate income. Such assessments constitute program income.

(ii) Special assessments to recover the non-CDBG portion may be made provided that CDBG funds are used to pay the special assessment in behalf of all properties owned and occupied by low and moderate income persons; except that CDBG funds need not be used to pay the special assessments in behalf of properties owned and occupied by moderate income persons if the grant recipient certifies that it does not have sufficient CDBG funds to pay the assessments in behalf of all of the low and moderate income owner-occupant persons. Funds collected through such special assessments are not program income.

(3) *Public improvements not initially assisted with CDBG funds.* The payment of special assessments with CDBG funds

---

[1] These circulars are available from the American Communities Center by calling the following toll-free numbers: (800) 998–9999 or (800) 483–2209 (TDD).

Ofc. of Asst. Secy., Comm. Planning, Develop., HUD §570.200

constitutes CDBG assistance to the public improvement. Therefore, CDBG funds may be used to pay special assessments provided:

(i) The installation of the public improvements was carried out in compliance with requirements applicable to activities assisted under this part including environmental, citizen participation and Davis-Bacon requirements;

(ii) The installation of the public improvement meets a criterion for national objectives in §570.208(a)(1), (b), or (c); and

(iii) The requirements of §570.200(c)(2)(ii) are met.

(d) *Consultant activities.* Consulting services are eligible for assistance under this part for professional assistance in program planning, development of community development objectives, and other general professional guidance relating to program execution. The use of consultants is governed by the following:

(1) *Employer-employee type of relationship.* No person providing consultant services in an employer-employee type of relationship shall receive more than a reasonable rate of compensation for personal services paid with CDBG funds. In no event, however, shall such compensation exceed the equivalent of the daily rate paid for Level IV of the Executive Schedule. Such services shall be evidenced by written agreements between the parties which detail the responsibilities, standards, and compensation.

(2) *Independent contractor relationship.* Consultant services provided under an independent contractor relationship are governed by the procurement requirements in 24 CFR 85.36, and are not subject to the compensation limitation of Level IV of the Executive Schedule.

(e) *Recipient determinations required as a condition of eligibility.* In several instances under this subpart, the eligibility of an activity depends on a special local determination. Recipients shall maintain documentation of all such determinations. A written determination is required for any activity carried out under the authority of §§570.201(f), 570.201(i)(2), 570.201(p), 570.201(q), 570.202(b)(3), 570.206(f), 570.209, 570.210, and 570.309.

(f) *Means of carrying out eligible activities.* (1) Activities eligible under this subpart, other than those authorized under §570.204(a), may be undertaken, subject to local law:

(i) By the recipient through:

(A) Its employees, or

(B) Procurement contracts governed by the requirements of 24 CFR 85.36; or

(ii) Through loans or grants under agreements with subrecipients, as defined at §570.500(c); or

(iii) By one or more public agencies, including existing local public agencies, that are designated by the chief executive officer of the recipient.

(2) Activities made eligible under §570.204(a) may only be undertaken by entities specified in that section.

(g) *Limitation on planning and administrative costs.* No more than 20 percent of the sum of any grant, plus program income, shall be expended for planning and program administrative costs, as defined in §§570.205 and 507.206, respectively. Recipients of entitlement grants under subpart D of this part shall conform with this requirement by limiting the amount of CDBG funds obligated for planning plus administration during each program year to an amount no greater than 20 percent of the sum of its entitlement grant made for that program year (if any) plus the program income received by the recipient and its subrecipients (if any) during that program year.

(h) *Reimbursement for pre-award costs.* The effective date of the grant agreement is the program year start date or the date that the consolidated plan is received by HUD, whichever is later. For a Section 108 loan guarantee, the effective date of the grant agreement is the date of HUD execution of the grant agreement amendment for the particular loan guarantee commitment.

(1) Prior to the effective date of the grant agreement, a recipient may incur costs or may authorize a subrecipient to incur costs, and then after the effective date of the grant agreement pay for those costs using its CDBG funds, provided that:

(i) The activity for which the costs are being incurred is included, prior to the costs being incurred, in a consolidated plan action plan, an amended

§ 570.200

consolidated plan action plan, or an application under subpart M of this part, except that a new entitlement grantee preparing to receive its first allocation of CDBG funds may incur costs necessary to develop its consolidated plan and undertake other administrative actions necessary to receive its first grant, prior to the costs being included in its consolidated plan;

(ii) Citizens are advised of the extent to which these pre-award costs will affect future grants;

(iii) The costs and activities funded are in compliance with the requirements of this part and with the Environmental Review Procedures stated in 24 CFR part 58;

(iv) The activity for which payment is being made complies with the statutory and regulatory provisions in effect at the time the costs are paid for with CDBG funds;

(v) CDBG payment will be made during a time no longer than the next two program years following the effective date of the grant agreement or amendment in which the activity is first included; and

(vi) The total amount of pre-award costs to be paid during any program year pursuant to this provision is no more than the greater of 25 percent of the amount of the grant made for that year or $300,000.

(2) Upon the written request of the recipient, HUD may authorize payment of pre-award costs for activities that do not meet the criteria at paragraph (h)(1)(v) or (h)(1)(vi) of this section, if HUD determines, in writing, that there is good cause for granting an exception upon consideration of the following factors, as applicable:

(i) Whether granting the authority would result in a significant contribution to the goals and purposes of the CDBG program;

(ii) Whether failure to grant the authority would result in undue hardship to the recipient or beneficiaries of the activity;

(iii) Whether granting the authority would not result in a violation of a statutory provision or any other regulatory provision;

(iv) Whether circumstances are clearly beyond the recipient's control; or

(v) Any other relevant considerations.

(i) *Urban Development Action Grant.* Grant assistance may be provided with Urban Development Action Grant funds, subject to the provisions of subpart G, for:

(1) Activities eligible for assistance under this subpart; and

(2) Notwithstanding the provisions of § 570.207, such other activities as the Secretary may determine to be consistent with the purposes of the Urban Development Action Grant program.

(j) *Faith-based activities.* (1) Organizations that are religious or faith-based are eligible, on the same basis as any other organization, to participate in the CDBG program. Neither the Federal government nor a State or local government receiving funds under CDBG programs shall discriminate against an organization on the basis of the organization's religious character or affiliation.

(2) Organizations that are directly funded under the CDBG program may not engage in inherently religious activities, such as worship, religious instruction, or proselytization, as part of the programs or services funded under this part. If an organization conducts such activities, the activities must be offered separately, in time or location, from the programs or services funded under this part, and participation must be voluntary for the beneficiaries of the HUD-funded programs or services.

(3) A religious organization that participates in the CDBG program will retain its independence from Federal, State, and local governments, and may continue to carry out its mission, including the definition, practice, and expression of its religious beliefs, provided that it does not use direct CDBG funds to support any inherently religious activities, such as worship, religious instruction, or proselytization. Among other things, faith-based organizations may use space in their facilities to provide CDBG-funded services, without removing religious art, icons, scriptures, or other religious symbols. In addition, a CDBG-funded religious organization retains its authority over its internal governance, and it may retain religious terms in its organization's name, select its board members

on a religious basis, and include religious references in its organization's mission statements and other governing documents.

(4) An organization that participates in the CDBG program shall not, in providing program assistance, discriminate against a program beneficiary or prospective program beneficiary on the basis of religion or religious belief.

(5) CDBG funds may not be used for the acquisition, construction, or rehabilitation of structures to the extent that those structures are used for inherently religious activities. CDBG funds may be used for the acquisition, construction, or rehabilitation of structures only to the extent that those structures are used for conducting eligible activities under this part. Where a structure is used for both eligible and inherently religious activities, CDBG funds may not exceed the cost of those portions of the acquisition, construction, or rehabilitation that are attributable to eligible activities in accordance with the cost accounting requirements applicable to CDBG funds in this part. Sanctuaries, chapels, or other rooms that a CDBG-funded religious congregation uses as its principal place of worship, however, are ineligible for CDBG-funded improvements. Disposition of real property after the term of the grant, or any change in use of the property during the term of the grant, is subject to government-wide regulations governing real property disposition (*see* 24 CFR parts 84 and 85).

(6) If a State or local government voluntarily contributes its own funds to supplement federally funded activities, the State or local government has the option to segregate the Federal funds or commingle them. However, if the funds are commingled, this section applies to all of the commingled funds.

[53 FR 34439, Sept. 6, 1988, as amended at 54 FR 47031, Nov. 8, 1989; 57 FR 27119, June 17, 1992; 60 FR 1943, Jan. 5, 1995; 60 FR 17445, Apr. 6, 1995; 60 FR 56910, Nov. 9, 1995; 61 FR 11476, Mar. 20, 1996; 61 FR 18674, Apr. 29, 1996; 65 FR 70215, Nov. 21, 2000; 68 FR 56404, Sept. 30, 2003; 69 FR 32778, June 10, 2004; 70 FR 76369, Dec. 23, 2005; 72 FR 46370, Aug. 17, 2007]

§ 570.201 Basic eligible activities.

CDBG funds may be used for the following activities:

(a) *Acquisition.* Acquisition in whole or in part by the recipient, or other public or private nonprofit entity, by purchase, long-term lease, donation, or otherwise, of real property (including air rights, water rights, rights-of-way, easements, and other interests therein) for any public purpose, subject to the limitations of § 570.207.

(b) *Disposition.* Disposition, through sale, lease, donation, or otherwise, of any real property acquired with CDBG funds or its retention for public purposes, including reasonable costs of temporarily managing such property or property acquired under urban renewal, provided that the proceeds from any such disposition shall be program income subject to the requirements set forth in § 570.504.

(c) *Public facilities and improvements.* Acquisition, construction, reconstruction, rehabilitation or installation of public facilities and improvements, except as provided in § 570.207(a), carried out by the recipient or other public or private nonprofit entities. (However, activities under this paragraph may be directed to the removal of material and architectural barriers that restrict the mobility and accessibility of elderly or severely disabled persons to public facilities and improvements, including those provided for in § 570.207(a)(1).) In undertaking such activities, design features and improvements which promote energy efficiency may be included. Such activities may also include the execution of architectural design features, and similar treatments intended to enhance the aesthetic quality of facilities and improvements receiving CDBG assistance, such as decorative pavements, railings, sculptures, pools of water and fountains, and other works of art. Facilities designed for use in providing shelter for persons having special needs are considered public facilities and not subject to the prohibition of new housing construction described in § 570.207(b)(3). Such facilities include shelters for the homeless; convalescent homes; hospitals, nursing homes; battered spouse shelters; halfway houses for run-away children, drug offenders or parolees; group homes for

§ 570.201

mentally retarded persons and temporary housing for disaster victims. In certain cases, nonprofit entities and subrecipients including those specified in § 570.204 may acquire title to public facilities. When such facilities are owned by nonprofit entities or subrecipients, they shall be operated so as to be open for use by the general public during all normal hours of operation. Public facilities and improvements eligible for assistance under this paragraph are subject to the policies in § 570.200(b).

(d) *Clearance and remediation activities.* Clearance, demolition, and removal of buildings and improvements, including movement of structures to other sites and remediation of known or suspected environmental contamination. Demolition of HUD-assisted or HUD-owned housing units may be undertaken only with the prior approval of HUD. Remediation may include project-specific environmental assessment costs not otherwise eligible under § 570.205.

(e) *Public services.* Provision of public services (including labor, supplies, and materials) including but not limited to those concerned with employment, crime prevention, child care, health, drug abuse, education, fair housing counseling, energy conservation, welfare (but excluding the provision of income payments identified under § 570.207(b)(4)), homebuyer downpayment assistance, or recreational needs. To be eligible for CDBG assistance, a public service must be either a new service or a quantifiable increase in the level of an existing service above that which has been provided by or on behalf of the unit of general local government (through funds raised by the unit or received by the unit from the State in which it is located) in the 12 calendar months before the submission of the action plan. (An exception to this requirement may be made if HUD determines that any decrease in the level of a service was the result of events not within the control of the unit of general local government.) The amount of CDBG funds used for public services shall not exceed paragraphs (e) (1) or (2) of this section, as applicable:

(1) The amount of CDBG funds used for public services shall not exceed 15 percent of each grant, except that for entitlement grants made under subpart D of this part, the amount shall not exceed 15 percent of the grant plus 15 percent of program income, as defined in § 570.500(a). For entitlement grants under subpart D of this part, compliance is based on limiting the amount of CDBG funds obligated for public service activities in each program year to an amount no greater than 15 percent of the entitlement grant made for that program year plus 15 percent of the program income received during the grantee's immediately preceding program year.

(2) A recipient which obligated more CDBG funds for public services than 15 percent of its grant funded from Federal fiscal year 1982 or 1983 appropriations (excluding program income and any assistance received under Public Law 98–8), may obligate more CDBG funds than allowable under paragraph (e)(1) of this section, so long as the total amount obligated in any program year does not exceed:

(i) For an entitlement grantee, 15% of the program income it received during the preceding program year; plus

(ii) A portion of the grant received for the program year which is the highest of the following amounts:

(A) The amount determined by applying the percentage of the grant it obligated for public services in the 1982 program year against the grant for its current program year;

(B) The amount determined by applying the percentage of the grant it obligated for public services in the 1983 program year against the grant for its current program year;

(C) The amount of funds it obligated for public services in the 1982 program year; or,

(D) The amount of funds it obligated for public services in the 1983 program year.

(f) *Interim assistance.* (1) The following activities may be undertaken on an interim basis in areas exhibiting objectively determinable signs of physical deterioration where the recipient has determined that immediate action is necessary to arrest the deterioration and that permanent improvements will be carried out as soon as practicable:

(i) The repairing of streets, sidewalks, parks, playgrounds, publicly owned utilities, and public buildings; and

(ii) The execution of special garbage, trash, and debris removal, including neighborhood cleanup campaigns, but not the regular curbside collection of garbage or trash in an area.

(2) In order to alleviate emergency conditions threatening the public health and safety in areas where the chief executive officer of the recipient determines that such an emergency condition exists and requires immediate resolution, CDBG funds may be used for:

(i) The activities specified in paragraph (f)(1) of this section, except for the repair of parks and playgrounds;

(ii) The clearance of streets, including snow removal and similar activities, and

(iii) The improvement of private properties.

(3) All activities authorized under paragraph (f)(2) of this section are limited to the extent necessary to alleviate emergency conditions.

(g) *Payment of non-Federal share.* Payment of the non-Federal share required in connection with a Federal grant-in-aid program undertaken as part of CDBG activities, provided, that such payment shall be limited to activities otherwise eligible and in compliance with applicable requirements under this subpart.

(h) *Urban renewal completion.* Payment of the cost of completing an urban renewal project funded under title I of the Housing Act of 1949 as amended. Further information regarding the eligibility of such costs is set forth in § 570.801.

(i) *Relocation.* Relocation payments and other assistance for permanently and temporarily relocated individuals families, businesses, nonprofit organizations, and farm operations where the assistance is (1) required under the provisions of § 570.606 (b) or (c); or (2) determined by the grantee to be appropriate under the provisions of § 570.606(d).

(j) *Loss of rental income.* Payments to housing owners for losses of rental income incurred in holding, for temporary periods, housing units to be used for the relocation of individuals and families displaced by program activities assisted under this part.

(k) *Housing services.* Housing services, as provided in section 105(a)(21) of the Act (42 U.S.C. 5305(a)(21)).

(l) *Privately owned utilities.* CDBG funds may be used to acquire, construct, reconstruct, rehabilitate, or install the distribution lines and facilities of privately owned utilities, including the placing underground of new or existing distribution facilities and lines.

(m) *Construction of housing.* CDBG funds may be used for the construction of housing assisted under section 17 of the United States Housing Act of 1937.

(n) *Homeownership assistance.* CDBG funds may be used to provide direct homeownership assistance to low- or moderate-income households in accordance with section 105(a) of the Act.

(o)(1) The provision of assistance either through the recipient directly or through public and private organizations, agencies, and other subrecipients (including nonprofit and for-profit subrecipients) to facilitate economic development by:

(i) Providing credit, including, but not limited to, grants, loans, loan guarantees, and other forms of financial support, for the establishment, stabilization, and expansion of microenterprises;

(ii) Providing technical assistance, advice, and business support services to owners of microenterprises and persons developing microenterprises; and

(iii) Providing general support, including, but not limited to, peer support programs, counseling, child care, transportation, and other similar services, to owners of microenterprises and persons developing microenterprises.

(2) Services provided this paragraph (o) shall not be subject to the restrictions on public services contained in paragraph (e) of this section.

(3) For purposes of this paragraph (o), "persons developing microenterprises" means such persons who have expressed interest and who are, or after an initial screening process are expected to be, actively working toward developing businesses, each of which is expected to be a microenterprise at the time it is formed.

(4) Assistance under this paragraph (o) may also include training, technical assistance, or other support services to increase the capacity of the recipient or subrecipient to carry out the activities under this paragraph (o).

(p) *Technical assistance.* Provision of technical assistance to public or nonprofit entities to increase the capacity of such entities to carry out eligible neighborhood revitalization or economic development activities. (The recipient must determine, prior to the provision of the assistance, that the activity for which it is attempting to build capacity would be eligible for assistance under this subpart C, and that the national objective claimed by the grantee for this assistance can reasonably be expected to be met once the entity has received the technical assistance and undertakes the activity.) Capacity building for private or public entities (including grantees) for other purposes may be eligible under § 570.205.

(q) *Assistance to institutions of higher education.* Provision of assistance by the recipient to institutions of higher education when the grantee determines that such an institution has demonstrated a capacity to carry out eligible activities under this subpart C.

[53 FR 34439, Sept. 6, 1988, as amended at 53 FR 31239, Aug. 17, 1988; 55 FR 29308, July 18, 1990; 57 FR 27119, June 17, 1992; 60 FR 1943, Jan. 5, 1995; 60 FR 56911, Nov. 9, 1995; 61 FR 18674, Apr. 29, 1996; 65 FR 70215, Nov. 21, 2000; 67 FR 47213, July 17, 2002; 71 FR 30034, May 24, 2006]

§ 570.202 Eligible rehabilitation and preservation activities.

(a) *Types of buildings and improvements eligible for rehabilitation assistance.* CDBG funds may be used to finance the rehabilitation of:

(1) Privately owned buildings and improvements for residential purposes; improvements to a single-family residential property which is also used as a place of business, which are required in order to operate the business, need not be considered to be rehabilitation of a commercial or industrial building, if the improvements also provide general benefit to the residential occupants of the building;

(2) Low-income public housing and other publicly owned residential buildings and improvements;

(3) Publicly or privately owned commercial or industrial buildings, except that the rehabilitation of such buildings owned by a private for-profit business is limited to improvement to the exterior of the building, abatement of asbestos hazards, lead-based paint hazard evaluation and reduction, and the correction of code violations;

(4) Nonprofit-owned nonresidential buildings and improvements not eligible under § 570.201(c); and

(5) Manufactured housing when such housing constitutes part of the community's permanent housing stock.

(b) *Types of assistance.* CDBG funds may be used to finance the following types of rehabilitation activities, and related costs, either singly, or in combination, through the use of grants, loans, loan guarantees, interest supplements, or other means for buildings and improvements described in paragraph (a) of this section, except that rehabilitation of commercial or industrial buildings is limited as described in paragraph (a)(3) of this section.

(1) Assistance to private individuals and entities, including profit making and nonprofit organizations, to acquire for the purpose of rehabilitation, and to rehabilitate properties, for use or resale for residential purposes;

(2) Labor, materials, and other costs of rehabilitation of properties, including repair directed toward an accumulation of deferred maintenance, replacement of principal fixtures and components of existing structures, installation of security devices, including smoke detectors and dead bolt locks, and renovation through alterations, additions to, or enhancement of existing structures and improvements, abatement of asbestos hazards (and other contaminants) in buildings and improvements that may be undertaken singly, or in combination;

(3) Loans for refinancing existing indebtedness secured by a property being rehabilitated with CDBG funds if such financing is determined by the recipient to be necessary or appropriate to achieve the locality's community development objectives;

(4) Improvements to increase the efficient use of energy in structures through such means as installation of storm windows and doors, siding, wall and attic insulation, and conversion, modification, or replacement of heating and cooling equipment, including the use of solar energy equipment;

(5) Improvements to increase the efficient use of water through such means as water savings faucets and shower heads and repair of water leaks;

(6) Connection of residential structures to water distribution lines or local sewer collection lines;

(7) For rehabilitation carried out with CDBG funds, costs of:

(i) Initial homeowner warranty premiums;

(ii) Hazard insurance premiums, except where assistance is provided in the form of a grant; and

(iii) Flood insurance premiums for properties covered by the Flood Disaster Protection Act of 1973, pursuant to § 570.605.

(8) Costs of acquiring tools to be lent to owners, tenants, and others who will use such tools to carry out rehabilitation;

(9) Rehabilitation services, such as rehabilitation counseling, energy auditing, preparation of work specifications, loan processing, inspections, and other services related to assisting owners, tenants, contractors, and other entities, participating or seeking to participate in rehabilitation activities authorized under this section, under section 312 of the Housing Act of 1964, as amended, under section 810 of the Act, or under section 17 of the United States Housing Act of 1937;

(10) Assistance for the rehabilitation of housing under section 17 of the United States Housing Act of 1937; and

(11) Improvements designed to remove material and architectural barriers that restrict the mobility and accessibility of elderly or severely disabled persons to buildings and improvements eligible for assistance under paragraph (a) of this section.

(c) *Code enforcement.* Costs incurred for inspection for code violations and enforcement of codes (e.g., salaries and related expenses of code enforcement inspectors and legal proceedings, but not including the cost of correcting the violations) in deteriorating or deteriorated areas when such enforcement together with public or private improvements, rehabilitation, or services to be provided may be expected to arrest the decline of the area.

(d) *Historic preservation.* CDBG funds may be used for the rehabilitation, preservation or restoration of historic properties, whether publicly or privately owned. Historic properties are those sites or structures that are either listed in or eligible to be listed in the National Register of Historic Places, listed in a State or local inventory of historic places, or designated as a State or local landmark or historic district by appropriate law or ordinance. Historic preservation, however, is not authorized for buildings for the general conduct of government.

(e) *Renovation of closed buildings.* CDBG funds may be used to renovate closed buildings, such as closed school buildings, for use as an eligible public facility or to rehabilitate such buildings for housing.

(f) *Lead-based paint activities.* Lead-based paint activities pursuant to § 570.608.

[53 FR 34439, Sept. 6, 1988; 53 FR 41330, Oct. 21, 1988, as amended at 60 FR 1944, Jan. 5, 1995; 60 FR 56911, Nov. 9, 1995; 64 FR 50225, Sept. 15, 1999; 71 FR 30035, May 24, 2006]

§ 570.203 Special economic development activities.

A recipient may use CDBG funds for special economic development activities in addition to other activities authorized in this subpart that may be carried out as part of an economic development project. Guidelines for selecting activities to assist under this paragraph are provided at § 570.209. The recipient must ensure that the appropriate level of public benefit will be derived pursuant to those guidelines before obligating funds under this authority. Special activities authorized under this section do not include assistance for the construction of new housing. Activities eligible under this section may include costs associated with project-specific assessment or remediation of known or suspected environmental contamination. Special economic development activities include:

§ 570.204

(a) The acquisition, construction, reconstruction, rehabilitation or installation of commercial or industrial buildings, structures, and other real property equipment and improvements, including railroad spurs or similar extensions. Such activities may be carried out by the recipient or public or private nonprofit subrecipients.

(b) The provision of assistance to a private for-profit business, including, but not limited to, grants, loans, loan guarantees, interest supplements, technical assistance, and other forms of support, for any activity where the assistance is appropriate to carry out an economic development project, excluding those described as ineligible in § 570.207(a). In selecting businesses to assist under this authority, the recipient shall minimize, to the extent practicable, displacement of existing businesses and jobs in neighborhoods.

(c) Economic development services in connection with activities eligible under this section, including, but not limited to, outreach efforts to market available forms of assistance; screening of applicants; reviewing and underwriting applications for assistance; preparation of all necessary agreements; management of assisted activities; and the screening, referral, and placement of applicants for employment opportunities generated by CDBG-eligible economic development activities, including the costs of providing necessary training for persons filling those positions.

[53 FR 34439, Sept. 6, 1988, as amended at 60 FR 1944, Jan. 5, 1995; 71 FR 30035, May 24, 2006]

§ 570.204 Special activities by Community-Based Development Organizations (CBDOs).

(a) *Eligible activities.* The recipient may provide CDBG funds as grants or loans to any CBDO qualified under this section to carry out a neighborhood revitalization, community economic development, or energy conservation project. The funded project activities may include those listed as eligible under this subpart, and, except as described in paragraph (b) of this section, activities not otherwise listed as eligible under this subpart. For purposes of qualifying as a project under paragraphs (a)(1), (a)(2), and (a)(3) of this section, the funded activity or activities may be considered either alone or in concert with other project activities either being carried out or for which funding has been committed. For purposes of this section:

(1) Neighborhood revitalization project includes activities of sufficient size and scope to have an impact on the decline of a geographic location within the jurisdiction of a unit of general local government (but not the entire jurisdiction) designated in comprehensive plans, ordinances, or other local documents as a neighborhood, village, or similar geographical designation; or the entire jurisdiction of a unit of general local government which is under 25,000 population;

(2) Community economic development project includes activities that increase economic opportunity, principally for persons of low- and moderate-income, or that stimulate or retain businesses or permanent jobs, including projects that include one or more such activities that are clearly needed to address a lack of affordable housing accessible to existing or planned jobs and those activities specified at 24 CFR 91.1(a)(1)(iii); activities under this paragraph may include costs associated with project-specific assessment or remediation of known or suspected environmental contamination;

(3) Energy conservation project includes activities that address energy conservation, principally for the benefit of the residents of the recipient's jurisdiction; and

(4) To carry out a project means that the CBDO undertakes the funded activities directly or through contract with an entity other than the grantee, or through the provision of financial assistance for activities in which it retains a direct and controlling involvement and responsibilities.

(b) *Ineligible activities.* Notwithstanding that CBDOs may carry out activities that are not otherwise eligible under this subpart, this section does not authorize:

(1) Carrying out an activity described as ineligible in § 570.207(a);

(2) Carrying out public services that do not meet the requirements of § 570.201(e), except that:

(i) Services carried out under this section that are specifically designed to increase economic opportunities through job training and placement and other employment support services, including, but not limited to, peer support programs, counseling, child care, transportation, and other similar services; and

(ii) Services of any type carried out under this section pursuant to a strategy approved by HUD under the provisions of 24 CFR 91.215(e) shall not be subject to the limitations in §570.201(e)(1) or (2), as applicable;

(3) Providing assistance to activities that would otherwise be eligible under §570.203 that do not meet the requirements of §570.209; or

(4) Carrying out an activity that would otherwise be eligible under §570.205 or §570.206, but that would result in the recipient's exceeding the spending limitation in §570.200(g).

(c) *Eligible CBDOs.* (1) A CBDO qualifying under this section is an organization which has the following characteristics:

(i) Is an association or corporation organized under State or local law to engage in community development activities (which may include housing and economic development activities) primarily within an identified geographic area of operation within the jurisdiction of the recipient, or in the case of an urban county, the jurisdiction of the county; and

(ii) Has as its primary purpose the improvement of the physical, economic or social environment of its geographic area of operation by addressing one or more critical problems of the area, with particular attention to the needs of persons of low and moderate income; and

(iii) May be either non-profit or for-profit, provided any monetary profits to its shareholders or members must be only incidental to its operations; and

(iv) Maintains at least 51 percent of its governing body's membership for low- and moderate-income residents of its geographic area of operation, owners or senior officers of private establishments and other institutions located in and serving its geographic area of operation, or representatives of low- and moderate-income neighborhood organizations located in its geographic area of operation; and

(v) Is not an agency or instrumentality of the recipient and does not permit more than one-third of the membership of its governing body to be appointed by, or to consist of, elected or other public officials or employees or officials of an ineligible entity (even though such persons may be otherwise qualified under paragraph (c)(1)(iv) of this section); and

(vi) Except as otherwise authorized in paragraph (c)(1)(v) of this section, requires the members of its governing body to be nominated and approved by the general membership of the organization, or by its permanent governing body; and

(vii) Is not subject to requirements under which its assets revert to the recipient upon dissolution; and

(viii) Is free to contract for goods and services from vendors of its own choosing.

(2) A CBDO that does not meet the criteria in paragraph (c)(1) of this section may also qualify as an eligible entity under this section if it meets one of the following requirements:

(i) Is an entity organized pursuant to section 301(d) of the Small Business Investment Act of 1958 (15 U.S.C. 681(d)), including those which are profit making; or

(ii) Is an SBA approved Section 501 State Development Company or Section 502 Local Development Company, or an SBA Certified Section 503 Company under the Small Business Investment Act of 1958, as amended; or

(iii) Is a Community Housing Development Organization (CHDO) under 24 CFR 92.2, designated as a CHDO by the HOME Investment Partnerships program participating jurisdiction, with a geographic area of operation of no more than one neighborhood, and has received HOME funds under 24 CFR 92.300 or is expected to receive HOME funds as described in and documented in accordance with 24 CFR 92.300(e).

(3) A CBDO that does not qualify under paragraph (c)(1) or (2) of this section may also be determined to qualify as an eligible entity under this section if the recipient demonstrates to the

satisfaction of HUD, through the provision of information regarding the organization's charter and by-laws, that the organization is sufficiently similar in purpose, function, and scope to those entities qualifying under paragraph (c)(1) or (2) of this section.

[60 FR 1944, Jan. 5, 1995, as amended at 71 FR 30035, May 24, 2006]

§ 570.205 Eligible planning, urban environmental design and policy-planning-management-capacity building activities.

(a) Planning activities which consist of all costs of data gathering, studies, analysis, and preparation of plans and the identification of actions that will implement such plans, including, but not limited to:

(1) Comprehensive plans;
(2) Community development plans;
(3) Functional plans, in areas such as:
(i) Housing, including the development of a consolidated plan;
(ii) Land use and urban environmental design;
(iii) Economic development;
(iv) Open space and recreation;
(v) Energy use and conservation;
(vi) Floodplain and wetlands management in accordance with the requirements of Executive Orders 11988 and 11990;
(vii) Transportation;
(viii) Utilities; and
(ix) Historic preservation.
(4) Other plans and studies such as:
(i) Small area and neighborhood plans;
(ii) Capital improvements programs;
(iii) Individual project plans (but excluding engineering and design costs related to a specific activity which are eligible as part of the cost of such activity under §§ 570.201–570.204);
(iv) The reasonable costs of general environmental, urban environmental design and historic preservation studies; and general environmental assessment- and remediation-oriented planning related to properties with known or suspected environmental contamination. However, costs necessary to comply with 24 CFR part 58, including project specific environmental assessments and clearances for activities eligible for assistance under this part, are eligible as part of the cost of such activities under §§ 570.201–570.204. Costs for such specific assessments and clearances may also be incurred under this paragraph but would then be considered planning costs for the purposes of § 570.200(g);

(v) Strategies and action programs to implement plans, including the development of codes, ordinances and regulations;

(vi) Support of clearinghouse functions, such as those specified in Executive Order 12372; and

(vii) Analysis of impediments to fair housing choice.

(viii) Developing an inventory of properties with known or suspected environmental contamination.

(5) [Reserved]

(6) Policy—planning—management—capacity building activities which will enable the recipient to:

(1) Determine its needs;
(2) Set long-term goals and short-term objectives, including those related to urban environmental design;
(3) Devise programs and activities to meet these goals and objectives;
(4) Evaluate the progress of such programs and activities in accomplishing these goals and objectives; and
(5) Carry out management, coordination and monitoring of activities necessary for effective planning implementation, but excluding the costs necessary to implement such plans.

[53 FR 34439, Sept. 6, 1988, as amended at 56 FR 56127, Oct. 31, 1991; 60 FR 1915, Jan. 5, 1995; 71 FR 30035, May 24, 2006]

§ 570.206 Program administrative costs.

Payment of reasonable administrative costs and carrying charges related to the planning and execution of community development activities assisted in whole or in part with funds provided under this part and, where applicable, housing activities (described in paragraph (g) of this section) covered in the recipient's housing assistance plan. This does not include staff and overhead costs directly related to carrying out activities eligible under § 570.201 through § 570.204, since those costs are eligible as part of such activities.

(a) *General management, oversight and coordination.* Reasonable costs of overall program management, coordination, monitoring, and evaluation. Such costs include, but are not necessarily limited to, necessary expenditures for the following:

(1) Salaries, wages, and related costs of the recipient's staff, the staff of local public agencies, or other staff engaged in program administration. In charging costs to this category the recipient may either include the entire salary, wages, and related costs allocable to the program of each person whose *primary* responsibilities with regard to the program involve program administration assignments, or the pro rata share of the salary, wages, and related costs of each person whose job includes *any* program administration assignments. The recipient may use only one of these methods during the program year (or the grant period for grants under subpart F). Program administration includes the following types of assignments:

(i) Providing local officials and citizens with information about the program;

(ii) Preparing program budgets and schedules, and amendments thereto;

(iii) Developing systems for assuring compliance with program requirements;

(iv) Developing interagency agreements and agreements with subrecipients and contractors to carry out program activities;

(v) Monitoring program activities for progress and compliance with program requirements;

(vi) Preparing reports and other documents related to the program for submission to HUD;

(vii) Coordinating the resolution of audit and monitoring findings;

(viii) Evaluating program results against stated objectives; and

(ix) Managing or supervising persons whose primary responsibilities with regard to the program include such assignments as those described in paragraph (a)(1)(i) through (viii) of this section.

(2) Travel costs incurred for official business in carrying out the program;

(3) Administrative services performed under third party contracts or agreements, including such services as general legal services, accounting services, and audit services; and

(4) Other costs for goods and services required for administration of the program, including such goods and services as rental or purchase of equipment, insurance, utilities, office supplies, and rental and maintenance (but not purchase) of office space.

(b) *Public information.* The provisions of information and other resources to residents and citizen organizations participating in the planning, implementation, or assessment of activities being assisted with CDBG funds.

(c) *Fair housing activities.* Provision of fair housing services designed to further the fair housing objectives of the Fair Housing Act (42 U.S.C. 3601–20) by making all persons, without regard to race, color, religion, sex, national origin, familial status or handicap, aware of the range of housing opportunities available to them; other fair housing enforcement, education, and outreach activities; and other activities designed to further the housing objective of avoiding undue concentrations of assisted persons in areas containing a high proportion of low and moderate income persons.

(d) [Reserved]

(e) *Indirect costs.* Indirect costs may be charged to the CDBG program under a cost allocation plan prepared in accordance with OMB Circular A–21, A–87, or A–122 as applicable.

(f) *Submission of applications for federal programs.* Preparation of documents required for submission to HUD to receive funds under the CDBG and UDAG programs. In addition, CDBG funds may be used to prepare applications for other Federal programs where the recipient determines that such activities are necessary or appropriate to achieve its community development objectives.

(g) *Administrative expenses to facilitate housing.* CDBG funds may be used for necessary administrative expenses in planning or obtaining financing for housing as follows: for entitlement recipients, assistance authorized by this paragraph is limited to units which are identified in the recipient's HUD approved housing assistance plan; for

§ 570.207

HUD-administered small cities recipients, assistance authorized by the paragraph is limited to facilitating the purchase or occupancy of existing units which are to be occupied by low and moderate income households, or the construction of rental or owner units where at least 20 percent of the units in each project will be occupied at affordable rents/costs by low and moderate income persons. Examples of eligible actions are as follows:

(1) The cost of conducting preliminary surveys and analysis of market needs;

(2) Site and utility plans, narrative descriptions of the proposed construction, preliminary cost estimates, urban design documentation, and "sketch drawings," but excluding architectural, engineering, and other details ordinarily required for construction purposes, such as structural, electrical, plumbing, and mechanical details;

(3) Reasonable costs associated with development of applications for mortgage and insured loan commitments, including commitment fees, and of applications and proposals under the Section 8 Housing Assistance Payments Program pursuant to 24 CFR parts 880–883;

(4) Fees associated with processing of applications for mortgage or insured loan commitments under programs including those administered by HUD, Farmers Home Administration (FmHA), Federal National Mortgage Association (FNMA), and the Government National Mortgage Association (GNMA);

(5) The cost of issuance and administration of mortgage revenue bonds used to finance the acquisition, rehabilitation or construction of housing, but excluding costs associated with the payment or guarantee of the principal or interest on such bonds; and

(6) Special outreach activities which result in greater landlord participation in Section 8 Housing Assistance Payments Program-Existing Housing or similar programs for low and moderate income persons.

(h) *Section 17 of the United States Housing Act of 1937.* Reasonable costs equivalent to those described in paragraphs (a), (b), (e) and (f) of this section for overall program management of the Rental Rehabilitation and Housing Development programs authorized under section 17 of the United States Housing Act of 1937, whether or not such activities are otherwise assisted with funds provided under this part.

(i) Whether or not such activities are otherwise assisted by funds provided under this part, reasonable costs equivalent to those described in paragraphs (a), (b), (e), and (f) of this section for overall program management of:

(1) A Federally designated Empowerment Zone or Enterprise Community; and

(2) The HOME program under title II of the Cranston-Gonzalez National Affordable Housing Act (42 U.S.C. 12701 note).

[53 FR 34439, Sept. 6, 1988; 53 FR 41330, Oct. 21, 1988, as amended at 54 FR 37411, Sept. 8, 1989; 60 FR 56912, Nov. 9, 1995; 69 FR 32778, June 10, 2004]

§ 570.207 Ineligible activities.

The general rule is that any activity that is not authorized under the provisions of §§ 570.201–570.206 is ineligible to be assisted with CDBG funds. This section identifies specific activities that are ineligible and provides guidance in determining the eligibility of other activities frequently associated with housing and community development.

(a) The following activities may not be assisted with CDBG funds:

(1) *Buildings or portions thereof, used for the general conduct of government* as defined at § 570.3(d) cannot be assisted with CDBG funds. This does not include, however, the removal of architectural barriers under § 570.201(c) involving any such building. Also, where acquisition of real property includes an existing improvement which is to be used in the provision of a building for the general conduct of government, the portion of the acquisition cost attributable to the land is eligible, provided such acquisition meets a national objective described in § 570.208.

(2) *General government expenses.* Except as otherwise specifically authorized in this subpart or under OMB Circular A-87, expenses required to carry out the regular responsibilities of the unit of general local government are not eligible for assistance under this part.

(3) *Political activities.* CDBG funds shall not be used to finance the use of facilities or equipment for political purposes or to engage in other partisan political activities, such as candidate forums, voter transportation, or voter registration. However, a facility originally assisted with CDBG funds may be used on an incidental basis to hold political meetings, candidate forums, or voter registration campaigns, provided that all parties and organizations have access to the facility on an equal basis, and are assessed equal rent or use charges, if any.

(b) The following activities may not be assisted with CDBG funds unless authorized under provisions of § 570.203 or as otherwise specifically noted herein or when carried out by an entity under the provisions of § 570.204.

(1) *Purchase of equipment.* The purchase of equipment with CDBG funds is generally ineligible.

(i) *Construction equipment.* The purchase of construction equipment is ineligible, but compensation for the use of such equipment through leasing, depreciation, or use allowances pursuant to OMB Circulars A–21, A–87 or A–122 as applicable for an otherwise eligible activity is an eligible use of CDBG funds. However, the purchase of construction equipment for use as part of a solid waste disposal facility is eligible under § 570.201(c).

(ii) *Fire protection equipment.* Fire protection equipment is considered for this purpose to be an integral part of a public facility and thus, purchase of such equipment would be eligible under § 570.201(c).

(iii) *Furnishings and personal property.* The purchase of equipment, fixtures, motor vehicles, furnishings, or other personal property not an integral structural fixture is generally ineligible. CDBG funds may be used, however, to purchase or to pay depreciation or use allowances (in accordance with OMB Circular A–21, A–87 or A–122, as applicable) for such items when necessary for use by a recipient or its subrecipients in the administration of activities assisted with CDBG funds, or when eligible as fire fighting equipment, or when such items constitute all or part of a public service pursuant to § 570.201(e).

(2) *Operating and maintenance expenses.* The general rule is that any expense associated with repairing, operating or maintaining public facilities, improvements and services is ineligible. Specific exceptions to this general rule are operating and maintenance expenses associated with public service activities, interim assistance, and office space for program staff employed in carrying out the CDBG program. For example, the use of CDBG funds to pay the allocable costs of operating and maintaining a facility used in providing a public service would be eligible under § 570.201(e), even if no other costs of providing such a service are assisted with such funds. Examples of ineligible operating and maintenance expenses are:

(i) Maintenance and repair of publicly owned streets, parks, playgrounds, water and sewer facilities, neighborhood facilities, senior centers, centers for persons with a disabilities, parking and other public facilities and improvements. Examples of maintenance and repair activities for which CDBG funds may not be used include the filling of pot holes in streets, repairing of cracks in sidewalks, the mowing of recreational areas, and the replacement of expended street light bulbs; and

(ii) Payment of salaries for staff, utility costs and similar expenses necessary for the operation of public works and facilities.

(3) *New housing construction.* For the purpose of this paragraph, activities in support of the development of low or moderate income housing including clearance, site assemblage, provision of site improvements and provision of public improvements and certain housing pre-construction costs set forth in § 570.206(g), are not considered as activities to subsidize or assist new residential construction. CDBG funds may not be used for the construction of new permanent residential structures or for any program to subsidize or assist such new construction, except:

(i) As provided under the last resort housing provisions set forth in 24 CFR part 42;

(ii) As authorized under § 570.201(m) or (n);

§ 570.208

(iii) When carried out by an entity pursuant to § 570.204(a);

(4) *Income payments.* The general rule is that CDBG funds may not be used for income payments. For purposes of the CDBG program, "income payments" means a series of subsistence-type grant payments made to an individual or family for items such as food, clothing, housing (rent or mortgage), or utilities, but excludes emergency grant payments made over a period of up to three consecutive months to the provider of such items or services on behalf of an individual or family.

[53 FR 34439, Sept. 6, 1988; 53 FR 41330, Oct. 21, 1988, as amended at 60 FR 1945, Jan. 5, 1995; 60 FR 56912, Nov. 9, 1995; 65 FR 70215, Nov. 21, 2000]

§ 570.208 Criteria for national objectives.

The following criteria shall be used to determine whether a CDBG-assisted activity complies with one or more of the national objectives as required under § 570.200(a)(2):

(a) *Activities benefiting low- and moderate-income persons.* Activities meeting the criteria in paragraph (a) (1), (2), (3), or (4) of this section as applicable, will be considered to benefit low and moderate income persons unless there is substantial evidence to the contrary. In assessing any such evidence, the full range of direct effects of the assisted activity will be considered. (The recipient shall appropriately ensure that activities that meet these criteria do not benefit moderate income persons to the exclusion of low income persons.)

(1) *Area benefit activities.* (i) An activity, the benefits of which are available to all the residents in a particular area, where at least 51 percent of the residents are low and moderate income persons. Such an area need not be coterminous with census tracts or other officially recognized boundaries but must be the entire area served by the activity. An activity that serves an area that is not primarily residential in character shall not qualify under this criterion.

(ii) For metropolitan cities and urban counties, an activity that would otherwise qualify under § 570.208(a)(1)(i), except that the area served contains less than 51 percent low- and moderate-income residents, will also be considered to meet the objective of benefiting low- and moderate-income persons where the proportion of such persons in the area is within the highest quartile of all areas in the recipient's jurisdiction in terms of the degree of concentration of such persons. This exception is inapplicable to non-entitlement CDBG grants in Hawaii. In applying this exception, HUD will determine the lowest proportion a recipient may use to qualify an area for this purpose, as follows:

(A) All census block groups in the recipient's jurisdiction shall be rank ordered from the block group of highest proportion of low and moderate income persons to the block group with the lowest. For urban counties, the rank ordering shall cover the entire area constituting the urban county and shall not be done separately for each participating unit of general local government.

(B) In any case where the total number of a recipient's block groups does not divide evenly by four, the block group which would be fractionally divided between the highest and second quartiles shall be considered to be part of the highest quartile.

(C) The proportion of low and moderate income persons in the last census block group in the highest quartile shall be identified. Any service area located within the recipient's jurisdiction and having a proportion of low and moderate income persons at or above this level shall be considered to be within the highest quartile.

(D) If block group data are not available for the entire jurisdiction, other data acceptable to the Secretary may be used in the above calculations.

(iii) An activity to develop, establish, and operate for up to two years after the establishment of, a uniform emergency telephone number system serving an area having less than the percentage of low- and moderate-income residents required under paragraph (a)(1)(i) of this section or (as applicable) paragraph (a)(1)(ii) of this section, provided the recipient obtains prior HUD approval. To obtain such approval, the recipient must:

(A) Demonstrate that the system will contribute significantly to the safety of the residents of the area. The request for approval must include a list of the emergency services that will participate in the emergency telephone number system;

(B) Submit information that serves as a basis for HUD to determine whether at least 51 percent of the use of the system will be by low- and moderate-income persons. As available, the recipient must provide information that identifies the total number of calls actually received over the preceding 12-month period for each of the emergency services to be covered by the emergency telephone number system and relates those calls to the geographic segment (expressed as nearly as possible in terms of census tracts, block numbering areas, block groups, or combinations thereof that are contained within the segment) of the service area from which the calls were generated. In analyzing this data to meet the requirements of this section, HUD will assume that the distribution of income among the callers generally reflects the income characteristics of the general population residing in the same geographic area where the callers reside. If HUD can conclude that the users have primarily consisted of low- and moderate-income persons, no further submission is needed by the recipient. If a recipient plans to make other submissions for this purpose, it may request that HUD review its planned methodology before expending the effort to acquire the information it expects to use to make its case;

(C) Demonstrate that other Federal funds received by the recipient are insufficient or unavailable for a uniform emergency telephone number system. For this purpose, the recipient must submit a statement explaining whether the lack of funds is due to the insufficiency of the amount of the available funds, restrictions on the use of such funds, or the prior commitment of funds by the recipient for other purposes; and

(D) Demonstrate that the percentage of the total costs of the system paid for by CDBG funds does not exceed the percentage of low- and moderate-income persons in the service area of the system. For this purpose, the recipient must include a description of the boundaries of the service area of the emergency telephone number system, the census divisions that fall within the boundaries of the service area (census tracts or block numbering areas), the total number of persons and the total number of low- and moderate-income persons within each census division, the percentage of low- and moderate-income persons within the service area, and the total cost of the system.

(iv) An activity for which the assistance to a public improvement that provides benefits to all the residents of an area is limited to paying special assessments (as defined in §570.200(c)) levied against residential properties owned and occupied by persons of low and moderate income.

(v) For purposes of determining qualification under this criterion, activities of the same type that serve different areas will be considered separately on the basis of their individual service area.

(vi) In determining whether there is a sufficiently large percentage of low- and moderate-income persons residing in the area served by an activity to qualify under paragraph (a)(1) (i), (ii), or (vii) of this section, the most recently available decennial census information must be used to the fullest extent feasible, together with the section 8 income limits that would have applied at the time the income information was collected by the Census Bureau. Recipients that believe that the census data does not reflect current relative income levels in an area, or where census boundaries do not coincide sufficiently well with the service area of an activity, may conduct (or have conducted) a current survey of the residents of the area to determine the percent of such persons that are low and moderate income. HUD will accept information obtained through such surveys, to be used in lieu of the decennial census data, where it determines that the survey was conducted in such a manner that the results meet standards of statistical reliability that are comparable to that of the decennial census data for areas of similar size. Where there is substantial evidence that provides a clear basis to believe that the use of the decennial census data would substantially overstate the proportion of persons residing there that are low and moderate income, HUD may require that the recipient rebut such evidence in order to demonstrate compliance with section 105(c)(2) of the Act.

(vii) Activities meeting the requirements of paragraph (d)(5)(i) of this section may be considered to qualify under this paragraph, provided that the area covered by the strategy is either a Federally-designated Empowerment Zone or Enterprise Community or primarily residential and contains a percentage of low- and moderate-income residents that is no less than the percentage computed by HUD pursuant to paragraph (a)(1)(ii) of this section or 70 percent, whichever is less, but in no event less than 51 percent. Activities meeting the requirements of paragraph (d)(6)(i) of this section may also be considered to qualify under paragraph (a)(1) of this section.

(2) *Limited clientele activities.* (i) An activity which benefits a limited clientele, at least 51 percent of whom are low- or moderate-income persons. (The following kinds of activities may not qualify under paragraph (a)(2) of this section: activities, the benefits of which are available to all the residents of an area; activities involving the acquisition, construction or rehabilitation of property for housing; or activities where the benefit to low- and moderate-income persons to be considered is the creation or retention of jobs, except as provided in paragraph (a)(2)(iv) of this section.) To qualify under paragraph (a)(2) of this section, the activity must meet one of the following tests:

(A) Benefit a clientele who are generally presumed to be principally low and moderate income persons. Activities that exclusively serve a group of persons in any one or a combination of the following categories may be presumed to benefit persons, 51 percent of whom are low- and moderate-income: abused children, battered spouses, elderly persons, adults meeting the Bureau of the Census' Current Population Reports definition of "severely disabled," homeless persons, illiterate adults, persons living with AIDS, and migrant farm workers; or

(B) Require information on family size and income so that it is evident that at least 51 percent of the clientele are persons whose family income does not exceed the low and moderate income limit; or

(C) Have income eligibility requirements which limit the activity exclusively to low and moderate income persons; or

(D) Be of such nature and be in such location that it may be concluded that the activity's clientele will primarily be low and moderate income persons.

(ii) An activity that serves to remove material or architectural barriers to the mobility or accessibility of elderly persons or of adults meeting the Bureau of the Census' Current Population Reports definition of "severely disabled" will be presumed to qualify under this criterion if it is restricted, to the extent practicable, to the removal of such barriers by assisting:

(A) The reconstruction of a public facility or improvement, or portion thereof, that does not qualify under paragraph (a)(1) of this section;

(B) The rehabilitation of a privately owned nonresidential building or improvement that does not qualify under paragraph (a)(1) or (4) of this section; or

(C) The rehabilitation of the common areas of a residential structure that contains more than one dwelling unit and that does not qualify under paragraph (a)(3) of this section.

(iii) A microenterprise assistance activity carried out in accordance with the provisions of § 570.201(o) with respect to those owners of microenterprises and persons developing microenterprises assisted under the activity during each program year who are low- and moderate-income persons. For purposes of this paragraph, persons determined to be low and moderate income may be presumed to continue to qualify as such for up to a three-year period.

(iv) An activity designed to provide job training and placement and/or other employment support services, including, but not limited to, peer support programs, counseling, child care, transportation, and other similar services, in which the percentage of low- and moderate-income persons assisted is less than 51 percent may qualify under this paragraph in the following limited circumstance:

(A) In such cases where such training or provision of supportive services assists business(es), the only use of CDBG assistance for the project is to provide the job training and/or supportive services; and

(B) The proportion of the total cost of the project borne by CDBG funds is no greater than the proportion of the total number of persons assisted who are low or moderate income.

(3) *Housing activities.* An eligible activity carried out for the purpose of providing or improving permanent residential structures which, upon completion, will be occupied by low- and moderate-income households. This would include, but not necessarily be limited to, the acquisition or rehabilitation of property by the recipient, a subrecipient, a developer, an individual homebuyer, or an individual homeowner; conversion of nonresidential structures; and new housing construction. If the structure contains two dwelling units, at least one must be so occupied, and if the structure contains more than two dwelling units, at least 51 percent of the units must be so occupied. Where two or more rental buildings being assisted are or will be located on the same or contiguous properties, and the buildings will be under common ownership and management, the grouped buildings may be considered for this purpose as a single structure. Where housing activities being assisted meet the requirements of paragraph §570.208 (d)(5)(ii) or (d)(6)(ii) of this section, all such housing may also be considered for this purpose as a single structure. For rental housing, occupancy by low and moderate income households must be at affordable rents to qualify under this criterion. The recipient shall adopt and make public its standards for determining "affordable rents" for this purpose. The following shall also qualify under this criterion:

(i) When less than 51 percent of the units in a structure will be occupied by low and moderate income households, CDBG assistance may be provided in the following limited circumstances:

(A) The assistance is for an eligible activity to reduce the development cost of the new construction of a multifamily, non-elderly rental housing project;

(B) Not less than 20 percent of the units will be occupied by low and moderate income households at affordable rents; and

(C) The proportion of the total cost of developing the project to be borne by CDBG funds is no greater than the proportion of units in the project that will be occupied by low and moderate income households.

(ii) When CDBG funds are used to assist rehabilitation eligible under §570.202(b)(9) or (10) in direct support of the recipient's Rental Rehabilitation program authorized under 24 CFR part 511, such funds shall be considered to benefit low and moderate income persons where not less than 51 percent of the units assisted, or to be assisted, by the recipient's Rental Rehabilitation program overall are for low and moderate income persons.

(iii) When CDBG funds are used for housing services eligible under §570.201(k), such funds shall be considered to benefit low- and moderate-income persons if the housing units for which the services are provided are HOME-assisted and the requirements at 24 CFR 92.252 or 92.254 are met.

(4) *Job creation or retention activities.* An activity designed to create or retain permanent jobs where at least 51 percent of the jobs, computed on a full time equivalent basis, involve the employment of low- and moderate-income persons. To qualify under this paragraph, the activity must meet the following criteria:

(i) For an activity that creates jobs, the recipient must document that at least 51 percent of the jobs will be held by, or will be available to, low- and moderate-income persons.

(ii) For an activity that retains jobs, the recipient must document that the jobs would actually be lost without the CDBG assistance and that either or both of the following conditions apply with respect to at least 51 percent of the jobs at the time the CDBG assistance is provided:

(A) The job is known to be held by a low- or moderate-income person; or

(B) The job can reasonably be expected to turn over within the following two years and that steps will be taken to ensure that it will be filled by, or made available to, a low- or moderate-income person upon turnover.

(iii) Jobs that are not held or filled by a low- or moderate-income person may be considered to be available to low- and moderate-income persons for these purposes only if:

(A) Special skills that can only be acquired with substantial training or work experience or education beyond high school are not a prerequisite to fill such jobs, or the business agrees to hire unqualified persons and provide training; and

(B) The recipient and the assisted business take actions to ensure that low- and moderate-income persons receive first consideration for filling such jobs.

(iv) For purposes of determining whether a job is held by or made available to a low- or moderate-income person, the person may be presumed to be a low- or moderate-income person if:

(A) He/she resides within a census tract (or block numbering area) that either:

(*1*) Meets the requirements of paragraph (a)(4)(v) of this section; or

(*2*) Has at least 70 percent of its residents who are low- and moderate-income persons; or

(B) The assisted business is located within a census tract (or block numbering area) that meets the requirements of paragraph (a)(4)(v) of this section and the job under consideration is to be located within that census tract.

(v) A census tract (or block numbering area) qualifies for the presumptions permitted under paragraphs (a)(4)(iv)(A)(*1*) and (B) of this section if it is either part of a Federally-designated Empowerment Zone or Enterprise Community or meets the following criteria:

(A) It has a poverty rate of at least 20 percent as determined by the most recently available decennial census information; and

(B) It does not include any portion of a central business district, as this term is used in the most recent Census of Retail Trade, unless the tract has a poverty rate of at least 30 percent as determined by the most recently available decennial census information; and

(C) It evidences pervasive poverty and general distress by meeting at least one of the following standards:

(*1*) All block groups in the census tract have poverty rates of at least 20 percent;

(*2*) The specific activity being undertaken is located in a block group that has a poverty rate of at least 20 percent; or

(*3*) Upon the written request of the recipient, HUD determines that the census tract exhibits other objectively determinable signs of general distress such as high incidence of crime, narcotics use, homelessness, abandoned housing, and deteriorated infrastructure or substantial population decline.

(vi) As a general rule, each assisted business shall be considered to be a separate activity for purposes of determining whether the activity qualifies under this paragraph, except:

(A) In certain cases such as where CDBG funds are used to acquire, develop or improve a real property (e.g., a business incubator or an industrial park) the requirement may be met by measuring jobs in the aggregate for all the businesses which locate on the property, provided such businesses are not otherwise assisted by CDBG funds.

(B) Where CDBG funds are used to pay for the staff and overhead costs of an entity making loans to businesses exclusively from non-CDBG funds, this requirement may be met by aggregating the jobs created by all of the businesses receiving loans during each program year.

(C) Where CDBG funds are used by a recipient or subrecipient to provide technical assistance to businesses, this requirement may be met by aggregating the jobs created or retained by all of the businesses receiving technical assistance during each program year.

(D) Where CDBG funds are used for activities meeting the criteria listed at §570.209(b)(2)(v), this requirement may be met by aggregating the jobs created or retained by all businesses for which CDBG assistance is obligated for such activities during the program year, except as provided at paragraph (d)(7) of this section.

(E) Where CDBG funds are used by a Community Development Financial Institution to carry out activities for the purpose of creating or retaining jobs, this requirement may be met by aggregating the jobs created or retained by all businesses for which CDBG assistance is obligated for such activities during the program year, except as provided at paragraph (d)(7) of this section.

(F) Where CDBG funds are used for public facilities or improvements which will result in the creation or retention of jobs by more than one business, this requirement may be met by aggregating the jobs created or retained by all such businesses as a result of the public facility or improvement.

(1) Where the public facility or improvement is undertaken principally for the benefit of one or more particular businesses, but where other businesses might also benefit from the assisted activity, the requirement may be met by aggregating only the jobs created or retained by those businesses for which the facility/improvement is principally undertaken, provided that the cost (in CDBG funds) for the facility/improvement is less than $10,000 per permanent full-time equivalent job to be created or retained by those businesses.

(2) In any case where the cost per job to be created or retained (as determined under paragraph (a)(4)(vi)(F)(1) of this section) is $10,000 or more, the requirement must be met by aggregating the jobs created or retained as a result of the public facility or improvement by all businesses in the service area of the facility/improvement. This aggregation must include businesses which, as a result of the public facility/improvement, locate or expand in the service area of the facility/improvement between the date the recipient identifies the activity in its action plan under part 91 of this title and the date one year after the physical completion of the facility/improvement. In addition, the assisted activity must comply with the public benefit standards at § 570.209(b).

(b) *Activities which aid in the prevention or elimination of slums or blight.* Activities meeting one or more of the following criteria, in the absence of substantial evidence to the contrary, will be considered to aid in the prevention or elimination of slums or blight:

(1) *Activities to address slums or blight on an area basis.* An activity will be considered to address prevention or elimination of slums or blight in an area if:

(i) The area, delineated by the recipient, meets a definition of a slum, blighted, deteriorated or deteriorating area under State or local law;

(ii) The area also meets the conditions in either paragraph (A) or (B):

(A) At least 25 percent of properties throughout the area experience one or more of the following conditions:

(*1*) Physical deterioration of buildings or improvements;

(*2*) Abandonment of properties;

(*3*) Chronic high occupancy turnover rates or chronic high vacancy rates in commercial or industrial buildings;

(*4*) Significant declines in property values or abnormally low property values relative to other areas in the community; or

(*5*) Known or suspected environmental contamination.

(B) The public improvements throughout the area are in a general state of deterioration.

(iii) Documentation is to be maintained by the recipient on the boundaries of the area and the conditions and standards used that qualified the area at the time of its designation. The recipient shall establish definitions of the conditions listed at § 570.208(b)(1)(ii)(A), and maintain records to substantiate how the area met the slums or blighted criteria. The designation of an area as slum or blighted under this section is required to be redetermined every 10 years for continued qualification. Documentation must be retained pursuant to the recordkeeping requirements contained at § 570.506 (b)(8)(ii).

(iv) The assisted activity addresses one or more of the conditions which contributed to the deterioration of the area. Rehabilitation of residential buildings carried out in an area meeting the above requirements will be considered to address the area's deterioration only where each such building rehabilitated is considered substandard under local definition before rehabilitation, and all deficiencies making a building substandard have been eliminated if less critical work on the building is undertaken. At a minimum, the local definition for this purpose must be such that buildings that it would render substandard would also fail to meet the housing quality standards for the Section 8 Housing Assistance Payments Program-Existing Housing (24 CFR 882.109).

(2) *Activities to address slums or blight on a spot basis.* The following activities may be undertaken on a spot basis to eliminate specific conditions of blight, physical decay, or environmental contamination that are not located in a slum or blighted area: acquisition; clearance; relocation; historic preservation; remediation of environmentally contaminated properties; or rehabilitation of buildings or improvements. However, rehabilitation must be limited to eliminating those conditions that are detrimental to public health and safety. If acquisition or relocation is undertaken, it must be a precursor to another eligible activity (funded with CDBG or other resources) that directly eliminates the specific conditions of blight or physical decay, or environmental contamination.

(3) *Activities to address slums or blight in an urban renewal area.* An activity will be considered to address prevention or elimination of slums or blight in an urban renewal area if the activity is:

(i) Located within an urban renewal project area or Neighborhood Development Program (NDP) action area; i.e., an area in which funded activities were authorized under an urban renewal Loan and Grant Agreement or an annual NDP Funding Agreement, pursuant to title I of the Housing Act of 1949; and

(ii) Necessary to complete the urban renewal plan, as then in effect, including *initial* land redevelopment permitted by the plan.

NOTE: Despite the restrictions in (b) (1) and (2) of this section, any rehabilitation activity which benefits low and moderate income persons pursuant to paragraph (a)(3) of this section can be undertaken without regard to the area in which it is located or the extent or nature of rehabilitation assisted.

(c) *Activities designed to meet community development needs having a particular urgency.* In the absence of substantial evidence to the contrary, an activity will be considered to address this objective if the recipient certifies that the activity is designed to alleviate existing conditions which pose a serious and immediate threat to the health or welfare of the community which are of recent origin or which recently became urgent, that the recipient is unable to finance the activity on its own, and that other sources of funding are not available. A condition will generally be considered to be of recent origin if it developed or became critical within 18 months preceding the certification by the recipient.

(d) *Additional criteria.* (1) Where the assisted activity is acquisition of real property, a preliminary determination of whether the activity addresses a national objective may be based on the planned use of the property after acquisition. A final determination shall be based on the actual use of the property, excluding any short-term, temporary use. Where the acquisition is for the purpose of clearance which will eliminate specific conditions of blight or physical decay, the clearance activity shall be considered the actual use of the property. However, any subsequent use or disposition of the cleared property shall be treated as a "change of use" under § 570.505.

(2) Where the assisted activity is relocation assistance that the recipient is required to provide, such relocation assistance shall be considered to address the same national objective as is addressed by the displacing activity. Where the relocation assistance is voluntary on the part of the grantee the recipient may qualify the assistance either on the basis of the national objective addressed by the displacing activity or on the basis that the recipients of the relocation assistance are low and moderate income persons.

(3) In any case where the activity undertaken for the purpose of creating or retaining jobs is a public improvement

and the area served is primarily residential, the activity must meet the requirements of paragraph (a)(1) of this section as well as those of paragraph (a)(4) of this section in order to qualify as benefiting low and moderate income persons.

(4) CDBG funds expended for planning and administrative costs under §570.205 and §570.206 will be considered to address the national objectives.

(5) Where the grantee has elected to prepare an area revitalization strategy pursuant to the authority of §91.215(e) of this title and HUD has approved the strategy, the grantee may also elect the following options:

(i) Activities undertaken pursuant to the strategy for the purpose of creating or retaining jobs may, at the option of the grantee, be considered to meet the requirements of this paragraph under the criteria at paragraph (a)(1)(vii) of this section in lieu of the criteria at paragraph (a)(4) of this section; and

(ii) All housing activities in the area for which, pursuant to the strategy, CDBG assistance is obligated during the program year may be considered to be a single structure for purposes of applying the criteria at paragraph (a)(3) of this section.

(6) Where CDBG-assisted activities are carried out by a Community Development Financial Institution whose charter limits its investment area to a primarily residential area consisting of at least 51 percent low- and moderate-income persons, the grantee may also elect the following options:

(i) Activities carried out by the Community Development Financial Institution for the purpose of creating or retaining jobs may, at the option of the grantee, be considered to meet the requirements of this paragraph under the criteria at paragraph (a)(1)(vii) of this section in lieu of the criteria at paragraph (a)(4) of this section; and

(ii) All housing activities for which the Community Development Financial Institution obligates CDBG assistance during the program year may be considered to be a single structure for purposes of applying the criteria at paragraph (a)(3) of this section.

(7) Where an activity meeting the criteria at §570.209(b)(2)(v) may also meet the requirements of either paragraph (d)(5)(i) or (d)(6)(i) of this section, the grantee may elect to qualify the activity under either the area benefit criteria at paragraph (a)(1)(vii) of this section or the job aggregation criteria at paragraph (a)(4)(vi)(D) of this section, but not both. Where an activity may meet the job aggregation criteria at both paragraphs (a)(4)(vi)(D) and (E) of this section, the grantee may elect to qualify the activity under either criterion, but not both.

[53 FR 34439, Sept. 6, 1988; 53 FR 41330, Oct. 21, 1988, as amended at 60 FR 1945, Jan. 5, 1995; 60 FR 17445, Apr. 6, 1995; 60 FR 56912, Nov. 9, 1995; 61 FR 18674, Apr. 29, 1996; 71 FR 30035, May 24, 2006; 72 FR 46370, Aug. 17, 2007]

§ 570.209 Guidelines for evaluating and selecting economic development projects.

The following guidelines are provided to assist the recipient to evaluate and select activities to be carried out for economic development purposes. Specifically, these guidelines are applicable to activities that are eligible for CDBG assistance under §570.203. These guidelines also apply to activities carried out under the authority of §570.204 that would otherwise be eligible under §570.203, were it not for the involvement of a Community-Based Development Organization (CBDO). (This would include activities where a CBDO makes loans to for-profit businesses.) These guidelines are composed of two components: guidelines for evaluating project costs and financial requirements; and standards for evaluating public benefit. The standards for evaluating public benefit are *mandatory*, but the guidelines for evaluating projects costs and financial requirements are not.

(a) *Guidelines and objectives for evaluating project costs and financial requirements.* HUD has developed guidelines that are designed to provide the recipient with a framework for financially underwriting and selecting CDBG-assisted economic development projects which are financially viable and will make the most effective use of the CDBG funds. These guidelines, also referred to as the underwriting guidelines, are published as appendix A to this part. The use of the underwriting guidelines published by HUD is not mandatory. However, grantees electing not to use these guidelines would be expected to conduct basic financial underwriting prior to the provision of CDBG financial assistance to a for-profit business. Where appropriate, HUD's underwriting guidelines recognize that different levels of review are appropriate to take into account differences in the size and scope of a proposed project, and in the case of a microenterprise or other small business to take into account the differences in the capacity and level of sophistication among businesses of differing sizes. Recipients are encouraged, when they develop their own programs and underwriting criteria, to also take these factors into account. The objectives of the underwriting guidelines are to ensure:

(1) That project costs are reasonable;

(2) That all sources of project financing are committed;

(3) That to the extent practicable, CDBG funds are not substituted for non-Federal financial support;

(4) That the project is financially feasible;

(5) That to the extent practicable, the return on the owner's equity investment will not be unreasonably high; and

(6) That to the extent practicable, CDBG funds are disbursed on a pro rata basis with other finances provided to the project.

(b) *Standards for evaluating public benefit.* The grantee is responsible for making sure that at least a minimum level of public benefit is obtained from the expenditure of CDBG funds under the categories of eligibility governed by these guidelines. The standards set forth below identify the types of public benefit that will be recognized for this purpose and the minimum level of each that must be obtained for the amount of CDBG funds used. Unlike the guidelines for project costs and financial requirements covered under paragraph (a) of this section, the use of the standards for public benefit is mandatory. Certain public facilities and improvements eligible under §570.201(c) of the regulations, which are undertaken for economic development purposes, are also subject to these standards, as specified in §570.208(a)(4)(vi)(F)(*2*).

(1) *Standards for activities in the aggregate.* Activities covered by these guidelines must, in the aggregate, either:

(i) Create or retain at least one full-time equivalent, permanent job per $35,000 of CDBG funds used; or

(ii) Provide goods or services to residents of an area, such that the number of low- and moderate-income persons residing in the areas served by the assisted businesses amounts to at least one low- and moderate-income person per $350 of CDBG funds used.

(2) *Applying the aggregate standards.* (i) A metropolitan city, an urban county, a non-entitlement CDBG grantee in Hawaii, or an Insular Area shall apply the aggregate standards under paragraph (b)(1) of this section to all applicable activities for which CDBG funds are first obligated within each single CDBG program year, without regard to the source year of the funds used for the activities. For Insular Areas, the preceding sentence applies to grants received in program years after Fiscal Year 2004. A grantee under the HUD-administered Small Cities Program, or Insular Areas CDBG grants prior to Fiscal Year 2005, shall apply the aggregate standards under paragraph (b)(1) of this section to all funds obligated for applicable activities from a given grant; program income obligated for applicable activities will, for these purposes, be aggregated with the most recent open grant. For any time period in which a community has no open HUD-administered or Insular Areas grants, the aggregate standards shall be applied to all applicable activities for which program income is obligated during that period.

(ii) The grantee shall apply the aggregate standards to the number of jobs to be created/retained, or to the number of persons residing in the area served (as applicable), as determined at the time funds are obligated to activities.

(iii) Where an activity is expected both to create or retain jobs and to provide goods or services to residents of an area, the grantee may elect to count the activity under either the jobs standard or the area residents standard, but not both.

(iv) Where CDBG assistance for an activity is limited to job training and

Ofc. of Asst. Secy., Comm. Planning, Develop., HUD § 570.209

placement and/or other employment support services, the jobs assisted with CDBG funds shall be considered to be created or retained jobs for the purposes of applying the aggregate standards.

(v) Any activity subject to these guidelines which meets one or more of the following criteria may, at the grantee's option, be excluded from the aggregate standards described in paragraph (b)(1) of this section:

(A) Provides jobs exclusively for unemployed persons or participants in one or more of the following programs:

(*1*) Jobs Training Partnership Act (JTPA);

(*2*) Jobs Opportunities for Basic Skills (JOBS); or

(*3*) Aid to Families with Dependent Children (AFDC);

(B) Provides jobs predominantly for residents of Public and Indian Housing units;

(C) Provides jobs predominantly for homeless persons;

(D) Provides jobs predominantly for low-skilled, low- and moderate-income persons, where the business agrees to provide clear opportunities for promotion and economic advancement, such as through the provision of training;

(E) Provides jobs predominantly for persons residing within a census tract (or block numbering area) that has at least 20 percent of its residents who are in poverty;

(F) Provides assistance to business(es) that operate(s) within a census tract (or block numbering area) that has at least 20 percent of its residents who are in poverty;

(G) Stabilizes or revitalizes a neighborhood that has at least 70 percent of its residents who are low- and moderate-income;

(H) Provides assistance to a Community Development Financial Institution that serve an area that is predominantly low- and moderate-income persons;

(I) Provides assistance to a Community-Based Development Organization serving a neighborhood that has at least 70 percent of its residents who are low- and moderate-income;

(J) Provides employment opportunities that are an integral component of a project designed to promote spatial deconcentration of low- and moderate-income and minority persons;

(K) With prior HUD approval, provides substantial benefit to low-income persons through other innovative approaches;

(L) Provides services to the residents of an area pursuant to a strategy approved by HUD under the provisions of § 91.215(e) of this title;

(M) Creates or retains jobs through businesses assisted in an area pursuant to a strategy approved by HUD under the provisions of § 91.215(e) of this title.

(N) Directly involves the economic development or redevelopment of environmentally contaminated properties.

(3) *Standards for individual activities.* Any activity subject to these guidelines which falls into one or more of the following categories will be considered by HUD to provide insufficient public benefit, and therefore may under no circumstances be assisted with CDBG funds:

(i) The amount of CDBG assistance exceeds either of the following, as applicable:

(A) $50,000 per full-time equivalent, permanent job created or retained; or

(B) $1,000 per low- and moderate-income person to which goods or services are provided by the activity.

(ii) The activity consists of or includes any of the following:

(A) General promotion of the community as a whole (as opposed to the promotion of specific areas and programs);

(B) Assistance to professional sports teams;

(C) Assistance to privately-owned recreational facilities that serve a predominantly higher-income clientele, where the recreational benefit to users or members clearly outweighs employment or other benefits to low- and moderate-income persons;

(D) Acquisition of land for which the specific proposed use has not yet been identified; and

(E) Assistance to a for-profit business while that business or any other business owned by the same person(s) or entity(ies) is the subject of unresolved findings of noncompliance relating to previous CDBG assistance provided by the recipient.

(4) *Applying the individual activity standards.* (i) Where an activity is expected both to create or retain jobs and to provide goods or services to residents of an area, it will be disqualified only if the amount of CDBG assistance exceeds both of the amounts in paragraph (b)(3)(i) of this section.

(ii) The individual activity standards in paragraph (b)(3)(i) of this section shall be applied to the number of jobs to be created or retained, or to the number of persons residing in the area served (as applicable), as determined at the time funds are obligated to activities.

(iii) Where CDBG assistance for an activity is limited to job training and placement and/or other employment support services, the jobs assisted with CDBG funds shall be considered to be created or retained jobs for the purposes of applying the individual activity standards in paragraph (b)(3)(i) of this section.

(c) *Amendments to economic development projects after review determinations.* If, after the grantee enters into a contract to provide assistance to a project, the scope or financial elements of the project change to the extent that a significant contract amendment is appropriate, the project should be reevaluated under these and the recipient's guidelines. (This would include, for example, situations where the business requests a change in the amount or terms of assistance being provided, or an extension to the loan payment period required in the contract.) If a reevaluation of the project indicates that the financial elements and public benefit to be derived have also substantially changed, then the recipient should make appropriate adjustments in the amount, type, terms or conditions of CDBG assistance which has been offered, to reflect the impact of the substantial change. (For example, if a change in the project elements results in a substantial reduction of the total project costs, it may be appropriate for the recipient to reduce the amount of total CDBG assistance.) If the amount of CDBG assistance provided to the project is increased, the amended project must still comply with the public benefit standards under paragraph (b) of this section.

(d) *Documentation.* The grantee must maintain sufficient records to demonstrate the level of public benefit, based on the above standards, that is actually achieved upon completion of the CDBG-assisted economic development activity(ies) and how that compares to the level of such benefit anticipated when the CDBG assistance was obligated. If the grantee's actual results show a pattern of substantial variation from anticipated results, the grantee is expected to take all actions reasonably within its control to improve the accuracy of its projections. If the actual results demonstrate that the recipient has failed the public benefit standards, HUD may require the recipient to meet more stringent standards in future years as appropriate.

[60 FR 1947, Jan. 5, 1995, as amended at 60 FR 17445, Apr. 6, 1995; 71 FR 30035, May 24, 2006; 72 FR 12535, Mar. 15, 2007; 72 FR 46370, Aug. 17, 2007]

§ 570.210 Prohibition on use of assistance for employment relocation activities.

(a) *Prohibition.* CDBG funds may not be used to directly assist a business, including a business expansion, in the relocation of a plant, facility, or operation from one LMA to another LMA if the relocation is likely to result in a significant loss of jobs in the LMA from which the relocation occurs.

(b) *Definitions.* The following definitions apply to this section:

(1) *Directly assist.* Directly assist means the provision of CDBG funds for activities pursuant to:

(i) § 570.203(b); or

(ii) §§ 570.201(a)—(d), 570.201(l), 570.203(a), or § 570.204 when the grantee, subrecipient, or, in the case of an activity carried out pursuant to § 570.204, a Community Based Development Organization (CDBO) enters into an agreement with a business to undertake one or more of these activities as a condition of the business relocating a facility, plant, or operation to the grantee's LMA. Provision of public facilities and indirect assistance that will provide benefit to multiple businesses does not fall under the definition of "directly assist," unless it includes the provision of infrastructure to aid a specific business that is the subject of an agreement with the specific assisted business.

(2) *Labor market area (LMA).* For metropolitan areas, an LMA is an area defined as such by the BLS. An LMA is an economically integrated geographic area within which individuals can live and find employment within a reasonable distance or can readily change employment without changing their place of residence. In addition, LMAs are nonoverlapping and geographically exhaustive. For metropolitan areas, grantees must use employment data, as defined by the BLS, for the LMA in which the affected business is currently located and from which current jobs may be lost. For non-metropolitan areas, an LMA is either an area defined by the BLS as an LMA, or a state may choose to combine non-metropolitan LMAs. States are required to define or reaffirm prior definitions of their LMAs on an annual basis and retain records to substantiate such areas prior to any business relocation that would be impacted by this rule. Metropolitan LMAs cannot be combined, nor can a non-metropolitan LMA be combined with a metropolitan LMA. For the HUD-administered Small Cities Program, each of the three participating counties in Hawaii will be considered to be its own LMA. Recipients of Fiscal Year 1999 Small Cities Program funding in New York will follow the requirements for State CDBG recipients.

(3) *Operation.* A business operation includes, but is not limited to, any equipment, employment opportunity, production capacity or product line of the business.

(4) *Significant loss of jobs.* (i) A loss of jobs is significant if: The number of jobs to be lost in the LMA in which the affected business is currently located is equal to or greater than one-tenth of one percent of the total number of persons in the labor force of that LMA; or in all cases, a loss of 500 or more jobs. Notwithstanding the aforementioned, a loss of 25 jobs or fewer does not constitute a significant loss of jobs.

(ii) A job is considered to be lost due to the provision of CDBG assistance if the job is relocated within three years of the provision of assistance to the business; or the time period within which jobs are to be created as specified by the agreement between the business and the recipient if it is longer than three years.

(c) *Written agreement.* Before directly assisting a business with CDBG funds, the recipient, subrecipient, or a CDBO (in the case of an activity carried out pursuant to §570.204) shall sign a written agreement with the assisted business. The written agreement shall include:

(1) *Statement.* A statement from the assisted business as to whether the assisted activity will result in the relocation of any industrial or commercial plant, facility, or operation from one LMA to another, and, if so, the number of jobs that will be relocated from each LMA;

(2) *Required information.* If the assistance will not result in a relocation covered by this section, a certification from the assisted business that neither it, nor any of its subsidiaries, has plans to relocate jobs at the time the agreement is signed that would result in a significant job loss as defined in this rule; and

(3) *Reimbursement of assistance.* The agreement shall provide for reimbursement of any assistance provided to, or expended on behalf of, the business in the event that assistance results in a relocation prohibited under this section.

(d) *Assistance not covered by this section.* This section does not apply to:

(1) *Relocation assistance.* Relocation assistance required by the Uniform Assistance and Real Property Acquisition Policies Act of 1970, (URA) (42 U.S.C. 4601–4655);

(2) *Microenterprises.* Assistance to microenterprises as defined by Section 102(a)(22) of the Housing and Community Development Act of 1974; and

(3) *Arms-length transactions.* Assistance to a business that purchases business equipment, inventory, or other physical assets in an arms-length transaction, including the assets of an existing business, provided that the purchase does not result in the relocation of the sellers' business operation (including customer base or list, goodwill, product lines, or trade names) from one LMA to another LMA and

§ 570.300

does not produce a significant loss of jobs in the LMA from which the relocation occurs.

[70 FR 76369, Dec. 23, 2005]

Subpart D—Entitlement Grants

SOURCE: 53 FR 34449, Sept. 6, 1988, unless otherwise noted.

§ 570.300 General.

This subpart describes the policies and procedures governing the making of community development block grants to entitlement communities and to non-entitlement counties in the State of Hawaii. The policies and procedures set forth in subparts A, C, J, K, and O of this part also apply to entitlement grantees and to non-entitlement grantees in the State of Hawaii. Sections 570.307 and 570.308 of this subpart do not apply to the Hawaii non-entitlement grantees.

[72 FR 46370, Aug. 17, 2007]

§ 570.301 Activity locations and float-funding.

The consolidated plan, action plan, and amendment submission requirements referred to in this section are those in 24 CFR part 91.

(a) For activities for which the grantee has not yet decided on a specific location, such as when the grantee is allocating an amount of funds to be used for making loans or grants to businesses or for residential rehabilitation, the description in the action plan or any amendment shall identify who may apply for the assistance, the process by which the grantee expects to select who will receive the assistance (including selection criteria), and how much and under what terms the assistance will be provided, or in the case of a planned public facility or improvement, how it expects to determine its location.

(b) *Float-funded activities and guarantees.* A recipient may use undisbursed funds in the line of credit and its CDBG program account that are budgeted in statements or action plans for one or more other activities that do not need the funds immediately, subject to the limitations described below. Such funds shall be referred to as the "float" for purposes of this section and the action plan. Each activity carried out using the float must meet all of the same requirements that apply to CDBG-assisted activities generally, and must be expected to produce program income in an amount at least equal to the amount of the float so used. Whenever the recipient proposes to fund an activity with the float, it must include the activity in its action plan or amend the action plan for the current program year. For purposes of this section, an activity that uses such funds will be called a "float-funded activity."

(1) Each float-funded activity must be individually listed and described as such in the action plan.

(2)(i) The expected time period between obligation of assistance for a float-funded activity and receipt of program income in an amount at least equal to the full amount drawn from the float to fund the activity may not exceed 2.5 years. An activity from which program income sufficient to recover the full amount of the float assistance is expected to be generated more than 2.5 years after obligation may not be funded from the float, but may be included in an action plan if it is funded from CDBG funds other than the float (e.g., grant funds or proceeds from an approved Section 108 loan guarantee).

(ii) Any extension of the repayment period for a float-funded activity shall be considered to be a new float-funded activity for these purposes and may be implemented by the grantee only if the extension is made subject to the same limitations and requirements as apply to a new float-funded activity.

(3) Unlike other projected program income, the full amount of income expected to be generated by a float-funded activity must be shown as a source of program income in the action plan containing the activity, whether or not some or all of the income is expected to be received in a future program year (in accordance with 24 CFR 91.220(g)(1)(ii)(D)).

(4) The recipient must also clearly declare in the action plan that identifies the float-funded activity the recipient's commitment to undertake one of the following options:

(i) Amend or delete activities in an amount equal to any default or failure to produce sufficient income in a timely manner. If the recipient makes this choice, it must include a description of the process it will use to select the activities to be amended or deleted and how it will involve citizens in that process; and it must amend the applicable statement(s) or action plan(s) showing those amendments or deletions promptly upon determining that the float-funded activity will not generate sufficient or timely program income;

(ii) Obtain an irrevocable line of credit from a commercial lender for the full amount of the float-funded activity and describe the lender and terms of such line of credit in the action plan that identifies the float-funded activity. To qualify for this purpose, such line of credit must be unconditionally available to the recipient in the amount of any shortfall within 30 days of the date that the float-funded activity fails to generate the projected amount of program income on schedule;

(iii) Transfer general local government funds in the full amount of any default or shortfall to the CDBG line of credit within 30 days of the float-funded activity's failure to generate the projected amount of the program income on schedule; or

(iv) A method approved in writing by HUD for securing timely return of the amount of the float funding. Such method must ensure that funds are available to meet any default or shortfall within 30 days of the float-funded activity's failure to generate the projected amount of the program income on schedule.

(5) When preparing an action plan for a year in which program income is expected to be received from a float-funded activity, and such program income has been shown in a prior statement or action plan, the current action plan shall identify the expected income and explain that the planned use of the income has already been described in prior statements or action plans, and shall identify the statements or action plans in which such descriptions may be found.

[60 FR 56913, Nov. 9, 1995]

§ 570.302 Submission requirements.

In order to receive its annual CDBG entitlement grant, a grantee must submit a consolidated plan in accordance with 24 CFR part 91. That part includes requirements for the content of the consolidated plan, for the process of developing the consolidated plan, including citizen participation provisions, for the submission date, for HUD approval, and for the amendment process.

(Approved by the Office of Management and Budget under control number 2506-0117)

[60 FR 1915, Jan. 5, 1995]

§ 570.303 Certifications.

The jurisdiction must make the certifications that are set forth in 24 CFR part 91 as part of the consolidated plan.

(Approved by the Office of Management and Budget under control number 2506-0117)

[60 FR 1915, Jan. 5, 1995]

§ 570.304 Making of grants.

(a) *Approval of grant.* HUD will approve a grant if the jurisdiction's submissions have been made and approved in accordance with 24 CFR part 91, and the certifications required therein are satisfactory to the Secretary. The certifications will be satisfactory to the Secretary for this purpose unless the Secretary has determined pursuant to subpart O of this part that the grantee has not complied with the requirements of this part, has failed to carry out its consolidated plan as provided under § 570.903, or has determined that there is evidence, not directly involving the grantee's past performance under this program, that tends to challenge in a substantial manner the grantee's certification of future performance. If the Secretary makes any such determination, however, further assurances may be required to be submitted by the grantee as the Secretary may deem warranted or necessary to find the grantee's certification satisfactory.

(b) *Grant agreement.* The grant will be made by means of a grant agreement executed by both HUD and the grantee.

(c) *Grant amount.* The Secretary will make a grant in the full entitlement amount, generally within the last 30 days of the grantee's current program year, unless:

(1) Either the consolidated plan is not received by August 16 of the federal fiscal year for which funds are appropriated or the consolidated plan is not approved under 24 CFR part 91, subpart F—in which case, the grantee will forfeit the entire entitlement amount; or

(2) The grantee's performance does not meet the performance requirements or criteria prescribed in subpart O and the grant amount is reduced.

[53 FR 34449, Sept. 6, 1988, as amended at 60 FR 1915, Jan. 5, 1995; 60 FR 16379, Mar. 30, 1995; 60 FR 56913, Nov. 9, 1995]

§ 570.307   Urban counties.

(a) *Determination of qualification.* The Secretary will determine the qualifications of counties to receive entitlements as urban counties upon receipt of qualification documentation from counties at such time, and in such manner and form as prescribed by HUD. The Secretary shall determine eligibility and applicable portions of each eligible county for purposes of fund allocation under section 106 of the Act on the basis of information available from the U.S. Bureau of the Census with respect to population and other pertinent demographic characteristics, and based on information provided by the county and its included units of general local government.

(b) *Qualification as an urban county.* (1) A county will qualify as an urban county if such county meets the definition at § 570.3(3). As necessitated by this definition, the Secretary shall determine which counties have authority to carry out essential community development and housing assistance activities in their included units of general local government without the consent of the local governing body and which counties must execute cooperation agreements with such units to include them in the urban county for qualification and grant calculation purposes.

(2) At the time of urban county qualification, HUD may refuse to recognize the cooperation agreement of a unit of general local government in an urban county where, based on past performance and other available information, there is substantial evidence that such unit does not cooperate in the implementation of the essential community development or housing assistance activities or where legal impediments to such implementation exist, or where participation by a unit of general local government in noncompliance with the applicable law in subpart K would constitute noncompliance by the urban county. In such a case, the unit of general local government will not be permitted to participate in the urban county, and its population or other needs characteristics will not be considered in the determination of whether the county qualifies as an urban county or in determining the amount of funds to which the urban county may be entitled. HUD will not take this action unless the unit of general local government and the county have been given an opportunity to challenge HUD's determination and to informally consult with HUD concerning the proposed action.

(c) *Essential activities.* For purposes of this section, the term "essential community development and housing assistance activities" means community renewal and lower income housing activities, specifically urban renewal and publicly assisted housing. In determining whether a county has the required powers, the Secretary will consider both its authority and, where applicable, the authority of its designated agency or agencies.

(d) *Period of qualification.* (1) The qualification by HUD of an urban county shall remain effective for three successive Federal fiscal years regardless of changes in its population during that period, except as provided under paragraph (f) of this section and except as provided under § 570.3(3) where the period of qualification shall be two successive Federal fiscal years.

(2) During the period of qualification, no included unit of general local government may withdraw from nor be removed from the urban county for HUD's grant computation purposes.

(3) If some portion of an urban county's unincorporated area becomes incorporated during the urban county qualification period, the newly incorporated unit of general local government shall not be excluded from the urban county nor shall it be eligible for

a separate grant under subpart D, F, or I until the end of the urban county's current qualification period, unless the urban county fails to receive a grant for any year during that qualification period.

(e) *Grant ineligibility of included units of general local government.* (1) An included unit of general local government cannot become eligible for an entitlement grant as a metropolitan city during the period of qualification of the urban county (even if it becomes a principal city of a metropolitan area or its population surpasses 50,000 during that period). Rather, such a unit of general local government shall continue to be included as part of the urban county for the remainder of the urban county's qualification period, and no separate grant amount shall be calculated for the included unit.

(2) An included unit of general local government which is part of an urban county shall be ineligible to apply for grants under subpart F, or to be a recipient of assistance under subpart I, during the entire period of urban county qualification.

(f) *Failure of an urban county to receive a grant.* Failure of an urban county to receive a grant during any year shall terminate the existing qualification of that urban county, and that county shall requalify as an urban county before receiving an entitlement grant in any successive Federal fiscal year. Such termination shall release units of general local government included in the urban county, in subsequent years, from the prohibition to receive grants under paragraphs (d)(3), (e)(1) and (e)(2) of this section. For this purpose an urban county shall be deemed to have received a grant upon having satisfied the requirements of sections 104 (a), (b), (c), and (d) of the Act, without regard to adjustments which may be made to this grant amount under section 104(e) or 111 of the Act.

(g) *Notifications of the opportunity to be excluded.* Any county seeking to qualify for an entitlement grant as an urban county for any Federal fiscal year shall notify each unit of general local government which is located, in whole or in part, within the county and which would otherwise be included in the urban county, but which is eligible to elect to have its population excluded from that of the urban county, that it has the opportunity to make such an election, and that such an election, or the failure to make such an election, shall be effective for the period for which the county qualifies as an urban county. These notifications shall be made by a date specified by HUD. A unit of general local government which elects to be excluded from participation as a part of the urban county shall notify the county and HUD in writing by a date specified by HUD. Such a unit of government may subsequently elect to participate in the urban county for the remaining one or two year period by notifying HUD and the county, in writing, of such election by a date specified by HUD.

[53 FR 34449, Sept. 6, 1988, as amended at 56 FR 56127, Oct. 31, 1991; 68 FR 69582, Dec. 12, 2003]

§ 570.308 Joint requests.

(a) *Joint requests and cooperation agreements.* (1) Any urban county and any metropolitan city located, in whole or in part, within that county may submit a joint request to HUD to approve the inclusion of the metropolitan city as a part of the urban county for purposes of planning and implementing a joint community development and housing program. Such a joint request shall only be considered if submitted at the time the county is seeking a three year qualification or requalification as an urban county. Such a joint request shall, upon approval by HUD, remain effective for the period for which the county is qualified as an urban county. An urban county may be joined by more than one metropolitan city, but a metropolitan city located in more than one urban county may only be included in one urban county for any program year. A joint request shall be deemed approved by HUD unless HUD notifies the city and the county of its disapproval and the reasons therefore within 30 days of receipt of the request by HUD.

(2) Each metropolitan city and urban county submitting a joint request shall submit an executed cooperation agreement to undertake or to assist in the undertaking of essential community

development and housing assistance activities, as defined in § 570.307(c).

(b) *Joint grant amount.* The grant amount for a joint recipient shall be the sum of the amounts authorized for the individual entitlement grantees, as described in section 106 of the Act. The urban county shall be the grant recipient.

(c) *Effect of inclusion.* Upon urban county qualification and HUD approval of the joint request and cooperation agreement, the metropolitan city shall be considered a part of the urban county for purposes of program planning and implementation for the period of the urban county qualification, and shall be treated the same as any other unit of general local government which is part of the urban county.

(d) *Submission requirements.* In requesting a grant under this part, the urban county shall make a single submission which meets the submission requirements of 24 CFR part 91 and covers all members of the joint recipient.

[53 FR 34449, Sept. 6, 1988, as amended at 60 FR 1915, Jan. 5, 1995]

§ 570.309 Restriction on location of activities.

CDBG funds may assist an activity outside the jurisdiction of the grantee only if the grantee determines that such an activity is necessary to further the purposes of the Act and the recipient's community development objectives, and that reasonable benefits from the activity will accrue to residents within the jurisdiction of the grantee. The grantee shall document the basis for such determination prior to providing CDBG funds for the activity.

[60 FR 56914, Nov. 9, 1995]

Subpart E—Special Purpose Grants

§ 570.400 General.

(a) *Applicability.* The policies and procedures set forth in subparts A, C, J, K, and O of this part shall apply to this subpart, except to the extent that they are specifically modified or augmented by the contents of this subpart, including specified exemptions described herein. The HUD Environmental Review Procedures contained in 24 CFR part 58 also apply to this subpart, unless otherwise specifically provided herein.

(b) *Data.* Wherever data are used in this subpart for selecting applicants for assistance or for determining grant amounts, the source of such data shall be the most recent information available from the U.S. Bureau of the Census which is referable to the same point or period of time.

(c) *Review of applications for discretionary assistance*—(1) *Review components.* An application for assistance under this subpart shall be reviewed by HUD to ensure that:

(i) The application is postmarked or received on or before any final date established by HUD;

(ii) The application is complete;

(iii) Required certifications have been included in the application; and

(iv) The application meets the specific program requirements listed in the FEDERAL REGISTER Notice published in connection with a competition for funding, and any other specific requirements listed under this subpart for each of the programs.

(2) *Timing and review.* HUD is not required by the Act to review and approve an application for assistance or a contract proposal within any specified time period. However, HUD will attempt to complete its review of any application/proposal within 75 days.

(3) *Notification to applicant/proposer.* HUD will notify the applicant/proposer in writing that the applicant/proposal has been approved, partially approved, or disapproved. If an application/proposal is partially approved or disapproved, the applicant/proposer will be informed of the basis for HUD's decision. HUD may make conditional approvals under § 570.304(d).

(d) *Program amendments.* (1) Recipients shall request prior written HUD approval for all program amendments involving changes in the scope or the location of approved activities.

(2) Any program amendments, whether or not they require HUD approval, must be fully documented in the recipient's records.

(e) *Performance reports.* Any performance report required of a discretionary

Ofc. of Asst. Secy., Comm. Planning, Develop., HUD § 570.401

assistance recipient shall be submitted in the form specified in this subpart, in the award document, or (if the report relates to a specific competition for an assistance award) in a form specified in a Notice published in the FEDERAL REGISTER.

(f) *Performance reviews and findings.* HUD may review the recipient's performance in carrying out the activities for which assistance is provided in a timely manner and in accordance with its approved application, all applicable requirements of this part and the terms of the assistance agreement. Findings of performance deficiencies may be cause for appropriate corrective and remedial actions under § 570.910.

(g) *Funding sanctions.* Following notice and opportunity for informal consultation, HUD may withhold, reduce or terminate the assistance where any corrective or remedial actions taken under § 570.910 fail to remedy a recipient's performance deficiencies, and the deficiencies are sufficiently substantial, in the judgment of HUD, to warrant sanctions.

(h) *Publication of availability of funds.* HUD will publish by Notice in the FEDERAL REGISTER each year the amount of funds available for the special purpose grants authorized by each section under this subpart.

[50 FR 37525, Sept. 16, 1985, as amended at 56 FR 18968, Apr. 24, 1991]

§ 570.401 Community adjustment and economic diversification planning assistance.

(a) *General*—(1) *Purpose.* The purpose of this program is to assist units of general local government in nonentitlement areas to undertake the planning of community adjustments and economic diversification activities, in response to physical, social, economic or governmental impacts on the communities generated by the actions of the Department of Defense (DoD) defined in paragraph (a)(2) of this section.

(2) *Impacts.* Funding under this section is available only to communities affected by one or more of the following DoD-related impacts:

(i) The proposed or actual establishment, realignment, or closure of a military installation;

(ii) The cancellation or termination of a DoD contract or the failure to proceed with an approved major weapon system program;

(iii) A publicly announced planned major reduction in DoD spending that would directly and adversely affect a unit of general local government and result in the loss of 1,000 or more full-time DoD and contractor employee positions over a five-year period in the unit of general local government and the surrounding area; or

(iv) The Secretary of HUD (in consultation with the Secretary of DoD) determines that an action described in paragraphs (a)(2)(i)–(iii) of this section is likely to have a direct and significant adverse consequence on the unit of general local government.

(3) *Form of awards.* Planning assistance will be awarded in the form of grants.

(4) *Program administration.* HUD will publish in the FEDERAL REGISTER early in each fiscal year the amount of funds to be available for that fiscal year for awards under this section. HUD will accept applications throughout the fiscal year, and will review and consider for funding each application according to the threshold and qualifying factors in paragraphs (f) and (g) of this section.

(b) *Definitions.* In addition to the definitions in § 570.3 of this part, the following definitions apply to this section:

(1) *Adjustment planning.* Generally, developing plans and proposals in direct response to contraction or expansion of the local economy, or changes in the physical development or the social conditions of the community, resulting from a DoD-generated impact. Typically, this planning includes one or more of the following tasks: Collecting, updating, and analyzing data; identifying problems; formulating solutions; proposing long- and short-term policies; recommending public- and private-sector actions to implement community adjustments and economic diversification activities; securing citizen involvement; and coordinating with Federal, State, and local entities with respect to the DoD-related impacts.

(2) *Community adjustment.* Any proposed action to change the physical,

economic, or social infrastructure within the jurisdiction or surrounding area, directly and appropriately in response to the DoD-generated impact.

(3) *Contract.* (i) Any defense contract in an amount not less than $5 million (without regard to the date on which the contract was awarded); and

(ii) Any subcontract that is entered into in connection with a contract (without regard to the effective date of the subcontract) and involves not less than $500,000.

(4) *Defense facility.* Any private facility producing goods or services pursuant to a defense contract.

(5) *DoD.* The Department of Defense.

(6) *Economic diversification activities.* Any public or private sector actions to change the local mix of industrial, commercial, and service sectors, or the mix of business ventures within a sector, that are intended to mitigate decline in the local economy resulting from DoD-generated impacts or, in the case of expansion of a military installation or a defense facility, that are intended to respond to new economic growth spawned by that expansion.

(7) *Military installation.* Any camp, post, station, base, yard, or other jurisdiction of a military department that is located within any of the several States, the District of Columbia, the Commonwealth of Puerto Rico, or Guam.

(8) *Realignment.* Any action that both reduces and relocates functions and civilian personnel positions, but does not include a reduction in force resulting from workload adjustments, reduced personnel or funding levels, or skill imbalances.

(9) *Section 107* means section 107 of the Housing and Community Development Act of 1974, 42 U.S.C. 5307. Section 107(b)(6) was added by section 801 of the Housing and Community Development Act of 1992 (Pub. L. 102–550, approved October 28, 1992).

(10) *Section 2391(b).* The Department of Defense adjustment planning program as set out in 10 U.S.C. 2391(b).

(11) *Small Cities CDBG Program.* The Community Development Block Grant program for nonentitlement areas in which the States have elected not to administer available program funds. The regulations governing this program are set out in subpart F of this part.

(12) *Surrounding area.* The labor market area as defined by the Bureau of Labor Statistics that:

(i) Includes all or part of the applicant's jurisdictions; and

(ii) Includes additional areas outside the jurisdiction.

(c) *Eligible applicants.* Any unit of general local government, excluding units of general government that are entitlement cities or are included in an urban county, and which does not include Indian Tribes.

(d) *Eligible activities.* Activities eligible for adjustment planning assistance include, generally:

(1) Initial assessments and quick studies of physical, social, economic, and fiscal impacts on the community;

(2) Preliminary identification of potential public and private sector actions needed for the community to initiate its response;

(3) If timely, modification of the applicant's current comprehensive plan or any functional plan, such as for housing, including shelter for the homeless, or for transportation or other physical infrastructure;

(4) If timely, modification of the applicant's current economic plans and programs, such as for business development, job training, or industrial or commercial development;

(5) Preparation for and conduct of initial community outreach activities to begin involving local citizens and the private sector in planning for adjustment and diversification;

(6) Environmental reviews related to DoD-related impacts;

(7) Initial identification of and coordination with Federal, State and local entities that may be expected to assist in the community's adjustment and economic development; and with State-designated enterprise zones, and Federal empowerment zones and enterprise communities when selected and announced.

(8) Any other planning activity that may enable the community to organize itself, establish a start-up capacity to plan, propose specific plans and programs, coordinate with appropriate public or private entities, or qualify more quickly for the more substantial

planning assistance available from DoD.

(e) *Ineligible activities.* Activities ineligible for adjustment planning assistance are:

(1) Base re-use planning.

(2) Site planning, architectural and engineering studies, feasibility and cost analyses and similar planning for specific projects to implement community adjustment or economic diversification, unless as last resort funding for those applicants which are unable to obtain planning assistance from other sources.

(3) Planning by communities which are encroaching on military installations.

(4) Demonstration planning activities intended to evolve new planning techniques for impacted communities.

(5) Any planning activity proposed to supplement or replace planning that has been or is being assisted by the DoD Sec. 2391(b) adjustment planning program.

(6) Any other planning activity the purpose of which is not demonstrably in direct response to a DOD-related impact triggered by one or more of the four criteria specified in paragraph (a)(2) of this section.

(f) *Threshold requirements.* No application will qualify for funding unless it meets the following requirements:

(1) Verification by HUD that the applicant is a unit of general government in a nonentitlement area.

(2) Verification by HUD and DoD that a triggering event described in paragraph (a)(2) of this section has occurred or will occur.

(3) With respect to communities affected by the 49 base closings and 28 realignments listed by the 1991 Base Closure and Realignment Commission, verification by DoD that it has provided no prior funding and that the applicant may benefit from start-up planning assistance from HUD.

(4) Determination by HUD that the proposed planning activities are eligible.

(5) Determination by HUD that the submission requirements in paragraph (h) of this section have been satisfied.

(g) *Qualifying factors.* HUD will make funding decisions on qualified applications on the basis of the factors listed below, in the order of such applications received, while program funds remain available. HUD will also request and consider advise from DoD's Office of Economic Assistance concerning the relative merits of each application.

(1) The adequacy of the applicant's initial assessment of actual or probable impacts on the community and the surrounding area;

(2) The adequacy and appropriateness of the start-up planning envisioned by the applicant in response to the impacts;

(3) The type, extent, and adequacy of coordination that the applicant has achieved, or plans to achieve, in order to undertake planning for community adjustment and economic diversification.

(4) The cost-effectiveness of the proposed budget to carry out the planning work envisioned by the applicant;

(5) The capability of the organization the applicant proposes to do the planning;

(6) The credentials and experience of the key staff the applicant proposes to do the planning;

(7) The presence of significant private sector impact, as measured by the extent to which the DoD-generated impact is projected to decrease or increase the employment base by 10% or more;

(8) The presence of significant public sector impact, as measured by the extent to which the DoD-generated impact is projected to decrease or increase the applicant's capital and operating budgets for the next fiscal year by 10% or more;

(9) The degree of urgency, to the extent that a suddenly announced action, e.g. a plant closing, is officially scheduled to occur within a year of the date of application.

(h) *Submission requirements.* Applicants may submit applications at any time to: Director, Office of Technical Assistance, room 7214, 451 Seventh Street, SW., Washington, DC 20410. Each application (an original and three copies) shall include the following:

(1) The Standard Form SF-424 as a face sheet, signed and dated by a person authorized to represent and contractually or otherwise commit the applicant;

§ 570.402

(2) A concise title and brief abstract of the proposed planning work, including the total cost;

(3) A narrative that:

(i) Documents one or more of the triggering events described in paragraph (a)(2) of this section that qualifies the applicant to apply for planning assistance for community adjustments and economic diversification;

(ii) Provides an initial assessment of actual or probable impacts on the applicant community and the surrounding area;

(iii) Provides an initial assessment of the type and extent of start-up planning envisioned by the applicant in response to the DoD-generated impact; and

(iv) Describes the measures by which the applicant has already coordinated, or plans to coordinate, with the DoD Office of Economic Assistance, the Economic Development Administration of the Department of Commerce, the Department of Labor, any military department, or any other appropriate Federal agency; appropriate State agencies, specifically including the agency administering the Small Cities CDBG Program; appropriate State-designated enterprise zones; appropriate Federal empowerment zones and enterprise communities, when selected and announced; appropriate other units of general local government in the nonentitlement area; appropriate businesses, corporations, and defense facilities concerned with impacts on the applicant community; and homeless nonprofit organizations, with respect to title V of the Stewart B. McKinney Act (42 U.S.C. 11411–11412), requiring the Federal property be considered for use in assisting the homeless.

(4) A Statement of Work describing the specific project tasks proposed to be undertaken in order to plan for community adjustment and economic diversification activities;

(5) A proposed budget showing the estimated costs and person-days of effort for each task, by cost categories, with supporting documentation of costs and a justification of the person-days of effort;

(6) A description of the qualifications of the proposed technical staff, including their names and resumes;

(7) A work plan that describes the schedule for accomplishing the tasks described in the Statement of Work, the time needed to do each task, and the elapsed time needed for all the tasks; and

(8) Other materials, as prescribed in the application kit; these materials will include required certifications dealing with: Drug-Free Workplace Requirements; Disclosure Regarding Payments to Influence Certain Federal Transactions; and Prohibition Regarding Excessive Force.

(i) *Approval procedures*—(1) *Acceptance.* HUD's acceptance of an application meeting the threshold requirements of paragraph (f) does not assure a commitment to provide funding or to provide the full amount requested. HUD may elect to negotiate both proposed tasks and budgets in order to promote more cost-effective planning.

(2) *Notification.* HUD will provide notification about whether a project will be funded, rejected, or held for further consideration by HUD and DoD.

(3) *Form of award.* HUD will award funds in the form of grants.

(4) *Administration.* Project administration will be governed by the terms of individual awards and by the following provisions of this part:

(i) Subpart A, § 570.5;

(ii) Subpart E, §§ 570.400(d), (e), (f), and (g);

(iii) Subpart J, §§ 570.500(c), 570.501, 570.502, 570.503, and 570.509;

(iv) Subpart K, §§ 570.601, 570.602, 570.609, 570.610, and 570.611.

The environmental review requirements of 24 CFR part 58 do not apply.

(Approved by the Office of Management and Budget under control number 2535–0084)

[59 FR 15016, Mar. 30, 1994]

§ 570.402 Technical assistance awards.

(a) *General.* (1) The purpose of the Community Development Technical Assistance Program is to increase the effectiveness with which States, units of general local government, and Indian tribes plan, develop, and administer assistance under title I and section 810 of the Act. Title I programs are the Entitlement Program (24 CFR part 570, subpart D); the section 108 Loan Guarantee Program (24 CFR part

570, subpart M); the Urban Development Action Grant Program (24 CFR part 570, subpart G); the HUD-administered Small Cities Program (24 CFR part 570, subpart F); the State-administered Program for Non-Entitlement Communities (24 CFR part 570, subpart I); the grants for Indian Tribes program (24 CFR part 571); and the Special Purpose Grants for Insular Areas, Community Development Work Study and Historically Black Colleges and Universities (24 CFR part 570, subpart E). The section 810 program is the Urban Homesteading Program (24 CFR part 590).

(2) Funding under this section is awarded for the provision of technical expertise in planning, managing or carrying out such programs including the activities being or to be assisted thereunder and other actions being or to be undertaken for the purpose of the program, such as increasing the effectiveness of public service and other activities in addressing identified needs, meeting applicable program requirements (e.g., citizen participation, non-discrimination, OMB Circulars), increasing program management or capacity building skills, attracting business or industry to CDBG assisted economic development sites or projects, assisting eligible CDBG subrecipients such as neighborhood nonprofits or small cities in how to obtain CDBG funding from cities and States. The provision of technical expertise in other areas which may have some tangential benefit or effect on a program is insufficient to qualify for funding.

(3) Awards may be made pursuant to HUD solicitations for assistance applications or procurement contract proposals issued in the form of a publicly available document which invites the submission of applications or proposals within a prescribed period of time. HUD may also enter into agreements with other Federal agencies for awarding the technical assistance funds:

(i) Where the Secretary determines that such funding procedures will achieve a particular technical assistance objective more effectively and the criteria for making the awards will be consistent with this section, or

(ii) The transfer of funds to the other Federal agency for use under the terms of the agreement is specifically authorized by law. The Department will not accept or fund unsolicited proposals.

(b) *Definitions.* (1) *Areawide planning organization* (APO) means an organization authorized by law or local agreement to undertake planning and other activities for a metropolitan or non-metropolitan area.

(2) *Technical assistance* means the facilitating of skills and knowledge in planning, developing and administering activities under title I and section 810 of the Act in entities that may need but do not possess such skills and knowledge, and includes assessing programs and activities under title I.

(c) *Eligible applicants.* Eligible applicants for award of technical assistance funding are:

(1) States, units of general local government, APOs, and Indian Tribes; and

(2) Public and private non-profit or for-profit groups, including educational institutions, qualified to provide technical assistance to assist such governmental units to carry out the title I or Urban Homesteading programs. An applicant group must be designated as a technical assistance provider to a unit of government's title I program or Urban Homesteading program by the chief executive officer of each unit to be assisted, unless the assistance is limited to conferences/workshops attended by more than one unit of government.

(d) *Eligible activities.* Activities eligible for technical assistance funding include:

(1) The provision of technical or advisory services;

(2) The design and operation of training projects, such as workshops, seminars, or conferences;

(3) The development and distribution of technical materials and information; and

(4) Other methods of demonstrating and making available skills, information and knowledge to assist States, units of general local government, or Indian Tribes in planning, developing, administering or assessing assistance under title I and Urban Homesteading programs in which they are participating or seeking to participate.

(e) *Ineligible activities.* Activities for which costs are ineligible under this section include:

(1) In the case of technical assistance for States, the cost of carrying out the administration of the State CDBG program for non-entitlement communities;

(2) The cost of carrying out the activities authorized under the title I and Urban Homesteading programs, such as the provision of public services, construction, rehabilitation, planning and administration, for which the technical assistance is to be provided;

(3) The cost of acquiring or developing the specialized skills or knowledge to be provided by a group funded under this section;

(4) Research activities;

(5) The cost of identifying units of governments needing assistance (except that the cost of selecting recipients of technical assistance under the provisions of paragraph (k) is eligible); or

(6) Activities designed primarily to benefit HUD, or to assist HUD in carrying out the Department's responsibilities; such as research, policy analysis of proposed legislation, training or travel of HUD staff, or development and review of reports to the Congress.

(f) *Criteria for competitive selection.* In determining whether to fund competitive applications or proposals under this section, the Department will use the following criteria:

(1) *For solicited assistance applications.* The Department will use two types of criteria for reviewing and selecting competitive assistance applications solicited by HUD:

(i) Evaluation criteria: These criteria will be used to rank applications according to weights which may vary with each competition:

(A) Probable effectiveness of the application in meeting needs of localities and accomplishing project objectives;

(B) Soundness and cost-effectiveness of the proposed approach;

(C) Capacity of the applicant to carry out the proposed activities in a timely and effective fashion;

(D) The extent to which the results may be transferable or applicable to other title I or Urban Homesteading program participants.

(ii) Program policy criteria: These factors may be used by the selecting official to select a range of projects that would best serve program objectives for a particular competition:

(A) Geographic distribution;

(B) Diversity of types and sizes of applicant entities; and

(C) Diversity of methods, approaches, or kinds of projects.

The Department will publish a Notice of Fund Availability (NOFA) in the FEDERAL REGISTER for each competition indicating the objective of the technical assistance, the amount of funding available, the application procedures, including the eligible applicants and activities to be funded, any special conditions applicable to the solicitation, including any requirements for a matching share or for commitments for CDBG or other title I funding to carry out eligible activities for which the technical assistance is to be provided, the maximum points to be awarded each evaluation criterion for the purpose of ranking applications, and any special factors to be considered in assigning the points to each evaluation criterion. The Notice will also indicate which program policy factors will be used, the impact of those factors on the selection process, the justification for their use and, if appropriate, the relative priority of each program policy factor.

(2) *For competitive procurement contract bids/proposals.* The Department's criteria for review and selection of solicited bids/proposals for procurement contracts will be described in its public announcement of the availability of an Invitation for Bids (IFB) or a Request for Proposals (RFP). The public notice, solicitation and award of procurement contracts, when used to acquire technical assistance, shall be procured in accordance with the Federal Acquisition Regulation (48 CFR chapter 1) and the HUD Acquisition Regulation (48 CFR chapter 24).

(g) *Submission procedures.* Solicited assistance applications shall be submitted in accordance with the time and place and content requirements described in the Department's NOFA. Solicited bids/proposals for procurement contracts shall be submitted in accordance with the requirements in the IFB or RFP.

(h) *Approval procedures*—(1) *Acceptance.* HUD's acceptance of an application or proposal for review does not imply a commitment to provide funding.

(2) *Notification.* HUD will provide notification of whether a project will be funded or rejected.

(3) *Form of award.* (i) HUD will award technical assistance funds as a grant, cooperative agreement or procurement contract, consistent with this section, the Federal Grant and Cooperative Agreement Act of 1977, 31 U.S.C. 6301–6308, the HUD Acquisition Regulation, and the Federal Acquisition Regulation.

(ii) When HUD's primary purpose is the transfer of technical assistance to assist the recipients in support of the title I or Section 810 programs, an assistance instrument (grant or cooperative agreement) will be used. A grant instrument will be used when substantial Federal involvement is not anticipated. A cooperative agreement will be used when substantial Federal involvement is anticipated. When a cooperative agreement is selected, the agreement will specify the nature of HUD's anticipated involvement in the project.

(iii) A contract will be used when HUD's primary purpose is to obtain a provider of technical assistance to act on the Department's behalf. In such cases the Department will define the specific tasks to be performed. However, nothing in this section shall preclude the Department from awarding a procurement contract in any other case when it is determined to be in the Department's best interests.

(4) *Administration.* Project administration will be governed by the terms of individual awards and relevant regulations. As a general rule, proposals will be funded to operate for one to two years, and periodic and final reports will be required.

(i) *Environmental and intergovernmental review.* The requirements for Environmental Reviews and Intergovernmental Reviews do not apply to technical assistance awards.

(j) *Selection of recipients of technical assistance.* Where under the terms of the funding award the recipient of the funding is to select the recipients of the technical assistance to be provided, the funding recipient shall publish, and publicly make available to potential technical assistance recipients, the availability of such assistance and the specific criteria to be used for the selection of the recipients to be assisted. Selected recipients must be entities participating or planning to participate in the title I or Urban Homesteading programs or activities for which the technical assistance is to be provided.

(Approved by the Office of Management and Budget under control numbers 2535–0085 and 2535–0084)

[56 FR 41938, Aug. 26, 1991]

§ 570.403 New Communities.

The regulations for New Communities grants in this section, that were effective immediately before April 19, 1996, will continue to govern the rights and obligations of recipients and HUD with respect to grants under the New Communities program.

[61 FR 11476, Mar. 20, 1996]

§ 570.404 Historically Black colleges and universities program.

(a) *General.* Grants under this section will be awarded to historically Black colleges and universities to expand their role and effectiveness in addressing community development needs, including neighborhood revitalization, housing and economic development in their localities, consistent with the purposes of title I of the Housing and Community Development Act of 1974.

(b) *Eligible applicants.* Only historically Black colleges and universities (as determined by the Department of Education in accordance with that Department's responsibilities under Executive Order 12677, dated April 28, 1989) are eligible to submit applications.

(c) *Eligible activities.* Activities that may be funded under this section are those eligible under §§ 570.201 through 570.207, provided that any activity which is required by State or local law to be carried out by a governmental entity may not be funded under this section. Notwithstanding the provisions of §§ 570.200(g), grants under this section

§ 570.404

are not subject to the 20 percent limitation on planning and program administration costs, as defined in §§ 570.205 and 570.206, respectively.

(d) *Applications.* Applications will only be accepted from eligible applicants in response to a Request for Applications (RFA) which will be issued either concurrently with or after the publication of a Notice of Funding Availability (NOFA) published in the FEDERAL REGISTER. The NOFA will describe any special objectives sought to be achieved by the funding to be provided, including any limitations on the type of activities to be funded to achieve the objectives, points to be awarded to each of the selection criteria listed in paragraph (e) of this section, and any special factors to be evaluated in assigning points under the selection factors to achieve the stated objectives. The NOFA will also state the deadline for the submission of applications, the total funding available for the competition, and the maximum amount of individual grants. The NOFA will include further information and instructions for the submission of acceptable applications to HUD.

(e) *Selection criteria.* Each application submitted under this section will be evaluated by HUD using the following criteria:

(1) The extent to which the applicant addresses the objectives published in the NOFA and the RFA.

(2) The extent to which the applicant demonstrates to HUD that the proposed activities will have a substantial impact in achieving the stated objectives.

(3) The special needs of the applicant or locality to be met in carrying out the proposed activities, particularly with respect to benefiting low- and moderate-income persons.

(4) The feasibility of the proposed activities, *i.e.*, their technical and financial feasibility, for achieving the stated objectives, including local support for activities proposed to be carried out in the locality and any matching funds proposed to be provided from other sources.

(5) The capability of the applicant to carry out satisfactorily the proposed activities in a timely fashion, including satisfactory performance in carrying out any previous HUD-assisted projects or activities.

(6) In the case of proposals/projects of approximately equal merit, HUD retains the right to exercise discretion in selecting projects in a manner that would best serve the program objectives, with consideration given to the needs of localities, types of activities proposed, an equitable geographical distribution, and program balance.

(f) *Certifications.* (1) Certifications required to be submitted by applicants shall be as prescribed in the RFA packages.

(2) In the absence of independent evidence which tends to challenge in a substantial manner the certifications made by the applicant, the required certifications will be accepted by HUD. If independent evidence is available to HUD, however, HUD may require further information or assurances to be submitted in order to determine whether the applicant's certifications are satisfactory.

(g) *Multiyear funding commitments.* (1) HUD may make funding commitments of up to five years, subject to the availability of appropriations. In determining the number of years for which a commitment will be made, HUD will consider the nature of the activities proposed, the capability of the recipient to carry out the proposed activities, and year-by-year funding requirements.

(2) Awards will be made on the basis of a 12-month period of performance. Once a recipient has been selected for a multi-year award, that recipient would not be required to compete in a competition for the subsequent funding years covered by the multi-year funding commitment. Recipients performing satisfactorily will be invited to submit applications for subsequent funding years in accordance with requirements outlined in the Notice of Funding Availability and Request for Grant Application. Subject to the availability of appropriations, subsequent-year funding will be determined by the following:

(i) The recipient has submitted all reports required for the previous year or years in a timely, complete and satisfactory manner in accordance with the terms and conditions of the grant.

Ofc. of Asst. Secy., Comm. Planning, Develop., HUD § 570.405

(ii) The recipient has submitted sufficient evidence to demonstrate successful completion of the tasks and deliverables of the grant. A determination of satisfactory performance will be made by HUD based upon evidence of task completions provided by the recipient, along with data from client feedback and site evaluations.

(iii) The recipient has submitted the next annual application.

(iv) The subsequent year's application is consistent with that described in the original application.

(3) Recipients participating in multi-year funding projects are not eligible to apply for additional grants for the same project or activity subject area for which they are receiving funds. Recipients are, however, eligible to compete for grants for other project or activity areas.

(h) *Selection and notification.* The HUD decision to approve, disapprove or conditionally approve an application shall be communicated in writing to the applicant.

(i) *Environmental and intergovernmental review.* The requirements for Intergovernmental Reviews do not apply to HBCU awards. HUD will conduct an environmental review in accordance with 24 CFR part 50 before giving its approval to a proposal.

[56 FR 18968, Apr. 24, 1991]

§ 570.405 The insular areas.

(a) *Eligible applicants.* Eligible applicants are Guam, the Virgin Islands, American Samoa, the Trust Territory of the Pacific Islands, and the Commonwealth of the Northern Mariana Islands.

(b) *Threshold requirements.* HUD shall review each grantee's progress on outstanding grants made under this section based on the grantee's performance report, the timeliness of close-outs and compliance with fund management requirements and pertinent regulations, taking into consideration the size of the grant and the degree and complexity of the program. If HUD determines upon such review that the applicant does not have the capacity effectively to administer a new grant, or a portion of a new grant, in addition to grants currently under administration, the applicant shall not be invited to submit an application for the current year's funding.

(c) *Previous audit findings and outstanding monetary obligations.* HUD shall not accept for review an application from an applicant that has either an outstanding audit finding for any HUD program, or an outstanding monetary obligation to HUD that is in arrears, or for which a repayment schedule has not been established and agreed to. The Field Office manager may waive this restriction if he or she finds that the applicant has made a good faith effort to clear the audit. In no instance, however, shall a waiver be provided when funds are due HUD, unless a satisfactory arrangement for repayment of the debt has been made and payments are current.

(d) *Criteria for funding.* The Secretary shall establish, for each fiscal year, an amount for which eligible applicants may apply. Grant amounts will be based on population of the applicant and its performance in previous years. In determining performance, HUD will consider program achievements and the applicant's effectiveness in using program funds. Effectiveness in using program funds shall be measured by reviewing audit, monitoring and performance reports.

(e) *Application and performance reporting.* Application and performance reporting requirements are as follows:

(1) Applicants must submit applications within 90 days of the notification of the grant amount from HUD.

(2) Applicants shall prepare and publish or post a proposed application in accordance with the citizen participation requirements of paragraph (h) of this section.

(3) Applicants shall submit to HUD a final application containing its community development objectives and activities. This application shall be submitted to the appropriate HUD office, together with the required certifications, in a form prescribed by HUD.

(4) Grant recipients must submit to HUD an annual performance report on progress achieved on previously funded grants. Grant recipients must submit the report at a time and in a format determined by HUD. The report should be

§ 570.405

made available to citizens in accordance with the requirements of paragraph (h)(1)(iv) of this section.

(f) *Costs incurred by the applicant.* (1) Notwithstanding any other provision of this part, HUD will not reimburse or recognize any costs incurred by an applicant before submission of the application to HUD.

(2) Normally, HUD will not reimburse or recognize costs incurred before HUD approval of the application for funding. However, under unusual circumstances, the Field office manager may consider and conditionally approve written requests to recognize and reimburse costs that will be incurred after submission of the application but before it is approved where failure to do so would impose undue or unreasonable hardship on the applicant. Conditional approvals will be made only before the costs are incurred and where the conditions for release of funds have been met in accordance with 24 CFR 58.22, and with the understanding that HUD has no obligation whatsoever to approve the application or to reimburse the applicant should the application be disapproved.

(g) *Criteria for conditional approval.* HUD may approve a grant subject to specified conditions. In any such case, the obligation and utilization of funds may be restricted. The reasons for the conditional appproval and the actions necessary to remove the conditions shall be specified. Failure of the applicant to satisfy the conditions may result in a termination of the grant. A conditional approval may be granted under any of the following circumstances:

(1) When local environmental reviews under 24 CFR part 58 have not yet been completed;

(2) To ensure that actual provision of other resources required to complete the proposed activities will be available within a reasonable period of time;

(3) To ensure that a project can be completed within its estimated costs;

(4) Where the grantee is required to satisfy an outstanding debt due to HUD under a payment plan executed between the grantee and the Department;

(5) Pending resolution of problems related to specific projects or the capability of the grantee to obtain resources needed to carry out, operate or maintain the project; or

(6) Pending approval of site and neighborhood standards for proposed housing projects.

(h) *Citizen participation.* (1) The applicant shall provide for appropriate citizen participation in the application and amendment process. The applicant must, at least, do each of the following:

(i) Furnish citizens with information concerning the amount of funds available for community development and housing activities and the range of activities that may be undertaken, including the estimated amount proposed to be used for activities that will benefit persons of low and moderate income, and the plans of the grantee for minimizing displacement of persons as a result of activities assisted with such funds and to assist persons actually displaced;

(ii) Hold one or more public hearings (scheduled at convenient times and places) to obtain the views of citizens on community development and housing needs;

(iii) Develop and publish or post the community development statement in such a manner as to afford affected citizens an opportunity to examine its contents and to submit comments;

(iv) Afford citizens an opportunity to review and comment on the applicant's performance under any community development block grant.

(2) Before submitting the application to HUD, the applicant shall certify that it has:

(i) Met the requirements of paragraph (h)(1) of this section;

(ii) Considered any comments and views expressed by citizens; and

(iii) If appropriate, modified the application accordingly and made the modified application available to citizens.

[50 FR 37526, Sept. 16, 1985, as amended at 60 FR 56914, Nov. 9, 1995; 61 FR 32269, June 21, 1996]

EFFECTIVE DATE NOTE: At 61 FR 32269, June 21, 1996, § 570.405(e)(4) was revised. This section contains information collection and recordkeeping requirements and will not become effective until approval has been given by the Office of Management and Budget.

§ 570.406 Formula miscalculation grants.

(a) *General.* Grants under this section will be made to States and units of general local government determined by the Secretary to have received insufficient amounts under section 106 of the Act as a result of a miscalculation of its share of funds under such section.

(b) *Application.* Since the grant is to correct a technical error in the formula amount which should have been awarded under section 106, no application is required.

(c) *Use of funds.* The use of funds shall be subject to the requirements, certifications and Final Statement otherwise applicable to the grantee's section 106 grant funds provided for the fiscal year in which the grant under this section is made.

(d) *Unavailability of funds.* If sufficient funds are not available to make the grant in the fiscal year in which the Secretary makes the determination required in paragraph (a) of this section, the grant will be made, subject to the availability of appropriations for this subpart, in the next fiscal year.

[56 FR 41940, Aug. 26, 1991]

§ 570.410 Special Projects Program.

(a) *Program objectives.* The Community Development Special Projects Program enables HUD to award grants to States and units of general local government, subject to availability of funds, for special projects that address community development activities or techniques consistent with the purposes of title I of the Housing and Community Development Act of 1974, as amended.

(b) *Eligible applicants.* Only States and units of general local government (as defined in § 570.3) are eligible to submit proposals or applications for Special Projects grants. Proposals or applications may be submitted by eligible applicants on behalf of themselves, on behalf of other eligible applicants, or jointly by more than one eligible applicant.

(c) *Eligible activities.* (1) Project activities that may be funded under this section are those eligible under 24 CFR part 570—Community Development Block Grants, subpart C—Eligible Activities. No more than twenty (20) percent of the funds awarded under this section may be used for overall program administration or planning activities eligible under §§ 570.205 and 570.206.

(2) The amount of funds awarded to a unit of general local government under this section that may be used for public service activities is limited. The applicant may use whichever of the following methods of calculation yields the highest amount:

(i) Fifteen percent of the special projects grant;

(ii) An amount equal to 15 percent of the sum of special project grant funds plus grant funds received for the same federal fiscal year under the Entitlement or State program, less the amount of the Entitlement or State program grant funds which will be used for other public service activities; or

(iii) In the case of an applicant that is an Entitlement grantee subject to the exception in § 570.201(e)(3), an amount equal to the amount of the Entitlement grant funds received for the same federal fiscal year that may be used for public service activities, less the amount of the Entitlement grant funds which will be used for other public service activities.

(d) *Proposals.* Eligible applicants may submit unsolicited proposals. HUD may ask proposers to submit additional information if necessary for evaluation. There is no HUD commitment to fund any unsolicited proposal regardless of its merit. If HUD elects to fund a proposal, it will request that the proposer submit a formal application.

(1) Three (3) copies of a proposal must be sent to the address stated in (3), below. Each proposal submitted pursuant to this section shall be evaluated by HUD using the following criteria:

(i) The extent to which the proposal satisfies purposes of this title and addresses a special community development need.

(ii) The eligibility of proposed activities.

(iii) The feasibility of the project; i.e., its technical and financial feasibility for achieving the goals stated in the proposal.

(iv) The capacity of the proposer to carry out satisfactorily the proposed project activities.

(2) If the proposal is submitted jointly by, or on behalf of, more than one eligible applicant, the proposal must:

(i) Contain a cooperation agreement signed by the Chief Executive Officer of each participating jurisdiction which specifies concurrence with the purpose and intent of the proposal and intent to comply with grant requirements;

(ii) Address problems faced by all jurisdictions listed in the proposal; and,

(iii) Be submitted by the lead jurisdiction. The lead jurisdiction shall be responsible for overall coordination and administration of the project.

(3) Unsolicited proposals may be submitted any time during the year. However, if there are no funds available for such proposals, they will be returned without review. Proposals shall contain a Standard Form 424 signed by the Chief Executive Officer of the State or unit of general local government. They shall be sent to: Department of Housing and Urban Development, Office of Community Planning and Development, 451 Seventh Street, SW., Washington, DC 20410, Attention: Director, Office of Program Policy Development, CPP.

(e) *Applications*. Applications are accepted only from eligible applicants in response to letters of solicitations, or to competition announcements published in Notices in the FEDERAL REGISTER. Submission requirements and criteria to be used by HUD to evaluate solicited applications and instructions regarding their submission shall be stated in each Notice or letter.

(f) *Certifications*. Applications shall contain the certifications required by 24 CFR 570.303, except that regarding citizen participation: The applicant must certify that citizens likely to be affected by the project, particularly low- and moderate-income persons, have been provided an opportunity to comment on the proposal or application. If the application is submitted jointly, or on behalf of more than one jurisdiction, each jurisdiction shall submit the required certifications.

(g) *Selection and notification*. The HUD decision to approve, disapprove or conditionally approve a proposal or application shall be communicated in writing to the applicant.

[47 FR 30054, July 12, 1982, as amended at 54 FR 31672, Aug. 1, 1989; 55 FR 29309, July 18, 1990; 56 FR 56127, Oct. 31, 1991]

§ 570.411 Joint Community Development Program.

(a) *General*. Grants under this section will be awarded to institutions of higher education or to States and local governments applying jointly with institutions of higher education. Institutions of higher education must demonstrate the capacity to carry out activities under title I of the Housing and Community Development Act of 1974. For ease of reference, this program may be called the Joint CD Program.

(b) *Definitions*.

Demonstrated capacity to carry out eligible activities under title I means recent satisfactory activity by the institution of higher education's staff designated to work on the program, including subcontractors and consultants firmly committed to work on the proposed activities, in title I programs or similar programs without the need for oversight by a State or unit of general local government.

Institution of higher education means a college or university granting 4-year degrees and accredited by a national or regional accrediting agency recognized by the U.S. Department of Education.

(c) *Eligible applicants*. Institutions of higher education or States and units of general local government jointly with institutions of higher education may apply. Institutions of higher education with demonstrated capacity to carry out eligible activities under title I may apply on their own, without the joint participation of a State or unit of general local government. States or unit of general local governments must file jointly with an institution of higher education. For these approved joint applications, the grant will be made to the State or unit of general local government and the institution of higher education jointly. If an eligible applicant is an institution of higher education, it will not be funded more than once for the same kinds of activities. These grantees may not receive funding under a subsequent NOFA if it has the same program objectives as the one under which the grantee previously received funding. However, a State or unit of general local government is eligible to apply if it files jointly with a different institution of higher education in each NOFA cycle. HUD may further limit the type of eligible applicant to be funded. Any such limitations will be contained in the Notice of Funding Availability described below in paragraph (h) of this section.

(d) *Role of participants in joint applications.* An institution of higher education and a State or unit of general local government may carry out eligible activities approved in joint applications. Where there are joint applicants, the grant will be made to both and both will be responsible for oversight, compliance, and performance. The application will have to clearly delineate the role of each applicant in the joint application. Any funding sanctions or other remedial actions by HUD for noncompliance or nonperformance, whether by the State or unit of general local government or by the institution of higher education, shall be taken against both grantees.

(e) *Eligible activities.* Activities that may be funded under this section are those eligible under 24 CFR part 570—Community Development Block Grants, subpart C—Eligible Activities. These activities may be designed to assist residents of colonias, as defined in section 916(d) of the Cranston-Gonzalez National Affordable Housing Act (42 U.S.C. 5306 note), to improve living conditions and standards within colonias. HUD may limit the activities to be funded. Any such limitations will be contained in the Notice of Funding Availability described in paragraph (h) of this section.

(f) *Applications.* Applications will only be accepted from eligible applicants in response to a publication of a Notice of Funding Availability (NOFA) published by HUD in the FEDERAL REGISTER.

(g) *Local approval.* (1) Where an institution of higher education is the applicant, each unit of general local government that is an entitlement jurisdiction where an activity is to take place must approve the activity and certify that the activity is consistent with its Consolidated Plan.

(2) Where a State is the joint applicant and it proposes to carry out an activity within the jurisdiction of one or more units of general local government, then each such unit must approve the activity and state that the activity is consistent with its Consolidated Plan.

(3) These approvals and findings must accompany each application and may take the form of a letter by the chief executive officer of each unit of general local government affected or a resolution of the legislative body of each such unit of general local government.

(h) *NOFA contents.* The NOFA will describe any special objectives sought to be achieved by the funding to be provided, including any limitations on the type of activities to be funded to achieve the objectives, any limitations on the type of eligible applicants, and points to be awarded to each of the selection criteria and any special factors to be evaluated in assigning points under the selection criteria to achieve the stated objectives. The NOFA will also state the deadline for the submission of applications, the total funding available for the competition, the period of performance and the maximum and minimum amount of individual grants. The NOFA will also state which of the various possible levels of competition HUD will use: national and/or regional or entitlement areas vs. nonentitlement areas; and States or units of general local government vs. institutions of higher education vs. institutions of higher education with a demonstrated capacity. The NOFA will include further information and instructions for the submission of acceptable applications to HUD.

(i) *Selection criteria.* Each application submitted under this section will be evaluated by HUD using the following criteria:

(1) The extent to which the applicant addresses the objectives published in the NOFA and demonstrates how the proposed activities will have a substantial impact in achieving the objectives.

(2) The extent of the needs to be addressed by the proposed activities, particularly with respect to benefiting low- and moderate-income persons and residents of colonias, where applicable.

(3) The feasibility of the proposed activities, i.e., their technical and financial feasibility, for achieving the stated objectives.

(4) The capability of the applicant to carry out satisfactorily the proposed activities in a timely fashion, including satisfactory performance in carrying out any previous HUD-assisted projects or activities.

(5) The extent of commitment to fair housing and equal opportunity, as indicated by such factors as previous HUD monitoring/compliance activity, actions to promote minority- and women-owned business enterprise, affirmatively furthering fair housing issues, and nondiscriminatory delivery of services.

(j) *Selection discretion.* HUD retains the right to exercise discretion in selecting projects in a manner that would best serve the program objectives, with consideration given to the needs of States and units of general local government and institutions of higher education, types of activities proposed, an equitable geographical distribution, and program balance. The NOFA will state whether HUD will use this discretion in any specific competition.

(k) *Certifications.* (1) Certifications, including those indicating that applicants have adhered to all civil rights requirements under subpart K of this part and the Americans with Disabilities Act of 1990, required to be submitted by applicants shall be as prescribed in the NOFA.

(2) In the absence of independent evidence which tends to challenge in a substantial manner the certifications made by the applicant, the required certifications will be accepted by HUD. However, if independent evidence is available, HUD may require further information or assurances to be submitted in order to determine whether the applicant's certifications are satisfactory.

(l) *Consolidated plan.* An applicant that proposes any housing activities as part of its application will be required to submit a certification that these activities are consistent with the Consolidated Plan of the jurisdiction to be served.

(m) *Citizen participation.* The citizen participation requirements of §§ 570.301, 570.431, 570.485(c) and 570.486(a) are modified to require the following: The applicant must certify that citizens likely to be affected by the project regardless of race, color, creed, sex, national origin, familial status, or handicap, particularly low- and moderate-income persons, have been provided an opportunity to comment on the proposal or application.

(n) *Environmental and Intergovernmental Review.* The requirements for Intergovernmental Reviews do not apply to these awards. When required, an environmental review in accordance with 24 CFR part 58 must be carried out by the State or unit of general local government when it is the applicant. HUD will conduct any required environmental review when an institution of higher education is the applicant.

(Approved by the Office of Management and Budget under control number 2535–0084)

[60 FR 15837, Mar. 27, 1995]

§ 570.415 Community Development Work Study Program.

(a) *Applicability and objectives.* HUD makes grants under CDWSP to institutions of higher education, either directly or through areawide planning organizations or States, for the purpose of providing assistance to economically disadvantaged and minority students who participate in a work study program while enrolled in full-time graduate programs in community and economic development, community planning, and community management. The primary objectives of the program are to attract economically disadvantaged and minority students to careers in community and economic development, community planning, and community management, and to provide a cadre of well-qualified professionals to plan, implement and administer local community development programs.

(b) *Definitions.* The following definitions apply to CDWSP:

Applicant means an institution of higher education, a State, or an areawide planning organization that submits an application for assistance under CDWSP.

Ofc. of Asst. Secy., Comm. Planning, Develop., HUD §570.415

Areawide planning organization (APO) means an organization authorized by law or by interlocal agreement to undertake planning and other activities for a metropolitan or nonmetropolitan area. For an organization operating in a nonmetropolitan area to be considered an APO, its jurisdiction must cover at least one county.

CDWSP means the Community Development Work Study Program.

Community building means community and economic development, community planning, community management, land use and housing activities.

Community building academic program or academic program means a graduate degree program whose purpose and focus is to educate students in community building. "Community building academic program" or "academic program" includes but is not limited to graduate degree programs in community and economic development, community planning, community management, public administration, public policy, urban economics, urban management, and urban planning. "Community building academic program" or "academic program" excludes social and humanistic fields such as law, economics (except for urban economics), education and history. "Community building academic program" or "academic program" excludes joint degree programs except where both joint degree fields have the purpose and focus of educating students in community building.

Economically disadvantaged and minority students means students who satisfy all applicable guidelines established at the participating institution of higher education to measure financial need for academic scholarship or loan assistance, including, but not limited to, students who are Black, American Indian/Alaskan Native, Hispanic, or Asian/Pacific Island, and including students with disabilities.

Institution of higher education means a public or private educational institution that offers a community building academic program and that is accredited by an accrediting agency or association recognized by the Secretary of Education under 34 CFR part 602.

Recipient means an approved applicant that executes a grant agreement with HUD.

Student means a student enrolled in an eligible full-time academic program. He/she must be a first-year student in a two-year graduate program. Students enrolled in Ph.D. programs are ineligible.

Student with disabilities means a student who meets the definition of "person with disabilities" in the Americans with Disabilities Act of 1990.

(c) *Assistance provided*—(1) *Types of assistance available.* HUD provides funding in the form of grants to recipients who make assistance available to eligible students. Grants are provided to cover the costs of student assistance and for an administrative allowance.

(i) *Student assistance.* Grants are made to recipients to cover the costs of assistance provided to eligible students in the form of student stipends, tuition support, and additional support.

(A) *Student stipend.* The amount of the student stipend is based upon the prevailing hourly rate for initial entry positions in community building and the number of hours worked by the student at the work placement assignment, except that the hourly rate used should be sufficiently high to allow a student to earn the full stipend without working over 20 hours per week during the school year and 40 hours per week during the summer. The amount of the stipend the student receives may not exceed the actual amount earned, up to $9,000 per year.

(B) *Tuition support and additional support.* The amount of support for tuition, fees, books, and travel related to the academic program, workplace assignment or conferences may not exceed actual costs incurred or $5,000 per year, whichever is higher. The conferences are limited to those dealing with community building, sponsored by professional organizations.

(ii) *Administrative allowance.* HUD provides an allowance to recipients to cover the administrative costs of the program. The administrative allowance is $1,000 per year for each student participating in the program.

(2) *Number of students assisted.* The minimum number of students that may

§ 570.415

be assisted is three students per participating institution of higher education. If an APO or State receives assistance for a program that is conducted by two or more institutions of higher education, each participating institution must have a minimum of three students in the program. The maximum number of students that may be assisted under CDWSP is five students per participating institution of higher education.

(d) *Recipient eligibility and responsibilities*—(1) *Recipient eligibility.* (i) The following organizations are eligible to apply for assistance under the program:

(A) *Institutions of higher education.* Institutions of higher education offering a community building academic program are eligible for assistance under CDWSP.

(B) *Areawide planning organizations and States.* An APO or a State may apply for assistance for a program to be conducted by two or more institutions of higher education. Institutions participating in an APO program must be located within the particular area that is served by the APO and is identified by the State law or interlocal agreement creating the APO. Institutions of higher education participating in a State program must be located within the State.

(ii) To be eligible in future funding competitions for CDWSP, recipients are required to maintain a 50-percent rate of graduation from a CDWSP-funded academic program.

(iii) If an institution of higher education that submits an individual application is also included in the application of an APO or State, then the separate individual application of the institution of higher education will be disregarded. Additionally, if an institution of higher education is included in the application of both an APO and a State, then the references to the institution in the application of the State will be stricken. The State's application will then be ineligible if fewer than two institutions of higher education remain as participants in the State's application.

(2) *Recipient responsibilities.* (i) The recipient is responsible for the administration of the program, for compliance with all program requirements, and for the coordination of program activities carried out by the work placement agencies and (if the recipient is an APO or State), by the participating institutions of higher education. The recipient must:

(A) Recruit and select students for participation in CDWSP. The recipient shall establish recruitment procedures that identify economically disadvantaged and minority students pursuing careers in community building, and make such students aware of the availability of assistance opportunities. Students must be selected before the beginning of the semester for which funding has been provided.

(B) Recruit and select work placement agencies, and negotiate and execute agreements covering each work placement assignment.

(C) Refer participating students to work placement agencies and assist students in the selection of work placement assignments.

(D) Assign sufficient staff to administer and supervise the program on a day-to-day basis, and, where the recipient is an APO or State, to monitor the activities of the work study coordinating committee.

(E) Encourage participating students to obtain employment for a minimum of two years after graduation with a unit of State or local government, Indian tribe or nonprofit organization engaged in community building.

(F) Maintain records by racial and ethnic categories for each economically disadvantaged student enrolled in the CDWSP.

(G) Keep records and make such reports as HUD may require.

(H) Comply with all other applicable Federal requirements.

(ii) If the recipient is an APO or State, the recipient must also:

(A) Establish a committee to coordinate activities between program participants, to advise the recipient on policy matters, to assist the recipient in ranking and selection of participating students, and to review disputes concerning compliance with program agreements and performance. The committee shall be chaired by a representative of the recipient, and shall include representatives of the participating institutions of higher education, work placement agencies, students, and HUD.

(B) Allocate the assistance awarded under the program to the participating institutions of higher education. APOs and States may not make fractional awards to institutions. (E.g., awards to institutions must assist a fixed number of students and not, for example, 6.5 students.)

(e) *Institutions of higher education.* Institutions of higher education participating in a program are responsible for providing its educational component. Where the recipient is an APO or State, the institution of higher education shall assist the APO or State in the administration and operation of the program. Responsibilities include assisting the recipient in the selection of students by determining the eligibility of students for the academic program, and by making the analysis of students under the financial need guidelines established by the institution. All institutions of higher education must comply with other applicable Federal requirements.

(f) *Work placement agencies eligibility and responsibilities*—(1) *Eligibility.* To be eligible to participate in the CDWSP, the work placement agencies must be involved in community building and must be an agency of a State or unit of local government, an APO, an Indian tribe, or a nonprofit organization.

(2) *Responsibilities.* Work placement agencies must:

(i) Provide practical experience and training in community building.

(ii) Consult with the institution of higher education (and the APO or State, where an APO or State is the recipient) to ensure that the student's work placement assignment provides the requisite experience and training to meet the required number of work hours specified in the student work placement agreement.

(iii) Provide a sufficient number of work placement assignments to provide participating students with a wide choice of work experience.

(iv) Require each student to devote 12-20 hours per week during the regular school year, or 35-40 hours a week during the summer, to the work placement assignment. Work placement agencies may provide flexibility in the work period, if such a schedule is consistent with the requirements of the student's academic program. However, a participating student may receive stipend payment only during the period that the student is placed with the work placement agency.

(v) Comply with all other applicable Federal requirements.

(vi) Maintain such records as HUD may require.

(g) *Student eligibility and responsibilities.* Students apply directly to recipients receiving grants under CDWSP. Students shall be selected in accordance with the following eligibility requirements and selection procedures.

(1) *Eligibility.* To be eligible for CDWSP, the student:

(i) Must satisfy all applicable guidelines established at the participating institution of higher education to measure financial need for academic scholarship or loan assistance.

(ii) Must be a full-time student enrolled in the first year of graduate study in a community building academic program at the participating institution of higher education. Individuals enrolled in doctoral programs are ineligible.

(iii) Must demonstrate an ability to maintain a satisfactory level of performance in the community building academic program and in work placement assignments, and to comply with the professional standards set by the recipient and the work placement agencies.

(iv) May not have previously participated in CDWSP.

(v) Must provide appropriate written evidence that he or she is lawfully admitted for permanent residence in the United States, if the individual is not a citizen.

(2) *Selection.* In selecting among eligible students, the recipient must consider the extent to which each student has demonstrated:

(i) Financial need under the applicable financial need guidelines established at the institution of higher education;

(ii) An interest in, and commitment to, a professional career in community building;

§ 570.415

(iii) The ability satisfactorily to complete academic and work placement responsibilities under CDWSP.

(3) *Student responsibilities.* Participating students must:

(i) Enroll in a two-year program. A student's academic and work placement responsibilities include: Full-time enrollment in an approved academic program; maintenance of a satisfactory level of performance in the community building academic program and in work placement assignments; and compliance with the professional conduct standards set by the recipient and the work placement agency. A satisfactory level of academic performance consists of maintaining a B average. A student's participation in CDWSP shall be terminated for failure to meet these responsibilities and standards. If a student's participation is terminated, the student is ineligible for further CDWSP assistance.

(ii) Agree to make a good-faith effort to obtain employment in community building with a unit of State or local government, an Indian tribe, or a nonprofit organization. The term of employment should be for at least two consecutive years following graduation from the academic program. If the student does not obtain such employment, the student is not required to repay the assistance received.

(h) *Notice of fund availability.* HUD will solicit grant applications from institutions of higher education, APO's and States by publishing a notice of fund availability in the FEDERAL REGISTER. The notice will:

(1) Explain how application packages (requests for grant applications) providing specific application requirements and guidance may be obtained;

(2) Specify the place for filing completed applications, and the date by which the applications must be physically received at that location;

(3) State the amount of funding available under the notice;

(4) Provide other appropriate program information and guidance.

(i) *Recipient selection process.* The selection process for applications under CDWSP consists of a threshold review, ranking of eligible applications and final selection.

(1) *Threshold.* To be eligible for ranking, applicants must meet each of the following threshold requirements:

(i) The application must be filed in the application form prescribed by HUD, and within the required time periods;

(ii) The applicant must demonstrate that it is eligible to participate;

(iii) The applicant must demonstrate that each institution of higher education participating in the program as a recipient has the required academic programs and faculty to carry out its activities under CDWSP. Each work placement agency must have the required staff and community building work study program to carry out its activities under CDWSP.

(2) *Rating.* All applications that meet the threshold requirements for applicant eligibility will be rated based on the following selection criteria:

(i) *Quality of academic program.* The quality of the academic program offered by the institution of higher education, including without limitation the:

(A) Quality of course offerings;

(B) Appropriateness of course offerings for preparing students for careers in community building; and

(C) Qualifications of faculty and percentage of their time devoted to teaching and research in community building.

(ii) *Rates of graduation.* The rates of graduation of students previously enrolled in a community building academic program at the institution of higher education, specifically including (where applicable) graduation rates from any previously funded CDWSP academic programs or similar programs.

(iii) *Extent of financial commitment.* The commitment and ability of the institution of higher education to assure that CDWSP students will receive sufficient financial assistance (including loans, where necessary) above and beyond the CDWSP funding to complete their academic program in a timely manner and without working in excess of 20 hours per week during the school year.

(iv) *Quality of work placement assignments.* The extent to which the participating students will receive a sufficient number and variety of work placement assignments, the assignments will provide practical and useful experience to students participating in the program, and the assignments will further the participating students' preparation for professional careers in community building.

(v) *Likelihood of fostering students' permanent employment in community building.* The extent to which the proposed program will lead participating students directly and immediately to permanent employment in community building, as indicated by, without limitation:

(A) The past success of the institution of higher education in placing its graduates (particularly CDWSP-funded and similar program graduates where applicable) in permanent employment in community building; and

(B) The amount of faculty and staff time and institutional resources devoted to assisting students (particularly students in CDWSP-funded and similar programs where applicable) in finding permanent employment in community building.

(vi) *Effectiveness of program administration.* The degree to which an applicant will be able effectively to coordinate and administer the program. HUD will allocate the maximum points available under this criterion equally among the following considerations set forth in paragraphs (i)(2)(vi) (A), (B), and (C) of this section, except that the maximum points available under this criterion will be allocated equally between the considerations set forth in paragraphs (i)(2)(vi) (A) and (B) of this section only where the applicant has not previously administered a CDWSP-funded program.

(A) The strength and clarity of the applicant's plan for placing CDWSP students on rotating work placement assignments and monitoring CDWSP students' progress both academically and in their work placement assignments;

(B) The degree to which the individual who will coordinate and administer the program has clear responsibility, ample available time, and sufficient authority to do so; and

(C) The effectiveness of the applicant's prior coordination and administration of a CDWSP-funded program, where applicable (including the timeliness and completeness of the applicant's compliance with CDWSP reporting requirements).

(vii) *Commitment to meeting economically disadvantaged and minority students' needs.* The applicant's commitment to meeting the needs of economically disadvantaged and minority students as demonstrated by policies and plans regarding, and past effort and success in, recruiting, enrolling and financially assisting economically disadvantaged and minority students. If the applicant is an APO or State, then HUD will consider the demonstrated commitment of each institution of higher education on whose behalf the APO or State is applying; HUD will then also consider the demonstrated commitment of the APO or State to recruit and hire economically disadvantaged and minority students.

(3) *Final selection.* Eligible applications will be considered for selection in their rank order. HUD may make awards out of rank order to achieve geographic diversity, and may provide assistance to support a number of students that is less than the number requested under applications in order to provide assistance to as many highly ranked applications as possible.

(j) *Agreements*—(1) *Grant agreement.* The responsibilities of the recipient under CDWSP will be incorporated in a grant agreement executed by HUD and the recipient.

(2) *Student agreement.* The recipient and each participating student must execute a written agreement incorporating their mutual responsibilities under CDWSP. The agreement must be executed before the student can be enrolled in the program. A student's participation in CDWSP shall be terminated for failure to meet the responsibilities and standards in the agreement.

(3) *Work placement assignment agreement.* The institution of higher education, the APO or state (if an APO or

State is the grant recipient), the participating student, and the work placement agency must execute a written agreement covering each work placement assignment. The agreement must address the responsibilities of each of the parties, the educational objectives, the nature of supervision, the standards of evaluation, and the student's time commitments under the work placement assignment.

(4) *APO (or state) and institution of higher education.* Where the recipient is an APO (or a State), the recipient and each participating institution of higher education must execute a written agreement incorporating their mutual responsibilities under CDWSP.

(k) *Grant administration*—(1) *Initial obligation of funds.* When HUD selects an application for funding, and notifies the recipient, HUD will obligate funds to cover the amount of the approved grant. The initial obligation of funds will provide for student grants for two years.

(2) *Disbursement.* Recipients will receive grant payments by direct deposit on a reimbursement basis. If that is not possible, grant payments will be made by U.S. Treasury checks.

(3) *Deobligation and recipient repayment.* (i) HUD may deobligate amounts for grants if proposed activities are not begun or completed within a reasonable time after selection.

(ii) If a student's participation in CDWSP is terminated before the completion of the two-year term of the student's program, the recipient may substitute another student to complete the two-year term of a student whose participation has terminated. The substituted student must have a sufficient number of academic credits to complete the degree program within the remaining portion of the terminated student's two-year term. With respect to any CDWSP grant, there is no requirement, regardless of the date of grant award, for students who are terminated from the CDWSP to repay tuition and additional assistance or for the grant recipient to repay such funds to HUD. Funds must still be otherwise expended consistent with CDWSP regulations and the grant agreement, or repayment may be required under paragraph (k)(3)(iii) of this section.

(iii) Consistent with OMB Circulars No. A–101 and A–110, HUD, in the grant agreement, will set forth in detail other circumstances under which funds may be deobligated, recipients may be liable for repayment, or other sanctions may be imposed.

(l) *Other Federal requirements*—(1) *Handicap provision.* Recipients must provide a statement certifying that no otherwise qualified handicapped person shall, solely by reason of handicap, be excluded from participation in, be denied the benefits of, or otherwise be subjected to discrimination under the CDWSP.

(2) *Nondiscrimination.* The recipient must adhere to the following nondiscrimination provisions: The requirements of title VIII of the Civil Rights Act of 1968, 42 U.S.C. 3600–20 (Fair Housing Act) and implementing regulations issued at subchapter A of title 24 of the Code of Federal Regulations; title VI of the Civil Rights Act of 1964 (42 U.S.C. 2000d–4) (Nondiscrimination in Federally Assisted Programs) and implementing regulations issued at 24 CFR part 1; section 504 of the Rehabilitation Act of 1973 (29 U.S.C. 794) and implementing regulations at 24 CFR part 8; Executive Order 11063 and implementing regulations at 24 CFR part 107; and the Age Discrimination Act of 1975 and implementing regulations at 24 CFR part 146.

[54 FR 27131, June 27, 1989, as amended at 61 FR 36458, July 10, 1996; 63 FR 31869, June 10, 1998]

§ 570.416 Hispanic-serving institutions work study program.

(a) *Applicability and objectives.* HUD makes grants under the Hispanic-serving Institutions Work Study Program (HSI-WSP) to public and private nonprofit Hispanic-serving Institutions (HSI's) of higher education for the purpose of providing assistance to economically disadvantaged and minority students who participate in a work study program while enrolled in full-time community college programs in community building, and to provide entry to pre-professional careers in these fields.

(b) *Definitions.* The following definitions apply to HSI-WSP:

§ 570.416

Applicant means a public or private non-profit Hispanic-serving institution of higher education that offers only two-year degree programs, including at least one community building academic degree program, and that applies for funding under HSI-WSP.

Community building means community and economic development, community planning, community management, public policy, urban economics, urban management, urban planning, land use planning, housing, and related fields. Related fields include, but are not limited to, administration of justice, child development, and human services.

Community building academic program or *academic program* means an undergraduate associate degree program whose purpose and focus is to educate students in community building. The terms "community building academic program" or "academic program" refer to the types of academic programs encompassed in the statutory phrase "community or economic development, community planning or community management." For purposes of HSI-WSP, such programs include, but are not limited to, associate degree programs in community and economic development, community planning, community management, public administration, public policy, urban economics, urban management, urban planning, land use planning, housing, and related fields of study. Related fields of study that promote community building, such as administration of justice, child development, and human services are eligible, while fields such as natural sciences, computer sciences, mathematics, accounting, electronics, engineering, and the humanities (such as English or history) would not be eligible. A transfer program (i.e., one that leads to transfer to a four-year institution of higher education for the student's junior year) in a community building academic discipline is eligible only if the student is required to declare his/her major in this discipline while at the community college.

Community building field means any of the fields of study eligible under a community building academic program.

Economically disadvantaged and minority students means students who satisfy all the applicable guidelines established at the participating institution of higher education to measure financial need for academic scholarship or loan assistance, including, but not limited to, students with disabilities and students who are Black, American Indian/Alaska Native, Hispanic, Asian/Pacific Islanders, where such students satisfy the financial needs guidelines defined above.

Hispanic-serving institution is an institution of higher education that certifies to the satisfaction of the Secretary that it meets the criteria set out at 20 U.S.C. 1059c(b)(1), including the following: An institution that has an enrollment of undergraduate full-time students that is at least 25 percent Hispanic; in which not less than 50 percent of the Hispanic students are low-income individuals (i.e., their families' taxable income for the preceding year did not exceed 150 percent of the poverty level) who are first generation college students; and in which another 25 percent are either low-income individuals or first generation college students.

HSI-WSP or *HSI-WSP program* means the Hispanic-serving Institutions Work Study program.

Institution of higher education means a public or private educational institution that offers two-year associate degrees in a community building academic program and that is accredited by an accrediting agency or association recognized by the Secretary of Education. Institutions offering BOTH four-year and two-year degrees are not eligible for HSI-WSP.

Recipient means an approved applicant that executes a grant agreement with HUD.

Student means a person attending the institution of higher education on a full-time basis, as defined by that institution and pursuing an eligible community building degree. Students must have attained no more than half of the credits required for their degree at the time they first receive assistance under HSI-WSP.

Student with disabilities means a student who meets the definition of a

§ 570.416

"person with disabilities" in the Americans with Disabilities Act of 1990.

(c) *Assistance provided*—(1) *Types of assistance available.* HUD provides funding in the form of grants to recipients who make assistance available to eligible students. Grants are provided to cover the costs of student assistance and for an administrative allowance.

(2) *Maximum amount of assistance.* The maximum amount that can be provided to a student is $13,200 a year, including $1,000 for an administrative allowance, subject to the 20% limitation described at 570.416(c)(4) below. HUD will not set maximums on how much should be spent to each eligible expenditure, other than for administrative costs. The institution must be able to document that the amounts paid are customary for that institution and that it has actually paid that amount to the students. If a student is receiving a Pell grant, he/she may not receive funding for the same educational support through HSI-WSP. However, HSI-WSP can substitute for all or part of the Pell grant.

(3) *Student assistance.* Grants are provided in the form of student stipends, tuition support, and additional support.

(i) *Student stipend.* The amount of the student stipend should be based on the hourly rate for initial entry positions in the community building field and the number of hours worked by the student at the work placement assignment. The stipend should be sufficiently high to allow the student to earn the full stipend, as determined by the recipient, without working over 20 hours per week during the school year and 40 hours per week during the summer.

(ii) *Tuition support.* The amount of tuition support may not exceed the tuition and required fees charged at the participating institution of higher education.

(iii) *Additional support.* The recipient may provide additional support for books, tutoring, and travel related to the academic program or work placement assignment. Costs associated with reasonable accommodations for students with disabilities including, but not limited to, interpreters for the deaf/hard of hearing, special equipment, and braille materials are eligible under this category.

(4) *Administrative allowance.* HUD provides an allowance to recipients to cover the administrative costs of the program. The administrative allowance is $1,000 per year for each student participating in the program; however, no more than 20 percent of the grant may be used for planning and program administrative costs.

(5) *Number of students assisted.* The minimum number of students that may be assisted is three students per participating institution of higher education. The maximum number of students that may be assisted is ten students per participating institution of higher education; however, a lower maximum or higher minimum may be established for a particular funding round by the NOFA announcing the availability of the funds.

(d) *Recipient eligibility and responsibilities*—(1) *Recipient eligibility.* Public or private Hispanic-serving institutions of higher education offering only undergraduate two-year degrees, including degrees in at least one community building academic program, are eligible for assistance under HSI-WSP. HSIs that offer BOTH two-year and four-year degrees are not eligible for HSI-WSP assistance.

(2) *Recipient responsibilities.* The recipient is responsible for administering the program, for compliance with all program requirements, and for coordination of program activities carried out by the work placement agencies. The recipient must:

(i) Recruit students for participation in HSI-WSP. The recipient shall establish recruitment procedures that identify eligible economically disadvantaged and minority students pursuing careers in community building, and make them aware of the availability of assistance opportunities. While the program is restricted to HSIs, the recipient may neither restrict the program to any particular minority group or groups, nor provide any preferential treatment in the selection process based on race or ethnicity. Only economically disadvantaged students, as defined herein, may be assisted.

(ii) Select students for participation in HSI-WSP. In selecting among the eligible students, the recipient must consider the extent to which each student has demonstrated financial need under the applicable guidelines established at the institution of higher education; an interest in, and commitment to, a career in community building; and the ability to satisfactorily complete the academic and work placement responsibilities under HSI-WSP. Students must be selected before the beginning of the semester for which funding is being provided. If a student's participation terminates, the student may not be replaced; the grant will be reduced by the amount of unused funds allotted for that student.

(iii) Provide the educational component for participating students.

(iv) Recruit and select work placement agencies, and negotiate and execute an agreement covering each work placement assignment.

(v) Refer participating students to work placement agencies and assist students in the selection of work placement assignments.

(vi) Assign sufficient staff to administer and supervise the program on a day-to-day basis.

(vii) Encourage participating students to either: obtain post-graduation employment with a unit of State or local government, an areawide planning organization (APO), Indian tribe or nonprofit organization engaged in community building; or transfer to a four-year institution of higher education to obtain a bachelor's degree in a community building academic discipline.

(viii) Maintain records by racial and ethnic categories for each economically disadvantaged and minority student participating in HSI-WSP.

(ix) Keep records and make such reports as HUD may require.

(x) Comply with all other applicable Federal requirements.

(e) *Work placement agencies eligibility and responsibilities*—(1) *Eligibility.* To be eligible to participate in HSI-WSP, the work placement agency must be an agency of a State or local government, an APO, an Indian tribe, or a private nonprofit organization involved in community building activities. A work placement site that is part of the institution of higher education (e.g., a child care center) can only be an eligible site if the services provided by that site are offered to people in the broader community outside the institution.

(2) *Responsibilities.* Work placement agencies must:

(i) Provide practical experience and training in the community building field to participating students through work placement assignments.

(ii) Consult with the institution of higher education to ensure that the student's work placement assignment provides the requisite experience and training to meet the required number of work hours specified in the student work placement agreement.

(iii) Provide a sufficient number and variety of work assignments to provide participating students with a wide choice of work experience.

(iv) Require each student to devote 12–20 hours per week during the regular school year, and 35–40 hours a week during the summer, to the work placement assignment. Work placement agencies may provide flexibility in the work period, if such a schedule is consistent with the requirements of the student's academic program. However, a participating student may receive a stipend payment only during the period when the student is placed with the work placement agency.

(v) Comply with all other applicable Federal requirements.

(vi) Maintain such records as HUD may require.

(f) *Student eligibility and responsibilities.* Students apply directly to recipients receiving grants under HSI-WSP.

(1) *Eligibility.* To be eligible for HSI-WSP, the student:

(i) Must satisfy all applicable guidelines established at the participating institution of higher education to measure financial need for academic scholarship or loan assistance.

(ii) Must be a full-time student enrolled in a community building associate degree program at the participating institution of higher education. The student must have attained no more than 50 percent of the credits required for his/her degree at the time the student first receives assistance under this program.

(iii) Must demonstrate an ability to maintain a satisfactory level of performance in community building academic program (i.e., maintain a B average, as defined by the institution) and in work placement assignments, and comply with the professional standards set by the recipient and the work placement agencies.

(iv) May not have previously participated in HSI-WSP.

(2) *Student responsibilities.* Participating students must:

(i) Enroll or be enrolled in a two-year community building associate degree program. A student's academic and work placement responsibilities include: Full-time enrollment in an approved academic program; maintenance of a satisfactory level of performance in the community building academic program and in work placement assignments; and compliance with the professional conduct standards set by the recipient and by the work placement agency. A satisfactory level of academic performance consists of maintaining a B average, as defined by the institution. A student's participation in HSI-WSP shall be terminated for failure to meet these responsibilities and standards. If the student's participation is terminated, the student is ineligible for further HSI-WSP assistance.

(ii) Devote 12–20 hours per week during the regular school year, and 35–40 hours a week during the summer, to the work placement assignment. Work placement agencies may provide flexibility in the work period, if such a schedule is consistent with the requirements of the student's academic program. However, a participating student may receive a stipend payment only during the period when the student is placed with the work placement agency.

(iii) Agree to make a good-faith effort to either: obtain employment in community building with a unit of State or local government, an APO, an Indian tribe, or a non-profit organization; or to transfer to a four-year institution of higher education to obtain a bachelor's degree in a community building academic discipline. However, if the student does not obtain such employment or transfer to a four-year institution, the student is not required to repay the assistance received.

(g) *Notice of funding availability.* HUD will solicit grant applications from eligible institutions of higher education by publishing a notice of funding availability in the FEDERAL REGISTER. The notice will:

(1) Explain how application kits providing specific application requirements and guidance may be obtained;

(2) Specify the place for filing completed applications, and the date by which applications must be physically received at that location;

(3) State the amount of funding available under the notice, which may include funds recaptured from previously awarded grants;

(4) Provide other appropriate program information and guidance.

(h) *Agreements.*—(1) *Grant agreement.* The responsibilities of the recipient under HSI-WSP will be incorporated in a grant agreement executed by HUD and the recipient.

(2) *Student agreement.* The recipient and each participating student must execute a written agreement incorporating their mutual responsibilities under HSI-WSP. The agreement must be executed before the student can be enrolled in the program. The Recipient shall terminate a student's participation in HSI-WSP for failure to meet the responsibilities and standards in the agreement.

(3) *Work placement assignment agreement.* The recipient, the student, and the work placement agency must execute a written agreement covering each work placement assignment. The agreement must address the responsibilities of each of the parties, the educational objectives, the nature of the supervision, the standards of evaluation, and the student's time commitments under the work placement assignment.

(i) *Grant administration*—(1) *Initial obligation of funds.* When HUD selects an application for funding, HUD will obligate funds to cover the amount of the approved grant. The term of the award will be for two calendar years, unless subsequently altered by HUD at its discretion for good cause.

(2) *Disbursement.* Recipients will receive grant payments by direct deposit

on a reimbursement basis. If that is not possible, grant payments will be made by U.S. Treasury checks.

(3) *Deobligation.* HUD may deobligate amounts for grants if proposed activities are not begun or completed within a reasonable period of time after selection.

(j) *Other Federal requirements*—(1) *Applicability of part 570.* HSI-WSP shall be subject to the policies and procedures set forth in subparts A, K, and O of 24 CFR part 570, as applicable, except as modified or limited under the provisions of this Notice. The provisions of subparts C and J of part 570 shall not apply to HSI-WSP.

(2) *Uniform Administrative requirements.* Recipients under HSI-WSP shall comply with the requirements and standards of OMB Circular No. A-22, "Cost Principles for Educational Institutions." Recipients that are private institutions of higher education shall comply with OMB Circular A-133, "Non-Federal Audit Requirements for Institutions of Higher Education and Other Nonprofit Institutions," which is implemented at 24 CFR part 45. Recipients that are public institutions of higher education shall comply with OMB Circular A-128, "Non-Federal Audit Requirements for State and Local Governments," which is implemented at 24 CFR part 44. Audits shall be conducted annually. In addition, all recipients under HSI-WSP shall comply with the provisions of OMB Circular A-110, "Uniform Administrative Requirements for Grants and Agreements With Institutions of Higher Education, Hospitals and Other Non-Profit Organizations," which is implemented at 24 CFR part 84. OMB Circular A-110 shall apply to recipients in its entirety.

[62 FR 17493, Apr. 9, 1997, as amended at 63 FR 9683, Feb. 25, 1998]

Subpart F—Small Cities, Non-Entitlement CDBG Grants in Hawaii and Insular Areas Programs

SOURCE: 62 FR 62914, Nov. 25, 1997, unless otherwise noted.

§ 570.420 General.

(a) *Administration of Non-entitlement CDBG funds in New York by HUD or Insular Areas*—(1) *Small cities.* The Act permits each state to elect to administer all aspects of the CDBG program annual fund allocation for the non-entitlement areas within its jurisdiction. All states except Hawaii have elected to administer the CDBG program for non-entitlement areas within their jurisdiction. This section is applicable only to active HUD-administered small cities grants in New York. The requirements for the non-entitlement CDBG grants in Hawaii are set forth in § 570.429 of this subpart. States that elected to administer the program after the close of Fiscal Year 1984 cannot return administration of the program to HUD. A decision by a state to discontinue administration of the program would result in the loss of CDBG funds for non-entitlement areas in that state and the reallocation of those funds to all states in the succeeding fiscal year.

(2) *Insular areas.* Title V of Public Law 108–186 amended the Act to move the insular areas funding authorization from sections 107(a) and (b) to section 106(a). This revision identified a specific portion of the CDBG allocation for insular areas that is separate from the distribution for special purpose grants, as well as from the Entitlement and State formula distribution. The insular areas of Guam, the Northern Mariana Islands, the Virgin Islands, and American Samoa are permitted to administer all aspects of their Community Development Block Grant (CDBG) program under section 106 of the Act in accordance with their final statement as further described at § 570.440.

(b) *Scope and applicability.* (1) This subpart describes the policies and procedures of the Small Cities program that apply to non-entitlement areas in states where HUD administers the CDBG program. HUD currently administers the Small Cities program in only two states—New York (for grants prior to FY 2000) and Hawaii (for non-entitlement CDBG grants in Hawaii). The Small Cities portion of this subpart addresses the requirements for New York Small Cities grants in §§ 570.421, 570.426,

§ 570.420

570.427, and 570.431. Section 570.429 identifies special procedures applicable to Hawaii.

(2) This subpart also describes the policies and procedures governing community development block grants to insular areas under section 106 of the Act. Sections 570.440 and 570.441 identify procedures applicable to the Insular Areas program under section 106 of the Act. Fund reservations for insular areas under section 107 of the Act shall remain governed by the policies and procedures described in section 107(a)(1)(A) of the Act and §§ 570.400 and 570.405 of this part.

(3) The policies and procedures set forth in the following identified subparts of this part apply to the HUD-administered Small Cities and Insular Areas programs, except as modified or limited under the provisions thereof or this subpart:

(i) Subpart A—General Provisions;
(ii) Subpart C—Eligible Activities;
(iii) Subpart J—Grant Administration;
(iv) Subpart K—Other Program Requirements;
(v) Subpart M—Loan Guarantees; and
(vi) Subpart O—Performance Reviews.

(c) *Abbreviated consolidated plan.* Applications for the HUD-administered Small Cities Program and the Insular Areas program under section 106 of the Act that contain housing activities must include a certification that the proposed housing activities are consistent with the applicant's consolidated plan as described at 24 CFR part 91.

(d) *National and primary objectives.* (1) Each activity funded through the Small Cities program and the Insular Areas program under section 106 of the Act must meet one of the following national objectives as defined under the criteria in § 570.208:

(i) Benefit low- and moderate-income families;
(ii) Aid in the prevention or elimination of slums or blight; or
(iii) Be an activity that the grantee certifies is designed to meet other community development needs having a particular urgency because existing conditions pose a serious and immediate threat to the health or welfare of the community and other financial resources are not available to meet such needs.

(2) In addition to the objectives described in paragraph (e)(1) of this section, with respect to grants made through the Small Cities program, not less than 70 percent of the total of grant funds from each grant and Section 108 loan guarantee funds received under subpart M of this part within a fiscal year must be expended for activities which benefit low- and moderate-income persons under the criteria of § 570.208(a) or of § 570.208(d)(5) or (6). In the case of multiyear plans in New York State approved in response to NOFAs published prior to calendar year 1997, not less than 70 percent of the total funding for grants approved pursuant to a multiyear plan for a time period of up to three years must be expended for activities which benefit low- and moderate-income persons. Thus, 70 percent of the grant for year 1 of a multiyear plan approved in response to NOFAs published prior to calendar year 1997 must meet the 70 percent requirement, 70 percent of the combined grants from years 1 and 2 must meet the requirement, and 70 percent of the combined grants from years 1, 2, and 3 must meet the requirement. In determining the percentage of funds expended for such activity, the provisions of § 570.200(a)(3)(i), (iii), (iv), and (v) shall apply.

(3) In addition to the objectives described in paragraph (e)(1) of this section, grants made through the Insular Areas program shall also comply with the primary objective of 70 percent benefit to low- and moderate-income persons. Insular area recipients must meet this requirement for each separate grant under section 107 of the Act. For grants made under section 106 of the Act, insular area recipients must ensure that over a period of time specified in their certifications not to exceed three years, not less than 70 percent of the aggregate of CDBG fund expenditures shall be for low- and moderate-income activities meeting the criteria under § 570.208(a) or under § 570.208(d)(5) or (6). See also § 570.200(a)(3) for further discussion of the primary objective.

(e) *Allocation of funds*—The allocation of appropriated funds for insular areas under section 106 of the Act shall be governed by the policies and procedures described in section 106(a)(2) of the Act and §§ 570.440, 570.441, and 570.442 of this subpart. The annual appropriations described in this section shall be distributed to insular areas on the basis of the ratio of the population of each insular area to the population of all insular areas.

[69 FR 32779, June 10, 2004, as amended at 72 FR 46370, Aug. 17, 2007]

§ 570.421 New York Small Cities Program design.

(a) *Selection system*—(1) *Competitive applications.* Each competitive application will be rated and scored against at least the following factors:

(i) Need-absolute number of persons in poverty as further explained in the NOFA;

(ii) Need-percent of persons in poverty as further explained in the NOFA;

(iii) Program Impact; and

(iv) Fair Housing and Equal Opportunity, which may include the applicant's Section 3 plan and implementation efforts with respect to actions to affirmatively further fair housing. The NOFA described in paragraph (b) of this section will contain a more detailed description of these factors, and the relative weight that each factor will be given.

(2) In addition HUD reserves the right to establish minimal thresholds for selection factors and otherwise select grants in accordance with § 570.425 and the applicable NOFA.

(3) *Imminent threats to public health and safety.* The criteria for these grants are described in § 570.424.

(4) *Repayment of Section 108 loans.* The criteria for these grants are described in § 570.432.

(5) *Economic development grants.* HUD intends to use the Section 108 loan guarantee program to the maximum extent feasible to fund economic development projects in the nonentitlement areas of New York. In the event that there are not enough Section 108 loan guarantee funds available to fund viable economic development projects, if a project needs a grant in addition to a loan guarantee to make it viable, or if the project does not meet the requirements of the Section 108 program but is eligible for a grant under this subpart, HUD may fund Economic Development applications as they are determined to be fundable in a specific amount by HUD up to the sum set aside for economic development projects in a notice of funding availability, notwithstanding paragraph (g) of this section. HUD also has the option in a NOFA of funding economic development activities on a competitive basis, as a competitive application as described in paragraph (a)(1) of this section. In order for an applicant to receive Small Cities grant funds on a noncompetitive basis, the field office must determine that the economic development project will have a substantial impact on the needs identified by the applicant.

(b) *Notice of funding availability.* HUD will issue one or more Notice(s) of Funding Availability (NOFA) each fiscal year which will indicate the amount of funds available, the annual grant limits per grantee, type of grants available, the application requirements, and the rating factors that will be used for those grants which are competitive. A NOFA may set forth, subject to the requirements of this subpart, additional selection criteria for all grants.

(c) *Eligible applicants.* (1) Eligible applicants in New York are units of general local government, excluding: Metropolitan cities, urban counties, units of general local government which are participating in urban counties or metropolitan cities, even if only part of the participating unit of government is located in the urban county or metropolitan city. Indian tribes are also ineligible for assistance under this subpart. An application may be submitted individually or jointly by eligible applicants.

(2) Counties, cities, towns, and villages may apply and receive funding for separate projects to be done in the same jurisdiction. Only one grant will be made under each funding round for the same type of project to be located within the jurisdiction of a unit of general local government (e.g., both the county and village cannot receive funding for a sewer system to be located in the same village, but the county can

receive funding for a sewer system that is located in the same village as a rehabilitation project for which the village receives funding). The NOFA will contain additional information on applicant eligibility.

(3) Counties may apply on behalf of units of general local government located within their jurisdiction when the unit of general local government has authorized the county to apply. At the time that the county submits its application for funding, it must submit a resolution by the governing body of the unit of local government that authorizes the county to submit an application on behalf of the unit of general local government. The county will be considered the grantee and will be responsible for executing all grant documents. The county is responsible for ensuring compliance with all laws, regulations, and Executive Orders applicable to the CDBG Program. HUD will deal exclusively with the county with respect to issues of program administration and performance, including remedial actions. The unit of general local government will be considered the grantee for the purpose of determining grant limits. The unit of general local government's statistics will be used for purposes of the selection factors referred to in § 570.421(a).

(d) *Public service activities cap.* Public service activities may be funded up to a maximum of fifteen (15) percent of a State's nonentitlement allocation for any fiscal year. HUD may award a grant to a unit of general local government for public service activities with up to 100 percent of the funds intended for public service activities. HUD will apply the 15 percent statewide cap to public service activities by funding public service activities in the highest rated applications in each NOFA until the cap is reached.

(e) *Activities outside an applicant's boundaries.* An applicant may conduct eligible CDBG activities outside its boundaries. These activities must be demonstrated to be appropriate to meeting the applicant's needs and objectives, and must be consistent with State and local law. This provision includes using funds provided under this subpart in a metropolitan city or an urban county.

(f) *Multiyear plans.* HUD will not make any new multiyear commitments for NOFAs published in calendar year 1997 or later. HUD will continue to honor the terms of the multiyear plans that were approved under the provisions of NOFAs published prior to calendar year 1997.

(g) *Maximum grant amount.* The maximum grant amount that will be awarded to a single unit of general local government in response to the annual Small Cities NOFA published in calendar year 1997 or later is $400,000, except that counties may apply for up to $600,000 in HUD-administered Small Cities funds. HUD may specify lower grant limits in the NOFA, which may include different limits for different types of grants available or different types of applicants. This paragraph (g) does not apply to multiyear plans that were approved under the provisions of NOFAs published prior to calendar year 1997, nor does it apply to grants awarded in connection with paragraphs (a)(3) through (a)(5) of this section. The maximum limits in this paragraph (g) apply to grants for economic development projects awarded under NOFAs in which there is no set-aside of funds for such projects.

§§ 570.422–425 [Reserved]

§ 570.426 Program income.

(a) The provisions of § 570.504(b) apply to all program income generated by a specific grant and received prior to grant closeout.

(b) If the unit of general local government has another ongoing CDBG grant at the time of closeout, the program income will be considered to be program income of the ongoing grant. The grantee can choose which grant to credit the program income to if it has multiple open CDBG grants.

(c) If the unit of general local government has no open ongoing CDBG grant at the time of closeout, program income of the unit of general local government or its subrecipients which amounts to less than $25,000 per year will not be considered to be program income unless needed to repay a Section 108 guaranteed loan. When more than $25,000 of program income is generated from one or more closed out grants in a year after closeout, the entire amount of the program income is subject to the requirements of this part. This will be a subject of the closeout agreement described in § 570.509(c).

§ 570.427 Program amendments.

(a) *HUD approval of certain program amendments.* Grantees shall request prior HUD approval for all program amendments involving new activities or alteration of existing activities that will significantly change the scope, location, or objectives of the approved activities or beneficiaries. Approval is subject to the amended activities meeting the requirements of this part and being able to be completed promptly.

(b) *Documentation of program amendments.* Any program amendments that do not require HUD approval must be fully documented in the grantee's records.

(c) *Citizen participation requirements.* Whenever an amendment requires HUD approval, the requirements for citizen participation in § 570.431 must be met.

[62 FR 62914, Nov. 25, 1997, as amended at 72 FR 46370, Aug. 17, 2007]

§ 570.428 [Reserved]

§ 570.429 Hawaii general and grant requirements.

(a) *General.* This section applies to non-entitlement CDBG grants in Hawaii. The non-entitlement counties in the State of Hawaii will be treated as entitlement grantees except for the calculation of allocations, and the source of their funding, which will be from section 106(d) of the Act.

(b) *Scope and applicability.* Except as modified or limited under the provisions thereof or this subpart, the policies and procedures outlined in subparts A, C, D, J, K, and O of this part apply to non-entitlement CDBG grants in Hawaii.

(c) *Grant amounts.* (1) For each eligible unit of general local government, a formula grant amount will be determined which bears the same ratio to the total amount available for the non-entitlement area of the State as the weighted average of the ratios between:

(i) The population of that eligible unit of general local government and the population of all eligible units of general local government in the non-entitlement areas of the State;

(ii) The extent of poverty in that eligible unit of general local government and the extent of poverty in all the eligible units of general local government in the nonentitlement areas of the State; and

(iii) The extent of housing overcrowding in that eligible unit of general local government and the extent of housing overcrowding in all the eligible units of general local government in the nonentitlement areas of the State.

(2) In determining the average of the ratios under this paragraph (c), the ratio involving the extent of poverty shall be counted twice and each of the other ratios shall be counted once. (0.25 + 0.50 + 0.25 = 1.00).

(d) *Reallocation.* (1) Any amounts that become available as a result of any reductions under subpart O of this part shall be reallocated in the same or future fiscal year to any remaining eligible applicants on a pro rata basis.

(2) Any formula grant amounts reserved for an applicant that chooses not to submit an application shall be reallocated to any remaining eligible applicants on a pro rata basis.

(3) No amounts shall be reallocated under paragraph (d) of this section in any fiscal year to any applicant whose grant amount was reduced under subpart O of this part.

(Approved by the Office of Management and Budget under control number 2506–0060)

[62 FR 62914, Nov. 25, 1997, as amended at 72 FR 46371, Aug. 17, 2007]

§ 570.431 Citizen participation.

(a) *General.* An applicant that is located in a nonentitlement area of a State that has not elected to distribute funds shall comply with the citizen participation requirements described in this section, including requirements for the preparation of the proposed application and the final application. The requirements for citizen participation do not restrict the responsibility or authority of the applicant for the development and execution of its community development program.

§ 570.431

(b) *Citizen participation plan.* The applicant must develop and follow a detailed citizen participation plan and must make the plan public. The plan must be completed and available before the application for assistance is submitted to HUD, and the applicant must certify that it is following the plan. The plan must set forth the applicant's policies and procedures for:

(1) Giving citizens timely notice of local meetings and reasonable and timely access to local meetings, information, and records relating to the grantee's proposed and actual use of CDBG funds including, but not limited to:

(i) The amount of CDBG funds expected to be made available for the coming year, including the grant and anticipated program income;

(ii) The range of activities that may be undertaken with those funds;

(iii) The estimated amount of those funds proposed to be used for activities that will benefit low- and moderate-income persons;

(iv) The proposed CDBG activities likely to result in displacement and the applicant's plans, consistent with the policies developed under § 570.606(b), for minimizing displacement of persons as a result of its proposed activities; and

(v) The types and levels of assistance the applicant plans to make available (or to require others to make available) to persons displaced by CDBG-funded activities, even if the applicant expects no displacement to occur;

(2) Providing technical assistance to groups representative of persons of low- and moderate-income that request assistance in developing proposals. The level and type of assistance to be provided is at the discretion of the applicant. The assistance need not include the provision of funds to the groups;

(3) Holding a minimum of two public hearings; for the purpose of obtaining citizens' views and formulating or responding to proposals and questions. Each public hearing must be conducted at a different stage of the CDBG program. Together, the hearings must address community development and housing needs, development of proposed activities and review of program performance. There must be reasonable notice of the hearings and the hearings must be held at times and accessible locations convenient to potential or actual beneficiaries, with reasonable accommodations including material in accessible formats for persons with disabilities. The applicant must specify in its plan how it will meet the requirement for hearings at times and locations convenient to potential or actual beneficiaries;

(4) Meeting the needs of non-English speaking residents in the case of public hearings where a significant number of non-English speaking residents can reasonably be expected to participate;

(5) Responding to citizen complaints and grievances, including the procedures that citizens must follow when submitting complaints and grievances. The applicant's policies and procedures must provide for timely written answers to written complaints and grievances within 15 working days of the receipt of the complaint, where practicable; and

(6) Encouraging citizen participation, particularly by low- and moderate-income persons who reside in slum or blighted areas, and in other areas in which CDBG funds are proposed to be used.

(c) *Publication of proposed application.* (1) The applicant shall publish a proposed application consisting of the proposed community development activities and community development objectives in order to afford affected citizens an opportunity to:

(i) Examine the application's contents to determine the degree to which they may be affected;

(ii) Submit comments on the proposed application; and

(iii) Submit comments on the performance of the applicant.

(2) The requirement for publishing in paragraph (c)(1) of this section may be met by publishing a summary of the proposed application in one or more newspapers of general circulation, and by making copies of the proposed application available at libraries, government offices, and public places. The summary must describe the contents and purpose of the proposed application, and must include a list of the locations where copies of the entire proposed application may be examined.

(d) *Preparation of a final application.* An applicant must prepare a final application. In the preparation of the final application, the applicant shall consider comments and views received related to the proposed application and may, if appropriate, modify the final application. The final application shall be made available to the public and shall include the community development objectives and projected use of funds, and the community development activities.

(e) *New York grantee amendments.* To assure citizen participation on program amendments to final applications that require HUD approval under §570.427, the grantee shall:

(1) Furnish citizens information concerning the amendment;

(2) Hold one or more public hearings to obtain the views of citizens on the proposed amendment;

(3) Develop and publish the proposed amendment in such a manner as to afford affected citizens an opportunity to examine the contents, and to submit comments on the proposed amendment;

(4) Consider any comments and views expressed by citizens on the proposed amendment and, if the grantee finds it appropriate, modify the final amendment accordingly; and

(5) Make the final amendment to the community development program available to the public before its submission to HUD.

§570.440 Application requirements for insular area grants funded under section 106.

(a) *Applicability.* The requirements of this section apply to insular grants funded under section 106 of the Act. An insular area jurisdiction may choose to prepare program statements following either:

(1) The abbreviated consolidated plan procedures described in this subpart and in 24 CFR 91.235; or

(2) The complete consolidated plan procedures applicable to local governments, discussed at 24 CFR 91.200 through 91.230.

(b) *Proposed statement.* An insular area jurisdiction shall prepare and publish a proposed statement and comply with the citizen participation requirements described in §570.441, if it submits an abbreviated consolidated plan under 24 CFR 91.235. The jurisdiction shall follow the citizen participation requirements of 24 CFR 91.105 and 91.100 (with the exception of §91.100(a)(4)), if it submits a complete consolidated plan.

(c) *Final statement.* The insular area jurisdiction shall submit to HUD a final statement describing its community development objectives and activities. The statement also must include a priority nonhousing community development plan in accordance with 24 CFR 91.235. This final statement shall be submitted, together with the required certifications, to the appropriate field office in a form prescribed by HUD.

(d) *Submission requirement.* Each insular area jurisdiction shall submit its final statement to HUD no later than 45 days before the start of its program year. Each jurisdiction may choose the start date for the annual period of its program year that most closely fits its own needs. HUD may grant an extension of the submission deadline for good cause.

(e) *Certifications.* The insular area jurisdiction's final statement must be accompanied by appropriate certifications as further described under 24 CFR 91.225. The jurisdiction should submit all general certifications, as well as all program certifications for each program from which it receives funding, if it submits a complete consolidated plan. For insular area jurisdictions receiving CDBG funds under an abbreviated consolidated plan, these certifications shall include at a minimum:

(1) The following general certifications described at §91.225(a) of this title: Affirmatively furthering fair housing; anti-displacement and relocation plan; drug-free workplace; anti-lobbying; authority of jurisdiction; consistency with plan; acquisition and relocation; and Section 3.

(2) The following CDBG certifications described at §91.225(b) of this title: Citizen participation; community development plan; following a plan; use of funds; excessive force; compliance with anti-discrimination laws; compliance with lead-based paint procedures; and compliance with laws.

§ 570.441

(f) *HUD action on final statement.* Following the review of the statement, HUD will promptly notify each jurisdiction of the action taken with regard to its statement. HUD will approve a grant if the jurisdiction's submissions have been made and approved in accordance with 24 CFR part 91, and if the certifications required in such submissions are satisfactory to HUD. The certifications will be satisfactory to HUD for this purpose, unless HUD determines pursuant to subpart O of this part that the jurisdiction has not complied with the requirements of this part, has failed to carry out its consolidated plan (or abbreviated consolidated plan) as provided under § 570.903, or has determined that there is evidence, not directly involving the jurisdiction's past performance under this program, that tends to challenge in a substantial manner the jurisdiction's certification of future performance. If HUD makes any such determination, however, further assurances may be required to be submitted by the jurisdiction as HUD may deem warranted or necessary to find the jurisdiction's certification satisfactory.

(g) *Reimbursement for pre-award costs.* Insular area jurisdictions may request reimbursement for pre-award costs in accordance with § 570.200(h).

(h) *Float funding.* An insular area jurisdiction may use undisbursed funds in the line of credit and its CDBG program account that are budgeted in final statements or action plans for one or more activities that do not need the funds immediately, subject to the limitations described in § 570.301(b).

(i) *Program amendments.* (1) The insular area jurisdiction's citizen participation plan (see § 570.441) must specify the criteria the jurisdiction will use for determining what changes in the jurisdiction's planned or actual activities will constitute a substantial amendment to its final statement. It must include changes in the use of CDBG funds from one eligible activity to another among the changes that qualify as a substantial amendment.

(2) The citizen participation plan must provide citizens with reasonable notice and an opportunity to comment on substantial amendments. The citizen participation plan must state how reasonable notice and an opportunity to comment will be given, as well as provide a period of not less than 30 days to receive comments on the substantial amendment before the amendment is implemented.

(3) The citizen participation plan shall require the jurisdiction to consider comments or views of citizens received in writing, or orally at public hearings, if any, in preparing the substantial amendment of its statement. A summary of comments or views not accepted and the reasons for non-acceptance shall be attached to the substantial amendment.

(4) Any program amendment, regardless of whether it is considered to be substantial, must be fully documented in the jurisdiction's records.

(j) *Performance reports.* Each insular area jurisdiction must submit annual performance reports in accordance with 24 CFR 91.520.

[69 FR 32780, June 10, 2004]

§ 570.441 Citizen participation—insular areas.

(a) *General.* An insular area jurisdiction submitting an abbreviated consolidated plan under 24 CFR 91.235 shall comply with the citizen participation requirements described in this section. An insular area jurisdiction submitting a complete consolidated plan in accordance with 24 CFR 91.200 through 91.230 shall follow the citizen participation requirements of § 91.100 and § 91.105, except for § 91.100(a)(4). For funding under section 106 of the Act, these requirements are applicable to all aspects of the Insular Areas program, including the preparation of the proposed statement and final statements as described in § 570.440. The requirements for citizen participation do not restrict the responsibility or authority of the jurisdiction for the development and execution of its community development program.

(b) *Citizen participation plan.* The insular area jurisdiction must develop and follow a detailed citizen participation plan and must make the plan public. The plan must be completed and available before the statement for assistance is submitted to HUD, and the jurisdiction must certify that it is following the plan. The plan must set

Ofc. of Asst. Secy., Comm. Planning, Develop., HUD § 570.441

forth the jurisdiction's policies and procedures for:

(1) Giving citizens timely notice of local meetings and reasonable and timely access to local meetings, information, and records relating to the grantee's proposed and actual use of CDBG funds including, but not limited to:

(i) The amount of CDBG funds expected to be made available for the coming year, including the grant and anticipated program income;

(ii) The range of activities that may be undertaken with those funds;

(iii) The estimated amount of those funds proposed to be used for activities that will benefit low- and moderate-income persons;

(iv) The proposed CDBG activities likely to result in displacement and the jurisdiction's plans, consistent with the policies developed under § 570.606(b), for minimizing displacement of persons as a result of its proposed activities; and

(v) The types and levels of assistance the jurisdiction plans to make available (or to require others to make available) to persons displaced by CDBG-funded activities, even if the jurisdiction expects no displacement to occur;

(2) Providing technical assistance to groups representative of persons of low- and moderate-income that request assistance in developing proposals. The level and type of assistance to be provided is at the discretion of the jurisdiction. The assistance need not include the provision of funds to the groups;

(3) Holding a minimum of two public hearings for the purpose of obtaining citizens' views and formulating or responding to proposals and questions. Each public hearing must be conducted at a different stage of the CDBG program. Together, the hearings must address community development and housing needs, development of proposed activities, and review of program performance. There must be reasonable notice of the hearings, and the hearings must be held at times and accessible locations convenient to potential or actual beneficiaries, with reasonable accommodations including material in accessible formats for persons with disabilities. The jurisdiction must specify in its plan how it will meet the requirement for hearings at times and locations convenient to potential or actual beneficiaries;

(4) Meeting the needs of non-English speaking residents in the case of public hearings where a significant number of non-English speaking residents can reasonably be expected to participate;

(5) Responding to citizen complaints and grievances, including the procedures that citizens must follow when submitting complaints and grievances. The jurisdiction's policies and procedures must provide for timely written answers to written complaints and grievances within 15 working days after the receipt of the complaint, where practicable; and

(6) Encouraging citizen participation, particularly by low- and moderate-income persons who reside in areas in which CDBG funds are proposed to be used.

(c) *Publication of proposed statement.* (1) The insular area jurisdiction shall publish a proposed statement consisting of the proposed community development activities and community development objectives in order to afford affected citizens an opportunity to:

(i) Examine the statement's contents to determine the degree to which they may be affected;

(ii) Submit comments on the proposed statement; and

(iii) Submit comments on the performance of the jurisdiction.

(2) The requirement for publishing in paragraph (c)(1) of this section may be met by publishing a summary of the proposed statement in one or more newspapers of general circulation and by making copies of the proposed statement available at libraries, government offices, and public places. The summary must describe the contents and purpose of the proposed statement and must include a list of the locations where copies of the entire proposed statement may be examined.

(d) *Preparation of a final statement.* An insular area jurisdiction must prepare a final statement. In the preparation of the final statement, the jurisdiction shall consider comments and views received relating to the proposed statement and may, if appropriate, modify the final statement. The final statement shall be made available to the public and shall include the community development objectives, projected use of funds, and the community development activities.

(e) *Program amendments.* To assure citizen participation on program amendments to final statements, the insular area grantee shall:

(1) Furnish citizens information concerning the amendment;

(2) Hold one or more public hearings to obtain the views of citizens on the proposed amendment;

(3) Develop and publish the proposed amendment in such a manner as to afford affected citizens an opportunity to examine the contents, and to submit comments on the proposed amendment;

(4) Consider any comments and views expressed by citizens on the proposed amendment and, if the grantee finds it appropriate, modify the final amendment accordingly; and

(5) Make the final amendment to the community development program available to the public before its submission to HUD.

(f) *Performance reports.* (1) The citizen participation plan must provide citizens with reasonable notice and an opportunity to comment on performance reports. The citizen participation plan must state how reasonable notice and an opportunity to comment will be given. The citizen participation plan must provide a period of not less than 15 days to receive comments on the performance report before it is to be submitted to HUD.

(2) The citizen participation plan shall require the jurisdiction to consider comments or views of citizens received in writing or orally at public hearings in preparing the performance report. A summary of these comments or views shall be attached to the performance report.

(g) *Application for loan guarantees.* Insular area jurisdictions intending to apply for the Section 108 Loan Guarantee program must ensure that they follow the applicable presubmission and citizen participation requirements of § 570.704.

[69 FR 32780, June 10, 2004]

§ 570.442 Reallocations-Insular Areas.

(a) Any Insular Area funds that become available as a result of reductions under subpart O of this part, shall be reallocated in the same or future fiscal year to any remaining eligible Insular Area grantees pro rata according to population.

(b) Any Insular Area grant funds for a fiscal year reserved for an applicant that chooses not to submit a final statement in accordance with § 570.440 to receive such funds, shall be reallocated in the same or future fiscal year to any remaining eligible Insular Area grantees pro rata according to population.

(c) No amounts shall be reallocated under this section in any fiscal year to any applicant whose grant amount in such fiscal year was reduced under subpart O of this part or who did not submit a final statement in accordance with § 570.440 for that fiscal year.

(d) Insular Area grantees receiving additional funds under this section will be evaluated for timeliness under § 570.902 based upon the original grant amount plus the additional funds received. Accordingly, references in § 570.902 to an Insular Area's grant amount for its current program year include such additional funds, and references to unexpended or undisbursed funds include such additional funds.

[72 FR 12536, Mar. 15, 2007]

Subpart G—Urban Development Action Grants

SOURCE: 47 FR 7983, Feb. 23, 1982, unless otherwise noted.

§ 570.450 Purpose.

The purpose of urban development action grants is to assist cities and urban counties that are experiencing severe economic distress to help stimulate economic development activity needed to aid in economic recovery.

This subpart G contains those regulations that are essential for the continued operation of this grant program.

[61 FR 11476, Mar. 20, 1996]

§ 570.456 Ineligible activities and limitations on eligible activities.

(a) Large cities and urban counties may not use assistance under this subpart for planning the project or developing the application. However, they may use entitlement community development block grant funds for this purpose, provided that the UDAG project meets the eligibility test of this part. Any small city which submits a project application which is selected for preliminary approval and for which legally binding grant agreement and for which a release of funds pursuant to 24 CFR part 58 has been issued may devote up to three (3) percent of the approved amount of its action grant to defray its actual costs in planning the project and preparing its application.

(b) Assistance under this subpart may not be used for public services as described in § 570.201(e).

(c)(1) No assistance may be provided under this subpart for speculative projects intended to facilitate the relocation of industrial or commercial plants or facilities from one area to another. The provisions of this paragraph (c)(1) shall not apply to a relocation of any such plant or facility within a metropolitan area.

(i) HUD will presume that a proposed project which includes speculative commercial or industrial space is intended to facilitate the relocation of a plant or facility from one area to another, if it is demonstrated to HUD's satisfaction that:

(A) The proposed project is reasonably proximate (i.e., within 50 miles) to an area from which there has been a significant current pattern of movement, to areas reasonably proximate, of jobs of the category for which such space is appropriate; and

(B) There is a likelihood of continuation of the pattern, based on measurable comparisons between the area from which the movement has been occurring and the area of the proposed project in terms of tax rates, energy costs, and similar relevant factors.

(ii) The restrictions established in this paragraph (c)(1) shall not apply if the Secretary determines that the relocation does not significantly and adversely affect the employment or economic base of the area from which the industrial or commercial plant or facility is to be relocated. However, the Secretary will not be required to make a determination whether there is a significant and adverse effect. If such a determination is undertaken, the Secretary will presume that there is a significant and adverse effect where the significant pattern of job movement and the likelihood of continuation of such a pattern has been from a distressed community.

(iii) The presumptions established in accordance with this paragraph (c)(1) are rebuttable by the applicant. However, the burden of overcoming the presumptions will be on the applicant.

(iv) The presumptions established in this paragraph (c)(1) will not apply if the speculative space contained in a commercial or industrial plant or facility included in a project constitutes a lesser percentage of the total space contained in that plant or facility than the threshold amounts specified below:

Size of plant or facility	Amount of speculative space
0 to 50,000 sq. ft.	10 percent.
50,001 to 250,000 sq. ft.	5,000 sq. ft. or 8 percent, whichever is greater.
250,001 to 1,000,000 sq. ft.	20,000 sq. ft. or 5 percent, whichever is greater.
1,000,001 or more sq. ft.	50,000 sq. ft. or 3 percent, whichever is greater.

(2) *Projects with identified intended occupants.* No assistance may be provided or utilized under this subpart for any project with identified intended occupants that is likely to facilitate:

(i) A relocation of any operation of an industrial or commercial plant or facility or other business establishment from any UDAG eligible jurisdiction; or

(ii) An expansion of any operation of an industrial or commercial plant or facility or other business establishment that results in a substantial reduction of any such operation in any UDAG eligible jurisdiction. The provisions of this paragraph (c)(2) shall not apply to a relocation of an operation or to an expansion of an operation within a metropolitan area. The provisions of this paragraph (c)(2) shall apply only to projects that do not have speculative space, or to projects that include both identified intended occupant space and speculative space.

(iii) *Significant and adverse effect.* The restrictions established in this paragraph (c)(2) shall not apply if the Secretary determines that the relocation or expansion does not significantly and adversely affect the employment or economic base of the UDAG eligible jurisdiction from which the relocation or expansion occurs. However, the Secretary will not be required to make a determination whether there is a significant and adverse effect. If such a determination is undertaken, among the factors which the Secretary will consider are:

(A) Whether it is reasonable to anticipate that there will be a significant net loss of jobs in the plant or facility being abandoned; and

(B) Whether an equivalent productive use will be made of the plant or facility being abandoned by the relocating or expanding operation, thus creating no deterioration of economic base.

(3) Within 90 days following notice of intent to withhold, deny or cancel assistance under paragraph (c) (1) or (2) of this section, the applicant may appeal in writing to the Secretary the withholding, denial or cancellation of assistance. The applicant will be notified and given an opportunity within a prescribed time for an informal consultation regarding the action.

(4) *Assistance for individuals adversely affected by prohibited relocations.* (i) Any amount withdrawn by, recaptured by, or paid to the Secretary because of a violation (or a settlement of an alleged violation) of this section (or any regulation issued or contractual provision entered into to carry out this section) by a project with identified intended occupants will be made available by the Secretary as a grant to the UDAG eligible jurisdiction from which the operation of an industrial or commercial plant or facility or other business establishment was relocated, or in which the operation was reduced.

(ii)(A) Any amount made available under this paragraph shall be used by the grantee to assist individuals who were employed by the operation involved before the relocation or reduction and whose employment or terms of employment were adversely affected by the relocation or reduction. The assistance shall include job training, job retraining, and job placement.

(B) If any amount made available to a grantee under this paragraph (c)(4) is more than is required to provide the assistance described in paragraph (c)(4)(ii)(A) of this section, the grantee shall use the excess amount to carry out community development activities eligible under section 105(a) of the Housing and Community Development Act of 1974.

(iii)(A) The provisions of this paragraph (c)(4) shall be applicable to any amount withdrawn by, recaptured by, or paid to the Secretary under this section, including any amount withdrawn, recaptured, or paid before the effective date of this paragraph.

(B) Grants may be made under this paragraph (c)(4) only to the extent of amounts provided in appropriation Acts.

(5) For purposes of this section, the following definitions apply:

(i) "Operation" means any plant, equipment, facility, substantial number of positions, substantial employment opportunities, production capacity, or product line.

(ii) "Metropolitan area" means a metropolitan area as defined in §570.3 and which consists of either a freestanding metropolitan area or a primary metropolitan statistical area where both primary and consolidated areas exist.

(iii) "Likely" means probably or reasonably to be expected, as determined by firm evidence such as resolutions of a corporation to close a plant or facility, notifications of closure to collective bargaining units, correspondence and notifications of corporate officials relative to a closure, and supportive evidence, such as newspaper articles and notices to employees regarding closure of a plant or facility. Consultant studies and marketing studies may be submitted as supportive evidence, but by themselves are not firm evidence.

(iv) "UDAG eligible jurisdiction" means a distressed community, a Pocket of Poverty, a Pocket of Poverty community, or an identifiable community described in section 119(p) of the Housing and Community Development Act of 1974.

(6) Notwithstanding any other provision of this subpart, nothing in this subpart may be construed to permit an inference or conclusion that the policy of the urban development action grant program is to facilitate the relocation of businesses from one area to another.

[47 FR 7983, Feb. 23, 1982, as amended at 53 FR 33028, Aug. 29, 1988; 54 FR 21169, May 16, 1989; 56 FR 56128, Oct. 31, 1991]

§ 570.457 Displacement, relocation, acquisition, and replacement of housing.

The displacement, relocation, acquisition, and replacement of housing requirements of § 570.606 apply to applicants under this subpart G.

[55 FR 29309, July 18, 1990]

§ 570.461 Post-preliminary approval requirements; lead-based paint.

The recipient may receive preliminary approval prior to the accomplishment of lead-based paint activities conducted pursuant to part 35, subparts A, B, J, K, and R of this title, but no funds will be released until such actions are complete and evidence of compliance is submitted to HUD.

[64 FR 50225, Sept. 15, 1999]

§ 570.463 Project amendments and revisions.

(a) *Pre-approval revisions to the application.* Applicants must submit to the HUD Area Office and to Central Office all revisions to the application. A revision is considered significant if it alters the scope, location, or scale of the project or changes the beneficiaries' population.

The applicant must hold at least one public hearing prior to making a significant revision to the application.

(b) *Post preliminary approval amendments.* Applicants receiving preliminary approval must submit to the HUD Central Office, a request for approval of any significant amendment. A copy of the request must also be submitted to the Area Office. A significant amendment involves new activities or alterations thereof which will change the scope, location, scale, or beneficiaries of such activities or which, as a result of a number of smaller changes, add up to an amount that exceeds ten percent of the grant. HUD approval of amendments may be granted to those requests which meet all of the following criteria:

(1) New or significantly altered activities must meet the criteria for selection applicable at the time of receipt of the program amendment.

(2) The recipient must have complied with all requirements of this subpart.

(3) The recipient may make amendments other than those requiring prior HUD approval as defined in paragraph (b) of this section but each recipient must notify both the Area and Central Offices of such changes.

[47 FR 7983, Feb. 23, 1982, as amended at 61 FR 11476, Mar. 20, 1996]

§ 570.464 Project closeout.

HUD will advise the recipient to initiate closeout procedures when HUD determines, in consultation with the recipient, that there are not impediments to closeout. Closeout shall be carried out in accordance with § 570.509 and applicable HUD guidelines.

[53 FR 8058, Mar. 11, 1988]

§ 570.465 Applicability of rules and regulations.

The provisions of subparts A, B, C, J, K, and O of this part 570 shall apply to this subpart except to the extent that they are modified or augmented by this subpart.

§ 570.466 Additional application submission requirements for Pockets of Poverty—employment opportunities.

Applicants for Action Grants under the Pockets of Poverty provision must describe the number and, to the extent possible, the types of new jobs (construction and permanent) that will be provided to the low- and moderate-income residents of the Pocket of Poverty as a direct result of the proposed project. If the application calls for job

§ 570.480

training programs (such as those related to the CETA program) or job recruiting services for the pocket's residents, then such proposed activities must be clearly and fully explained. HUD requires applicants to ensure that at least 75 percent of whatever permanent jobs initially result from the project are provided to low- and moderate-income persons and that at least 51 percent of whatever permanent jobs initially result from the project are provided to low- and moderate-income residents from the pocket. HUD encourages applicants to ensure that at least 20 percent of all permanent jobs are filled by persons from the pocket qualified to participate in the CETA program on a continuous basis. HUD requires all applicants to continuously use best efforts to ensure that at least 75 percent of all permanent jobs resulting from any Action Grant-assisted project are provided to low- and moderate-income persons and that at least 51 percent of all permanent jobs resulting from any Action Grant-assisted project are provided to low- and moderate-income residents from the pocket. The application should clearly describe how the applicant intends to meet initial and continuous job requirements. Private participating parties must meet these employment requirements in the aggregate. To enable the private participants to do so, lease agreements executed by a private participating party shall include:

(a) Provisions requiring lessees to follow hiring practices that the private participating party has determined will enable it to meet these requirements in the aggregate; and

(b) Provisions that will enable the private participating party to declare a default under the lease agreement if the lessees do not follow such practices.

[61 FR 11476, Mar. 20, 1996]

Subpart H [Reserved]

Subpart I—State Community Development Block Grant Program

SOURCE: 57 FR 53397, Nov. 9, 1992, unless otherwise noted.

§ 570.480 General.

(a) This subpart describes policies and procedures applicable to states that elect to receive Community Development Block Grant funds for distribution to units of general local government in the state's nonentitlement areas under the Housing and Community Development Act of 1974. Other subparts of part 570 are not applicable to the State CDBG Program, except as expressly provided otherwise.

(b) HUD's authority for the waiver of regulations and for the suspension of requirements to address damage in a Presidentially-declared disaster area is described in 24 CFR part 5 and in section 122 of the Act, respectively.

(c) In exercising the Secretary's obligation and responsibility to review a state's performance, the Secretary will give maximum feasible deference to the state's interpretation of the statutory requirements and the requirements of this regulation, provided that these interpretations are not plainly inconsistent with the Act and the Secretary's obligation to enforce compliance with the intent of the Congress as declared in the Act. The Secretary will not determine that a state has failed to carry out its certifications in compliance with requirements of the Act (and this regulation) unless the Secretary finds that procedures and requirements adopted by the state are insufficient to afford reasonable assurance that activities undertaken by units of general local government were not plainly inappropriate to meeting the primary objectives of the Act, this regulation, and the state's community development objectives.

(d) Administrative action taken by the Secretary that is not explicitly and fully part of this regulation shall only apply to a specific case or issue at a specific time, and shall not be generally applicable to the state-administered CDBG program.

(e) Religious organizations are eligible to participate under the State CDBG Program as provided in § 570.200(j).

[57 FR 53397, Nov. 9, 1992, as amended at 61 FR 11477, Mar. 20, 1996; 61 FR 54921, Oct. 22, 1996; 69 FR 41718, July 9, 2004]

§ 570.481 Definitions.

(a) Except for terms defined in applicable statutes or this subpart, the Secretary will defer to a state's definitions, provided that these definitions are explicit, reasonable and not plainly inconsistent with the Act. As used in this subpart, the following terms shall have the meaning indicated:

(1) *Act* means title I of the Housing and Community Development Act of 1974 (42 U.S.C. 5301 *et seq.*).

(2) *CDBG funds* means Community Development Block Grant funds, in the form of grants under this subpart and program income, and loans guaranteed by the state under section 108 of the Act.

(b) [Reserved]

[57 FR 53397, Nov. 9, 1992, as amended at 61 FR 5209, Feb. 9, 1996]

§ 570.482 Eligible activities.

(a) *General.* The choice of activities on which block grant funds are expended represents the determination by state and local participants, developed in accordance with the state's program design and procedures, as to which approach or approaches will best serve these interests. The eligible activities are listed at section 105(a) of the Act.

(b) *Special assessments under the CDBG program.* The following policies relate to special assessments under the CDBG program:

(1) *Public improvements initially assisted with CDBG funds.* Where CDBG funds are used to pay all or part of the cost of a public improvement, special assessments may be imposed as follows:

(i) Special assessments to recover the *CDBG funds* may be made only against properties owned and occupied by persons *not* of low and moderate income. These assessments constitute program income.

(ii) Special assessments to recover the *non-CDBG* portion may be made, provided that CDBG funds are used to pay the special assessment in behalf of all properties owned and occupied by low and moderate income persons; except that CDBG funds need not be used to pay the special assessments in behalf of properties owned and occupied by moderate income persons if, when permitted by the state, the unit of general local government certifies that it does not have sufficient CDBG funds to pay the assessments in behalf of all of the low and moderate income owner-occupant persons. Funds collected through such special assessments are not program income.

(2) *Public improvements not initially assisted with CDBG funds.* CDBG funds may be used to pay special assessments levied against property when this form of assessment is used to recover the capital cost of eligible public improvements initially financed solely from sources other than CDBG funds. The payment of special assessments with CDBG funds constitutes CDBG assistance to the public improvement. Therefore, CDBG funds may be used to pay special assessments, provided that:

(i) The installation of the public improvements was carried out in compliance with requirements applicable to activities assisted under this subpart, including labor, environmental and citizen participation requirements;

(ii) The installation of the public improvement meets a criterion for national objectives. (See § 570.483(b)(1), (c), and (d).)

(iii) The requirements of § 570.482(b)(1)(ii) are met.

(c) *Special eligibility provisions.* (1) Microenterprise development activities eligible under section 105(a)(23) of the Housing and Community Development Act of 1974, as amended (42 U.S.C. 5301 *et seq.*) (the Act) may be carried out either through the recipient directly or through public and private organizations, agencies, and other subrecipients (including nonprofit and for-profit subrecipients).

(2) *Provision of public services.* The following activities shall not be subject to the restrictions on public services under section 105(a)(8) of the Act:

(i) Support services provided under section 105(a)(23) of the Act, and paragraph (c) of this section;

(ii) Services carried out under the provisions of section 105(a)(15) of the Act, that are specifically designed to increase economic opportunities through job training and placement and other employment support services, including, but not limited to, peer support programs, counseling, child care, transportation, and other similar services; and

(iii) Services of any type carried out under the provisions of section 105(a)(15) of the Act pursuant to a strategy approved by a state under the provisions of §91.315(e)(2) of this title.

(3) *Environmental cleanup and economic development or redevelopment of contaminated properties.* Remediation of known or suspected environmental contamination may be undertaken under the authority of section 205 of Public Law 105–276 and section 105(a)(4) of the Act. Economic development activities carried out under sections 105(a)(14), (a)(15), or (a)(17) of the Act may include costs associated with project-specific assessment or remediation of known or suspected environmental contamination.

(d) [Reserved]

(e) *Guidelines and objectives for evaluating project costs and financial requirements*—(1) *Applicability.* The following guidelines, also referred to as the underwriting guidelines, are provided to assist the recipient to evaluate and select activities to be carried out for economic development purposes. Specifically, these guidelines are applicable to activities that are eligible for CDBG assistance under section 105(a)(17) of the Act, economic development activities eligible under section 105(a)(14) of the Act, and activities that are part of a community economic development project eligible under section 105(a)(15) of the Act. The use of the underwriting guidelines published by HUD is not mandatory. However, states electing not to use these guidelines would be expected to ensure that the state or units of general local government conduct basic financial underwriting prior to the provision of CDBG financial assistance to a for-profit business.

(2) *Objectives.* The underwriting guidelines are designed to provide the recipient with a framework for financially underwriting and selecting CDBG-assisted economic development projects which are financially viable and will make the most effective use of the CDBG funds. Where appropriate, HUD's underwriting guidelines recognize that different levels of review are appropriate to take into account differences in the size and scope of a proposed project, and in the case of a microenterprise or other small business to take into account the differences in the capacity and level of sophistication among businesses of differing sizes. Recipients are encouraged, when they develop their own programs and underwriting criteria, to also take these factors into account. These underwriting guidelines are published as appendix A to this part. The objectives of the underwriting guidelines are to ensure:

(i) That project costs are reasonable;

(ii) That all sources of project financing are committed;

(iii) That to the extent practicable, CDBG funds are not substituted for non-Federal financial support;

(iv) That the project is financially feasible;

(v) That to the extent practicable, the return on the owner's equity investment will not be unreasonably high; and

(vi) That to the extent practicable, CDBG funds are disbursed on a pro rata basis with other finances provided to the project.

(f) *Standards for evaluating public benefit*—(1) *Purpose and applicability.* The grantee is responsible for making sure that at least a minimum level of public benefit is obtained from the expenditure of CDBG funds under the categories of eligibility governed by these standards. The standards set forth below identify the types of public benefit that will be recognized for this purpose and the minimum level of each that must be obtained for the amount of CDBG funds used. These standards are applicable to activities that are eligible for CDBG assistance under section 105(a)(17) of the Act, economic development activities eligible under section 105(a)(14) of the Act, and activities that are part of a community economic development project eligible under section 105(a)(15) of the Act. Certain public facilities and improvements eligible under section 105(a)(2) of the Act, which are undertaken for economic development purposes, are also subject to these standards, as specified in §570.483(b)(4)(vi)(F)(*2*). Unlike the guidelines for project costs and financial requirements covered under paragraph (a) of this section, the use of the standards for public benefit is mandatory.

(2) *Standards for activities in the aggregate.* Activities covered by these standards must, in the aggregate, either:

(i) Create or retain at least one full-time equivalent, permanent job per $35,000 of CDBG funds used; or

(ii) Provide goods or services to residents of an area, such that the number of low- and moderate-income persons residing in the areas served by the assisted businesses amounts to at least one low- and moderate-income person per $350 of CDBG funds used.

(3) *Applying the aggregate standards.* (i) A state shall apply the aggregate standards under paragraph (e)(2) of this section to all funds distributed for applicable activities from each annual grant. This includes the amount of the annual grant, any funds reallocated by HUD to the state, any program income distributed by the state and any guaranteed loan funds made under the provisions of subpart M of this part covered in the method of distribution in the final statement for a given annual grant year.

(ii) The grantee shall apply the aggregate standards to the number of jobs to be created/retained, or to the number of persons residing in the area served (as applicable), as determined at the time funds are obligated to activities.

(iii) Where an activity is expected both to create or retain jobs and to provide goods or services to residents of an area, the grantee may elect to count the activity under either the jobs standard or the area residents standard, but not both.

(iv) Where CDBG assistance for an activity is limited to job training and placement and/or other employment support services, the jobs assisted with CDBG funds shall be considered to be created or retained jobs for the purposes of applying the aggregate standards.

(v) Any activity subject to these standards which meets one or more of the following criteria may, at the grantee's option, be excluded from the aggregate standards described in paragraph (f)(2) of this section:

(A) Provides jobs exclusively for unemployed persons or participants in one or more of the following programs:

(*1*) Jobs Training Partnership Act (JTPA);

(*2*) Jobs Opportunities for Basic Skills (JOBS); or

(*3*) Aid to Families with Dependent Children (AFDC);

(B) Provides jobs predominantly for residents of Public and Indian Housing units;

(C) Provides jobs predominantly for homeless persons;

(D) Provides jobs predominantly for low-skilled, low- and moderate-income persons, where the business agrees to provide clear opportunities for promotion and economic advancement, such as through the provision of training;

(E) Provides jobs predominantly for persons residing within a census tract (or block numbering area) that has at least 20 percent of its residents who are in poverty;

(F) Provides assistance to business(es) that operate(s) within a census tract (or block numbering area) that has at least 20 percent of its residents who are in poverty;

(G) Stabilizes or revitalizes a neighborhood income that has at least 70 percent of its residents who are low- and moderate-income;

(H) Provides assistance to a Community Development Financial Institution (as defined in the Community Development Banking and Financial Institutions Act of 1994, (12 U.S.C. 4701 note)) serving an area that has at least 70 percent of its residents who are low- and moderate-income;

(I) Provides assistance to an organization eligible to carry out activities under section 105(a)(15) of the Act serving an area that has at least 70 percent of its residents who are low- and moderate-income;

(J) Provides employment opportunities that are an integral component of a project designed to promote spatial deconcentration of low- and moderate-income and minority persons;

(K) With prior HUD approval, provides substantial benefit to low-income persons through other innovative approaches;

(L) Provides services to the residents of an area pursuant to a strategy approved by the State under the provisions of § 91.315(e)(2) of this title;

(M) Creates or retains jobs through businesses assisted in an area pursuant to a strategy approved by the State under the provisions of § 91.315(e)(2) of this title.

(N) Directly involves the economic development or redevelopment of environmentally contaminated properties.

(4) *Standards for individual activities.* Any activity subject to these standards which falls into one or more of the following categories will be considered by HUD to provide insufficient public benefit, and therefore may under no circumstances be assisted with CDBG funds:

(i) The amount of CDBG assistance exceeds either of the following, as applicable:

(A) $50,000 per full-time equivalent, permanent job created or retained; or

(B) $1,000 per low- and moderate-income person to which goods or services are provided by the activity.

(ii) The activity consists of or includes any of the following:

(A) General promotion of the community as a whole (as opposed to the promotion of specific areas and programs);

(B) Assistance to professional sports teams;

(C) Assistance to privately-owned recreational facilities that serve a predominantly higher-income clientele, where the recreational benefit to users or members clearly outweighs employment or other benefits to low- and moderate-income persons;

(D) Acquisition of land for which the specific proposed use has not yet been identified; and

(E) Assistance to a for-profit business while that business or any other business owned by the same person(s) or entity(ies) is the subject of unresolved findings of noncompliance relating to previous CDBG assistance provided by the recipient.

(5) *Applying the individual activity standards.* (i) Where an activity is expected both to create or retain jobs and to provide goods or services to residents of an area, it will be disqualified only if the amount of CDBG assistance exceeds both of the amounts in paragraph (f)(4)(i) of this section.

(ii) The individual activity tests in paragraph (f)(4)(i) of this section shall be applied to the number of jobs to be created or retained, or to the number of persons residing in the area served (as applicable), as determined at the time funds are obligated to activities.

(iii) Where CDBG assistance for an activity is limited to job training and placement and/or other employment support services, the jobs assisted with CDBG funds shall be considered to be created or retained jobs for the purposes of applying the individual activity standards in paragraph (f)(4)(i) of this section.

(6) *Documentation.* The state and its grant recipients must maintain sufficient records to demonstrate the level of public benefit, based on the above standards, that is actually achieved upon completion of the CDBG-assisted economic development activity(ies) and how that compares to the level of such benefit anticipated when the CDBG assistance was obligated. If a state grant recipient's actual results show a pattern of substantial variation from anticipated results, the state and its recipient are expected to take those actions reasonably within their respective control to improve the accuracy of the projections. If the actual results demonstrate that the state has failed the public benefit standards, HUD may require the state to meet more stringent standards in future years as appropriate.

(g) *Amendments to economic development projects after review determinations.* If, after the grantee enters into a contract to provide assistance to a project, the scope or financial elements of the project change to the extent that a significant contract amendment is appropriate, the project should be reevaluated under these and the recipient's guidelines. (This would include, for example, situations where the business requests a change in the amount or terms of assistance being provided, or an extension to the loan payment period required in the contract.) If a reevaluation of the project indicates that the financial elements and public benefit to be derived have also substantially changed, then the recipient should make appropriate adjustments in the amount, type, terms or conditions of CDBG assistance which has been offered, to reflect the impact of the substantial change. (For example, if a change in the project elements results in a substantial reduction of the total project costs, it may be appropriate for the recipient to reduce the amount of total CDBG assistance.) If the amount of CDBG assistance provided to the project is increased, the amended project must still comply with the public benefit standards under paragraph (f) of this section.

(h) *Prohibition on use of assistance for employment relocation activities*—(1) *Prohibition.* CDBG funds may not be used to directly assist a business, including a business expansion, in the relocation of a plant, facility, or operation from one labor market area (LMA) to another LMA if the relocation is likely to result in a significant loss of jobs in the LMA from which the relocation occurs.

(2) *Definitions.* The following definitions apply to the section:

(i) *Directly assist.* Directly assist means the provision of CDBG funds to a business pursuant to section 105(a)(15) or (17) of the Housing and Community Development Act of 1974 (42 U.S.C. 5301 et seq). Direct assistance also includes assistance under section 105(a)(1), (2), (4), (7), and (14) of the Housing and Community Development Act of 1974, when the state's grantee, subrecipient, or nonprofit entity eligible under section 105(a)(15) enters into an agreement with a business to undertake one or more of these activities as a condition of the business relocating a facility, plant, or operation to the LMA. Provision of public facilities and indirect assistance that will provide benefit to multiple businesses does not fall under the definition of "directly assist," unless it includes the provision of infrastructure to aid a specific business that is the subject of an agreement with the specific assisted business.

(ii) *Labor market area (LMA).* For metropolitan areas, an LMA is an area defined as such by the U.S. Bureau of Labor Statistics (BLS). An LMA is an economically integrated geographic area within which individuals can live and find employment within a reasonable distance or can readily change employment without changing their place of residence. In addition, LMAs are nonoverlapping and geographically exhaustive. For metropolitan areas, grantees must use employment data, as defined by the BLS, for the LMA in which the affected business is currently located and from which current jobs may be lost. For non-metropolitan areas, grantees must use employment data, as defined by the BLS, for the LMA in which the assisted business is currently located and from which current jobs may be lost. For non-metropolitan areas, a LMA is either an area defined by the BLS as an LMA, or a state may choose to combine non-metropolitan LMAs. States are required to define or reaffirm prior definitions of their LMAs on an annual basis and retain records to substantiate such areas prior to any business relocation that would be impacted by this rule. Metropolitan LMAs cannot be combined, nor can a non-metropolitan LMA be combined with a metropolitan LMA. For the Insular Areas, each jurisdiction will be considered to be an LMA. For the HUD-administered Small Cities Program, each of the three participating counties in Hawaii will be considered to be its own LMA. Recipients of Fiscal Year 1999 Small Cities Program funding in New York will follow the requirements for State CDBG recipients.

(iii) *Operation.* A business operation includes, but is not limited to, any equipment, employment opportunity, production capacity, or product line of the business.

(iv) *Significant loss of jobs.* (A) A loss of jobs is significant if: The number of jobs to be lost in the LMA in which the affected business is currently located is equal to or greater than one-tenth of one percent of the total number of persons in the labor force of that LMA; or in all cases, a loss of 500 or more jobs. Notwithstanding the aforementioned, a loss of 25 jobs or fewer does not constitute a significant loss of jobs.

(B) A job is considered to be lost due to the provision of CDBG assistance if the job is relocated within three years from the date the assistance is provided to the business or the time period

§ 570.483

within which jobs are to be created as specified by the agreement among the business, the recipient, and the state (as applicable) if it is longer than three years.

(3) *Written agreement.* Before directly assisting a business with CDBG funds, the recipient, subrecipient, or (in the case of any activity carried out pursuant to 105(a)(15)) nonprofit entity shall sign a written agreement with the assisted business. The written agreement shall include:

(i) *Statement.* A statement from the assisted business as to whether the assisted activity will result in the relocation of any industrial or commercial plant, facility, or operation from one LMA to another and, if so, the number of jobs that will be relocated from each LMA;

(ii) *Required certification.* If the assistance will not result in a relocation covered by this section, a certification from the assisted business that neither it, nor any of its subsidiaries, has plans to relocate jobs at the time the agreement is signed that would result in a significant job loss as defined in this rule; and

(iii) *Reimbursement of assistance.* The agreement shall provide for reimbursement to the recipient of any assistance provided to, or expended on behalf of, the business in the event that assistance results in a relocation prohibited under this section.

(4) *Assistance not covered by this paragraph.* This paragraph does not apply to:

(i) *Relocation assistance.* Relocation assistance required by the Uniform Assistance and Real Property Acquisition Policies Act of 1970 (URA), (42 U.S.C. 4601–4655); optional relocation assistance under section 105(a)(11), as implemented at 570.606(d);

(ii) *Microenterprises.* Assistance to microenterprises as defined by section 102(a)(22) of the Housing and Community Development Act of 1974; and

(iii) *Arms-length transactions.* Assistance to a business that purchases business equipment, inventory, or other physical assets in an arms-length transaction, including the assets of an existing business, provided that the purchase does not result in the relocation of the sellers' business operation (including customer base or list, goodwill, product lines, or trade names) from one LMA to another LMA and does not produce a significant loss of jobs in the LMA from which the relocation occurs.

[57 FR 53397, Nov. 9, 1992, as amended at 60 FR 1949, Jan. 5, 1995; 61 FR 54921, Oct. 22, 1996; 70 FR 76370, Dec. 23, 2005; 71 FR 30035, May 24, 2006]

§ 570.483 Criteria for national objectives.

(a) *General.* The following criteria shall be used to determine whether a CDBG assisted activity complies with one or more of the national objectives as required to section 104(b)(3) of the Act. (HUD is willing to consider a waiver of these requirements in accordance with § 570.480(b)).

(b) *Activities benefiting low and moderate income persons.* An activity will be considered to address the objective of benefiting low and moderate income persons if it meets one of the criteria in paragraph (b) of this section, unless there is substantial evidence to the contrary. In assessing any such evidence, the full range of direct effects of the assisted activity will be considered. The activities, when taken as a whole, must not benefit moderate income persons to the exclusion of low income persons:

(1) *Area benefit activities.* (i) An activity, the benefits of which are available to all the residents in a particular area, where at least 51 percent of the residents are low and moderate income persons. Such an area need not be coterminous with census tracts or other officially recognized boundaries but must be the entire area served by the activity. Units of general local government may, at the discretion of the state, use either HUD-provided data comparing census data with appropriate low and moderate income levels or survey data that is methodologically sound. An activity that serves an area that is not primarily residential in character shall not qualify under this criterion.

(ii) An activity, where the assistance is to a public improvement that provides benefits to all the residents of an area, that is limited to paying special assessments levied against residential properties owned and occupied by persons of low and moderate income.

(iii)(A) An activity to develop, establish and operate (not to exceed two years after establishment), a uniform emergency telephone number system serving an area having less than 51 percent of low and moderate income residents, when the system has not been made operational before the receipt of CDBG funds, provided a prior written determination is obtained from HUD. HUD's determination will be based upon certifications by the State that:

(1) The system will contribute significantly to the safety of the residents of the area. The unit of general local government must provide the state a list of jurisdictions and unincorporated areas to be served by the system and a list of the emergency services that will participate in the emergency telephone number system;

(2) At least 51 percent of the use of the system will be by low and moderate income persons. The state's certification may be based upon information which identifies the total number of calls actually received over the preceding twelve-month period for each of the emergency services to be covered by the emergency telephone number system and relates those calls to the geographic segment (expressed as nearly as possible in terms of census tracts, enumeration districts, block groups, or combinations thereof that are contained within the segment) of the service area from which the calls were generated. In analyzing this data to meet the requirements of this section, the state will assume that the distribution of income among callers generally reflects the income characteristics of the general population residing in the same geographic area where the callers reside. Alternatively, the state's certification may be based upon other data, agreed to by HUD and the state, which shows that over the preceding twelve-month period the users of all the services to be included in the emergency telephone number system consisted of at least 51 percent low and moderate income persons.

(3) Other federal funds received by the unit of general local government are insufficient or unavailable for a uniform emergency telephone number system. The unit of general local government must submit a statement explaining whether the problem is caused by the insufficiency of the amount of such funds, the restrictions on the use of such funds, or the prior commitment of such funds for other purposes by the unit of general local government.

(4) The percentage of the total costs of the system paid for by CDBG funds does not exceed the percentage of low and moderate income persons in the service area of the system. The unit of general local government must include a description of the boundaries of the service area of the system; the census tracts or enumeration districts within the boundaries; the total number of persons and the total number of low and moderate income persons in each census tract or enumeration district, and the percentage of low and moderate income persons in the service area; and the total cost of the system.

(B) The certifications of the state must be submitted along with a brief statement describing the factual basis upon which the certifications were made.

(iv) Activities meeting the requirements of paragraph (e)(4)(i) of this section may be considered to qualify under paragraph (b)(1) of this section.

(v) HUD will consider activities meeting the requirements of paragraph (e)(5)(i) of this section to qualify under paragraph (b)(1) of this section, provided that the area covered by the strategy meets one of the following criteria:

(A) The area is in a Federally-designated Empowerment Zone or Enterprise Community;

(B) The area is primarily residential and contains a percentage of low and moderate income residents that is no less than 70 percent;

(C) All of the census tracts (or block numbering areas) in the area have poverty rates of at least 20 percent, at least 90 percent of the census tracts (or block numbering areas) in the area have poverty rates of at least 25 percent, and the area is primarily residential. (If only part of a census tract or block numbering area is included in a strategy area, the poverty rate shall be computed for those block groups (or

§ 570.483

any part thereof) which are included in the strategy area.)

(D) Upon request by the State, HUD may grant exceptions to the 70 percent low and moderate income or 25 percent poverty minimum thresholds on a case-by-case basis. In no case, however, may a strategy area have both a percentage of low and moderate income residents less than 51 percent and a poverty rate less than 20 percent.

(2) *Limited clientele activities.* (i) An activity which benefits a limited clientele, at least 51 percent of whom are low and moderate income persons. The following kinds of activities may not qualify under paragraph (b)(2) of this section:

(A) Activities, the benefits of which are available to all the residents of an area;

(B) Activities involving the acquisition, construction or rehabilitation of property for housing; or

(C) Activities where the benefit to low- and moderate-income persons to be considered is the creation or retention of jobs, except as provided in paragraph (b)(2)(v) of this section.

(ii) To qualify under paragraph (b)(2) of this section, the activity must meet one or the following tests:

(A) It must benefit a clientele who are generally presumed to be principally low and moderate income persons. Activities that exclusively serve a group of persons in any one or a combination of the following categories may be presumed to benefit persons, 51 percent of whom are low and moderate income: abused children, battered spouses, elderly persons, adults meeting the Bureau of the Census' Current Population Reports definition of "severely disabled," homeless persons, illiterate adults, persons living with AIDS, and migrant farm workers; or

(B) It must require information on family size and income so that it is evident that at least 51 percent of the clientele are persons whose family income does not exceed the low and moderate income limit; or

(C) It must have income eligibility requirements which limit the activity exclusively to low and moderate income persons; or

(D) It must be of such a nature, and be in such a location, that it may be concluded that the activity's clientele will primarily be low and moderate income persons.

(iii) An activity that serves to remove material or architectural barriers to the mobility or accessibility of elderly persons or of adults meeting the Bureau of the Census' Current Population Reports definition of "severely disabled" will be presumed to qualify under this criterion if it is restricted, to the extent practicable, to the removal of such barriers by assisting:

(A) The reconstruction of a public facility or improvement, or portion thereof, that does not qualify under § 570.483(b)(1);

(B) The rehabilitation of a privately owned nonresidential building or improvement that does not qualify under § 570.483(b) (1) or (4); or

(C) The rehabilitation of the common areas of a residential structure that contains more than one dwelling unit and that does not qualify under § 570.483(b)(3).

(iv) A microenterprise assistance activity (carried out in accordance with the provisions of section 105(a)(23) of the Act or § 570.482(c) and limited to microenterprises) with respect to those owners of microenterprises and persons developing microenterprises assisted under the activity who are low- and moderate-income persons. For purposes of this paragraph, persons determined to be low and moderate income may be presumed to continue to qualify as such for up to a three-year period.

(v) An activity designed to provide job training and placement and/or other employment support services, including, but not limited to, peer support programs, counseling, child care, transportation, and other similar services, in which the percentage of low- and moderate-income persons assisted is less than 51 percent may qualify under this paragraph in the following limited circumstances:

(A) In such cases where such training or provision of supportive services is an integrally-related component of a larger project, the only use of CDBG assistance for the project is to provide the job training and/or supportive services; and

(B) The proportion of the total cost of the project borne by CDBG funds is no greater than the proportion of the total number of persons assisted who are low or moderate income.

(3) *Housing activities.* An eligible activity carried out for the purpose of providing or improving permanent residential structures that, upon completion, will be occupied by low and moderate income households. This would include, but not necessarily be limited to, the acquisition or rehabilitation of property by the unit of general local government, a subrecipient, an entity eligible to receive assistance under section 105(a)(15) of the Act, a developer, an individual homebuyer, or an individual homeowner; conversion of non-residential structures; and new housing construction. If the structure contains two dwelling units, at least one must be so occupied, and if the structure contains more than two dwelling units, at least 51 percent of the units must be so occupied. If two or more rental buildings being assisted are or will be located on the same or contiguous properties, and the buildings will be under common ownership and management, the grouped buildings may be considered for this purpose as a single structure. If housing activities being assisted meet the requirements of paragraph (e)(4)(ii) or (e)(5)(ii) of this section, all such housing may also be considered for this purpose as a single structure. For rental housing, occupancy by low and moderate income households must be at affordable rents to qualify under this criterion. The unit of general local government shall adopt and make public its standards for determining "affordable rents" for this purpose. The following shall also qualify under this criterion:

(i) When less than 51 percent of the units in a structure will be occupied by low and moderate income households, CDBG assistance may be provided in the following limited circumstances:

(A) The assistance is for an eligible activity to reduce the development cost of the new construction of a multifamily, non-elderly rental housing project; and

(B) Not less than 20 percent of the units will be occupied by low and moderate income households at affordable rents; and

(C) The proportion of the total cost of developing the project to be borne by CDBG funds is no greater than the proportion of units in the project that will be occupied by low and moderate income households.

(ii) Where CDBG funds are used to assist rehabilitation delivery services or in direct support of the unit of general local government's Rental Rehabilitation Program authorized under 24 CFR part 511, the funds shall be considered to benefit low and moderate income persons where not less than 51 percent of the units assisted, or to be assisted, by the Rental Rehabilitation Program overall are for low and moderate income persons.

(iii) When CDBG funds are used for housing services eligible under section 105(a)(21) of the Act, such funds shall be considered to benefit low and moderate income persons if the housing units for which the services are provided are HOME-assisted and the requirements of § 92.252 or § 92.254 of this title are met.

(4) *Job creation or retention activities.* (i) An activity designed to create permanent jobs where at least 51 percent of the jobs, computed on a full time equivalent basis, involve the employment of low and moderate income persons. For an activity that creates jobs, the unit of general local government must document that at least 51 percent of the jobs will be held by, or will be made available to low and moderate income persons.

(ii) For an activity that retains jobs, the unit of general local government must document that the jobs would actually be lost without the CDBG assistance and that either or both of the following conditions apply with respect to at least 51 percent of the jobs at the time the CDBG assistance is provided: The job is known to be held by a low or moderate income person; or the job can reasonably be expected to turn over within the following two years and that it will be filled by, or that steps will be taken to ensure that it is made available to, a low or moderate income person upon turnover.

(iii) Jobs will be considered to be available to low and moderate income persons for these purposes only if:

(A) Special skills that can only be acquired with substantial training or work experience or education beyond high school are not a prerequisite to fill such jobs, or the business agrees to hire unqualified persons and provide training; and

(B) The unit of general local government and the assisted business take actions to ensure that low and moderate income persons receive first consideration for filling such jobs.

(iv) For purposes of determining whether a job is held by or made available to a low- or moderate-income person, the person may be presumed to be a low- or moderate-income person if:

(A) He/she resides within a census tract (or block numbering area) that either:

(*1*) Meets the requirements of paragraph (b)(4)(v) of this section; or

(*2*) Has at least 70 percent of its residents who are low- and moderate-income persons; or

(B) The assisted business is located within a census tract (or block numbering area) that meets the requirements of paragraph (b)(4)(v) of this section and the job under consideration is to be located within that census tract.

(v) A census tract (or block numbering area) qualifies for the presumptions permitted under paragraphs (b)(4)(iv) (A)(*1*) and (B) of this section if it is either part of a Federally-designated Empowerment Zone or Enterprise Community or meets the following criteria:

(A) It has a poverty rate of at least 20 percent as determined by the most recently available decennial census information;

(B) It does not include any portion of a central business district, as this term is used in the most recent Census of Retail Trade, unless the tract has a poverty rate of at least 30 percent as determined by the most recently available decennial census information; and

(C) It evidences pervasive poverty and general distress by meeting at least one of the following standards:

(*1*) All block groups in the census tract have poverty rates of at least 20 percent;

(*2*) The specific activity being undertaken is located in a block group that has a poverty rate of at least 20 percent; or

(*3*) Upon the written request of the recipient, HUD determines that the census tract exhibits other objectively determinable signs of general distress such as high incidence of crime, narcotics use, homelessness, abandoned housing, and deteriorated infrastructure or substantial population decline.

(vi) As a general rule, each assisted business shall be considered to be a separate activity for purposes of determining whether the activity qualifies under this paragraph, except:

(A) In certain cases such as where CDBG funds are used to acquire, develop or improve a real property (e.g., a business incubator or an industrial park) the requirement may be met by measuring jobs in the aggregate for all the businesses that locate on the property, provided the businesses are not otherwise assisted by CDBG funds.

(B) Where CDBG funds are used to pay for the staff and overhead costs of an entity specified in section 105(a)(15) of the Act making loans to businesses exclusively from non-CDBG funds, this requirement may be met by aggregating the jobs created by all of the businesses receiving loans during any one-year period.

(C) Where CDBG funds are used by a recipient or subrecipient to provide technical assistance to businesses, this requirement may be met by aggregating the jobs created or retained by all of the businesses receiving technical assistance during any one-year period.

(D) Where CDBG funds are used for activities meeting the criteria listed at § 570.482(f)(3)(v), this requirement may be met by aggregating the jobs created or retained by all businesses for which CDBG assistance is obligated for such activities during any one-year period, except as provided at paragraph (e)(6) of this section.

(E) Where CDBG funds are used by a Community Development Financial Institution to carry out activities for the purpose of creating or retaining jobs, this requirement may be met by aggregating the jobs created or retained by all businesses for which CDBG assistance is obligated for such activities during any one-year period, except as provided at paragraph (e)(6) of this section.

(F) Where CDBG funds are used for public facilities or improvements which will result in the creation or retention of jobs by more than one business, this requirement may be met by aggregating the jobs created or retained by all such businesses as a result of the public facility or improvement.

(*1*) Where the public facility or improvement is undertaken principally for the benefit of one or more particular businesses, but where other businesses might also benefit from the assisted activity, the requirement may be met by aggregating only the jobs created or retained by those businesses for which the facility/improvement is principally undertaken, provided that the cost (in CDBG funds) for the facility/improvement is less than $10,000 per permanent full-time equivalent job to be created or retained by those businesses.

(*2*) In any case where the cost per job to be created or retained (as determined under paragraph (b)(4)(vi)(F)(*1*) of this section) is $10,000 or more, the requirement must be met by aggregating the jobs created or retained as a result of the public facility or improvement by all businesses in the service area of the facility/improvement. This aggregation must include businesses which, as a result of the public facility/improvement, locate or expand in the service area of the public facility/improvement between the date the state awards the CDBG funds to the recipient and the date one year after the physical completion of the public facility/improvement. In addition, the assisted activity must comply with the public benefit standards at § 570.482(f).

(5) *Planning-only activities.* An activity involving planning (when such activity is the only activity for which the grant to the unit of general local government is given, or if the planning activity is unrelated to any other activity assisted by the grant) if it can be documented that at least 51 percent of the persons who would benefit from implementation of the plan are low and moderate income persons. Any such planning activity for an area or a community composed of persons of whom at least 51 percent are low and moderate income shall be considered to meet this national objective.

(c) *Activities which aid in the prevention or elimination of slums or blight.* Activities meeting one or more of the following criteria, in the absence of substantial evidence to the contrary, will be considered to aid in the prevention or elimination of slums or blight:

(1) *Activities to address slums or blight on an area basis.* An activity will be considered to address prevention or elimination of slums or blight in an area if the state can determine that:

(i) The area, delineated by the unit of general local government, meets a definition of a slum, blighted, deteriorated or deteriorating area under state or local law;

(ii) The area also meets the conditions in either paragraph (c)(1)(ii)(A) or(c)(1)(ii)(B) of this section.

(A) At least 25 percent of properties throughout the area experience one or more of the following conditions:

(*1*) Physical deterioration of buildings or improvements;

(*2*) Abandonment of properties;

(*3*) Chronic high occupancy turnover rates or chronic high vacancy rates in commercial or industrial buildings;

(*4*) Significant declines in property values or abnormally low property values relative to other areas in the community; or

(*5*) Known or suspected environmental contamination.

(B) The public improvements throughout the area are in a general state of deterioration.

(iii) The assisted activity addresses one or more of the conditions which contributed to the deterioration of the area. Rehabilitation of residential buildings carried out in an area meeting the above requirements will be considered to address the area's deterioration only where each such building rehabilitated is considered substandard before rehabilitation, and all deficiencies making a building substandard have been eliminated if less critical work on the building is also undertaken. The State shall ensure that the unit of general local government has developed minimum standards for building quality which may take into account local conditions.

§ 570.483

(iv) The state keeps records sufficient to document its findings that a project meets the national objective of prevention or elimination of slums and blight. The state must establish definitions of the conditions listed at § 570.483(c)(1)(ii)(A) and maintain records to substantiate how the area met the slums or blighted criteria. The designation of an area as slum or blighted under this section is required to be redetermined every 10 years for continued qualification. Documentation must be retained pursuant to the recordkeeping requirements contained at § 570.490.

(2) *Activities to address slums or blight on a spot basis.* The following activities can be undertaken on a spot basis to eliminate specific conditions of blight, physical decay, or environmental contamination that are not located in a slum or blighted area: Acquisition; clearance; relocation; historic preservation; remediation of environmentally contaminated properties; or rehabilitation of buildings or improvements. However, rehabilitation must be limited to eliminating those conditions that are detrimental to public health and safety. If acquisition or relocation is undertaken, it must be a precursor to another eligible activity (funded with CDBG or other resources) that directly eliminates the specific conditions of blight or physical decay, or environmental contamination.

(3) *Planning only activities.* An activity involving planning (when the activity is the only activity for which the grant to the unit of general local government is given, or the planning activity is unrelated to any other activity assisted by the grant) if the plans are for a slum or blighted area, or if all elements of the planning are necessary for and related to an activity which, if funded, would meet one of the other criteria of elimination of slums or blight.

(d) *Activities designed to meet community development needs having a particular urgency.* In the absence of substantial evidence to the contrary, an activity will be considered to address this objective if the unit of general local government certifies, and the state determines, that the activity is designed to alleviate existing conditions which pose a serious and immediate threat to the health or welfare of the community which are of recent origin or which recently became urgent, that the unit of general local government is unable to finance the activity on its own, and that other sources of funding are not available. A condition will generally be considered to be of recent origin if it developed or became urgent within 18 months preceding the certification by the unit of general local government.

(e) *Additional criteria.* (1) In any case where the activity undertaken is a public improvement and the activity is clearly designed to serve a primarily residential area, the activity must meet the requirements of paragraph (b)(1) of this section whether or not the requirements of paragraph (b)(4) of this section are met in order to qualify as benefiting low and moderate income persons.

(2) Where the assisted activity is acquisition of real property, a preliminary determination of whether the activity addresses a national objective may be based on the planned use of the property after acquisition. A final determination shall be based on the actual use of the property, excluding any short-term, temporary use. Where the acquisition is for the purpose of clearance which will eliminate specific conditions of blight or physical decay, the clearance activity shall be considered the actual use of the property. However, any subsequent use or disposition of the cleared property shall be treated as a "change of use" under § 570.489(j).

(3) Where the assisted activity is relocation assistance that the unit of general local government is required to provide, the relocation assistance shall be considered to address the same national objective as is addressed by the displacing activity. Where the relocation assistance is voluntary, the unit of general local government may qualify the assistance either on the basis of the national objective addressed by the displacing activity or, if the relocation assistance is to low and moderate income persons, on the basis of the national objective of benefiting low and moderate income persons.

(4) Where CDBG-assisted activities are carried out by a Community Development Financial Institution whose charter limits its investment area to a primarily residential area consisting of at least 51 percent low- and moderate-income persons, the unit of general local government may also elect the following options:

(i) Activities carried out by the Community Development Financial Institution for the purpose of creating or retaining jobs may, at the option of the unit of general local government, be considered to meet the requirements of this paragraph under the criteria at paragraph (b)(1)(iv) of this section in lieu of the criteria at paragraph (b)(4) of this section; and

(ii) All housing activities for which the Community Development Financial Institution obligates CDBG assistance during any one-year period may be considered to be a single structure for purposes of applying the criteria at paragraph (b)(3) of this section.

(5) If the unit of general local government has elected to prepare a community revitalization strategy pursuant to the authority of § 91.315(e)(2) of this title, and the State has approved the strategy, the unit of general local government may also elect the following options:

(i) Activities undertaken pursuant to the strategy for the purpose of creating or retaining jobs may, at the option of the grantee, be considered to meet the requirements of paragraph (b) of this section under the criteria at § 570.483(b)(1)(v) instead of the criteria at § 570.483(b)(4); and

(ii) All housing activities in the area undertaken pursuant to the strategy may be considered to be a single structure for purposes of applying the criteria at paragraph (b)(3) of this section.

(6) If an activity meeting the criteria in § 570.482(f)(3)(v) also meets the requirements of either paragraph (e)(4)(i) or (e)(5)(i) of this section, the unit of general local government may elect to qualify the activity either under the area benefit criteria at paragraph (b)(1)(iv) or (v) of this section or under the job aggregation criteria at paragraph (b)(4)(vi)(D) of this section, but not under both. Where an activity may meet the job aggregation criteria at both paragraphs (b)(4)(vi)(D) and (E) of this section, the unit of general local government may elect to qualify the activity under either criterion, but not both.

(f) *Planning and administrative costs.* CDBG funds expended for eligible planning and administrative costs by units of general local government in conjunction with other CDBG assisted activities will be considered to address the national objectives.

[57 FR 53397, Nov. 9, 1992, as amended at 60 FR 1951, Jan. 5, 1995; 60 FR 17445, Apr. 6, 1995; 61 FR 54921, Oct. 22, 1996; 71 FR 30036, May 24, 2006]

§ 570.484 Overall benefit to low and moderate income persons.

(a) *General.* The State must certify that, in the aggregate, not less than 70 percent of the CDBG funds received by the state during a period specified by the state, not to exceed three years, will be used for activities that benefit persons of low and moderate income. The period selected and certified to by the state shall be designated by fiscal year of annual grants, and shall be for one, two or three consecutive annual grants. The period shall be in effect until all included funds are expended. No CDBG funds may be included in more than one period selected, and all CDBG funds received must be included in a selected period.

(b) *Computation of 70 percent benefit.* Determination that a state has carried out its certification under paragraph (a) of this section requires evidence that not less than 70 percent of the aggregate of the designated annual grant(s), any funds reallocated by HUD to the state, any distributed program income and any guaranteed loan funds under the provisions of subpart M of this part covered in the method of distribution in the final statement or statements for the designated annual grant year or years have been expended for activities meeting criteria as provided in § 570.483(b) for activities benefiting low and moderate income persons. In calculating the percentage of funds expended for such activities:

(1) All CDBG funds included in the period selected and certified to by the state shall be accounted for, except for funds used by the State, or by the units

§ 570.485

of general local government, for program administration, or for planning activities other than those which must meet a national objective under § 570.483 (b)(5) or (c)(3).

(2) Any funds expended by a state for the purpose of repayment of loans guaranteed under the provisions of subpart M of this part shall be excepted from inclusion in this calculation.

(3) Except as provided in paragraph (b)(4) of this section, CDBG funds expended for an eligible activity meeting the criteria for activities benefiting low and moderate income persons shall count in their entirety towards meeting the 70 percent benefit to persons of low and moderate income requirement.

(4) Funds expended for the acquisition, new construction or rehabilitation of property for housing that qualifies under § 570.483(b)(3) shall be counted for this purpose, but shall be limited to an amount determined by multiplying the total cost (including CDBG and non-CDBG costs) of the acquisition, construction or rehabilitation by the percent of units in such housing to be occupied by low and moderate income persons, except that the amount counted shall not exceed the amount of CDBG funds provided.

§ 570.485 Making of grants.

(a) *Required submissions.* In order to receive its annual CDBG grant under this subpart, a State must submit a consolidated plan in accordance with 24 CFR part 91. That part includes requirements for the content of the consolidated plan, for the process of developing the plan, including citizen participation provisions, for the submission date, for HUD approval, and for the amendment process.

(b) *Failure to make submission.* The state's failure to make the submission required by paragraph (a) of this section within the prescribed deadline constitutes the state's election not to receive and distribute amounts allocated for its nonentitlement areas for the applicable fiscal year. Funds will be either:

(1) Administered by HUD pursuant to subpart F of this part if the state has not administered the program in any previous fiscal year; or

(2) Reallocated to all states in the succeeding fiscal year according to the formula of section 106(d) of the Act, if the state administered the program in any previous year.

(c) *Approval of grant.* HUD will approve a grant if the State's submissions have been made and approved in accordance with 24 CFR part 91, and the certifications required therein are satisfactory to the Secretary. The certifications will be satisfactory to the Secretary for this purpose unless the Secretary has determined pursuant to § 570.493 that the State has not complied with the requirements of this subpart, or has determined that there is evidence, not directly involving the State's past performance under this program, that tends to challenge in a substantial manner the State's certification of future performance. If the Secretary makes any such determination, however, the State may be required to submit further assurances as the Secretary may deem warranted or necessary to find the grantee's certification satisfactory.

[57 FR 53397, Nov. 9, 1992, as amended at 60 FR 1916, Jan. 5, 1995; 61 FR 54922, Oct. 22, 1996]

§ 570.486 Local government requirements.

(a) *Citizen participation requirements of a unit of general local government.* Each unit of general local government shall meet the following requirements as required by the state at § 91.115(e) of this title.

(1) Provide for and encourage citizen participation, particularly by low and moderate income persons who reside in slum or blighted areas and areas in which CDBG funds are proposed to be used;

(2) Ensure that citizens will be given reasonable and timely access to local meetings, information, and records relating to the unit of local government's proposed and actual use of CDBG funds;

(3) Furnish citizens information, including but not limited to:

(i) The amount of CDBG funds expected to be made available for the current fiscal year (including the grant and anticipated program income);

(ii) The range of activities that may be undertaken with the CDBG funds;

Ofc. of Asst. Secy., Comm. Planning, Develop., HUD § 570.487

(iii) The estimated amount of the CDBG funds proposed to be used for activities that will meet the national objective of benefit to low and moderate income persons; and

(iv) The proposed CDBG activities likely to result in displacement and the unit of general local government's antidisplacement and relocation plans required under § 570.488.

(4) Provide technical assistance to groups representative of persons of low and moderate income that request assistance in developing proposals in accordance with the procedures developed by the state. Such assistance need not include providing funds to such groups;

(5) Provide for a minimum of two public hearings, each at a different stage of the program, for the purpose of obtaining citizens' views and responding to proposals and questions. Together the hearings must cover community development and housing needs, development of proposed activities and a review of program performance. The public hearings to cover community development and housing needs must be held before submission of an application to the state. There must be reasonable notice of the hearings and they must be held at times and locations convenient to potential or actual beneficiaries, with accommodations for the handicapped. Public hearings shall be conducted in a manner to meet the needs of non-English speaking residents where a significant number of non-English speaking residents can reasonably be expected to participate;

(6) Provide citizens with reasonable advance notice of, and opportunity to comment on, proposed activities in an application to the state and, for grants already made, activities which are proposed to be added, deleted or substantially changed from the unit of general local government's application to the state. Substantially changed means changes made in terms of purpose, scope, location or beneficiaries as defined by criteria established by the state.

(7) Provide citizens the address, phone number, and times for submitting complaints and grievances, and provide timely written answers to written complaints and grievances, within 15 working days where practicable.

(b) *Activities serving beneficiaries outside the jurisdiction of the unit of general local government.* CDBG-funded activities may serve beneficiaries outside the jurisdiction of the unit of general local government that receives the grant, provided the unit of general local government determines that the activity is meeting its needs in accordance with section 106(d)(2)(D) of the Act.

[57 FR 53397, Nov. 9, 1992, as amended at 61 FR 54922, Oct. 22, 1996]

§ 570.487 Other applicable laws and related program requirements.

(a) *General.* Certain statutes are expressly made applicable to activities assisted under the Act by the Act itself, while other laws not referred to in the Act may be applicable to such activities by their own terms. Certain statutes or executive orders that may be applicable to activities assisted under the Act by their own terms are administered or enforced by governmental officials, departments or agencies other than HUD. Paragraphs (d) and (c) of this section contain two of the requirements expressly made applicable to CDBG activities by the Act itself.

(b) *Affirmatively furthering fair housing.* The Act requires the state to certify to the satisfaction of HUD that it will affirmatively further fair housing. The act also requires each unit of general local government to certify that it will affirmatively further fair housing. The certification that the State will affirmatively further fair housing shall specifically require the State to assume the responsibility of fair housing planning by:

(1) Conducting an analysis to identify impediments to fair housing choice within the State;

(2) Taking appropriate actions to overcome the effects of any impediments identified through that analysis;

(3) Maintaining records reflecting the analysis and actions in this regard; and

(4) Assuring that units of local government funded by the State comply with their certifications to affirmatively further fair housing.

(c) *Lead-Based Paint Poisoning Prevention Act.* States shall devise, adopt and

§ 570.488

carry out procedures with respect to CDBG assistance that fulfill the objectives and requirements of the Lead-Based Paint Poisoning Prevention Act (42 U.S.C. 4821–4846), the Residential Lead-Based Paint Hazard Reduction Act of 1992 (42 U.S.C. 4851–4856), and implementing regulations at part 35, subparts A, B, J, K, and R of this title.

(d) States shall comply with section 3 of the Housing and Urban Development Act of 1968 (12 U.S.C. 1701u) and the implementing regulations in 24 CFR part 135. Section 3 requires that employment and other economic opportunities arising in connection with housing rehabilitation, housing construction, or other public construction projects shall, to the greatest extent feasible, and consistent with existing Federal, State, and local laws and regulations, be given to low- and very low-income persons.

(e) *Architectural Barriers Act and the Americans with Disabilities Act.* The Architectural Barriers Act of 1968 (42 U.S.C. 4151–4157) requires certain Federal and Federally-funded buildings and other facilities to be designed, constructed, or altered in accordance with standards that ensure accessibility to, and use by, physically handicapped people. A building or facility designed, constructed, or altered with funds allocated or reallocated under this subpart after November 21, 1996 and that meets the definition of *residential structure* as defined in 24 CFR 40.2, or the definition of *building* as defined in 41 CFR 101–19.602(a), is subject to the requirements of the Architectural Barriers Act of 1968 and shall comply with the Uniform Federal Accessibility Standards. For general type buildings, these standards are in appendix A to 41 CFR part 101–19.6. For residential structures, these standards are available from the Department of Housing and Urban Development, Office of Fair Housing and Equal Opportunity, Disability Rights Division, Room 5240, 451 Seventh Street, SW, Washington, DC 20410; telephone (202) 708–2333 (voice) or (202) 708–1734 (TTY) (these are not toll-free numbers).

[57 FR 53397, Nov. 9, 1992, as amended at 59 FR 33894, June 30, 1994; 60 FR 1916, Jan. 5, 1995; 61 FR 54922, Oct. 22, 1996; 64 FR 50225, Sept. 15, 1999]

§ 570.488 **Displacement, relocation, acquisition, and replacement of housing.**

The requirements for States and state recipients with regard to the displacement, relocation, acquisition, and replacement of housing are in § 570.606 and 24 CFR part 42.

[61 FR 11477, Mar. 20, 1996]

§ 570.489 **Program administrative requirements.**

(a) *Administrative and planning costs*—(1) *State administrative costs.* (i) The state is responsible for the administration of all CDBG funds. The state shall pay from its own resources all administrative costs incurred by the state in carrying out its responsibilities under this subpart, except that the state may use CDBG funds to pay such costs in an amount not to exceed $100,000 plus 50 percent of such costs in excess of $100,000. States are therefore required to match such costs in excess of $100,000 on a dollar for dollar basis. The amount of CDBG funds used to pay such costs in excess of $100,000 shall not exceed 2 percent of the aggregate of the state's annual grant, program income received by units of general local government (whether retained by the unit of general local government or paid to the State) and funds reallocated by HUD to the state.

(ii) For determining the amount of CDBG funds available in past years for administrative costs incurred by the state, the following schedule applies:

(A) $100,000 per annual grant beginning with FY 1984 allocations;

(B) Two percent of program income returned by units of general local government to the State after August 21, 1985; and

(C) Two percent of program income received by units of general local government after February 11, 1991.

(iii) The state has the option of selecting its approach for demonstrating compliance with this requirement. Regardless of the approach selected by the state, the state will be required to pay its 50 percent of administrative costs in excess of $100,000 in the same amount and at the same time at which it draws CDBG funds for such costs after the expenditure of the $100,000. Any state for which it is determined

Ofc. of Asst. Secy., Comm. Planning, Develop., HUD § 570.489

that matching costs contributions are in arrears on the use of CDBG funds for administrative costs will be required to bring matching cost expenditures up to the level of CDBG expenditures for such costs within one year of the effective date of this subpart. A state grant may not be closed out if the state's matching cost contribution is not at least equal to the amount of CDBG funds in excess of $100,000 expended for administration. Funds from any year's grant may be used to pay administrative costs associated with any other year's grant. The two approaches are:

(A) Cumulative accounting of administrative costs incurred by the state since its assumption of the Program. Under this approach, the state will identify, for each grant it has received, the CDBG funds eligible to be used for administrative costs as well as the maximum amount of matching funds which the state is required to pay. The amounts will then be aggregated for all grants received. The state must keep records demonstrating the actual amount of CDBG funds from each grant received which was used for administrative costs as well as matching amounts paid by the state. These amounts will also be aggregated for all grants received. The state will be considered to be in compliance with the requirement if the aggregate of actual amounts spent for administrative costs does not exceed the maximum amount allowable and the amount which the state has paid in matching funds is at least equal to the amount of CDBG funds in excess of $100,000 (for each applicable allocation) drawn for administrative purposes. Any administrative amounts associated with a particular state grant shall be deducted from the aggregate totals upon closeout of that state grant.

(B) An accounting process developed and implemented by the state which provides sufficient information to demonstrate that the requirements of this subsection are met.

(2) The state may not charge fees of any entity for processing or considering any application for CDBG fund, or for carrying out its responsibilities under this subpart.

(3) The state and its funded units of general local government shall not expend for planning, management and administrative costs more than 20 percent of the aggregate amount of the annual grant, plus program income and funds reallocated by HUD to the State which are distributed during the time the final Statement for the annual grant is in effect. Administrative costs are those described at §570.489(a)(1) for states, and for units of general local government those described at sections 105(a)(12) and (a)(13) of the Act.

(b) *Reimbursement of pre-agreement costs.* The state may permit, in accordance with such procedures as the State may establish, a unit of local government to incur costs for CDBG activities before the establishment of a formal grant relationship between the State and the unit of general local government and to charge these pre-agreement costs to the grant, provided that the activities are eligible and undertaken in accordance with the requirements of this subpart and 24 CFR part 58.

(c) *Federal grant payments*—(1) *Payments.* The state shall be paid in advance in accordance with Treasury Circular 1075 (31 CFR part 205). The State shall use procedures to minimize the time elapsing between the transfer of grant funds and disbursement of funds by the State to units of general local government. Units of general local government shall also use procedures to minimize the time elapsing between the transfer of funds by the State and disbursement for CDBG activities.

(2) *Interest on advances.* Interest earned by units of general local government on grant funds before disbursement of the funds for activities is not program income and must be returned to the Treasury, except that the unit of general local government may keep interest amounts of up $100 per year for administrative expenses. However, the state shall not be held accountable for interest earned on grants for which payments are made in accordance with paragraph (c)(1) of this section pending disbursement for CDBG activities.

(d) *Fiscal controls and accounting procedures.* (1) A state shall have fiscal and administrative requirements for expending and accounting for all funds received under this subpart. These requirements must be available for Federal inspection and must:

(i) Be sufficiently specific to ensure that funds received under this subpart are used in compliance with all applicable statutory and regulatory provisions;

(ii) Ensure that funds received under this subpart are only spent for reasonable and necessary costs of operating programs under this subpart; and

(iii) Ensure that funds received under this subpart are not used for general expenses required to carry out other responsibilities of state and local governments.

(2) A state may satisfy this requirement by:

(i) Using fiscal and administrative requirements applicable to the use of its own funds;

(ii) Adopting new fiscal and administrative requirements; or

(iii) Applying the provisions in 24 CFR part 85 "Uniform Administrative Requirements for Grants and Cooperative Agreements to State and Local Governments."

(e) *Program income.* (1) For the purposes of this subpart, "program income" is defined as gross income received by a state, a unit of general local government or a subrecipient of a unit of general local government that was generated from the use of CDBG funds, except as provided in paragraph (e)(2) of this section. When income is generated by an activity that is only partially assisted with CDBG funds, the income shall be prorated to reflect the percentage of CDBG funds used (e.g., a single loan supported by CDBG funds and other funds; a single parcel of land purchased with CDBG funds and other funds). Program income includes, but is not limited to, the following:

(i) Proceeds from the disposition by sale or long term lease of real property purchased or improved with CDBG funds;

(ii) Proceeds from the disposition of equipment purchased with CDBG funds;

(iii) Gross income from the use or rental of real or personal property acquired by the unit of general local government or a subrecipient of a unit of general local government with CDBG funds; less the costs incidental to the generation of the income;

(iv) Gross income from the use or rental of real property owned by the unit of general local government or a subrecipient of a unit of general local government, that was constructed or improved with CDBG funds, less the costs incidental to the generation of the income;

(v) Payments of principal and interest on loans made using CDBG funds;

(vi) Proceeds from the sale of loans made with CDBG funds;

(vii) Proceeds from the sale of obligations secured by loans made with CDBG funds;

(viii) Interest earned on funds held in a revolving fund account;

(ix) Interest earned on program income pending disposition of the income;

(x) Funds collected through special assessments made against properties owned and occupied by households *not* of low and moderate income, where the special assessments are used to recover all or part of the CDBG portion of a public improvement; and

(xi) Gross income paid to a unit of general local government or subrecipient from the ownership interest in a for-profit entity acquired in return for the provision of CDBG assistance.

(2) "Program income" does not include the following:

(i) The total amount of funds which is less than $25,000 received in a single year that is retained by a unit of general local government and its subrecipients;

(ii) Amounts generated by activities eligible under section 105(a)(15) of the Act and carried out by an entity under the authority of section 105(a)(15) of the Act;

(iii) Amounts generated by activities that are financed by a loan guaranteed under section 108 of the Act and meet one or more of the public benefit criteria specified at §570.482(f)(3)(v) or are carried out in conjunction with a grant under section 108(q) of the Act in an area determined by HUD to meet the eligibility requirements for designation as an Urban Empowerment Zone pursuant to 24 CFR part 597, subpart B. Such exclusion shall not apply if CDBG funds are used to repay the guaranteed loan. When such a guaranteed loan is partially repaid with CDBG funds, the amount generated shall be prorated to reflect the percentage of CDBG funds used. Amounts generated by activities financed with loans guaranteed under section 108 of the Act which are not defined as program income shall be treated as miscellaneous revenue and shall not be subject to any of the requirements of this part. However, such treatment shall not affect the right of the Secretary to require the section 108 borrower to pledge such amounts as security for the guaranteed loan. The determination whether such amounts shall constitute program income shall be governed by the provisions of the contract required at § 570.705(b)(1).

(3) The state may permit the unit of general local government which receives or will receive program income to retain the program income, subject to the requirements of paragraph (e)(3)(ii) of this section, or the state may require the unit of general local government to pay the program income to the state. The state, however, must permit the unit of general local government to retain the program income if the program income will be used to continue the activity from which the program income was derived. The state will determine when an activity will be considered to be continued.

(i) *Program income paid to the state.* Program income that is paid to the state is treated as additional CDBG funds subject to the requirements of this subpart and must be distributed to units of general local government in accordance with the method of distribution in the state's final Statement. To the maximum extent feasible, program income shall be distributed before the state makes additional withdrawals from the Treasury, except as provided in paragraph (f) of this section.

(ii) *Program income retained by a unit of general local government.* (A) Program income that is received and retained by the unit of general local government before closeout of the grant that generated the program income is treated as additional CDBG funds and is subject to all applicable requirements of this subpart.

(B) Program income that is received and retained by the unit of general local government after closeout of the grant that generated the program income is not subject to the requirements of this subpart, except:

(1) If the unit of general local government has another ongoing CDBG grant from the state at the time of closeout, the program income continues to be subject to the requirements of this subpart as long as there is an ongoing grant; and

(2) If program income is used to continue the activity that generated the program income, the requirements of this subpart apply to the program income as long as the unit of general local government uses the program income to continue the activity;

(3) The state may extend the period of applicability of the requirements of this subpart.

(C) The state shall require units of general local government, to the maximum extent feasible, to disburse program income that is subject to the requirements of this subpart before requesting additional funds from the state for activities, except as provided in paragraph (f) of this section.

(f) *Revolving funds.* (1) The state may permit units of general local government to establish revolving funds to carry out specific, identified activities. A revolving fund, for this purpose, is a separate fund (with a set of accounts that are independent of other program accounts) established to carry out specific activities which, in turn, generate payments to the fund for use in carrying out such activities. These payments to the revolving fund are program income and must be substantially disbursed from the revolving fund before additional grant funds are drawn from the Treasury for revolving fund activities. Such program income is not required to be disbursed for non-revolving fund activities.

(2) The state may establish a revolving fund to distribute funds to units of general local government to carry out specific, identified activities. A revolving fund, for this purpose, is a separate fund (with a set of accounts that are independent of other program accounts) established to fund grants to units of general local government to

carry out specific activities which, in turn, generate payments to the fund for additional grants to units of general local government to carry out such activities. Program income in the revolving fund must be disbursed from the fund before additional grant funds are drawn from the Treasury for payments to units of general local government which could be funded from the revolving fund.

(3) A revolving fund established by either the State or unit of general local government shall not be directly funded or capitalized with grant funds.

(g) *Procurement.* When procuring property or services to be paid for in whole or in part with CDBG funds, the state shall follow its procurement policies and procedures. The state shall establish requirements for procurement policies and procedures for units of general local government, based on full and open competition. Methods of procurement (e.g., small purchase, sealed bids/formal advertising, competitive proposals, and noncompetitive proposals) and their applicability shall be specified by the state. Cost plus a percentage of cost and percentage of construction costs methods of contracting shall not be used. The policies and procedures shall also include standards of conduct governing employees engaged in the award or administration of contracts. (Other conflicts of interest are covered by §570.489(h).) The state shall ensure that all purchase orders and contracts include any clauses required by Federal statutes, executive orders and implementing regulations.

(h) *Conflict of interest*—(1) *Applicability.* (i) In the procurement of supplies, equipment, construction, and services by the States, units of local general governments, and subrecipients, the conflict of interest provisions in paragraph (g) of this section shall apply.

(ii) In all cases not governed by paragraph (g) of this section, this paragraph (h) shall apply. Such cases include the acquisition and disposition of real property and the provision of assistance with CDBG funds by the unit of general local government or its subrecipients, to individuals, businesses and other private entities.

(2) *Conflicts prohibited.* Except for eligible administrative or personnel costs, the general rule is that no persons described in paragraph (h)(3) of this section who exercise or have exercised any functions or responsibilities with respect to CDBG activities assisted under this subpart or who are in a position to participate in a decision-making process or gain inside information with regard to such activities, may obtain a financial interest or benefit from the activity, or have an interest or benefit from the activity, or have an interest in any contract, subcontract or agreement with respect thereto, or the proceeds thereunder, either for themselves or those with whom they have family or business ties, during their tenure or for one year thereafter.

(3) *Persons covered.* The conflict of interest provisions for paragraph (h)(2) of this section apply to any person who is an employee, agent, consultant, officer, or elected official or appointed official of the state, or of a unit of general local government, or of any designated public agencies, or subrecipients which are receiving CDBG funds.

(4) *Exceptions: Thresholds requirements.* Upon written request by the State, an exception to the provisions of paragraph (h)(2) of this section involving an employee, agent, consultant, officer, or elected official or appointed official of the state may be granted by HUD on a case-by-case basis. In all other cases, the state may grant such an exception upon written request of the unit of general local government provided the state shall fully document its determination in compliance with all requirements of paragraph (h)(4) of this section including the state's position with respect to each factor at paragraph (h)(5) of this section and such documentation shall be available for review by the public and by HUD. An exception may be granted after it is determined that such an exception will serve to further the purpose of the Act and the effective and efficient administration of the program or project of the state or unit of general local government as appropriate. An exception may be considered only after the state or unit of general local government, as

appropriate, has provided the following:

(i) A disclosure of the nature of the conflict, accompanied by an assurance that there has been public disclosure of the conflict and a description of how the public disclosure was made; and

(ii) An opinion of the attorney for the state or the unit of general local government, as appropriate, that the interest for which the exception is sought would not violate state or local law.

(5) *Factors to be considered for exceptions.* In determining whether to grant a requested exception after the requirements of paragraph (h)(4) of this section have been satisfactorily met, the cumulative effect of the following factors, where applicable, shall be considered:

(i) Whether the exception would provide a significant cost benefit or an essential degree of expertise to the program or project which would otherwise not be available;

(ii) Whether an opportunity was provided for open competitive bidding or negotiation;

(iii) Whether the person affected is a member of a group or class of low or moderate income persons intended to be the beneficiaries of the assisted activity, and the exception will permit such person to receive generally the same interests or benefits as are being made available or provided to the group or class;

(iv) Whether the affected person has withdrawn from his or her functions or responsibilities, or the decisionmaking process with respect to the specific assisted activity in question;

(v) Whether the interest or benefit was present before the affected person was in a position as described in paragraph (h)(3) of this section;

(vi) Whether undue hardship will result either to the State or the unit of general local government or the person affected when weighed against the public interest served by avoiding the prohibited conflict; and

(vii) Any other relevant considerations.

(i) *Closeout of grants to units of general local government.* The State shall establish requirements for timely closeout of grants to units of general local government and shall take action to ensure the timely closeout of such grants.

(j) *Change of use of real property.* The standards described in this section apply to real property within the unit of general local government's control (including activities undertaken by subrecipients) which was acquired or improved in whole or in part using CDBG funds in excess of the threshold for small purchase procurement (24 CFR 85.36, "Administrative Requirements for Grants and Cooperative Agreements to State, Local and Federally Recognized Indian Tribal Governments"). These standards shall apply from the date CDBG funds are first spent for the property until five years after closeout of the unit of general local government's grant.

(1) A unit of general local governments may not change the use or planned use of any such property (including the beneficiaries of such use) from that for which the acquisition or improvement was made, unless the unit of general local government provides affected citizens with reasonable notice of and opportunity to comment on any proposed change, and either:

(i) The new use of the property qualifies as meeting one of the national objectives and is not a building for the general conduct of government; or

(ii) The requirements in paragraph (j)(2) of this section are met.

(2) If the unit of general local government determines, after consultation with affected citizens, that it is appropriate to change the use of the property to a use which does not qualify under paragraph (j)(1) of this section, it may retain or dispose of the property for the changed use if the unit of general local government's CDBG program is reimbursed or the state's CDBG program is reimbursed, at the discretion of the state. The reimbursement shall be in the amount of the current fair market value of the property, less any portion of the value attributable to expenditures of non-CDBG funds for acquisition of, and improvements to, the property, except that if the change in use occurs after grant closeout but within 5 years of such closeout, the unit of general local government shall

§ 570.490

make the reimbursement to the State's CDBG program account.

(3) Following the reimbursement of the CDBG program in accordance with paragraph (j)(2) of this section, the property no longer will be subject to any CDBG requirements.

(k) *Accountability for real and personal property.* The State shall establish and implement requirements, consistent with State law and the purposes and requirements of this subpart (including paragraph (j) of this section) governing the use, management, and disposition of real and personal property acquired with CDBG funds.

(l) *Debarment and suspension.* The requirements in 2 CFR part 2424 are applicable. CDBG funds may not be provided to excluded or disqualified persons.

(m) *Audits.* Audits of the state and units of general local government shall be conducted in accordance with 24 CFR part 44 which implements the Single Audit Act (31 U.S.C. 7501–07). States shall develop and administer an audits management system to ensure that audits of units of general local government are conducted in accordance with 24 CFR part 44.

[57 FR 53397, Nov. 9, 1992, as amended at 60 FR 1952, Jan. 5, 1995; 61 FR 54922, Oct. 22, 1996; 67 FR 15112, Mar. 29, 2002; 72 FR 73496, Dec. 27, 2007]

§ 570.490 Recordkeeping requirements.

(a) *State records.* (1) The state shall establish and maintain such records as may be necessary to facilitate review and audit by HUD of the state's administration of CDBG funds under § 570.493. The content of records maintained by the state shall be as jointly agreed upon by HUD and the states and sufficient to enable HUD to make the determinations described at § 570.493. For fair housing and equal opportunity purposes, and as applicable, such records shall include data on the racial, ethnic, and gender characteristics of persons who are applicants for, participants in, or beneficiaries of the program. The records shall also permit audit of the states in accordance with 24 CFR part 85.

(2) The state shall keep records to document its funding decisions reached under the method of distribution described in 24 CFR 91.320(j)(1), including all the criteria used to select applications from local governments for funding and the relative importance of the criteria (if applicable), regardless of the organizational level at which final funding decisions are made, so that they can be reviewed by HUD, the Inspector General, the Government Accountability Office, and citizens pursuant to the requirements of § 570.490(c).

(b) *Unit of general local government's record.* The State shall establish recordkeeping requirements for units of general local government receiving CDBG funds that are sufficient to facilitate reviews and audits of such units of general local government under §§ 570.492 and 570.493. For fair housing and equal opportunity purposes, and as applicable, such records shall include data on the racial, ethnic, and gender characteristics of persons who are applicants for, participants in, or beneficiaries of the program.

(c) *Access to records.* (1) Representatives of HUD, the Inspector General, and the General Accounting Office shall have access to all books, accounts, records, reports, files, and other papers, or property pertaining to the administration, receipt and use of CDBG funds and necessary to facilitate such reviews and audits.

(2) The State shall provide citizens with reasonable access to records regarding the past use of CDBG funds and ensure that units of general local government provide citizens with reasonable access to records regarding the past use of CDBG funds consistent with State or local requirements concerning the privacy of personal records.

(d) *Record retention.* Records of the State and units of general local government, including supporting documentation, shall be retained for the greater of three years from closeout of the grant to the state, or the period required by other applicable laws and regulations as described in § 570.487 and § 570.488.

[57 FR 53397, Nov. 9, 1992, as amended at 71 FR 6971, Feb. 9, 2006]

§ 570.491 Performance and evaluation report.

The annual performance and evaluation report shall be submitted in accordance with 24 CFR part 91.

(Approved by the Office of Management and Budget under control number 2506–0117)

[60 FR 1916, Jan. 5, 1995]

§ 570.492 State's reviews and audits.

(a) The state shall make reviews and audits including on-site reviews, of units of general local government as may be necessary or appropriate to meet the requirements of section 104(e)(2) of the Act.

(b) In the case of noncompliance with these requirements, the State shall take such actions as may be appropriate to prevent a continuance of the deficiency, mitigate any adverse effects or consequences and prevent a recurrence. The state shall establish remedies for units of general local government noncompliance.

§ 570.493 HUD's reviews and audits.

(a) *General.* At least on an annual basis, HUD shall make such reviews and audits as may be necessary or appropriate to determine:

(1) Whether the state has distributed CDBG funds to units of general local government in a timely manner in conformance to the method of distribution described in its action plan under part 91 of this title;

(2) Whether the state has carried out its certifications in compliance with the requirements of the Act and this subpart and other applicable laws; and

(3) Whether the state has made reviews and audits of the units of general local government required by § 570.492.

(b) *Information considered.* In conducting performance reviews and audits, HUD will rely primarily on information obtained from the state's performance report, records maintained by the state, findings from on-site monitoring, audit reports, and the status of the state's unexpended grant funds. HUD may also consider relevant information on the state's performance gained from other sources, including litigation, citizens' comments, and other information provided by the state. A State's failure to maintain records in accordance with § 570.490 may result in a finding that the State has failed to meet the applicable requirement to which the record pertains.

[57 FR 53397, Nov. 9, 1992, as amended at 61 FR 54922, Oct. 22, 1996]

§ 570.494 Timely distribution of funds by states.

(a) States are encouraged to adopt and achieve a goal of obligating and announcing 95 percent of funds to units of general local government within 12 months of the state signing its grant agreement with HUD.

(b) HUD will review each state to determine if the state has distributed CDBG funds in a timely manner. The state's distribution of CDBG funds is timely if:

(1) All of the state's annual grant (excluding state administration) has been obligated and announced to units of general local government within 15 months of the state signing its grant agreement with HUD; and

(2) Recaptured funds and program income received by the state are expeditiously obligated and announced to units of general local government.

(c) HUD may collect necessary information from states to determine whether CDBG funds have been distributed in a timely manner.

§ 570.495 Reviews and audits response.

(a) If HUD's review and audit under § 570.493 results in a negative determination, or if HUD otherwise determines that a state or unit of general local government has failed to comply with any requirement of this subpart, the state will be given an opportunity to contest the finding and will be requested to submit a plan for corrective action. If the state is unsuccessful in contesting the validity of the finding to the satisfaction of HUD, or if the state's plan for corrective action is not satisfactory to HUD, HUD may take one or more of the following actions to prevent a continuation of the deficiency; mitigate, to the extent possible, the adverse effects or consequence of the deficiency; or prevent a recurrence of the deficiency:

(1) Issue a letter of warning that advises the State of the deficiency and

puts the state on notice that additional action will be taken if the deficiency is not corrected or is repeated;

(2) Advise the state that additional information or assurances will be required before acceptance of one or more of the certifications required for the succeeding year grant;

(3) Advise the state to suspend or terminate disbursement of funds for a deficient activity or grant;

(4) Advise the state to reimburse its grant in any amounts improperly expended;

(5) Change the method of payment to the state from an advance basis to a reimbursement basis;

(6) Based on the state's current failure to comply with a requirement of this subpart which will affect the use of the succeeding year grant, condition the use of the succeeding fiscal years grant funds upon appropriate corrective action by the state. When the use of funds is conditioned, HUD shall specify the reasons for the conditions and the actions necessary to satisfy the conditions.

(b)(1) Whenever HUD determines that a state or unit of general local government which is a recipient of CDBG funds has failed to comply with section 109 of the Act (nondiscrimination requirements), HUD shall notify the governor of the State or chief executive officer of the unit of general local government of the noncompliance and shall request the governor or the chief executive officer to secure compliance. If within a reasonable time, not to exceed sixty days, the governor or chief executive officer fails or refuses to secure compliance, HUD may take the following action:

(i) Refer the matter to the Attorney General with a recommendation that an appropriate civil action be instituted;

(ii) Exercise the powers and functions provided by title VI of the Civil Rights Act of 1964 (42 U.S.C. 2000d–2000d–7);

(iii) Exercise the powers and functions provided for in § 570.496; or

(iv) Take such other action as may be provided by law.

(2) When a matter is referred to the Attorney General pursuant to paragraph (b)(1)(i) of this section, or whenever HUD has reason to believe that a State or unit of general local government is engaged in a pattern or practice in violation of the provisions of section 109 of the Act, the Attorney General may bring a civil action in any appropriate United States district court for such relief as may be appropriate, including injunctive relief.

§ 570.496 Remedies for noncompliance; opportunity for hearing.

(a) *General.* Action pursuant to this section will be taken only after at least one of the corrective or remedial actions specified in § 570.495 has been taken, and only then if the State or unit of general local government has not made an appropriate or timely response.

(b) *Remedies.* (1) If HUD finds after reasonable notice and opportunity for hearing that a State or unit of general local government has failed to comply with any provision of this subpart, until HUD is satisfied that there is no longer failure to comply, HUD shall:

(i) Terminate payments to the state;

(ii) Reduce payments for current or future grants to the state by an amount equal to the amount of CDBG funds distributed or used without compliance with the requirements of this subpart;

(iii) Limit the availability of payments to the state to activities not affected by the failure to comply or to activities designed to overcome the failure to comply;

(iv) Based on the state's failure to comply with a requirement of this subpart (other than the state's current failure to comply which will affect the use of the succeeding year grant), condition the use of the grant funds upon appropriate corrective action by the state specified by HUD; or

(v) With respect to a CDBG grant awarded by the state to a unit of general local government, withhold, reduce, or withdraw the grant, require the state to withhold, reduce, or withdraw the grant, or take other action as appropriate, except that CDBG funds expended on eligible activities shall not be recaptured or deducted from future CDBG grants to such unit of general local government.

(2) HUD may on due notice suspend payments at any time after the

issuance of a notice of opportunity for hearing pursuant to paragraph (d) of this section, pending such hearing and a final decision, to the extent HUD determines such action necessary to prevent a continuation of the noncompliance.

(c) In lieu of, or in addition to, the action authorized by paragraph (b) of this section, if HUD has reason to believe that the state or unit of general local government has failed to comply substantially with any provision of this subpart, HUD may:

(1) Refer the matter to the Attorney General of the United States with a recommendation that an appropriate civil action be instituted; and

(2) Upon such a referral, the Attorney General may bring a civil action in any United States district court having venue thereof for such relief as may be appropriate, including an action to recover the amount of the CDBG funds which was not expended in accordance with this subpart, or for mandatory or injunctive relief.

(d) *Proceedings.* When HUD proposes to take action pursuant to this section, the respondent in the proceedings will be the state. At the option of HUD, a unit of general local government may also be a respondent. These procedures are to be followed before imposition of a sanction described in paragraph (b)(1) of this section:

(1) *Notice of opportunity for hearing.* HUD shall notify the respondent in writing of the proposed action and of the opportunity for a hearing. The notice shall be sent to the respondent by first class mail and shall provide notice:

(i) In a manner which is adequate to allow the respondent to prepare its response, the basis upon which HUD determined that the respondent failed to comply with a provision of this subpart;

(ii) That the hearing procedures are governed by these rules;

(iii) That the respondent has 14 days from receipt of the notice within which to provide a written request for a hearing to the Docket Clerk, Office of Administrative Law Judges, and the address and telephone number of the Docket Clerk;

(iv) Of the action which HUD proposes to take and that the authority for this action is § 570.496 of this subpart;

(v) That if the respondent fails to request a hearing within the time specified, HUD's determination that the respondent failed to comply with a provision of this subpart shall be final and HUD may proceed to take the proposed action.

(2) *Initiation of hearing.* The respondent shall be allowed 14 days from receipt of the notice within which to notify HUD in writing of its request for a hearing. If no request is received within the time specified, HUD's determination that the respondent failed to comply with a provision of this subpart shall be final and HUD may proceed to take the proposed action.

(3) *Administrative Law Judge.* Proceedings conducted under these rules shall be presided over by an Administrative Law Judge (ALJ), appointed as provided by section 11 of the Administrative Procedure Act (5 U.S.C. 3105). The case shall be referred to the ALJ by HUD at the time a hearing is requested. The ALJ shall promptly notify the parties of the time and place at which the hearing will be held. The ALJ shall conduct a fair and impartial hearing and take all action necessary to avoid delay in the disposition of proceedings and to maintain order. The ALJ shall have all powers necessary to those ends, including but not limited to the power:

(i) To administer oaths and affirmations;

(ii) To issue subpoenas as authorized by law;

(iii) To rule upon offers of proof and receive relevant evidence;

(iv) To order or limit discovery before the hearing as the interests of justice may require;

(v) To regulate the course of the hearing and the conduct of the parties and their counsel;

(vi) To hold conferences for the settlement or simplification of the issues by consent of the parties;

(vii) To consider and rule upon all procedural and other motions appropriate in adjudicative proceedings; and

(viii) To make and file initial determinations.

(4) *Ex parte communications.* An ex parte communication is any communication with an ALJ, direct or indirect, oral or written, concerning the merits or procedures of any pending proceeding which is made by a party in the absence of any other party. Ex parte communications are prohibited except where the purpose and content of the communication have been disclosed in advance or simultaneously to all parties, or the communication is a request for information concerning the status of the case. Any ALJ who receives an ex parte communication which the ALJ knows or has reason to believe is unauthorized shall promptly place the communication, or its substance, in all files and shall furnish copies to all parties. Unauthorized ex parte communications shall not be taken into consideration in deciding any matter in issue.

(5) *The hearing.* All parties shall have the right to be represented at the hearing by counsel. The ALJ shall conduct the proceedings in an expeditious manner while allowing the parties to present all oral and written evidence which tends to support their respective positions, but the ALJ shall exclude irrelevant, immaterial or unduly repetitious evidence. HUD has the burden of proof in showing by a preponderance of evidence that the respondent failed to comply with a provision of this subpart. Each party shall be allowed to cross-examine adverse witnesses and to rebut and comment upon evidence presented by the other party. Hearings shall be open to the public. So far as the orderly conduct of the hearing permits, interested persons other than the parties may appear and participate in the hearing.

(6) *Transcripts.* Hearings shall be recorded and transcribed only by a reporter under the supervision of the ALJ. The original transcript shall be a part of the record and shall constitute the sole official transcript. Respondents and the public, at their own expense, shall obtain copies of the transcript.

(7) *The ALJ's decisions.* At the conclusion of the hearing, the ALJ shall give the parties a reasonable opportunity to submit proposed findings and conclusions and supporting reasons therefor. Generally, within 60 days after the conclusion of the hearing, the ALJ shall prepare a written decision which includes a Statement of findings and conclusions, and the reasons or basis therefor, on all the material issues of fact, law or discretion presented on the record and the appropriate sanction or denial thereof. The decision shall be based on consideration of the whole record or those parts thereof cited by a party and supported by and in accordance with the reliable, probative, and substantial evidence. A copy of the decision shall be furnished to the parties immediately by first class mail and shall include a notice that any requests for review by the Secretary must be made in writing to the Secretary within 30 days of the receipt of the decision.

(8) *Record.* The transcript of testimony and exhibits, together with the decision of the ALJ and all papers and requests filed in the proceeding, constitutes the exclusive record for decision and, on payment of its reasonable cost, shall be made available to the parties. After reaching the initial decision, the ALJ shall certify to the complete record and forward the record to the Secretary.

(9) *Review by the Secretary.* The decision by the ALJ shall constitute the final decision of HUD unless, within 30 days after the receipt of the decision, either the respondent or the Assistant Secretary for Community Planning and Development files an exception and request for review by the Secretary. The excepting party must transmit simultaneously to the Secretary and the other party the request for review and the bases of the party's exceptions to the findings of the ALJ. The other party shall be allowed 30 days from receipt of the exception to provide the Secretary and the excepting party with a written reply. The Secretary shall then review the record of the case, including the exceptions and the reply. On the basis of such review, the Secretary shall issue a written determination, including a Statement of the rationale therefor, affirming, modifying or revoking the decision of the ALJ. The Secretary's decision shall be made and transmitted to the parties within 60 days after the decision of the ALJ was furnished to the parties.

(10) *Judicial review.* The respondent may seek judicial review of HUD's decision pursuant to section 111(c) of the Act.

[74 FR 4636, Jan. 26, 2009]

§ 570.497 Condition of State election to administer State CDBG Program.

Pursuant to section 106(d)(2)(A)(i) of the Act, a State has the right to elect, in such manner and at such time as the Secretary may prescribe, to administer funds allocated under subpart A of this part for use in nonentitlement areas of the State. After January 26, 1995, any State which elects to administer the allocation of CDBG funds for use in nonentitlement areas of the State in any year must, in addition to all other requirements of this subpart, submit a pledge by the State in accordance with section 108(d)(2) of the Act, and in a form acceptable to HUD, of any future CDBG grants it may receive under subpart A and this subpart. Such pledge shall be for the purpose of assuring repayment of any debt obligations (as defined in § 570.701), in accordance with their terms, that HUD may have guaranteed in the respective State on behalf of any nonentitlement public entity (as defined in § 570.701) or its designated public agency prior to the State's election.

[59 FR 66604, Dec. 27, 1994]

Subpart J—Grant Administration

Source: 53 FR 8058, Mar. 11, 1988, unless otherwise noted.

§ 570.500 Definitions.

For the purposes of this subpart, the following terms shall apply:

(a) *Program income* means gross income received by the recipient or a subrecipient directly generated from the use of CDBG funds, except as provided in paragraph (a)(4) of this section.

(1) Program income includes, but is not limited to, the following:

(i) Proceeds from the disposition by sale or long-term lease of real property purchased or improved with CDBG funds;

(ii) Proceeds from the disposition of equipment purchased with CDBG funds;

(iii) Gross income from the use or rental of real or personal property acquired by the recipient or by a subrecipient with CDBG funds, less costs incidental to generation of the income;

(iv) Gross income from the use or rental of real property, owned by the recipient or by a subrecipient, that was constructed or improved with CDBG funds, less costs incidental to generation of the income;

(v) Payments of principal and interest on loans made using CDBG funds, except as provided in paragraph (a)(3) of this section;

(vi) Proceeds from the sale of loans made with CDBG funds;

(vii) Proceeds from sale of obligations secured by loans made with CDBG funds;

(viii) [Reserved]

(ix) Interest earned on program income pending its disposition; and

(x) Funds collected through special assessments made against properties owned and occupied by households *not* of low and moderate income, where the assessments are used to recover all or part of the CDBG portion of a public improvement.

(2) Program income does not include income earned (except for interest described in § 570.513) on grant advances from the U.S. Treasury. The following items of income earned on grant advances must be remitted to HUD for transmittal to the U.S. Treasury, and will not be reallocated under section 106(c) or (d) of the Act:

(i) Interest earned from the investment of the initial proceeds of a grant advance by the U.S. Treasury;

(ii) Interest earned on loans or other forms of assistance provided with CDBG funds that are used for activities determined by HUD either to be ineligible or to fail to meet a national objective in accordance with the requirements of subpart C of this part, or that fail substantially to meet any other requirement of this part; and

(iii) Interest earned on the investment of amounts reimbursed to the CDBG program account prior to the use of the reimbursed funds for eligible purposes.

(3) The calculation of the amount of program income for the recipient's

§ 570.500

CDBG program as a whole (i.e., comprising activities carried out by a grantee and its subrecipients) shall exclude payments made by subrecipients of principal and/or interest on CDBG-funded loans received from grantees if such payments are made using program income received by the subrecipient. (By making such payments, the subrecipient shall be deemed to have transferred program income to the grantee.) The amount of program income derived from this calculation shall be used for reporting purposes, for purposes of applying the requirement under § 570.504(b)(2)(iii), and in determining limitations on planning and administration and public services activities to be paid for with CDBG funds.

(4) Program income does not include:

(i) Any income received in a single program year by the recipient and all its subrecipients if the total amount of such income does not exceed $25,000; and

(ii) Amounts generated by activities that are financed by a loan guaranteed under section 108 of the Act and meet one or more of the public benefit criteria specified at § 570.209(b)(2)(v) or are carried out in conjunction with a grant under section 108(q) in an area determined by HUD to meet the eligibility requirements for designation as an Urban Empowerment Zone pursuant to 24 CFR part 597, subpart B. Such exclusion shall not apply if CDBG funds are used to repay the guaranteed loan. When such a guaranteed loan is partially repaid with CDBG funds, the amount generated shall be prorated to reflect the percentage of CDBG funds used. Amounts generated by activities financed with loans guaranteed under section 108 which are not defined as program income shall be treated as miscellaneous revenue and shall not be subject to any of the requirements of this part, except that the use of such funds shall be limited to activities that are located in a revitalization strategy area and implement a HUD approved area revitalization strategy pursuant to § 91.215(e) of this title. However, such treatment shall not affect the right of the Secretary to require the section 108 borrower to pledge such amounts as security for the guaranteed loan. The determination whether such amounts shall constitute program income shall be governed by the provisions of the contract required at § 570.705(b)(1).

(5) Examples of other receipts that are not considered program income are proceeds from fund raising activities carried out by subrecipients receiving CDBG assistance (the costs of fundraising are generally unallowable under the applicable OMB circulars referenced in 24 CFR 84.27), funds collected through special assessments used to recover the non-CDBG portion of a public improvement, and proceeds from the disposition of real property acquired or improved with CDBG funds when the disposition occurs after the applicable time period specified in § 570.503(b)(8) for subrecipient-controlled property, or in § 570.505 for recipient-controlled property.

(b) *Revolving fund* means a separate fund (with a set of accounts that are independent of other program accounts) established for the purpose of carrying out specific activities which, in turn, generate payments to the fund for use in carrying out the same activities. Each revolving loan fund's cash balance must be held in an interest-bearing account, and any interest paid on CDBG funds held in this account shall be considered interest earned on grant advances and must be remitted to HUD for transmittal to the U.S. Treasury no less frequently than annually. (Interest paid by borrowers on eligible loans made from the revolving loan fund shall be program income and treated accordingly.)

(c) *Subrecipient* means a public or private nonprofit agency, authority, or organization, or a for-profit entity authorized under § 570.201(o), receiving CDBG funds from the recipient or another subrecipient to undertake activities eligible for such assistance under subpart C of this part. The term excludes an entity receiving CDBG funds from the recipient under the authority of § 570.204, unless the grantee explicitly designates it as a subrecipient. The term includes a public agency designated by a unit of general local government to receive a loan guarantee under subpart M of this part, but does not include contractors providing supplies, equipment, construction, or services subject to the procurement requirements in 24 CFR 85.36 or 84.40, as applicable.

[53 FR 8058, Mar. 11, 1988, as amended at 57 FR 27120, June 17, 1992; 60 FR 1952, Jan. 5, 1995; 60 FR 17445, Apr. 6, 1995; 60 FR 56914, Nov. 9, 1995]

§ 570.501 Responsibility for grant administration.

(a) One or more public agencies, including existing local public agencies, may be designated by the chief executive officer of the recipient to undertake activities assisted by this part. A public agency so designated shall be subject to the same requirements as are applicable to subrecipients.

(b) The recipient is responsible for ensuring that CDBG funds are used in accordance with all program requirements. The use of designated public agencies, subrecipients, or contractors does not relieve the recipient of this responsibility. The recipient is also responsible for determining the adequacy of performance under subrecipient agreements and procurement contracts, and for taking appropriate action when performance problems arise, such as the actions described in § 570.910. Where a unit of general local government is participating with, or as part of, an urban county, or as part of a metropolitan city, the recipient is responsible for applying to the unit of general local government the same requirements as are applicable to subrecipients, except that the five-year period identified under § 570.503(b)(8)(i) shall begin with the date that the unit of general local government is no longer considered by HUD to be a part of the metropolitan city or urban county, as applicable, instead of the date that the subrecipient agreement expires.

[53 FR 8058, Mar. 11, 1988, as amended at 57 FR 27120, June 17, 1992]

§ 570.502 Applicability of uniform administrative requirements.

(a) Recipients and subrecipients that are governmental entities (including public agencies) shall comply with the requirements and standards of OMB Circular No. A-87, "Cost Principles for State, Local, and Indian Tribal Governments"; OMB Circular A-128, "Audits of State and Local Governments" (implemented at 24 CFR part 44); and with the following sections of 24 CFR part 85 "Uniform Administrative Requirements for Grants and Cooperative Agreements to State and Local Governments" or the related CDBG provision, as specified in this paragraph:

(1) Section 85.3, "Definitions";
(2) Section 85.6, "Exceptions";
(3) Section 85.12, "Special grant or subgrant conditions for 'high-risk' grantees";
(4) Section 85.20, "Standards for financial management systems," except paragraph (a);
(5) Section 85.21, "Payment," except as modified by § 570.513;
(6) Section 85.22, "Allowable costs";
(7) Section 85.26, "Non-federal audits";
(8) Section 85.32, "Equipment," except in all cases in which the equipment is sold, the proceeds shall be program income;
(9) Section 85.33, "Supplies";
(10) Section 85.34, "Copyrights";
(11) Section 85.35, "Subawards to debarred and suspended parties";
(12) Section 85.36, "Procurement," except paragraph (a);
(13) Section 85.37, "Subgrants";
(14) Section 85.40, "Monitoring and reporting program performance," except paragraphs (b) through (d) and paragraph (f);
(15) Section 85.41, "Financial reporting," except paragraphs (a), (b), and (e);
(16) Section 85.42, "Retention and access requirements for records," except that the period shall be four years;
(17) Section 85.43, "Enforcement";
(18) Section 85.44, "Termination for convenience";
(19) Section 85.51 "Later disallowances and adjustments" and
(20) Section 85.52, "Collection of amounts due."

(b) Subrecipients, except subrecipients that are governmental entities, shall comply with the requirements and standards of OMB Circular No. A-122, "Cost Principles for Non-profit Organizations," or OMB Circular No. A-21, "Cost Principles for Educational Institutions," as applicable, and OMB Circular A-133, "Audits of Institutions

§ 570.503

of Higher Education and Other Non-profit Institutions" (as set forth in 24 CFR part 45). Audits shall be conducted annually. Such subrecipients shall also comply with the following provisions of the Uniform Administrative requirements of OMB Circular A-110 (implemented at 24 CFR part 84, "Uniform Administrative Requirements for Grants and Agreements With Institutions of Higher Education, Hospitals and Other Non-Profit Organizations") or the related CDBG provision, as specified in this paragraph:

(1) Subpart A—"General";

(2) Subpart B—"Pre-Award Requirements," except for § 84.12, "Forms for Applying for Federal Assistance";

(3) Subpart C—"Post-Award Requirements," except for:

(i) Section 84.22, "Payment Requirements." Grantees shall follow the standards of §§ 85.20(b)(7) and 85.21 in making payments to subrecipients;

(ii) Section 84.23, "Cost Sharing and Matching";

(iii) Section 84.24, "Program Income." In lieu of § 84.24, CDBG subrecipients shall follow § 570.504;

(iv) Section 84.25, "Revision of Budget and Program Plans";

(v) Section 84.32, "Real Property." In lieu of § 84.32, CDBG subrecipients shall follow § 570.505;

(vi) Section 84.34(g), "Equipment." In lieu of the disposition provisions of § 84.34(g), the following applies:

(A) In all cases in which equipment is sold, the proceeds shall be program income (prorated to reflect the extent to which CDBG funds were used to acquire the equipment); and

(B) Equipment not needed by the subrecipient for CDBG activities shall be transferred to the recipient for the CDBG program or shall be retained after compensating the recipient;

(vii) Section 84.51 (b), (c), (d), (e), (f), (g), and (h), "Monitoring and Reporting Program Performance";

(viii) Section 84.52, "Financial Reporting";

(ix) Section 84.53(b), "Retention and access requirements for records." Section 84.53(b) applies with the following exceptions:

(A) The retention period referenced in § 84.53(b) pertaining to individual CDBG activities shall be four years; and

(B) The retention period starts from the date of submission of the annual performance and evaluation report, as prescribed in 24 CFR 91.520, in which the specific activity is reported on for the final time rather than from the date of submission of the final expenditure report for the award;

(x) Section 84.61, "Termination." In lieu of the provisions of § 84.61, CDBG subrecipients shall comply with § 570.503(b)(7); and

(4) Subpart D—"After-the-Award Requirements," except for § 84.71, "Closeout Procedures."

[53 FR 8058, Mar. 11, 1988, as amended at 60 FR 1916, Jan. 5, 1995; 60 FR 56915, Nov. 9, 1995]

§ 570.503 Agreements with subrecipients.

(a) Before disbursing any CDBG funds to a subrecipient, the recipient shall sign a written agreement with the subrecipient. The agreement shall remain in effect during any period that the subrecipient has control over CDBG funds, including program income.

(b) At a minimum, the written agreement with the subrecipient shall include provisions concerning the following following items:

(1) *Statement of work.* The agreement shall include a description of the work to be performed, a schedule for completing the work, and a budget. These items shall be in sufficient detail to provide a sound basis for the recipient effectively to monitor performance under the agreement.

(2) *Records and reports.* The recipient shall specify in the agreement the particular records the subrecipient must maintain and the particular reports the subrecipient must submit in order to assist the recipient in meeting its recordkeeping and reporting requirements.

(3) *Program income.* The agreement shall include the program income requirements set forth in § 570.504(c). The agreement shall also specify that, at the end of the program year, the grantee may require remittance of all or part of any program income balances (including investments thereof) held by the subrecipient (except those needed

for immediate cash needs, cash balances of a revolving loan fund, cash balances from a lump sum drawdown, or cash or investments held for section 108 security needs).

(4) *Uniform administrative requirements.* The agreement shall require the subrecipient to comply with applicable uniform administrative requirements, as described in §570.502.

(5) *Other program requirements.* The agreement shall require the subrecipient to carry out each activity in compliance with all Federal laws and regulations described in subpart K of these regulations, except that:

(i) The subrecipient does not assume the recipient's environmental responsibilities described at §570.604; and

(ii) The subrecipient does not assume the recipient's responsibility for initiating the review process under the provisions of 24 CFR part 52.

(6) *Suspension and termination.* The agreement shall specify that, in accordance with 24 CFR 85.43, suspension or termination may occur if the subrecipient materially fails to comply with any term of the award, and that the award may be terminated for convenience in accordance with 24 CFR 85.44.

(7) *Reversion of assets.* The agreement shall specify that upon its expiration the subrecipient shall transfer to the recipient any CDBG funds on hand at the time of expiration and any accounts receivable attributable to the use of CDBG funds. It shall also include provisions designed to ensure that any real property under the subrecipient's control that was acquired or improved in whole or in part with CDBG funds (including CDBG funds provided to the subrecipient in the form of a loan) in excess of $25,000 is either:

(i) Used to meet one of the national objectives in §570.208 (formerly §570.901) until five years after expiration of the agreement, or for such longer period of time as determined to be appropriate by the recipient; or

(ii) Not used in accordance with paragraph (b)(7)(i) of this section, in which event the subrecipient shall pay to the recipient an amount equal to the current market value of the property less any portion of the value attributable to expenditures of non-CDBG funds for the acquisition of, or improvement to, the property. The payment is program income to the recipient. (No payment is required after the period of time specified in paragraph (b)(7)(i) of this section.)

[53 FR 8058, Mar. 11, 1988, as amended at 53 FR 41331, Oct. 21, 1988; 57 FR 27120, June 17, 1992; 60 FR 56915, Nov. 9, 1995; 68 FR 56405, Sept. 30, 2003]

§ 570.504 **Program income.**

(a) *Recording program income.* The receipt and expenditure of program income as defined in §570.500(a) shall be recorded as part of the financial transactions of the grant program.

(b) *Disposition of program income received by recipients.* (1) Program income received before grant closeout may be retained by the recipient if the income is treated as additional CDBG funds subject to all applicable requirements governing the use of CDBG funds.

(2) If the recipient chooses to retain program income, that program income shall be disposed of as follows:

(i) Program income in the form of repayments to, or interest earned on, a revolving fund as defined in §570.500(b) shall be substantially disbursed from the fund before additional cash withdrawals are made from the U.S. Treasury for the same activity. (This rule does not prevent a lump sum disbursement to finance the rehabilitation of privately owned properties as provided for in §570.513.)

(ii) Substantially all other program income shall be disbursed for eligible activities before additional cash withdrawals are made from the U.S. Treasury.

(iii) At the end of each program year, the aggregate amount of program income cash balances and any investment thereof (except those needed for immediate cash needs, cash balances of a revolving loan fund, cash balances from a lump-sum drawdown, or cash or investments held for section 108 loan guarantee security needs) that, as of the last day of the program year, exceeds one-twelfth of the most recent grant made pursuant to §570.304 shall be remitted to HUD as soon as practicable thereafter, to be placed in the recipient's line of credit. This provision applies to program income cash balances and investments thereof held by the grantee and its subrecipients. (This provision shall be applied for the first time at the end of the program year for which Federal Fiscal Year 1996 funds are provided.)

(3) Program income on hand at the time of closeout shall continue to be subject to the eligibility requirements in subpart C and all other applicable provisions of this part until it is expended.

(4) Unless otherwise provided in any grant closeout agreement, and subject to the requirements of paragraph (b)(5) of this section, income received after closeout shall not be governed by the provisions of this part, except that, if at the time of closeout the recipient has another ongoing CDBG grant received directly from HUD, funds received after closeout shall be treated as program income of the ongoing grant program.

(5) If the recipient does not have another ongoing grant received directly from HUD at the time of closeout, income received after closeout from the disposition of real property or from loans outstanding at the time of closeout shall not be governed by the provisions of this part, except that such income shall be used for activities that meet one of the national objectives in § 570.901 and the eligibility requirements described in section 105 of the Act.

(c) *Disposition of program income received by subrecipients.* The written agreement between the recipient and the subrecipient, as required by § 570.503, shall specify whether program income received is to be returned to the recipient or retained by the subrecipient. Where program income is to be retained by the subrecipient, the agreement shall specify the activities that will be undertaken with the program income and that all provisions of the written agreement shall apply to the specified activities. When the subrecipient retains program income, transfers of grant funds by the recipient to the subrecipient shall be adjusted according to the principles described in paragraphs (b)(2) (i) and (ii) of this section. Any program income on hand when the agreement expires, or received after the agreement's expiration, shall be paid to the recipient as required by § 570.503(b)(8).

(d) *Disposition of certain program income received by urban counties.* Program income derived from urban county program activities undertaken by or within the jurisdiction of a unit of general local government which thereafter terminates its participation in the urban county shall continue to be program income of the urban county. The urban county may transfer the program income to the unit of general local government, upon its termination of urban county participation, provided that the unit of general local government has become an entitlement grantee and agrees to use the program income in its own CDBG entitlement program.

[53 FR 8058, Mar. 11, 1988, as amended at 60 FR 56915, Nov. 9, 1995]

§ 570.505 Use of real property.

The standards described in this section apply to real property within the recipient's control which was acquired or improved in whole or in part using CDBG funds in excess of $25,000. These standards shall apply from the date CDBG funds are first spent for the property until five years after closeout of an entitlement recipient's participation in the entitlement CDBG program or, with respect to other recipients, until five years after the closeout of the grant from which the assistance to the property was provided.

(a) A recipient may not change the use or planned use of any such property (including the beneficiaries of such use) from that for which the acquisition or improvement was made unless the recipient provides affected citizens with reasonable notice of, and opportunity to comment on, any proposed change, and either:

(1) The new use of such property qualifies as meeting one of the national objectives in § 570.208 (formerly § 570.901) and is not a building for the general conduct of government; or

(2) The requirements in paragraph (b) of this section are met.

(b) If the recipient determines, after consultation with affected citizens, that it is appropriate to change the use of the property to a use which does not qualify under paragraph (a)(1) of this section, it may retain or dispose of the property for the changed use if the recipient's CDBG program is reimbursed in the amount of the current fair market value of the property, less any portion of the value attributable to expenditures of non-CDBG funds for acquisition of, and improvements to, the property.

(c) If the change of use occurs after closeout, the provisions governing income from the disposition of the real property in §570.504(b)(4) or (5), as applicable, shall apply to the use of funds reimbursed.

(d) Following the reimbursement of the CDBG program in accordance with paragraph (b) of this section, the property no longer will be subject to any CDBG requirements.

[53 FR 8058, Mar. 11, 1988, as amended at 53 FR 41331, Oct. 21, 1988]

§ 570.506 Records to be maintained.

Each recipient shall establish and maintain sufficient records to enable the Secretary to determine whether the recipient has met the requirements of this part. At a minimum, the following records are needed:

(a) Records providing a full description of each activity assisted (or being assisted) with CDBG funds, including its location (if the activity has a geographical locus), the amount of CDBG funds budgeted, obligated and expended for the activity, and the provision in subpart C under which it is eligible.

(b) Records demonstrating that each activity undertaken meets one of the criteria set forth in §570.208. (Where information on income by family size is required, the recipient may substitute evidence establishing that the person assisted qualifies under another program having income qualification criteria at least as restrictive as that used in the definitions of "low and moderate income person" and "low and moderate income household" (as applicable) at §570.3, such as Job Training Partnership Act (JTPA) and welfare programs; or the recipient may substitute evidence that the assisted person is homeless; or the recipient may substitute a copy of a verifiable certification from the assisted person that his or her family income does not exceed the applicable income limit established in accordance with §570.3; or the recipient may substitute a notice that the assisted person is a referral from a state, county or local employment agency or other entity that agrees to refer individuals it determines to be low and moderate income persons based on HUD's criteria and agrees to maintain documentation supporting these determinations.) Such records shall include the following information:

(1) For each activity determined to benefit low and moderate income persons, the income limits applied and the point in time when the benefit was determined.

(2) For each activity determined to benefit low and moderate income persons based on the area served by the activity:

(i) The boundaries of the service area;

(ii) The income characteristics of families and unrelated individuals in the service area; and

(iii) If the percent of low and moderate income persons in the service area is less than 51 percent, data showing that the area qualifies under the exception criteria set forth at §570.208(a)(1)(ii).

(3) For each activity determined to benefit low and moderate income persons because the activity involves a facility or service designed for use by a limited clientele consisting exclusively or predominantly of low and moderate income persons:

(i) Documentation establishing that the facility or service is designed for the particular needs of or used exclusively by senior citizens, adults meeting the Bureau of the Census' Current Population Reports definition of "severely disabled," persons living with AIDS, battered spouses, abused children, the homeless, illiterate adults, or migrant farm workers, for which the regulations provide a presumption concerning the extent to which low- and moderate-income persons benefit; or

(ii) Documentation describing how the nature and, if applicable, the location of the facility or service establishes that it is used predominantly by low and moderate income persons; or

(iii) Data showing the size and annual income of the family of each person receiving the benefit.

(4) For each activity carried out for the purpose of providing or improving housing which is determined to benefit low and moderate income persons:

(i) A copy of a written agreement with each landlord or developer receiving CDBG assistance indicating the total number of dwelling units in each multifamily structure assisted and the number of those units which will be occupied by low and moderate income households after assistance;

(ii) The total cost of the activity, including both CDBG and non-CDBG funds.

(iii) For each unit occupied by a low and moderate income household, the size and income of the household;

(iv) For rental housing only:

(A) The rent charged (or to be charged) after assistance for each dwelling unit in each structure assisted; and

(B) Such information as necessary to show the affordability of units occupied (or to be occupied) by low and moderate income households pursuant to criteria established and made public by the recipient;

(v) For each property acquired on which there are no structures, evidence of commitments ensuring that the criteria in § 570.208(a)(3) will be met when the structures are built;

(vi) Where applicable, records demonstrating that the activity qualifies under the special conditions at § 570.208(a)(3)(i);

(vii) For any homebuyer assistance activity qualifying under § 570.201(e), 570.201(n), or 570.204, identification of the applicable eligibility paragraph and evidence that the activity meets the eligibility criteria for that provision; for any such activity qualifying under § 570.208(a), the size and income of each homebuyer's household; and

(viii) For a § 570.201(k) housing services activity, identification of the HOME project(s) or assistance that the housing services activity supports, and evidence that project(s) or assistance meet the HOME program income targeting requirements at 24 CFR 92.252 or 92.254.

(5) For each activity determined to benefit low and moderate income persons based on the creation of jobs, the recipient shall provide the documentation described in either paragraph (b)(5)(i) or (ii) of this section.

(i) Where the recipient chooses to document that at least 51 percent of the jobs will be available to low and moderate income persons, documentation for each assisted business shall include:

(A) A copy of a written agreement containing:

(1) A commitment by the business that it will make at least 51 percent of the jobs available to low and moderate income persons and will provide training for any of those jobs requiring special skills or education;

(2) A listing by job title of the permanent jobs to be created indicating which jobs will be available to low and moderate income persons, which jobs require special skills or education, and which jobs are part-time, if any; and

(3) A description of actions to be taken by the recipient and business to ensure that low and moderate income persons receive first consideration for those jobs; and

(B) A listing by job title of the permanent jobs filled, and which jobs of those were available to low and moderate income persons, and a description of how first consideration was given to such persons for those jobs. The description shall include what hiring process was used; which low and moderate income persons were interviewed for a particular job; and which low and moderate income persons were hired.

(ii) Where the recipient chooses to document that at least 51 percent of the jobs will be held by low and moderate income persons, documentation for each assisted business shall include:

(A) A copy of a written agreement containing:

(1) A commitment by the business that at least 51 percent of the jobs, on a full-time equivalent basis, will be held by low and moderate income persons; and

(2) A listing by job title of the permanent jobs to be created, identifying which are part-time, if any;

(B) A listing by job title of the permanent jobs filled and which jobs were initially held by low and moderate income persons; and

Ofc. of Asst. Secy., Comm. Planning, Develop., HUD § 570.506

(C) For each such low and moderate income person hired, the size and annual income of the person's family prior to the person being hired for the job.

(6) For each activity determined to benefit low and moderate income persons based on the retention of jobs:

(i) Evidence that in the absence of CDBG assistance jobs would be lost;

(ii) For each business assisted, a listing by job title of permanent jobs retained, indicating which of those jobs are part-time and (where it is known) which are held by low and moderate income persons at the time the CDBG assistance is provided. Where applicable, identification of any of the retained jobs (other than those known to be held by low and moderate income persons) which are projected to become available to low and moderate income persons through job turnover within two years of the time CDBG assistance is provided. Information upon which the job turnover projections were based shall also be included in the record;

(iii) For each retained job claimed to be held by a low and moderate income person, information on the size and annual income of the person's family;

(iv) For jobs claimed to be available to low and moderate income persons based on job turnover, a description covering the items required for "available to" jobs in paragraph (b)(5) of this section; and

(v) Where jobs were claimed to be available to low and moderate income persons through turnover, a listing of each job which has turned over to date, indicating which of those jobs were either taken by, or available to, low and moderate income persons. For jobs made available, a description of how first consideration was given to such persons for those jobs shall also be included in the record.

(7) For purposes of documenting, pursuant to paragraph (b)(5)(i)(B), (b)(5)(ii)(C), (b)(6)(iii) or (b)(6)(v) of this section, that the person for whom a job was either filled by or made available to a low- or moderate-income person based upon the census tract where the person resides or in which the business is located, the recipient, in lieu of maintaining records showing the person's family size and income, may substitute records showing either the person's address at the time the determination of income status was made or the address of the business providing the job, as applicable, the census tract in which that address was located, the percent of persons residing in that tract who either are in poverty or who are low- and moderate-income, as applicable, the data source used for determining the percentage, and a description of the pervasive poverty and general distress in the census tract in sufficient detail to demonstrate how the census tract met the criteria in § 570.208(a)(4)(v), as applicable.

(8) For each activity determined to aid in the prevention or elimination of slums or blight based on addressing one or more of the conditions which qualified an area as a slum or blighted area:

(i) The boundaries of the area; and

(ii) A description of the conditions which qualified the area at the time of its designation in sufficient detail to demonstrate how the area met the criteria in § 570.208(b)(1).

(9) For each residential rehabilitation activity determined to aid in the prevention or elimination of slums or blight in a slum or blighted area:

(i) The local definition of "substandard";

(ii) A pre-rehabilitation inspection report describing the deficiencies in each structure to be rehabilitated; and

(iii) Details and scope of CDBG assisted rehabilitation, by structure.

(10) For each activity determined to aid in the prevention or elimination of slums or blight based on the elimination of specific conditions of blight or physical decay not located in a slum or blighted area:

(i) A description of the specific condition of blight or physical decay treated; and

(ii) For rehabilitation carried out under this category, a description of the specific conditions detrimental to public health and safety which were identified and the details and scope of the CDBG assisted rehabilitation by structure.

(11) For each activity determined to aid in the prevention or elimination of slums or blight based on addressing slums or blight in an urban renewal area, a copy of the Urban Renewal

§ 570.506

Plan, as in effect at the time the activity is carried out, including maps and supporting documentation.

(12) For each activity determined to meet a community development need having a particular urgency:

(i) Documentation concerning the nature and degree of seriousness of the condition requiring assistance;

(ii) Evidence that the recipient certified that the CDBG activity was designed to address the urgent need;

(iii) Information on the timing of the development of the serious condition; and

(iv) Evidence confirming that other financial resources to alleviate the need were not available.

(c) Records that demonstrate that the recipient has made the determinations required as a condition of eligibility of certain activities, as prescribed in §§ 570.201(f), 570.201(i)(2), 570.201(p), 570.201(q), 570.202(b)(3), 570.206(f), 570.209, 570.210, and 570.309.

(d) Records which demonstrate compliance with § 570.505 regarding any change of use of real property acquired or improved with CDBG assistance.

(e) Records that demonstrate compliance with the citizen participation requirements prescribed in 24 CFR part 91, subpart B, for entitlement recipients, or in 24 CFR part 91, subpart C, for HUD-administered small cities recipients.

(f) Records which demonstrate compliance with the requirements in § 570.606 regarding acquisition, displacement, relocation, and replacement housing.

(g) Fair housing and equal opportunity records containing:

(1) Documentation of the analysis of impediments and the actions the recipient has carried out with its housing and community development and other resources to remedy or ameliorate any impediments to fair housing choice in the recipient's community.

(2) Data on the extent to which each racial and ethnic group and single-headed households (by gender of household head) have applied for, participated in, or benefited from, any program or activity funded in whole or in part with CDBG funds. Such information shall be used only as a basis for further investigation as to compliance with nondiscrimination requirements. No recipient is required to attain or maintain any particular statistical measure by race, ethnicity, or gender in covered programs.

(3) Data on employment in each of the recipient's operating units funded in whole or in part with CDBG funds, with such data maintained in the categories prescribed on the Equal Employment Opportunity Commission's EEO-4 form; and documentation of any actions undertaken to assure equal employment opportunities to all persons regardless of race, color, national origin, sex or handicap in operating units funded in whole or in part under this part.

(4) Data indicating the race and ethnicity of households (and gender of single heads of households) displaced as a result of CDBG funded activities, together with the address and census tract of the housing units to which each displaced household relocated. Such information shall be used only as a basis for further investigation as to compliance with nondiscrimination requirements. No recipient is required to attain or maintain any particular statistical measure by race, ethnicity, or gender in covered programs.

(5) Documentation of actions undertaken to meet the requirements of § 570.607(b) which implements section 3 of the Housing Development Act of 1968, as amended (12 U.S.C. 1701U) relative to the hiring and training of low and moderate income persons and the use of local businesses.

(6) Data indicating the racial/ethnic character of each business entity receiving a contract or subcontract of $25,000 or more paid, or to be paid, with CDBG funds, data indicating which of those entities are women's business enterprises as defined in Executive Order 12138, the amount of the contract or subcontract, and documentation of recipient's affirmative steps to assure that minority business and women's business enterprises have an equal opportunity to obtain or compete for contracts and subcontracts as sources of supplies, equipment, construction and services. Such affirmative steps may include, but are not limited to, technical assistance open to all businesses but designed to enhance opportunities

for these enterprises and special outreach efforts to inform them of contract opportunities. Such steps shall not include preferring any business in the award of any contract or subcontract solely or in part on the basis of race or gender.

(7) Documentation of the affirmative action measures the recipient has taken to overcome prior discrimination, where the courts or HUD have found that the recipient has previously discriminated against persons on the ground of race, color, national origin or sex in administering a program or activity funded in whole or in part with CDBG funds.

(h) Financial records, in accordance with the applicable requirements listed in §570.502, including source documentation for entities not subject to parts 84 and 85 of this title. Grantees shall maintain evidence to support how the CDBG funds provided to such entities are expended. Such documentation must include, to the extent applicable, invoices, schedules containing comparisons of budgeted amounts and actual expenditures, construction progress schedules signed by appropriate parties (e.g., general contractor and/or a project architect), and/or other documentation appropriate to the nature of the activity.

(i) Agreements and other records related to lump sum disbursements to private financial institutions for financing rehabilitation as prescribed in §570.513; and

(j) Records required to be maintained in accordance with other applicable laws and regulations set forth in subpart K of this part.

(Approved by the Office of Management and Budget under control number 2506–0077)

[53 FR 34454, Sept. 6, 1988; 53 FR 41330, Oct. 21, 1988, as amended at 60 FR 1916, 1953, Jan. 5, 1995; 60 FR 56915, Nov. 9, 1995; 61 FR 18674, Apr. 29, 1996; 64 FR 38813, July 19, 1999; 70 FR 76370, Dec. 23, 2005]

§570.507 Reports.

(a) *Performance and evaluation report*—(1) *Entitlement grant recipients and HUD-administered small cities recipients in Hawaii.* The annual performance and evaluation report shall be submitted in accordance with 24 CFR part 91.

(2) *HUD-administered Small Cities recipients in New York, and Hawaii recipients for pre-FY 1995 grants*—(i) *Content.* Each performance and evaluation report must contain completed copies of all forms and narratives prescribed by HUD, including a summary of the citizen comments received on the report.

(ii) *Timing.* The performance and evaluation report on each grant shall be submitted:

(A) No later than October 31 for all grants executed before April 1 of the same calendar year. The first report should cover the period from the execution of the grant until September 30. Reports on grants made after March 31 of a calendar year will be due October 31 of the following calendar year, and the reports will cover the period of time from the execution of the grant until September 30 of the calendar year following grant execution. After the initial submission, the performance and evaluation report will be submitted annually on October 31 until completion of the activities funded under the grant;

(B) Hawaii grantees will submit their small cities performance and evaluation report for each pre-FY 1995 grant no later than 90 days after the completion of their most recent program year. After the initial submission, the performance and evaluation report will be submitted annually until completion of the activities funded under the grant; and

(C) No later than 90 days after the criteria for grant closeout, as described in §570.509(a), have been met.

(iii) *Citizen comments on the report.* Each recipient shall make copies of the performance and evaluation report available to its citizens in sufficient time to permit the citizens to comment on the report before its submission to HUD. Each recipient may determine the specific manner and times the report will be made available to citizens consistent with the preceding sentence.

(b) *Equal employment opportunity reports.* Recipients of entitlement grants or HUD-administered small cities grants shall submit to HUD each year a report (HUD/EEO-4) on recipient employment containing data as of June 30.

§ 570.508

(c) *Minority business enterprise reports.* Recipients of entitlement grants, HUD-administered small cities grants or Urban Development Action Grants shall submit to HUD, by April 30, a report on contracts and subcontract activity during the first half of the fiscal year and by October 31 a report on such activity during the second half of the year.

(d) *Other reports.* Recipients may be required to submit such other reports and information as HUD determines are necessary to carry out its responsibilities under the Act or other applicable laws.

(Approved by the Office of Management and Budget under control numbers 2506–0077 for paragraph (a) and 2529–0008 for paragraph (b) and 2506–0066 for paragraph (c))

[53 FR 34456, Sept. 6, 1988, as amended at 60 FR 1916, Jan. 5, 1995; 61 FR 32269, June 21, 1996]

§ 570.508 Public access to program records.

Notwithstanding 24 CFR 85.42(f), recipients shall provide citizens with reasonable access to records regarding the past use of CDBG funds, consistent with applicable State and local laws regarding privacy and obligations of confidentiality.

§ 570.509 Grant closeout procedures.

(a) *Criteria for closeout.* A grant will be closed out when HUD determines, in consultation with the recipient, that the following criteria have been met:

(1) All costs to be paid with CDBG funds have been incurred, with the exception of closeout costs (e.g., audit costs) and costs resulting from contingent liabilities described in the closeout agreement pursuant to paragraph (c) of this section. Contingent liabilities include, but are not limited to, third-party claims against the recipient, as well as related administrative costs.

(2) With respect to activities (such as rehabilitation of privately owned properties) which are financed by means of escrow accounts, loan guarantees, or similar mechanisms, the work to be assisted with CDBG funds (but excluding program income) has actually been completed.

(3) Other responsibilities of the recipient under the grant agreement and applicable laws and regulations appear to have been carried out satisfactorily or there is no further Federal interest in keeping the grant agreement open for the purpose of securing performance.

(b) *Closeout actions.* (1) Within 90 days of the date it is determined that the criteria for closeout have been met, the recipient shall submit to HUD a copy of the final performance and evaluation report described in 24 CFR part 91. If an acceptable report is not submitted, an audit of the recipient's grant activities may be conducted by HUD.

(2) Based on the information provided in the performance report and other relevant information, HUD, in consultation with the recipient, will prepare a closeout agreement in accordance with paragraph (c) of this section.

(3) HUD will cancel any unused portion of the awarded grant, as shown in the signed grant closeout agreement. Any unused grant funds disbursed from the U.S. Treasury which are in the possession of the recipient shall be refunded to HUD.

(4) Any costs paid with CDBG funds which were not audited previously shall be subject to coverage in the recipient's next single audit performed in accordance with 24 CFR part 44. The recipient may be required to repay HUD any disallowed costs based on the results of the audit, or on additional HUD reviews provided for in the closeout agreement.

(c) *Closeout agreement.* Any obligations remaining as of the date of the closeout shall be covered by the terms of a closeout agreement. The agreement shall be prepared by the HUD field office in consultation with the recipient. The agreement shall identify the grant being closed out, and include provisions with respect to the following:

(1) Identification of any closeout costs or contingent liabilities subject to payment with CDBG funds after the closeout agreement is signed;

(2) Identification of any unused grant funds to be canceled by HUD;

(3) Identification of any program income on deposit in financial institutions at the time the closeout agreement is signed;

(4) Description of the recipient's responsibility after closeout for:

(i) Compliance with all program requirements, certifications and assurances in using program income on deposit at the time the closeout agreement is signed and in using any other remaining CDBG funds available for closeout costs and contingent liabilities;

(ii) Use of real property assisted with CDBG funds in accordance with the principles described in § 570.505;

(iii) Compliance with requirements governing program income received subsequent to grant closeout, as described in § 570.504(b)(4) and (5); and

(iv) Ensuring that flood insurance coverage for affected property owners is maintained for the mandatory period;

(5) Other provisions appropriate to any special circumstances of the grant closeout, in modification of or in addition to the obligations in paragraphs (c)(1) through (4) of this section. The agreement shall authorize monitoring by HUD, and shall provide that findings of noncompliance may be taken into account by HUD, as unsatisfactory performance of the recipient, in the consideration of any future grant award under this part.

(d) *Status of consolidated plan after closeout.* Unless otherwise provided in a closeout agreement, the Consolidated Plan will remain in effect after closeout until the expiration of the program year covered by the last approved consolidated plan.

(e) *Termination of grant for convenience.* Grant assistance provided under this part may be terminated for convenience in whole or in part before the completion of the assisted activities, in accordance with the provisions of 24 CFR 85.44. The recipient shall not incur new obligations for the terminated portions after the effective date, and shall cancel as many outstanding obligations as possible. HUD shall allow full credit to the recipient for those portions of obligations which could not be canceled and which had been properly incurred by the recipient in carrying out the activities before the termination. The closeout policies contained in this section shall apply in such cases, except where the approved grant is terminated in its entirety. Responsibility for the environmental review to be performed under 24 CFR part 50 or 24 CFR part 58, as applicable, shall be determined as part of the closeout process.

(f) *Termination for cause.* In cases in which the Secretary terminates the recipient's grant under the authority of subpart O of this part, or under the terms of the grant agreement, the closeout policies contained in this section shall apply, except where the approved grant is cancelled in its entirety. The provisions in 24 CFR 85.43(c) on the effects of termination shall also apply. HUD shall determine whether an environmental assessment or finding of inapplicability is required, and if such review is required, HUD shall perform it in accordance with 24 CFR part 50.

[53 FR 8058, Mar. 11, 1988, as amended at 56 FR 56128, Oct. 31, 1991; 60 FR 1916, Jan. 5, 1995; 60 FR 16379, Mar. 30, 1995]

§ 570.510 Transferring projects from urban counties to metropolitan cities.

Section 106(c)(3) of the Act authorizes the Secretary to transfer unobligated grant funds from an urban county to a new metropolitan city, provided: the city was an included unit of general local government in the urban county immediately before its qualification as a metropolitan city; the funds to be transferred were received by the county before the qualification of the city as a metropolitan city; the funds to be transferred had been programmed by the urban county for use in the city before such qualification; and the city and county agree to transfer responsibility for the administration of the funds being transferred from the county's letter of credit to the city's letter of credit. The following rules apply to the transfer of responsibility for an activity from an urban county to the new metropolitan city.

(a) The urban county and the metropolitan city must execute a legally binding agreement which shall specify:

(1) The amount of funds to be transferred from the urban county's letter of

credit to the metropolitan city's letter of credit;

(2) The activities to be carried out by the city with the funds being transferred;

(3) The county's responsibility for all expenditures and unliquidated obligations associated with the activities before the time of transfer, including a statement that responsibility for all audit and monitoring findings associated with those expenditures and obligations shall remain with the county;

(4) The responsibility of the metropolitan city for all other audit and monitoring findings;

(5) How program income (if any) from the activities specified shall be divided between the metropolitan city and the urban county; and

(6) Such other provisions as may be required by HUD.

(b) Upon receipt of a request for the transfer of funds from an urban county to a metropolitan city and a copy of the executed agreement, HUD, in consultation with the Department of the Treasury, shall establish a date upon which the funds shall be transferred from the letter of credit of the urban county to the letter of credit of the metropolitan city, and shall take all necessary actions to effect the requested transfer of funds.

(c) HUD shall notify the metropolitan city and urban county of any special audit and monitoring rules which apply to the transferred funds when the date of the transfer is communicated to the city and the county.

§ 570.511 Use of escrow accounts for rehabilitation of privately owned residential property.

(a) *Limitations.* A recipient may withdraw funds from its letter of credit for immediate deposit into an escrow account for use in funding loans and grants for the rehabilitation of privately owned residential property under § 570.202(a)(1). The following additional limitations apply to the use of escrow accounts for residential rehabilitation loans and grants closed after September 7, 1990:

(1) The use of escrow accounts under this section is limited to loans and grants for the rehabilitation of primarily residential properties containing no more than four dwelling units (and accessory neighborhood-scale non-residential space within the same structure, if any, *e.g.*, a store front below a dwelling unit).

(2) An escrow account shall not be used unless the contract between the property owner and the contractor selected to do the rehabilitation work specifically provides that payment to the contractor shall be made through an escrow account maintained by the recipient, by a subrecipient as defined in § 570.500(c), by a public agency designated under § 570.501(a), or by an agent under a procurement contact governed by the requirements of 24 CFR 85.36. No deposit to the escrow account shall be made until after the contract has been executed between the property owner and the rehabilitation contractor.

(3) All funds withdrawn under this section shall be deposited into one interest earning account with a financial institution. Separate bank accounts shall not be established for individual loans and grants.

(4) The amount of funds deposited into an escrow account shall be limited to the amount expected to be disbursed within 10 working days from the date of deposit. If the escrow account, for whatever reason, at any time contains funds exceeding 10 days cash needs, the grantee immediately shall transfer the excess funds to its program account. In the program account, the excess funds shall be treated as funds erroneously drawn in accordance with the requirements of U.S. Treasury Financial Manual, paragraph 6–2075.30.

(5) Funds deposited into an escrow account shall be used only to pay the actual costs of rehabilitation incurred by the owner under the contract with a private contractor. Other eligible costs related to the rehabilitation loan or grant, *e.g.*, the recipient's administrative costs under § 570.206 or rehabilitation services costs under § 570.202(b)(9), are not permissible uses of escrowed funds. Such other eligible rehabilitation costs shall be paid under normal CDBG payment procedures (*e.g.*, from withdrawals of grant funds under the recipient's letter of credit with the Treasury).

(b) *Interest.* Interest earned on escrow accounts established in accordance with this section, less any service charges for the account, shall be remitted to HUD at least quarterly but not more frequently than monthly. Interest earned on escrow accounts is not required to be remitted to HUD to the extent the interest is attributable to the investment of program income.

(c) *Remedies for noncompliance.* If HUD determines that a recipient has failed to use an escrow account in accordance with this section, HUD may, in addition to imposing any other sanctions provided for under this part, require the recipient to discontinue the use of escrow accounts, in whole or in part.

[55 FR 32369, Aug. 8, 1990]

§ 570.512 [Reserved]

§ 570.513 Lump sum drawdown for financing of property rehabilitation activities.

Subject to the conditions prescribed in this section, recipients may draw funds from the letter of credit in a lump sum to establish a rehabilitation fund in one or more private financial institutions for the purpose of financing the rehabilitation of privately owned properties. The fund may be used in conjunction with various rehabilitation financing techniques, including loans, interest subsidies, loan guarantees, loan reserves, or such other uses as may be approved by HUD consistent with the objectives of this section. The fund may also be used for making grants, but only for the purpose of leveraging non-CDBG funds for the rehabilitaton of the same property.

(a) *Limitation on drawdown of grant funds.* (1) The funds that a recipient deposits to a rehabilitation fund shall not exceed the grant amount that the recipient reasonably expects will be required, together with anticipated program income from interest and loan repayments, for the rehabilitation activities during the period specified in the agreement to undertake activities, based on either:

(i) Prior level of rehabilitation activity; or

(ii) Rehabilitation staffing and management capacity during the period specified in the agreement to undertake activities.

(2) No grant funds may be deposited under this section solely for the purpose of investment, notwithstanding that the interest or other income is to be used for the rehabilitation activities.

(3) The recipient's rehabilitation program administrative costs and the administrative costs of the financial institution may not be funded through lump sum drawdown. Such costs must be paid from periodic letter of credit withdrawals in accordance with standard procedures or from program income, other than program income generated by the lump sum distribution.

(b) *Standards to be met.* The following standards shall apply to all lump sum drawdowns of CDBG funds for rehabilitation:

(1) *Eligible rehabilitation activities.* The rehabilitation fund shall be used to finance the rehabilitation of privately owned properties eligible under the general policies in § 570.200 and the specific provisions of either § 570.202, including the acquisition of properties for rehabilitation, or § 570.203.

(2) *Requirements for agreement.* The recipient shall execute a written agreement with one or more private financial institutions for the operation of the rehabilitation fund. The agreement shall specify the obligations and responsibilities of the parties, the terms and conditions on which CDBG funds are to be deposited and used or returned, the anticipated level of rehabilitation activities by the financial institution, the rate of interest and other benefits to be provided by the financial institution in return for the lump sum deposit, and such other terms as are necessary for compliance with the provisions of this section. Upon execution of the agreement, a copy must be provided to the HUD field office for its record and use in monitoring. Any modifications made during the term of the agreement must also be provided to HUD.

(3) *Period to undertake activities.* The agreement must provide that the rehabilitation fund may only be used for authorized activities during a period of no more than two years. The lump sum

deposit shall be made only after the agreement is fully executed.

(4) *Time limit on use of deposited funds.* Use of the deposited funds for rehabilitation financing assistance must start (e.g., first loan must be made, subsidized or guaranteed) within 45 days of the deposit. In addition, substantial disbursements from the fund must occur within 180 days of the receipt of the deposit. (Where CDBG funds are used as a guarantee, the funds that must be substantially disbursed are the guaranteed funds.) For a recipient with an agreement specifying two years to undertake activities, the disbursement of 25 percent of the fund (deposit plus any interest earned) within 180 days will be regarded as meeting this requirement. If a recipient with an agreement specifying two years to undertake activities determines that it has had substantial disbursement from the fund within the 180 days although it had not met this 25 percent threshold, the justification for the recipient's determination shall be included in the program file. Should use of deposited funds not start within 45 days, or substantial disbursement from such fund not occur within 180 days, the recipient may be required by HUD to return all or part of the deposited funds to the recipient's letter of credit.

(5) *Program activity.* Recipients shall review the level of program activity on a yearly basis. Where activity is substantially below that anticipated, program funds shall be returned to the recipient's letter of credit.

(6) *Termination of agreement.* In the case of substantial failure by a private financial institution to comply with the terms of a lump sum drawdown agreement, the recipient shall terminate its agreement, provide written justification for the action, withdraw all unobligated deposited funds from the private financial institution, and return the funds to the recipient's letter of credit.

(7) *Return of unused deposits.* At the end of the period specified in the agreement for undertaking activities, all unobligated deposited funds shall be returned to the recipient's letter of credit unless the recipient enters into a new agreement conforming to the requirements of this section. In addition, the recipient shall reserve the right to withdraw any unobligated deposited funds required by HUD in the exercise of corrective or remedial actions authorized under §570.910(b), §570.911, §570.912 or §570.913.

(8) *Rehabilitation loans made with non-CDBG funds.* If the deposited funds or program income derived from deposited funds are used to subsidize or guarantee repayment of rehabilitation loans made with non-CDBG funds, or to provide a supplemental loan or grant to the borrower of the non-CDBG funds, the rehabilitation activities are considered to be CDBG-assisted activities subject to the requirements applicable to such activities, except that repayment of non-CDBG funds shall not be treated as program income.

(9) *Provision of consideration.* In consideration for the lump sum deposit by the recipient in a private financial institution, the deposit must result in appropriate benefits in support of the recipient's local rehabilitation program. Minimum requirements for such benefits are:

(i) Grantees shall require the financial institution to pay interest on the lump sum deposit.

(A) The interest rate paid by the financial institution shall be no more than three points below the rate on one year Treasury obligations at constant maturity.

(B) When an agreement sets a fixed interest rate for the entire term of the agreement, the rate should be based on the rate at the time the agreement is excuted.

(C) The agreement may provide for an interest rate that would fluctuate periodically during the term of the agreement, but at no time shall the rate be established at more than three points below the rate on one year Treasury obligations at constant maturity.

(ii) In addition to the payment of interest, at least one of the following benefits must be provided by the financial institution:

(A) Leverage of the deposited funds so that the financial institution commits private funds for loans in the rehabilitation program in an amount substantially in excess of the amount of the lump sum deposit;

(B) Commitment of private funds by the financial institution for rehabilitation loans at below market interest rates, at higher than normal risk, or with longer than normal repayment periods; or

(C) Provision of administrative services in support of the rehabilitation program by the participating financial institution at no cost or at lower than actual cost.

(c) *Program income.* Interest earned on lump sum deposits and payments on loans made from such deposits are program income and, during the period of the agreement, shall be used for rehabilitation activities under the provisions of this section.

(d) *Outstanding findings.* Notwithstanding any other provision of this section, no recipient shall enter into a new agreement during any period of time in which an audit or monitoring finding on a previous lump sum drawdown agreement remains unresolved.

(e) *Prior notification.* The recipient shall provide the HUD field office with written notification of the amount of funds to be distributed to a private financial institution before distribution under the provisions of this section.

(f) *Recordkeeping requirements.* The recipient shall maintain in its files a copy of the written agreement and related documents establishing conformance with this section and concerning performance by a financial institution in accordance with the agreement.

Subpart K—Other Program Requirements

SOURCE: 53 FR 34456, Sept. 6, 1988, unless otherwise noted.

§ 570.600 General.

(a) This subpart K enumerates laws that the Secretary will treat as applicable to grants made under section 106 of the Act, other than grants to states made pursuant to section 106(d) of the Act, for purposes of the Secretary's determinations under section 104(e)(1) of the Act, including statutes expressly made applicable by the Act and certain other statutes and Executive Orders for which the Secretary has enforcement responsibility. This subpart K applies to grants made under the Insular Areas Program in § 570.405 and § 570.440 with the exception of § 570.612. The absence of mention herein of any other statute for which the Secretary does not have direct enforcement responsibility is not intended to be taken as an indication that, in the Secretary's opinion, such statute or Executive Order is not applicable to activities assisted under the Act. For laws that the Secretary will treat as applicable to grants made to states under section 106(d) of the Act for purposes of the determination required to be made by the Secretary pursuant to section 104(e)(2) of the Act, see § 570.487.

(b) This subpart also sets forth certain additional program requirements which the Secretary has determined to be applicable to grants provided under the Act as a matter of administrative discretion.

(c) In addition to grants made pursuant to section 106(b) and 106(d)(2)(B) of the Act (subparts D and F, respectively), the requirements of this subpart K are applicable to grants made pursuant to sections 107 and 119 of the Act (subparts E and G, respectively), and to loans guaranteed pursuant to subpart M.

[53 FR 34456, Sept. 6, 1988, as amended at 61 FR 11477, Mar. 20, 1996; 72 FR 12536, Mar. 15, 2007]

§ 570.601 Public Law 88–352 and Public Law 90–284; affirmatively furthering fair housing; Executive Order 11063.

(a) The following requirements apply according to sections 104(b) and 107 of the Act:

(1) Public Law 88–352, which is title VI of the Civil Rights Act of 1964 (42 U.S.C. 2000d *et seq.*), and implementing regulations in 24 CFR part 1.

(2) Public Law 90–284, which is the Fair Housing Act (42 U.S.C. 3601–3620). In accordance with the Fair Housing Act, the Secretary requires that grantees administer all programs and activities related to housing and community development in a manner to affirmatively further the policies of the Fair Housing Act. Furthermore, in accordance with section 104(b)(2) of the Act, for each community receiving a grant

§ 570.602

under subpart D of this part, the certification that the grantee will affirmatively further fair housing shall specifically require the grantee to assume the responsibility of fair housing planning by conducting an analysis to identify impediments to fair housing choice within its jurisdiction, taking appropriate actions to overcome the effects of any impediments identified through that analysis, and maintaining records reflecting the analysis and actions in this regard.

(b) Executive Order 11063, as amended by Executive Order 12259 (3 CFR, 1959–1963 Comp., p. 652; 3 CFR, 1980 Comp., p. 307) (Equal Opportunity in Housing), and implementing regulations in 24 CFR part 107, also apply.

[61 FR 11477, Mar. 20, 1996]

§ 570.602 Section 109 of the Act.

Section 109 of the Act requires that no person in the United States shall on the grounds of race, color, national origin, religion, or sex be excluded from participation in, be denied the benefits of, or be subjected to discrimination under any program or activity receiving Federal financial assistance made available pursuant to the Act. Section 109 also directs that the prohibitions against discrimination on the basis of age under the Age Discrimination Act and the prohibitions against discrimination on the basis of disability under Section 504 shall apply to programs or activities receiving Federal financial assistance under Title I programs. The policies and procedures necessary to ensure enforcement of section 109 are codified in 24 CFR part 6.

[64 FR 3802, Jan. 25, 1999]

§ 570.603 Labor standards.

(a) Section 110(a) of the Act contains labor standards that apply to nonvolunteer labor financed in whole or in part with assistance received under the Act. In accordance with section 110(a) of the Act, the Contract Work Hours and Safety Standards Act (40 U.S.C. 327 et seq.) also applies. However, these requirements apply to the rehabilitation of residential property only if such property contains not less than 8 units.

(b) The regulations in 24 CFR part 70 apply to the use of volunteers.

[61 FR 11477, Mar. 20, 1996]

§ 570.604 Environmental standards.

For purposes of section 104(g) of the Act, the regulations in 24 CFR part 58 specify the other provisions of law which further the purposes of the National Environmental Policy Act of 1969, and the procedures by which grantees must fulfill their environmental responsibilities. In certain cases, grantees assume these environmental review, decisionmaking, and action responsibilities by execution of grant agreements with the Secretary.

[61 FR 11477, Mar. 20, 1996]

§ 570.605 National Flood Insurance Program.

Notwithstanding the date of HUD approval of the recipient's application (or, in the case of grants made under subpart D of this part or HUD-administered small cities recipients in Hawaii, the date of submission of the grantee's consolidated plan, in accordance with 24 CFR part 91), section 202(a) of the Flood Disaster Protection Act of 1973 (42 U.S.C. 4106) and the regulations in 44 CFR parts 59 through 79 apply to funds provided under this part 570.

[61 FR 11477, Mar. 20, 1996]

§ 570.606 Displacement, relocation, acquisition, and replacement of housing.

(a) *General policy for minimizing displacement.* Consistent with the other goals and objectives of this part, grantees (or States or state recipients, as applicable) shall assure that they have taken all reasonable steps to minimize the displacement of persons (families, individuals, businesses, nonprofit organizations, and farms) as a result of activities assisted under this part.

(b) *Relocation assistance for displaced persons at URA levels.* (1) A displaced person shall be provided with relocation assistance at the levels described in, and in accordance with the requirements of 49 CFR part 24, which contains the government-wide regulations implementing the Uniform Relocation

Assistance and Real Property Acquisition Policies Act of 1970 (URA) (42 U.S.C. 4601–4655).

(2) *Displaced person.* (i) For purposes of paragraph (b) of this section, the term "*displaced person*" means any person (family, individual, business, nonprofit organization, or farm) that moves from real property, or moves his or her personal property from real property, permanently and involuntarily, as a direct result of rehabilitation, demolition, or acquisition for an activity assisted under this part. A permanent, involuntary move for an assisted activity includes a permanent move from real property that is made:

(A) After notice by the grantee (or the state recipient, if applicable) to move permanently from the property, if the move occurs after the initial official submission to HUD (or the State, as applicable) for grant, loan, or loan guarantee funds under this part that are later provided or granted.

(B) After notice by the property owner to move permanently from the property, if the move occurs after the date of the submission of a request for financial assistance by the property owner (or person in control of the site) that is later approved for the requested activity.

(C) Before the date described in paragraph (b)(2)(i)(A) or (B) of this section, if either HUD or the grantee (or State, as applicable) determines that the displacement directly resulted from acquisition, rehabilitation, or demolition for the requested activity.

(D) After the "initiation of negotiations" if the person is the tenant-occupant of a dwelling unit and any one of the following three situations occurs:

(*1*) The tenant has not been provided with a reasonable opportunity to lease and occupy a suitable decent, safe, and sanitary dwelling in the same building/complex upon the completion of the project, including a monthly rent that does not exceed the greater of the tenant's monthly rent and estimated average utility costs before the initiation of negotiations or 30 percent of the household's average monthly gross income; or

(*2*) The tenant is required to relocate temporarily for the activity but the tenant is not offered payment for all reasonable out-of-pocket expenses incurred in connection with the temporary relocation, including the cost of moving to and from the temporary location and any increased housing costs, or other conditions of the temporary relocation are not reasonable; and the tenant does not return to the building/complex; or

(*3*) The tenant is required to move to another unit in the building/complex, but is not offered reimbursement for all reasonable out-of-pocket expenses incurred in connection with the move.

(ii) Notwithstanding the provisions of paragraph (b)(2)(i) of this section, the term "*displaced person-*" does not include:

(A) A person who is evicted for cause based upon serious or repeated violations of material terms of the lease or occupancy agreement. To exclude a person on this basis, the grantee (or State or state recipient, as applicable) must determine that the eviction was not undertaken for the purpose of evading the obligation to provide relocation assistance under this section;

(B) A person who moves into the property after the date of the notice described in paragraph (b)(2)(i)(A) or (B) of this section, but who received a written notice of the expected displacement before occupancy.

(C) A person who is not displaced as described in 49 CFR 24.2(g)(2).

(D) A person who the grantee (or State, as applicable) determines is not displaced as a direct result of the acquisition, rehabilitation, or demolition for an assisted activity. To exclude a person on this basis, HUD must concur in that determination.

(iii) A grantee (or State or state recipient, as applicable) may, at any time, request HUD to determine whether a person is a displaced person under this section.

(3) *Initiation of negotiations.* For purposes of determining the type of replacement housing assistance to be provided under paragraph (b) of this section, if the displacement is the direct result of privately undertaken rehabilitation, demolition, or acquisition of real property, the term "*initiation of negotiations*" means the execution of the grant or loan agreement between

§ 570.607

the grantee (or State or state recipient, as applicable) and the person owning or controlling the real property.

(c) *Residential antidisplacement and relocation assistance plan.* The grantee shall comply with the requirements of 24 CFR part 42, subpart B.

(d) *Optional relocation assistance.* Under section 105(a)(11) of the Act, the grantee may provide (or the State may permit the state recipient to provide, as applicable) relocation payments and other relocation assistance to persons displaced by activities that are not subject to paragraph (b) or (c) of this section. The grantee may also provide (or the State may also permit the state recipient to provide, as applicable) relocation assistance to persons receiving assistance under paragraphs (b) or (c) of this section at levels in excess of those required by these paragraphs. Unless such assistance is provided under State or local law, the grantee (or state recipient, as applicable) shall provide such assistance only upon the basis of a written determination that the assistance is appropriate (see, e.g., 24 CFR 570.201(i), as applicable). The grantee (or state recipient, as applicable) must adopt a written policy available to the public that describes the relocation assistance that the grantee (or state recipient, as applicable) has elected to provide and that provides for equal relocation assistance within each class of displaced persons.

(e) *Acquisition of real property.* The acquisition of real property for an assisted activity is subject to 49 CFR part 24, subpart B.

(f) *Appeals.* If a person disagrees with the determination of the grantee (or the state recipient, as applicable) concerning the person's eligibility for, or the amount of, a relocation payment under this section, the person may file a written appeal of that determination with the grantee (or state recipient, as applicable). The appeal procedures to be followed are described in 49 CFR 24.10. In addition, a low- or moderate-income household that has been displaced from a dwelling may file a written request for review of the grantee's decision to the HUD Field Office. For purposes of the State CDBG program, a low- or moderate-income household may file a written request for review of the state recipient's decision with the State.

(g) *Responsibility of grantee or State.* (1) The grantee (or State, if applicable) is responsible for ensuring compliance with the requirements of this section, notwithstanding any third party's contractual obligation to the grantee to comply with the provisions of this section. For purposes of the State CDBG program, the State shall require state recipients to certify that they will comply with the requirements of this section.

(2) The cost of assistance required under this section may be paid from local public funds, funds provided under this part, or funds available from other sources.

(3) The grantee (or State and state recipient, as applicable) must maintain records in sufficient detail to demonstrate compliance with the provisions of this section.

(Approved by the Office of Management and Budget under OMB control number 2506–0102)

[61 FR 11477, Mar. 20, 1996, as amended at 61 FR 51760, Oct. 3, 1996]

§ 570.607 **Employment and contracting opportunities.**

To the extent that they are otherwise applicable, grantees shall comply with:

(a) Executive Order 11246, as amended by Executive Orders 11375, 11478, *12086*, and 12107 (3 CFR 1964–1965 Comp. p. 339; 3 CFR, 1966–1970 Comp., p. 684; 3 CFR, 1966–1970., p. 803; 3 CFR, 1978 Comp., p. 230; 3 CFR, 1978 Comp., p. 264 (Equal Employment Opportunity), and Executive Order 13279 (Equal Protection of the Laws for Faith-Based and Community Organizations), 67 FR 77141, 3 CFR, 2002 Comp., p. 258; and the implementing regulations at 41 CFR chapter 60; and

(b) Section 3 of the Housing and Urban Development Act of 1968 (12 U.S.C. 1701u) and implementing regulations at 24 CFR part 135.

[68 FR 56405, Sept. 30, 2003]

§ 570.608 **Lead-based paint.**

The Lead-Based Paint Poisoning Prevention Act (42 U.S.C. 4821–4846), the Residential Lead-Based Paint Hazard Reduction Act of 1992 (42 U.S.C. 4851–4856), and implementing regulations at part 35, subparts A, B, J, K, and R of this part apply to activities under this program.

[64 FR 50226, Sept. 15, 1999]

§ 570.609 Use of debarred, suspended or ineligible contractors or subrecipients.

The requirements set forth in 24 CFR part 5 apply to this program.

[61 FR 5209, Feb. 9, 1996]

§ 570.610 Uniform administrative requirements and cost principles.

The recipient, its agencies or instrumentalities, and subrecipients shall comply with the policies, guidelines, and requirements of 24 CFR part 85 and OMB Circulars A-87, A-110 (implemented at 24 CFR part 84), A-122, A-133 (implemented at 24 CFR part 45), and A-128[2] (implemented at 24 CFR part 44), as applicable, as they relate to the acceptance and use of Federal funds under this part. The applicable sections of 24 CFR parts 84 and 85 are set forth at § 570.502.

[60 FR 56916, Nov. 9, 1995]

§ 570.611 Conflict of interest.

(a) *Applicability.* (1) In the procurement of supplies, equipment, construction, and services by recipients and by subrecipients, the conflict of interest provisions in 24 CFR 85.36 and 24 CFR 84.42, respectively, shall apply.

(2) In all cases not governed by 24 CFR 85.36 and 84.42, the provisions of this section shall apply. Such cases include the acquisition and disposition of real property and the provision of assistance by the recipient or by its subrecipients to individuals, businesses, and other private entities under eligible activities that authorize such assistance (e.g., rehabilitation, preservation, and other improvements of private properties or facilities pursuant to § 570.202; or grants, loans, and other assistance to businesses, individuals, and other private entities pursuant to § 570.203, 570.204, 570.455, or 570.703(i)).

(b) *Conflicts prohibited.* The general rule is that no persons described in paragraph (c) of this section who exercise or have exercised any functions or responsibilities with respect to CDBG activities assisted under this part, or who are in a position to participate in a decisionmaking process or gain inside information with regard to such activities, may obtain a financial interest or benefit from a CDBG-assisted activity, or have a financial interest in any contract, subcontract, or agreement with respect to a CDBG-assisted activity, or with respect to the proceeds of the CDBG-assisted activity, either for themselves or those with whom they have business or immediate family ties, during their tenure or for one year thereafter. For the UDAG program, the above restrictions shall apply to all activities that are a part of the UDAG project, and shall cover any such financial interest or benefit during, or at any time after, such person's tenure.

(c) *Persons covered.* The conflict of interest provisions of paragraph (b) of this section apply to any person who is an employee, agent, consultant, officer, or elected official or appointed official of the recipient, or of any designated public agencies, or of subrecipients that are receiving funds under this part.

(d) *Exceptions.* Upon the written request of the recipient, HUD may grant an exception to the provisions of paragraph (b) of this section on a case-by-case basis when it has satisfactorily met the threshold requirements of (d)(1) of this section, taking into account the cumulative effects of paragraph (d)(2) of this section.

(1) *Threshold requirements.* HUD will consider an exception only after the recipient has provided the following documentation:

(i) A disclosure of the nature of the conflict, accompanied by an assurance that there has been public disclosure of the conflict and a description of how the public disclosure was made; and

(ii) An opinion of the recipient's attorney that the interest for which the exception is sought would not violate State or local law.

(2) *Factors to be considered for exceptions.* In determining whether to grant a requested exception after the recipient has satisfactorily met the requirements of paragraph (d)(1) of this section, HUD shall conclude that such an

---

[2] See footnote 1 at § 570.200(a)(5).

exception will serve to further the purposes of the Act and the effective and efficient administration of the recipient's program or project, taking into account the cumulative effect of the following factors, as applicable:

(i) Whether the exception would provide a significant cost benefit or an essential degree of expertise to the program or project that would otherwise not be available;

(ii) Whether an opportunity was provided for open competitive bidding or negotiation;

(iii) Whether the person affected is a member of a group or class of low- or moderate-income persons intended to be the beneficiaries of the assisted activity, and the exception will permit such person to receive generally the same interests or benefits as are being made available or provided to the group or class;

(iv) Whether the affected person has withdrawn from his or her functions or responsibilities, or the decisionmaking process with respect to the specific assisted activity in question;

(v) Whether the interest or benefit was present before the affected person was in a position as described in paragraph (b) of this section;

(vi) Whether undue hardship will result either to the recipient or the person affected when weighed against the public interest served by avoiding the prohibited conflict; and

(vii) Any other relevant considerations.

[60 FR 56916, Nov. 9, 1995]

§ 570.612 Executive Order 12372.

(a) *General.* Executive Order 12372, Intergovernmental Review of Federal Programs, and the Department's implementing regulations at 24 CFR part 52, allow each State to establish its own process for review and comment on proposed Federal financial assistance programs.

(b) *Applicability.* Executive Order 12372 applies to the CDBG Entitlement program and the UDAG program. The Executive Order applies to all activities proposed to be assisted under UDAG, but it applies to the Entitlement program only where a grantee proposes to use funds for the planning or construction (reconstruction or installation) of water or sewer facilities. Such facilities include storm sewers as well as all sanitary sewers, but do not include water and sewer lines connecting a structure to the lines in the public right-of-way or easement. It is the responsibility of the grantee to initiate the Executive Order review process if it proposes to use its CDBG or UDAG funds for activities subject to review.

§ 570.613 Eligibility restrictions for certain resident aliens.

(a) *Restriction.* Certain newly legalized aliens, as described in 24 CFR part 49, are not eligible to apply for benefits under covered activities funded by the programs listed in paragraph (e) of this section. "Benefits" under this section means financial assistance, public services, jobs and access to new or rehabilitated housing and other facilities made available under covered activities funded by programs listed in paragraph (e) of this section. "Benefits" do not include relocation services and payments to which displacees are entitled by law.

(b) *Covered activities.* "Covered activities" under this section means activities meeting the requirements of § 570.208(a) that either:

(1) Have income eligibility requirements limiting the benefits exclusively to low and moderate income persons; or

(2) Are targeted geographically or otherwise to primarily benefit low and moderate income persons (excluding activities serving the public at large, such as sewers, roads, sidewalks, and parks), and that provide benefits to persons on the basis of an application.

(c) *Limitation on coverage.* The restrictions under this section apply only to applicants for new benefits not being received by covered resident aliens as of the effective date of this section.

(d) *Compliance.* Compliance can be accomplished by obtaining certification as provided in 24 CFR 49.20.

(e) *Programs affected.* (1) The Community Development Block Grant program for small cities, administered under subpart F of part 570 of this title until closeout of the recipient's grant.

(2) The Community Development Block Grant program for entitlement

grants, administered under subpart D of part 570 of this title.

(3) The Community Development Block Grant program for States, administered under subpart I of part 570 of this title until closeout of the unit of general local government's grant by the State.

(4) The Urban Development Action Grants program, administered under subpart G of part 570 of this title until closeout of the recipient's grant.

[55 FR 18494, May 2, 1990]

§ 570.614 Architectural Barriers Act and the Americans with Disabilities Act.

(a) The Architectural Barriers Act of 1968 (42 U.S.C. 4151–4157) requires certain Federal and Federally funded buildings and other facilities to be designed, constructed, or altered in accordance with standards that insure accessibility to, and use by, physically handicapped people. A building or facility designed, constructed, or altered with funds allocated or reallocated under this part after December 11, 1995, and that meets the definition of "residential structure" as defined in 24 CFR 40.2 or the definition of "building" as defined in 41 CFR 101–19.602(a) is subject to the requirements of the Architectural Barriers Act of 1968 (42 U.S.C. 4151–4157) and shall comply with the Uniform Federal Accessibility Standards (appendix A to 24 CFR part 40 for residential structures, and appendix A to 41 CFR part 101–19, subpart 101–19.6, for general type buildings).

(b) The Americans with Disabilities Act (42 U.S.C. 12131; 47 U.S.C. 155, 201, 218 and 225) (ADA) provides comprehensive civil rights to individuals with disabilities in the areas of employment, public accommodations, State and local government services, and telecommunications. It further provides that discrimination includes a failure to design and construct facilities for first occupancy no later than January 26, 1993, that are readily accessible to and usable by individuals with disabilities. Further, the ADA requires the removal of architectural barriers and communication barriers that are structural in nature in existing facilities, where such removal is readily achievable—that is, easily accomplishable and able to be carried out without much difficulty or expense.

[60 FR 56917, Nov. 9, 1995]

Subpart L [Reserved]

Subpart M—Loan Guarantees

SOURCE: 59 FR 66604, Dec. 27, 1994, unless otherwise noted.

§ 570.700 Purpose.

This subpart contains requirements governing the guarantee under section 108 of the Act of debt obligations as defined in § 570.701.

§ 570.701 Definitions.

Borrower means the public entity or its designated public agency that issues debt obligations under this subpart.

Debt obligation means a promissory note or other obligation issued by a public entity or its designated public agency and guaranteed by HUD under this subpart, or a trust certificate or other obligation offered by HUD or by a trust or other offeror approved for purposes of this subpart by HUD which is guaranteed by HUD under this subpart and is based on and backed by a trust or pool composed of notes or other obligations issued by public entities or their designated public agencies and guaranteed or eligible for guarantee by HUD under this subpart.

Designated public agency means a public agency designated by a public entity to issue debt obligations as borrower under this subpart.

Entitlement public entity means a metropolitan city or an urban county receiving a grant under subpart D of this part.

Guaranteed loan funds means the proceeds payable to the borrower from the issuance of debt obligations under this subpart.

Nonentitlement public entity means any unit of general local government in a nonentitlement area.

Public entity shall have the meaning provided for the term *"Eligible public entity"* in section 108(o) of the Act.

State-assisted public entity means a unit of general local government in a nonentitlement area which is assisted

§ 570.702

by a State as required in § 570.704(b)(9) and § 570.705(b)(2).

[59 FR 66604, Dec. 27, 1994, as amended at 61 FR 11481, Mar. 20, 1996]

§ 570.702 Eligible applicants.

The following public entities may apply for loan guarantee assistance under this subpart.

(a) Entitlement public entities.

(b) Nonentitlement public entities that are assisted in the submission of applications by States that administer the CDBG program (under subpart I of this part). Such assistance shall consist, at a minimum, of the certifications required under § 570.704(b)(9) (and actions pursuant thereto).

(c) Nonentitlement public entities eligible to apply for grant assistance under subpart F of this part.

§ 570.703 Eligible activities.

Guaranteed loan funds may be used for the following activities, provided such activities meet the requirements of § 570.200. However, guaranteed loan funds may not be used to reimburse the CDBG program account or line of credit for costs incurred by the public entity or designated public agency and paid with CDBG grant funds or program income.

(a) Acquisition of improved or unimproved real property in fee or by long-term lease, including acquisition for economic development purposes.

(b) Rehabilitation of real property owned or acquired by the public entity or its designated public agency.

(c) Payment of interest on obligations guaranteed under this subpart.

(d) Relocation payments and other relocation assistance for individuals, families, businesses, nonprofit organizations, and farm operations who must relocate permanently or temporarily as a result of an activity financed with guaranteed loan funds, where the assistance is:

(1) Required under the provisions of § 570.606(b) or (c); or

(2) Determined by the public entity to be appropriate under the provisions of § 570.606(d).

(e) Clearance, demolition, and removal, including movement of structures to other sites and remediation of properties with known or suspected environmental contamination, of buildings and improvements on real property acquired or rehabilitated pursuant to paragraphs (a) and (b) of this section. Remediation may include project-specific environmental assessment costs not otherwise eligible under § 570.205.

(f) Site preparation, including construction, reconstruction, installation of public and other site improvements, utilities or facilities (other than buildings), or remediation of properties (remediation can include project-specific environmental assessment costs not otherwise eligible under § 570.205) with known or suspected environmental contamination, which is:

(1) Related to the redevelopment or use of the real property acquired or rehabilitated pursuant to paragraphs (a) and (b) of this section, or

(2) For an economic development purpose.

(g) Payment of issuance, underwriting, servicing, trust administration and other costs associated with private sector financing of debt obligations under this subpart.

(h) Housing rehabilitation eligible under § 570.202.

(i) The following economic development activities:

(1) Activities eligible under § 570.203; and

(2) Community economic development projects eligible under § 570.204.

(j) Construction of housing by nonprofit organizations for homeownership under section 17(d) of the United States Housing Act of 1937 (Housing Development Grants Program, 24 CFR part 850) or title VI of the Housing and Community Development Act of 1987 (Nehemiah Housing Opportunity Grants Program, 24 CFR part 280).

(k) A debt service reserve to be used in accordance with requirements specified in the contract entered into pursuant to § 570.705(b)(1).

(1) Acquisition, construction, reconstruction, rehabilitation or historic preservation, or installation of public facilities (except for buildings for the general conduct of government) to the extent eligible under § 570.201(c), including public streets, sidewalks, other site improvements and public utilities, and remediation of known or suspected

environmental contamination in conjunction with these activities. Remediation may include project-specific environmental assessment costs not otherwise eligible under § 570.205.

(m) In the case of applications by public entities which are, or which contain, "colonias" as defined in section 916 of the Cranston-Gonzalez National Affordable Housing Act (42 U.S.C. 5306 note), as amended by section 810 of the Housing and Community Development Act of 1992, acquisition, construction, reconstruction, rehabilitation or installation of public works and site or other improvements which serve the colonia.

[59 FR 66604, Dec. 27, 1994, as amended at 61 FR 11481, Mar. 20, 1996; 71 FR 30036, May 24, 2006]

§ 570.704 Application requirements.

(a) *Presubmission and citizen participation requirements.* (1) Before submission of an application for loan guarantee assistance to HUD, the public entity must:

(i) Develop a proposed application that includes the following items:

(A) The community development objectives the public entity proposes to pursue with the guaranteed loan funds.

(B) The activities the public entity proposes to carry out with the guaranteed loan funds. Each activity must be described in sufficient detail, including the specific provision of § 570.703 under which it is eligible and the national objective to be met, amount of guaranteed loan funds expected to be used, and location, to allow citizens to determine the degree to which they will be affected. The proposed application must indicate which activities are expected to generate program income. The application must also describe where citizens may obtain additional information about proposed activities.

(C) A description of the pledge of grants required under § 570.705(b)(2). In the case of applications by State-assisted public entities, the description shall note that pledges of grants will be made by the State and by the public entity.

(ii) Fulfill the applicable requirements in its citizen participation plan developed in accordance with § 570.704(a)(2).

(iii) Publish community-wide its proposed application so as to afford affected citizens an opportunity to examine the application's contents and to provide comments on the proposed application.

(iv) Prepare its final application. Once the public entity has held the public hearing and published the proposed application as required by paragraphs (a)(1)(ii) and (iii) of this section, respectively, the public entity must consider any such comments and views received and, if the public entity deems appropriate, modify the proposed application. Upon completion, the public entity must make the final application available to the public. The final application must describe each activity in sufficient detail to permit a clear understanding of the nature of each activity, as well as identify the specific provision of § 570.703 under which it is eligible, the national objective to be met, and the amount of guaranteed loan funds to be used. The final application must also indicate which activities are expected to generate program income.

(v) If an application for loan guarantee assistance is to be submitted by an entitlement or nonentitlement public entity simultaneously with the public entity's submission for its grant, the public entity shall include and identify in its proposed and final consolidated plan the activities to be undertaken with the guaranteed loan funds, the national objective to be met by each of these activities, the amount of any program income expected to be received during the program year, and the amount of guaranteed loan funds to be used. The public entity shall also include in the consolidated plan a description of the pledge of grants, as required under § 570.705(b)(2). In such cases the proposed and final application requirements of paragraphs (a)(1)(i), (iii), and (iv) of this section will be deemed to have been met.

(2) *Citizen participation plan.* The public entity must develop and follow a detailed citizen participation plan and make the plan public. The plan must be completed and available before the application is submitted to HUD. The plan may be the citizen plan required for the consolidated plan, modified to include guaranteed loan funds. The

§ 570.704

public entity is not required to hold a separate public hearing for its consolidated plan and for the guaranteed loan funds to obtain citizens' views on community development and housing needs. The plan must set forth the public entity's policies and procedures for:

(i) Giving citizens timely notice of local meetings and reasonable and timely access to local meetings, information, and records relating to the public entity's proposed and actual use of guaranteed loan funds, including, but not limited to:

(A) The amount of guaranteed loan funds expected to be made available for the coming year, including program income anticipated to be generated by the activities carried out with guaranteed loan funds;

(B) The range of activities that may be undertaken with guaranteed loan funds;

(C) The estimated amount of guaranteed loan funds (including program income derived therefrom) proposed to be used for activities that will benefit low and moderate income persons;

(D) The proposed activities likely to result in displacement and the public entity's plans, consistent with the policies developed under § 570.606 for minimizing displacement of persons as a result of its proposed activities.

(ii) Providing technical assistance to groups representative of persons of low and moderate income that request assistance in developing proposals. The level and type of assistance to be provided is at the discretion of the public entity. Such assistance need not include the provision of funds to such groups.

(iii) Holding a minimum of two public hearings, each at a different stage of the public entity's program, for the purpose of obtaining the views of citizens and formulating or responding to proposals and questions. Together the hearings must address community development and housing needs, development of proposed activities and review of program performance. At least one of these hearings must be held before submission of the application to obtain the views of citizens on community development and housing needs. Reasonable notice of the hearing must be provided and the hearing must be held at times and locations convenient to potential or actual beneficiaries, with accommodation for the handicapped. The public entity must specify in its plan how it will meet the requirement for a hearing at times and locations convenient to potential or actual beneficiaries.

(iv) Meeting the needs of non-English speaking residents in the case of public hearings where a significant number of non-English speaking residents can reasonably be expected to participate.

(v) Providing affected citizens with reasonable advance notice of, and opportunity to comment on, proposed activities not previously included in an application and activities which are proposed to be deleted or substantially changed in terms of purpose, scope, location, or beneficiaries. The criteria the public entity will use to determine what constitutes a substantial change for this purpose must be described in the citizen participation plan.

(vi) Responding to citizens' complaints and grievances, including the procedures that citizens must follow when submitting complaints and grievances. The public entity's policies and procedures must provide for timely written answers to written complaints and grievances within 15 working days of the receipt of the complaint, where practicable.

(vii) Encouraging citizen participation, particularly by low and moderate income persons who reside in slum or blighted areas, and other areas in which guaranteed loan funds are proposed to be used.

(b) *Submission requirements.* An application for loan guarantee assistance may be submitted at any time. The application (or consolidated plan) shall be submitted to the appropriate HUD Office and shall be accompanied by the following:

(1) A description of how each of the activities to be carried out with the guaranteed loan funds meets one of the criteria in § 570.208.

(2) A schedule for repayment of the loan which identifies the sources of repayment, together with a statement identifying the entity that will act as borrower and issue the debt obligations.

(3) A certification providing assurance that the public entity possesses the legal authority to make the pledge of grants required under § 570.705(b)(2).

(4) A certification providing assurance that the public entity has made efforts to obtain financing for activities described in the application without the use of the loan guarantee, the public entity will maintain documentation of such efforts for the term of the loan guarantee, and the public entity cannot complete such financing consistent with the timely execution of the program plans without such guarantee.

(5)–(6) [Reserved]

(7) The anti-lobbying statement required under 24 CFR part 87 (appendix A).

(8) Certifications by the public entity that:

(i) It possesses the legal authority to submit the application for assistance under this subpart and to use the guaranteed loan funds in accordance with the requirements of this subpart.

(ii) Its governing body has duly adopted or passed as an official act a resolution, motion or similar official action:

(A) Authorizing the person identified as the official representative of the public entity to submit the application and amendments thereto and all understandings and assurances contained therein, and directing and authorizing the person identified as the official representative of the public entity to act in connection with the application to provide such additional information as may be required; and

(B) Authorizing such official representative to execute such documents as may be required in order to implement the application and issue debt obligations pursuant thereto (provided that the authorization required by this paragraph (B) may be given by the local governing body after submission of the application but prior to execution of the contract required by § 570.705(b);

(iii) Before submission of its application to HUD, the public entity has:

(A) Furnished citizens with information required by § 570.704(a)(2)(i);

(B) Held at least one public hearing to obtain the views of citizens on community development and housing needs; and

(C) Prepared its application in accordance with § 570.704(a)(1)(iv) and made the application available to the public.

(iv) It is following a detailed citizen participation plan which meets the requirements described in § 570.704(a)(2).

(v) The public entity will affirmatively further fair housing, and the guaranteed loan funds will be administered in compliance with:

(A) Title VI of the Civil Rights Act of 1964 (42 U.S.C. 2000d et seq.); and

(B) The Fair Housing Act (42 U.S.C. 3601–3619).

(vi)(A) (For entitlement public entities only.) In the aggregate, at least 70 percent of all CDBG funds, as defined at § 570.3, to be expended during the one, two, or three consecutive years specified by the public entity for its CDBG program will be for activities which benefit low and moderate income persons, as described in criteria at § 570.208(a).

(B) (For nonentitlement public entities eligible under subpart F of this part only.) It will comply with primary and national objectives requirements, as applicable under subpart F of this part.

(vii) It will comply with the requirements governing displacement, relocation, real property acquisition, and the replacement of low and moderate income housing described in § 570.606.

(viii) It will comply with the requirements of § 570.200(c)(2) with regard to the use of special assessments to recover the capital costs of activities assisted with guaranteed loan funds.

(ix) (Where applicable, the public entity may also include the following additional certification.) It lacks sufficient resources from funds provided under this subpart or program income to allow it to comply with the provisions of § 570.200(c)(2), and it must therefore assess properties owned and occupied by moderate income persons, to recover the guaranteed loan funded portion of the capital cost without paying such assessments in their behalf from guaranteed loan funds.

(x) It will comply with the other provisions of the Act and with other applicable laws.

(9) In the case of an application submitted by a State-assisted public entity, certifications by the State that:

(i) It agrees to make the pledge of grants required under § 570.705(b)(2).

(ii) It possesses the legal authority to make such pledge.

(iii) At least 70 percent of the aggregate use of CDBG grant funds received by the State, guaranteed loan funds, and program income during the one, two, or three consecutive years specified by the State for its CDBG program will be for activities that benefit low and moderate income persons.

(iv) It agrees to assume the responsibilities described in § 570.710.

(c) *HUD review and approval of applications.* (1) HUD will normally accept the certifications submitted with the application. HUD may, however, consider relevant information which challenges the certifications and require additional information or assurances from the public entity or State as warranted by such information.

(2) The HUD Office shall review the application for compliance with requirements specified in this subpart and forward the application together with its recommendation for approval or disapproval of the requested loan guarantee to HUD Headquarters.

(3) HUD may disapprove an application, or may approve loan guarantee assistance for an amount less than requested, for any of the following reasons:

(i) HUD determines that the guarantee constitutes an unacceptable financial risk. Factors that will be considered in assessing financial risk shall include, but not be limited to, the following:

(A) The length of the proposed repayment period;

(B) The ratio of expected annual debt service requirements to expected annual grant amount;

(C) The likelihood that the public entity or State will continue to receive grant assistance under this part during the proposed repayment period;

(D) The public entity's ability to furnish adequate security pursuant to § 570.705(b), and

(E) The amount of program income the proposed activities are reasonably estimated to contribute toward repayment of the guaranteed loan.

(ii) The requested loan amount exceeds any of the limitations specified under § 570.705(a).

(iii) Funds are not available in the amount requested.

(iv) The performance of the public entity, its designated public agency or State under this part is unacceptable.

(v) Activities to be undertaken with the guaranteed loan funds are not eligible under § 570.703.

(vi) Activities to be undertaken with the guaranteed loan funds do not meet the criteria in § 570.208 for compliance with one of the national objectives of the Act.

(4) HUD will notify the public entity in writing that the loan guarantee request has either been approved, reduced or disapproved. If the request is reduced or disapproved, the public entity shall be informed of the specific reasons for reduction or disapproval. If the request is approved, HUD shall issue an offer of commitment to guarantee debt obligations of the borrower identified in the application subject to compliance with this part, including the requirements under § 570.705(b), (d), (g) and (h) for securing and issuing debt obligations, the conditions for release of funds described in paragraph (d) of this section, and such other conditions as HUD may specify in the commitment documents in a particular case.

(5) *Amendments.* If the public entity wishes to carry out an activity not previously described in its application or to substantially change the purpose, scope, location, or beneficiaries of an activity, the amendment must be approved by HUD. Amendments by State-assisted public entities must also be approved by the State. The public entity shall follow the citizen participation requirements for amendments in § 570.704(a)(2).

(d) *Environmental review.* The public entity shall comply with HUD environmental review procedures (24 CFR part 58) for the release of funds for each project carried out with loan guarantee assistance. These procedures set forth the regulations, policies, responsibilities and procedures governing the carrying out of environmental review responsibilities of public entities. All public entities, including nonentitlement public entities, shall submit the request for release of funds and related certification for each project to be assisted with guaranteed loan funds to the appropriate HUD Field Office.

(e) *Displacement, relocation, acquisition, and replacement of housing.* The public entity (or the designated public agency) shall comply with the displacement, relocation, acquisition, and replacement of low/moderate-income housing requirements in § 570.606 in connection with any activity financed in whole or in part with guaranteed loan funds.

[59 FR 66604, Dec. 27, 1994, as amended at 60 FR 1917, Jan. 5, 1995; 61 FR 11481, Mar. 20, 1996; 69 FR 32781, June 10, 2004; 72 FR 73496, Dec. 27, 2008]

§ 570.705 Loan requirements.

(a) *Limitations on commitments.* (1) If loan guarantee commitments have been issued in any fiscal year in an aggregate amount equal to 50 percent of the amount approved in an appropriation act for that fiscal year, HUD may limit the amount of commitments any one public entity may receive during such fiscal year as follows (except that HUD will not decrease commitments already issued):

(i) The amount any one entitlement public entity may receive may be limited to $35,000,000.

(ii) The amount any one nonentitlement public entity may receive may be limited to $7,000,000.

(iii) The amount any one public entity may receive may be limited to such amount as is necessary to allow HUD to give priority to applications containing activities to be carried out in areas designated as empowerment zones/enterprise communities by the Federal Government or by any State.

(2) In addition to the limitations specified in paragraph (a)(1) of this section, the following limitations shall apply.

(i) *Entitlement public entities.* No commitment to guarantee shall be made if the total unpaid balance of debt obligations guaranteed under this subpart (excluding any amount defeased under the contract entered into under § 570.705(b)(1)) on behalf of the public entity would thereby exceed an amount equal to five times the amount of the most recent grant made pursuant to § 570.304 to the public entity.

(ii) *State-assisted public entities.* No commitment to guarantee shall be made if the total unpaid balance of debt obligations guaranteed under this subpart (excluding any amount defeased under the contract entered into under § 570.705(b)(1)) on behalf of the public entity and all other State-assisted public entities in the State would thereby exceed an amount equal to five times the amount of the most recent grant received by such State under subpart I.

(iii) *Nonentitlement public entities eligible under subpart F of this part.* No commitment to guarantee shall be made with respect to a nonentitlement public entity in an insular area or the State of Hawaii if the total unpaid balance of debt obligations guaranteed under this subpart (excluding any amount defeased under the contract entered into under § 570.705(b)(1)) on behalf of the public entity would thereby exceed an amount equal to five times the amount of the most recent grant made pursuant to § 570.429 or § 570.440 (as applicable) to the public entity.

(A) The most recent grant approved for the public entity pursuant to subpart F of this part,

(B) The average of the most recent three grants approved for the public entity pursuant to subpart F of this part, excluding any grant in the same fiscal year as the commitment, or

(C) The average amount of grants made under subpart F of this part to units of general local government in New York State in the previous fiscal year.

(b) *Security requirements.* To assure the repayment of debt obligations and the charges incurred under paragraph (g) of this section and as a condition for receiving loan guarantee assistance, the public entity (and State and designated public agency, as applicable) shall:

(1) Enter into a contract for loan guarantee assistance with HUD, in a form acceptable to HUD, including provisions for repayment of debt obligations guaranteed hereunder;

(2) Pledge all grants made or for which the public entity or State may become eligible under this part; and

(3) Furnish, at the discretion of HUD, such other security as may be deemed appropriate by HUD in making such guarantees. Other security shall be required for all loans with repayment periods of ten years or longer. Such other security shall be specified in the contract entered into pursuant to §570.705(b)(1). Examples of other security HUD may require are:

(i) Program income as defined in §570.500(a);

(ii) Liens on real and personal property;

(iii) Debt service reserves; and

(iv) Increments in local tax receipts generated by activities carried out with the guaranteed loan funds.

(c) *Use of grants for loan repayment.* Notwithstanding any other provision of this part:

(1) Community Development Block Grants allocated pursuant to section 106 of the Act (including program income derived therefrom) may be used for:

(i) Paying principal and interest due (including such issuance, servicing, underwriting, or other costs as may be incurred under paragraph (g) of this section) on the debt obligations guaranteed under this subpart;

(ii) Defeasing such debt obligations; and

(iii) Establishing debt service reserves as additional security pursuant to paragraph (b)(3) of this section.

(2) HUD may apply grants pledged pursuant to paragraph (b)(2) of this section to any amounts due under the debt obligations, the payment of costs incurred under paragraph (g) of this section, or to the purchase or defeasance of such debt obligations, in accordance with the terms of the contract required by paragraph (b)(1) of this section.

(d) *Debt obligations.* Debt obligations guaranteed under this subpart shall be in the form and denominations prescribed by HUD. Such debt obligations may be issued and sold only under such terms and conditions as may be prescribed by HUD. HUD may prescribe the terms and conditions of debt obligations, or of their issuance and sale, by regulation or by contractual arrangements authorized by section 108(r)(4) of the Act and paragraph (h) of this section. Unless specifically provided otherwise in the contract for loan guarantee assistance required under paragraph (b) of this section, debt obligations shall not constitute general obligations of any public entity or State secured by its full faith and credit.

(e) *Taxable obligations.* Interest earned on debt obligations under this subpart shall be subject to Federal taxation as provided in section 108(j) of the Act.

(f) *Loan repayment period.* The term of debt obligations under this subpart shall not exceed twenty years.

(g) *Issuance, underwriting, servicing, and other costs.* Each public entity or its designated public agency issuing debt obligations under this subpart must pay the issuance, underwriting, servicing, trust administration and other costs associated with the private sector financing of the debt obligations. Such costs are payable out of the guaranteed loan funds and shall be secured under paragraph (b) of this section.

(h) *Contracting with respect to issuance and sale of debt obligations; effect of other laws.* No State or local law, and no Federal law, shall preclude or limit HUD's exercise of:

(1) The power to contract with respect to public offerings and other sales of debt obligations under this subpart upon such terms and conditions as HUD deems appropriate;

(2) The right to enforce any such contract by any means deemed appropriate by HUD;

(3) Any ownership rights of HUD, as applicable, in debt obligations under this subpart.

[59 FR 66604, Dec. 27, 1994, as amended at 69 FR 32782, June 10, 2004]

§570.706 Federal guarantee; subrogation.

Section 108(f) of the Act provides for the incontestability of guarantees by HUD under subpart M of this part in the hands of a holder of such guaranteed obligations. If HUD pays a claim under a guarantee made under section 108 of the Act, HUD shall be fully subrogated for all the rights of the holder of the guaranteed debt obligation with respect to such obligation.

[61 FR 11481, Mar. 20, 1996]

§ 570.707 Applicability of rules and regulations.

(a) *Entitlement public entities.* The provisions of subparts A, C, J, K and O of this part applicable to entitlement grants shall apply equally to guaranteed loan funds and other CDBG funds, except to the extent they are specifically modified or augmented by the provisions of this subpart.

(b) *State-assisted public entities.* The provisions of subpart I of this part, and the requirements the State imposes on units of general local government receiving Community Development Block Grants or program income to the extent applicable, shall apply equally to guaranteed loan funds and Community Development Block Grants (including program income derived therefrom) administered by the State under the CDBG program, except to the extent they are specifically modified or augmented by the provisions of this subpart.

(c) *Nonentitlement public entities eligible under subpart F of this part.* The provisions of subpart F of this part shall apply equally to guaranteed loan funds and other CDBG funds, except to the extent they are specifically modified or augmented by the provisions of this subpart.

§ 570.708 Sanctions.

(a) *Non-State assisted public entities.* The performance review procedures described in subpart O of this part apply to all public entities receiving guaranteed loan funds other than State-assisted public entities. Performance deficiencies in the use of guaranteed loan funds made available to such public entities (or program income derived therefrom) or violations of the contract entered into pursuant to § 570.705(b)(1) may result in the imposition of a sanction authorized pursuant to § 570.900(b)(7) against pledged CDBG grants. In addition, upon a finding by HUD that the public entity has failed to comply substantially with any provision of the Act with respect to either the pledged grants or the guaranteed loan funds or program income, HUD may take action against the pledged grants as provided in § 570.913 and/or may take action as provided in the contract for loan guarantee assistance.

(b) *State-assisted public entities.* Performance deficiencies in the use of guaranteed loan funds (or program income derived therefrom) or violations of the contract entered into pursuant to § 570.705(b)(1) may result in an action authorized pursuant to § 570.495 or § 570.496. In addition, upon a finding by HUD that the State or public entity has failed to comply substantially with any provision of the Act with respect to the pledged CDBG nonentitlement funds, the guaranteed loan funds, or program income, HUD may take action against the pledged funds as provided in § 570.496 and/or may take action as provided in the contract.

§ 570.709 Allocation of loan guarantee assistance.

Of the amount approved in any appropriation act for guarantees under this subpart in any fiscal year, 70 percent shall be allocated for entitlement public entities and 30 percent shall be allocated for nonentitlement public entities. HUD need not comply with these percentage requirements in any fiscal year to the extent that there is an absence of applications approvable under this subpart from entitlement or nonentitlement public entities.

§ 570.710 State responsibilities.

The State is responsible for choosing public entities that it will assist under this subpart. States are free to develop procedures and requirements for determining which activities will be assisted, subject to the requirements of this subpart. Upon approval by HUD of an application from a State-assisted public entity, the State will be principally responsible, subject to HUD oversight under subpart I of this part, for ensuring that the public entity complies with all applicable requirements governing the use of the guaranteed loan funds. Notwithstanding the State's responsibilities described in this section, HUD may take any action necessary for ensuring compliance with requirements affecting the security interests of HUD with respect to the guaranteed loan.

Subpart N—Urban Renewal Provisions

SOURCE: 41 FR 20524, May 18, 1976, unless otherwise noted.

§ 570.800 Urban renewal regulations.

The regulations governing urban renewal projects and neighborhood development programs in subpart N of this part, that were effective immediately before April 19, 1996, will continue to govern the rights and obligations of recipients and HUD with respect to such projects and programs.

[61 FR 11481, Mar. 20, 1996]

Subpart O—Performance Reviews

SOURCE: 53 FR 34466, Sept. 6, 1988, unless otherwise noted.

§ 570.900 General.

(a) *Performance review authorities*—(1) *Entitlement, Insular Areas, and HUD-administered Small Cities performance reviews.* Section 104(e)(1) of the Act requires that the Secretary shall, at least on an annual basis, make such reviews and audits as may be necessary or appropriate to determine whether the recipient has carried out its activities in a timely manner, whether the recipient has carried out those activities and its certifications in accordance with the requirements and the primary objectives of the Act and with other applicable laws, and whether the recipient has a continuing capacity to carry out those activities in a timely manner.

(2) *Urban Development Action Grant (UDAG) performance reviews.* Section 119(g) of the Act requires the Secretary, at least on an annual basis, to make such reviews and audits of recipients of Urban Development Action Grants as necessary to determine whether the recipient's progress in carrying out the approved activities is substantially in accordance with the recipient's approved plans and timetables.

(b) *Performance review procedures.* This paragraph describes the review procedures the Department will use in conducting the performance reviews required by sections 104(e) and 119(g) of the Act:

(1) The Department will determine the performance of each entitlement, Insular Areas, and HUD-administered small cities recipient in accordance with section 104(e)(1) of the Act by reviewing for compliance with the requirements described in § 570.901 and by applying the performance criteria described in §§ 570.902 and 570.903 relative to carrying out activities in a timely manner. The review criteria in § 570.904 will be used to assist in determining if the recipient's program is being carried out in compliance with civil rights requirements.

(2) The Department will review UDAG projects and activities to determine whether such projects and activities are being carried out substantially in accordance with the recipient's approved plans and schedules. The Department will also review to determine if the recipient has carried out its UDAG program in accordance with all other requirements of the Grant Agreement and with all applicable requirements of this part.

(3) In conducting performance reviews, HUD will primarily rely on information obtained from the recipient's performance report, records maintained, findings from monitoring, grantee and subrecipient audits, audits and surveys conducted by the HUD Inspector General, and financial data regarding the amount of funds remaining in the line of credit plus program income. HUD may also consider relevant information pertaining to a recipient's performance gained from other sources, including litigation, citizen comments, and other information provided by or concerning the recipient. A recipient's failure to maintain records in the prescribed manner may result in a finding that the recipient has failed to meet the applicable requirement to which the record pertains.

(4) If HUD determines that a recipient has not met a civil rights review criterion in § 570.904, the recipient will be provided an opportunity to demonstrate that it has nonetheless met the applicable civil rights requirement.

(5) If HUD finds that a recipient has failed to comply with a program requirement or has failed to meet a performance criterion in §570.902 or §570.903, HUD will give the recipient an opportunity to provide additional information concerning the finding.

(6) If, after considering any additional information submitted by a recipient, HUD determines to uphold the finding, HUD may advise the recipient to undertake appropriate corrective or remedial actions as specified in §570.910. HUD will consider the recipient's capacity as described in §570.905 prior to selecting the corrective or remedial actions.

(7) If the recipient fails to undertake appropriate corrective or remedial actions which resolve the deficiency to the satisfaction of the Secretary, the Secretary may impose a sanction pursuant to §570.911, 570.912, or 570.913, as applicable.

[53 FR 34466, Sept. 6, 1988, as amended at 60 FR 56917, Nov. 9, 1995; 72 FR 12536, Mar. 15, 2007]

§ 570.901 Review for compliance with the primary and national objectives and other program requirements.

HUD will review each entitlement, Insular Areas, and HUD-administered small cities recipient's program to determine if the recipient has carried out its activities and certifications in compliance with:

(a) The requirement described at §570.200(a)(3) that, consistent with the primary objective of the Act, not less than 70 percent of the aggregate amount of CDBG funds received by the recipient shall be used over the period specified in its certification for activities that benefit low and moderate income persons;

(b) The requirement described at §570.200(a)(2) that each CDBG assisted activity meets the criteria for one or more of the national objectives described at §570.208;

(c) All other activity eligibility requirements defined in subpart C of this part;

(d) For entitlement grants and non-entitlement CDBG grants in Hawaii, the submission requirements of 24 CFR part 91 and the displacement policy requirements at §570.606;

(e) For HUD-administered Small Cities grants in New York, the citizen participation requirements at §570.431, the amendment requirements at §570.427, and the displacement policy requirements of §570.606;

(f) For Insular Areas Program grants only, the application and amendment requirements at §570.440, the citizen participation requirements at §570.441, the displacement policy requirements of §570.606, and the lead-based paint requirements of 24 CFR 35.940;

(g) The grant administration requirements described in subpart J;

(h) Other applicable laws and program requirements described in subpart K; and

(i) Where applicable, the requirements pertaining to loan guarantees (subpart M) and urban renewal completions (subpart N).

[53 FR 34466, Sept. 6, 1988, as amended at 60 FR 1917, Jan. 5, 1995; 60 FR 56917, Nov. 9, 1995; 72 FR 12536, Mar. 15, 2007; 72 FR 46371, Aug. 17, 2007]

§ 570.902 Review to determine if CDBG-funded activities are being carried out in a timely manner.

HUD will review the performance of each entitlement, HUD-administered small cities, and Insular Areas recipient to determine whether each recipient is carrying out its CDBG-assisted activities in a timely manner.

(a) *Entitlement recipients and Non-entitlement CDBG grantees in Hawaii.* (1) Before the funding of the next annual grant and absent contrary evidence satisfactory to HUD, HUD will consider an entitlement recipient or a non-entitlement CDBG grantee in Hawaii to be failing to carry out its CDBG activities in a timely manner if:

(i) Sixty days prior to the end of the grantee's current program year, the amount of entitlement grant funds available to the recipient under grant agreements but undisbursed by the U.S. Treasury is more than 1.5 times the entitlement grant amount for its current program year; and

(ii) The grantee fails to demonstrate to HUD's satisfaction that the lack of timeliness has resulted from factors beyond the grantee's reasonable control.

(2) Notwithstanding that the amount of funds in the line of credit indicates that the recipient is carrying out its activities in a timely manner pursuant to paragraph (a)(1) of this section, HUD may determine that the recipient is not carrying out its activities in a timely manner if:

(i) The amount of CDBG program income the recipient has on hand 60 days prior to the end of its current program year, together with the amount of funds in its CDBG line of credit, exceeds 1.5 times the entitlement grant amount for its current program year; and.

(ii) The grantee fails to demonstrate to HUD's satisfaction that the lack of timeliness has resulted from factors beyond the grantee's reasonable control.

(3) In determining the appropriate corrective action to take with respect to a HUD determination that a recipient is not carrying out its activities in a timely manner pursuant to paragraphs (a)(1) or (a)(2) of this section, HUD will consider the likelihood that the recipient will expend a sufficient amount of funds over the next program year to reduce the amount of unexpended funds to a level that will fall within the standard described in paragraph (a)(1) of this section when HUD next measures the grantee's timeliness performance. For these purposes, HUD will take into account the extent to which funds on hand have been obligated by the recipient and its subrecipients for specific activities at the time the finding is made and other relevant information.

(b) *HUD-administered Small Cities program in New York.* The Department will, absent substantial evidence to the contrary, deem a HUD-administered Small Cities recipient in New York to be carrying out its CDBG-funded activities in a timely manner if the schedule for carrying out its activities, as contained in the approved application (including any subsequent amendment(s)), is being substantially met.

(c) *Insular Areas recipients.* (1) Before the funding of the next annual grant and absent contrary evidence satisfactory to HUD, HUD will consider an Insular Areas recipient to be failing to carry out its CDBG activities in a timely manner if:

(i) Sixty days prior to the end of the grantee's current program year, the amount of Insular Area grant funds available to the recipient under grant agreements but undisbursed by the U.S. Treasury is more than 2.0 times the Insular Area's grant amount for its current program year; and

(ii) The grantee fails to demonstrate to HUD's satisfaction that the lack of timeliness has resulted from factors beyond the grantee's reasonable control.

(2) Notwithstanding that the amount of funds in the line of credit indicates that the Insular Area recipient is carrying out its activities in a timely manner pursuant to paragraph (c)(1) of this section, HUD may determine that the recipient is not carrying out its activities in a timely manner if:

(i) The amount of CDBG program income the recipient has on hand 60 days prior to the end of its current program year, together with the amount of funds in its CDBG line of credit, exceeds 2.0 times the Insular Area's grant amount for its current program year; and

(ii) The grantee fails to demonstrate to HUD's satisfaction that the lack of timeliness has resulted from factors beyond the grantee's reasonable control.

(3) In determining the appropriate corrective action to take with respect to a HUD determination that a recipient is not carrying out its activities in a timely manner pursuant to paragraphs (c)(1) or (c)(2) of this section, HUD will consider the likelihood that the recipient will expend a sufficient amount of funds over the next program year to reduce the amount of unexpended funds to a level that will fall within the standards described in paragraphs (c)(1) and (2) of this section when HUD next measures the grantee's timeliness performance. For these purposes, HUD will take into account the extent to which funds on hand have been obligated by the recipient and its sub-recipients for specific activities at the time the finding is made and other relevant information.

(4) If a recipient is determined to be untimely pursuant to paragraphs (c)(1)

or (c)(2) of this section in one year, and the recipient is again determined to be untimely in the following year, HUD may reduce the recipient's next grant by 100 percent of the amount in excess of twice the Insular Area's most recent CDBG grant, unless HUD determines that the untimeliness resulted from factors outside of the grantee's reasonable control.

(5) The first review under paragraphs (c)(1) and (c)(2) of this section will take place 60 days prior to the conclusion of the Fiscal Year 2006 program year.

[53 FR 34466, Sept. 6, 1988, as amended at 60 FR 56917, Nov. 9, 1995; 72 FR 12536, Mar. 15, 2007; 72 FR 46371, Aug. 17, 2007]

§ 570.903 Review to determine if the recipient is meeting its consolidated plan responsibilities.

The consolidated plan, action plan, and amendment submission requirements referred to in this section are in 24 CFR part 91. For the purpose of this section, the term consolidated plan includes an abbreviated consolidated plan that is submitted pursuant to 24 CFR 91.235.

(a) *Review timing and purpose.* HUD will review the consolidated plan performance of each entitlement, Insular Areas, and Hawaii HUD-administered Small Cities grant recipient prior to acceptance of a grant recipient's annual certification under 24 CFR 91.225(b)(3) to determine whether the recipient followed its HUD-approved consolidated plan for the most recently completed program year, and whether activities assisted with CDBG funds during that period were consistent with that consolidated plan, except that grantees are not bound by the consolidated plan with respect to the use or distribution of CDBG funds to meet non-housing community development needs.

(b) *Following a consolidated plan.* The recipient will be considered to be following its consolidated plan if it has taken all of the planned actions described in its action plan. This includes, but is not limited to:

(1) Pursuing all resources that the grantee indicated it would pursue;

(2) Providing certifications of consistency, when requested to do so by applicants for HUD programs for which the grantee indicated that it would support application by other entities, in a fair and impartial manner; and

(3) Not hindering implementation of the consolidated plan by action or willful inaction.

(c) *Disapproval.* If HUD determines that a recipient has not met the criteria outlined in paragraph (b) of this section, HUD will notify the recipient and provide the recipient up to 45 days to demonstrate to the satisfaction of the Secretary that it has followed its consolidated plan. HUD will consider all relevant circumstances and the recipient's actions and lack of actions affecting the provision of assistance covered by the consolidated plan within its jurisdiction. Failure to so demonstrate in a timely manner will be cause for HUD to find that the recipient has failed to meet its certification. A complete and specific response by the recipient shall describe:

(1) Any factors beyond the control of the recipient that prevented it from following its consolidated plan, and any actions the recipient has taken or plans to take to alleviate such factors; and

(2) Actions taken by the recipient, if any, beyond those described in the consolidated plan performance report to facilitate following the consolidated plan, including the effects of such actions.

(d) *New York HUD-administered Small Cities.* New York HUD-administered grantees shall follow the provisions of paragraph (b) of this section for their abbreviated or full consolidated plan to the extent that the provisions of paragraph (b) of this section are applicable. If the grantee does not comply with the requirements of paragraph (b) of this section, and does not provide HUD with an acceptable explanation, HUD may decide, in accordance with the requirements of the notice of fund availability, that the grantee does not meet threshold requirements to apply for a new small cities grant.

[60 FR 56918, Nov. 9, 1995, as amended at 72 FR 12537, Mar. 15, 2007]

§ 570.904 Equal opportunity and fair housing review criteria.

(a) *General.* (1) Where the criteria in this section are met, the Department will presume that the recipient has carried out its CDBG-funded program in accordance with civil rights certifications and civil rights requirements of the Act relating to equal employment opportunity, equal opportunity in services, benefits and participation, and is affirmatively furthering fair housing unless:

(i) There is evidence which shows, or from which it is reasonable to infer, that the recipient, motivated by considerations of race, color, religion where applicable, sex, national origin, age or handicap, has treated some persons less favorably than others, or

(ii) There is evidence that a policy, practice, standard or method of administration, although neutral on its face, operates to deny or affect adversely in a significantly disparate way the provision of employment or services, benefits or participation to persons of a particular race, color, religion where applicable, sex, national origin, age or handicap, or fair housing to persons of a particular race, color, religion, sex, or national origin, or

(iii) Where the Secretary required a further assurance pursuant to §570.304 in order to accept the recipient's prior civil rights certification, the recipient has failed to meet any such assurance.

(2) In such instances, or where the review criteria in this section are not met, the recipient will be afforded an opportunity to present evidence that it has not failed to carry out the civil rights certifications and fair housing requirements of the Act. The Secretary's determination of whether there has been compliance with the applicable requirements will be made based on a review of the recipient's performance, evidence submitted by the recipient, and all other available evidence. The Department may also initiate separate compliance reviews under title VI of the Civil Rights Act of 1964 or section 109 of the Act.

(b) *Review for equal opportunity.* Title VI of the Civil Rights Act of 1964 (42 U.S.C. 2000d *et seq.*), and implementing regulations in 24 CFR part 1, together with section 109 of the Act (see §570.602), prohibit discrimination in any program or activity funded in whole or in part with funds made available under this part.

(1) *Review for equal employment opportunity.* The Department will presume that a recipient's hiring and employment practices have been carried out in compliance with its equal opportunity certifications and requirements of the Act. This presumption may be rebutted where, based on the totality of circumstances, there has been a deprivation of employment, promotion, or training opportunities by a recipient to any person within the meaning of section 109. The extent to which persons of a particular race, gender, or ethnic background are represented in the workforce may in certain circumstances be considered, together with complaints, performance reviews, and other information.

(2) *Review of equal opportunity in services, benefits and participation.* The Department will presume a recipient is carrying out its programs and activities in accordance with the civil rights certifications and requirements of the Act. This presumption may be rebutted where, based on the totality of circumstances, there has been a deprivation of services, benefits, or participation in any program or activity funded in whole or in part with block grant funds by a recipient to any person within the meaning of section 109. The extent to which persons of a particular race, gender, or ethnic background participate in a program or activity may in certain circumstances be considered, together with complaints, performance reviews, and other information.

(c) *Fair housing review criteria.* See the requirements in the Fair Housing Act (42 U.S.C. 3601–20), as well as §570.601(a), which sets forth the grantee's responsibility to certify that it will affirmatively further fair housing.

(d) *Actions to use minority and women's business firms.* The Department will review a recipient's performance to determine if it has administered its activities funded with assistance under this part in a manner to encourage use of minority and women's business enterprises described in Executive Orders 11625, 12432 and 12138, and 24 CFR 85.36(e). In making this review, the Department will determine if the grantee has taken actions required under §85.36(e) of this chapter, and will review the effectiveness of those actions in accomplishing the objectives of § 85.36(e) of this chapter and the Executive Orders. No recipient is required by this part to attain or maintain any particular statistical level of participation in its contracting activities by race, ethnicity, or gender of the contractor's owners or managers.

[53 FR 34466, Sept. 6, 1988; 53 FR 41330, Oct. 21, 1988, as amended at 54 FR 37411, Sept. 9, 1989; 60 FR 1917, Jan. 5, 1995; 61 FR 11482, Mar. 20, 1996]

§ 570.905 Review of continuing capacity to carry out CDBG funded activities in a timely manner.

If HUD determines that the recipient has not carried out its CDBG activities and certifications in accordance with the requirements and criteria described in § 570.901 or 570.902, HUD will undertake a further review to determine whether or not the recipient has the continuing capacity to carry out its activities in a timely manner. In making the determination, the Department will consider the nature and extent of the recipient's performance deficiencies, types of corrective actions the recipient has undertaken and the success or likely success of such actions.

§ 570.906 Review of urban counties.

In reviewing the performance of an urban county, HUD will hold the county accountable for the actions or failures to act of any of the units of general local government participating in the urban county. Where the Department finds that a participating unit of government has failed to cooperate with the county to undertake or assist in undertaking an essential community development or assisted housing activity and that such failure results, or is likely to result, in a failure of the urban county to meet any requirement of the program or other applicable laws, the Department may prohibit the county's use of funds made available under this part for that unit of government. HUD will also consider any such failure to cooperate in its review of a future cooperation agreement between the county and such included unit of government described at § 570.307(b)(2).

§§ 570.907–570.909 [Reserved]

§ 570.910 Corrective and remedial actions.

(a) *General.* Consistent with the procedures described in § 570.900(b), the Secretary may take one or more of the actions described in paragraph (b) of this section. Such actions shall be designed to prevent a continuation of the performance deficiency; mitigate, to the extent possible, the adverse effects or consequences of the deficiency; and prevent a recurrence of the deficiency.

(b) *Actions authorized.* The following lists the actions that HUD may take in response to a deficiency identified during the review of a recipient's performance:

(1) Issue a letter of warning advising the recipient of the deficiency and putting the recipient on notice that additional action will be taken if the deficiency is not corrected or is repeated;

(2) Recommend, or request the recipient to submit, proposals for corrective actions, including the correction or removal of the causes of the deficiency, through such actions as:

(i) Preparing and following a schedule of actions for carrying out the affected CDBG activities, consisting of schedules, timetables and milestones necessary to implement the affected CDBG activities;

(ii) Establishing and following a management plan which assigns responsibilities for carrying out the actions identified in paragraph (b)(2)(i) of this section;

(iii) For entitlement and Insular Areas recipients, canceling or revising affected activities that are no longer feasible to implement due to the deficiency and re-programming funds from such affected activities to other eligible activities (pursuant to the citizen participation requirements in 24 CFR part 91); or

(iv) Other actions which will serve to prevent a continuation of the deficiency, mitigate (to the extent possible) the adverse effects or consequences of the deficiency, and prevent a recurrence of the deficiency;

(3) Advise the recipient that a certification will no longer be acceptable and that additional assurances will be required;

§ 570.911

(4) Advise the recipient to suspend disbursement of funds for the deficient activity;

(5) Advise the recipient to reimburse its program account or letter of credit in any amounts improperly expended and reprogram the use of the funds in accordance with applicable requirements;

(6) Change the method of payment to the recipient from a letter of credit basis to a reimbursement basis;

(7) In the case of claims payable to HUD or the U.S. Treasury, institute collection procedures pursuant to subpart B of 24 CFR part 17; and

(8) In the case of an entitlement or Insular Areas recipient, condition the use of funds from a succeeding fiscal year's allocation upon appropriate corrective action by the recipient. The failure of the recipient to undertake the actions specified in the condition may result in a reduction, pursuant to § 570.911, of the entitlement or Insular Areas recipient's annual grant by up to the amount conditionally granted.

[53 FR 34466, Sept. 6, 1988, as amended at 60 FR 1917, Jan. 5, 1995; 72 FR 12537, Mar. 15, 2007]

§ 570.911 Reduction, withdrawal, or adjustment of a grant or other appropriate action.

(a) *Opportunity for an informal consultation.* Prior to a reduction, withdrawal, or adjustment of a grant or other appropriate action, taken pursuant to paragraph (b), (c), or (d) of this section, the recipient shall be notified of such proposed action and given an opportunity within a prescribed time period for an informal consultation.

(b) *Entitlement grants, Non-entitlement CDBG grants in Hawaii, and Insular Areas grants.* Consistent with the procedures described in § 570.900(b), the Secretary may make a reduction in the entitlement, non-entitlement CDBG grants in Hawaii, or Insular Areas grant amount either for the succeeding program year or, if the grant had been conditioned, up to the amount that had been conditioned. The amount of the reduction shall be based on the severity of the deficiency and may be for the entire grant amount.

(c) *HUD-administered small cities grants.* Consistent with the procedures described in § 570.900(b), the Secretary may adjust, reduce or withdraw the grant or take other actions as appropriate, except that funds already expended on eligible approved activities shall not be recaptured or deducted from future grants.

(d) *Urban Development Action Grants.* Consistent with the procedures described in § 570.900(b), the Secretary may adjust, reduce or withdraw the grant or take other actions as appropriate, except that funds already expended on eligible approved activities shall not be recaptured or deducted from future grants made to the recipient.

[61 FR 11481, Mar. 20, 1996, as amended at 72 FR 12537, Mar. 15, 2007; 72 FR 46371, Aug. 17, 2007]

§ 570.912 Nondiscrimination compliance.

(a) Whenever the Secretary determines that a unit of general local government which is a recipient of assistance under this part has failed to comply with § 570.602, the Secretary shall notify the governor of such State or chief executive officer of such unit of general local government of the noncompliance and shall request the governor or the chief executive officer to secure compliance. If within a reasonable period of time, not to exceed sixty days, the governor or chief executive officer fails or refuses to secure compliance, the Secretary is authorized to:

(1) Refer the matter to the Attorney General with a recommendation that an appropriate civil action be instituted;

(2) Exercise the powers and functions provided by title VI of the Civil Rights Act of 1964 (42 U.S.C. 2000d);

(3) Exercise the powers and functions provided for in § 570.913; or

(4) Take such other action as may be provided by law.

(b) When a matter is referred to the Attorney General pursuant to paragraph (a)(1) of this section, or whenever the Secretary has reason to believe that a State or a unit of general local government is engaged in a pattern or practice in violation of the provisions of § 570.602, the Attorney General may bring a civil action in any appropriate United States district court for such relief as may be appropriate, including injunctive relief.

§ 570.913 Other remedies for noncompliance.

(a) *Action to enforce compliance.* When the Secretary acts to enforce the civil rights provisions of Section 109, as described in § 570.602 and 24 CFR part 6, the procedures described in 24 CFR parts 6 and 180 apply. If the Secretary finds, after reasonable notice and opportunity for hearing, that a recipient has failed to comply substantially with any other provisions of this part, the provisions of this section apply. The Secretary, until he/she is satisfied that there is no longer any such failure to comply, shall:

(1) Terminate payments to the recipient;

(2) Reduce payments to the recipient by an amount equal to the amount of such payments which were not expended in accordance with this part; or

(3) Limit the availability of payments to programs or activities not affected by such failure to comply.

Provided, however, that the Secretary may on due notice suspend payments at any time after the issuance of a notice of opportunity for hearing pursuant to paragraph (c)(1) of this section, pending such hearing and a final decision, to the extent the Secretary determines such action necessary to preclude the further expenditure of funds for activities affected by such failure to comply.

(b) In lieu of, or in addition to, any action authorized by paragraph (a) of this section, the Secretary may, if he/she has reason to believe that a recipient has failed to comply substantially with any provision of this part;

(1) Refer the matter to the Attorney General of the United States with a recommendation that an appropriate civil action be instituted; and

(2) Upon such a referral, the Attorney General may bring a civil action in any United States district court having venue thereof for such relief as may be appropriate, including an action to recover the amount of the assistance furnished under this part which was not expended in accordance with it, or for mandatory or injunctive relief;

(c) *Proceedings.* When the Secretary proposes to take action pursuant to this section, the respondent is the unit of general local government or State receiving assistance under this part. These procedures are to be followed prior to imposition of a sanction described in paragraph (a) of this section:

(1) *Notice of opportunity for hearing:* The Secretary shall notify the respondent in writing of the proposed action and of the opportunity for a hearing. The notice shall:

(i) Specify, in a manner which is adequate to allow the respondent to prepare its response, allegations with respect to a failure to comply substantially with a provision of this part;

(ii) State that the hearing procedures are governed by these rules;

(iii) State that a hearing may be requested within 10 days from receipt of the notice and the name, address and telephone number of the person to whom any request for hearing is to be addressed:

(iv) Specify the action which the Secretary proposes to take and that the authority for this action is section 111(a) of the Act;

(v) State that if the respondent fails to request a hearing within the time specified a decision by default will be rendered against the respondent; and

(vi) Be sent to the respondent by certified mail, return receipt requested.

(2) *Initiation of hearing.* The respondent shall be allowed at least 10 days from receipt of the notice within which to notify HUD of its request for a hearing. If no request is received within the time specified, the Secretary may proceed to make a finding on the issue of compliance with this part and to take the proposed action.

(3) *Administrative Law Judge.* Proceedings conducted under these rules shall be presided over by an Administrative Law Judge (ALJ), appointed as provided by section 11 of the Administrative Procedures Act (5 U.S.C. 3105). The case shall be referred to the ALJ by the Secretary at the time a hearing is requested. The ALJ shall promptly notify the parties of the time and place at which the hearing will be held. The ALJ shall conduct a fair and impartial hearing and take all action necessary

§ 570.913

to avoid delay in the disposition of proceedings and to maintain order. The ALJ shall have all powers necessary to those ends, including but not limited to the power to:

(i) Administer oaths and affirmations;

(ii) Issue subpoenas as authorized by law;

(iii) Rule upon offers of proof and receive relevant evidence;

(iv) Order or limit discovery prior to the hearing as the interests of justice may require;

(v) Regulate the course of the hearing and the conduct of the parties and their counsel;

(vi) Hold conferences for the settlement or simplification of the issues by consent of the parties;

(vii) Consider and rule upon all procedural and other motions appropriate in adjudicative proceedings; and

(viii) Make and file initial determinations.

(4) *Ex parte communications.* An ex parte communication is any communication with an ALJ, direct or indirect, oral or written, concerning the merits or procedures of any pending proceeding which is made by a party in the absence of any other party. Ex parte communications are prohibited except where the purpose and content of the communication have been disclosed in advance or simultaneously to all parties, or the communication is a request for information concerning the status of the case. Any ALJ who receives an ex parte communication which the ALJ knows or has reason to believe is unauthorized shall promptly place the communication, or its substance, in all files and shall furnish copies to all parties. Unauthorized ex parte communications shall not be taken into consideration in deciding any matter in issue.

(5) *The hearing.* All parties shall have the right to be represented at the hearing by counsel. The ALJ shall conduct the proceedings in an expeditious manner while allowing the parties to present all oral and written evidence which tends to support their respective positions, but the ALJ shall exclude irrelevant, immaterial or unduly repetitious evidence. The Department has the burden of proof in showing by a preponderance of the evidence that the respondent failed to comply substantially with a provision of this part. Each party shall be allowed to cross-examine adverse witnesses and to rebut and comment upon evidence presented by the other party. Hearings shall be open to the public. So far as the orderly conduct of the hearing permits, interested persons other than the parties may appear and participate in the hearing.

(6) *Transcripts.* Hearing shall be recorded and transcribed only by a reporter under the supervision of the ALJ. The orginal transcript shall be a part of the record and shall constitute the sole official transcript. Respondents and the public, at their own expense, may obtain copies of the transcript.

(7) *The ALJ's decision.* At the conclusion of the hearing, the ALJ shall give the parties a reasonable opportunity to submit proposed findings and conclusions and supporting reasons therefor. Within 25 days after the conclusion of the hearing, the ALJ shall prepare a written decision which includes a statement of findings and conclusions, and the reasons or basis therefor, on all the material issues of fact, law or discretion presented on the record and the appropriate sanction or denial thereof. The decision shall be based on consideration of the whole record or those parts thereof cited by a party and supported by and in accordance with the reliable, probative, and substantial evidence. A copy of the decision shall be furnished to the parties immediately by certified mail, return receipt requested, and shall include a notice that any requests for review by the Secretary must be made in writing to the Secretary within 30 days of the receipt of the decision.

(8) *The record.* The transcript of testimony and exhibits, together with the decision of the ALJ and all papers and requests filed in the proceeding, constitutes the exclusive record for decision and, on payment of its reasonable cost, shall be made available to the parties. After reaching his/her initial decision, the ALJ shall certify to the complete record and forward the record to the Secretary.

(9) *Review by the Secretary.* The decision by the ALJ shall constitute the final decision of the Secretary unless, within 30 days after the receipt of the decision, either the respondent or the Assistant Secretary for Community Planning and Development files an exception and request for review by the Secretary. The excepting party must transmit simultaneously to the Secretary and the other party the request for review and the basis of the party's exceptions to the findings of the ALJ. The other party shall be allowed 30 days from receipt of the exception to provide the Secretary and the excepting party with a written reply. The Secretary shall then review the record of the case, including the exceptions and the reply. On the basis of such review, the Secretary shall issue a written determination, including a statement of the reasons or basis therefor, affirming, modifying or revoking the decision of the ALJ. The Secretary's decision shall be made and transmitted to the parties within 80 days after the decision of the ALJ was furnished to the parties.

(10) *Judicial review.* The respondent may seek judicial review of the Secretary's decision pursuant to section 111(c) of the Act.

[53 FR 34466, Sept. 6, 1988, as amended at 64 FR 3802, Jan. 25, 1999]

APPENDIX A TO PART 570—GUIDELINES AND OBJECTIVES FOR EVALUATING PROJECT COSTS AND FINANCIAL REQUIREMENTS

I. *Guidelines and Objectives for Evaluating Project Costs and Financial Requirements.* HUD has developed the following guidelines that are designed to provide the recipient with a framework for financially underwriting and selecting CDBG-assisted economic development projects which are financially viable and will make the most effective use of the CDBG funds. *The use of these underwriting guidelines as published by HUD is not mandatory.* However, grantees electing not to use these underwriting guidelines would be expected to conduct basic financial underwriting prior to the provision of CDBG financial assistance to a for-profit business. States electing not to use these underwriting guidelines would be expected to ensure that the state or units of general local government conduct basic financial underwriting prior to the provision of CDBG financial assistance to a for-profit business.

II. Where appropriate, HUD's underwriting guidelines recognize that different levels of review are appropriate to take into account differences in the size and scope of a proposed project, and in the case of a microenterprise or other small business to take into account the differences in the capacity and level of sophistication among businesses of differing sizes.

III. Recipients are encouraged, when they develop their own programs and underwriting criteria, to also take these factors into account. For example, a recipient administering a program providing only technical assistance to small businesses might choose to apply underwriting guidelines to the technical assistance program as a whole, rather than to each instance of assistance to a business. Given the nature and dollar value of such a program, a recipient might choose to limit its evaluation to factors such as the extent of need for this type of assistance by the target group of businesses and the extent to which this type of assistance is already available.

IV. The objectives of the underwriting guidelines are to ensure:

(1) that project costs are reasonable;
(2) that all sources of project financing are committed;
(3) that to the extent practicable, CDBG funds are not substituted for non-Federal financial support;
(4) that the project is financially feasible;
(5) that to the extent practicable, the return on the owner's equity investment will not be unreasonably high; and
(6) that to the extent practicable, CDBG funds are disbursed on a pro rata basis with other finances provided to the project.

i. Project costs are reasonable. i. Reviewing costs for reasonableness is important. It will help the recipient avoid providing either too much or too little CDBG assistance for the proposed project. Therefore, it is suggested that the grantee obtain a breakdown of all project costs and that each cost element making up the project be reviewed for reasonableness. The amount of time and resources the recipient expends evaluating the reasonableness of a cost element should be commensurate with its cost. For example, it would be appropriate for an experienced reviewer looking at a cost element of less than $10,000 to judge the reasonableness of that cost based upon his or her knowledge and common sense. For a cost element in excess of $10,000, it would be more appropriate for the reviewer to compare the cost element with a third-party, fair-market price quotation for that cost element. Third-party price quotations may also be used by a reviewer to help determine the reasonableness of cost elements below $10,000 when the reviewer evaluates projects infrequently or if the reviewer is less experienced in cost estimations. If a recipient does not use third-party price quotations to verify cost elements, then the recipient would need to conduct its own cost analysis using appropriate cost estimating manuals or services.

ii. The recipient should pay particular attention to any cost element of the project that will be carried out through a non-arms-length transaction. A non-arms-length transaction occurs when the entity implementing the CDBG assisted activity procures goods or services from itself or from another party with whom there is a financial interest or family relationship. If abused, non-arms-length transactions misrepresent the true cost of the project.

2. *Commitment of all project sources of financing.* The recipient should review all projected sources of financing necessary to carry out the economic development project. This is to ensure that time and effort is not wasted on assessing a proposal that is not able to proceed. To the extent practicable, prior to the commitment of CDBG funds to the project, the recipient should verify that: sufficient sources of funds have been identified to finance the project; all participating parties providing those funds have affirmed their intention to make the funds available; and the participating parties have the financial capacity to provide the funds.

3. *Avoid substitution of CDBG funds for non-Federal financial support.* i. The recipient should review the economic development project to ensure that, to the extent practicable, CDBG funds will not be used to substantially reduce the amount of non-Federal financial support for the activity. This will help the recipient to make the most efficient use of its CDBG funds for economic development. To reach this determination, the recipient's reviewer would conduct a financial underwriting analysis of the project, including reviews of appropriate projections of revenues, expenses, debt service and returns on equity investments in the project. The extent of this review should be appropriate for the size and complexity of the project and should use industry standards for similar projects, taking into account the unique factors of the project such as risk and location.

ii. Because of the high cost of underwriting and processing loans, many private financial lenders do not finance commercial projects that are less than $100,000. A recipient should familiarize itself with the lending practices of the financial institutions in its community. If the project's total cost is one that would normally fall within the range that financial institutions participate, then the recipient should normally determine the following:

A. *Private debt financing*—whether or not the participating private, for-profit business (or other entity having an equity interest) has applied for private debt financing from a commercial lending institution and whether that institution has completed all of its financial underwriting and loan approval actions resulting in either a firm commitment of its funds or a decision not to participate in the project; and

B. *Equity participation*—whether or not the degree of equity participation is reasonable given general industry standards for rates of return on equity for similar projects with similar risks and given the financial capacity of the entrepreneur(s) to make additional financial investments.

iii. If the recipient is assisting a microenterprise owned by a low- or moderate-income person(s), in conducting its review under this paragraph, the recipient might only need to determine that non-Federal sources of financing are not available (at terms appropriate for such financing) in the community to serve the low- or moderate-income entrepreneur.

4. *Financial feasibility of the project.* i. The public benefit a grantee expects to derive from the CDBG assisted project (the subject of separate regulatory standards) will not materialize if the project is not financially feasible. To determine if there is a reasonable chance for the project's success, the recipient should evaluate the financial viability of the project. A project would be considered financially viable if all of the assumptions about the project's market share, sales levels, growth potential, projections of revenue, project expenses and debt service (including repayment of the CDBG assistance if appropriate) were determined to be realistic and met the project's break-even point (which is generally the point at which all revenues are equal to all expenses). Generally speaking, an economic development project that does not reach this break-even point over time is not financially feasible. The following should be noted in this regard:

A. some projects make provisions for a negative cash flow in the early years of the project while space is being leased up or sales volume built up, but the project's projections should take these factors into account and provide sources of financing for such negative cash flow; and

B. it is expected that a financially viable project will also project sufficient revenues to provide a reasonable return on equity investment. The recipient should carefully examine any project that is not economically able to provide a reasonable return on equity investment. Under such circumstances, a business may be overstating its real equity investment (actual costs of the project may be overstated as well), or it may be overstating some of the project's operating expenses in the expectation that the difference will be taken out as profits, or the business may be overly pessimistic in its market share and revenue projections and has downplayed its profits.

ii. In addition to the financial underwriting reviews carried out earlier, the recipient should evaluate the experience and capacity of the assisted business owners to manage an assisted business to achieve the projections. Based upon its analysis of these factors, the recipient should identify those elements, if any, that pose the greatest risks contributing to the project's lack of financial feasibility.

5. *Return on equity investment.* To the extent practicable, the CDBG assisted activity should provide not more than a reasonable return on investment to the owner of the assisted activity. This will help ensure that the grantee is able to maximize the use of its CDBG funds for its economic development objectives. However, care should also be taken to avoid the situation where the owner is likely to receive too small a return on his/her investment, so that his/her motivation remains high to pursue the business with vigor. The amount, type and terms of the CDBG assistance should be adjusted to allow the owner a reasonable return on his/her investment given industry rates of return for that investment, local conditions and the risk of the project.

6. *Disbursement of CDBG funds on a pro rata basis.* To the extent practicable, CDBG funds used to finance economic development activities should be disbursed on a pro rata basis with other funding sources. Recipients should be guided by the principle of not placing CDBG funds at significantly greater risk than non-CDBG funds. This will help avoid the situation where it is learned that a problem has developed that will block the completion of the project, even though all or most of the CDBG funds going in to the project have already been expended. When this happens, a recipient may be put in a position of having to provide additional financing to complete the project or watch the potential loss of its funds if the project is not able to be completed. When the recipient determines that it is not practicable to disburse CDBG funds on a pro rata basis, the recipient should consider taking other steps to safeguard CDBG funds in the event of a default, such as insisting on securitizing assets of the project.

[60 FR 1953, Jan. 5, 1995]

PART 572—HOPE FOR HOMEOWNERSHIP OF SINGLE FAMILY HOMES PROGRAM (HOPE 3)

Subpart A—General

Sec.
572.1 Overview of HOPE 3.
572.5 Definitions.
572.10 Section 8 assistance.

Subpart B—Homeownership Program Requirements—Implementation Grants

572.100 Acquisition and rehabilitation of eligible properties; rehabilitation standards.
572.105 Financing the purchase of properties by eligible families.
572.110 Identifying and selecting eligible families for homeownership.
572.115 Transfer of homeownership interests.
572.120 Affordability standards.
572.125 Replacement reserves.
572.130 Restrictions on resale by initial homeowners.
572.135 Use of proceeds from sales to eligible families, resale proceeds, and program income.
572.140 Third party rights.
572.145 Displacement prohibited; protection of nonpurchasing residents.

Subpart C—Grants

572.200 Planning grants.
572.205 Planning grants—eligible activities.
572.210 Implementation grants.
572.215 Implementation grants—eligible activities.
572.220 Implementation grants—matching requirements.
572.225 Grant agreements; corrective and remedial actions.
572.230 Cash and Management Information (C/MI) System.
572.235 Amendments.

Subpart D—Selection Process

572.300 Notices of funding availability (NOFAs); grant applications.
572.315 Rating criteria for planning grants.

Subpart E—Other Federal Requirements

572.400 Consolidated plan.
572.405 Nondiscrimination and equal opportunity requirements.
572.410 Environmental procedures and standards.
572.415 Conflict of interest.
572.420 Miscellaneous requirements.
572.425 Recordkeeping and reports; audit of recipients.

AUTHORITY: 42 U.S.C. 3535(d) and 12891.

SOURCE: 58 FR 36526, July 7, 1993, unless otherwise noted.

Subpart A—General

§ 572.1 Overview of HOPE 3.

The purpose of the HOPE for Homeownership of Single Family Homes program (HOPE 3) is to provide homeownership opportunities for eligible families to purchase Federal, State, and local government-owned single family properties. HOPE 3 provides grants to eligible applicants to plan and implement homeownership programs designed to meet the needs of low-income first-time homebuyers.

[58 FR 36526, July 7, 1993, as amended at 61 FR 48797, Sept. 16, 1996]

§ 572.5 Definitions.

The terms *HUD, Indian Housing Authority (IHA), NAHA, 1937 Act, NOFA,* and *Public Housing Agency (PHA)* are defined in 24 CFR part 5.

Administrative costs means reasonable and necessary costs, as described and valued in accordance with OMB Circular No. A-87 or A-122[1] as applicable, incurred by a recipient in carrying out a homeownership program under this part. For purposes of complying with the 15 percent limitation in § 572.215(o), administrative costs do not include the costs of activities that are separately eligible under § 572.215.

Applicant means a private nonprofit organization; a cooperative association; or a public body in cooperation with a private nonprofit organization that applies for a HOPE 3 grant under this part. A cooperative association is an eligible applicant only for eligible property it proposes to acquire and transfer ownership interests to eligible families under a homeownership program.

Consolidated plan means the document that is submitted to HUD that serves as the planning document of the jurisdiction, in accordance with 24 CFR part 91.

Cooperating entity means a private nonprofit organization or public body that the lead applicant has designed in its application to carry out certain functions in the HOPE 3 program. The responsibilities of a cooperating entity must be specified in a memorandum of agreement signed by the lead applicant and the cooperating entity.

Cooperative association means an association organized and existing under applicable State, local, territorial, or tribal law primarily for the purpose of acquiring, owning, and operating housing for its members or shareholders, as applicable.

Displaced homemaker means as the term is defined in 42 U.S.C. 12704. The individual must not have worked full-time, full-year in the labor force for at least 2 years.

Eligible family means a low-income family who is a first-time homebuyer.

Eligible property means a single residential property, containing no more than four units, that is owned or held by HUD, the Secretary of Veterans Affairs, the Secretary of Agriculture, the Secretary of Defense, the Secretary of Transportation, the Resolution Trust Corporation, the Federal Deposit Insurance Corporation, the General Services Administration, or any other Federal agency; a State or local government (including any in rem property); or a PHA/IHA (excluding public or Indian housing under the 1937 Act). This definition includes individual condominium units located in multifamily structures owned or held by an eligible source and properties held by institutions within the jurisdiction of the Resolution Trust Corporation. All cooperative units acquired under HOPE 3 must be located in properties containing no more than four units to qualify as eligible property under this part. In the case of two- to four-unit property, only property that may be divided so each unit may be acquired by an eligible family is eligible, except as provided in § 572.115(c). For purposes of this definition, the term State or local government means any entity included in the first sentence of the definition of public body.

First-time homebuyer means as the term is defined in 42 U.S.C. 12704.

Homeownership program means a program for homeownership meeting the requirements under this part. The program must provide for acquisition by eligible families of ownership interests in the units in an eligible property

---

[1] See § 572.420(a) concerning the availability of OMB Circulars.

under an ownership arrangement approved by HUD under this part. All eligible properties assisted under the program must be initially acquired by eligible families.

Lead applicant means an eligible applicant designated in a HOPE 3 application to assume legal responsibility as the recipient and execute the grant agreement.

Lease-purchase means

(1) An agreement, enforceable under State (or territorial) and local law, between the recipient or its designee and an eligible family under which the family:

(i) Obtains the right to occupy a unit in an eligible property, subject to the payment of rent and other reasonable lease conditions, for a period of not more than two years, except as provided in §572.115(a)(2); and

(ii) At the end of such two years has the right to purchase the unit under the terms stated in the lease-purchase agreement, including the completion of any additional rehabilitation required during the lease-purchase period.

(2) A lease-purchase agreement qualifies as a transfer of the unit to the eligible family for purposes of the deadline for transfer in §572.115(a), but it is not otherwise an "ownership interest" under this part. The interest that the family acquires at the end of the two-year lease-purchase period must be an ownership interest under this part, and the terms and conditions of the purchase of such interest must meet the affordability requirements of this part.

Low-income family means a family or individual qualifying as a low-income family under 24 CFR part 813 (where the recipient is not a PHA/IHA), part 913 (where the recipient is a PHA), or part 905 (where the recipient is an Indian tribe or IHA). A low-income family is generally defined as a family whose annual income does not exceed 80 percent of median income for the area, as determined by HUD with adjustment for family size. HUD may establish income limits higher or lower than 80 percent of median income for the area on the basis of its finding that such variations are necessary because of prevailing construction costs or unusually high or low family incomes.

Ownership interest means ownership by an eligible family by fee simple title to a unit in an eligible property (including a condominium unit), ownership of shares of or membership in a cooperative, or another form of ownership proposed and justified by the applicant and approved by HUD pursuant to §572.115(b).

Private nonprofit organization means any nonprofit organization that

(1) Is organized and exists under applicable Federal, State, territorial, local, or tribal law;

(2) Has no part of its net earnings inuring to the benefit of any individual, corporation, or other entity;

(3) Has a voluntary board;

(4) Has an accounting system or has designated a fiscal agent in accordance with requirements established by HUD;

(5) Practices nondiscrimination in the provision of assistance;

(6) Is a tax exempt entity under section 501(c) of the Internal Revenue Code of 1986 (26 U.S.C. 501(c)), or for a private nonprofit organization in the Commonwealth of Puerto Rico, is a tax-exempt entity under Puerto Rico law;

(7) Is privately controlled and has a governing body that is controlled 51 percent or more by private individuals acting in a private capacity. An individual is considered to be acting in a private capacity if the individual is not an employee of a public body, is not appointed by or acting as the representative of a public body (including the applicant or recipient), and is not being paid by a public body (including the applicant or recipient) while performing functions in connection with the nonprofit organization.

Program income means income earned from the program as described in parts 84 and 85 of this title, as applicable, except that program income does not include proceeds from the sale and resale of properties. Such sale and resale proceeds, and interest earned by the recipient or its designee on those proceeds, are governed by §572.135(a) through (c).

Public body means any State of the United States; any city, county, town, township, parish, village, or other general purpose political subdivision of a State; the Commonwealth of Puerto

§ 572.10

Rico, the District of Columbia, Guam, the Northern Mariana Islands, the Virgin Islands, American Samoa, or a general purpose political subdivision thereof; any Indian tribe, as defined in title I of the Housing and Community Development Act of 1974; any public agency or instrumentality of any of the foregoing jurisdictions that is created by or pursuant to State, territorial, local, or tribal law, including a State or local Housing Finance Agency; and any PHA or IHA. For purposes of this definition, an organization that meets the requirements of paragraphs (1) and (2) of the definition of private nonprofit organization, but is controlled 51 percent or more by public officials acting in their official capacities, may qualify as a public body.

Recipient means the lead applicant that is approved by HUD to receive a HOPE 3 grant and is legally responsible for the grant.

Single parent means as the term is defined in 42 U.S.C. 12896.

[58 FR 36526, July 7, 1993, as amended at 60 FR 36018, July 12, 1995; 61 FR 5209, Feb. 9, 1996; 61 FR 48797, Sept. 16, 1996; 62 FR 34145, June 24, 1997]

§ 572.10 Section 8 assistance.

Assistance under section 8 of the 1937 Act and other rental assistance to the homebuyer will be terminated not later than the date an eligible family acquires an ownership interest in an eligible property or executes a lease-purchase agreement for the property.

Subpart B—Homeownership Program Requirements—Implementation Grants

§ 572.100 Acquisition and rehabilitation of eligible properties; rehabilitation standards.

(a) *Minimum number of properties.* (1) Each homeownership program must involve acquisition of at least ten units in eligible properties by eligible families.

(2) A homeownership program may not result in appreciably reducing in the locality the number of affordable rental housing units of the type to be assisted that would be available to residents currently residing in the types of properties proposed for use under the program or to families who would be eligible to reside in the properties.

(b) *Maximum acquisition costs.* The cost of acquiring an eligible property (by a recipient or other entity for transfer to eligible families or by an eligible family from a recipient or directly from an eligible source) may not exceed the as-is fair market value of the property, plus reasonable and customary closing costs charged for comparable transactions in the market area. The as-is fair market value of a property must be determined in accordance with a recent appraisal conducted under procedures consistent with appraisal standards published by The Appraisal Foundation in the current edition of "Uniform Standards of Professional Appraisal Practice."

(c) *Maximum cost of acquisition and rehabilitation.* The cost of acquisition and rehabilitation paid for from grant funds or credited as match may not exceed 80 percent of the maximum amount that may be insured in the area under section 203(b) of the National Housing Act, plus reasonable and customary closing costs charged for comparable transactions in the market area.

(d) *Rehabilitation standards.* (1) The recipient is responsible to assure that rehabilitation of eligible property meets local codes applicable to rehabilitation of work in the jurisdiction (but not less than the housing quality standards established under the Section 8 rental voucher program, described in § 982.401 of this title). Rehabilitation must also include work necessary to meet applicable federal requirements, including lead-based paint requirements set forth at part 35, subparts A, B, J, K, and R of this title.

(2) The property must be rehabilitated to a level that makes it marketable for homeownership in the market area to families with incomes at or below 80 percent of the median for the area. Luxury items (fixtures, equipment, and landscaping of a type or quality that substantially exceeds that customarily used in the locality for properties of the same general type as that being rehabilitated) are not eligible expenses. HUD reserves the right to disapprove improvements or amenities

to be paid for from nonprogram funds that it determines are unsuitable for the HOPE 3 program.

(3) Rehabilitation costs must comply with the cost standards established by HUD (see paragraph (c) of this section for applicable cost limitations covering both acquisition and rehabilitation). If improvements are made to an eligible property beyond those that qualify as eligible costs, the applicant must assure that the entire cost of the excess improvements will be covered by funds other than the HOPE 3 grant and any amounts contributed toward the match, and that the affordability of the property will not be impaired.

(4) Higher standards may be proposed by the applicant or required by lenders.

(5) The applicant must adopt written rehabilitation standards.

(e) *Rehabilitation and transfer of units.* (1) The unit must be free from any defects that pose a danger to life, health, or safety before transfer of an ownership interest in the unit to the family or occupancy of a unit by an eligible family under a lease-purchase agreement. The recipient must inspect, or ensure inspection of, each unit to determine that it does not pose an imminent threat to the life, health, or safety of residents and that the property has passed recent fire and other applicable safety inspections conducted by appropriate local officials.

(2) The unit must, not later than 2 years after transfer of an ownership interest in the unit to an eligible family, or execution of a lease-purchase agreement for the unit, meet minimum rehabilitation standards under paragraph (d)(1) of this section. The recipient must inspect, or ensure inspection of, each unit to determine that it meets the rehabilitation standards required under paragraph (d)(1) of this section.

[58 FR 36526, July 7, 1993, as amended at 62 FR 34145, June 24, 1997; 64 FR 50226, Sept. 15, 1999]

§ 572.105 Financing the purchase of properties by eligible families.

(a) *Types of financing.* (1) Financing may include use of the implementation grant to permit transfer of an ownership interest in a unit to an eligible family for less than fair market value or with assisted financing; or other sources of financing (subject to requirements that apply to those sources), including, but not limited to, conventional mortgage loans, mortgage loans insured under title II of the National Housing Act, and mortgage loans under other available programs, such as Veterans Administration (VA), Farmers Home Administration (FmHA), and Resolution Trust Corporation (RTC) seller-assisted financing.

(2) *FHA single family mortgage insurance requirements.* All regulatory requirements and underwriting procedures established for FHA single family mortgage insurance apply to mortgages insured by FHA on properties assisted under the HOPE 3 program. Exceptions in the regulations specifically for homebuyers under the HOPE 3 program are:

(i) The eligible family/mortgagor may obtain a loan for the down payment from a corporation or another person under conditions satisfactory to HUD (24 CFR 203.19(b) and 234.28(c));

(ii) A second mortgage may be placed against the property even though the entity holding a second mortgage is not a Federal, State, or local government agency, if the entity is designated in the homeownership plan of an applicant for an implementation grant (24 CFR 203.32(b) and 234.55(b)); and

(iii) Certain restrictions on conveyance may be permissible. Property with restrictions that do not comply with FHA regulations will be ineligible for FHA mortgage insurance, notwithstanding HUD approval under § 572.130(e).

(b) *Financial assistance to homebuyers.* Recipients may provide assistance to, or on behalf of, eligible families to make acquisition and rehabilitation of eligible properties affordable. This may include interest rate reductions ("interest rate buy-downs"), payment of all or a portion of closing costs, down payments, mortgage insurance premiums, and other expenses, and other forms of assistance approved by HUD. No mechanisms to financially assist homebuyers that would require grant recipients to make lump sum deposits of HOPE 3 grant funds will be permitted.

§ 572.110 Identifying and selecting eligible families for homeownership.

(a) *Selection procedures.* (1) Recipients must establish written equitable procedures for identifying and selecting eligible families to participate in the homeownership program, consistent with the affordability standards in § 572.120. Except for Indian tribes and IHAs as described in § 572.405(a)(2), the recipient must have a procedure to carry out its affirmative fair marketing responsibilities, described in § 572.405(e), that apply whenever homeownership opportunities are made available to other than current residents of the property. These procedures must include specific steps to inform potential applicants and solicit applications from eligible families in the housing market area who are least likely to apply for the program without special outreach.

(2) The written selection procedures must provide for selection only of families that are creditworthy and have the financial capacity to handle the anticipated costs of homeownership. Any family determined not to have paid the appropriate amount of tenant contribution under a HUD housing assistance program must be required to resolve any deficiency before being selected for homeownership.

(b) *Preferences.* (1) In making selections for the program, each recipient must give first preference to qualified residents who legally occupied units on the date the recipient's application for the implementation grant was submitted to HUD and to persons residing in the units at the time the properties are selected. If the unit occupied by a former resident on the date the implementation grant application was submitted to HUD is occupied by a different resident at the time of property selection, a vacant unit under this program must be offered to the former resident at the earliest possible time.

(2) In the case of vacant properties for which the preferences in paragraph (b)(1) of this section do not apply, recipients must give a first preference to otherwise qualified eligible families who reside in public or Indian housing under the 1937 Act. Recipients must use whatever measures are considered appropriate to inform residents of public and Indian housing developments within the housing market area of the preference, such as informing resident councils, PHAs, and IHAs, or other appropriate measures.

(3) Recipients must give a second preference to otherwise qualified eligible families who have completed participation in one of the following economic self-sufficiency programs: Project Self-Sufficiency, Operation Bootstrap, Family Self-Sufficiency, JOBS, and any other Federal, State, territorial, or local program approved by HUD as equivalent.

(c) *Responsibilities of selected families.* (1) Each eligible family selected for homeownership must certify at the time it acquires an ownership interest in the unit (or enters into a lease-purchase agreement for the unit) that it intends to occupy the unit as its principal residence during the six-year period from the date it acquires ownership interest in the unit, unless the recipient determines that the family is required to move outside the market area due to a change in employment or an emergency situation or the family sells its ownership interest. The family may permit others to rent space (such as a basement area or a spare bedroom) in the unit occupied by the family as its principal residence. (See § 572.115(c) concerning the rental of units in a multi-unit property purchased by a homebuyer under this part.)

(2) Any homebuyer that violates the agreement made under paragraph (c)(1) of this section shall be subject to penalties as provided in the transfer documents, as prescribed by HUD.

(3) Each eligible family selected for the program must participate in counseling and training of homebuyers and homeowners regarding the general rights and responsibilities of homeownership.

(d) *Social security numbers; wage and claims information.* As a condition of eligibility for homeownership under this part, at the time a family applies for howeownership, the recipient (or other appropriate entity) must:

(1) Require the family to meet the requirements for the disclosure and verification of social security numbers, as provided by part 5, subpart B, of this title; and

(2) Require the family to sign and submit consent forms for the obtaining of wage and claim information from State Wage Information Collection Agencies, as provided by part 5, subpart B, of this title.

(e) *Notification of rejected applicant families.* Recipients or another appropriate entity must promptly notify in writing any rejected applicant family of the grounds for any rejection.

[58 FR 36526, July 7, 1993, as amended at 61 FR 11118, Mar. 18, 1996; 61 FR 48797, Sept. 16, 1996]

§ 572.115 **Transfer of homeownership interests.**

(a) *Deadline for transfer.* (1) All units in eligible properties (including in rem properties) must be transferred to eligible families within two years of the effective date of the implementation grant agreement, except as otherwise provided for multi-unit properties in paragraph (c) of this section. The transfer must involve either:

(i) Acquisition by an eligible family of an ownership interest in a unit; or

(ii) Execution of a lease-purchase agreement for a unit.

(2) The HUD Field Office may approve a request for an extension of the deadline in paragraph (a)(1) of this section on a per-program or per-unit basis if the Field Office determines that all program activities will be completed in accordance with the timing requirements of § 572.210(f) (including any extension granted under § 572.210(f)).

(b) *Form of ownership.* (1) Forms of ownership interests acquired by eligible families under this part may include fee simple ownership (including condominium ownership), cooperative ownership, or another form of ownership interest proposed and justified by the applicant and approved by HUD. HUD will not approve other forms of ownership that would substantially limit the ability of homeowners to realize financial appreciation in the value of their homes as determined by HUD. The type of ownership interest must be consistent with any applicable State (or territorial), local, or tribal law.

(2) The ownership interest may be subject only to:

(i) The restrictions on resale required or approved under § 572.130;

(ii) Mortgages, deeds of trust, or other liens or instruments securing the eligible family's purchase money financing as approved by the recipient; or

(iii) Any other restrictions or encumbrances that do not impair the good and marketable nature of title to the ownership interest except as otherwise approved by the recipient. In approving the terms of an eligible family's purchase money financing or any other encumbrances on the property under paragraphs (b)(2)(ii) and (iii) of this section, the recipient shall not approve financing terms that do not comply with the affordability standards in § 572.120, or mortgage terms and conditions or other encumbrances that in effect constitute resale restrictions that would not be approved by HUD under this part.

(3) Mutual housing is eligible only to the extent it provides for the transfer of ownership interests to eligible families.

(c) *Transfer of multi-unit properties.* (1) In the case of a two-to-four unit property, only property that may be divided so that an ownership interest in each unit may be acquired by an eligible family is eligible. HUD may grant an exception to this requirement on a program-by-program basis when it determines that such an exception will serve to further the purposes of the HOPE 3 program.

(2) HUD Headquarters will consider and may approve an exception under the following circumstances:

(i) The reasonably projected net rental income will be included in the determination of the appraised value of the property at the time of the homebuyer's purchase;

(ii) The rent charged by the owner will not exceed the Fair Market Rent established by HUD for the area;

(iii) The recipient will provide the homebuyer with counseling and training in property management, and will approve the form of lease used by the homebuyer; and

(iv) The recipient will include the family's potential net rental income in calculating the family's initial affordability in accordance with § 572.120 of this part.

[58 FR 36526, July 7, 1993, as amended at 61 FR 48797, Sept. 16, 1996]

§ 572.120 Affordability standards.

(a) *Initial affordability.* (1) The monthly expenditure for principal, interest, taxes, and insurance by an eligible family that is required under the financing both for the acquisition and for the rehabilitation in accordance with § 572.100(d) of a unit (whether the required rehabilitation occurs before or after the family takes title) must be not less than 20 percent and not more than 30 percent of one-twelfth of the annual income of the family used for the purpose of determining eligibility under § 572.110(a). (For the purpose of determining affordability of the family, the recipient may, at its option, adjust downward the annual incomes of eligible families using reasonable standards and procedures consistently applied.) HUD may approve a justified request for a floor lower than 20 percent to avoid undue hardship to families, such as where the cost of utilities is high.

(2) The 30 percent cap on monthly payments includes closing costs only if closing costs are included in the costs of principal and interest, or are otherwise required to be paid by the homeowner over time after acquisition.

(3) Applicants are encouraged to consider the additional monthly costs of utilities and other monthly housing costs, such as condominium and cooperative fees, in determining whether the family can afford to purchase a unit.

(b) *Continued affordability.* The recipient must develop a plan demonstrating reasonable efforts to ensure continued affordability by homeowners in the eligible property. Financing that would impair the continued affordability of the property for homebuyers, such as a mortgage that is not fully amortizing (*e.g.*, a "balloon" mortgage) may not be used. The plan should take into account such program features as long-term financing at reasonable terms, energy conservation, and improvements that will entail low-cost maintenance.

[58 FR 36526, July 7, 1993, as amended at 60 FR 36018, July 12, 1995]

§ 572.125 Replacement reserves.

(a) *Purpose.* A single replacement reserve may be established for the homeownership program only if HUD determines it is necessary to prevent severe financial hardship to families caused by the failure of a major system or component of the property that would render the unit substandard. Initially, the reserve must be justified by the applicant and approved by HUD as part of the program budget in the application or an amended application.

(b) *Need for reserve account.* In determining the need for a replacement reserve, the applicant or recipient must demonstrate that the financial status of eligible families is insufficient to meet the needs for which the reserve is established, and that the amount proposed for the reserve is reasonable, taking into account the following factors:

(1) The size of the implementation grant and the amount of matching contributions;

(2) The availability of insurance, and the home maintenance and repair capabilities of the families; and

(3) The condition and age of the properties and each of their major systems and components (including at least the heating, plumbing, and electrical systems, the roof, foundation, windows, exterior walls, and common area, if any).

(c) *Drawdown of reserve funds.* Replacement reserve funds may only be drawn down under the Cash and Management Information System when specifically needed to assist a homeowner. At time of program closeout, all funds approved for a replacement reserve may be drawn down to fund a reserve account. The account may not exceed six years estimated replacement cost needs for the properties transferred under the homeownership program.

(d) *Administration of the reserve account.* The recipient must identify the entity that will administer the replacement reserve account at time of program closeout. The entity responsible

Ofc. of Asst. Secy., Comm. Planning, Develop., HUD § 572.130

for administering the account must be bonded and approved by HUD. The account must be interest bearing, if possible, and interest earned thereon must be used for the purposes for which the account is established. Unused funds at the end of the term of the account must be treated as program income in accordance with § 572.135(d).

§ 572.130 Restrictions on resale by initial homeowners.

(a) *Right to transfer.* A homeowner may transfer the homeowner's ownership interest in the unit, subject only to the right to purchase under paragraph (b) of this section; the requirement for the purchaser to execute a promissory note, if required under paragraph (d) of this section; and the limitation on the amount of sales proceeds a family may retain upon sale within the first six years, as required under paragraph (c) of this section.

(b) *Right to purchase.* (1) Where a cooperative has jurisdiction over the unit, it has the prior right to purchase the ownership interest in the unit from the initial homeowner for the amount and on the terms specified in a firm contract between the homeowner and a prospective buyer. The cooperative association has 10 days after receiving notice of the firm contract to decide whether to exercise its right and 60 additional days to complete closing of the purchase.

(2) If no cooperative has jurisdiction over the unit and if the prospective buyer is not a low-income family, the recipient or a PHA/IHA with jurisdiction for the area in which the unit is located, whichever is specified in the documents under which the initial family acquires an ownership interest in the unit, has the prior right to purchase the ownership interest in the unit for the amount and on the terms specified in a firm contract between the recipient and a prospective buyer. The recipient or PHA/IHA has 10 days after receiving notice of the firm contract to decide whether to exercise its right and 60 additional days to complete closing of the purchase.

(3) Where a recipient, cooperative, or PHA/IHA exercises a right to purchase, it must resell the unit to an eligible family promptly.

(4) Unless otherwise provided in the property transfer documents, none of the provisions of paragraph (b) of this section apply in the case of liquidation of a security interest in the property. If FHA has insured a mortgage on the property, the provisions of paragraph (b) of this section shall not apply upon occurrence of an event requiring termination under 24 CFR 203.41(c)(2) or 234.66(c)(2).

(c) *Limitation on equity interest an initial homeowner may retain from sale during first six years.* (1) The HOPE program is designed to assure that an initial or subsequent homeowner does not receive any undue profit from acquiring a unit under the program and that, to the extent the sales price is sufficient, an initial homeowner recovers the equity interest in the property. With respect to any sale by an initial homeowner during the first six years after acquisition, the family may retain only the amount computed under this paragraph. Any excess must be distributed as provided in § 572.135(b). The amount of equity an initial homeowner has in the property is determined by computing the sum of the following:

(i) The contribution to equity paid by the family (such as any downpayment (in the form of cash or the value of sweat equity) and any amount paid towards principal on a mortgage loan during the period of ownership);

(ii) The value of any improvements (not including normal or routine maintenance) installed at the expense of the family during the family's tenure as owner (including improvements made through sweat equity), as determined by the recipient or other entity specified in the approved application based on evidence of amounts spent on the improvements, including the cost of material and labor (or the value of the sweat equity); and

(iii) The appreciated value, determined by applying the Consumer Price Index (Urban Consumers) or other HUD approved index against the contribution to equity under paragraphs (d)(i) and (ii) of this section.

(2) The recipient (or other entity) may, at the time of initial sale, enter into an agreement with the family to set a maximum amount which this appreciation may not exceed.

§ 572.130

(3) Amounts that count towards a family's equity may not also count towards the match.

(d) *Promissory note.* (1) If the purchase price of the unit (adjusted, if applicable as described in this paragraph) paid by the initial homebuyer is less than the fair market value of the property (based on an appraisal of the value of the unit after rehabilitation to applicable program standards conducted in accordance with the appraisal requirements in § 572.100(b)), the initial homeowner must, at closing, execute a non-amortizing, nonrecourse, noninterest-bearing promissory note, in a form acceptable to HUD, equal to the difference between such fair market value of the unit and the adjusted purchase price, together with a security instrument securing the obligation of the note and recorded in local land records or other applicable system of recordation appropriate to the type of security interest being recorded. The note must be payable to the recipient or other entity designated in the approved homeownership plan. In determining the amount of the promissory note and for that purpose only, the purchase price must be adjusted by deducting all substantial amounts of financial assistance with respect to the family's acquisition or rehabilitation of the unit that would result in an undue profit to the family if it were to sell the unit at the beginning of the 7th year of homeownership. (See paragraph (c) of this section for an additional restriction on return to the homeowner on resales during the first six years.) For this purpose, "substantial financial assistance" includes all forms of assistance or subsidy from HOPE 3 resources that reduce the cash return (sales proceeds) received by the recipient for the unit below its appraised after-rehabilitation fair market value by more than a total of $4,000, including (without limitation) discounted purchase prices, downpayment assistance, and rehabilitation or purchase money grants or loans that are not repayable on an amortizing basis. Financing to homeowners provided from HOPE 3 resources may not be assumed by subsequent homebuyers.

(2) With respect to a sale by an initial homeowner, the note must require payment upon sale by the initial homeowner, to the extent proceeds of the sale remain after paying off other outstanding debt secured by the property that was incurred for the purpose of acquisition or property improvement, paying any other amounts due in connection with the sale (such as closing costs and transfer taxes), and paying the family the amount of its equity in the property, computed in accordance with paragraph (c) of this section.

(3) With respect to a sale by an initial homeowner after the first six years after acquisition, through the 20th year, the amount payable under the note must be reduced by $1/168$ of the original principal amount of the note for each full month of ownership by the family after the end of the sixth year. The homeowner may retain all other proceeds of the sale.

(4) Where a subsequent purchaser during the 20-year period, measured by the term of the initial promissory note, purchases the property for less than the then current fair market value (determined in accordance with the appraisal requirements in § 572.100(b)), the purchaser must also execute at closing a promissory note and mortgage (to be recorded as stated in paragraph (d)(1) of this section) payable to the recipient or its designee, for the amount of the discount (but no more than the amount payable at the time of the sale on the promissory note by the seller). The term of the promissory note must be the period remaining of the original 20-year period. The note must require payment upon sale by the subsequent homeowner, to the extent proceeds of the sale remain after covering costs of the sale, paying off other outstanding debt secured by the property that was incurred for the purpose of acquisition or property improvement, and paying any other amounts due in connection with the sale. The amount payable on the note must be reduced by a percentage of the original principal amount of the note for each full month of ownership by the subsequent homeowner. The percentage must be computed by determining the percentage of the term of the promissory note the homeowner has owned the property. The remainder may be retained by the subsequent homeowner selling the property.

Ofc. of Asst. Secy., Comm. Planning, Develop., HUD § 572.145

(e) *Additional restrictions.* Notwithstanding paragraph (a) of this section, an applicant may propose in its application, and HUD may approve, additional reasonable restrictions on the resale of units under the program. HUD does not encourage additional restrictions, but HUD approval will be based on a review of the individual circumstances. However, HUD will not approve restrictions that it determines will substantially limit the ability of homeowners to realize financial appreciation in the value of their homes.

[58 FR 36526, July 7, 1993, as amended at 61 FR 48798, Sept. 16, 1996]

§ 572.135 **Use of proceeds from sales to eligible families, resale proceeds, and program income.**

(a) *Proceeds from sales.* The recipient or another entity approved by HUD must use the proceeds, if any, from the initial sale for costs of their HOPE 3 program, including additional homeownership opportunities eligible under the HOPE 3 program, improvements to properties under the HOPE 3 program, business opportunities for low-income families participating in the HOPE 3 program, supportive services related to the HOPE 3 program, and other activities approved by HUD, either as part of the approved application or later on request. Such proceeds include the full consideration received by the recipient or other entity for the property, including principal and interest on purchase money loans from HOPE 3 funds or match.

(b) *Resale proceeds.* Fifty percent of any portion of the net sales proceeds that may not be retained by the homeowner under § 572.130(c), (d), and (e) must be paid to the recipient, or another entity approved by HUD, for use for additional homeownership opportunities eligible under the HOPE 3 program, improvements to properties under the HOPE 3 program, business opportunities for homeowners under the HOPE 3 program, supportive services related to the HOPE 3 program, and other activities approved by HUD in the approved homeownership program or later on request. The remaining 50 percent must be collected by the recipient and returned to HUD within 15 days of the sale for use under the HOPE 3 program, subject to any limitations contained in appropriations Acts.

(c) *Requirements for use of sale and resale proceeds.* Sale and resale proceeds must be committed for approved activities within one year of receipt. All sale and resale proceeds must be accounted for by the recipient, and 50 percent of all resale proceeds received by the recipient must be returned to HUD, as described in paragraph (b) of this section. Recipients may use up to 15 percent of their sale and resale proceeds for administrative expenses to expand their HOPE 3 program and provide additional homeownership opportunities. Recipients must retain records on the use of these funds to the same level of detail as required of grant funds under the HOPE 3 system or whatever records HUD otherwise prescribes. The recipient, and any other entity approved by HUD to administer the sale and resale proceeds, remain responsible to comply with the requirements of this part, or such other requirements as HUD may prescribe (consistent with then applicable law) in closeout procedures or agreements.

(d) *Program income.* Any program income, as defined in § 572.5, received by the recipient may be added to the funds committed to the grant agreement by HUD and the recipient, in accordance with the requirements of parts 84 and 85 of this title, as applicable.

[58 FR 36526, July 7, 1993, as amended at 60 FR 36018, July 12, 1995; 62 FR 34145, June 24, 1997]

§ 572.140 **Third party rights.**

The rights of third parties are governed by 42 U.S.C. 12895(d) and apply to the requirements of this part.

[61 FR 48798, Sept. 16, 1996]

§ 572.145 **Displacement prohibited; protection of nonpurchasing residents.**

(a) *Displacement prohibited.* (1) No person may be displaced from his or her dwelling as a direct result of a homeownership program under this part. This does not preclude terminations of tenancy for violation of the terms of occupancy of the unit. Each resident of

§ 572.200

an eligible property on the date the application for an implementation grant was submitted to HUD and each resident at the time the property is selected must be given an opportunity to become a homeowner under this program if the resident qualifies as an eligible family and meets other program requirements. If the resident does not qualify or does not elect to move, the property is not eligible. The protections provided to residents under this section do not apply to the former owner of the property if the property is acquired from him or her as a result of a tax or mortgage foreclosure.

(2) In addition to any applicable sanctions under the grant agreement, a violation of paragraph (a)(1) of this section may trigger a requirement to provide relocation assistance in accordance with the Uniform Relocation Assistance and Real Property Acquisition Policies Act of 1970 and government-wide implementing regulations at 49 CFR part 24.

(b) *Relocation assistance for residents who elect to move.* The recipient must offer each nonpurchasing resident who elects to move relocation assistance in accordance with the approved homeownership program. The program must provide, at least, the following assistance:

(1) Advisory services, including timely information, counseling (including the provision of information on a resident's rights under the Fair Housing Act), and referrals to suitable, affordable, decent, safe, and sanitary alternative housing;

(2) Payment for actual, reasonable moving expenses; and

(3) Financial assistance sufficient to permit relocation to suitable, affordable, decent, safe, and sanitary housing. This requirement is met if the family is provided the opportunity to relocate to suitable, decent, safe, and sanitary housing for which the monthly rent and estimated average utility costs do not exceed the greater of 30 percent of the person's income or the person's monthly rent before relocation and the estimated average monthly utility costs. The homeownership program must specify the period for which replacement housing assistance will be provided to persons who do not receive assistance through a Section 8 rental certificate or voucher or other housing program subsidy.

(c) *Temporary relocation.* The recipient must provide each resident of an eligible property, who is required to relocate temporarily to permit work to be carried out, with suitable, decent, safe, and sanitary housing for the temporary period and must reimburse the resident for all reasonable out-of-pocket expenses incurred in connection with the temporary relocation, including the costs of moving to and from the temporarily occupied housing and any increase in monthly costs of rent and utilities.

(d) *Notice of relocation assistance.* As soon as feasible, each recipient must give each resident of an eligible property a written description of the applicable provisions of this section.

Subpart C—Grants

§ 572.200 Planning grants.

Any planning grants made by HUD under the HOPE 3 program will continue to be governed by the provisions in this section in effect immediately before October 16, 1996. When or before HUD announces the availability of funds for planning grants under this part, these provisions will be recodified.

[61 FR 48798, Sept. 16, 1996]

§ 572.205 Planning grants—eligible activities.

Any planning grants made by HUD under the HOPE 3 program will continue to be governed by the provisions in this section in effect immediately before October 16, 1996. When or before HUD announces the availability of funds for planning grants under this part, these provisions will be recodified.

[61 FR 48798, Sept. 16, 1996]

§ 572.210 Implementation grants.

(a) *General authority.* Any implementation grants for the purpose of carrying out homeownership programs approved under this part will be awarded using a selection process and selection criteria to be published in a NOFA.

(b) *Deadline for completion.* A recipient must spend all implementation grant amounts within 4 years from the effective date of the grant agreement. The appropriate HUD field office may approve a request to extend the deadline when it determines that an extension is warranted. A previously approved grant amount may not be amended to increase the grant amount.

(c) *Program closeout.* Recipients will comply with closeout procedures as issued by HUD.

[62 FR 34145, June 24, 1997]

§ 572.215 Implementation grants—eligible activities.

Implementation grants may be used for the reasonable costs of eligible activities necessary to carry out a homeownership program under this part. Only costs incurred on or after the effective date of an implementation grant agreement qualify for funding under this part. Eligible activities include:

(a) *Acquisition of eligible properties by the recipient.* Acquisition of eligible properties for the purpose of transferring ownership interests to eligible families in a homeownership program under this part, in accordance with § 572.100. (Where the applicant owns the eligible property or where HUD otherwise determines that an "arms length" relationship for acquisition does not exist, program funds may not be used for acquisition of the property for the program. However, if the property is owned by an eligible source, it may be donated as match in accordance with § 572.220(b)(4).)

(b) *Recipient closing costs.* Customary and reasonable closing costs of the buyer associated with the purchase of eligible properties under the program.

(c) *Financial assistance to homebuyers.* Provision of assistance to families to make acquisition and rehabilitation of eligible properties affordable, in accordance with § 572.105(b).

(d) *Rehabilitation.* Rehabilitation of the eligible property covered by the homeownership program, in accordance with standards and cost limitations established by HUD in § 572.100.

(e) *Architectural and engineering work.* Architectural and engineering work, and related professional services required to prepare architectural plans or drawings, write-ups, specifications or inspections, including lead-based paint evaluation.

(f) *Relocation.* Relocation of residents in eligible properties who elect to move, in accordance with § 572.145(b).

(g) *Temporary relocation of homebuyers.* Temporary relocation of residents during rehabilitation, in accordance with § 572.145(c).

(h) *Legal fees.* Customary and reasonable costs of professional legal services.

(i) *Replacement reserves.* A single replacement reserve for the properties under the program if necessary, in accordance with § 572.125.

(j) *Homebuyer outreach and selection.* Reasonable and necessary costs of marketing the program to potential homebuyers and of identifying and selecting homebuyers under the program. These costs may include costs related to implementing the affirmative fair housing marketing strategy required under § 572.110.

(k) *Counseling and training.* Counseling and training of only those homebuyers (and their alternates) and homeowners selected under the homeownership program. This may include such subjects as personal financial management, home maintenance, home repair, construction skills (especially where the eligible family will do some of the rehabilitation), property management for owners of multi-unit properties, and the general rights and responsibilities of homeownership.

(l) *Property management and holding costs.* Reasonable and necessary costs related to properly maintaining and securing eligible properties after acquisition or donation and before sale to an eligible homebuyer. These costs may include property insurance expenses, security costs, property taxes, utility charges, and other costs related to sound property management of recipient-owned properties before sale under the program. These costs may not be charged relative to eligible properties donated to the program by the recipient or another entity that HUD determines does not have an "arm's length" relationship with the recipient.

(m) *Recipient training needs.* Defraying costs for ongoing training needs of the recipient for courses of instruction that are directly related to developing and carrying out the homeownership program.

(n) *Economic development.* Economic development activities that promote economic self-sufficiency of homebuyers and homeowners under the homeownership program. The economic development activities must be directly related to the homeownership program, and may only benefit families and individuals who are homeowners or who have been selected as homebuyers under the program. These costs are limited to job training or retraining and day care costs of those participating in job training and retraining activities approved under the HOPE 3 program. The recipient must enter into written agreements with the providers of economic development services specifying the services to be provided, including estimates of the numbers of homebuyers and homeowners to be assisted. The aggregate amount of planning and implementation grants that may be used for economic development activities related to any one program may not exceed $250,000.

(o) *Administrative costs.* Reasonable and necessary costs, as described and valued in accordance with the OMB Circular Nos. A-87 or A-122, as applicable, incurred by a recipient in carrying out the HOPE 3 program. The total amount that may be spent on administrative activities from the implementation grant and any contribution toward the match may not exceed 15 percent of the amount of the grant. For purposes of complying with the 15 percent limitation, administrative costs do not include the cost of activities that are separately eligible under this section.

(p) *Other activities.* Other activities proposed by the applicant, to the extent the applicant justifies them as necessary for the proposed homeownership program and HUD approves them.

[58 FR 36526, July 7, 1993, as amended at 64 FR 50226, Sept. 15, 1999]

§ 572.220 **Implementation grants— matching requirements.**

(a) *General requirements.* (1) Except as provided in paragraph (a)(3) of this section, each recipient must assure that matching contributions equal to not less than 33 percent (or 25 percent for grants awarded after April 11, 1994) of the amount of the implementation grant shall be provided from non-Federal sources to carry out the homeownership program. Amounts contributed to the match must be used for eligible activities or in accordance with the requirements of this section.

(2) All contributions toward eligible activities to be counted toward the match must be provided no later than the deadline for completion of program activities established in accordance with § 572.210(f), except as permitted under paragraphs (b)(1)(iv) and (b)(3) of this section.

(3) When the recipient is an IHA, and the IHA (acting in that capacity) has not received, and will not receive, amounts under title I of the Housing and Community Development Act of 1974 for the fiscal year in which HUD obligates HOPE grant funds, the match requirements under this section will not apply.

(b) *Form.* Contributions may only be in the form of:

(1) *Cash contributions.* (i) Cash contributions from non-Federal resources contributed permanently for uses under the HOPE 3 program by the applicant, non-Federal public entities, private entities, or individuals, except that a cash contribution in the form of a down payment made by an eligible family may not count as a matching contribution. Funds will be considered permanently contributed if all principal, interest, and any other return on the contribution are used for eligible activities in accordance with program requirements.

(ii) Non-Federal resources may include:

(A) Contribution of trust funds held by Federal agencies for Indian tribes;

(B) PHA section 8 operating reserve funds, where approved by HUD;

(C) Income from a Federal grant earned after the end of the award period, if no Federal programmatic requirements govern the disposition of the program income.

(D) Amounts, determined in accordance with paragraph (b)(1)(iv)(B) of this section, that have been requested by

Ofc. of Asst. Secy., Comm. Planning, Develop., HUD § 572.220

the applicant in an application submitted to the Federal Housing Finance Board for assistance under its affordable housing program, so long as the application is approved within 30 days of HUD's conditional approval of the HOPE 3 application.

(iii) Non-Federal resources may not include:

(A) Funds from a Community Development Block Grant under section 106(b) or section 106(d), respectively, of the Housing and Community Development Act of 1974, except to the extent permitted for administrative expenses under paragraph (b)(2) of this section;

(B) Federal tax expenditures, including low-income housing tax credits.

(iv) The grant equivalent of a below-market interest rate loan to the homebuyer from non-Federal resources, where all repayments, interest, and other return will not be permanently contributed to the HOPE 3 program, may be counted as a cash contribution. The grant equivalent of a below market interest rate loan must be calculated in accordance with paragraphs (b)(1)(iv) (A) and (B) of this section—

(A) If the loan is made from proceeds of obligations issued by or on behalf of a public body that are exempt from taxation by the United States, the contribution is the present discounted cash value of the difference between payments to be made on the borrowed funds and payments to be received on the loan to the homebuyer, based on a discount rate equal to the interest rate on the borrowed funds;

(B) If the loan is made from funds other than under paragraph (b)(1)(iv)(A) of this section, the contribution is the present discounted cash value of the yield forgone, calculated based on a discount rate approved or prescribed by HUD. In determining the yield forgone, the recipient must use as a measure of a market yield one of the following, as appropriate:

(*1*) With respect to housing financed with a fixed interest rate mortgage, a rate equal to the 10-year Treasury note rate plus 200 basis points; or

(*2*) With respect to housing financed with an adjustable interest rate mortgage, a rate equal to the one-year Treasury bill rate plus 250 basis points.

(v) Cash contributions may also be made from sales proceeds from the Turnkey III Homeownership and Mutual Help programs, as approved by HUD, or an approved homeownership program under section 5(h) of the 1937 Act.

(2) *Administrative costs.* (i) Contributions of eligible administrative services up to a value equal to 7 percent of the amount of the implementation grant. This limitation is in addition to the 15 percent limitation on administrative costs (see § 572.215(o)).

(ii) If an applicant proposes to contribute administrative services, HUD will automatically approve an applicant's assurances for matching purposes that it will pay eligible administrative costs from non-Federal sources in an amount up to 7 percent of the implementation grant, and will not require further documentation of those expenditures for purposes of the HOPE 3 program. If a recipient uses more than 8 percent of its implementation grant to pay administrative costs, the amount credited toward the match will be reduced to less than 7 percent to stay within the 15 percent limitation.

(iii) Non-Federal resources, for the purposes of counting contributions for administrative costs, may include funds from a Community Development Block Grant under section 106(b) or section 106(d) of the Housing and Community Development Act of 1974 and are subject to the recordkeeping and documentation requirements of that program.

(3) *Taxes, fees, and other charges.* (i) The present value of taxes, fees, or other charges that are normally and customarily imposed but are waived, forgone, or deferred in a manner that facilitates the implementation of a homeownership program assisted under this part. Only amounts that would have been imposed after the date a property is acquired by a recipient or other entity for transfer to eligible families, the effective date of the implementation grant agreement if the recipient already owns the property, or the date after an eligible property is acquired directly from an eligible source by an eligible family, as applicable, may be counted towards the match.

(ii) Amounts that would be waived, forgone, or deferred for longer than 20 years from the date a family acquires homeownership interests in the unit may not be counted towards the match.

(iii) The present value of taxes, fees, or other charges waived, forgone, or deferred must be computed by discounting the estimated amount that would be otherwise payable over the time period (up to 20 years) based on a discount rate approved or prescribed by HUD.

(iv) Where the match includes amounts under paragraph (b)(3) of this section, the documents transferring the homeownership interest to the family must evidence the contribution, to the extent the contribution has not already been received.

(4) *Real property.* Real property contributed for use under an approved homeownership program. To the extent properties were acquired with Federal resources or are donated directly to the program from Federal sources, their value is not an eligible match contribution.

(i) The as-is fair market value of eligible property may be counted as a contribution toward the match, determined in accordance with a recent appraisal conducted under procedures established or approved by HUD. The maximum value contributed will be limited as provided in § 572.100.

(ii) When eligible real property is sold to the recipient or its designee from non-Federal sources at a price below fair market value, the differential between the fair market value and the discounted sales price may be counted toward the match.

(iii) Vacant land from any non-Federal source located on existing streets with available utilities (which need not include laterals) may be contributed for use under the program, but only if a structure acquired or donated from an eligible HOPE 3 source will be moved onto it. The total amount of the contribution and any amount paid from HOPE 3 funds for acquisition of the structure, moving, and rehabilitation costs must be within the limits provided in § 572.100.

(5) *Infrastructure.* The fair market value of investment (as approved by HUD), not made with Federal resources, in on-site and off-site infrastructure that directly contributes to a homeownership program. The infrastructure investment may be counted toward the match only if it was completed no earlier than 12 months before the deadline date set by HUD in the NOFA for receipt of implementation grant applications. Investment in infrastructure may include such activities as new or repaired utility laterals connecting eligible property to the main line and new or rebuilt walkways, sidewalks, or curbs on or contiguous to the eligible property. If the investment in infrastructure also benefits other properties, only the share of the costs directly benefiting the eligible property under the homeownership program may be counted toward the match.

(6) *Donated labor.* All donated labor, including sweat equity provided by a homebuyer or homeowner, to be valued at $10 an hour or at a rate promulgated by HUD in the NOFA, except for donated professional labor, as approved by HUD, including professional labor by homebuyers and homeowners. The donated professional labor will be valued at the fair market value of the work completed. Professional labor is work ordinarily performed by the donor for payment, such as work by attorneys, electricians, carpenters, and architects that is equivalent to work they do in their occupations. Sweat equity may be counted towards the match only if it is not also counted toward a family's equity.

(7) *Donated materials and supplies.* Donated materials and supplies may be counted toward the match contribution at their fair market value. The recipient must maintain a written enumeration of what donated materials and supplies are being used in the program, as well as documentation of their cost or value.

(8) *Other in-kind contributions.* The reasonable value of in-kind contributions proposed by the applicant in the application and approved by HUD. In reviewing proposed in-kind contributions, HUD will review to ensure:

(i) The proposed contribution is to be used for an eligible activity under the proposed homeownership program;

(ii) The application demonstrates that the proposed in-kind contribution will actually be provided; and

(iii) The proposed value of the contribution is reasonable. In determining whether the value is reasonable, HUD will generally consider the amount such contribution would otherwise cost the program.

[58 FR 36526, July 7, 1993, as amended at 60 FR 36018, July 12, 1995; 61 FR 48798, Sept. 16, 1996]

§ 572.225 Grant agreements; corrective and remedial actions.

(a) *Terms and conditions.* After HUD approves an application for a planning grant or an implementation grant under this part, it will enter into a grant agreement with the recipient setting forth the amount of the grant and applicable terms and conditions. The grant agreement will be effective for purposes of this part and funds may be disbursed under the Cash and Management Information (C/MI) System, described in § 572.230, after the grant agreement has been executed by the authorized official of the recipient and HUD. Among other things, the grant agreement will provide that the recipient agrees:

(1) To carry out the program in accordance with the provisions of this part, applicable law, the approved application, and all other applicable requirements; and

(2) To comply with such other terms and conditions, including recordkeeping and reports, as HUD may establish for the purposes of administering, monitoring, and evaluating the program in an effective and efficient manner.

(b) *Corrective and remedial actions.* (1) HUD may withhold, withdraw, or recapture any portion of a grant, terminate the grant agreement, or take other appropriate action authorized under the grant agreement, if HUD determines that the recipient is failing to carry out the approved homeownership program in accordance with the terms of the approved application and this part, including failure to provide the contributions toward the match. Corrective or remedial actions that HUD may instruct the recipient to undertake include:

(i) Preparing and following a schedule of actions or a management plan for properly completing the approved activities;

(ii) Cancelling or revising the affected activities before expending grant funds for them, revising the grant budget as necessary, and substituting other eligible activities;

(iii) Discontinuing draws under the C/MI System, and not incurring further costs for the affected activities;

(iv) Reimbursing its HOPE 3 program account in the amount not used in accordance with this part and the grant agreement; and

(v) In the case of implementation grants, making additional matching contributions in substitution for contributions not in compliance with this part and the grant agreement or submitting to HUD acceptable evidence that matching contributions sufficient to meet the total match required under this part and the grant agreement will be made, before additional draws are made.

(2) If HUD determines that the recipient is not complying with the corrective or remedial actions agreed upon with the recipient, or as otherwise authorized in the grant agreement, HUD may implement the following additional corrective and remedial actions:

(i) Changing the method of payment under the C/MI System to a reimbursement basis;

(ii) Suspending the recipient's authority to make draws under the C/MI System for affected activities;

(iii) Reducing (deobligating) the grant in the amount affected by the performance deficiency, including, in the case of implementation grants, failure to furnish matching contributions in the required amount;

(iv) Terminating the grant for all further activities and initiating close-out procedures;

(v) Taking action against the recipient under 2 CFR part 2424 with respect to future HOPE 3, HUD, or federal grant awards; and

(vi) Taking any other remedial action legally available.

§ 572.230

(3) If the amount of grant funds that has been disbursed under the C/MI System exceeds the amount finally determined by HUD to be authorized (including any authorized deobligation), the recipient must repay such excess amount to HUD, and will have no right to reclaim or reuse such excess amount.

(c) *Failure to complete and transfer a property to a homebuyer.* If a property assisted under this part or credited as match is not completed and transferred to homebuyers as required under this part, whether voluntarily by the recipient or otherwise, grant expenditures on the property are considered ineligible, and HOPE 3 funds for acquisition and rehabilitation must be repaid to the program account. Preliminary costs (such as architectural and engineering, inspection, and appraisal fees) expended before acquisition are considered general program expenses and need not be repaid.

(d) *Failure to provide homeownership opportunities under an implementation grant.* Failure to provide at least 70 percent of the number of homeownership opportunities proposed in the application for an implementation grant within the timeframe specified in § 572.210(f) may result in remedial actions, as described in paragraph (b) of this section, being taken by HUD, including requiring repayment of all or part of the grant.

[58 FR 36526, July 7, 1993, as amended at 72 FR 73496, Dec. 27, 2007]

§ 572.230 **Cash and Management Information (C/MI) System.**

Disbursement of HOPE 3 grant funds is managed through HUD's Cash and Management Information (C/MI) System for the HOPE 3 program. Funds that may be disbursed through the C/MI System include funds awarded to the recipient and obligated through the grant approval letter issued by HUD. HOPE 3 funds are drawn down by the recipient or its authorized designee from a United States Treasury account for the program, using the Treasury Automated Clearinghouse (ACH) System. Any drawdown of HOPE 3 funds from the United States Treasury account is conditioned upon the submission of satisfactory information about the program and compliance with other procedures specified by HUD in HUD's forms and issuances concerning the C/MI System.

[62 FR 34145, June 24, 1997]

§ 572.235 **Amendments.**

Amendments to the approved program must be documented or approved by HUD in accordance with instructions provided by HUD.

Subpart D—Selection Process

§ 572.300 **Notices of funding availability (NOFAs); grant applications.**

When funds are made available for planning grants or implementation grants under this part, HUD will publish a NOFA in the FEDERAL REGISTER, in accordance with the requirements of part 4 of this title, and will select applications for funding on a competitive basis as provided in the applicable NOFA.

[62 FR 34145, June 24, 1997]

§ 572.315 **Rating criteria for planning grants.**

Any planning grants made by HUD under the HOPE 3 program will continue to be governed by the provisions in this section in effect immediately before October 16, 1996. When or before HUD announces the availability of funds for planning grants under this part, these provisions will be recodified.

[61 FR 48798, Sept. 16, 1996]

Subpart E—Other Federal Requirements

§ 572.400 **Consolidated plan.**

Applicants must provide a certification of consistency with the approved consolidated plan, in accordance with 24 CFR 91.510.

[60 FR 36018, July 12, 1995]

§ 572.405 **Nondiscrimination and equal opportunity requirements.**

In addition to the nondiscrimination and equal opportunity requirements set forth in 24 CFR part 5, the following requirements apply to homeownership programs under this part:

(a) *Modification of fair housing and nondiscrimination requirements for Indian tribes and IHAs.* (1) The Indian Civil Rights Act (25 U.S.C. 1301 *et seq.*) applies to tribes when they exercise their powers of self-government. Thus, it is applicable in all cases when an IHA has been established by exercise of such powers. In the case of the IHA established pursuant to State law, the applicability of the Indian Civil Rights Act shall be determined on a case-by-case basis. Development subject to the Indian Civil Rights Act must be developed and operated in compliance with its provisions and all implementing HUD requirements, instead of title VI and the Fair Housing Act and their implementing regulations.

(2) In the case of Indian tribes and IHAs, compliance with the requirements of this section shall be to the maximum extent consistent, but not in derogation of, the Indian Self-Determination and Education Assistance Act (25 U.S.C. 450e(b)).

(b) *Affirmative fair housing marketing.* The recipient must adopt a strategy for informing and soliciting applications from people who are least likely to apply, because of race, color, religion, sex, disability, familial status, or national origin, for the program without special outreach, consistent with the affirmative fair housing marketing requirements. (See 24 CFR 92.351 for an example of an affirmative strategy.) Paragraph (b) of this section does not apply to Indian tribes and IHAs, as described in paragraph (a)(1) of this section.

(c) *Authority for collection of racial, ethnic, and gender data.* HUD requires submission of racial, ethnic, and gender data under this part under the authority of section 562 of the Housing and Community Development Act of 1987 and section 808(e)(6) of the Fair Housing Act.

(d) *Faith-based activities.* (1) Organizations that are religious or faith-based are eligible, on the same basis as any other organization, to participate in the HOPE 3 program. Neither the Federal government nor a State or local government receiving funds under HOPE 3 programs shall discriminate against an organization on the basis of the organization's religious character or affiliation.

(2) Organizations that are directly funded under the HOPE 3 program may not engage in inherently religious activities, such as worship, religious instruction, or proselytization, as part of the programs or services funded under this part. If an organization conducts such activities, the activities must be offered separately, in time or location, from the programs or services funded under this part, and participation must be voluntary for the beneficiaries of the HUD-funded programs or services.

(3) A religious organization that participates in the HOPE 3 program will retain its independence from Federal, State, and local governments, and may continue to carry out its mission, including the definition, practice, and expression of its religious beliefs, provided that it does not use direct HOPE 3 funds to support any inherently religious activities, such as worship, religious instruction, or proselytization. Among other things, faith-based organizations may use space in their facilities to provide HOPE 3-funded services, without removing religious art, icons, scriptures, or other religious symbols. In addition, a HOPE 3-funded religious organization retains its authority over its internal governance, and it may retain religious terms in its organization's name, select its board members on a religious basis, and include religious references in its organization's mission statements and other governing documents.

(4) An organization that participates in the HOPE 3 program shall not, in providing program assistance, discriminate against a program beneficiary or prospective program beneficiary on the basis of religion or religious belief.

(5) HOPE 3 funds may not be used for the acquisition, construction, or rehabilitation of structures to the extent that those structures are used for inherently religious activities. HOPE 3 funds may be used for the acquisition, construction, or rehabilitation of structures only to the extent that those structures are used for conducting eligible activities under this part. Where a structure is used for both

§ 572.410

eligible and inherently religious activities, HOPE 3 funds may not exceed the cost of those portions of the acquisition, construction, or rehabilitation that are attributable to eligible activities in accordance with the cost accounting requirements applicable to HOPE 3 funds in this part. Sanctuaries, chapels, or other rooms that a HOPE 3-funded religious congregation uses as its principal place of worship, however, are ineligible for HOPE 3-funded improvements. Disposition of real property after the term of the grant, or any change in use of the property during the term of the grant, is subject to government-wide regulations governing real property disposition (see 24 CFR parts 84 and 85).

(6) If a State or local government voluntarily contributes its own funds to supplement federally funded activities, the State or local government has the option to segregate the Federal funds or commingle them. However, if the funds are commingled, this section applies to all of the commingled funds.

[58 FR 36526, July 7, 1993, as amended at 59 FR 33894, June 30, 1994; 61 FR 5209, Feb. 9, 1996; 68 FR 56405, Sept. 30, 2003]

§ 572.410 Environmental procedures and standards.

(a) *Planning grants.* HUD has determined that its approval of applications for planning grants under this part is categorically excluded from environmental review and compliance requirements of the National Environmental Policy Act of 1969 (NEPA) and that other Federal environmental laws and authorities listed in 24 CFR 50.4 are not applicable.

(b) *Implementation grants.* (1) Recipients of implementation grants must comply with the applicable environmental laws and authorities at 24 CFR 50.4 and must:

(i) Supply HUD with information necessary for it to perform any necessary environmental review of the property (or neighborhood);

(ii) Carry out mitigating measures required by HUD or select alternate eligible property; and

(iii) Not acquire or otherwise carry out program activities with respect to any eligible property until HUD approval for the property (or neighborhood) is received.

(2) Before any amounts under this part are used to acquire or rehabilitate an eligible property, HUD must determine whether the proposed activities trigger applicability thresholds for the applicable Federal environmental laws and authorities. These may apply when the property is:

(i) Located within designated coastal barriers;

(ii) Listed on, or eligible for listing on, the National Register of Historic Places; or is located within, or adjacent to, an historic district;

(iii) Located near hazardous operations handling fuels or chemicals of an explosive or flammable nature;

(iv) Contaminated by toxic chemicals or radioactive materials;

(v) Located within a runway clear zone at a civil airport or within a clear zone or accident potential zone at a military airfield; or

(vi) Located within a special flood hazard area or within a location requiring flood insurance protection.

(3) A recipient may choose to make the threshold reviews itself or with assistance from State or local governments or qualified persons or to refer the property to HUD for threshold review. Where the recipient makes the threshold review itself, it must submit the result to HUD.

(4) If a recipient chooses not to make the threshold reviews, it must submit information to HUD to permit HUD to make the review.

(5) If HUD determines on the basis of the recipient's threshold review or HUD's threshold review that one or more of the thresholds are exceeded, HUD will conduct an environmental review of that issue and, if appropriate, establish mitigating measures that the recipient must carry out for the property unless it decides to select an alternate property.

§ 572.415 Conflict of interest.

(a) *Conflict of interest.* In addition to the conflict of interest requirements in OMB Circular A–110[1] and 24 CFR part 85, no person who is an employee,

---

[1] See § 572.425(b) concerning availability of OMB Circulars.

agent, consultant, officer, or elected or appointed official of the recipient or cooperating entity named in the application and who exercises or has exercised any functions or responsibilities with respect to assisted activities, or who is in a position to participate in a decision-making process or gain inside information with regard to such activities, may obtain a financial interest or benefit from the activity, or have an interest in any contract, subcontract, or agreement with respect thereto, or the proceeds thereunder, either for himself or herself or for those with whom he or she has family or business ties, during his or her tenure or for one year thereafter, except that a resident of an eligible property may acquire an ownership interest.

(b) *Exception.* HUD may grant an exception to the exclusion in paragraph (a) of this section on a case-by-case basis when it determines that such an exception will serve to further the purposes of the HOPE 3 program and the effective and efficient administration of the local homeownership program. An exception may be considered only after the applicant or recipient has provided a disclosure of the nature of the conflict, accompanied by an assurance that there has been public disclosure of the conflict, a description of how the public disclosure was made, and an opinion of the applicant's or recipient's attorney that the interest for which the exception is sought would not violate State or local law. In determining whether to grant a requested exception, HUD will consider the cumulative effect of the following factors, where applicable:

(1) Whether the exception would provide a significant cost benefit or an essential degree of expertise to the local homeownership program that would otherwise not be available;

(2) Whether an opportunity was provided for open competitive bidding or negotiation;

(3) Whether the person affected is a member of a group or class intended to be the beneficiaries of the activity and the exception will permit such person to receive generally the same interests or benefits as are being made available or provided to the group or class;

(4) Whether the affected person has withdrawn from his or her functions or responsibilities, or the decisionmaking process, with respect to the specific activity in question;

(5) Whether the interest or benefit was present before the affected person was in a position as described in paragraph (b) of this section;

(6) Whether undue hardship will result either to the applicant, recipient, or the person affected when weighed against the public interest served by avoiding the prohibited conflict; and

(7) Any other relevant considerations.

§ 572.420 **Miscellaneous requirements.**

(a) *Application of OMB Circulars.* (1) The policies, guidelines, and requirements of OMB Circular Nos. A-87 (Cost Principles Applicable to Grants, Contracts and Other Agreements with State and Local Governments) and 24 CFR part 85 (Administrative Requirements for Grants and Cooperative Agreements to State, Local and Federally Recognized Indian Tribal Governments) apply to the award, acceptance, and use of assistance under this part by applicable entities, and to the remedies for non-compliance, except where inconsistent with the provisions of NAHA, other Federal statutes, or this part. Part 84 of this title (Grants and Agreements with Institutions of Higher Education, Hospitals, and Other Nonprofit Organizations) and OMB Circular Nos. A-122 (Cost Principles Applicable to Grants, Contract and Other Agreements with Nonprofit Institutions) and, as applicable, A-21 (Cost Principles for Educational Institutions) apply to the acceptance and use of assistance under this part by covered organizations, except where inconsistent with the provisions of Federal statutes or this part. Recipients are also subject to the audit requirements of OMB Circular A-128 (Audits of State and Local Governments) implemented at 24 CFR part 44, and OMB Circular A-133 (Audits of Institutions of Higher Learning and Other Nonprofit Institutions), implemented at 24 CFR part 45, as applicable.

(2) Copies of OMB Circulars may be obtained from E.O.P. Publications,

§ 572.425

room 2200, New Executive Office Building, Washington, DC 20503, telephone (202) 395–7332 (this is not a toll-free number). There is a limit of two free copies.

(b) *Requirements in 24 CFR part 5.* The Disclosure requirements; provisions on Debarred, suspended or ineligible contractors; and Drug-Free Workplace requirements, as identified in § 5.105 (b), (c), and (d) of this title, apply to this program.

(c)–(d) [Reserved]

(e) *Labor standards.* If other Federal programs are used in connection with the HOPE 3 homeownership program, labor standards requirements apply to the extent required by such other Federal programs.

(f) *Flood insurance.* Pursuant to the Flood Disaster Protection Act of 1973 (42 U.S.C. 4001–4128), the recipient may not provide financial assistance for acquisition or rehabilitation of properties located in an area identified by the Federal Emergency Management Agency (FEMA) as having special flood hazards, unless:

(1) The community in which the area is situated is participating in the National Flood Insurance program (see 44 CFR parts 59 through 79), or less than one year has passed since FEMA notification regarding such hazards; and

(2) Flood insurance is obtained as a condition of the acquisition or rehabilitation of the property.

(g) *Coastal Barrier Resources Act.* Pursuant to the Coastal Barrier Resources Act (16 U.S.C. 3601), HUD will not approve use of properties in the Coastal Barrier Resources System.

(h) *Lead-based paint activities.* The Lead-Based Paint Poisoning Prevention Act (42 U.S.C. 4821–4846), the Residential Lead-Based Paint Hazard Reduction Act of 1992 (42 U.S.C. 4851–4856), and implementing regulations at part 35, subparts A, B, J, K and R of this title apply to activities under these programs.

[58 FR 36526, July 7, 1993, as amended at 59 FR 2738, Jan. 19, 1994; 61 FR 48798, Sept. 16, 1996; 62 FR 34145, June 24, 1997; 64 FR 50226, Sept. 15, 1999]

§ 572.425 Recordkeeping and reports; audit of recipients.

(a) *General records.* Each recipient must keep records that will facilitate an effective audit to determine compliance with program requirements and that fully disclose:

(1) The amount and disposition by the recipient of the planning and implementation grants received under this part, including sufficient records that document the reasonableness and necessity of each expenditure;

(2) The amount and disposition of proceeds from financing obtained in connection with the program, sales to eligible families, and any funds recaptured upon sale by the homeowner;

(3) The total cost of the homeownership program;

(4) The amount and nature of any other assistance, including cash, property, services, or other items contributed as a condition of receiving an implementation grant;

(5) The cost or other value of all in-kind contributions towards the match required by § 572.220; and

(6) Any other proceeds received for, or otherwise used in connection with, the homeownership program under this part.

(b) *Family size and income; racial, ethnic, and gender data.* The recipient must maintain records on the family size and income, and racial, ethnic, and gender characteristics of families who apply for homeownership and families who become homeowners.

(c) *Selection procedures.* The recipient must maintain a copy of its procedures for identifying and selecting eligible families in accordance with § 572.110, and records documenting the eligibility of each family selected for homeownership.

(d) *Rehabilitation standards.* The recipient must maintain written rehabilitation standards required by § 572.100(d)(5).

(e) *Cooperative and condominium agreements.* The recipient must maintain a copy of any condominium and cooperative association agreements for properties under a homeownership program approved under this part.

(f) *Amounts available for reuse.* The recipient must keep and make available to HUD all records necessary to calculate accurately payments due to HUD under § 572.135(b) and (c).

(g) *Access by HUD and the Comptroller General.* For purposes of audit, examination, monitoring, and evaluation, each recipient must give HUD (including any duly authorized representatives and the Inspector General) and the Comptroller General of the United States (and any duly authorized representatives) access to any books, documents, papers, and records of the recipient that are pertinent to assistance received under this part, including all records required to be kept under this section.

(h) *Reports.* The recipient must submit reports required by HUD.

(Approved by the Office of Management and Budget, with respect to implementation grants, under control number 2506-0128)

PART 573—LOAN GUARANTEE RECOVERY FUND

Sec.
573.1   Authority and purpose.
573.2   Definitions.
573.3   Eligible activities.
573.4   Loan term.
573.5   Underwriting standards and availability of loan guarantee assistance.
573.6   Submission requirements.
573.7   Loan guarantee agreement.
573.8   Environmental procedures and standards.
573.9   Other requirements.
573.10   Fees for guaranteed loans.
573.11   Record access and recordkeeping.

AUTHORITY: Pub. L. 104–155, 110 Stat. 1392, 18 U.S.C. 241 note; 42 U.S.C. 3535(d).

SOURCE: 61 FR 47405, Sept. 6, 1996, unless otherwise noted.

§ 573.1 Authority and purpose.

Section 4 of the Church Arson Prevention Act of 1996 (Pub. L. 104–155, approved July 3, 1996) authorizes HUD to guarantee loans made by financial institutions to certain nonprofit organizations to finance activities designed to remedy the damage and destruction to real and personal property caused by acts of arson or terrorism. This part establishes the general procedures and requirements that apply to HUD's guarantee of these loans.

§ 573.2 Definitions.

The following definitions are only applicable to loan guarantees under this part, and are not criminal definitions.

Act means "The Church Arson Prevention Act of 1996" (Pub. L. 104–155, approved July 3, 1996).

Arson means a fire or explosion causing damage to (or destruction of) real or personal property that a Qualified Certification Official determines, or reasonably believes, to be deliberately set.

Borrower means an organization described in section 501(c)(3) of the Internal Revenue Code of 1986, as amended, whose property has been damaged or destroyed as a result of an act of arson or terrorism and that incurs a debt obligation to a financial institution for the purpose of carrying out activities eligible under his part.

Financial Institution means a lender which may be a bank, trust company, savings and loan association, credit union, mortgage company, or other issuer regulated by the Federal Deposit Insurance Corporation, the Office of Thrift Supervision, the Credit Union Administration, or the U.S. Comptroller of the Currency. A Financial Institution may also be a Pension Fund.

Guarantee means an obligation of the United States Government guaranteeing payment of the outstanding principal loan amount, in whole or in part, plus interest thereon, on a debt obligation of the Borrower to a Financial Institution upon failure of the Borrower to repay the debt.

Guaranteed Loan Funds means funds received by the borrower from the Financial Institution to finance eligible activities under this part, the repayment of which is guaranteed by HUD.

Loan Guarantee Agreement means an agreement between a Financial Institution and the Secretary detailing the rights, responsibilities, procedures, terms, and conditions under which a loan provided by a Financial Institution to a Borrower may be guaranteed under section 4 of the Act.

Qualified Certification Official (QCO)— (1) *For the purpose of certifying an act of arson.* A State or local official authorized to investigate possible acts of arson. For the purposes of this definition, such an official is authorized to

§ 573.3

execute an Official Incident Report or its equivalent and may be an official or employee of such agencies as the local fire department, the local police department, or the State Fire Marshall Office or its equivalent. The term "Qualified Certification Official" also includes HUD, which will consult with the Bureau of Alcohol, Tobacco, and Firearms of the Department of the Treasury in making its determinations.

(2) *For the purpose of certifying an act of terrorism.* The Secretary or his designee, in consultation with the Federal Bureau of Investigation, shall determine whether an act of violence is a terrorist act or is reasonably believed to be a terrorist act.

Section 4 Guaranteed Loan means a HUD guaranteed loan made by a Financial Institution to a Borrower for the purpose of carrying out eligible activities to address damage or destruction caused by acts of arson or terrorism.

Terrorism means an act of violence causing damage to (or destruction of) real or personal property that the Secretary or his designee, in consultation with the Federal Bureau of Investigation, determines to be, or reasonably believes to be, a terrorist act, as defined by applicable Federal law or guidelines.

§ 573.3 Eligible activities.

Guaranteed Loan Funds may be used by a Borrower for the following activities when it is certified in accordance with § 573.6(e) that the activity is necessary to address damage caused by an act or acts of arson or terrorism as certified in accordance with § 573.6(f):

(a) Acquisition of improved or unimproved real property in fee or under long term lease.

(b) Acquisition and installation of personal property.

(c) Rehabilitation of real property owner, acquired, or leased by the Borrower.

(d) Construction, reconstruction, or replacement of real property improvement.

(e) Clearance, demolition, and removal, including movement of structures to other sites, of buildings, fixtures and improvements on real property.

(f) Site preparation, including construction, reconstruction, or installation of site improvements, utilities, or facilities, which is related to the activities described in paragraph (a), (c), or (d) of this section.

(g) Architectural, engineering, and similar services necessary to develop plans in connection with activities financed under paragraph (a), (b), (c), or (d) of this section.

(h) Acquisition, installation and restoration of security systems.

(i) Loans for refinancing existing indebtedness secured by a property which has been or will be acquired, constructed, rehabilitated or reconstructed, if such financing is determined to be appropriate to achieve the objectives of the Act and this part.

(j) Other necessary project costs such as insurance, bonding, legal fees, appraisals, surveys, relocation, closing costs, etc., paid or incurred by the Borrower in connection with the completion of the above activities.

[61 FR 47405, Sept. 6, 1996, as amended at 62 FR 24574, May 6, 1997]

§ 573.4 Loan term.

The term of the loan to be guaranteed by HUD under this part may not exceed 20 years.

§ 573.5 Underwriting standards and availability of loan guarantee assistance.

(a) HUD may, in its discretion, accept the underwriting standards of the Financial Institution making a loan to a Borrower.

(b) HUD will not make the loan guarantee unless it determines that the guaranteed loan is an acceptable financial risk under HUD's generally applicable loan underwriting standards based on the following:

(1) The Borrower's ability to pay debt service; and

(2) The value of the collateral assigned or pledged as security for the repayment of the loan.

(c) The provision of a loan guarantee to a Financial Institution and the amount of the guarantee do not depend in any way on the purpose, function, or identity of the organization to which the Financial Institution has made, or intends to make, a Section 4 Guaranteed Loan.

(d) HUD may disapprove a request for loan guarantee assistance based on the availability of funding.

(e) HUD may decline any Financial Institution's participation if its underwriting criteria are insufficient to make the guarantee an acceptable financial risk, or if the proposed interest rates or fees are unacceptable. HUD expects the proposed interest rates to take into account the value of the Federal guarantee.

(f) HUD may limit the availability of Guaranteed Loan Funds to geographic areas having the greatest need, as determined by a needs analysis of the most current available date conducted by HUD.

(g) Other requirements associated with the underwriting standards and guidelines shall be contained in the Loan Guarantee Agreement.

§ 573.6 Submission requirements.

A Financial Institution seeking a Section 4 Guaranteed Loan must submit to HUD the following documentation:

(a) A statement that the institution is a Financial Institution as defined at § 573.2.

(b) A statement that the Borrower is eligible as defined at § 573.2.

(c) A description of each eligible activity for which the loan is requested.

(d) A statement of other available funds to be used to finance the eligible activities (e.g., insurance proceeds).

(e) A certification by the Borrower that the activities to be assisted resulted from an act of arson or terrorism which is the subject of the certification described in paragraph (f) of this section.

(f) A certification by a QCO that the damage or destruction to be remedied by the use of the Guaranteed Loan Funds resulted from an act of arson or terrorism.

(g) The environmental documentation required by § 573.8.

(h) A narrative of the institution's underwriting standards used in reviewing the Borrower's loan request.

(i) The interest rate on the loan and fees the lender intends to use in connection with the loan; and

(j) The percentage of the loan for which a guarantee is requested.

§ 573.7 Loan guarantee agreement.

(a) The rights and responsibilities with respect to the guaranteed loan shall be substantially described in an agreement entered into between the Financial Institution, as the lender, and the Secretary, as the guarantor, which agreement shall provide that:

(1) The lender has submitted or will submit a request for loan guarantee assistance that is accompanied by the Borrower's request for a loan to carry out eligible activities described in § 573.3;

(2) The lender will require the Borrower to execute a promissory note promising to repay the guaranteed loan in accordance with the terms thereof;

(3) The lender will require the Borrower to provide collateral security, to an extent and in a form, acceptable to HUD;

(4) HUD reserves the right to limit loan guarantees to loans financing the replacement of damaged property with comparable new property;

(5) The lender will follow certain claim procedures to be specified by HUD in connection with any defaults, including appropriate notification of default as required by HUD;

(6) The lender will follow procedures for payment under the guarantee whereby the lender will be paid (up to the amount of guarantee) the amount owed to the lender less any amount recovered from the underlying collateral security for the loan; and

(7) The lender will act as the fiscal agent for the loan, servicing the guaranteed loan, maintaining loan documents, and receiving the Borrower's payments of principal and interest. The Borrower and the lender may be required to execute a fiscal agency agreement.

(b) In addition, the agreement shall contain other requirements, terms, and conditions required or approved by HUD.

§ 573.8 Environmental procedures and standards.

The environmental review requirements at 24 CFR part 50 are applicable to this part.

§ 573.8

(a) *Environmental procedures.* Before any lender's submission requesting a loan guarantee for the acquisition, rehabilitation, or construction of real property can be selected for a loan guarantee, HUD shall determine whether any environmental thresholds are exceeded in accordance with 24 CFR part 50, which implements the National Environmental Policy Act (NEPA) and the related Federal environmental laws and authorities listed under 24 CFR 50.4. To assist in complying with environmental requirements, Borrowers are encouraged to select sites that are free of environmental hazards and are to provide HUD with environmental data needed to make a determination of compliance. For successful Borrowers, the costs for preparing the environmental data are eligible as project costs.

(1) If HUD determines that one or more of the thresholds are exceeded, HUD shall conduct a compliance review of the issue and, if appropriate, establish mitigating measures that the applicant shall carry out for the property.

(2) The lender's submissions under § 573.6 shall provide HUD with:

(i) Documentation for environmental threshold review; and

(ii) Any previously issued environmental reviews prepared by local, State, or other Federal agencies for the proposed property.

(3) In providing the above information, the Borrower is encouraged to contact the local community development agency to obtain any previously issued environmental reviews for the proposed property as well as for other relevant information that can be used in the applicant documentation for the environmental threshold review.

(4) HUD reserves the right to disqualify any request where one or more environmental thresholds are exceeded if HUD determines that the compliance review cannot be satisfactorily completed.

(5) If Guaranteed Loan Funds are requested for acquisition, rehabilitation, or construction, Borrowers and Financial Institutions are prohibited from committing or expending State, local, or other funds to undertake property acquisition, rehabilitation or construction under this part until HUD issues a letter of commitment notifying the lender of HUD approval of the loan guarantee.

(b) *Environmental thresholds.* HUD shall determine whether a NEPA environmental assessment is required. Also, HUD shall determine whether the proposed property triggers thresholds for the applicable Federal environmental laws and authorities listed under 24 CFR 50.4 as follows:

(1) For minor rehabilitation of a building and acquisition of any property, Federal environmental laws and authorities may apply when the property is:

(i) Located within designated coastal barrier resources;

(ii) Contaminated by toxic chemicals or radioactive materials;

(iii) Located within a floodplain;

(iv) A building for which flood insurance protection is required;

(v) Located within a runway clear zone at a civil airport or within a clear zone or accident potential zone at a military airfield; or

(vi) Listed on, or eligible for listing on, the National Register of Historic Places; located within, or adjacent to, an historic district, or is a property whose area of potential effects includes a historic district or property.

(2) For major rehabilitation of a building or for new construction or rebuilding, and environmental assessment under NEPA is required and, in addition to paragraph (b)(1)(i) through (vi) of this section, other Federal environmental laws and authorities may apply when the property:

(i) Affects coastal zone management;

(ii) Is located near hazardous industrial operations handling fuels or chemicals of an explosive or flammable nature;

(iii) Affects a sole source aquifer;

(iv) Affects endangered species;

(v) Is located within a designated wetland; or

(vi) Is located in a high noise area.

(c) *Qualified data sources.* The environmental threshold information provided by applicants mut be from qualified data sources. A qualified data source means any Federal, State, or local agency with expertise or experience in environmental protection (e.g., the local community development agency; the local planning agency; the State environmental protection agency; or the State Historic Preservation Officer) or any other source qualified to provide reliable information on the particular property.

(d) *Definition.* Minor rehabilitation means proposed fixing and repairs:

(1) Whose estimated cost is less than 75 percent of the estimated cost of replacement after completion;

(2) That does not involve changes in land use from residential to nonresidential, or from nonresidential to residential; and

(3) In the case of residential properties, that does not increase density more than 20 percent.

(e) *Project consultants.* In achieving compliance with these procedures, Borrower's architectural and engineering consultants shall consider these environmental factors and provide information in their plan narratives as to how their construction plans conform with the above environmental factors. To facilitate HUD's compliance with part 50, the Borrower is required to submit the consultant's information and plan narrative discussing the pertinent environmental factors under this section.

§ 573.9 Other requirements.

(a) *Nondiscrimination and equal opportunity.* The nondiscrimination and equal opportunity requirements described in 24 CFR part 5, subpart A apply to this part.

(b) *24 CFR part 84.* The provisions of 24 CFR part 84 apply to guaranteed loans under this part.

(c) *Lead-based paint.* Housing assisted under this part is subject to the lead-based paint requirements described in part 35, subparts A, B, E, G, and R of this title.

(d) *Labor standards*—(1) *Davis-Bacon.* All laborers and mechanics employed by contractors or subcontractors in the performance of construction work financed in whole or in part with Guaranteed Loan Funds under this part shall be paid wages at rates not less than those prevailing on similar construction in the locality as determined by the Secretary of Labor in accordance with the Davis-Bacon Act, as amended (40 U.S.C. 276a–276a–5). This paragraph shall apply to the rehabilitation of residential property only if such property contains not less than 8 units.

(2) *Volunteers.* The provisions of paragraph (d)(1) of this section shall not apply to volunteers under the conditions set forth in 24 CFR part 70. In applying part 70, loan guarantees under this part shall be treated as a program for which there is a statutory exemption for volunteers.

(3) *Labor standards.* Any contract, subcontract, or building loan agreement executed for a project subject to Davis-Bacon wage rates under paragraph (d)(1) of this section shall comply with all labor standards and provisions of 29 CFR parts 1, 3 and 5 that would be applicable to a loan guarantee program to which Davis-Bacon wage rates are made applicable by statute.

[61 FR 47405, Sept. 6, 1996, as amended at 64 FR 50226, Sept. 15, 1999]

§ 573.10 Fees for guaranteed loans.

(a) No fees will be assessed by HUD for its guaranty of a loan under this part.

(b) The lender may assess the Borrower loan origination fees or other charges provided that such fees and charges are those charged by the lender to its other customers for similar transactions, and are no higher than those charged by the lender for similar transactions.

§ 573.11 Record access and recordkeeping.

Records pertaining to the loans made by the Financial Institution shall be held for the life of the loan. A lender with a Section 4 Guaranteed Loan shall allow HUD, the Comptroller General of the United States, and their authorized representatives access from time to time to any documents, papers or files which are pertinent to the guaranteed loan, and to inspect and make copies of such records which relate to any Section 4 Loan. Any inspection will be made during the lender's regular business hours or any other mutually convenient time.

PART 574—HOUSING OPPORTUNITIES FOR PERSONS WITH AIDS

Subpart A—General

Sec.
574.3 Definitions.

Subpart B—Formula Entitlements

574.100 Eligible applicants.
574.110 Overview of formula allocations.
574.120 Responsibility of applicant to serve EMSA.
574.130 Formula allocations.
574.190 Reallocation of grant amounts.

Subpart C—Competitive Grants

574.200 Amounts available for competitive grants.
574.210 Eligible applicants.
574.240 Application requirements.
574.260 Amendments.

Subpart D—Uses of Grant Funds

574.300 Eligible activities.
574.310 General standards for eligible housing activities.
574.320 Additional standards for rental assistance.
574.330 Additional standards for short-term supported housing.
574.340 Additional standards for community residences.

Subpart E—Special Responsibilities of Grantees and Project Sponsors

574.400 Prohibition of substitution of funds.
574.410 Capacity.
574.420 Cooperation.
574.430 Fee prohibitions.
574.440 Confidentiality.
574.450 Financial records.

Subpart F—Grant Administration

574.500 Responsibility for grant administration.
574.510 Environmental procedures and standards.
574.520 Performance reports.
574.530 Recordkeeping.
574.540 Deobligation of funds.

Subpart G—Other Federal Requirements

574.600 Cross-reference.
574.603 Nondiscrimination and equal opportunity.
574.605 Applicability of OMB circulars.
574.625 Conflict of interest.
574.630 Displacement, relocation and real property acquisition.
574.635 Lead-based paint.
574.640 Flood insurance protection.
574.645 Coastal barriers.
574.650 Audit.
574.655 Wage rates.

AUTHORITY: 42 U.S.C. 3535(d) and 12901–12912.

SOURCE: 57 FR 61740, Dec. 28, 1992, unless otherwise noted.

Subpart A—General

§ 574.3 Definitions.

The terms *Grantee* and *Secretary* are defined in 24 CFR part 5.

Acquired immunodeficiency syndrome (AIDS) or related diseases means the disease of acquired immunodeficiency syndrome or any conditions arising from the etiologic agent for acquired immunodeficiency syndrome, including infection with the human immunodeficiency virus (HIV).

Administrative costs mean costs for general management, oversight, coordination, evaluation, and reporting on eligible activities. Such costs do not include costs directly related to carrying out eligible activities, since those costs are eligible as part of the activity delivery costs of such activities.

Applicant means a State or city applying for a formula allocation as described under § 574.100 or a State, unit of general local government, or a nonprofit organization applying for a competitive grant as described under § 574.210.

City has the meaning given it in section 102(a) of the Housing and Community Development Act of 1974 (42 U.S.C. 5302).

Eligible Metropolitan Statistical Area (EMSA) means a metropolitan statistical area that has a population of more than 500,000 and has more than 1,500 cumulative cases of AIDS.

Eligible person means a person with acquired immunodeficiency syndrome or related diseases who is a low-income individual, as defined in this section, and the person's family. A person with AIDS or related diseases or a family member regardless of income is eligible to receive housing information services, as described in § 574.300(b)(1). Any person living in proximity to a community residence is eligible to participate in that residence's community outreach and educational activities regarding AIDS or related diseases, as provided in § 574.300(b)(9).

Eligible State means a State that has:

(1) More than 1,500 cumulative cases of AIDS in those areas of the State outside of eligible metropolitan statistical areas that are eligible to be funded through a qualifying city; and

(2) A consolidated plan prepared, submitted, and approved in accordance with 24 CFR part 91 that covers the assistance to be provided under this part. (A State may carry out activities anywhere in the State, including within an EMSA.)

Family means a household composed of two or more related persons. The term family also includes one or more eligible persons living with another person or persons who are determined to be important to their care or well being, and the surviving member or members of any family described in this definition who were living in a unit assisted under the HOPWA program with the person with AIDS at the time of his or her death.

Low-income individual has the meaning given it in section 853(3) of the AIDS Housing Opportunity Act (42 U.S.C. 12902).

Metropolitan statistical area has the meaning given it in section 853(5) of the AIDS Housing Opportunity Act (42.U.S.C. 12902).

Nonprofit organization means any nonprofit organization (including a State or locally chartered, nonprofit organization) that:

(1) Is organized under State or local laws;

(2) Has no part of its net earnings inuring to the benefit of any member, founder, contributor, or individual;

(3) Has a functioning accounting system that is operated in accordance with generally accepted accounting principles, or has designated an entity that will maintain such an accounting system; and

(4) Has among its purposes significant activities related to providing services or housing to persons with acquired immunodeficiency syndrome or related diseases.

Non-substantial rehabilitation means rehabilitation that involves costs that are less than or equal to 75 percent of the value of the building after rehabilitation.

Population means total resident population based on data compiled by the U.S. Census and referable to the same point in time.

Project sponsor means any nonprofit organization or governmental housing agency that receives funds under a contract with the grantee to carry out eligible activities under this part. The selection of project sponsors is not subject to the procurement requirements of 24 CFR 85.36.

Qualifying city means a city that is the most populous unit of general local government in an eligible metropolitan statistical area (EMSA) and that has a consolidated plan prepared, submitted, and approved in accordance with 24 CFR part 91 that covers the assistance to be provided under this part.

Rehabilitation means the improvement or repair of an existing structure, or an addition to an existing structure that does not increase the floor area by more than 100 percent.

State has the meaning given it in section 853(9) of the AIDS Housing Opportunity Act (42 U.S.C. 12902).

Substantial rehabilitation means rehabilitation that involves costs in excess of 75 percent of the value of the building after rehabilitation.

Unit of general local government means any city, town, township, parish, county, village, or other general purpose political subdivision of a State; Guam, the Northern Mariana Islands, the Virgin Islands, American Samoa, the Federated States of Micronesia and Palau, the Marshall Islands, or a general purpose political subdivision thereof; and any agency or instrumentality thereof that is established pursuant to legislation and designated by the chief executive to act on behalf of the jurisdiction with regard to provisions of the National Affordable Housing Act.

[57 FR 61740, Dec. 28, 1992, as amended at 59 FR 17199, Apr. 11, 1994; 60 FR 1917, Jan. 5, 1995; 61 FR 5209, Feb. 9, 1996; 61 FR 7963, Feb. 29, 1996]

Subpart B—Formula Entitlements

§ 574.100 Eligible applicants.

(a) Eligible States and qualifying cities, as defined in § 574.3, qualify for formula allocations under HOPWA.

(b) HUD will notify eligible States and qualifying cities of their formula eligibility and allocation amounts and EMSA service areas annually.

[57 FR 61740, Dec. 28, 1992, as amended at 59 FR 17199, Apr. 11, 1994; 60 FR 1917, Jan. 5, 1995]

§ 574.110 Overview of formula allocations.

The formula grants are awarded upon submission and approval of a consolidated plan, pursuant to 24 CFR part 91, that covers the assistance to be provided under this part. Certain states and cities that are the most populous unit of general local government in eligible metropolitan statistical areas will receive formula allocations based on their State or metropolitan population and proportionate number of cases of persons with AIDS. They will receive funds under this part (providing they comply with 24 CFR part 91) for eligible activities that address the housing needs of persons with AIDS or related diseases and their families (see § 574.130(b)).

[61 FR 7963, Feb. 29, 1996]

§ 574.120 Responsibility of applicant to serve EMSA.

The EMSA's applicant shall serve eligible persons who live anywhere within the EMSA, except that housing assistance shall be provided only in localities within the EMSA that have a consolidated plan prepared, submitted, and approved in accordance with 24 CFR part 91 that covers the assistance to be provided under this part. In allocating grant amounts among eligible activities, the EMSA's applicant shall address needs of eligible persons who reside within the metropolitan statistical area, including those not within the jurisdiction of the applicant.

[60 FR 1917, Jan. 5, 1995]

§ 574.130 Formula allocations.

(a) *Data sources.* HUD will allocate funds based on the number of cases of acquired immunodeficiency syndrome reported to and confirmed by the Director of the Centers for Disease Control, and on population data provided by the U.S. Census. The number of cases of acquired immunodeficiency syndrome used for this purpose shall be the number reported as of March 31 of the fiscal year immediately preceding the fiscal year for which the amounts are appropriated and allocated.

(b) *Distribution of appropriated funds for entitlement awards.* (1) Seventy-five percent of the funds allocated under the formula is distributed to qualifying cities and eligible States, as described in § 574.100, based on each metropolitan statistical area's or State's proportionate share of the cumulative number of AIDS cases in all eligible metropolitan statistical areas and eligible States.

(2) The remaining twenty-five percent is allocated among qualifying cities, but not States, where the per capita incidence of AIDS for the year, April 1 through March 31, preceding the fiscal year of the appropriation is higher than the average for all metropolitan statistical areas with more than 500,000 population. Each qualifying city's allocation reflects its EMSA's proportionate share of the high incidence factor among EMSA's with higher than average per capita incidence of AIDS. The high incidence factor is computed by multiplying the population of the metropolitan statistical area by the difference between its twelve-month-per-capita-incidence rate and the average rate for all metropolitan statistical areas with more than 500,000 population. The EMSA's proportionate share is determined by dividing its high incidence factor by the sum of the high incidence factors for all EMSA's with higher than average per capita incidence of AIDS.

(c) *Minimum grant.* No grant awarded under paragraph (b) of this section shall be less than $200,000. Therefore, if the calculations under paragraph (b) of this section would result in any eligible metropolitan statistical area or eligible State receiving less than $200,000, the amount allocated to that entity is increased to $200,000 and allocations to entities in excess of $200,000 are proportionately reduced by the amount of the increase.

§ 574.190 Reallocation of grant amounts.

If an eligible State or qualifying city does not submit a consolidated plan in a timely fashion, in accordance with 24 CFR part 91, that provides for use of its allocation of funding under this part, the funds allocated to that jurisdiction will be added to the funds available for formula allocations to other jurisdictions in the current fiscal year. Any formula funds that become available as a result of deobligations or the imposition of sanctions as provided for in § 574.540 will be added to the funds available for formula allocations in the next fiscal year.

[57 FR 61740, Dec. 28, 1992, as amended at 60 FR 1918, Jan. 5, 1995]

Subpart C—Competitive Grants

§ 574.200 Amounts available for competitive grants.

(a) The Department will set aside 10 percent of the amounts appropriated under this program to fund on a competitive basis:

(1) Special projects of national significance; and

(2) Other projects submitted by States and localities that do not qualify for formula grants.

(b) Any competitively awarded funds that become available as a result of deobligations or the imposition of sanctions, as provided in § 574.540, will be added to the funds available for competitive grants in the next fiscal year.

(c) The competitive grants are awarded based on applications, as described in subpart C of this part, submitted in response to a Notice of Funding Availability published in the FEDERAL REGISTER. All States and units of general local government and nonprofit organizations are eligible to apply for competitive grants to fund projects of national significance. Only those States and units of general local government that do not qualify for formula allocations are eligible to apply for competitive grants to fund other projects.

(d) If HUD makes a procedural error in a funding competition that, when corrected, would warrant funding of an otherwise eligible application, HUD will select that application for potential funding when sufficient funds become available.

[57 FR 61740, Dec. 28, 1992, as amended at 61 FR 7963, Feb. 29, 1996]

§ 574.210 Eligible applicants.

(a) All States, units of general local government, and nonprofit organizations, may apply for grants for projects of national significance.

(b) Only those States and units of general local government that do not qualify for formula grants, as described in § 574.100; may apply for grants for other projects as described in § 574.200(a)(2).

(c) Except for grants for projects of national significance, nonprofit organizations are not eligible to apply directly to HUD for a grant but may receive funding as a project sponsor under contract with a grantee.

§ 574.240 Application requirements.

Applications must comply with the provisions of the Department's Notice of Funding Availability (NOFA) for the fiscal year published in the FEDERAL REGISTER in accordance with 24 CFR part 12. The rating criteria, including the point value for each, are described in the NOFA, including criteria determined by the Secretary.

[61 FR 7963, Feb. 29, 1996]

§ 574.260 Amendments.

(a) After an application has been selected for funding, any change that will significantly alter the scope, location, service area, or objectives of an activity or the number of eligible persons served must be justified to HUD and approved by HUD. Whenever any other amendment to the application is made, the grantee must provide a copy to HUD.

(b) Each amendment request must contain a description of the revised proposed use of funds. Funds may not be expended for the revised proposed use of funds until:

(1) HUD accepts the revised proposed use; and

(2) For amendments to acquire, rehabilitate, convert, lease, repair or construct properties to provide housing, an environmental review of the revised proposed use of funds has been completed in accordance with § 574.510.

(Approved by the Office of Management and Budget under control number 2506-0133)

Subpart D—Uses of Grant Funds

§ 574.300 Eligible activities.

(a) *General.* Subject to applicable requirements described in §§ 574.310, 574.320, 574.330, and 574.340, HOPWA funds may be used to assist all forms of housing designed to prevent homelessness including emergency housing, shared housing arrangements, apartments, single room occupancy (SRO) dwellings, and community residences. Appropriate supportive services, as required by § 574.310(a), must be provided as part of any HOPWA assisted housing, but HOPWA funds may also be used to provide services independently of any housing activity.

(b) *Activities.* The following activities may be carried out with HOPWA funds:

(1) Housing information services including, but not limited to, counseling, information, and referral services to assist an eligible person to locate, acquire, finance and maintain housing. This may also include fair housing counseling for eligible persons who may encounter discrimination on the basis of race, color, religion, sex, age, national origin, familial status, or handicap;

(2) Resource identification to establish, coordinate and develop housing assistance resources for eligible persons (including conducting preliminary research and making expenditures necessary to determine the feasibility of specific housing-related initiatives);

(3) Acquisition, rehabilitation, conversion, lease, and repair of facilities to provide housing and services;

(4) New construction (for single room occupancy (SRO) dwellings and community residences only).

(5) Project- or tenant-based rental assistance, including assistance for shared housing arrangements;

(6) Short-term rent, mortgage, and utility payments to prevent the homelessness of the tenant or mortgagor of a dwelling;

(7) Supportive services including, but not limited to, health, mental health, assessment, permanent housing placement, drug and alcohol abuse treatment and counseling, day care, personal assistance, nutritional services, intensive care when required, and assistance in gaining access to local, State, and Federal government benefits and services, except that health services may only be provided to individuals with acquired immunodeficiency syndrome or related diseases and not to family members of these individuals;

(8) Operating costs for housing including maintenance, security, operation, insurance, utilities, furnishings, equipment, supplies, and other incidental costs;

(9) Technical assistance in establishing and operating a community residence, including planning and other pre-development or pre-construction expenses and including, but not limited to, costs relating to community outreach and educational activities regarding AIDS or related diseases for persons residing in proximity to the community residence;

(10) Administrative expenses:

(i) Each grantee may use not more than 3 percent of the grant amount for its own administrative costs relating to administering grant amounts and allocating such amounts to project sponsors; and

(ii) Each project sponsor receiving amounts from grants made under this program may use not more than 7 percent of the amounts received for administrative costs.

(11) For competitive grants only, any other activity proposed by the applicant and approved by HUD.

(c) *Faith-based activities.* (1) Organizations that are religious or faith-based are eligible, on the same basis as any other organization, to participate in the HOPWA program. Neither the Federal government nor a State or local government receiving funds under HOPWA programs shall discriminate against an organization on the basis of the organization's religious character or affiliation.

(2) Organizations that are directly funded under the HOPWA program may not engage in inherently religious activities, such as worship, religious instruction, or proselytization, as part of the programs or services funded under this part. If an organization conducts such activities, the activities must be offered separately, in time or location, from the programs or services funded under this part, and participation must be voluntary for the beneficiaries of the HUD-funded programs or services.

(3) An organization that participates in the HOPWA program will retain its independence from Federal, State, and local governments, and may continue to carry out its mission, including the definition, practice, and expression of its religious beliefs, provided that it does not use direct HOPWA funds to support any inherently religious activities, such as worship, religious instruction, or proselytization. Among other things, faith-based organizations may use space in their facilities to provide HOPWA-funded services, without removing religious art, icons, scriptures, or other religious symbols. In addition, a HOPWA-funded religious organization retains its authority over its internal governance, and it may retain religious terms in its organization's name, select its board members on a religious basis, and include religious references in its organization's mission statements and other governing documents.

(4) An organization that participates in the HOPWA program shall not, in providing program assistance, discriminate against a program beneficiary or prospective program beneficiary on the basis of religion or religious belief.

(5) HOPWA funds may not be used for the acquisition, construction, or rehabilitation of structures to the extent that those structures are used for inherently religious activities. HOPWA funds may be used for the acquisition, construction, or rehabilitation of structures only to the extent that those structures are used for conducting eligible activities under this part. Where a structure is used for both eligible and inherently religious activities, HOPWA funds may not exceed the cost of those portions of the acquisition, construction, or rehabilitation that are attributable to eligible activities in accordance with the cost accounting requirements applicable to HOPWA funds in this part. Sanctuaries, chapels, or other rooms that a HOPWA-funded religious congregation uses as its principal place of worship, however, are ineligible for HOPWA-funded improvements. Disposition of real property after the term of the grant, or any change in use of the property during the term of the grant, is subject to government-wide regulations governing real property disposition (see 24 CFR parts 84 and 85).

(6) If a State or local government voluntarily contributes its own funds to supplement federally funded activities, the State or local government has the option to segregate the Federal funds or commingle them. However, if the funds are commingled, this section applies to all of the commingled funds.

[57 FR 61740, Dec. 28, 1992, as amended at 59 FR 17200, Apr. 11, 1994; 68 FR 56405, Sept. 30, 2003]

§ 574.310 General standards for eligible housing activities.

All grantees using grant funds to provide housing must adhere to the following standards:

(a)(1) *General.* The grantee shall ensure that qualified service providers in the area make available appropriate supportive services to the individuals assisted with housing under this subpart. Supportive services are described in § 574.300(b)(7). For any individual with acquired immunodeficiency syndrome or a related disease who requires more intensive care than can be provided in housing assisted under this subpart, the grantee shall provide for locating a care provider who can appropriately care for the individual and for referring the individual to the care provider.

(2) *Payments.* The grantee shall ensure that grant funds will not be used to make payments for health services for any item or service to the extent that payment has been made, or can reasonably be expected to be made, with respect to that item or service:

(i) Under any State compensation program, under an insurance policy, or under any Federal or State health benefits program; or

(ii) By an entity that provides health services on a prepaid basis.

(b) *Housing quality standards.* All housing assisted under § 574.300(b) (3), (4), (5), and (8) must meet the applicable housing quality standards outlined below.

(1) *State and local requirements.* Each recipient of assistance under this part must provide safe and sanitary housing that is in compliance with all applicable State and local housing codes, licensing requirements, and any other requirements in the jurisdiction in which the housing is located regarding the condition of the structure and the operation of the housing.

(2) *Habitability standards.* Except for such variations as are proposed by the locality and approved by HUD, recipients must meet the following requirements:

(i) *Structure and materials.* The structures must be structurally sound so as not to pose any threat to the health and safety of the occupants and so as to protect the residents from hazards.

(ii) *Access.* The housing must be accessible and capable of being utilized without unauthorized use of other private properties. Structures must provide alternate means of egress in case of fire.

(iii) *Space and security.* Each resident must be afforded adequate space and security for themselves and their belongings. An acceptable place to sleep must be provided for each resident.

(iv) *Interior air quality.* Every room or space must be provided with natural or mechanical ventilation. Structures must be free of pollutants in the air at levels that threaten the health of residents.

(v) *Water supply.* The water supply must be free from contamination at levels that threaten the health of individuals.

(vi) *Thermal environment.* The housing must have adequate heating and/or cooling facilities in proper operating condition.

(vii) *Illumination and electricity.* The housing must have adequate natural or artificial illumination to permit normal indoor activities and to support the health and safety of residents. Sufficient electrical sources must be provided to permit use of essential electrical appliance while assuring safety from fire.

(viii) *Food preparation and refuse disposal.* All food preparation areas must contain suitable space and equipment to store, prepare, and serve food in a sanitary manner.

(ix) *Sanitary condition.* The housing and any equipment must be maintained in sanitary condition.

(c) *Minimum use period for structures.* (1) Any building or structure assisted with amounts under this part must be maintained as a facility to provide housing or assistance for individuals with acquired immunodeficiency syndrome or related diseases:

(i) For a period of not less than 10 years, in the case of assistance provided under an activity eligible under § 574.300(b) (3) and (4) involving new construction, substantial rehabilitation or acquisition of a building or structure; or

(ii) For a period of not less than 3 years in the cases involving non-substantial rehabilitation or repair of a building or structure.

(2) Waiver of minimum use period. HUD may waive the minimum use period of a building or structure as stipulated in paragraph (c)(1) of this section if the grantee can demonstrate, to the satisfaction of HUD, that:

(i) The assisted structure is no longer needed to provide supported housing or assistance, or the continued operation of the structure for such purposes is no longer feasible; and

(ii) The structure will be used to benefit individuals or families whose incomes do not exceed 80 percent of the median income for the area, as determined by HUD with adjustments for smaller and larger families, if the Secretary finds that such variations are necessary because of construction costs or unusually high or low family incomes.

(d) *Resident rent payment.* Except for persons in short-term supported housing, each person receiving rental assistance under this program or residing in any rental housing assisted under this program must pay as rent, including utilities, an amount which is the higher of:

(1) 30 percent of the family's monthly adjusted income (adjustment factors include the age of the individual, medical expenses, size of family and child care expenses and are described in detail in 24 CFR 5.609). The calculation of the family's monthly adjusted income must include the expense deductions provided in 24 CFR 5.611(a), and for eligible persons, the calculation of monthly adjusted income also must include the disallowance of earned income as provided in 24 CFR 5.617, if applicable;

(2) 10 percent of the family's monthly gross income; or

(3) If the family is receiving payments for welfare assistance from a public agency and a part of the payments, adjusted in accordance with the family's actual housing costs, is specifically designated by the agency to meet the family's housing costs, the portion of the payment that is designated for housing costs.

(e) *Termination of assistance*—(1) *Surviving family members.* With respect to the surviving member or members of a family who were living in a unit assisted under the HOPWA program with the person with AIDS at the time of his or her death, housing assistance and supportive services under the HOPWA program shall continue for a grace period following the death of the person with AIDS. The grantee or project sponsor shall establish a reasonable grace period for continued participation by a surviving family member, but that period may not exceed one year from the death of the family member with AIDS. The grantee or project sponsor shall notify the family of the duration of their grace period and may assist the family with information on other available housing programs and with moving expenses.

(2) *Violation of requirements*—(i) *Basis.* Assistance to participants who reside in housing programs assisted under this part may be terminated if the participant violates program requirements or conditions of occupancy. Grantees must ensure that supportive services are provided, so that a participant's assistance is terminated only in the most severe cases.

(ii) *Procedure.* In terminating assistance to any program participant for violation of requirements, grantees must provide a formal process that recognizes the rights of individuals receiving assistance to due process of law. This process at minimum, must consist of:

(A) Serving the participant with a written notice containing a clear statement of the reasons for termination;

(B) Permitting the participant to have a review of the decision, in which the participant is given the opportunity to confront opposing witnesses, present written objections, and be represented by their own counsel, before a person other than the person (or a subordinate of that person) who made or approved the termination decision; and

(C) Providing prompt written notification of the final decision to the participant.

(Paragraph (c) approved by the Office of Management and Budget under control number 2506–0133)

[57 FR 61740, Dec. 28, 1992, as amended at 59 FR 17200, Apr. 11, 1994; 61 FR 7963, Feb. 29, 1996; 66 FR 6225, Jan. 19, 2001]

§ 574.320 Additional standards for rental assistance.

(a) If grant funds are used to provide rental assistance, the following additional standards apply:

(1) *Maximum subsidy.* The amount of grant funds used to pay monthly assistance for an eligible person may not exceed the difference between:

(i) The lower of the rent standard or reasonable rent for the unit; and

(ii) The resident's rent payment calculated under § 574.310(d).

(2) *Rent standard.* The rent standard shall be established by the grantee and shall be no more than the published section 8 fair market rent (FMR) or the HUD-approved community-wide exception rent for the unit size. However, on a unit by unit basis, the grantee may increase that amount by up to 10 percent for up to 20 percent of the units assisted.

(3) *Rent reasonableness.* The rent charged for a unit must be reasonable in relation to rents currently being charged for comparable units in the private unassisted market and must not be in excess of rents currently being charged by the owner for comparable unassisted units.

§ 574.330

(b) With respect to shared housing arrangements, the rent charged for an assisted family or individual shall be in relation to the size of the private space for that assisted family or individual in comparison to other private space in the shared unit, excluding common space. An assisted family or individual may be assigned a pro rata portion based on the ratio derived by dividing the number of bedrooms in their private space by the number of bedrooms in the unit. Participation in shared housing arrangements shall be voluntary.

[57 FR 61740, Dec. 28, 1992, as amended at 61 FR 7963, Feb. 29, 1996]

§ 574.330 Additional standards for short-term supported housing.

Short-term supported housing includes facilities to provide temporary shelter to eligible individuals as well as rent, mortgage, and utilities payments to enable eligible individuals to remain in their own dwellings. If grant funds are used to provide such short-term supported housing assistance, the following additional standards apply:

(a) *Time limits.* (1) A short-term supported housing facility may not provide residence to any individual for more than 60 days during any six month period. Rent, mortgage, and utilities payments to prevent the homelessness of the tenant or mortgagor of a dwelling may not be provided to such an individual for these costs accruing over a period of more than 21 weeks in any 52 week period. These limitations do not apply to rental assistance provided under § 574.300(b)(5).

(2) *Waiver of time limitations.* HUD may waive, as it determines appropriate, the limitations of paragraph (a)(1) and will favorably consider a waiver based on the good faith effort of a project sponsor to provide permanent housing under subsection (c).

(b) *Residency limitations*—(1) *Residency.* A short-term supported facility may not provide shelter or housing at any single time for more than 50 families or individuals;

(2) *Waiver of residency limitations.* HUD may waive, as it determines appropriate, the limitations of paragraph (b)(1) of this section.

(c) *Placement.* A short-term supported housing facility assisted under this part must, to the maximum extent practicable, provide each individual living in such housing the opportunity for placement in permanent housing or in a living environment appropriate to his or her health and social needs.

(d) *Assistance to continue independent living.* In addition to the supportive services provided when an individual is relocated to a short-term supported housing facility, supportive services may be provided to individuals when they remain in their residence because the residence is appropriate to the needs of the individual. In the latter case, a rent, mortgage and utilities payments program assisted under this part shall provide, when reasonable, supportive services specifically designed to maintain the individual in such residence.

(e) *Case management services.* A program assisted under this section shall provide each assisted individual with an opportunity, if eligible, to receive case management services from the appropriate social service agencies.

(Paragraph (b) approved by the Office of Management and Budget under control number 2506–0133)

[57 FR 61740, Dec. 28, 1992, as amended at 59 FR 17200, Apr. 11, 1994]

§ 574.340 Additional standards for community residences.

(a) A community residence is a multiunit residence designed for eligible persons to provide a lower cost residential alternative to institutional care; to prevent or delay the need for such care; to provide a permanent or transitional residential setting with appropriate services to enhance the quality of life for those who are unable to live independently; and to enable such persons to participate as fully as possible in community life.

(b) If grant funds are used to provide a community residence, except for planning and other expenses preliminary to construction or other physical improvement for a community residence, the grantee must, prior to the expenditure of such funds, obtain and keep on file the following certifications:

(1) *A services agreement.* (i) A certification that the grantee will itself provide services as required by § 574.310(a) to eligible persons assisted by the community residence; or

(ii) A certification that the grantee has entered into a written agreement with a project sponsor or contracted service provider to provide services as required by § 574.310(a) to eligible persons assisted by the community residence;

(2) *The adequacy of funding.* (i) A certification that the grantee has acquired sufficient funding for these services; or

(ii) A certification that the grantee has on file an analysis of the service level needed for each community residence, a statement of which grantee agency, project sponsor, or service provider will provide the needed services, and a statement of how the services will be funded; and

(3) *Capability.* (i) A certification that the grantee is qualified to provide the services; or

(ii) A certification that the project sponsor or the service provider is qualified to provide the services.

[57 FR 61740, Dec. 28, 1992, as amended at 59 FR 17200, Apr. 11, 1994]

Subpart E—Special Responsibilities of Grantees and Project Sponsors

§ 574.400 Prohibition of substitution of funds.

Amounts received from grants under this part may not be used to replace other amounts made available or designated by State or local governments through appropriations for use for the purposes of this part.

§ 574.410 Capacity.

The grantee shall ensure that any project sponsor with which the grantee contracts to carry out an activity under this part has the capacity and capability to effectively administer the activity.

§ 574.420 Cooperation.

(a) The grantee shall agree, and shall ensure that each project sponsor agrees, to cooperate and coordinate in providing assistance under this part with the agencies of the relevant State and local governments responsible for services in the area served by the grantee for eligible persons and other public and private organizations and agencies providing services for such eligible persons.

(b) A grantee that is a State shall obtain the approval of the unit of general local government in which a project is to be located before entering into a contract with a project sponsor to carry out an activity authorized under this part.

(c) A grantee that is a city receiving a formula allocation for an EMSA shall coordinate with other units of general local government located within the metropolitan statistical area to address needs within that area.

§ 574.430 Fee prohibitions.

The grantee shall agree, and shall ensure that each project sponsor agrees, that no fee, except rent, will be charged of any eligible person for any housing or services provided with amounts from a grant under this part.

§ 574.440 Confidentiality.

The grantee shall agree, and shall ensure that each project sponsor agrees, to ensure the confidentiality of the name of any individual assisted under this part and any other information regarding individuals receiving assistance.

§ 574.450 Financial records.

The grantee shall agree, and shall ensure that each project sponsor agrees, to maintain and make available to HUD for inspection financial records sufficient, in HUD's determination, to ensure proper accounting and disbursing of amounts received from a grant under this part.

Subpart F—Grant Administration

§ 574.500 Responsibility for grant administration.

(a) *General.* Grantees are responsible for ensuring that grants are administered in accordance with the requirements of this part and other applicable laws. Grantees are responsible for ensuring that their respective project

§ 574.510

sponsors carry out activities in compliance with all applicable requirements.

(b) *Grant agreement.* The grant agreement will provide that the grantee agrees, and will ensure that each project sponsor agrees, to:

(1) Operate the program in accordance with the provisions of these regulations and other applicable HUD regulations;

(2) Conduct an ongoing assessment of the housing assistance and supportive services required by the participants in the program;

(3) Assure the adequate provision of supportive services to the participants in the program; and

(4) Comply with such other terms and conditions, including recordkeeping and reports (which must include racial and ethnic data on participants) for program monitoring and evaluation purposes, as HUD may establish for purposes of carrying out the program in an effective and efficient manner.

(c) *Enforcement.* HUD will enforce the obligations in the grant agreement in accordance with the provisions of 24 CFR 85.43. A grantee will be provided an opportunity for informal consultation before HUD will exercise any remedies authorized in paragraph (a) of that section.

§ 574.510 Environmental procedures and standards.

(a) Activities under this part are subject to HUD environmental regulations in part 58 of this title, except that HUD will perform an environmental review in accordance with part 50 of this title for any competitive grant for Fiscal Year 2000.

(b) The recipient, its project partners and their contractors may not acquire, rehabilitate, convert, lease, repair, dispose of, demolish, or construct property for a project under this part, or commit or expend HUD or local funds for such eligible activities under this part, until the responsible entity (as defined in § 58.2 of this title) has completed the environmental review procedures required by part 58 and the environmental certification and RROF have been approved (or HUD has performed an environmental review and the recipient has received HUD approval of the property). HUD will not release grant funds if the recipient or any other party commits grant funds (*i.e.*, incurs any costs or expenditures to be paid or reimbursed with such funds) before the recipient submits and HUD approves its RROF (where such submission is required).

(c) For activities under a grant to a nonprofit entity that would generally be subject to review under part 58, HUD may make a finding in accordance with § 58.11(d) and may itself perform the environmental review under the provisions of part 50 of this title if the recipient nonprofit entity objects in writing to the responsible entity's performing the review under part 58. Irrespective of whether the responsible entity in accord with part 58 (or HUD in accord with part 50) performs the environmental review, the recipient shall supply all available, relevant information necessary for the responsible entity (or HUD, if applicable) to perform for each property any environmental review required by this part. The recipient also shall carry out mitigating measures required by the responsible entity (or HUD, if applicable) or select alternate eligible property.

[68 FR 56130, Sept. 29, 2003]

§ 574.520 Performance reports.

(a) *Formula grants.* For a formula grant recipient, the performance reporting requirements are specified in 24 CFR part 91.

(b) *Competitive grants.* A grantee shall submit to HUD annually a report describing the use of the amounts received, including the number of individuals assisted, the types of assistance provided, and any other information that HUD may require. Annual reports are required until all grant funds are expended.

[60 FR 1918, Jan. 5, 1995]

§ 574.530 Recordkeeping.

Each grantee must ensure that records are maintained for a four-year period to document compliance with the provisions of this part. Grantees must maintain current and accurate data on the race and ethnicity of program participants.

[57 FR 61740, Dec. 28, 1992, as amended at 60 FR 1918, Jan. 5, 1995]

§ 574.540 Deobligation of funds.

HUD may deobligate all or a portion of the amounts approved for eligible activities if such amounts are not expended in a timely manner, or the proposed activity for which funding was approved is not provided in accordance with the approved application or action plan and the requirements of this regulation. HUD may deobligate any amount of grant funds that have not been expended within a three-year period from the date of the signing of the grant agreement. The grant agreement may set forth other circumstances under which funds may be deobligated or sanctions imposed.

[61 FR 7963, Feb. 29, 1996]

Subpart G—Other Federal Requirements

§ 574.600 Cross-reference.

The Federal requirements set forth in 24 CFR part 5 apply to this program as specified in this subpart.

[61 FR 5209, Feb. 9, 1996]

§ 574.603 Nondiscrimination and equal opportunity.

Within the population eligible for this program, the nondiscrimination and equal opportunity requirements set forth in 24 CFR part 5 and the following requirements apply:

(a) *Fair housing requirements.* (1) Grantees and project sponsors shall comply with the applicable provisions of the Americans with Disabilities Act (42 U.S.C. 12101–12213) and implementing regulations at 28 CFR part 35 (States and local government grantees) and part 36 (public accommodations and requirements for certain types of short-term housing assistance).

(2) Executive Order 11246, as amended by Executive Orders 11375, 11478, 12086, and 12107 (3 CFR, 1964–1965 Comp., p. 339; 3 CFR, 1966–1970 Comp., p. 684; 3 CFR, 1966–1970 Comp., p. 803; 3 CFR 1978 Comp., p. 230; and 3 CFR, 1978 Comp., p. 264) (Equal Employment Opportunity) does not apply to this program.

(b) *Affirmative outreach.* A grantee or project sponsor must adopt procedures to ensure that all persons who qualify for the assistance, regardless of their race, color, religion, sex, age, national origin, familial status, or handicap, know of the availability of the HOPWA program, including facilities and services accessible to persons with a handicap, and maintain evidence of implementation of the procedures.

[57 FR 61740, Dec. 28, 1992, as amended at 59 FR 33894, June 30, 1994. Redesignated and amended at 61 FR 5209, Feb. 9, 1996; 61 FR 7964, Feb. 29, 1996]

§ 574.605 Applicability of OMB circulars.

The policies, guidelines, and requirements of 24 CFR part 85 (codified pursuant to OMB Circular No. A–102) and OMB Circular No. A–87 apply with respect to the acceptance and use of funds under the program by States and units of general local government, including public agencies, and Circulars Nos. A–110 and A–122 apply with respect to the acceptance and use of funds under the program by private non-profit entities. (Copies of OMB Circulars may be obtained from E.O.P. Publications, room 2200, New Executive Office Building, Washington, DC 20503, telephone (202) 395–7332. (This is not a toll-free number.) There is a limit of two free copies.

§ 574.625 Conflict of interest.

(a) In addition to the conflict of interest requirements in OMB Circular A–102 and 24 CFR 85.36(b)(3), no person who is an employee, agent, consultant, officer, or elected or appointed official of the grantee or project sponsor and who exercises or has exercised any functions or responsibilities with respect to assisted activities, or who is in a position to participate in a decision making process or gain inside information with regard to such activities, may obtain a financial interest or benefit from the activity, or have an interest in any contract, subcontract, or agreement with respect thereto, or the proceeds thereunder, either for himself or herself or for those with whom he or she has family or business ties, during his or her tenure or for one year thereafter.

(b) *Exceptions: Threshold requirements.* Upon the written request of the recipient, HUD may grant an exception to the provisions of paragraph (a) of this

§ 574.630

section when it determines that the exception will serve to further the purposes of the HOPWA program and the effective and efficient administration of the recipient's program or project. An exception may be considered only after the recipient has provided the following:

(1) A disclosure of the nature of the conflict, accompanied by an assurance that there has been public disclosure of the conflict and a description of how the public disclosure was made; and

(2) An opinion of the recipient's attorney that the interest for which the exception is sought would not violate State or local law.

(c) *Factors to be considered for exceptions.* In determining whether to grant a requested exception after the recipient has satisfactorily met the requirements of paragraph (b) of this section, HUD will consider the cumulative effect of the following factors, where applicable:

(1) Whether the exception would provide a significant cost benefit or an essential degree of expertise to the program or project that would otherwise not be available;

(2) Whether the person affected is a member of a group or class of eligible persons and the exception will permit such person to receive generally the same interests or benefits as are being made available or provided to the group or class;

(3) Whether the affected person has withdrawn from his or her functions or responsibilities, or the decisionmaking process with respect to the specific assisted activity in question;

(4) Whether the interest or benefit was present before the affected person was in a position as described in paragraph (a) of this section;

(5) Whether undue hardship will result either to the recipient or the person affected when weighed against the public interest served by avoiding the prohibited conflict; and

(6) Any other relevant considerations.

§ 574.630 Displacement, relocation and real property acquisition.

(a) *Minimizing displacement.* Consistent with the other goals and objectives of this part, grantees and project sponsors must assure that they have taken all reasonable steps to minimize the displacement of persons (families, individuals, businesses, nonprofit organizations, and farms) as a result of a project assisted under this part.

(b) *Relocation assistance for displaced persons.* A displaced person (defined in paragraph (f) of this section) must be provided relocation assistance at the levels described in, and in accordance with the requirements of, the Uniform Relocation Assistance and Real Property Acquisition Policies Act of 1970 (URA) (42 U.S.C. 4601–4655) and implementing regulations at 49 CFR part 24.

(c) *Real property acquisition requirements.* The acquisition of real property for a project is subject to the URA and the requirements described in 49 CFR part 24, subpart B.

(d) *Appeals.* A person who disagrees with the grantee's or project sponsor's determination concerning whether the person qualifies as a "displaced person," or the amount of relocation assistance for which the person is eligible, may file a written appeal of that determination with the grantee. A low-income person who is dissatisfied with the grantee's determination on his or her appeal may submit a written request for review of that determination to the HUD Field Office.

(e) *Responsibility of grantee.* (1) Each grantee shall certify (i.e., provide assurance of compliance as required by 49 CFR part 24) that it will comply with the URA, the regulations at 49 CFR part 24, and the requirements of this section, and shall ensure such compliance notwithstanding any third party's contractual obligation to the grantee to comply with these provisions.

(2) The cost of required relocation assistance is an eligible project cost in the same manner and to the same extent as other project costs. Such costs also may be paid for with funds available from other sources.

(3) The grantee shall maintain records in sufficient detail to demonstrate compliance with these provisions.

(f) *Definition of displaced person.* (1) For purposes of this section, the term "displaced person" means a person (family, individual, business, nonprofit organization, or farm) that moves from real property, or moves personal property from real property, permanently, as a direct result of acquisition, rehabilitation, or demolition for a project assisted under this part. This includes any permanent, involuntary move for an assisted project including any permanent move for an assisted project, including any permanent move from the real property that is made:

(i) After notice by the grantee, project sponsor, or property owner to move permanently from the property, if the move occurs on or after the date that the grantee submits to HUD an application for assistance that is later approved and funded;

(ii) Before the submission of the application to HUD, if the grantee, project sponsor, or HUD determines that the displacement resulted directly from acquisition, rehabilitation, or demolition for the assisted project; or

(iii) By a tenant-occupant of a dwelling unit, if any one of the following three situations occurs:

(A) The tenant moves after the "initiation of negotiations" and the move occurs before the tenant has been provided written notice offering him or her the opportunity to lease and occupy a suitable, decent, safe and sanitary dwelling in the same building/complex, under reasonable terms and conditions, upon completion of the project. Such reasonable terms and conditions include a monthly rent and estimated average monthly utility costs that do not exceed the greater of:

(*1*) The tenant's monthly rent before the initiation of negotiations and estimated average utility costs, or

(*2*) 30 percent of gross household income; or

(B) The tenant is required to relocate temporarily, does not return to the building/complex and either:

(*1*) The tenant is not offered payment for all reasonable out-of-pocket expenses incurred in connection with the temporary relocation, or

(*2*) Other conditions of the temporary relocation are not reasonable; or

(C) The tenant is required to move to another unit in the same building/complex but is not offered reimbursement for all reasonable out-of-pocket expenses incurred in connection with the move, or other conditions of the move are not reasonable.

(2) Notwithstanding the provisions of paragraph (f)(1) of this section, a person does not qualify as a "displaced person" (and is not eligible for relocation assistance under the URA or this section), if:

(i) The person has been evicted for serious or repeated violation of the terms and conditions of the lease or occupancy agreement, violation or applicable Federal, State or local law, or other good cause, and HUD determines that the eviction was not undertaken for the purposes of evading the obligation to provide relocation assistance;

(ii) The person moved into the property after the submission of the application and, before signing a lease and commencing occupancy, was provided written notice of the project, its possible impact on the person (e.g., the person may be displaced, temporarily relocated, or suffer a rent increase) and the fact that the person would not qualify as a "displaced person" (or for any assistance provided under this section), if the project is approved;

(iii) The person is ineligible under 49 CFR 24.2(g)(2); or

(iv) HUD determines that the person was not displaced as a direct result of acquisition, rehabilitation, or demolition for the project.

(3) The grantee or project sponsor may request, at any time, HUD's determination of whether a displacement is or would be covered under this section.

(g) *Definition of initiation of negotiations.* For purposes of determining the formula for computing the replacement housing assistance to be provided to a residential tenant displaced as a direct result of privately undertaken rehabilitation, demolition, or acquisition of the real property, the term "initiation of negotiations" means the execution of the agreement between the grantee and the project sponsor.

§ 574.635 **Lead-based paint.**

The Lead-Based Paint Poisoning Prevention Act (42 U.S.C. 4821–4846), the Residential Lead-Based Paint Hazard Reduction Act of 1992 (42 U.S.C. 4851–4856), and implementing regulations at part 35, subparts A, B, H, J, K, M, and

§ 574.640

R of this part apply to activities under this program.

[64 FR 50226, Sept. 15, 1999]

§ 574.640 Flood insurance protection.

No property to be assisted under this part may be located in an area that has been identified by the Federal Emergency Management Agency (FEMA) as having special flood hazards, unless:

(a)(1) The community in which the area is situated is participating in the National Flood Insurance Program and the regulations thereunder (44 CFR parts 59 through 79); or

(2) Less than a year has passed since FEMA notification regarding such hazards; and

(b) The grantee will ensure that flood insurance on the structure is obtained in compliance with section 102(a) of the Flood Disaster Protection Act of 1973 (42 U.S.C. 4001 et seq.).

§ 574.645 Coastal barriers.

In accordance with the Coastal Barrier Resources Act, 16 U.S.C. 3501, no financial assistance under this part may be made available within the Coastal Barrier Resources System.

§ 574.650 Audit.

The financial management system used by a State or unit of general local government that is a grantee must provide for audits in accordance with 24 CFR part 44. A nonprofit organization that is a grantee or a project sponsor is subject to the audit requirements set forth in 24 CFR part 45.

§ 574.655 Wage rates.

The provisions of the Davis-Bacon Act (40 U.S.C. 276a–276a–5) do not apply to this program, except where funds received under this part are combined with funds from other Federal programs that are subject to the Act.

[59 FR 17201, Apr. 11, 1994]

PART 576—EMERGENCY SHELTER GRANTS PROGRAM: STEWART B. McKINNEY HOMELESS ASSISTANCE ACT

Subpart A—General

Sec.
576.1 Applicability and purpose.
576.3 Definitions.
576.5 Allocation of grant amounts.

Subpart B—Eligible Activities

576.21 Eligible activities.
576.23 Faith-based activities.
576.25 Who may carry out eligible activities.

Subpart C—Award and Use of Grant Amounts

576.31 Application requirements.
576.33 Review and approval of applications.
576.35 Deadlines for using grant amounts.

Subpart D—Reallocations

576.41 Reallocation; lack of approved consolidated plan—formula cities and counties.
576.43 Reallocation of grant amounts; lack of approved consolidated plan—States, territories, and Indian tribes.
576.45 Reallocation of grant amounts; returned or unused amounts.

Subpart E—Program Requirements

576.51 Matching funds.
576.53 Use as an emergency shelter.
576.55 Building standards.
576.56 Homeless assistance and participation.
576.57 Other Federal requirements.
576.59 Relocation and acquisition.

Subpart F—Grant Administration

576.61 Responsibility for grant administration.
576.63 Method of payment.
576.65 Recordkeeping.
576.67 Sanctions.

AUTHORITY: 42 U.S.C. 3535(d) and 11376.

SOURCE: 54 FR 46799, Nov. 7, 1989, unless otherwise noted.

Subpart A—General

§ 576.1 Applicability and purpose.

This part implements the Emergency Shelter Grants program contained in subtitle B of title IV of the Stewart B. McKinney Homeless Assistance Act (42

Ofc. of Asst. Secy., Comm. Planning, Develop., HUD § 576.3

U.S.C. 11371–11378). The program authorizes the Secretary to make grants to States, units of general local government, territories, and Indian tribes (and to private nonprofit organizations providing assistance to homeless individuals in the case of grants made with reallocated amounts) for the rehabilitation or conversion of buildings for use as emergency shelter for the homeless, for the payment of certain operating expenses and essential services in connection with emergency shelters for the homeless, and for homeless prevention activities. The program is designed to be the first step in a continuum of assistance to enable homeless individuals and families to move toward independent living as well as to prevent homelessness.

[61 FR 51548, Oct. 2, 1996]

§ 576.3 Definitions.

The terms *Grantee* and *HUD* are defined in 24 CFR part 5.

Administrative costs means as the term is defined in § 583.135(b) of this part, except that the exclusion relates to the costs of carrying out eligible activities under § 576.21(a).

Consolidated plan means the plan prepared in accordance with part 91 of this title. An approved consolidated plan means a consolidated plan that has been approved by HUD in accordance with part 91 of this title.

Conversion means a change in the use of a building to an emergency shelter for the homeless under this part, where the cost of conversion and any rehabilitation costs exceed 75 percent of the value of the building after conversion.

Emergency shelter means any facility, the primary purpose of which is to provide temporary or transitional shelter for the homeless in general or for specific populations of the homeless.

Essential services includes services concerned with employment, health, drug abuse, and education and may include (but are not limited to):

(1) Assistance in obtaining permanent housing.

(2) Medical and psychological counseling and supervision.

(3) Employment counseling.

(4) Nutritional counseling.

(5) Substance abuse treatment and counseling.

(6) Assistance in obtaining other Federal, State, and local assistance including mental health benefits; employment counseling; medical assistance; Veteran's benefits; and income support assistance such as Supplemental Security Income benefits, Aid to Families with Dependent Children, General Assistance, and Food Stamps;

(7) Other services such as child care, transportation, job placement and job training; and

(8) Staff salaries necessary to provide the above services.

Formula city or county means a metropolitan city or urban county that is eligible to receive an allocation of grant amounts under § 576.5.

Homeless means as the term is defined in 42 U.S.C. 11302.

Homeless prevention means activities or programs designed to prevent the incidence of homelessness, including (but not limited to):

(1) Short-term subsidies to defray rent and utility arrearages for families that have received eviction or utility termination notices;

(2) Security deposits or first month's rent to permit a homeless family to move into its own apartment;

(3) Mediation programs for landlord-tenant disputes;

(4) Legal services programs for the representation of indigent tenants in eviction proceedings;

(5) Payments to prevent foreclosure on a home; and

(6) Other innovative programs and activities designed to prevent the incidence of homelessness.

Indian tribe means as the term is defined in 42 U.S.C. 5302(a).

Major rehabilitation means rehabilitation that involves costs in excess of 75 percent of the value of the building before rehabilitation.

Metropolitan city means a city that was classified as a metropolitan city under 42 U.S.C. 5302(a) for the fiscal year immediately preceding the fiscal year for which emergency shelter grant amounts are made available.

Nonprofit recipient means any private nonprofit organization providing assistance to the homeless, to which a State or unit of general local government distributes emergency shelter grant amounts.

§ 576.5

Obligated means that the grantee or State recipient, as appropriate, has placed orders, awarded contracts, received services, or entered similar transactions that require payment from the grant amount. Grant amounts that a unit of general local government or State awards to a private nonprofit organization by a written agreement or letter of award requiring payment from the grant amount are obligated.

Private nonprofit organization means as the term is defined in 42 U.S.C. 11371.

Rehabilitation means the labor, materials, tools, and other costs of improving buildings, other than minor or routine repairs. The term includes where the use of a building is changed to an emergency shelter and the cost of this change and any rehabilitation costs does not exceed 75 percent of the value of the building before the change in use.

Renovation means rehabilitation that involves costs of 75 percent or less of the value of the building before rehabilitation.

Responsible entity means as the term is defined in § 58.2 of this title, as applied though § 58.1(b)(3) of this title and § 576.57(e).

State means each of the several States and the Commonwealth of Puerto Rico.

Territory means each of the following: the Virgin Islands, Guam, American Samoa, the Northern Mariana Islands, Palau (Trust Territory of the Pacific), and any other territory or possession of the United States.

State recipient means any unit of general local government or nonprofit organization to which a State makes available emergency shelter grant amounts.

Unit of general local government means any city, county, town, township, parish, village, or other general purpose political subdivision of a State.

Urban county means a county that was classified as an urban county under 42 U.S.C. 5302(a) for the fiscal year immediately preceding the fiscal year for which emergency shelter grant amounts are made available.

Value of the building means the monetary value assigned to a building by an independent real estate appraiser, or as otherwise reasonably established by the grantee or the State recipient.

[54 FR 46799, Nov. 7, 1989, as amended at 56 FR 56128, Oct. 31, 1991; 60 FR 1918, Jan. 5, 1995; 61 FR 5210, Feb. 9, 1996; 61 FR 51548, Oct. 2, 1996]

§ 576.5 Allocation of grant amounts.

(a) *Territories.* HUD will set aside for allocation to the territories an amount equal to 0.2 percent of the total amount of each appropriation under this part in any fiscal year. HUD will allocate this set-aside amount to each territory based upon its proportionate share of the total population of all territories.

(b) *States, metropolitan cities, urban counties, and Indian tribes.* HUD will allocate the amounts that remain after the set-aside to territories under paragraph (a) of this section, to States, metropolitan cities, urban counties, and Indian tribes, as provided in 42 U.S.C. 11373. HUD will subsequently distribute the amount set aside for Indian tribes under this paragraph as provided in § 576.31.

(c) *Notification of allocation amount.* HUD will notify in writing each State, metropolitan city, urban county, and territory that is eligible to receive an allocation under this section of the amount of its allocation.

[61 FR 51549, Oct. 2, 1996]

Subpart B—Eligible Activities

§ 576.21 Eligible activities.

(a) *Eligible activities.* Emergency shelter grant amounts may be used for one or more of the following activities relating to emergency shelter for the homeless:

(1) Renovation, major rehabilitation, or conversion of buildings for use as emergency shelters for the homeless;

(2) Provision of essential services to the homeless, subject to the limitations in paragraph (b) of this section;

(3) Payment for shelter maintenance, operation, rent, repairs, security, fuel, equipment, insurance, utilities, food, and furnishings. Not more than 10 percent of the grant amount may be used for costs of staff;

(4) Developing and implementing homeless prevention activities, subject

to the limitations in 42 U.S.C. 11374(a)(4) and paragraph (c) of this section. Grant funds may be used under this paragraph to assist families that have received eviction notices or notices of termination of utility services only if the conditions stated in 42 U.S.C. 11374(a)(4) are met; and

(5) Administrative costs, in accordance with 42 U.S.C. 11378.

(b) *Limitations on provision of essential services.* (1) Grant amounts provided by HUD to units of general local government, territories, or Indian tribes, and grant amounts provided by a State to State recipients, may be used to provide an essential service under paragraph (a)(2) of this section only if the service is a new service, or is a quantifiable increase in the level of a service above that which the unit of general local government (or, in the case of a nonprofit organization, the unit of general local government in which the proposed activities are to be located), territory, or Indian tribe, as applicable, provided with local funds during the 12 calendar months immediately before the grantee or State recipient received initial grant amounts.

(2) Limits on the use of assistance for essential services established in 42 U.S.C. 11374(a)(2) are applicable even when the unit of local government, territory, or Indian tribe provides some or all of its grant funds to a nonprofit recipient. This limitation may be waived in accordance with 42 U.S.C. 11374.

(c) *Limitation on homeless prevention activities.* Limits on the use of assistance for homeless prevention activities established in 42 U.S.C. 11374(a)(4) are applicable even when the unit of local government, territory, or Indian tribe provides some or all of its grant funds to a nonprofit recipient.

[61 FR 51549, Oct. 2, 1996]

§ 576.23 Faith-based activities.

(a) Organizations that are religious or faith-based are eligible, on the same basis as any other organization, to participate in the Emergency Shelter Grants program. Neither the Federal government nor a State or local government receiving funds under Emergency Shelter Grants programs shall discriminate against an organization on the basis of the organization's religious character or affiliation.

(b) Organizations that are directly funded under the Emergency Shelter Grants program may not engage in inherently religious activities, such as worship, religious instruction, or proselytization as part of the programs or services funded under this part. If an organization conducts such activities, the activities must be offered separately, in time or location, from the programs or services funded under this part, and participation must be voluntary for the beneficiaries of the HUD-funded programs or services.

(c) A religious organization that participates in the Emergency Shelter Grants program will retain its independence from Federal, State, and local governments, and may continue to carry out its mission, including the definition, practice, and expression of its religious beliefs, provided that it does not use direct Emergency Shelter Grants funds to support any inherently religious activities, such as worship, religious instruction, or proselytization. Among other things, faith-based organizations may use space in their facilities to provide Emergency Shelter Grants-funded services, without removing religious art, icons, scriptures, or other religious symbols. In addition, an Emergency Shelter Grants-funded religious organization retains its authority over its internal governance, and it may retain religious terms in its organization's name, select its board members on a religious basis, and include religious references in its organization's mission statements and other governing documents.

(d) An organization that participates in the Emergency Shelter Grants program shall not, in providing program assistance, discriminate against a program beneficiary or prospective program beneficiary on the basis of religion or religious belief.

(e) Emergency shelter grants may not be used for the rehabilitation of structures to the extent that those structures are used for inherently religious activities. Emergency shelter grants may be used for the rehabilitation of structures only to the extent that those structures are used for conducting eligible activities under this

§ 576.25

part. Where a structure is used for both eligible and inherently religious activities, emergency shelter grants may not exceed the cost of those portions of the rehabilitation that are attributable to eligible activities in accordance with the cost accounting requirements applicable to emergency shelter grants in this part. Sanctuaries, chapels, or other rooms that an Emergency Shelter Grants-funded religious congregation uses as its principal place of worship, however, are ineligible for Emergency Shelter Grants-funded improvements. Disposition of real property after the term of the grant, or any change in use of the property during the term of the grant, is subject to government-wide regulations governing real property disposition (*see* 24 CFR parts 84 and 85).

(f) If a State or local government voluntarily contributes its own funds to supplement federally funded activities, the State or local government has the option to segregate the Federal funds or commingle them. However, if the funds are commingled, this section applies to all of the commingled funds.

[68 FR 56406, Sept. 30, 2003]

§ 576.25 Who may carry out eligible activities.

(a) *Generally.* As provided in 42 U.S.C. 11373 eligible activities may be carried out by all State recipients and grantees, except States.

(b) *States.* All of a State's formula allocation, except for administrative costs, must be made available to the following entities:

(1) Units of general local government in the State, which may include formula cities and counties even if such cities and counties receive grant amounts directly from HUD; or

(2) Private nonprofit organizations, in accordance with 42 U.S.C. 11373(c).

(c) *Nonprofit recipients.* Units of general local government, territories, and Indian tribes may distribute all or part of their grant amounts to nonprofit recipients to be used for emergency shelter grant activities.

[61 FR 51549, 51550, Oct. 2, 1996]

Subpart C—Award and Use of Grant Amounts

Source: 54 FR 46799, Nov. 7, 1989, unless otherwise noted. Redesignated at 61 FR 51550, Oct. 2, 1996.

§ 576.31 Application requirements.

(a) *Indian tribes.* After funds are set aside for allocation to Indian tribes under § 576.5, HUD will publish a Notice of Funding Availability (NOFA) in the FEDERAL REGISTER. The NOFA will specify the requirements and procedures applicable to the allocation and competitive awarding of these set-aside funds to eligible Indian tribe applicants.

(b) *States, territories, and formula cities and counties.* To receive emergency shelter grant amounts, a State, territory, or formula city or county must:

(1) Submit documentation required under this part, part 5 of this title, or any other applicable provisions of Federal law; and

(2) Submit and obtain HUD approval of a consolidated plan that includes activities to be funded under this part. This consolidated plan serves as the jurisdiction's application for funding under this part.

[61 FR 51550, Oct. 2, 1996]

§ 576.33 Review and approval of applications.

(a) *Conditional grant.* HUD may make a conditional grant restricting the obligation and use of emergency shelter grant amounts. Conditional grants may be made where there is substantial evidence that there has been, or there will be, a failure to meet the requirements of this part. In such a case, the reason for the conditional grant, the action necessary to remove the condition, and the deadline for taking those actions will be specified. Failure to satisfy the condition may result in imposition of a sanction under § 576.69, or in any other action authorized under applicable Federal law.

(b) *Grant agreement.* The grant will be made by means of a grant agreement executed by HUD and the grantee. HUD will not disburse funds before the grant agreement is fully executed.

[54 FR 46799, Nov. 7, 1989, as amended at 60 FR 1918, Jan. 5, 1995. Redesignated and amended at 61 FR 51550, Oct. 2, 1996]

§ 576.35 Deadlines for using grant amounts.

(a)(1) *States.* Each State must make available to its State recipients all emergency shelter grant amounts that it was allocated under § 576.5 within 65 days of the date of the grant award by HUD. Funds set aside by a State for homeless prevention activities under § 576.21(a)(4) must be made available to State recipients within 180 days of the grant award by HUD.

(2) *State recipients*—(i) *Obligation of grant funds.* Each State recipient must have its grant amounts obligated (as that term is defined at § 576.3) within 180 days of the date on which the State made the grant amounts available to the State recipient. In the case of grants for homeless prevention activities under § 576.21(a)(4), State recipients are required to obligate grant amounts within 30 days of the date on which the State made the grant amounts available to the State recipient.

(ii) *Expenditure of grant funds.* Each State recipient must spend all of its grant amounts within 24 months of the date on which the State made the grant amounts available to the State recipient. In the case of grants for homeless prevention activities, State recipients must spend such sums within 180 days of the date on which the State made the grant amounts available to the recipient.

(b) *Formula cities and counties, territories and Indian tribes—Expenditure of grant funds.* Each formula city or county, territory, and Indian tribe must spend all of the grant amounts it was allocated or awarded under § 576.5 or 576.31 within 24 months of the date of the grant award by HUD.

(c) *Failure to meet deadlines.* (1) Any emergency shelter grant amounts that are not made available or obligated within the applicable time periods specified in paragraph (a)(1) or (b) of this section will be reallocated under § 576.45.

(2) The State must recapture any grant amounts that a State recipient does not obligate and spend within the time periods specified in paragraph (a)(2) of this section. The State, at its option, must make these amounts and other amounts returned to the State (except amounts referred to in § 576.22(b)(6) available as soon as practicable to other units of general local government for use within the time period specified in paragraph (a)(2) of this section or to HUD for reallocation under § 576.45.

[54 FR 46799, Nov. 7, 1989. Redesignated and amended at 61 FR 51550, Oct. 2, 1996]

Subpart D—Reallocations

SOURCE: 54 FR 46799, Nov. 7, 1989, unless otherwise noted. Redesignated at 61 FR 51550, Oct. 2, 1996.

§ 576.41 Reallocation; lack of approved consolidated plan—formula cities and counties.

(a) *Applicability.* This section applies where a formula city or county fails to submit or obtain HUD approval of its consolidated plan within 90 days of the date upon which amounts under this part first become available for allocation in any fiscal year.

(b) *Grantee.* HUD will make available to the State in which the city or county is located the amounts that a city or county referred to in paragraph (a) of this section would have received.

(c) *Notification of availability.* The responsible HUD field office will promptly notify the State of the availability of any reallocation amounts under this section.

(d) *Eligibility for reallocation amounts.* In order to receive reallocation amounts under this section, the State must:

(1) Execute a grant agreement with HUD for the fiscal year for which the amounts to be reallocated were initially made available.

(2) If necessary, submit an amendment to its application for that fiscal year for the reallocation amounts it wishes to receive. The amendment must be submitted to the responsible HUD field office no later than 30 days after notification is given to the State under paragraph (c) of this section.

(e) *Amendment review and approval.* (1) Section 576.33 governs the review and

§ 576.43

approval of application amendments under this section. HUD will endeavor to make grant awards within 30 days of the application amendment deadline, or as soon thereafter as practicable.

(2) Program activities represented by proposed amendments are subject to environmental review under § 576.57 in the same manner as original proposals.

(f) *Deadlines for using reallocated grant amounts.* Section 576.35 governs the use of amounts reallocated under this section.

(g) *Amounts that cannot be reallocated.* Any grant amounts that cannot be reallocated to a State under this section will be reallocated as provided by § 576.43. Amounts that are reallocated under this section, but that are returned or unused, will be reallocated under § 576.45.

[54 FR 46799, Nov. 7, 1989, as amended at 56 FR 56128, Oct. 31, 1991; 60 FR 1918, Jan. 5, 1995. Redesignated and amended at 61 FR 51551, Oct. 2, 1996]

§ 576.43 Reallocation of grant amounts; lack of approved consolidated plan—States, territories, and Indian tribes.

(a) *Applicability.* This section applies when:

(1) A State, territory, or Indian tribe fails to obtain approval of its consolidated plan within 90 days of the date upon which amounts under this part first become available for allocation in any fiscal year; or

(2) Grant amounts cannot be reallocated to a State under § 576.41.

(b) *Grantees.* (1) HUD will reallocate the amounts that a State or Indian tribe referred to in paragraph (a)(1) of this section would have received:

(i) In accordance with 42 U.S.C. 11373(d)(3); and

(ii) If grant amounts remain, then to territories that demonstrate extraordinary need or large numbers of homeless individuals.

(2) HUD will make available the amounts that a territory under paragraph (a)(1) of this section would have received to other territories that demonstrate extraordinary need or large numbers of homeless individuals.

(c) *Notification of funding availability.* HUD will make reallocations to States and Indian tribes under this section by direct notification or FEDERAL REGISTER notice that will set forth the terms and conditions under which amounts under this section are to be reallocated and grant awards made. In the case of reallocations to Territories, the responsible HUD field office will promptly notify each Territory of any reallocation amounts under this section, and indicate the terms and conditions under which reallocation amounts are to be made available and grant awards made.

(d) *Eligibility for reallocation amounts.* In order to receive reallocation amounts under this section, the formula city or county, State, territory, or Indian tribe must:

(1) Submit an amendment, in accordance with 24 CFR part 91, to its consolidated plan for that program year to cover activities for the reallocation amount it wishes to receive; and

(2) Execute a grant agreement with HUD for the fiscal year for which the amounts to be reallocated were initially made available.

(e) *Review and approval.* (1) Section 576.53, and such additional requirements as HUD may specify in the notification under paragraph (c) of this section, govern the review and approval of application amendments under this section. HUD will rank the amendments and make grant awards under this section on the basis of the following factors:

(i) The nature and extent of the unmet homeless need within the jurisdiction in which the grant amounts will be used;

(ii) The extent to which the proposed activities address this need; and

(iii) The ability of the grantee to carry out the proposed activities promptly.

(2) HUD will endeavor to make grant awards within 30 days of the application amendment deadline, or as soon thereafter as practicable.

(f) *Grant amounts.* HUD may make a grant award for less than the amount applied for or for fewer than all of the activities identified in the application amendment.

(g) *Deadlines for using reallocated amounts.* Section 576.35 governs the use of amounts reallocated under this section.

(h) *Amounts not reallocated.* Any grant amounts that are not reallocated under this section, or that are reallocated, but are unused, will be reallocated under § 576.45(d). Any amounts that are reallocated, but are returned, will be reallocated under § 576.45(c).

[54 FR 46799, Nov. 7, 1989, as amended at 56 FR 56129, Oct. 31, 1991; 60 FR 1918, Jan. 5, 1995. Redesignated and amended at 61 FR 51551, Oct. 2, 1996]

§ 576.45 Reallocation of grant amounts; returned or unused amounts.

(a) *General.* From time to time, HUD will reallocate emergency shelter grant amounts that are returned or unused, as those terms are defined in paragraph (f) of this section. HUD will make reallocations under this section by direct notification or FEDERAL REGISTER Notice that will set forth the terms and conditions under which the grant amounts are to be reallocated and grant awards are to be made.

(b) *FEMA boards.* HUD may use State and local boards established under the Emergency Food and Shelter Program administered by the Federal Emergency Management Agency, as a resource to identify potential applicants for reallocated grant amounts.

(c) *Reallocation—returned grant amounts*—(1) *States and formula cities and counties.* HUD will endeavor to reallocate returned emergency shelter grant amounts that were initially allocated under § 576.5 to a State or a formula city or county, for use within the same jurisdiction. Reallocation of these grant amounts is subject to the following requirements:

(i) Returned grant amounts that were allocated to a State will be made available (A) first, to units of general local government within the State and (B) if grant amounts remain, then to other States.

(ii) Returned grant amounts that were allocated to a formula city or county will be made available:

(A) First, for use in the city or county, to units of general local government that are authorized under applicable law to carry out activities serving the homeless in the jurisdiction;

(B) If grant amounts remain, then to the State in which the city or county is located;

(C) If grant amounts remain, to units of general local government in the State; and

(D) If grant amounts remain, to other States.

(2) *Indian tribes.* Returned grant amounts that were allocated to an Indian tribe will be made available to other Indian tribes.

(3) *Territories.* Returned grant amounts that were allocated to a territory will be made available, first, to other territories and, if grant amounts remain, then to States.

(4) *Further reallocation:* States, formula cities and counties, territories, and Indian tribes. HUD will reallocate under paragraph (e) of this section any grant amounts that remain after applying the preceding provisions of paragraph (c) of this section or that are returned to HUD after reallocation under those provisions.

(5) The responsible HUD field office will announce the availability of returned grant amounts. The announcement will establish deadlines for submitting applications, and will set out other terms and conditions relating to grant awards, consistent with this part. The announcement will specify the application documents to be submitted.

(6) The responsible HUD field office may establish maximum grant amounts, considering the grant amounts available, and will rank the applications using the criteria in paragraph (e) of this section.

(7) HUD may make a grant award for less than the amount applied for or for fewer than all of the activities identified in the application, based on competing demands for grant amounts and the extent to which the respective activities address the needs of the homeless.

(8) HUD will endeavor to make grant awards within 30 days of the application deadline or as soon thereafter as practicable.

(9) Grants awarded under this section are subject to environmental review under § 576.57.

(d) *Reallocation—unused grant amounts.* Unused grant amounts will be added to the appropriation for the fiscal year immediately following the fiscal year in which the amounts become

§ 576.51

available to HUD for reallocation, and will be allocated in accordance with the provisions of § 576.5 of this part.

(e) *Selection criteria.* HUD will award grants under paragraph (c) of this section based on consideration of the following criteria:

(1) The nature and extent of the unmet homeless need within the jurisdiction in which the grant amounts will be used;

(2) The extent to which the proposed activities address this need; and

(3) The ability of the grantee to carry out the proposed activities promptly.

(f) *Definitions—returned or unused grant amounts.* (1) For purposes of this section, emergency shelter grant amounts are considered "returned" when they become available for reallocation because a jurisdiction does not execute a grant agreement with HUD for them.

(2) For purposes of this section, emergency shelter grant amounts are considered "unused" (i.e., Federal deobligation):

(i) When they become available for reallocation by HUD after a grantee has executed a grant agreement with HUD for those amounts; or

(ii) The amounts remain after reallocation under § 576.43 or paragraph (c) of this section.

[54 FR 46799, Nov. 7, 1989, as amended at 57 FR 54507, Nov. 19, 1992; 60 FR 1918, Jan. 5, 1995. Redesignated and amended at 61 FR 51551, Oct. 2, 1996]

Subpart E—Program Requirements

SOURCE: 54 FR 46799, Nov. 7, 1989, unless otherwise noted. Redesignated at 61 FR 51550, Oct. 2, 1996.

§ 576.51 Matching funds.

(a) *General.* (1) Each grantee, other than a territory, must match the funding provided by HUD under this part as set forth in 42 U.S.C. 11375. This statute provides that a grantee may use funds from any source, including any other federal source (but excluding the specific statutory subtitle from which ESG funds are provided), as well as State, local, and private sources, provided that funds from the other source are not statutorily prohibited to be used as a match.

(2) The first $100,000 of any assistance provided to a recipient that is a State is not required to be matched, but the benefit of the unmatched amount must be shared as provided in 42 U.S.C. 11375(c)(4). Matching funds must be provided after the date of the grant award to the grantee. Funds used to match a previous ESG grant may not be used to match a subsequent grant award under this part. A grantee may comply with this requirement by providing the matching funds itself, or through matching funds or voluntary efforts provided by any State recipient or nonprofit recipient (as appropriate).

(3) It is the responsibility of the grantee to ensure that any funds used as matching funds are eligible under the laws governing the funds to be used as matching funds for a grant awarded under this program.

(b) *Calculating the matching amount.* In calculating the amount of matching funds, in accordance with 42 U.S.C. 11375(a)(3), the time contributed by volunteers shall be determined at the rate of $5 per hour. For purposes of this paragraph, the grantee will determine the value of any donated material or building, or of any lease, using a method reasonably calculated to establish a fair market value.

[61 FR 51552, Oct. 2, 1996, as amended at 73 FR 75325, Dec. 11, 2008]

§ 576.53 Use as an emergency shelter.

(a)(1) *Restrictions and definition.* Period of use restrictions applicable to assistance provided under this part are governed by 42 U.S.C. 11375(a). Use of grant amounts for developing and implementing homeless prevention activities does not trigger period of use requirements.

(2) For purposes of the requirements under this section, the term *same general population* means either the same types of homeless persons originally served with ESG assistance (i.e., battered spouses, runaway children, families, or mentally ill individuals), or persons in the same geographic area.

(b) *Calculating the applicable period.* The 3- and 10-year periods applicable under paragraph (a) of this section begin to run:

(1) In the case of a building that was not operated as an emergency shelter

for the homeless before receipt of grant amounts under this part, on the date of initial occupancy as an emergency shelter for the homeless.

(2) In the case of a building that was operated as an emergency shelter before receipt of grant amounts under this part, on the date that grant amounts are first obligated for the shelter.

[54 FR 46799, Nov. 7, 1989. Redesignated and amended at 61 FR 51552, Oct. 2, 1996]

§ 576.55 Building standards.

(a) Any building for which emergency shelter grant amounts are used for conversion, major rehabilitation, rehabilitation, or renovation must meet local government safety and sanitation standards.

(b) For projects of 15 or more units, when rehabilitation costs are:

(1) 75 percent or more of the replacement cost of the building, that project must meet the requirements of §8.23(a) of this title; or

(2) Less than 75 percent of the replacement cost of the building, that project must meet the requirements of §8.23(b) of this title.

[61 FR 51552, Oct. 2, 1996]

§ 576.56 Homeless assistance and participation.

(a) *Assistance.* (1) Grantees and recipients must assure that homeless individuals and families are given assistance in obtaining:

(i) Appropriate supportive services, including permanent housing, medical health treatment, mental health treatment, counseling, supervision, and other services essential for achieving independent living; and

(ii) Other Federal, State, local, and private assistance available for such individuals.

(2) Requirements to ensure confidentiality of records pertaining to the provision of family violence prevention or treatment services with assistance under this part are set forth in 42 U.S.C. 11375(c)(5).

(3) Grantees and recipients may, in accordance with 42 U.S.C. 11375(e), terminate assistance provided under this part to an individual or family who violates program requirements.

(b) *Participation.* (1) Each unit of local government, Indian tribe, and nonprofit recipient that receives funds under this part must provide for the participation of homeless individuals on its policymaking entity in accordance with 42 U.S.C. 11375(d).

(2) Each State, territory, Indian tribe, unit of local government, and nonprofit recipient that receives funds under this part must involve homeless individuals and families in providing work or services pertaining to facilities or activities assisted under this part, in accordance with 42 U.S.C. 11375(c)(7).

[61 FR 51552, Oct. 2, 1996]

§ 576.57 Other Federal requirements.

In addition to the Federal requirements set forth in 24 CFR part 5, use of emergency shelter grant amounts must comply with the following requirements:

(a) *Nondiscrimination and equal opportunity.* The nondiscrimination and equal opportunity requirements at 24 CFR part 5 are modified as follows:

(1) *Rehabilitation Act requirements.* HUD's regulations at 24 CFR part 8 implement section 504 of the Rehabilitation Act of 1973 (29 U.S.C. 794). For purposes of the emergency shelter grants program, the term "dwelling units" in 24 CFR part 8 shall include sleeping accommodations.

(2) Use of emergency shelter grant amounts must also comply with the requirement that the grantee or the State recipient make known that use of the facilities and services is available to all on a nondiscriminatory basis. If the procedures that the grantee or recipient intends to use to make known the availability of the facilities and services are unlikely to reach persons of any particular race, color, religion, sex, age, national origin, familial status, or disability who may qualify for such facilities and services, the grantee or recipient must establish additional procedures that will ensure that such persons are made aware of the facilities and services. Grantees

§ 576.57

and recipients must also adopt procedures which will make available to interested persons information concerning the location of services and facilities that are accessible to persons with disabilities.

(b) *Applicability of OMB Circulars.*[1] The policies, guidelines, and requirements of 24 CFR part 85 (codified pursuant to OMB Circular No. A–102) and OMB Circular No. A–87, as they relate to the acceptance and use of emergency shelter grant amounts by States and units of general local government, and Nos. A–110 and A–122 as they relate to the acceptance and use of emergency shelter grant amounts by private non-profit organizations.

(c) The Lead-Based Paint Poisoning Prevention Act (42 U.S.C. 4821–4846), the Residential Lead-Based Paint Hazard Reduction Act of 1992 (42 U.S.C. 4851–4856), and implementing regulations at part 35, subparts A, B, J, K, and R of this title apply to activities under this program.

(d) *Conflicts of interest.* In addition to the conflict of interest requirements in OMB Circulars A–102 and A–110, no person—

(1)(i) Who is an employee, agent, consultant, officer, or elected or appointed official of the grantee, State recipient, or nonprofit recipient (or of any designated public agency) that receives emergency shelter grant amounts and

(ii) Who exercises or has exercised any functions or responsibilities with respect to assisted activities, or

(2) Who is in a position to participate in a decisionmaking process or gain inside information with regard to such activities, may obtain a personal or financial interest or benefit from the activity, or have an interest in any contract, subcontract, or agreement with respect thereto, or the proceeds thereunder, either for him or herself or for those with whom he or she has family or business ties, during his or her tenure, or for one year thereafter. HUD may grant an exception to this exclusion as provided in § 570.611 (d) and (e) of this chapter.

---

[1] OMB Circulars referenced in this section are available at the Entitlement Cities Division, Room 7282, Department of Housing and Urban Development, 451 Seventh Street, SW., Washington, DC 20410.

24 CFR Ch. V (4–1–09 Edition)

(e) *Environmental review responsibilities*—(1) *Generally.* Responsible entities must assess the environmental effects of each application under part 58 of this title. An applicant must include in its application an assurance that the applicant will assume all the environmental review responsibility that would otherwise be performed by HUD as the responsible Federal official under the National Environmental Policy Act of 1969 (NEPA) and related authorities listed in part 58 of this title. The grant award is subject to completion of the environmental responsibilities set out in part 58 of this title within a reasonable time period after notification of the award. This provision does not preclude the applicant from enclosing its environmental certification and Request for Release of Funds with its application.

(2) *Awards to States.* In the case of emergency shelter grants to States that are distributed to:

(i) Units of general local government, the unit of general local government shall be the responsible entity, and the State will assume HUD's functions with regard to the release of funds; or

(ii) Nonprofit organizations, the State shall be the responsible entity, and HUD will perform functions regarding release of funds under part 58 of this title.

(3) *Release of funds.* HUD will not release funds for an eligible activity if the grantee, recipient, or any other party commits emergency shelter grant funds before the grantee submits, and HUD approves, any required Request for Release of Funds.

(f) *Audit.* The financial management systems used by a State, formula city or county, governmental entity, or an Indian tribe that is a grantee under this program must provide for audits in accordance with part 44 of this title. A private nonprofit organization is subject to the audit requirements of OMB Circular A–133, as set forth in part 45 of this title. (OMB Circulars are available from the Executive Office of the President, Publication Service, 725 17th Street, NW., Suite G–2200, Washington, DC 20503, Telephone, 202–395–7332.)

(g) *Audit.* The financial management system used by a State or unit of general local government that is a grantee or State recipient must provide for audits in accordance with 24 CFR part 44. A private nonprofit organization is subject to the audit requirements of OMB Circular A-133, as set forth in 24 CFR part 45.

(h) *Lobbying and disclosure requirements.* The disclosure requirements and prohibitions of 42 U.S.C. 3537a and 3545 and 31 U.S.C. 1352 (the Byrd Amendment), and the implementing regulations at parts 4 and 87 of this title.

(i) *Davis-Bacon Act.* The provisions of the Davis-Bacon Act (40 U.S.C. 276a–276a–5) do not apply to this program.

(j) *Intergovernmental review.* The requirements of Executive Order 12372 and the regulations issued under the order at 24 CFR part 52, to the extent provided by FEDERAL REGISTER notice in accordance with 24 CFR 52.3.

[54 FR 46799, Nov. 7, 1989, as amended at 57 FR 33256, July 27, 1992; 61 FR 5210, Feb. 9, 1996. Redesignated and amended at 61 FR 51552, Oct. 2, 1996; 64 FR 50226, Sept. 15, 1999]

§ 576.59 Relocation and acquisition.

(a) *Minimizing displacement.* Consistent with the other goals and objectives of this part, grantees and recipients must assure that they have taken all reasonable steps to minimize the displacement of persons (families, individuals, businesses, nonprofit organizations, and farms) as a result of a project assisted under this part.

(b) *Relocation assistance for displaced persons.* A displaced person (defined in paragraph (f)(1) of this section) must be provided relocation assistance at the levels described in, and in accordance with, 49 CFR part 24, which contains the government-wide regulations implementing the Uniform Relocation Assistance and Real Property Acquisition Policies Act of 1970 (URA) (42 U.S.C. 4601–4655).

(c) *Real property acquisition requirements.* The acquisition of real property for a project is subject to the URA and the requirements described in 49 CFR part 24, subpart B.

(d) *Responsibility of grantees and recipients.* Each grantee and recipient must assure that it will comply with the URA, the regulations at 49 CFR part 24, and the requirements of this section. The cost of assistance required by this section may be paid from local public funds, funds provided in accordance with this part, or funds available from other sources.

(e) *Appeals.* A person who disagrees with the grantee's or recipient's determination concerning a payment or other assistance required by this section may file a written appeal of that determination with the grantee or recipient. The appeal procedures to be followed are described in 49 CFR 24.10.

(f) *Definition*—(1) *Displaced person.* (i) The term "displaced person" means a person (family, individual, business, nonprofit organization, or farm) that moves from real property, or moves personal property from real property, permanently and involuntarily, as a direct result of acquisition, rehabilitation, or demolition for a project assisted under this part. Permanent, involuntary moves for an assisted project include:

(A) A permanent move from the real property (building or complex) following notice by the grantee, recipient or property owner to move permanently from the property, if the move occurs on or after the date that the grantee or recipient submits to HUD an application for assistance that is later approved and funded;

(B) A permanent move from the real property that occurs before the submission of the application to HUD, if the grantee, recipient or HUD determines that the displacement resulted directly from acquisition, rehabilitation, or demolition for the project, or

(C) A permanent move from the real property by a tenant-occupant of a dwelling unit that occurs after the execution of the agreement between the recipient and HUD if:

(*1*) The tenant has not been provided a reasonable opportunity to lease and occupy a suitable, decent, safe and sanitary dwelling in the same building/complex following the completion of the project at a rent, including estimated average utility costs, that does not exceed the greater of the tenant's rent and estimated average utility costs before the initiation of negotiations, or 30 percent of gross household income; or

(*2*) The tenant has been required to relocate temporarily but the tenant is not offered payment for all reasonable

§ 576.61

out-of-pocket expenses incurred in connection with the temporary relocation or other conditions of the temporary relocation are not reasonable, and the tenant does not return to the building/complex; or

(3) The tenant is required to move to another unit in the same building/complex but is not offered reimbursement for all reasonable out-of-pocket expenses incurred in connection with the move.

(ii) A person does not qualify as a "displaced person" if:

(A) The person has been evicted for cause based upon a serious or repeated violation of material terms of the lease or occupancy agreement and HUD determines that the eviction was not undertaken for the purpose of evading the obligation to provide relocation assistance;

(B) The person moved into the property after the submission of the application and, before commencing occupancy, received written notice of the expected displacement;

(C) The person is ineligible under 49 CFR 24.2(g)(2); or

(D) HUD determines that the person was not displaced as a direct result of acquisition, rehabilitation, or demolition for the project.

(iii) The grantee or recipient may, at any time, request a HUD determination of whether a displacement is or would be covered under this section.

(2) Initiation of negotiations. For purposes of determining the type of replacement housing payment to be made to a residential tenant displaced as a direct result of privately undertaken rehabilitation, demolition, or acquisition of the real property, the term "initiation of negotiations" means the execution of the agreement between the grantee and HUD.

(Approved by the Office of Management and Budget under OMB control number 2506–0089)

[54 FR 46799, Nov. 7, 1989, as amended at 54 FR 52397, Dec. 21, 1989. Redesignated at 61 FR 51553, Oct. 2, 1996]

Subpart F—Grant Administration

SOURCE: 54 FR 46799, Nov. 7, 1989, unless otherwise noted. Redesignated at 61 FR 51550, Oct. 2, 1996.

§ 576.61 Responsibility for grant administration.

Grantees are responsible for ensuring that emergency shelter grant amounts are administered in accordance with the requirements of this part and other applicable laws. The State, territory, Indian tribe, or unit of local government is responsible for ensuring that its recipients carry out the recipients' emergency shelter grant programs in compliance with all applicable requirements in the case of:

(a) A State making grant amounts available to State recipients; or

(b) A territory, Indian tribe, or unit of general local government distributing grant amounts to nonprofit recipients.

[54 FR 46799, Nov. 7, 1989. Redesignated and amended at 61 FR 51553, Oct. 2, 1996]

§ 576.63 Method of payment.

Payments are made to a grantee upon its request after the grant agreement has been fully executed, and may include a working capital advance for 30 days' cash needs or an advance of $5,000, whichever is greater. Thereafter, the grantee will be reimbursed for the amount of its actual cash disbursements. If a grantee requests a working capital advance, it must base the request on a realistic, firm estimate of the amounts required to be disbursed over the 30-day period in payment of eligible activity costs.

[54 FR 46799, Nov. 7, 1989. Redesignated and amended at 61 FR 51553, Oct. 2, 1996]

§ 576.65 Recordkeeping.

(a) Each grantee must ensure that records are maintained for a 4-year period to document compliance with the provisions of this part.

(b) Requirements to ensure confidentiality of records pertaining to the provision of family violence prevention or treatment services with assistance under this part are set forth in 42 U.S.C. 11375(c)(5).

[61 FR 51553, Oct. 2, 1996]

§ 576.67 Sanctions.

(a) HUD sanctions. If HUD determines that a grantee is not complying with the requirements of this part or of

Ofc. of Asst. Secy., Comm. Planning, Develop., HUD §581.1

other applicable Federal law, HUD may (in addition to any remedies that may otherwise be available) take any of the following sanctions, as appropriate:

(1) Issue a warning letter that further failure to comply with such requirements will result in a more serious sanction;

(2) Condition a future grant;

(3) Direct the grantee to stop the incurring of costs with grant amounts;

(4) Require that some or all of the grant amounts be remitted to HUD;

(5) Reduce the level of funds the grantee would otherwise be entitled to receive; or

(6) Elect not to provide future grant funds to the grantee until appropriate actions are taken to ensure compliance.

(b) *State sanctions.* If a State determines that a State recipient is not complying with the requirements of this part or other applicable Federal laws, the State must take appropriate actions, which may include the actions described in paragraph (a) of this section. Any grant amounts that become available to a State as a result of a sanction under this section must, at the option of the State, be made available (as soon as practicable) to other nonprofit organizations or units of general local government located in the State for use within the time periods specified in §576.35(a)(2), or to HUD for reallocation under §576.45(d).

(c) *Reallocations.* Any grant amounts that become available to HUD as a result of the imposition of a sanction under this section will be reallocated under §576.45(d).

[54 FR 46799, Nov. 7, 1989. Redesignated and amended at 61 FR 51553, Oct. 2, 1996]

PART 581—USE OF FEDERAL REAL PROPERTY TO ASSIST THE HOMELESS

Sec.
581.1 Definitions.
581.2 Applicability.
581.3 Collecting the information.
581.4 Suitability determination.
581.5 Real property reported excess to GSA.
581.6 Suitability criteria.
581.7 Determination of availability.
581.8 Public notice of determination.
581.9 Application process.
581.10 Action on approved applications.
581.11 Unsuitable properties.
581.12 No applications approved.
581.13 Waivers.

AUTHORITY: 42 U.S.C. 11411 note; 42 U.S.C. 3535(d).

SOURCE: 56 FR 23794, 23795, May 24, 1991, unless otherwise noted.

§581.1 Definitions.

Applicant means any representative of the homeless which has submitted an application to the Department of Health and Human Services to obtain use of a particular suitable property to assist the homeless.

Checklist or property checklist means the form developed by HUD for use by landholding agencies to report the information to be used by HUD in making determinations of suitability.

Classification means a property's designation as unutilized, underutilized, excess, or surplus.

Day means one calendar day including weekends and holidays.

Eligible organization means a State, unit of local government or a private non-profit organization which provides assistance to the homeless, and which is authorized by its charter or by State law to enter into an agreement with the Federal government for use of real property for the purposes of this subpart. Representatives of the homeless interested in receiving a deed for a particular piece of surplus Federal property must be section 501(c)(3) tax exempt.

Excess property means any property under the control of any Federal executive agency that is not required for the agency's needs or the discharge of its responsibilities, as determined by the head of the agency pursuant to 40 U.S.C. 483.

GSA means the General Services Administration.

HHS means the Department of Health and Human Services.

Homeless means:

(1) An individual or family that lacks a fixed, regular, and adequate nighttime residence; and

(2) An individual or family that has a primary nighttime residence that is:

(i) A supervised publicly or privately operated shelter designed to provide temporary living accommodations (including welfare hotels, congregate shelters, and transitional housing for the mentally ill);

(ii) An institution that provides a temporary residence for individuals intended to be institutionalized; or

(iii) A public or private place not designed for, or ordinarily used as, a regular sleeping accommodation for human beings. This term does not include any individual imprisoned or otherwise detained under an Act of the Congress or a State law.

HUD means the Department of Housing and Urban Development.

ICH means the Interagency Council on the Homeless.

Landholding agency means a Federal department or agency with statutory authority to control real property.

Lease means an agreement between either the Department of Health and Human Services for surplus property, or landholding agencies in the case of non-excess properties or properties subject to the Base Closure and Realignment Act (Public Law 100–526; 10 U.S.C. 2687), and the applicant, giving rise to the relationship of lessor and lessee for the use of Federal real property for a term of at least one year under the conditions set forth in the lease document.

Non-profit organization means an organization no part of the net earnings of which inures to the benefit of any member, founder, contributor, or individual; that has a voluntary board; that has an accounting system or has designated an entity that will maintain a functioning accounting system for the organization in accordance with generally accepted accounting procedures; and that practices nondiscrimination in the provision of assistance.

Permit means a license granted by a landholding agency to use unutilized or underutilized property for a specific amount of time under terms and conditions determined by the landholding agency.

Property means real property consisting of vacant land or buildings, or a portion thereof, that is excess, surplus, or designated as unutilized or underutilized in surveys by the heads of landholding agencies conducted pursuant to section 202(b)(2) of the Federal Property and Administrative Services Act of 1949 (40 U.S.C. 483(b)(2).)

Regional homeless coordinator means a regional coordinator of the Interagency Council on the Homeless.

Representative of the homeless means a State or local government agency, or private nonprofit organization which provides, or proposes to provide, services to the homeless.

Screen means the process by which GSA surveys Federal agencies, or State, local and non-profit entities, to determine if any such entity has an interest in using excess Federal property to carry out a particular agency mission or a specific public use.

State homeless coordinator means a state contact person designated by a state to receive and disseminate information and communications received from the Interagency Council on the Homeless in accordance with section 210(a) of the Stewart B. McKinney Act of 1987, as amended.

Suitable property means that HUD has determined that a particular property satisfies the criteria listed in § 581.6.

Surplus property means any excess real property not required by any Federal landholding agency for its needs or the discharge of its responsibilities, as determined by the Administrator of GSA.

Underutilized means an entire property or portion thereof, with or without improvements which is used only at irregular periods or intermittently by the accountable landholding agency for current program purposes of that agency, or which is used for current program purposes that can be satisfied with only a portion of the property.

Unsuitable property means that HUD has determined that a particular property does not satisfy the criteria in § 581.6.

Unutilized property means an entire property or portion thereof, with or without improvements, not occupied for current program purposes for the accountable executive agency or occupied in caretaker status only.

§ 581.2 Applicability.

(a) This part applies to Federal real property which has been designated by Federal landholding agencies as unutilized, underutilized, excess or surplus

Ofc. of Asst. Secy., Comm. Planning, Develop., HUD § 581.4

and is therefore subject to the provisions of title V of the McKinney Act (42 U.S.C. 11411).

(b) The following categories of properties are not subject to this subpart (regardless of whether they may be unutilized or underutilized).

(1) Machinery and equipment.

(2) Government-owned, contractor-operated machinery, equipment, land, and other facilities reported excess for sale only to the using contractor and subject to a continuing military requirement.

(3) Properties subject to special legislation directing a particular action.

(4) Properties subject to a court order.

(5) Property not subject to survey requirements of Executive Order 12512 (April 29, 1985).

(6) Mineral rights interests.

(7) Air space interests.

(8) Indian Reservation land subject to section 202(a)(2) of the Federal Property and Administrative Service Act of 1949, as amended.

(9) Property interests subject to reversion.

(10) Easements.

(11) Property purchased in whole or in part with Federal funds if title to the property is not held by a Federal landholding agency as defined in this part.

§ 581.3 Collecting the information.

(a) *Canvass of landholding agencies.* On a quarterly basis, HUD will canvass landholding agencies to collect information about property described as unutilized, underutilized, excess, or surplus, in surveys conducted by the agencies under section 202 of the Federal Property and Administrative Services Act (40 U.S.C. 483), Executive Order 12512, and 41 CFR part 101–47.800. Each canvass will collect information on properties not previously reported and about property reported previously the status or classification of which has changed or for which any of the information reported on the property checklist has changed.

(1) HUD will request descriptive information on properties sufficient to make a reasonable determination, under the criteria described below, of the suitability of a property for use as a facility to assist the homeless.

(2) HUD will direct landholding agencies to respond to requests for information within 25 days of receipt of such requests.

(b) *Agency annual report.* By December 31 of each year, each landholding agency must notify HUD regarding the current availability status and classification of each property controlled by the agency that:

(1) Was included in a list of suitable properties published that year by HUD, and

(2) Remains available for application for use to assist the homeless, or has become available for application during that year.

(c) *GSA inventory.* HUD will collect information, in the same manner as described in paragraph (a) of this section, from GSA regarding property that is in GSA's current inventory of excess or surplus property.

(d) *Change in status.* If the information provided on the property checklist changes subsequent to HUD's determination of suitability, and the property remains unutilized, underutilized, excess or surplus, the landholding agency shall submit a revised property checklist in response to the next quarterly canvass. HUD will make a new determination of suitability and, if it differs from the previous determination, republish the property information in the FEDERAL REGISTER. For example, property determined unsuitable for national security concerns may no longer be subject to security restrictions, or property determined suitable may subsequently be found to be contaminated.

EFFECTIVE DATE NOTE: At 56 FR 23794, 23795, May 24, 1991, part 581 was added, effective on May 24, 1991, except for § 581.3 which will not become effective until approved by the District Court for the District of Columbia, pending further proceedings.

§ 581.4 Suitability determination.

(a) *Suitability determination.* Within 30 days after the receipt of information from landholding agencies regarding properties which were reported pursuant to the canvass described in § 581.3(a), HUD will determine, under

§ 581.5

criteria set forth in § 581.6, which properties are suitable for use as facilities to assist the homeless and report its determination to the landholding agency. Properties that are under lease, contract, license, or agreement by which a Federal agency retains a real property interest or which are scheduled to become unutilized or underutilized will be reviewed for suitability no earlier than six months prior to the expected date when the property will become unutilized or underutilized, except that properties subject to the Base Closure and Realignment Act may be reviewed up to eighteen months prior to the expected date when the property will become unutilized or underutilized.

(b) *Scope of suitability.* HUD will determine the suitability of a property for use as a facility to assist the homeless without regard to any particular use.

(c) *Environmental information.* HUD will evaluate the environmental information contained in property checklists forwarded to HUD by the landholding agencies solely for the purpose of determining suitability of properties under the criteria in § 581.6.

(d) *Written record of suitability determination.* HUD will assign an identification number to each property reviewed for suitability. HUD will maintain a written public record of the following:

(1) The suitability determination for a particular piece of property, and the reasons for that determination; and

(2) The landholding agency's response to the determination pursuant to the requirements of § 581.7(a).

(e) *Property determined unsuitable.* Property that is reviewed by HUD under this section and that is determined unsuitable for use to assist the homeless may not be made available for any other purpose for 20 days after publication in the FEDERAL REGISTER of a Notice of unsuitability to allow for review of the determination at the request of a representative of the homeless.

(f) *Procedures for appealing unsuitability determinations.* (1) To request review of a determination of unsuitability, a representative of the homeless must contact HUD within 20 days of publication of notice in the FEDERAL REGISTER that a property is unsuitable. Requests may be submitted to HUD in writing or by calling 1–800–927–7588 (Toll Free). Written requests must be received no later than 20 days after notice of unsuitability is published in the FEDERAL REGISTER.

(2) Requests for review of a determination of unsuitability may be made only by representatives of the homeless, as defined in § 581.1.

(3) The request for review must specify the grounds on which it is based, i.e., that HUD has improperly applied the criteria or that HUD has relied on incorrect or incomplete information in making the determination (e.g., that property is in a floodplain but not in a floodway).

(4) Upon receipt of a request to review a determination of unsuitability, HUD will notify the landholding agency that such a request has been made, request that the agency respond with any information pertinent to the review, and advise the agency that it should refrain from initiating disposal procedures until HUD has completed its reconsideration regarding unsuitability.

(i) HUD will act on all requests for review within 30 days of receipt of the landholding agency's response and will notify the representative of the homeless and the landholding agency in writing of its decision.

(ii) If a property is determined suitable as a result of the review, HUD will request the landholding agency's determination of availability pursuant to § 581.7(a), upon receipt of which HUD will promptly publish the determination in the FEDERAL REGISTER. If the determination of unsuitability stands, HUD will inform the representative of the homeless of its decision.

§ 581.5 Real property reported excess to GSA.

(a) Each landholding agency must submit a report to GSA of properties it determines excess. Each landholding agency must also provide a copy of HUD's suitability determination, if any, including HUD's identification number for the property.

(b) If a landholding agency reports a property to GSA which has been reviewed by HUD for homeless assistance suitability and HUD determined the property suitable, GSA will screen the property pursuant to §581.5(g) and will advise HUD of the availability of the property for use by the homeless as provided in §581.5(e). In lieu of the above, GSA may submit a new checklist to HUD and follow the procedures in §581.5(c) through §581.5(g).

(c) If a landholding agency reports a property to GSA which has not been reviewed by HUD for homeless assistance suitability, GSA will complete a property checklist, based on information provided by the landholding agency, and will forward this checklist to HUD for a suitability determination. This checklist will reflect any change in classification, i.e., from unutilized or underutilized to excess.

(d) Within 30 days after GSA's submission, HUD will advise GSA of the suitability determination.

(e) When GSA receives a letter from HUD listing suitable excess properties in GSA's inventory, GSA will transmit to HUD within 45 days a response which includes the following for each identified property:

(1) A statement that there is no other compelling Federal need for the property, and therefore, the property will be determined surplus; or

(2) A statement that there is further and compelling Federal need for the property (including a full explanation of such need) and that, therefore, the property is not presently available for use to assist the homeless.

(f) When an excess property is determined suitable and available and notice is published in the FEDERAL REGISTER, GSA will concurrently notify HHS, HUD, State and local government units, known homeless assistance providers that have expressed interest in the particular property, and other organizations, as appropriate, concerning suitable properties.

(g) Upon submission of a Report of Excess to GSA, GSA may screen the property for Federal use. In addition, GSA may screen State and local governmental units and eligible nonprofit organizations to determine interest in the property in accordance with current regulations. (See 41 CFR 101-47.203-5, 101-47.204-1 and 101-47.303-2.)

(h) The landholding agency will retain custody and accountability and will protect and maintain any property which is reported excess to GSA as provided in 41 CFR 101-47.402.

§ 581.6 Suitability criteria.

(a) All properties, buildings and land will be determined suitable unless a property's characteristics include one or more of the following conditions:

(1) *National security concerns.* A property located in an area to which the general public is denied access in the interest of national security (e.g., where a special pass or security clearance is a condition of entry to the property) will be determined unsuitable. Where alternative access can be provided for the public without compromising national security, the property will not be determined unsuitable on this basis.

(2) *Property containing flammable or explosive materials.* A property located within 2000 feet of an industrial, commercial or Federal facility handling flammable or explosive material (excluding underground storage) will be determined unsuitable. Above ground containers with a capacity of 100 gallons or less, or larger containers which provide the heating or power source for the property, and which meet local safety, operation, and permitting standards, will not affect whether a particular property is determined suitable or unsuitable. Underground storage, gasoline stations and tank trucks are not included in this category and their presence will not be the basis of an unsuitability determination unless there is evidence of a threat to personal safety as provided in paragraph (a)(5) of this section.

(3) *Runway clear zone and military airfield clear zone.* A property located within an airport runway clear zone or military airfield clear zone will be determined unsuitable.

(4) *Floodway.* A property located in the floodway of a 100 year floodplain will be determined unsuitable. If the floodway has been contained or corrected, or if only an incidental portion of the property not affecting the use of the remainder of the property is in the floodway, the property will not be determined unsuitable.

§ 581.7

(5) *Documented deficiencies.* A property with a documented and extensive condition(s) that represents a clear threat to personal physical safety will be determined unsuitable. Such conditions may include, but are not limited to, contamination, structural damage or extensive deterioration, friable asbestos, PCB's, or natural hazardous substances such as radon, periodic flooding, sinkholes or earth slides.

(6) *Inaccessible.* A property that is inaccessible will be determined unsuitable. An inaccessible property is one that is not accessible by road (including property on small off-shore islands) or is land locked (e.g., can be reached only by crossing private property and there is no established right or means of entry).

§ 581.7 Determination of availability.

(a) Within 45 days after receipt of a letter from HUD pursuant to § 581.4(a), each landholding agency must transmit to HUD a statement of one of the following:

(1) In the case of unutilized or underutilized property:

(i) An intention to declare the property excess,

(ii) An intention to make the property available for use to assist the homeless, or

(iii) The reasons why the property cannot be declared excess or made available for use to assist the homeless. The reasons given must be different than those listed as suitability criteria in § 581.6.

(2) In the case of excess property which had previously been reported to GSA:

(i) A statement that there is no compelling Federal need for the property, and that, therefore, the property will be determined surplus; or

(ii) A statement that there is a further and compelling Federal need for the property (including a full explanation of such need) and that, therefore, the property is not presently available for use to assist the homeless.

§ 581.8 Public notice of determination.

(a) No later than 15 days after the last 45 day period has elapsed for receiving responses from the landholding agencies regarding availability, HUD will publish in the FEDERAL REGISTER a list of all properties reviewed, including a description of the property, its address, and classification. The following designations will be made:

(1) Properties that are suitable and available.

(2) Properties that are suitable and unavailable.

(3) Properties that are suitable and to be declared excess.

(4) Properties that are unsuitable.

(b) Information about specific properties can be obtained by contacting HUD at the following toll free number, 1–800–927–7588.

(c) HUD will transmit to the ICH a copy of the list of all properties published in the FEDERAL REGISTER. The ICH will immediately distribute to all state and regional homeless coordinators area-relevant portions of the list. The ICH will encourage the state and regional homeless coordinators to disseminate this information widely.

(d) No later than February 15 of each year, HUD shall publish in the FEDERAL REGISTER a list of all properties reported pursuant to § 581.3(b).

(e) HUD shall publish an annual list of properties determined suitable but which agencies reported unavailable including the reasons such properties are not available.

(f) Copies of the lists published in the FEDERAL REGISTER will be available for review by the public in the HUD headquarters building library (room 8141); area-relevant portions of the lists will be available in the HUD regional offices and in major field offices.

§ 581.9 Application process.

(OMB approval number 09370191)

(a) *Holding period.* (1) Properties published as available for application for use to assist the homeless shall not be available for any other purpose for a period of 60 days beginning on the date of publication. Any representative of the homeless interested in any underutilized, unutilized, excess or surplus Federal property for use as a facility to assist the homeless must send to HHS a written expression of interest in that property within 60 days after the property has been published in the FEDERAL REGISTER.

(2) If a written expression of interest to apply for suitable property for use to assist the homeless is received by HHS within the 60 day holding period, such property may not be made available for any other purpose until the date HHS or the appropriate landholding agency has completed action on the application submitted pursuant to that expression of interest.

(3) The expression of interest should identify the specific property, briefly describe the proposed use, include the name of the organization, and indicate whether it is a public body or a private non-profit organization. The expression of interest must be sent to the Division of Health Facilities Planning (DHFP) of the Department of Health and Human Services at the following address:

Director, Division of Health Facilities Planning, Public Health Service, room 17A-10, Parklawn Building, 5600 Fishers Lane, Rockville, Maryland 20857.

HHS will notify the landholding agency (for unutilized and underutilized properties) or GSA (for excess and surplus properties) when an expression of interest has been received for a particular property.

(4) An expression of interest may be sent to HHS any time after the 60 day holding period has expired. In such a case, an application submitted pursuant to this expression of interest may be approved for use by the homeless if:

(i) No application or written expression of interest has been made under any law for use of the property for any purpose; and

(ii) In the case of excess or surplus property, GSA has not received a bona fide offer to purchase that property or advertised for the sale of the property by public auction.

(b) *Application requirements.* Upon receipt of an expression of interest, DHFP will send an application packet to the interested entity. The application packet requires the applicant to provide certain information, including the following—

(1) *Description of the applicant organization.* The applicant must document that it satisfies the definition of a "representative of the homeless," as specified in § 581.1 of this subpart. The applicant must document its authority to hold real property. Private non-profit organizations applying for deeds must document that they are section 501(c)(3) tax-exempt.

(2) *Description of the property desired.* The applicant must describe the property desired and indicate that any modifications made to the property will conform to local use restrictions except for local zoning regulations.

(3) *Description of the proposed program.* The applicant must fully describe the proposed program and demonstrate how the program will address the needs of the homeless population to be assisted. The applicant must fully describe what modifications will be made to the property before the program becomes operational.

(4) *Ability to finance and operate the proposed program.* The applicant must specifically describe all anticipated costs and sources of funding for the proposed program. The applicant must indicate that it can assume care, custody, and maintenance of the property and that it has the necessary funds or the ability to obtain such funds to carry out the approved program of use for the property.

(5) *Compliance with non-discrimination requirements.* Each applicant and lessee under this part must certify in writing that it will comply with the requirements of the Fair Housing Act (42 U.S.C. 3601–3619) and implementing regulations; and as applicable, Executive Order 11063 (Equal Opportunity in Housing) and implementing regulations; title VI of the Civil Rights Act of 1964 (42 U.S.C. 2000d to d–4) (Nondiscrimination in Federally Assisted Programs) and implementing regulations; the prohibitions against discrimination on the basis of age under the Age Discrimination Act of 1975 (42 U.S.C. 6101–6107) and implementing regulations; and the prohibitions against otherwise qualified individuals with handicaps under section 504 of the Rehabilitation Act of 1973 (29 U.S.C. 794) and implementing regulations. The applicant must state that it will not discriminate on the basis of race, color, national origin, religion, sex, age, familial status, or handicap in the use of

the property, and will maintain the required records to demonstrate compliance with Federal laws.

(6) *Insurance.* The applicant must certify that it will insure the property against loss, damage, or destruction in accordance with the requirements of 45 CFR 12.9.

(7) *Historic preservation.* Where applicable, the applicant must provide information that will enable HHS to comply with Federal historic preservation requirements.

(8) *Environmental information.* The applicant must provide sufficient information to allow HHS to analyze the potential impact of the applicant's proposal on the environment, in accordance with the instructions provided with the application packet. HHS will assist applicants in obtaining any pertinent environmental information in the possession of HUD, GSA, or the landholding agency.

(9) *Local government notification.* The applicant must indicate that it has informed the applicable unit of general local government responsible for providing sewer, water, police, and fire services, in writing of its proposed program.

(10) *Zoning and local use restrictions.* The applicant must indicate that it will comply with all local use restrictions, including local building code requirements. Any applicant which applies for a lease or permit for a particular property is not required to comply with local zoning requirements. Any applicant applying for a deed of a particular property, pursuant to §581.9(b)(3), must comply with local zoning requirements, as specified in 45 CFR part 12.

(c) *Scope of evaluations.* Due to the short time frame imposed for evaluating applications, HHS' evaluation will, generally, be limited to the information contained in the application.

(d) *Deadline.* Completed applications must be received by DHFP, at the above address, within 90 days after an expression of interest is received from a particular applicant for that property. Upon written request from the applicant, HHS may grant extensions, provided that the appropriate landholding agency concurs with the extension. Because each applicant will have a different deadline based on the date the applicant submitted an expression of interest, applicants should contact the individual landholding agency to confirm that a particular property remains available prior to submitting an application.

(e) *Evaluations.* (1) Upon receipt of an application, HHS will review it for completeness, and, if incomplete, may return it or ask the applicant to furnish any missing or additional required information prior to final evaluation of the application.

(2) HHS will evaluate each completed application within 25 days of receipt and will promptly advise the applicant of its decision. Applications are evaluated on a first-come, first-serve basis. HHS will notify all organizations which have submitted expressions of interest for a particular property regarding whether the first application received for that property has been approved or disapproved. All applications will be reviewed on the basis of the following elements, which are listed in descending order of priority, except that paragraphs (e)(2)(iv) and (e)(2)(v) of this section are of equal importance.

(i) *Services offered.* The extent and range of proposed services, such as meals, shelter, job training, and counseling.

(ii) *Need.* The demand for the program and the degree to which the available property will be fully utilized.

(iii) *Implementation time.* The amount of time necessary for the proposed program to become operational.

(iv) *Experience.* Demonstrated prior success in operating similar programs and recommendations attesting to that fact by Federal, State, and local authorities.

(v) *Financial ability.* The adequacy of funding that will likely be available to run the program fully and properly and to operate the facility.

(3) Additional evaluation factors may be added as deemed necessary by HHS. If additional factors are added, the application packet will be revised to include a description of these additional factors.

(4) If HHS receives one or more competing applications for a property within 5 days of the first application HHS

will evaluate all completed applications simultaneously. HHS will rank approved applications based on the elements listed in § 581.8(e)(2), and notify the landholding agency, or GSA, as appropriate, of the relative ranks.

§ 581.10 Action on approved applications.

(a) *Unutilized and underutilized properties.* (1) When HHS approves an application, it will so notify the applicant and forward a copy of the application to the landholding agency. The landholding agency will execute the lease, or permit document, as appropriate, in consultation with the applicant.

(2) The landholding agency maintains the discretion to decide the following:

(i) The length of time the property will be available. (Leases and permits will be for a period of at least one year unless the applicant requests a shorter term.)

(ii) Whether to grant use of the property via a lease or permit;

(iii) The terms and conditions of the lease or permit document.

(b) *Excess and surplus properties.* (1) When HHS approves an application, it will so notify the applicant and request that GSA assign the property to HHS for leasing. Upon receipt of the assignment, HHS will execute a lease in accordance with the procedures and requirements set out in 45 CFR part 12. In accordance with 41 CFR 101–47.402, custody and accountability of the property will remain throughout the lease term with the agency which initially reported the property as excess.

(2) Prior to assignment to HHS, GSA may consider other Federal uses and other important national needs; however, in deciding the disposition of surplus real property, GSA will generally give priority of consideration to uses to assist the homeless. GSA may consider any competing request for the property made under section 203(k) of the Federal Property and Administrative Services Act of 1949 (40 U.S.C. 484(k)) that is so meritorious and compelling that it outweighs the needs of the homeless, and HHS may likewise consider any competing request made under subsection 203(k)(1) of that law.

(3) Whenever GSA or HHS decides in favor of a competing request over a request for property for homeless assistance use as provided in paragraph (b)(2) of this section, the agency making the decision will transmit to the appropriate committees of the Congress an explanatory statement which details the need satisfied by conveyance of the surplus property, and the reasons for determining that such need was so meritorious and compelling as to outweigh the needs of the homeless.

(4) *Deeds.* Surplus property may be conveyed to representatives of the homeless pursuant to section 203(k) of the Federal Property and Administrative Services Act of 1949 (40 U.S.C. 484(k)(1), and section 501(f) of the McKinney Act as amended, 42 U.S.C. 11411. Representatives of the homeless must complete the application packet pursuant to the requirements of § 581.9 of this part and in accordance with the requirements of 45 CFR part 12.

(c) *Completion of lease term and reversion of title.* Lessees and grantees will be responsible for the protection and maintenance of the property during the time that they possess the property. Upon termination of the lease term or reversion of title to the Federal government, the lessee or grantee will be responsible for removing any improvements made to the property and will be responsible for restoration of the property. If such improvements are not removed, they will become the property of the Federal government. GSA or the landholding agency, as appropriate, will assume responsibility for protection and maintenance of a property when the lease terminates or title reverts.

§ 581.11 Unsuitable properties.

The landholding agency will defer, for 20 days after the date that notice of a property is published in the FEDERAL REGISTER, action to dispose of properties determined unsuitable for homeless assistance. HUD will inform landholding agencies or GSA if appeal of an unsuitability determination is filed by a representative of the homeless pursuant to § 581.4(f)(4). HUD will advise the agency that it should refrain from initiating disposal procedures until HUD has completed its reconsideration process regarding unsuitability. Thereafter, or if no appeal has been filed after 20

§ 581.12

days, GSA or the appropriate landholding agency may proceed with disposal action in accordance with applicable law.

§ 581.12 No applications approved.

(a) At the end of the 60 day holding period described in § 581.9(a), HHS will notify GSA, or the landholding agency, as appropriate, if an expression of interest has been received for a particular property. Where there is no expression of interest, GSA or the landholding agency, as appropriate, will proceed with disposal in accordance with applicable law.

(b) Upon advice from HHS that all applications have been disapproved, or if no completed applications or requests for extensions have been received by HHS within 90 days from the date of the last expression of interest, disposal may proceed in accordance with applicable law.

§ 581.13 Waivers.

The Secretary may waive any requirement of this part that is not required by law, whenever it is determined that undue hardship would result from applying the requirement, or where application of the requirement would adversely affect the purposes of the program. Each waiver will be in writing and will be supported by documentation of the pertinent facts and grounds. The Secretary periodically will publish notice of granted waivers in the FEDERAL REGISTER.

PART 582—SHELTER PLUS CARE

Subpart A—General

Sec.
582.1 Purpose and scope.
582.5 Definitions.

Subpart B—Assistance Provided

582.100 Program component descriptions.
582.105 Rental assistance amounts and payments.
582.110 Matching requirements.
582.115 Limitations on assistance.
582.120 Consolidated plan.

Subpart C—Application and Grant Award

582.200 Application and grant award.
582.230 Environmental review.

Subpart D—Program Requirements

582.300 General operation.
582.305 Housing quality standards; rent reasonableness.
582.310 Resident rent.
582.315 Occupancy agreements.
582.320 Termination of assistance to participants.
582.325 Outreach activities.
582.330 Nondiscrimination and equal opportunity requirements.
582.335 Displacement, relocation, and real property acquisition.
582.340 Other Federal requirements.

Subpart E—Administration

582.400 Grant agreement.
582.405 Program changes.
582.410 Obligation and deobligation of funds.

AUTHORITY: 42 U.S.C. 3535(d) and 11403–11407b.

SOURCE: 58 FR 13892, Mar. 15, 1993, unless otherwise noted.

Subpart A—General

§ 582.1 Purpose and scope.

(a) *General.* The Shelter Plus Care program (S+C) is authorized by title IV, subtitle F, of the Stewart B. McKinney Homeless Assistance Act (the McKinney Act) (42 U.S.C. 11403–11407b). S+C is designed to link rental assistance to supportive services for hard-to-serve homeless persons with disabilities (primarily those who are seriously mentally ill; have chronic problems with alcohol, drugs, or both; or have acquired immunodeficiency syndrome (AIDS) and related diseases) and their families. The program provides grants to be used for rental assistance for permanent housing for homeless persons with disabilities. Rental assistance grants must be matched in the aggregate by supportive services that are equal in value to the amount of rental assistance and appropriate to the needs of the population to be served. Recipients are chosen on a competitive basis nationwide.

(b) *Components.* Rental assistance is provided through four components described in § 582.100. Applicants may apply for assistance under any one of the four components, or a combination.

[58 FR 13892, Mar. 15, 1993, as amended at 61 FR 51169, Sept. 30, 1996]

§ 582.5 Definitions.

The terms *Fair Market Rent (FMR), HUD, Public Housing Agency (PHA), Indian Housing Authority (IHA),* and *Secretary* are defined in 24 CFR part 5.

As used in this part:

Acquired immunodeficiency syndrome (AIDS) and related diseases has the meaning given in section 853 of the AIDS Housing Opportunity Act (42 U.S.C. 12902).

Applicant has the meaning given in section 462 of the McKinney Act (42 U.S.C. 11403g).

Eligible person means a homeless person with disabilities (primarily persons who are seriously mentally ill; have chronic problems with alcohol, drugs, or both; or have AIDS and related diseases) and, if also homeless, the family of such a person. To be eligible for assistance, persons must be very low income, except that low-income individuals may be assisted under the SRO component in accordance with 24 CFR 813.105(b).

Homeless or *homeless individual* has the meaning given in section 103 of the McKinney Act (42 U.S.C. 11302).

Indian tribe has the meaning given in section 102 of the Housing and Community Development Act of 1974 (42 U.S.C. 5302).

Low-income means an annual income not in excess of 80 percent of the median income for the area, as determined by HUD. HUD may establish income limits higher or lower than 80 percent of the median income for the area on the basis of its finding that such variations are necessary because of the prevailing levels of construction costs or unusually high or low family incomes.

Nonprofit organization has the meaning given in section 104 of the Cranston-Gonzalez National Affordable Housing Act (42 U.S.C. 12704). The term nonprofit organization also includes a community mental health center established as a public nonprofit organization.

Participant means an eligible person who has been selected to participate in S+C.

Person with disabilities means a household composed of one or more persons at least one of whom is an adult who has a disability.

(1) A person shall be considered to have a disability if such person has a physical, mental, or emotional impairment which is expected to be of long-continued and indefinite duration; substantially impedes his or her ability to live independently; and is of such a nature that such ability could be improved by more suitable housing conditions.

(2) A person will also be considered to have a disability if he or she has a developmental disability, which is a severe, chronic disability that—

(i) Is attributable to a mental or physical impairment or combination of mental and physical impairments;

(ii) Is manifested before the person attains age 22;

(iii) Is likely to continue indefinitely;

(iv) Results in substantial functional limitations in three or more of the following areas of major life activity:

(A) Self-care;

(B) Receptive and expressive language;

(C) Learning;

(D) Mobility;

(E) Self-direction;

(F) Capacity for independent living; and

(G) Economic self-sufficiency; and

(v) Reflects the person's need for a combination and sequence of special, interdisciplinary, or generic care, treatment, or other services which are of lifelong or extended duration and are individually planned and coordinated.

(3) Notwithstanding the preceding provisions of this definition, the term *person with disabilities* includes, except in the case of the SRO component, two or more persons with disabilities living together, one or more such persons living with another person who is determined to be important to their care or well-being, and the surviving member or members of any household described in the first sentence of this definition who were living, in a unit assisted under this part, with the deceased member of the household at the time of his or her death. (In any event, with respect to the surviving member or members of a household, the right to rental assistance under this part will terminate at the end of the grant period

under which the deceased member was a participant.)

Recipient means an applicant approved to receive a S+C grant.

Seriously mentally ill has the meaning given in section 462 of the McKinney Act (42 U.S.C. 11403g).

Single room occupancy (SRO) housing means a unit for occupancy by one person, which need not but may contain food preparation or sanitary facilities, or both.

Sponsor means a nonprofit organization which owns or leases dwelling units and has contracts with a recipient to make such units available to eligible homeless persons and receives rental assistance payments under the SRA component.

State has the meaning given in section 462 of the McKinney Act (42 U.S.C. 11403g).

Supportive service provider, or *service provider*, means a person or organization licensed or otherwise qualified to provide supportive services, either for profit or not for profit.

Supportive services means assistance that—

(1) Addresses the special needs of eligible persons; and

(2) Provides appropriate services or assists such persons in obtaining appropriate services, including health care, mental health treatment, alcohol and other substance abuse services, child care services, case management services, counseling, supervision, education, job training, and other services essential for achieving and maintaining independent living.

(Inpatient acute hospital care does not qualify as a supportive service.).

Unit of general local government has the meaning given in section 102 of the Housing and Community Development Act of 1974 (42 U.S.C. 5302).

Very low-income means an annual income not in excess of 50 percent of the median income for the area, as determined by HUD, with adjustments for smaller and larger families. HUD may establish income limits higher or lower than 50 percent of the median income for the area on the basis of its finding that such variations are necessary because of unusually high or low family incomes.

[61 FR 51169, Sept. 30, 1996; 62 FR 13539, Mar. 21, 1997]

Subpart B—Assistance Provided

§ 582.100 Program component descriptions.

(a) *Tenant-based rental assistance (TRA).* Tenant-based rental assistance provides grants for rental assistance which permit participants to choose housing of an appropriate size in which to reside. Participants retain the rental assistance if they move. Where necessary to facilitate the coordination of supportive services, grant recipients may require participants to live in a specific area for their entire period of participation or in a specific structure for the first year and in a specific area for the remainder of their period of participation. Recipients may not define the area in a way that violates the Fair Housing Act or the Rehabilitation Act of 1973. The term of the grant between HUD and the grant recipient for TRA is five years.

(b) *Project-based rental assistance (PRA).* Project-based rental assistance provides grants for rental assistance to the owner of an existing structure, where the owner agrees to lease the subsidized units to participants. Participants do not retain rental assistance if they move. Rental subsidies are provided to the owner for a period of either five or ten years. To qualify for ten years of rental subsidies, the owner must complete at least $3,000 of eligible rehabilitation for each unit (including the unit's prorated share of work to be accomplished on common areas or systems), to make the structure decent, safe and sanitary. This rehabilitation must be completed with in 12 months of the grant award.

(c) *Sponsor-based rental assistance (SRA).* Sponsor-based rental assistance provides grants for rental assistance through contracts between the grant recipient and sponsor organizations. A sponsor may be a private, nonprofit organization or a community mental health agency established as a public nonprofit organization. Participants reside in housing owned or leased by the sponsor. The term of the grant between HUD and the grant recipient for SRA is five years.

(d) *Moderate rehabilitation for single room occupancy dwellings (SRO).* (1) The SRO component provides grants for rental assistance in connection with the moderate rehabilitation of single room occupancy housing units. Resources to initially fund the cost of rehabilitating the dwellings must be obtained from other sources. However, the rental assistance covers operating expenses of the rehabilitated SRO units occupied by homeless persons, including debt service to retire the cost of the moderate rehabilitation over a ten-year period.

(2) SRO housing must be in need of moderate rehabilitation and must meet the requirements of 24 CFR 882.803(a). Costs associated with rehabilitation of common areas may be included in the calculation of the cost for assisted units based on the proportion of the number of units to be assisted under this part to the total number of units.

(3) SRO assistance may also be used for efficiency units selected for rehabilitation under this program, but the gross rent (contract rent plus any utility allowance) for those units will be no higher than for SRO units (i.e., 75 percent of the 0-bedroom Moderate Rehabilitation Fair Market Rent).

(4) The requirements regarding maintenance, operation, and inspections described in 24 CFR 882.806(b)(4) and 882.808(n) must be met.

(5) *Governing regulations.* Except where there is a conflict with any requirement under this part or where specifically provided, the SRO component will be governed by the regulations set forth in 24 CFR part 882, subpart H.

§ 582.105 Rental assistance amounts and payments.

(a) *Eligible activity.* S+C grants may be used for providing rental assistance for housing occupied by participants in the program and administrative costs as provided for in paragraph (e) of this section, except that the housing may not be currently receiving Federal funding for rental assistance or operating costs under other HUD programs. Recipients may design a housing program that includes a range of housing types with differing levels of supportive services. Rental assistance may include security deposits on units in an amount up to one month's rent.

(b) *Amount of the grant.* The amount of the grant is based on the number and size of units proposed by the applicant to be assisted over the grant period. The grant amount is calculated by multiplying the number of units proposed times the applicable Fair Market Rent (FMR) of each unit times the term of the grant.

(c) *Payment of grant.* (1) The grant amount will be reserved for rental assistance over the grant period. An applicant's grant request is an estimate of the amount needed for rental assistance. Recipients will make draws from the reserved amount to pay the actual costs of rental assistance for program participants. For TRA, on demonstration of need, up to 25 percent of the total rental assistance awarded may be spent in any one of the five years, or a higher percentage if approved by HUD, where the applicant provides evidence satisfactory to HUD that it is financially committed to providing the housing assistance described in the application for the full five-year period.

(2) A recipient must serve at least as many participants as shown in its application. Where the grant amount reserved for rental assistance over the grant period exceeds the amount that will be needed to pay the actual costs of rental assistance, due to such factor as contract rents being lower than FMRs and participants are being able to pay a portion of the rent, recipients may use the remaining funds for the costs of administering the housing assistance, as described in paragraph (e) of this section, for damage to property, as described in paragraph (f) of this section, for covering the costs of rent increases, or for serving a great number of participants.

(d) *Vacancies.* (1) If a unit assisted under this part is vacated before the expiration of the occupancy agreement described in § 582.315 of this part, the assistance for the unit may continue for a maximum of 30 days from the end of the month in which the unit was vacated, unless occupied by another eligible person. No additional assistance

§ 582.110

will be paid until the unit is occupied by another eligible person.

(2) As used in this paragraph (d), the term "vacate" does not include brief periods of inpatient care, not to exceed 90 days for each occurrence.

(e) *Administrative costs.* (1) Up to eight percent of the grant amount may be used to pay the costs of administering the housing assistance. Recipients may contract with another entity approved by HUD to administer the housing assistance.

(2) Eligible administrative activities include processing rental payments to landlords, examining participant income and family composition, providing housing information and assistance, inspecting units for compliance with housing quality standards, and receiving into the program new participants. This administrative allowance does not include the cost of administering the supportive services or the grant (*e.g.,* costs of preparing the application, reports or audits required by HUD), which are not eligible activities under a S+C grant.

(f) *Property damage.* Recipients may use grant funds in an amount up to one month's rent to pay for any damage to housing due to the action of a participant.

[58 FR 13892, Mar. 15, 1993, as amended at 61 FR 51170, Sept. 30, 1996]

§ 582.110 Matching requirements.

(a) *Matching rental assistance with supportive services.* (1) To qualify for rental assistance grants, an applicant must certify that it will provide or ensure the provision of supportive services, including funding the services itself if the planned resources do not become available for any reason, appropriate to the needs of the population being served, and at least equal in value to the aggregate amount of rental assistance funded by HUD. The supportive services may be newly created for the program or already in operation, and may be provided or funded by other Federal, State, local, or private programs in accordance with 42 U.S.C. 11403b. This statute provides that a recipient may use funds from any source, including any other Federal source (but excluding the specific statutory subtitle from which S+C funds are provided), as well as State, local, and private sources, provided that funds from the other source are not statutorily prohibited to be used as a match.

(2) Only services that are provided after the execution of the grant agreement may count toward the match.

(3) It is the responsibility of the recipient to ensure that any funds or services used to satisfy the matching requirements of this section are eligible under the laws governing the funds or services to be used as matching funds or services for a grant awarded under this program.

(b) *Availability to participants.* Recipients must give reasonable assurances that supportive services will be available to participants for the entire term of the rental assistance. The value of the services provided to a participant, however, does not have to equal the amount of rental assistance provided that participant, nor does the value have to be equal to the amount of rental assistance on a year-to-year basis.

(c) *Calculating the value of supportive services.* In calculating the amount of the matching supportive services, applicants may count:

(1) Salaries paid to staff of the recipient to provide supportive services to S+C participants;

(2) The value of supportive services provided by other persons or organizations to S+C participants;

(3) The value of time and services contributed by volunteers at the rate of $10.00 an hour, except for donated professional services which may be counted at the customary charge for the service provided (professional services are services ordinarily performed by donors for payment, such as the services of health professionals, that are equivalent to the services they provide in their occupations);

(4) The value of any lease on a building used for the provision of supportive services, provided the value included in the match is no more than the prorated share used for the program; and

(5) The cost of outreach activities, as described in § 582.325(a) of this part.

[58 FR 13892, Mar. 15, 1993, as amended at 73 FR 75325, Dec. 11, 2008]

§ 582.115 Limitations on assistance.

(a) *Current occupants.* Current occupants of the real property are not eligible for assistance under this part. However, as described in § 582.335, persons displaced as a direct result of acquisition, rehabilitation, or demolition for a project under the S+C program are eligible for and must be provided relocation assistance at Uniform Relocation Act levels.

(b) *Amount of assistance provided within a jurisdiction.* HUD will limit the amount of assistance provided within the jurisdiction of any one unit of local government to no more than 10 percent of the amount available.

(c) *Faith-based activities.* (1) Organizations that are religious or faith-based are eligible, on the same basis as any other organization, to participate in the S+C program. Neither the Federal government nor a State or local government receiving funds under S+C programs shall discriminate against an organization on the basis of the organization's religious character or affiliation.

(2) Organizations that are directly funded under the S+C program may not engage in inherently religious activities, such as worship, religious instruction, or proselytization as part of the programs or services funded under this part. If an organization conducts such activities, the activities must be offered separately, in time or location, from the programs or services funded under this part, and participation must be voluntary for the beneficiaries of the HUD-funded programs or services.

(3) A religious organization that participates in the S+C program will retain its independence from Federal, State, and local governments, and may continue to carry out its mission, including the definition, practice and expression of its religious beliefs, provided that it does not use direct S+C funds to support any inherently religious activities, such as worship, religious instruction, or proselytization. Among other things, faith-based organizations may use space in their facilities to provide S+C-funded services, without removing religious art, icons, scriptures, or other religious symbols. In addition, an S+C-funded religious organization retains its authority over its internal governance, and it may retain religious terms in its organization's name, select its board members on a religious basis, and include religious references in its organization's mission statements and other governing documents.

(4) An organization that participates in the S+C program shall not, in providing program assistance, discriminate against a program beneficiary or prospective program beneficiary on the basis of religion or religious belief.

(5) If a State or local government voluntarily contributes its own funds to supplement federally funded activities, the State or local government has the option to segregate the Federal funds or commingle them. However, if the funds are commingled, this section applies to all of the commingled funds.

(d) *Maintenance of effort.* No assistance received under this part (or any State or local government funds used to supplement this assistance) may be used to replace funds provided under any State or local government assistance programs previously used, or designated for use, to assist persons with disabilities, homeless persons, or homeless persons with disabilities.

[58 FR 13892, Mar. 15, 1993, as amended at 68 FR 56407, Sept. 30, 2003]

§ 582.120 Consolidated plan.

(a) *Applicants that are States or units of general local government.* The applicant must have a HUD-approved complete or abbreviated consolidated plan, in accordance with 24 CFR part 91, and must submit a certification that the application for funding is consistent with the HUD-approved consolidated plan. Funded applicants must certify in a grant agreement that they are following the HUD-approved consolidated plan. If the applicant is a State, and the project will be located in a unit of general local government that is required to have, or has, a complete consolidated plan, or that is applying for Shelter Plus Care assistance under the same Notice of Fund Availability (NOFA) and will have an abbreviated consolidated plan with respect to that application, the State also must submit a certification by the unit of general local government that the State's application is consistent with the unit

§ 582.200

of general local government's HUD-approved consolidated plan.

(b) *Applicants that are not States or units of general local government.* The applicant must submit a certification by the jurisdiction in which the proposed project will be located that the jurisdiction is following its HUD-approved consolidated plan and the applicant's application for funding is consistent with the jurisdiction's HUD-approved consolidated plan. The certification must be made by the unit of general local government or the State, in accordance with the consistency certification provisions of the consolidated plan regulations, 24 CFR part 91, subpart F.

(c) *Indian tribes and the Insular Areas of Guam, the U.S. Virgin Islands, American Samoa, and the Northern Mariana Islands.* These entities are not required to have a consolidated plan or to make consolidated plan certifications. An application by an Indian tribe or other applicant for a project that will be located on a reservation of an Indian tribe will not require a certification by the tribe or the State. However, where an Indian tribe is the applicant for a project that will not be located on a reservation, the requirement for a certification under paragraph (b) of this section will apply.

(d) *Timing of consolidated plan certification submissions.* Unless otherwise set forth in the NOFA, the required certification that the application for funding is consistent with the HUD-approved consolidated plan must be submitted by the funding application submission deadline announced in the NOFA.

[60 FR 16379, Mar. 30, 1995]

Subpart C—Application and Grant Award

§ 582.200 Application and grant award.

(a) *Review.* When funds are made available for assistance, HUD will publish a notice of fund availability in the FEDERAL REGISTER in accordance with the requirements of 24 CFR part 4. Applications will be reviewed and screened in accordance with the guidelines, rating criteria and procedures published in the notice.

(b) *Rating criteria.* HUD will award funds based on the criteria specified in section 455(a)(1) through (8) of the McKinney Act (42 U.S.C. 11403d(1)—11403d(8)) and on the following criteria authorized by section 455(a)(9) of the McKinney Act (42 U.S.C. 11403d(9)):

(1) The extent to which the applicant has demonstrated coordination with other Federal, State, local, private and other entities serving homeless persons in the planning and operation of the project, to the extent practicable;

(2) Extent to which the project targets homeless persons living in emergency shelters, supportive housing for homeless persons, or in places not designed for, or ordinarily used as, a regular sleeping accommodation for human beings;

(3) Quality of the project; and

(4) Extent to which the program will serve homeless persons who are seriously mentally ill, have chronic alcohol and/or drug abuse problems, or have AIDS and related diseases.

(Approved by the Office of Management and Budget under control number 2506–0118)

[61 FR 51170, Sept. 30, 1996]

§ 582.230 Environmental review.

(a) Activities under this part are subject to HUD environmental regulations in part 58 of this title, except that HUD will perform an environmental review in accordance with part 50 of this title prior to its approval of any conditionally selected applications from PHAs for Fiscal Year 2000 and prior years for other than the SRO component. For activities under a grant to a PHA that generally would be subject to review under part 58, HUD may make a finding in accordance with § 58.11(d) and may itself perform the environmental review under the provisions of part 50 of this title if the recipient PHA objects in writing to the responsible entity's performing the review under part 58. Irrespective of whether the responsible entity in accord with part 58 (or HUD in accord with part 50) performs the environmental review, the recipient shall supply all available, relevant information necessary for the responsible entity (or HUD, if applicable) to perform for each property any environmental review required by this part.

The recipient also shall carry out mitigating measures required by the responsible entity (or HUD, if applicable) or select alternate eligible property. HUD may eliminate from consideration any application that would require an Environmental Impact Statement (EIS).

(b) The recipient, its project partners and their contractors may not acquire, rehabilitate, convert, lease, repair, dispose of, demolish, or construct property for a project under this part, or commit or expend HUD or local funds for such eligible activities under this part, until the responsible entity (as defined in § 58.2 of this title) has completed the environmental review procedures required by part 58 and the environmental certification and RROF have been approved or HUD has performed an environmental review under part 50 and the recipient has received HUD approval of the property. HUD will not release grant funds if the recipient or any other party commits grant funds (*i.e.,* incurs any costs or expenditures to be paid or reimbursed with such funds) before the recipient submits and HUD approves its RROF (where such submission is required).

[68 FR 56130, Sept. 29, 2003]

Subpart D—Program Requirements

§ 582.300 General operation.

(a) *Participation of homeless individuals.* (1) Each recipient must provide for the consultation and participation of not less than one homeless individual or formerly homeless individual on the board of directors or other equivalent policy-making entity of the recipient, to the extent that the entity considers and makes policies and decisions regarding any housing assisted under this part or services for the participants. This requirement is waived if the applicant is unable to meet the requirement and presents a plan, which HUD approves, to otherwise consult with homeless or formerly homeless individuals in considering and making such policies and decisions. Participation by such an individual who also is a participant under the program does not constitute a conflict of interest under § 582.340(b) of this part.

(2) To the maximum extent practicable, each recipient must involve homeless individuals and families, through employment, volunteer services, or otherwise, in constructing or rehabilitating housing assisted under this part and in providing supportive services required under § 582.215 of this part.

(b) *Ongoing assessment of housing and supportive services.* Each recipient of assistance must conduct an ongoing assessment of the housing assistance and supportive services required by the participants, and make adjustments as appropriate.

(c) *Adequate supportive services.* Each recipient must assure that adequate supportive services are available to participants in the program.

(d) *Records and reports.* (1) Each recipient must keep any records and, within the timeframe required, make any reports (including those pertaining to race, ethnicity, gender, and disability status data) that HUD may require.

(2) Each recipient must keep on file, and make available to the public on request, a description of the procedures used to select sponsors under the SRA component and buildings under the SRO, SRA, and PRA components.

(3) Each recipient must develop, and make available to the public upon request, its procedures for managing the rental housing assistance funds provided by HUD. At a minimum, such procedures must describe how units will be identified and selected; how the responsibility for inspections will be handled; the process for deciding which unit a participant will occupy; how participants will be placed in, or assisted in finding appropriate housing; how rent calculations will be made and the amount of rental assistance payments determined; and what safeguards will be used to prevent the misuse of funds.

(Approved by the Office of Management and Budget under control number 2506–0118)

[58 FR 13892, Mar. 15, 1993, as amended at 61 FR 51171, Sept. 30, 1996]

§ 582.305 Housing quality standards; rent reasonableness.

(a) *Housing quality standards.* Housing assisted under this part must meet the applicable housing quality standards (HQS) under § 982.401 of this title—except that § 982.401(j) of this title does not apply and instead part 35, subparts A, B, K and R of this title apply—and, for SRO under § 882.803(b) of this title. Before any assistance will be provided on behalf of a participant, the recipient, or another entity acting on behalf of the recipient (other than the owner of the housing), must physically inspect each unit to assure that the unit meets the HQS. Assistance will not be provided for units that fail to meet the HQS, unless the owner corrects any deficiencies within 30 days from the date of the lease agreement and the recipient verifies that all deficiencies have been corrected. Recipients must also inspect all units at least annually during the grant period to ensure that the units continue to meet the HQS.

(b) *Rent reasonableness.* HUD will only provide assistance for a unit for which the rent is reasonable. For TRA, PRA, and SRA, it is the responsibility of the recipient to determine whether the rent charged for the unit receiving rental assistance is reasonable in relation to rents being charged for comparable unassisted units, taking into account the location, size, type, quality, amenities, facilities, and management and maintenance of each unit, as well as not in excess of rents currently being charged by the same owner for comparable unassisted units. For SRO, rents are calculated in accordance with 24 CFR 882.805(g).

[58 FR 13892, Mar. 15, 1993, as amended at 61 FR 51171, Sept. 30, 1996; 64 FR 50226, Sept. 15, 1999]

§ 582.310 Resident rent.

(a) *Amount of rent.* Each participant must pay rent in accordance with section 3(a)(1) of the U.S. Housing Act of 1937 (42 U.S.C. 1437a(a)(1)), except that in determining the rent of a person occupying an intermediate care facility assisted under title XIX of the Social Security Act, the gross income of this person is the same as if the person were being assisted under title XVI of the Social Security Act.

(b) *Calculating income.* (1) Income of participants must be calculated in accordance with 24 CFR 5.609 and 24 CFR 5.611(a).

(2) Recipients must examine a participant's income initially, and at least annually thereafter, to determine the amount of rent payable by the participant. Adjustments to a participant's rental payment must be made as necessary.

(3) As a condition of participation in the program, each participant must agree to supply the information or documentation necessary to verify the participant's income. Participants must provide the recipient information at any time regarding changes in income or other circumstances that may result in changes to a participant's rental payment.

[66 FR 6225, Jan. 19, 2001]

§ 582.315 Occupancy agreements.

(a) *Initial occupancy agreement.* Participants must enter into an occupancy agreement for a term of at least one month. The occupancy agreement must be automatically renewable upon expiration, except on prior notice by either party.

(b) *Terms of agreement.* In addition to standard lease provisions, the occupancy agreement may also include a provision requiring the participant to take part in the supportive services provided through the program as a condition of continued occupancy.

§ 582.320 Termination of assistance to participants.

(a) *Termination of assistance.* The recipient may terminate assistance to a participant who violates program requirements or conditions of occupancy. Recipients must exercise judgment and examine all extenuating circumstances in determining when violations are serious enough to warrant termination, so that a participant's assistance is terminated only in the most severe cases. Recipients are not prohibited from resuming assistance to a participant whose assistance has been terminated.

(b) *Due process.* In terminating assistance to a participant, the recipient must provide a formal process that recognizes the rights of individuals receiving assistance to due process of law. This process, at a minimum, must consist of:

(1) Written notice to the participant containing a clear statement of the reasons for termination;

(2) A review of the decision, in which the participant is given the opportunity to present written or oral objections before a person other than the person (or a subordinate of that person) who made or approved the termination decision; and

(3) Prompt written notice of the final decision to the participant.

§ 582.325 Outreach activities.

Recipients must use their best efforts to ensure that eligible hard-to-reach persons are served by S+C. Recipients are expected to make sustained efforts to engage eligible persons so that they may be brought into the program. Outreach should be primarily directed toward eligible persons who have a nighttime residence that is an emergency shelter or a public or private place not designed for, or ordinarily used as, a regular sleeping accommodation for human beings (*e.g.*, persons living in cars, streets, and parks). Outreach activities are considered to be a supportive service, and the value of such activities that occur after the execution of the grant agreement may be included in meeting the matching requirement.

§ 582.330 Nondiscrimination and equal opportunity requirements.

(a) *General.* Recipients may establish a preference as part of their admissions procedures for one or more of the statutorily targeted populations (*i.e.*, seriously mentally ill, alcohol or substance abusers, or persons with AIDS and related diseases). However, other eligible disabled homeless persons must be considered for housing designed for the target population unless the recipient can demonstrate that there is sufficient demand by the target population for the units, and other eligible disabled homeless persons would not benefit from the primary supportive services provided.

(b) *Compliance with requirements.* (1) In addition to the nondiscrimination and equal opportunity requirements set forth in 24 CFR part 5, recipients serving a designated population of homeless persons must, within the designated population, comply with the prohibitions against discrimination against handicapped individuals under section 503 of the Rehabilitation Act of 1973 (29 U.S.C. 794) and implementing regulations at 41 CFR chapter 60–741.

(2) The nondiscrimination and equal opportunity requirements set forth at part 5 of this title are modified as follows:

(i) The Indian Civil Rights Act (25 U.S.C. 1301 *et seq.*) applies to tribes when they exercise their powers of self-government, and to IHAs when established by the exercise of such powers. When an IHA is established under State law, the applicability of the Indian Civil Rights Act will be determined on a case-by-case basis. Projects subject to the Indian Civil Rights Act must be developed and operated in compliance with its provisions and all implementing HUD requirements, instead of title VI and the Fair Housing Act and their implementing regulations.

(ii) [Reserved]

(c) *Affirmative outreach.* (1) If the procedures that the recipient intends to use to make known the availability of the program are unlikely to reach persons of any particular race, color, religion, sex, age, national origin, familial status, or handicap who may qualify for assistance, the recipient must establish additional procedures that will ensure that interested persons can obtain information concerning the assistance.

(2) The recipient must adopt procedures to make available information on the existence and locations of facilities and services that are accessible to persons with a handicap and maintain evidence of implementation of the procedures.

(d) The accessibility requirements, reasonable modification, and accommodation requirements of the Fair Housing Act and of section 504 of the Rehabilitation Act of 1973, as amended.

[58 FR 13892, Mar. 15, 1993, as amended at 61 FR 5210, Feb. 9, 1996]

§ 582.335 Displacement, relocation, and real property acquisition.

(a) *Minimizing displacement.* Consistent with the other goals and objectives of this part, recipients must assure that they have taken all reasonable steps to minimize the displacement of persons (families, individuals, businesses, nonprofit organizations, and farms) as a result of supportive housing assisted under this part.

(b) *Relocation assistance for displaced persons.* A displaced person (defined in paragraph (f) of this section) must be provided relocation assistance at the levels described in, and in accordance with, the requirements of the Uniform Relocation Assistance and Real Property Acquisition Policies Act of 1970 (URA) (42 U.S.C. 4601–4655) and implementing regulations at 49 CFR part 24.

(c) *Real property acquisition requirements.* The acquisition of real property for supportive housing is subject to the URA and the requirements described in 49 CFR part 24, subpart B.

(d) *Responsibility of recipient.* (1) The recipient must certify (*i.e.*, provide assurance of compliance) that it will comply with the URA, the regulations at 49 CFR part 24, and the requirements of this section, and must ensure such compliance notwithstanding any third party's contractual obligation to the recipient to comply with these provisions.

(2) The cost of required relocation assistance is an eligible project cost in the same manner and to the same extent as other project costs. Such costs also may be paid for with local public funds or funds available from other sources.

(3) The recipient must maintain records in sufficient detail to demonstrate compliance with provisions of this section.

(e) *Appeals.* A person who disagrees with the recipient's determination concerning whether the person qualifies as a "displaced person," or the amount of relocation assistance for which the person is eligible, may file a written appeal of that determination with the recipient. A low-income person who is dissatisfied with the recipient's determination on his or her appeal may submit a written request for review of that determination to the HUD field office.

(f) *Definition of displaced person.* (1) For purposes of this section, the term "displaced person" means a person (family, individual, business, nonprofit organization, or farm) that moves from real property, or moves personal property from real property permanently as a direct result of acquisition, rehabilitation, or demolition for supportive housing project assisted under this part. The term "displaced person" includes, but may not be limited to:

(i) A person that moves permanently from the real property after the property owner (or person in control of the site) issues a vacate notice or refuses to renew an expiring lease, if the move occurs on or after:

(A) The date that the recipient submits to HUD an application for assistance that is later approved and funded, if the recipient has control of the project site; or

(B) The date that the recipient obtains control of the project site, if such control is obtained after the submission of the application to HUD.

(ii) Any person, including a person who moves before the date described in paragraph (f)(1)(i) of this section, if the recipient or HUD determines that the displacement resulted directly from acquisition, rehabilitation, or demolition for the assisted project.

(iii) A tenant-occupant of a dwelling unit who moves permanently from the building/complex on or after the date of the "initiation of negotiations" (see paragraph (g) of this section) if the move occurs before the tenant has been provided written notice offering him or her the opportunity to lease and occupy a suitable, decent, safe and sanitary dwelling in the same building/complex, under reasonable terms and conditions, upon completion of the project. Such reasonable terms and conditions must include a monthly rent and estimated average monthly utility costs that do not exceed the greater of:

(A) The tenant's monthly rent before the initiation of negotiations and estimated average utility costs, or

(B) 30 percent of gross household income. If the initial rent is at or near the maximum, there must be a reasonable basis for concluding at the time the project is initiated that future rent increases will be modest.

(iv) A tenant of a dwelling who is required to relocate temporarily, but does not return to the building/complex, if either:

(A) A tenant is not offered payment for all reasonable out-of-pocket expenses incurred in connection with the temporary relocation, or

(B) Other conditions of the temporary relocation are not reasonable.

(v) A tenant of a dwelling who moves from the building/complex permanently after he or she has been required to move to another unit in the same building/complex, if either:

(A) The tenant is not offered reimbursement for all reasonable out-of-pocket expenses incurred in connection with the move; or

(B) Other conditions of the move are not reasonable.

(2) Notwithstanding the provisions of paragraph (f)(1) of this section, a person does not qualify as a "displaced person" (and is not eligible for relocation assistance under the URA or this section), if:

(i) The person has been evicted for serious or repeated violation of the terms and conditions of the lease or occupancy agreement, violation of applicable Federal, State, or local or tribal law, or other good cause, and HUD determines that the eviction was not undertaken for the purpose of evading the obligation to provide relocation assistance;

(ii) The person moved into the property after the submission of the application and, before signing a lease and commencing occupancy, was provided written notice of the project, its possible impact on the person (e.g., the person may be displaced, temporarily relocated, or suffer a rent increase) and the fact that the person would not qualify as a "displaced person" (or for any assistance provided under this section), if the project is approved;

(iii) The person is ineligible under 49 CFR 24.2(g)(2); or

(iv) HUD determines that the person was not displaced as a direct result of acquisition, rehabilitation, or demolition for the project.

(3) The recipient may request, at any time, HUD's determination of whether a displacement is or would be covered under this section.

(g) *Definition of initiation of negotiations.* For purposes of determining the formula for computing the replacement housing assistance to be provided to a residential tenant displaced as a direct result of privately undertaken rehabilitation, demolition, or acquisition of the real property, the term "initiation of negotiations" means the execution of the agreement between the recipient and HUD, or selection of the project site, if later.

§ 582.340 **Other Federal requirements.**

In addition to the Federal requirements set forth in 24 CFR part 5, the following requirements apply to this program:

(a) *OMB Circulars.*[1] (1) The policies, guidelines, and requirements of OMB Circular No. A-87 (Cost Principles Applicable to Grants, Contracts and Other Agreements with State and Local Governments) and 24 CFR part 85 apply to the acceptance and use of assistance under the program by governmental entities, and OMB Circular Nos. A-110 (Grants and Cooperative Agreements with Institutions of Higher Education, Hospitals, and Other Nonprofit Organizations) and 24 CFR part 84 and A-122 (Cost Principles Applicable to Grants, Contracts and Other Agreements with Nonprofit Institutions) apply to the acceptance and use of assistance by private nonprofit organizations, except where inconsistent with provisions of the McKinney Act, other Federal statutes, or this part.

(2) The financial management systems used by recipients under this program must provide for audits in accordance with the provisions of 24 CFR part 44. Private nonprofit organizations who are subrecipients are subject to the audit requirements of 24 CFR part 45. HUD may perform or require additional audits as it finds necessary or appropriate.

(b) *Conflict of interest.* (1) In addition to the conflict of interest requirements

---

[1] Copies of OMB Circulars may be obtained from E.O.P. Publications, room 2200, New Executive Office Building, Washington, DC 20503, telephone (202) 395-7332. (This is not a toll-free number.) There is a limit of two free copies.

in 24 CFR part 85, no person who is an employee, agent, consultant, officer, or elected or appointed official of the recipient and who exercises or has exercised any functions or responsibilities with respect to assisted activities, or who is in a position to participate in a decisionmaking process or gain inside information with regard to such activities, may obtain a personal or financial interest or benefit from the activity, or have an interest in any contract, subcontract, or agreement with respect thereto, or the proceeds thereunder, either for himself or herself or for those with whom he or she has family or business ties, during his or her tenure or for one year thereafter. Participation by homeless individuals who also are participants under the program in policy or decisionmaking under § 582.300 of this part does not constitute a conflict of interest.

(2) Upon the written request of the recipient, HUD may grant an exception to the provisions of paragraph (b)(1) of this section on a case-by-case basis when it determine that the exception will serve to further the purposes of the program and the effective and efficient administration of the recipient's project. An exception may be considered only after the recipient has provided the following:

(i) For States, units of general local governments, PHAs and IHAs, a disclosure of the nature of the conflict, accompanied by an assurance that there has been public disclosure of the conflict and a description of how the public disclosure was made; and

(ii) For all recipients, an opinion of the recipient's attorney that the interest for which the exception is sought would not violate State or local law.

(3) In determining whether to grant a requested exception after the recipient has satisfactorily met the requirement of paragraph (b)(2) of this section, HUD will consider the cumulative effect of the following factors, where applicable:

(i) Whether the exception would provide a significant cost benefit or an essential degree of expertise to the project which would otherwise not be available;

(ii) Whether the person affected is a member of a group or class of eligible persons and the exception will permit such person to receive generally the same interests or benefits as are being made available or provided to the group or class;

(iii) Whether the affected person has withdrawn from his or her functions or responsibilities, or the decisionmaking process with respect to the specific assisted activity in question;

(iv) Whether the interest or benefit was present before the affected person was in a position as described in paragraph (b)(1) of this section;

(v) Whether undue hardship will result either to the recipient or the person affected when weighed against the public interest served by avoiding the prohibited conflict; and

(vi) Any other relevant considerations.

[58 FR 13892, Mar. 15, 1993, as amended at 61 FR 5210, Feb. 9, 1996; 61 FR 51171, Sept. 30, 1996; 62 FR 13539, Mar. 21, 1997]

Subpart E—Administration

§ 582.400 Grant agreement.

(a) *General.* The grant agreement will be between HUD and the recipient. HUD will hold the recipient responsible for the overall administration of the program, including overseeing any subrecipients or contractors. Under the grant agreement, the recipient must agree to operate the program in accordance with the provisions of this part and other applicable HUD regulations.

(b) *Enforcement.* HUD will enforce the obligations in the grant agreement through such action as may be necessary, including recapturing assistance awarded under the program.

§ 582.405 Program changes.

(a) *Changes.* HUD must approve, in writing, any significant changes to an approved program. Significant changes that require approval include, but are not limited to, a change in sponsor , a change in the project site for SRO or PRA with rehabilitation projects, and a change in the type of persons with disabilities to be served. Depending on the nature of the change, HUD may require a new certification of consistency with the CHAS (see § 582.120).

(b) *Approval.* Approval for such changes is contingent upon the application ranking remaining high enough to have been competitively selected for funding in the year the application was selected.

§ 582.410 **Obligation and deobligation of funds.**

(a) *Obligation of funds.* When HUD and the applicant execute a grant agreement, HUD will obligate funds to cover the amount of the approved grant. The recipient will be expected to carry out the activities as proposed in the application. After the initial obligation of funds, HUD is under no obligation to make any upward revisions to the grant amount for any approved assistance.

(b) *Deobligation.* (1) HUD may deobligate all or a portion of the approved grant amount if such amount is not expended in a timely manner, or the proposed housing for which funding was approved or the supportive services proposed in the application are not provided in accordance with the approved application, the requirements of this part, and other applicable HUD regulations. The grant agreement may set forth other circumstances under which funds may be deobligated, and other sanctions may be imposed.

(2) HUD may readvertise, in a notice of fund availability, the availability of funds that have been deobligated, or may reconsider applications that were submitted in response to the most recently published notice of fund availability and select applications for funding with the deobligated funds. Such selections would be made in accordance with the selection process described in § 582.220 of this part. Any selections made using deobligated funds will be subject to applicable appropriation act requirements governing the use of deobligated funding authority.

(Approved by the Office of Management and Budget under control number 2506–0118)

PART 583—SUPPORTIVE HOUSING PROGRAM

Subpart A—General

Sec.
583.1 Purpose and scope.

583.5 Definitions.

Subpart B—Assistance Provided

583.100 Types and uses of assistance.
583.105 Grants for acquisition and rehabilitation.
583.110 Grants for new construction.
583.115 Grants for leasing.
583.120 Grants for supportive service costs.
583.125 Grants for operating costs.
583.130 Commitment of grant amounts for leasing, supportive services, and operating costs.
583.135 Administrative costs.
583.140 Technical assistance.
583.145 Matching requirements.
583.150 Limitations on use of assistance.
583.155 Consolidated plan.

Subpart C—Application and Grant Award Process

583.200 Application and grant award.
583.230 Environmental review.
583.235 Renewal grants.

Subpart D—Program Requirements

583.300 General operation.
583.305 Term of commitment; repayment of grants; prevention of undue benefits.
583.310 Displacement, relocation, and acquisition.
583.315 Resident rent.
583.320 Site control.
583.325 Nondiscrimination and equal opportunity requirements.
583.330 Applicability of other Federal requirements.

Subpart E—Administration

583.400 Grant agreement.
583.405 Program changes.
583.410 Obligation and deobligation of funds.

AUTHORITY: 42 U.S.C. 11389 and 3535(d).

SOURCE: 58 FR 13871, Mar. 15, 1993, unless otherwise noted.

Subpart A—General

§ 583.1 **Purpose and scope.**

(a) *General.* The Supportive Housing Program is authorized by title IV of the Stewart B. McKinney Homeless Assistance Act (the McKinney Act) (42 U.S.C. 11381–11389). The Supportive Housing program is designed to promote the development of supportive housing and supportive services, including innovative approaches to assist homeless persons in the transition from homelessness, and to promote the provision of supportive housing to homeless persons to enable them to live as independently as possible.

(b) *Components.* Funds under this part may be used for:

(1) Transitional housing to facilitate the movement of homeless individuals and families to permanent housing;

(2) Permanent housing that provides long-term housing for homeless persons with disabilities;

(3) Housing that is, or is part of, a particularly innovative project for, or alternative methods of, meeting the immediate and long-term needs of homeless persons; or

(4) Supportive services for homeless persons not provided in conjunction with supportive housing.

[58 FR 13871, Mar. 15, 1993, as amended at 61 FR 51175, Sept. 30, 1996]

§ 583.5 Definitions.

As used in this part:

Applicant is defined in section 422(1) of the McKinney Act (42 U.S.C. 11382(1)). For purposes of this definition, governmental entities include those that have general governmental powers (such as a city or county), as well as those that have limited or special powers (such as public housing agencies).

Consolidated plan means the plan that a jurisdiction prepares and submits to HUD in accordance with 24 CFR part 91.

Date of initial occupancy means the date that the supportive housing is initially occupied by a homeless person for whom HUD provides assistance under this part. If the assistance is for an existing homeless facility, the *date of initial occupancy* is the date that services are first provided to the residents of supportive housing with funding under this part.

Date of initial service provision means the date that supportive services are initially provided with funds under this part to homeless persons who do not reside in supportive housing. This definition applies only to projects funded under this part that do not provide supportive housing.

Disability is defined in section 422(2) of the McKinney Act (42 U.S.C. 11382(2)).

Homeless person means an individual or family that is described in section 103 of the McKinney Act (42 U.S.C. 11302).

Metropolitan city is defined in section 102(a)(4) of the Housing and Community Development Act of 1974 (42 U.S.C. 5302(a)(4)). In general, metropolitan cities are those cities that are eligible for an entitlement grant under 24 CFR part 570, subpart D.

New construction means the building of a structure where none existed or an addition to an existing structure that increases the floor area by more than 100 percent.

Operating costs is defined in section 422(5) of the McKinney Act (42 U.S.C. 11382(5)).

Outpatient health services is defined in section 422(6) of the McKinney Act (42 U.S.C. 11382(6)).

Permanent housing for homeless persons with disabilities is defined in section 424(c) of the McKinney Act (42 U.S.C. 11384(c)).

Private nonprofit organization is defined in section 422(7) (A), (B), and (D) of the McKinney Act (42 U.S.C. 11382(7) (A), (B), and (D)). The organization must also have a functioning accounting system that is operated in accordance with generally accepted accounting principles, or designate an entity that will maintain a functioning accounting system for the organization in accordance with generally accepted accounting principles.

Project is defined in sections 422(8) and 424(d) of the McKinney Act (42 U.S.C. 11382(8), 11384(d)).

Recipient is defined in section 422(9) of the McKinney Act (42 U.S.C. 11382(9)).

Rehabilitation means the improvement or repair of an existing structure or an addition to an existing structure that does not increase the floor area by more than 100 percent. Rehabilitation does not include minor or routine repairs.

State is defined in section 422(11) of the McKinney Act (42 U.S.C. 11382(11)).

Supportive housing is defined in section 424(a) of the McKinney Act (42 U.S.C. 11384(a)).

Supportive services is defined in section 425 of the McKinney Act (42 U.S.C. 11385).

Transitional housing is defined in section 424(b) of the McKinney Act (42 U.S.C. 11384(b)). See also § 583.300(j).

Tribe is defined in section 102 of the Housing and Community Development Act of 1974 (42 U.S.C. 5302).

Urban county is defined in section 102(a)(6) of the Housing and Community Development Act of 1974 (42 U.S.C. 5302(a)(6)). In general, urban counties are those counties that are eligible for an entitlement grant under 24 CFR part 570, subpart D.

[61 FR 51175, Sept. 30, 1996]

Subpart B—Assistance Provided

§ 583.100 Types and uses of assistance.

(a) *Grant assistance.* Assistance in the form of grants is available for acquisition of structures, rehabilitation of structures, acquisition and rehabilitation of structures, new construction, leasing, operating costs for supportive housing, and supportive services, as described in §§ 583.105 through 583.125. Applicants may apply for more than one type of assistance.

(b) *Uses of grant assistance.* Grant assistance may be used to:

(1) Establish new supportive housing facilities or new facilities to provide supportive services;

(2) Expand existing facilities in order to increase the number of homeless persons served;

(3) Bring existing facilities up to a level that meets State and local government health and safety standards;

(4) Provide additional supportive services for residents of supportive housing or for homeless persons not residing in supportive housing;

(5) Purchase HUD-owned single family properties currently leased by the applicant for use as a homeless facility under 24 CFR part 291; and

(6) Continue funding supportive housing where the recipient has received funding under this part for leasing, supportive services, or operating costs.

(c) *Structures used for multiple purposes.* Structures used to provide supportive housing or supportive services may also be used for other purposes, except that assistance under this part will be available only in proportion to the use of the structure for supportive housing or supportive services.

(d) *Technical assistance.* HUD may offer technical assistance, as described in § 583.140.

[58 FR 13871, Mar. 15, 1993, as amended at 59 FR 36891, July 19, 1994]

§ 583.105 Grants for acquisition and rehabilitation.

(a) *Use.* HUD will grant funds to recipients to:

(1) Pay a portion of the cost of the acquisition of real property selected by the recipients for use in the provision of supportive housing or supportive services, including the repayment of any outstanding debt on a loan made to purchase property that has not been used previously as supportive housing or for supportive services;

(2) Pay a portion of the cost of rehabilitation of structures, including cost-effective energy measures, selected by the recipients to provide supportive housing or supportive services; or

(3) Pay a portion of the cost of acquisition and rehabilitation of structures, as described in paragraphs (a)(1) and (2) of this section.

(b) *Amount.* The maximum grant available for acquisition, rehabilitation, or acquisition and rehabilitation is the lower of:

(1) $200,000; or

(2) The total cost of the acquisition, rehabilitation, or acquisition and rehabilitation minus the applicant's contribution toward the cost.

(c) *Increased amounts.* In areas determined by HUD to have high acquisition and rehabilitation costs, grants of more than $200,000, but not more than $400,000, may be available.

§ 583.110 Grants for new construction.

(a) *Use.* HUD will grant funds to recipients to pay a portion of the cost of new construction, including cost-effective energy measures and the cost of land associated with that construction, for use in the provision of supportive housing. If the grant funds are used for new construction, the applicant must demonstrate that the costs associated with new construction are substantially less than the costs associated with rehabilitation or that there is a lack of available appropriate units that could be rehabilitated at a cost less than new construction. For purposes of

§ 583.115

this cost comparison, costs associated with rehabilitation or new construction may include the cost of real property acquisition.

(b) *Amount.* The maximum grant available for new construction is the lower of:

(1) $400,000; or

(2) The total cost of the new construction, including the cost of land associated with that construction, minus the applicant's contribution toward the cost of same.

§ 583.115 Grants for leasing.

(a) *General.* HUD will provide grants to pay (as described in § 583.130 of this part) for the actual costs of leasing a structure or structures, or portions thereof, used to provide supportive housing or supportive services for up to five years.

(b)(1) *Leasing structures.* Where grants are used to pay rent for all or part of structures, the rent paid must be reasonable in relation to rents being charged in the area for comparable space. In addition, the rent paid may not exceed rents currently being charged by the same owner for comparable space.

(2) *Leasing individual units.* Where grants are used to pay rent for individual housing units, the rent paid must be reasonable in relation to rents being charged for comparable units, taking into account the location, size, type, quality, amenities, facilities, and management services. In addition, the rents may not exceed rents currently being charged by the same owner for comparable unassisted units, and the portion of rents paid with grant funds may not exceed HUD-determined fair market rents. Recipients may use grant funds in an amount up to one month's rent to pay the non-recipient landlord for any damages to leased units by homeless participants.

[58 FR 13871, Mar. 15, 1993, as amended at 59 FR 36891, July 19, 1994]

§ 583.120 Grants for supportive services costs.

(a) *General.* HUD will provide grants to pay (as described in § 583.130 of this part) for the actual costs of supportive services for homeless persons for up to five years. All or part of the supportive services may be provided directly by the recipient or by arrangement with public or private service providers.

(b) *Supportive services costs.* Costs associated with providing supportive services include salaries paid to providers of supportive services and any other costs directly associated with providing such services. For a transitional housing project, supportive services costs also include the costs of services provided to former residents of transitional housing to assist their adjustment to independent living. Such services may be provided for up to six months after they leave the transitional housing facility.

[58 FR 13871, Mar. 15, 1993, as amended at 59 FR 36891, July 19, 1994]

§ 583.125 Grants for operating costs.

(a) *General.* HUD will provide grants to pay a portion (as described in § 583.130) of the actual operating costs of supportive housing for up to five years.

(b) *Operating costs.* Operating costs are those associated with the day-to-day operation of the supportive housing. They also include the actual expenses that a recipient incurs for conducting on-going assessments of the supportive services needed by residents and the availability of such services; relocation assistance under § 583.310, including payments and services; and insurance.

(c) *Recipient match requirement for operating costs.* Assistance for operating costs will be available for up to 75 percent of the total cost in each year of the grant term. The recipient must pay the percentage of the actual operating costs not funded by HUD. At the end of each operating year, the recipient must demonstrate that it has met its match requirement of the costs for that year.

[58 FR 13871, Mar. 15, 1993, as amended at 61 FR 51175, Sept. 30, 1996; 65 FR 30823, May 12, 2000]

§ 583.130 Commitment of grant amounts for leasing, supportive services, and operating costs.

Upon execution of a grant agreement covering assistance for leasing, supportive services, or operating costs, HUD will obligate amounts for a period not to exceed five operating years. The

Ofc. of Asst. Secy., Comm. Planning, Develop., HUD § 583.150

total amount obligated will be equal to an amount necessary for the specified years of operation, less the recipient's share of operating costs.

(Approved by the Office of Management and Budget under OMB control number 2506-0112)

[59 FR 36891, July 19, 1994]

§ 583.135 Administrative costs.

(a) *General.* Up to five percent of any grant awarded under this part may be used for the purpose of paying costs of administering the assistance.

(b) *Administrative costs.* Administrative costs include the costs associated with accounting for the use of grant funds, preparing reports for submission to HUD, obtaining program audits, similar costs related to administering the grant after the award, and staff salaries associated with these administrative costs. They do not include the costs of carrying out eligible activities under §§ 583.105 through 583.125.

[58 FR 13871, Mar. 15, 1993, as amended at 61 FR 51175, Sept. 30, 1996]

§ 583.140 Technical assistance.

(a) *General.* HUD may set aside funds annually to provide technical assistance, either directly by HUD staff or indirectly through third-party providers, for any supportive housing project. This technical assistance is for the purpose of promoting the development of supportive housing and supportive services as part of a continuum of care approach, including innovative approaches to assist homeless persons in the transition from homelessness, and promoting the provision of supportive housing to homeless persons to enable them to live as independently as possible.

(b) *Uses of technical assistance.* HUD may use these funds to provide technical assistance to prospective applicants, applicants, recipients, or other providers of supportive housing or services for homeless persons, for supportive housing projects. The assistance may include, but is not limited to, written information such as papers, monographs, manuals, guides, and brochures; person-to-person exchanges; and training and related costs.

(c) *Selection of providers.* From time to time, as HUD determines the need, HUD may advertise and competitively select providers to deliver technical assistance. HUD may enter into contracts, grants, or cooperative agreements, when necessary, to implement the technical assistance.

[59 FR 36892, July 19, 1994]

§ 583.145 Matching requirements.

(a) *General.* The recipient must match the funds provided by HUD for grants for acquisition, rehabilitation, and new construction with an equal amount of funds from other sources.

(b) *Cash resources.* The matching funds must be cash resources provided to the project by one or more of the following: the recipient, the Federal government, State and local governments, and private resources, in accordance with 42 U.S.C. 11386. This statute provides that a recipient may use funds from any source, including any other Federal source (but excluding the specific statutory subtitle from which Supportive Housing Program funds are provided), as well as State, local, and private sources, provided that funds from the other source are not statutorily prohibited to be used as a match. It is the responsibility of the recipient to ensure that any funds used to satisfy the matching requirements of this section are eligible under the laws governing the funds to be used as matching funds for a grant awarded under this program.

(c) *Maintenance of effort.* State or local government funds used in the matching contribution are subject to the maintenance of effort requirements described at § 583.150(a).

[58 FR 13871, Mar. 15, 1993, as amended at 73 FR 75326, Dec. 11, 2008]

§ 583.150 Limitations on use of assistance.

(a) *Maintenance of effort.* No assistance provided under this part (or any State or local government funds used to supplement this assistance) may be used to replace State or local funds previously used, or designated for use, to assist homeless persons.

(b) *Faith-based activities.* (1) Organizations that are religious or faith-based are eligible, on the same basis as any other organization, to participate in the Supportive Housing Program. Neither the Federal government nor a State or local government receiving funds under Supportive Housing programs shall discriminate against an organization on the basis of the organization's religious character or affiliation.

(2) Organizations that are directly funded under the Supportive Housing Program may not engage in inherently religious activities, such as worship, religious instruction, or proselytization as part of the programs or services funded under this part. If an organization conducts such activities, the activities must be offered separately, in time or location, from the programs or services funded under this part, and participation must be voluntary for the beneficiaries of the HUD-funded programs or services.

(3) A religious organization that participates in the Supportive Housing Program will retain its independence from Federal, State, and local governments, and may continue to carry out its mission, including the definition, practice, and expression of its religious beliefs, provided that it does not use direct Supportive Housing Program funds to support any inherently religious activities, such as worship, religious instruction, or proselytization. Among other things, faith-based organizations may use space in their facilities to provide Supportive Housing Program-funded services, without removing religious art, icons, scriptures, or other religious symbols. In addition, a Supportive Housing Program-funded religious organization retains its authority over its internal governance, and it may retain religious terms in its organization's name, select its board members on a religious basis, and include religious references in its organization's mission statements and other governing documents.

(4) An organization that participates in the Supportive Housing Program shall not, in providing program assistance, discriminate against a program beneficiary or prospective program beneficiary on the basis of religion or religious belief.

(5) Program funds may not be used for the acquisition, construction, or rehabilitation of structures to the extent that those structures are used for inherently religious activities. Program funds may be used for the acquisition, construction, or rehabilitation of structures only to the extent that those structures are used for conducting eligible activities under this part. Where a structure is used for both eligible and inherently religious activities, program funds may not exceed the cost of those portions of the acquisition, construction, or rehabilitation that are attributable to eligible activities in accordance with the cost accounting requirements applicable to Supportive Housing Program funds in this part. Sanctuaries, chapels, or other rooms that a Supportive Housing Program-funded religious congregation uses as its principal place of worship, however, are ineligible for Supportive Housing Program-funded improvements. Disposition of real property after the term of the grant, or any change in use of the property during the term of the grant, is subject to government-wide regulations governing real property disposition (*see* 24 CFR parts 84 and 85).

(6) If a State or local government voluntarily contributes its own funds to supplement federally funded activities, the State or local government has the option to segregate the Federal funds or commingle them. However, if the funds are commingled, this section applies to all of the commingled funds.

(c) *Participant control of site.* Where an applicant does not propose to have control of a site or sites but rather proposes to assist a homeless family or individual in obtaining a lease, which may include assistance with rent payments and receiving supportive services, after which time the family or individual remains in the same housing without further assistance under this part, that applicant may not request assistance for acquisition, rehabilitation, or new construction.

[58 FR 13871, Mar. 15, 1993, as amended at 59 FR 36892, July 19, 1993; 68 FR 56407, Sept. 30, 2003]

§ 583.155 Consolidated plan.

(a) *Applicants that are States or units of general local government.* The applicant must have a HUD-approved complete or abbreviated consolidated plan, in accordance with 24 CFR part 91, and

Ofc. of Asst. Secy., Comm. Planning, Develop., HUD § 583.230

must submit a certification that the application for funding is consistent with the HUD-approved consolidated plan. Funded applicants must certify in a grant agreement that they are following the HUD-approved consolidated plan.

(b) *Applicants that are not States or units of general local government.* The applicant must submit a certification by the jurisdiction in which the proposed project will be located that the applicant's application for funding is consistent with the jurisdiction's HUD-approved consolidated plan. The certification must be made by the unit of general local government or the State, in accordance with the consistency certification provisions of the consolidated plan regulations, 24 CFR part 91, subpart F.

(c) *Indian tribes and the Insular Areas of Guam, the U.S. Virgin Islands, American Samoa, and the Northern Mariana Islands.* These entities are not required to have a consolidated plan or to make consolidated plan certifications. An application by an Indian tribe or other applicant for a project that will be located on a reservation of an Indian tribe will not require a certification by the tribe or the State. However, where an Indian tribe is the applicant for a project that will not be located on a reservation, the requirement for a certification under paragraph (b) of this section will apply.

(d) *Timing of consolidated plan certification submissions.* Unless otherwise set forth in the NOFA, the required certification that the application for funding is consistent with the HUD-approved consolidated plan must be submitted by the funding application submission deadline announced in the NOFA.

[60 FR 16380, Mar. 30, 1995]

Subpart C—Application and Grant Award Process

§ 583.200 **Application and grant award.**

When funds are made available for assistance, HUD will publish a notice of funding availability (NOFA) in the FEDERAL REGISTER, in accordance with the requirements of 24 CFR part 4. HUD will review and screen applications in accordance with the requirements in section 426 of the McKinney Act (42 U.S.C. 11386) and the guidelines, rating criteria, and procedures published in the NOFA.

[61 FR 51176, Sept. 30, 1996]

§ 583.230 **Environmental review.**

(a) Activities under this part are subject to HUD environmental regulations in part 58 of this title, except that HUD will perform an environmental review in accordance with part 50 of this title prior to its approval of any conditionally selected applications for Fiscal Year 2000 and prior years that were received directly from private non-profit entities and governmental entities with special or limited purpose powers. For activities under a grant that generally would be subject to review under part 58, HUD may make a finding in accordance with § 58.11(d) and may itself perform the environmental review under the provisions of part 50 of this title if the recipient objects in writing to the responsible entity's performing the review under part 58. Irrespective of whether the responsible entity in accord with part 58 (or HUD in accord with part 50) performs the environmental review, the recipient shall supply all available, relevant information necessary for the responsible entity (or HUD, if applicable) to perform for each property any environmental review required by this part. The recipient also shall carry out mitigating measures required by the responsible entity (or HUD, if applicable) or select alternate eligible property. HUD may eliminate from consideration any application that would require an Environmental Impact Statement (EIS).

(b) The recipient, its project partners and their contractors may not acquire, rehabilitate, convert, lease, repair, dispose of, demolish or construct property for a project under this part, or commit or expend HUD or local funds for such eligible activities under this part, until the responsible entity (as defined in § 58.2 of this title) has completed the environmental review procedures required by part 58 and the environmental certification and RROF have been approved or HUD has performed an environmental review under part 50 and the recipient has received HUD approval of the property. HUD will not release grant funds if the recipient or any other party commits grant funds (*i.e.*, incurs any costs or expenditures to be paid or reimbursed with such funds) before the recipient submits and HUD approves its RROF (where such submission is required).

[68 FR 56131, Sept. 29, 2003]

§ 583.235 Renewal grants.

(a) *General.* Grants made under this part, and grants made under subtitles C and D (the Supportive Housing Demonstration and SAFAH, respectively) of the Stewart B. McKinney Homeless Assistance Act as in effect before October 28, 1992, may be renewed on a non-competitive basis to continue ongoing leasing, operations, and supportive services for additional years beyond the initial funding period. To be considered for renewal funding for leasing, operating costs, or supportive services, recipients must submit a request for such funding in the form specified by HUD, must meet the requirements of this part, and must submit requests within the time period established by HUD.

(b) *Assistance available.* The first renewal will be for a period of time not to exceed the difference between the end of the initial funding period and ten years from the date of initial occupancy or the date of initial service provision, as applicable. Any subsequent renewal will be for a period of time not to exceed five years. Assistance during each year of the renewal period, subject to maintenance of effort requirements under § 583.150(a) may be for:

(1) Up to 50 percent of the actual operating and leasing costs in the final year of the initial funding period;

(2) Up to the amount of HUD assistance for supportive services in the final year of the initial funding period; and

(3) An allowance for cost increases.

(c) *HUD review.* (1) HUD will review the request for renewal and will evaluate the recipient's performance in previous years against the plans and goals established in the initial application for assistance, as amended. HUD will approve the request for renewal unless the recipient proposes to serve a population that is not homeless, or the recipient has not shown adequate progress as evidenced by an unacceptably slow expenditure of funds, or the recipient has been unsuccessful in assisting participants in achieving and maintaining independent living. In determining the recipient's success in assisting participants to achieve and maintain independent living, consideration will be given to the level and type of problems of participants. For recipients with a poor record of success, HUD will also consider the recipient's willingness to accept technical assistance and to make changes suggested by technical assistance providers. Other factors which will affect HUD's decision to approve a renewal request include the following: a continuing history of inadequate financial management accounting practices, indications of mismanagement on the part of the recipient, a drastic reduction in the population served by the recipient, program changes made by the recipient without prior HUD approval, and loss of project site.

(2) HUD reserves the right to reject a request from any organization with an outstanding obligation to HUD that is in arrears or for which a payment schedule has not been agreed to, or whose response to an audit finding is overdue or unsatisfactory.

(3) HUD will notify the recipient in writing that the request has been approved or disapproved.

(Approved by the Office of Management and Budget under control number 2506–0112)

Subpart D—Program Requirements

§ 583.300 General operation.

(a) *State and local requirements.* Each recipient of assistance under this part must provide housing or services that are in compliance with all applicable State and local housing codes, licensing requirements, and any other requirements in the jurisdiction in which the project is located regarding the condition of the structure and the operation of the housing or services.

(b) *Habitability standards.* Except for such variations as are proposed by the recipient and approved by HUD, supportive housing must meet the following requirements:

(1) *Structure and materials.* The structures must be structurally sound so as not to pose any threat to the health

and safety of the occupants and so as to protect the residents from the elements.

(2) *Access.* The housing must be accessible and capable of being utilized without unauthorized use of other private properties. Structures must provide alternate means of egress in case of fire.

(3) *Space and security.* Each resident must be afforded adequate space and security for themselves and their belongings. Each resident must be provided an acceptable place to sleep.

(4) *Interior air quality.* Every room or space must be provided with natural or mechanical ventilation. Structures must be free of pollutants in the air at levels that threaten the health of residents.

(5) *Water supply.* The water supply must be free from contamination.

(6) *Sanitary facilities.* Residents must have access to sufficient sanitary facilities that are in proper operating condition, may be used in privacy, and are adequate for personal cleanliness and the disposal of human waste.

(7) *Thermal environment.* The housing must have adequate heating and/or cooling facilities in proper operating condition.

(8) *Illumination and electricity.* The housing must have adequate natural or artificial illumination to permit normal indoor activities and to support the health and safety of residents. Sufficient electrical sources must be provided to permit use of essential electrical appliances while assuring safety from fire.

(9) *Food preparation and refuse disposal.* All food preparation areas must contain suitable space and equipment to store, prepare, and serve food in a sanitary manner.

(10) *Sanitary condition.* The housing and any equipment must be maintained in sanitary condition.

(11) *Fire safety.* (i) Each unit must include at least one battery-operated or hard-wired smoke detector, in proper working condition, on each occupied level of the unit. Smoke detectors must be located, to the extent practicable, in a hallway adjacent to a bedroom. If the unit is occupied by hearing-impaired persons, smoke detectors must have an alarm system designed for hearing-impaired persons in each bedroom occupied by a hearing-impaired person.

(ii) The public areas of all housing must be equipped with a sufficient number, but not less than one for each area, of battery-operated or hard-wired smoke detectors. Public areas include, but are not limited to, laundry rooms, community rooms, day care centers, hallways, stairwells, and other common areas.

(c) *Meals.* Each recipient of assistance under this part who provides supportive housing for homeless persons with disabilities must provide meals or meal preparation facilities for residents.

(d) *Ongoing assessment of supportive services.* Each recipient of assistance under this part must conduct an ongoing assessment of the supportive services required by the residents of the project and the availability of such services, and make adjustments as appropriate.

(e) *Residential supervision.* Each recipient of assistance under this part must provide residential supervision as necessary to facilitate the adequate provision of supportive services to the residents of the housing throughout the term of the commitment to operate supportive housing. Residential supervision may include the employment of a full- or part-time residential supervisor with sufficient knowledge to provide or to supervise the provision of supportive services to the residents.

(f) *Participation of homeless persons.* (1) Each recipient must provide for the participation of homeless persons as required in section 426(g) of the McKinney Act (42 U.S.C. 11386(g)). This requirement is waived if an applicant is unable to meet it and presents a plan for HUD approval to otherwise consult with homeless or formerly homeless persons in considering and making policies and decisions. See also § 583.330(e).

(2) Each recipient of assistance under this part must, to the maximum extent practicable, involve homeless individuals and families, through employment, volunteer services, or otherwise, in constructing, rehabilitating, maintaining, and operating the project and

§ 583.305

in providing supportive services for the project.

(g) *Records and reports.* Each recipient of assistance under this part must keep any records and make any reports (including those pertaining to race, ethnicity, gender, and disability status data) that HUD may require within the timeframe required.

(h) *Confidentiality.* Each recipient that provides family violence prevention or treatment services must develop and implement procedures to ensure:

(1) The confidentiality of records pertaining to any individual services; and

(2) That the address or location of any project assisted will not be made public, except with written authorization of the person or persons responsible for the operation of the project.

(i) *Termination of housing assistance.* The recipient may terminate assistance to a participant who violates program requirements. Recipients should terminate assistance only in the most severe cases. Recipients may resume assistance to a participant whose assistance was previously terminated. In terminating assistance to a participant, the recipient must provide a formal process that recognizes the rights of individuals receiving assistance to due process of law. This process, at a minimum, must consist of:

(1) Written notice to the participant containing a clear statement of the reasons for termination;

(2) A review of the decision, in which the participant is given the opportunity to present written or oral objections before a person other than the person (or a subordinate of that person) who made or approved the termination decision; and

(3) Prompt written notice of the final decision to the participant.

(j) *Limitation of stay in transitional housing.* A homeless individual or family may remain in transitional housing for a period longer than 24 months, if permanent housing for the individual or family has not been located or if the individual or family requires additional time to prepare for independent living. However, HUD may discontinue assistance for a transitional housing project if more than half of the homeless individuals or families remain in that project longer than 24 months.

(k) *Outpatient health services.* Outpatient health services provided by the recipient must be approved as appropriate by HUD and the Department of Health and Human Services (HHS). Upon receipt of an application that proposes the provision of outpatient health services, HUD will consult with HHS with respect to the appropriateness of the proposed services.

(l) *Annual assurances.* Recipients who receive assistance only for leasing, operating costs or supportive services costs must provide an annual assurance for each year such assistance is received that the project will be operated for the purpose specified in the application.

(Approved by the Office of Management and Budget under control number 2506–0112)

[58 FR 13871, Mar. 15, 1993, as amended at 59 FR 36892, July 19, 1994; 61 FR 51176, Sept. 30, 1996]

§ 583.305 Term of commitment; repayment of grants; prevention of undue benefits.

(a) *Term of commitment and conversion.* Recipients must agree to operate the housing or provide supportive services in accordance with this part and with sections 423 (b)(1) and (b)(3) of the McKinney Act (42 U.S.C. 11383(b)(1), 11383(b)(3)).

(b) *Repayment of grant and prevention of undue benefits.* In accordance with section 423(c) of the McKinney Act (42 U.S.C. 11383(c)), HUD will require recipients to repay the grant unless HUD has authorized conversion of the project under section 423(b)(3) of the McKinney Act (42 U.S.C. 11383(b)(3)).

[61 FR 51176, Sept. 30, 1996]

§ 583.310 Displacement, relocation, and acquisition.

(a) *Minimizing displacement.* Consistent with the other goals and objectives of this part, recipients must assure that they have taken all reasonable steps to minimize the displacement of persons (families, individuals, businesses, nonprofit organizations, and farms) as a result of supportive housing assisted under this part.

(b) *Relocation assistance for displaced persons.* A displaced person (defined in paragraph (f) of this section) must be provided relocation assistance at the levels described in, and in accordance with, the requirements of the Uniform Relocation Assistance and Real Property Acquisition Policies Act of 1970 (URA) (42 U.S.C. 4601–4655) and implementing regulations at 49 CFR part 24.

(c) *Real property acquisition requirements.* The acquisition of real property for supportive housing is subject to the URA and the requirements described in 49 CFR part 24, subpart B.

(d) *Responsibility of recipient.* (1) The recipient must certify (*i.e.,* provide assurance of compliance) that it will comply with the URA, the regulations at 49 CFR part 24, and the requirements of this section, and must ensure such compliance notwithstanding any third party's contractual obligation to the recipient to comply with these provisions.

(2) The cost of required relocation assistance is an eligible project cost in the same manner and to the same extent as other project costs. Such costs also may be paid for with local public funds or funds available from other sources.

(3) The recipient must maintain records in sufficient detail to demonstrate compliance with provisions of this section.

(e) *Appeals.* A person who disagrees with the recipient's determination concerning whether the person qualifies as a "displaced person," or the amount of relocation assistance for which the person is eligible, may file a written appeal of that determination with the recipient. A low-income person who is dissatisfied with the recipient's determination on his or her appeal may submit a written request for review of that determination to the HUD field office.

(f) *Definition of displaced person.* (1) For purposes of this section, the term "displaced person" means a person (family, individual, business, nonprofit organization, or farm) that moves from real property, or moves personal property from real property permanently as a direct result of acquisition, rehabilitation, or demolition for supportive housing projects assisted under this part. The term "displaced person" includes, but may not be limited to:

(i) A person that moves permanently from the real property after the property owner (or person in control of the site) issues a vacate notice, or refuses to renew an expiring lease in order to evade the responsibility to provide relocation assistance, if the move occurs on or after the date the recipient submits to HUD the application or application amendment designating the project site.

(ii) Any person, including a person who moves before the date described in paragraph (f)(1)(i) of this section, if the recipient or HUD determines that the displacement resulted directly from acquisition, rehabilitation, or demolition for the assisted project.

(iii) A tenant-occupant of a dwelling unit who moves permanently from the building/complex on or after the date of the "initiation of negotiations" (see paragraph (g) of this section) if the move occurs before the tenant has been provided written notice offering him or her the opportunity to lease and occupy a suitable, decent, safe and sanitary dwelling in the same building/complex, under reasonable terms and conditions, upon completion of the project. Such reasonable terms and conditions must include a monthly rent and estimated average monthly utility costs that do not exceed the greater of:

(A) The tenant's monthly rent before the initiation of negotiations and estimated average utility costs, or

(B) 30 percent of gross household income. If the initial rent is at or near the maximum, there must be a reasonable basis for concluding at the time the project is initiated that future rent increases will be modest.

(iv) A tenant of a dwelling who is required to relocate temporarily, but does not return to the building/complex, if either:

(A) A tenant is not offered payment for all reasonable out-of-pocket expenses incurred in connection with temporary relocation, or

(B) Other conditions of the temporary relocation are not reasonable.

§ 583.315

(v) A tenant of a dwelling who moves from the building/complex permanently after he or she has been required to move to another unit in the same building/complex, if either:

(A) The tenant is not offered reimbursement for all reasonable out-of-pocket expenses incurred in connection with the move; or

(B) Other conditions of the move are not reasonable.

(2) Notwithstanding the provisions of paragraph (f)(1) of this section, a person does not qualify as a "displaced person" (and is not eligible for relocation assistance under the URA or this section), if:

(i) The person has been evicted for serious or repeated violation of the terms and conditions of the lease or occupancy agreement, violation of applicable Federal, State, or local or tribal law, or other good cause, and HUD determines that the eviction was not undertaken for the purpose of evading the obligation to provide relocation assistance;

(ii) The person moved into the property after the submission of the application and, before signing a lease and commencing occupancy, was provided written notice of the project, its possible impact on the person (e.g., the person may be displaced, temporarily relocated, or suffer a rent increase) and the fact that the person would not qualify as a "displaced person" (or for any assistance provided under this section), if the project is approved;

(iii) The person is ineligible under 49 CFR 24.2(g)(2); or

(iv) HUD determines that the person was not displaced as a direct result of acquisition, rehabilitation, or demolition for the project.

(3) The recipient may request, at any time, HUD's determination of whether a displacement is or would be covered under this section.

(g) *Definition of initiation of negotiations.* For purposes of determining the formula for computing the replacement housing assistance to be provided to a residential tenant displaced as a direct result of privately undertaken rehabilitation, demolition, or acquisition of the real property, the term "initiation of negotiations" means the execution of the agreement between the recipient and HUD.

(h) *Definition of project.* For purposes of this section, the term "project" means an undertaking paid for in whole or in part with assistance under this part. Two or more activities that are integrally related, each essential to the others, are considered a single project, whether or not all component activities receive assistance under this part.

[58 FR 13871, Mar. 15, 1993, as amended at 59 FR 36892, July 19, 1994]

§ 583.315 Resident rent.

(a) *Calculation of resident rent.* Each resident of supportive housing may be required to pay as rent an amount determined by the recipient which may not exceed the highest of:

(1) 30 percent of the family's monthly adjusted income (adjustment factors include the number of people in the family, age of family members, medical expenses and child care expenses). The calculation of the family's monthly adjusted income must include the expense deductions provided in 24 CFR 5.611(a), and for persons with disabilities, the calculation of the family's monthly adjusted income also must include the disallowance of earned income as provided in 24 CFR 5.617, if applicable;

(2) 10 percent of the family's monthly gross income; or

(3) If the family is receiving payments for welfare assistance from a public agency and a part of the payments, adjusted in accordance with the family's actual housing costs, is specifically designated by the agency to meet the family's housing costs, the portion of the payment that is designated for housing costs.

(b) *Use of rent.* Resident rent may be used in the operation of the project or may be reserved, in whole or in part, to assist residents of transitional housing in moving to permanent housing.

(c) *Fees.* In addition to resident rent, recipients may charge residents reasonable fees for services not paid with grant funds.

[58 FR 13871, Mar. 15, 1993, as amended at 59 FR 36892, July 19, 1994; 66 FR 6225, Jan. 19, 2001]

§ 583.320 Site control.

(a) *Site control.* (1) Where grant funds will be used for acquisition, rehabilitation, or new construction to provide supportive housing or supportive services, or where grant funds will be used for operating costs of supportive housing, or where grant funds will be used to provide supportive services except where an applicant will provide services at sites not operated by the applicant, an applicant must demonstrate site control before HUD will execute a grant agreement (*e.g.*, through a deed, lease, executed contract of sale). If such site control is not demonstrated within one year after initial notification of the award of assistance under this part, the grant will be deobligated as provided in paragraph (c) of this section.

(2) Where grant funds will be used to lease all or part of a structure to provide supportive housing or supportive services, or where grant funds will be used to lease individual housing units for homeless persons who will eventually control the units, site control need not be demonstrated.

(b) *Site change.* (1) A recipient may obtain ownership or control of a suitable site different from the one specified in its application. Retention of an assistance award is subject to the new site's meeting all requirements under this part for suitable sites.

(2) If the acquisition, rehabilitation, acquisition and rehabilitation, or new construction costs for the substitute site are greater than the amount of the grant awarded for the site specified in the application, the recipient must provide for all additional costs. If the recipient is unable to demonstrate to HUD that it is able to provide for the difference in costs, HUD may deobligate the award of assistance.

(c) *Failure to obtain site control within one year.* HUD will recapture or deobligate any award for assistance under this part if the recipient is not in control of a suitable site before the expiration of one year after initial notification of an award.

§ 583.325 Nondiscrimination and equal opportunity requirements.

(a) *General.* Notwithstanding the permissibility of proposals that serve designated populations of disabled homeless persons, recipients serving a designated population of disabled homeless persons are required, within the designated population, to comply with these requirements for nondiscrimination on the basis of race, color, religion, sex, national origin, age, familial status, and disability.

(b) *Nondiscrimination and equal opportunity requirements.* The nondiscrimination and equal opportunity requirements set forth at part 5 of this title apply to this program. The Indian Civil Rights Act (25 U.S.C. 1301 et seq.) applies to tribes when they exercise their powers of self-government, and to Indian housing authorities (IHAs) when established by the exercise of such powers. When an IHA is established under State law, the applicability of the Indian Civil Rights Act will be determined on a case-by-case basis. Projects subject to the Indian Civil Rights Act must be developed and operated in compliance with its provisions and all implementing HUD requirements, instead of title VI and the Fair Housing Act and their implementing regulations.

(c) *Procedures.* (1) If the procedures that the recipient intends to use to make known the availability of the supportive housing are unlikely to reach persons of any particular race, color, religion, sex, age, national origin, familial status, or handicap who may qualify for admission to the housing, the recipient must establish additional procedures that will ensure that such persons can obtain information concerning availability of the housing.

(2) The recipient must adopt procedures to make available information on the existence and locations of facilities and services that are accessible to persons with a handicap and maintain evidence of implementation of the procedures.

(d) *Accessibility requirements.* The recipient must comply with the new construction accessibility requirements of the Fair Housing Act and section 504 of the Rehabilitation Act of 1973, and the reasonable accommodation and rehabilitation accessibility requirements of section 504 as follows:

(1) All new construction must meet the accessibility requirements of 24

CFR 8.22 and, as applicable, 24 CFR 100.205.

(2) Projects in which costs of rehabilitation are 75 percent or more of the replacement cost of the building must meet the requirements of 24 CFR 8.23(a). Other rehabilitation must meet the requirements of 24 CFR 8.23(b).

[58 FR 13871, Mar. 15, 1993, as amended at 59 FR 33894, June 30, 1994; 61 FR 5210, Feb. 9, 1996; 61 FR 51176, Sept. 30, 1996]

§ 583.330 Applicability of other Federal requirements.

In addition to the requirements set forth in 24 CFR part 5, use of assistance provided under this part must comply with the following Federal requirements:

(a) *Flood insurance.* (1) The Flood Disaster Protection Act of 1973 (42 U.S.C. 4001–4128) prohibits the approval of applications for assistance for acquisition or construction (including rehabilitation) for supportive housing located in an area identified by the Federal Emergency Management Agency (FEMA) as having special flood hazards, unless:

(i) The community in which the area is situated is participating in the National Flood Insurance Program (see 44 CFR parts 59 through 79), or less than a year has passed since FEMA notification regarding such hazards; and

(ii) Flood insurance is obtained as a condition of approval of the application.

(2) Applicants with supportive housing located in an area identified by FEMA as having special flood hazards and receiving assistance for acquisition or construction (including rehabilitation) are responsible for assuring that flood insurance under the National Flood Insurance Program is obtained and maintained.

(b) The Coastal Barrier Resources Act of 1982 (16 U.S.C. 3501 *et seq.*) may apply to proposals under this part, depending on the assistance requested.

(c) *Applicability of OMB Circulars.* The policies, guidelines, and requirements of OMB Circular No. A–87 (Cost Principles Applicable to Grants, Contracts and Other Agreements with State and Local Governments) and 24 CFR part 85 apply to the award, acceptance, and use of assistance under the program by governmental entities, and OMB Circular Nos. A–110 (Grants and Cooperative Agreements with Institutions of Higher Education, Hospitals, and Other Nonprofit Organizations) and A–122 (Cost Principles Applicable to Grants, Contracts and Other Agreements with Nonprofit Institutions) apply to the acceptance and use of assistance by private nonprofit organizations, except where inconsistent with the provisions of the McKinney Act, other Federal statutes, or this part. (Copies of OMB Circulars may be obtained from E.O.P. Publications, room 2200, New Executive Office Building, Washington, DC 20503, telephone (202) 395–7332. (This is not a toll-free number.) There is a limit of two free copies.

(d) *Lead-based paint.* The Lead-Based Paint Poisoning Prevention Act (42 U.S.C. 4821–4846), the Residential Lead-Based Paint Hazard Reduction Act of 1992 (42 U.S.C. 4851–4856), and implementing regulations at part 35, subparts A, B, J, K, and R of this title apply to activities under this program.

(e) *Conflicts of interest.* (1) In addition to the conflict of interest requirements in 24 CFR part 85, no person who is an employee, agent, consultant, officer, or elected or appointed official of the recipient and who exercises or has exercised any functions or responsibilities with respect to assisted activities, or who is in a position to participate in a decisionmaking process or gain inside information with regard to such activities, may obtain a personal or financial interest or benefit from the activity, or have an interest in any contract, subcontract, or agreement with respect thereto, or the proceeds thereunder, either for himself or herself or for those with whom he or she has family or business ties, during his or her tenure or for one year thereafter. Participation by homeless individuals who also are participants under the program in policy or decisionmaking under § 583.300(f) does not constitute a conflict of interest.

(2) Upon the written request of the recipient, HUD may grant an exception to the provisions of paragraph (e)(1) of this section on a case-by-case basis when it determines that the exception will serve to further the purposes of the program and the effective and efficient administration of the recipient's

project. An exception may be considered only after the recipient has provided the following:

(i) For States and other governmental entities, a disclosure of the nature of the conflict, accompanied by an assurance that there has been public disclosure of the conflict and a description of how the public disclosure was made; and

(ii) For all recipients, an opinion of the recipient's attorney that the interest for which the exception is sought would not violate State or local law.

(3) In determining whether to grant a requested exception after the recipient has satisfactorily met the requirement of paragraph (e)(2) of this section, HUD will consider the cumulative effect of the following factors, where applicable:

(i) Whether the exception would provide a significant cost benefit or an essential degree of expertise to the project which would otherwise not be available;

(ii) Whether the person affected is a member of a group or class of eligible persons and the exception will permit such person to receive generally the same interests or benefits as are being made available or provided to the group or class;

(iii) Whether the affected person has withdrawn from his or her functions or responsibilities, or the decisionmaking process with respect to the specific assisted activity in question;

(iv) Whether the interest or benefit was present before the affected person was in a position as described in paragraph (e)(1) of this section;

(v) Whether undue hardship will result either to the recipient or the person affected when weighed against the public interest served by avoiding the prohibited conflict; and

(vi) Any other relevant considerations.

(f) *Audit.* The financial management systems used by recipients under this program must provide for audits in accordance with 24 CFR part 44 or part 45, as applicable. HUD may perform or require additional audits as it finds necessary or appropriate.

(g) Davis-Bacon Act. The provisions of the Davis-Bacon Act do not apply to this program.

[58 FR 13871, Mar. 15, 1993, as amended at 61 FR 5211, Feb. 9, 1996; 64 FR 50226, Sept. 15, 1999]

Subpart E—Administration

§ 583.400 Grant agreement.

(a) *General.* The duty to provide supportive housing or supportive services in accordance with the requirements of this part will be incorporated in a grant agreement executed by HUD and the recipient.

(b) *Enforcement.* HUD will enforce the obligations in the grant agreement through such action as may be appropriate, including repayment of funds that have already been disbursed to the recipient.

§ 583.405 Program changes.

(a) *HUD approval.* (1) A recipient may not make any significant changes to an approved program without prior HUD approval. Significant changes include, but are not limited to, a change in the recipient, a change in the project site, additions or deletions in the types of activities listed in § 583.100 of this part approved for the program or a shift of more than 10 percent of funds from one approved type of activity to another, and a change in the category of participants to be served. Depending on the nature of the change, HUD may require a new certification of consistency with the consolidated plan (see § 583.155).

(2) Approval for changes is contingent upon the application ranking remaining high enough after the approved change to have been competitively selected for funding in the year the application was selected.

(b) *Documentation of other changes.* Any changes to an approved program that do not require prior HUD approval must be fully documented in the recipient's records.

[58 FR 13871, Mar. 15, 1993, as amended at 61 FR 51176, Sept. 30, 1996]

§ 583.410 Obligation and deobligation of funds.

(a) *Obligation of funds.* When HUD and the applicant execute a grant agreement, funds are obligated to cover the amount of the approved assistance under subpart B of this part. The recipient will be expected to carry out the supportive housing or supportive services activities as proposed in the application.

(b) *Increases.* After the initial obligation of funds, HUD will not make revisions to increase the amount obligated.

(c) *Deobligation.* (1) HUD may deobligate all or parts of grants for acquisition, rehabilitation, acquisition and rehabilitation, or new construction:

(i) If the actual total cost of acquisition, rehabilitation, acquisition and rehabilitation, or new construction is less than the total cost anticipated in the application; or

(ii) If proposed activities for which funding was approved are not begun within three months or residents do not begin to occupy the facility within nine months after grant execution.

(2) HUD may deobligate the amounts for annual leasing costs, operating costs or supportive services in any year:

(i) If the actual leasing costs, operating costs or supportive services for that year are less than the total cost anticipated in the application; or

(ii) If the proposed supportive housing operations are not begun within three months after the units are available for occupancy.

(3) The grant agreement may set forth in detail other circumstances under which funds may be deobligated, and other sanctions may be imposed.

(4) HUD may:

(i) Readvertise the availability of funds that have been deobligated under this section in a notice of fund availability under § 583.200, or

(ii) Award deobligated funds to applications previously submitted in response to the most recently published notice of fund availability, and in accordance with subpart C of this part.

PART 585—YOUTHBUILD PROGRAM

Subpart A—General

Sec.
585.1 Authority.
585.2 Program purpose.
585.3 Program components.
585.4 Definitions.

Subpart B [Reserved]

Subpart C—Youthbuild Planning Grants

585.201 Purpose.
585.202 Award limits.
585.203 Grant term.
585.204 Locational considerations.
585.205 Eligible activities.

Subpart D—Youthbuild Implementation Grants

585.301 Purpose.
585.302 Award limits.
585.303 Grant term.
585.304 Locational considerations.
585.305 Eligible activities.
585.306 Designation of costs.
585.307 Environmental procedures and standards.
585.308 Relocation assistance and real property acquisition.
585.309 Project-related restrictions applicable to Youthbuild residential rental housing.
585.310 Project-related restrictions applicable to Youthbuild transitional housing for the homeless.
585.311 Project-related restrictions applicable to Youthbuild homeownership housing.
585.312 Wages, labor standards, and nondiscrimination.
585.313 Labor standards.

Subpart E—Administration

585.401 Recordkeeping by recipients.
585.402 Grant agreement.
585.403 Reporting requirements.
585.404 Program changes.
585.405 Obligation and deobligation of funds.
585.406 Faith-based activities.

Subpart F—Applicability of Other Federal Requirements

585.501 Application of OMB Circulars.
585.502 Certifications.
585.503 Conflict of interest.
585.504 Use of debarred, suspended, or ineligible contractors.

AUTHORITY: 42 U.S.C. 3535(d) and 8011.

SOURCE: 60 FR 9737, Feb. 21, 1995, unless otherwise noted.

Subpart A—General

§ 585.1 Authority.

(a) *General.* The Youthbuild program is authorized under subtitle D of title IV of the National Affordable Housing Act (42 U.S.C. 8011), as added by section 164 of the Housing and Community Development Act of 1992 (Pub. L. 102–550).

(b) *Authority restriction.* No provision of the Youthbuild program may be construed to authorize any agency, officer, or employee of the United States to exercise any direction, supervision, or control over the curriculum, program of instruction, administration, or personnel of any educational institution, school, or school system, or over the selection of library resources, textbooks, or other printed or published instructional materials used by any educational institution or school system participating in a Youthbuild program.

§ 585.2 Program purpose.

The purposes of the Youthbuild program are set out in section 451 of the National Affordable Housing Act (42 U.S.C. 12899) ("NAHA").

[61 FR 52187, Oct. 4, 1996]

§ 585.3 Program components.

A Youthbuild implementation program uses comprehensive and multidisciplinary approaches designed to prepare young adults who have dropped out of high school for educational and employment opportunities by employing them as construction trainees on work sites for housing designated for homeless persons and low- and very low-income families. A Youthbuild planning grant is designed to give recipients sufficient time and financial resources to develop a comprehensive Youthbuild program that can be effectively implemented. Youthbuild programs must contain the three components described in paragraphs (a), (b) and (d) of this section. Other activities described in paragraph (c) of this section are optional:

(a) *Educational services*, including:

(1) Services and activities designed to meet the basic educational needs of participants. For example, a Youthbuild program may include basic skills instruction and remedial education, bilingual education for individuals with limited English proficiency, secondary educational services and activities designed to lead to the attainment of a high school diploma or its equivalency (GED), or counseling and assistance in attaining post-secondary education and required financial aid;

(2) Vocational classroom courses geared to construction terminology and concepts; and

(3) Strategies to coordinate with local trade unions and apprenticeship programs where possible.

(b) *Leadership training, counseling and other support activities*, including:

(1) Activities designed to develop employment and leadership skills, including support for youth councils;

(2) Counseling services to assist trainees in personal, health, housing, child care, family or legal problems and/or referral services to appropriate social service resources;

(3) Support services and stipends necessary to enable individuals to participate in the program and, for a period not to exceed 12 months after completion of training, to assist participants through continued support services;

(4) Job development and placement activities and post-graduation follow-up assistance; and

(5) Pre-employment training plan aimed at developing job seeking skills.

(c) *Other activities.* A local program may be designed to include other, special activities such as:

(1) Entrepreneurial training and courses in small business development;

(2) Assistance to correct learning disabilities; or

(3) Drivers' education courses.

(d) *On-site training*, through actual housing rehabilitation and/or construction work. This component must include:

(1) Access to housing sites where construction/ rehabilitation work is being carried out;

(2) Work site training plan for a closely supervised construction site;

(3) Construction or rehabilitation plan and timetable; and

(4) Approaches to work site safety.

(e) The Youthbuild implementation program must be structured so that 50 percent of each full-time participant's time is spent in educational services

§ 585.4

and activities (paragraphs (a), (b), and (c) of this section) and 50 percent is spent in on-site training (paragraph (d) of this section). Youthbuild planning grant applications must contain strategies, plans and approaches to be used during the planning process to ultimately implement these program requirements.

§ 585.4 Definitions.

The terms "adjusted income," "community based organization," "homeless individual," "housing development agency," "Indian tribe," "individual who has dropped out of high school," "institution of higher education," "limited-English proficiency," "low-income family," "offender," "State," and "very low-income family" are defined in section 457 of NAHA.

The terms *Secretary* and *1937 Act* are defined in 24 CFR part 5.

1992 Act means the Housing and Community Development Act of 1992.

Access to housing applies to Youthbuild implementation grants required to document that the program has access to the housing project(s) for young adult on-site training, e.g. program participants have permission to work on the housing site.

Applicable residential rental housing quality standards shall mean those standards of the applicable HUD or other Federal, State or local program providing assistance for residential rental housing involved in a Youthbuild implementation grant as used under section 455(a), Youthbuild Program Requirements, of the Act.

Applicant means a public or private nonprofit agency, including:

(1) A community-based organization;

(2) An administrative entity designated under section 103(b)(1)(B) of the Job Training Partnership Act;

(3) A community action agency;

(4) A State or local housing development agency;

(5) A community development corporation;

(6) A public and/or Indian housing authority and resident management corporations, resident councils and resident organizations;

(7) A State or local youth service or conservation corps; and

(8) Any other entity (including States, units of general local government, and Indian Tribes) eligible to provide education and employment training.

Combined Youthbuild application means the submission by an applicant of a single application to HUD for a planning and implementation grant request for one Youthbuild program.

Consolidated Plan means the document that is submitted to HUD that serves as the planning documents (comprehensive housing affordability strategy and community development plan) of the jurisdiction and an application for funding under any of the Community Planning and Development formula grant programs which is prepared in accordance with the process described in 24 CFR part 91.

Full-time participation for program eligible participants is limited to not less than 6 months and not more than 24 months.

Graduates are those participants who have completed the full-time education/on-site training components of a Youthbuild program and who are eligible to take advantage of meaningful opportunities in continued education, in owning their own businesses, in meaningful employment or in other means by which the participant can attain economic self-sufficiency.

Homeless Act means the Stewart B. McKinney Homeless Assistance Act, as amended, (42 U.S.C. 11301 et seq.).

JTPA means the Job Training Partnership Act (P.L. 102-235), as amended.

Participant means:

(1) An individual who is:

(i) 16 to 24 years of age, inclusive, at time of enrollment;

(ii) A very low-income individual or a member of a very low-income family; and

(iii) An individual who has dropped out of high school.

(2) An exception of not more than 25 percent of all full-time participants is permitted for young adults who do not meet the program's income or educational requirements but who have educational needs despite attainment of a high school diploma or its equivalent.

Private nonprofit organization means any private nonprofit organization that:
(1) Is organized and exists under Federal, State, local, or tribal law;
(2) Has no part of its earnings inuring to the benefit of any individual, corporation, or other entity;
(3) Has a voluntary board;
(4) Has an accounting system or has designated a fiscal agent in accordance with requirements established by HUD; and
(5) Practices nondiscrimination in the provision of assistance.

Project-related restrictions mean Youthbuild housing restrictions applicable only in cases where a Youthbuild implementation grant is providing assistance to residential rental, transitional or homeownership housing projects for specific costs relating to property acquisition, architectural and engineering fees, construction, rehabilitation, operating costs, or replacement reserves.

Recipient means any entity that receives assistance under this part.

Related facilities include cafeterias or dining halls, community rooms or buildings, child care centers, appropriate recreation facilities, and other essential service facilities that are physically attached to the housing to be constructed or rehabilitated. Related facilities which stand alone are not appropriate construction sites for trainees.

Title IV means title IV of the National Affordable Housing Act, as amended (42 U.S.C. 1437).

Transitional housing means a project that has as its purpose facilitating the movement of homeless individuals and families to permanent housing within a reasonable amount of time (usually 24 months). Transitional housing includes housing primarily designed to serve deinstitutionalized homeless individuals and other homeless individuals with mental or physical disabilities and homeless families with children.

Useful life shall mean a period of 10 years upon construction completion and issuance of an occupancy permit applicable to a residential rental, transitional or homeownership property acquired, constructed or rehabilitated (including architectural and engineering fees), or maintained (i.e., operating costs or replacement reserves), in whole or in part, with Youthbuild implementation grant funds (as used in section 455(a), Youthbuild Program Requirements, of the Act).

[60 FR 9737, Feb. 21, 1995, as amended at 61 FR 5211, Feb. 9, 1996; 61 FR 52187, Oct. 4, 1996]

Subpart B [Reserved]

Subpart C—Youthbuild Planning Grants

§ 585.201 Purpose.

HUD will award Youthbuild planning grants to eligible applicants for the purpose of developing Youthbuild programs in accordance with subtitle D of title IV of the National Affordable Housing Act. Applications will be selected in a national competition in accordance with the selection process described in the current NOFA.

§ 585.202 Award limits.

Maximum awards. The maximum amount of a Youthbuild planning grant is $150,000 unless a lower amount is established in the NOFA. HUD may for good cause approve a grant in a higher amount.

§ 585.203 Grant term.

Funds awarded for planning grants are expected to be used within 12 months of the effective date of the planning grant agreement. The award of a Youthbuild planning grant does not obligate HUD to fund the implementation of the program upon completion of the approved planning activities (unless the companion implementation grant was submitted as a combined application and funded in the implementation grant competition).

§ 585.204 Locational considerations.

HUD will not approve multiple applications for planning grants in the same jurisdiction unless it determines that the jurisdiction is sufficiently large to justify approval of more than one application.

§ 585.205 Eligible activities.

Planning grant activities to develop a Youthbuild program may include:

§ 585.301

(a) The undertaking of studies and research efforts to determine the feasibility and need for a Youthbuild program in a selected location including whether a proposed program can meet the education and training needs of young adults, aid in the expansion of affordable housing to meet the needs of the community, and achieve financial feasibility;

(b) The formation and establishment of a consortium among Federal, State, or local training and education programs, service providers, housing programs and providers including but not limited to homeless providers, housing owners, developers, and other organizations necessary for the establishment of a Youthbuild program;

(c) The preliminary identification and potential selection of housing for the Youthbuild program including an assessment of the type of housing program to be used and the method by which program participants will have access to the housing project;

(d) The planning and identification of resources required for basic skills instruction and education, job training and job development, leadership and employment skills development, counseling, referral, and other related support services that will be provided as part of the Youthbuild program;

(e) The preparation of an application for an implementation grant.

(f) Preliminary architectural and engineering (A & E) work for the Youthbuild proposed housing including:

(1) The development of cost and time estimates associated with the amount of work to be done through new construction or the rehabilitation of existing housing;

(2) Technical studies to evaluate environmental problems and to determine whether mitigation is feasible on the potential site; and

(3) The identification and initiation of the permit process required to commence work on the selected site.

(g) The planning and development of multi-disciplinary educational and employment training curricula, leadership development training, counseling, and other supportive services and activities for the Youthbuild program including the identification and training of staff assigned to each program component;

(h) The identification and establishment of relationships with local unions, apprenticeship programs, housing owners, local employers and public or private community organizations for job training, development, and placement opportunities;

(i) *Administration.* Youthbuild funds for administrative costs may not exceed 15 percent of the total amount of Youthbuild program and project costs or such higher percentage as HUD determines is necessary to support capacity development by a private nonprofit organization.

Subpart D—Youthbuild Implementation Grants

§ 585.301 Purpose.

HUD will award Youthbuild implementation grants to eligible applicants for the purpose of carrying out Youthbuild programs in accordance with subtitle D of title IV of the National Affordable Housing Act. Applications will be selected in a national competition in accordance with the selection process described in the current NOFA.

§ 585.302 Award limits.

Maximum awards. The maximum award for a Youthbuild implementation grant will be defined in the NOFA for each competition and may vary by competition. HUD may for good cause approve a grant in a higher amount than the specified limit.

§ 585.303 Grant term.

Funds awarded for implementation grants are expected to be used within 30 months of the effective date of the implementation grant agreement.

§ 585.304 Locational considerations.

Each application for an implementation grant may only include activities to carry out one Youthbuild program, i.e., to start a new Youthbuild program or to fund new classes of Youthbuild participants for an existing program. The same applicant organization may submit more than one application in the current competition if the proposed programs are in different jurisdictions. HUD will not approve multiple applications for implementation grants in the same jurisdiction unless it determines that the jurisdiction is sufficiently large to justify approval of more than one application.

§ 585.305 Eligible activities.

Implementation grant activities to conduct a Youthbuild program may include:

(a) Acquisition of housing and related facilities to be used for the purposes of providing homeownership, residential rental housing, or transitional housing for the homeless and low- and very low-income persons and families;

(b) Architectural and engineering work associated with Youthbuild housing;

(c) Construction of housing and related facilities to be used for the purposes of providing homeownership, residential rental housing, or transitional housing for the homeless and low- and very low-income persons and families;

(d) Rehabilitation of housing and related facilities to be used for the purposes of providing homeownership, residential rental housing, or transitional housing for the homeless and low- and very low-income persons and families, including lead-based paint activities; in accordance with part 35 of this title;

(e) Operating expenses and replacement reserves for the housing assisted in the Youthbuild program;

(f) Relocation payments and other assistance required to comply with § 585.308, legal fees, and construction management;

(g) Outreach and recruitment activities, emphasizing special outreach efforts to be undertaken to recruit eligible young women (including young women with dependent children);

(h) Education and job training services and activities including work experience, basic skills instruction and remedial education, bilingual education; secondary education leading to the attainment of a high school diploma or its equivalent; counseling and assistance in attaining post-secondary education and required financial aid;

(i) Wages, benefits and need-based stipends provided to participants;

(j) Leadership development, counseling, support services, and development of employment skills;

(k) Defraying costs for the ongoing training and technical assistance needs of the recipient that are related to developing and carrying out a Youthbuild program;

(l) Job placement (including entrepreneurial training and business development), counseling, and support services for a period not to exceed 12 months after completion of training to assist participants; and

(m) *Administration.* Youthbuild funds for administrative costs may not exceed 15 percent of the total amount of Youthbuild program and project costs or such higher percentage as HUD determines is necessary to support capacity development by a private nonprofit organization.

[60 FR 9737, Feb. 21, 1995, as amended at 64 FR 50226, Sept. 15, 1999]

§ 585.306 Designation of costs.

The following budget items are to be considered training or other costs under the Youthbuild implementation grant and should not be considered costs associated with acquisition, rehabilitation, or new construction for the purposes of §§ 585.307, 585.309, 585.310, and 585.311.

(a) Trainees' tools and clothing.
(b) Participant stipends and wages.
(c) On-site trainee supervisors.
(d) Construction management.
(e) Relocation costs.
(f) Legal fees.
(g) Clearance and demolition.

§ 585.307 Environmental procedures and standards.

(a) *Environmental procedures.* Applicants are encouraged to select hazard-free and problem-free properties for their Youthbuild projects. Environmental procedures apply to HUD approval of implementation grants when the applicant proposes to use Youthbuild funds to cover any costs for the lease, acquisition, rehabilitation, or new construction of real property that is proposed for housing project development. Environmental procedures do not apply to HUD approval of implementation grants when applicants propose to use their Youthbuild funds

§ 585.307

solely to cover any costs for classroom and/or on-the-job construction training and supportive services. For those applicants that propose to use their Youthbuild funds to cover any costs of the lease, acquisition, rehabilitation, or new construction of real property, the applicant shall submit all relevant environmental information in its application to support HUD decision-making in accordance with the following environmental procedures and standards.

(1) Before any Youthbuild implementation application that requests funds for acquisition, rehabilitation, or construction can be selected for funding, HUD shall determine whether any environmental thresholds are exceeded in accordance with 24 CFR part 50, which implements the National Environmental Policy Act (NEPA) and the related Federal environmental laws and authorities listed under 24 CFR 50.4.

(i) If HUD determines that one or more of the thresholds are exceeded, HUD shall conduct a compliance review of the issue and, if appropriate, establish mitigating measures that the applicant shall carry out for the property;

(ii) In performing its review, HUD may use previously issued environmental reviews prepared by local, State, or other Federal agencies for the proposed property;

(iii)(A) The application for the Youthbuild implementation grant shall provide HUD with:

(*1*) Applicant documentation for environmental threshold review; and

(*2*) Any previously issued environmental reviews prepared by local, State, or other Federal agencies for the proposed property.

(B) The applicant is encouraged to contact the local community development agency to obtain any previously issued environmental reviews for the proposed property as well as for other relevant information that can be used in the applicant documentation for the environmental threshold review. In using previous reviews by other sources, HUD must, however, conduct the environmental analysis and prepare the environmental review and be responsible for any required environmental findings.

(2) HUD reserves the right to disqualify any application where one or more environmental thresholds are exceeded if HUD determines that the compliance review cannot be conducted and satisfactorily completed within the HUD review period for applications.

(3) If Youthbuild funds are requested for acquisition, rehabilitation, or construction, applicants are prohibited from committing or expending State, local or other funds to undertake property acquisition (including lease), rehabilitation or construction under this program until notification of grant award.

(b) *Environmental thresholds.* HUD shall determine whether a NEPA environmental assessment is required. Also, HUD shall determine whether the proposed property triggers thresholds for the applicable Federal environmental laws and authorities listed under 24 CFR 50.4 as follows:

(1) For minor rehabilitation of a building and any property acquisition (including lease), Federal environmental laws and authorities may apply when the property is:

(i) Located within designated coastal barrier resources;

(ii) Contaminated by toxic chemicals or radioactive materials;

(iii) Located within a floodplain;

(iv) A building for which flood insurance protection is required;

(v) Located within a runway clear zone at a civil airport or within a clear zone or accident potential zone at a military airfield; or

(vi) Listed on, or eligible for listing on, the National Register of Historic Places; located within, or adjacent to, an historic district, or is a property whose area of potential effects includes a historic district or property.

(2) For major rehabilitation of a building and also for substantial improvement in floodplains, in addition to paragraphs (b)(1)(i) through (vi) of this section, other Federal environmental laws and authorities may apply when the property:

(i) Has significant impact to the human environment;

(ii) Is a project involving five or more dwelling units severely noise-impacted; or

(iii) Affects coastal zone management.

(3) For new construction, conversion or increase in dwelling unit density, in addition to paragraphs (b)(1)(i) through (vi) and paragraphs (b)(2)(i) through (iii) of this section, other Federal environmental laws and authorities may apply when the property:

(i) Is located near hazardous industrial operations handling fuels or chemicals of an explosive or flammable nature;

(ii) Affects a sole source aquifer;

(iii) Affects endangered species; or

(iv) Is located within a designated wetland.

(c) *Qualified data sources.* The environmental threshold information provided by applicants must be from qualified data sources. A qualified data source means any Federal, State, or local agency with expertise or experience in environmental protection (e.g., the local community development agency; the local planning agency; the State environmental protection agency; the State Historic Preservation Officer) or any other source qualified to provide reliable information on the particular property.

(d) *Minor rehabilitation* means proposed fixing and repairs:

(1) Whose estimated cost is less than 75 percent of the property value after completion;

(2) That does not involve changes in land use from residential to nonresidential, or from nonresidential to residential;

(3) That does not involve the demolition of one or more buildings, or parts of a building, containing the primary use served by the property; and

(4) That does not increase unit density more than 20 percent.

§ 585.308 Relocation assistance and real property acquisition.

The Youthbuild program is subject to the provisions of the Uniform Relocation Assistance and Real Property Acquisition Policies Act of 1970, as amended (URA) and implementing regulations at 49 CFR part 24. HUD Handbook 1378, Tenant Assistance, Relocation and Real Property Acquisition, available from the Relocation and Real Estate Division at the address listed in this section, describes these policies and procedures. Any occupied property used in a Youthbuild program is subject to the URA regardless of the source of the property or construction funds. The URA requires recipients to provide relocation assistance to persons (families, individuals, businesses, and nonprofit organizations) that are displaced as a direct result of acquisition, rehabilitation or demolition for an assisted project. Property occupants who are not displaced also have certain rights. Therefore, if a proposed Youthbuild implementation program involves occupied property, before submitting the application the applicant should consult with staff of the Relocation and Real Estate Division, Office of Community Planning and Development, Department of Housing and Urban Development, Room 7154, 451 Seventh Street, SW, Washington, DC 20410; telephone: (202) 708–0336. TDD: (202) 708–1455. Fax: (202) 708–1744. (These are not toll-free numbers.)

§ 585.309 Project-related restrictions applicable to Youthbuild residential rental housing.

Where the award of a Youthbuild implementation grant includes the eligible activities of acquisition, architectural and engineering fees, construction, rehabilitation, operating costs or replacement reserves for residential rental units, and where the costs for these activities are to be funded, in whole or in part, from the Youthbuild grant award, the recipient shall be required to comply with the following Youthbuild project-related restrictions for a period of not less than 10 years:

(a) *Occupancy by low- and very low-income families.* (1) For the 10 year period of the residential rental Youthbuild project, the recipient or rightful owner will be required to maintain at least a 90 percent level of occupancy for individuals and families with incomes less than 60 percent of the area median income, adjusted for family size—"the 90 percent category." The recipient or rightful owner must offer each available rental unit to the 60 percent of area median income group for an advertising period of not less than 90 days upon each vacancy occurrence throughout the 10 year period. Community-

§ 585.309

wide advertisements for tenants of this income group must be conducted.

(2) In order to maintain the financial stability of the project and to provide flexibility in averting long-term vacancies in the 90 percent category, the rightful owner is permitted, under certain circumstances described below, to execute temporary two year leases with individuals and families with incomes between 60 and 80 percent of the area median income. This temporary deviation is permitted when no qualifying tenant (with an income of 60 percent or less of median) leases the unit upon the end of the 90 day advertising period. The owner may then advertise the unit to individuals and families with incomes less than 80 percent of the area median income, adjusted for family size, for another advertisement period of 90 days. Temporary leases for tenants whose incomes are between 60 and 80 percent of the area median income (exclusive of the 10 percent allowance) shall be limited to two years. Temporary tenants are not covered by Youthbuild tenant protections regarding termination of tenancy (paragraph (b)(2) of this section), tenant selection plan (paragraph (b)(4) of this section) and tenant participation plan (paragraph (d) of this section).

(3) The remaining 10 percent of the units must be made available to and occupied by low-income families—"the 10 percent category." The income test must be conducted for both the 90 percent and 10 percent categories only at time of entry for each unit available for occupancy.

(b) *Tenant protections.* Upon submission of the implementation grant application, the applicant or rightful owner of the residential rental units covered under this paragraph shall certify to the following tenant protections:

(1) *Lease.* As part of the Youthbuild implementation grant application, the applicant or rightful owner of the property shall provide a model lease containing terms and conditions acceptable to HUD. The model lease shall become an addendum to the executed grant agreement and shall remain in force for a period of 10 years. The lease between a tenant and the owner of residential rental housing shall be for a period of not less than one year, unless otherwise mutually agreed to by the tenant and the owner, and shall contain such terms and conditions as HUD determines to be appropriate. Any change to a lease must be approved by HUD.

(2) *Termination of tenancy.* Upon submission of the implementation grant application, the applicant or other rightful owner of the property must certify that the following restrictions will be applied to all lease terminations initiated by the owner. The restrictions must state that an owner shall not terminate the tenancy or refuse to renew the lease of a tenant occupying a Youthbuild residential rental housing unit except for serious or repeated violations of the terms and conditions of the lease, or for violation of applicable Federal, State, or local laws, or for other good cause. Any termination or refusal to renew the lease must be preceded by not less than 30 days by the owner's service upon the tenant of a written notice specifying the grounds for the action. With regard to leases for tenants in units controlled by public housing authorities, 24 CFR part 966 shall take precedence over this provision.

(3) *Maintenance and replacements.* Upon submission of the implementation grant application, the applicant or rightful owner of Youthbuild residential rental housing must certify that the premises will be maintained in compliance with all applicable housing quality standards and local code requirements for the 10 year period. HUD's section 8 housing quality standards apply when no other public assistance is involved other than the Youthbuild grant. In other cases, the applicable HUD or other Federal, State or local program guidelines shall apply.

(4) *Tenant selection.* The applicant or rightful owner of Youthbuild residential rental housing must develop and adopt a tenant selection plan containing selection policies and criteria that are consistent with HUD requirements. The tenant selection plan shall remain in force for the 10 year period. Upon submission of the implementation grant application, the applicant or owner of the property must certify

that the plan complies with the following HUD requirements:

(i) The plan is consistent with the purpose of providing housing for homeless and very low-income families and individuals;

(ii) The plan is reasonably related to program eligibility and the applicant's or owner's ability to perform the obligations of the lease;

(iii) The plan gives reasonable consideration to the housing needs of families that would qualify for a preference under section 6(c)(4)(A) of the United States Housing Act of 1937;

(iv) The plan provides for the selection of tenants from a written waiting list in the chronological order of their application, to the extent practicable, and for the prompt notification in writing of any rejected applicant of the grounds for any rejection; and

(v) The plan acknowledges that a family holding tenant-based assistance under section 8 of the United States Housing Act of 1937 will not be refused tenancy because of the status of the prospective tenant as a holder of such assistance.

(c) *Limitation on rental payments.* Upon submission of the implementation grant application, the applicant or other rightful owner of Youthbuild residential rental housing project involved in a Youthbuild program shall certify that tenants in each rental unit shall be not required to pay rent in excess of the amount provided under section 3(a) of the United States Housing Act of 1937.

(d) *Tenant participation plan.* The Youthbuild program shall require a tenant participation plan applicable to the rightful owner of Youthbuild residential rental housing, provided such owner is a nonprofit public or private organization. Upon submission of the implementation grant application, the nonprofit owner shall certify that the tenant participation plan is the plan to be adopted and followed for tenant participation in management decisions for the 10 year period.

(e) *Limitations on profit.* Youthbuild residential rental housing projects meeting the requirements of this section shall be restricted from producing profit in excess of the limitations set out in sections 455(c)(1) and (2) of NAHA.

(f) *Restrictions on conveyance.* Conveyance restrictions apply to Youthbuild residential rental housing project(s) meeting the requirements of this section. Ownership of the property may not be conveyed unless the instrument of conveyance requires a subsequent owner to comply with the same restrictions imposed upon the original owner for the balance of the 10 year period.

(g) *Ten year restriction.* The restrictions listed in paragraphs (a) through (f) of this section shall remain in force for a period of not less than 10 years after construction completion and issuance of an occupancy permit for all Youthbuild residential rental housing projects receiving Youthbuild assistance.

(Approved by the Office of Management and Budget under control number 2506–0142)

[60 FR 9737, Feb. 21, 1995, as amended at 61 FR 52187, Oct. 4, 1996]

§ 585.310 Project-related restrictions applicable to Youthbuild transitional housing for the homeless.

Where the award of a Youthbuild implementation grant includes the eligible activities of acquisition, architectural and engineering fees, construction, rehabilitation, operating costs or replacement reserves of transitional housing units, and where the costs for these activities are funded, in whole or in part, with Youthbuild grant funds, the housing project shall be required to comply with the following Youthbuild project-related restrictions:

(a) *Limitations on profit.* Youthbuild residential rental housing projects meeting the requirements of this section shall be restricted from producing profit in excess of the limitations set out in sections 455(c)(1) and (2) of NAHA.

(b) *Restrictions on conveyance.* Conveyance restrictions apply to Youthbuild transitional housing projects meeting the requirements of this section. Ownership of the property may not be conveyed unless the instrument of conveyance requires a subsequent owner to comply with the same restrictions imposed upon the original owner for the balance of the 10 year period.

§ 585.311

(c) *Program requirements for transitional housing.* (1) Youthbuild transitional housing projects meeting the requirements of this section shall adhere to the requirements regarding service delivery, housing standards and rent limitations applicable to comparable housing receiving assistance under the Transitional Housing component of the Supportive Housing Program (title IV of the Stewart B. McKinney Homeless Assistance Act).

(2) The Secretary may waive these requirements to permit the conversion of a Youthbuild transitional housing project to a permanent housing project only if such housing complies with the Youthbuild project-related restrictions for residential rental housing projects found in § 585.309.

(d) *Ten year restriction.* The restrictions listed in paragraphs (a) through (c) of this section shall remain in force for a period of not less than 10 years after construction completion and issuance of an occupancy permit for a Youthbuild transitional housing project receiving Youthbuild assistance.

[60 FR 9737, Feb. 21, 1995, as amended at 61 FR 52187, Oct. 4, 1996]

§ 585.311 Project-related restrictions applicable to Youthbuild homeownership housing.

Where the award of a Youthbuild implementation grant includes the eligible activities of acquisition, architectural and engineering fees, construction, or rehabilitation of homeownership housing, and where the costs for these activities are to be funded, in whole or in part, with Youthbuild grant funds, the housing project shall be required to comply with the following Youthbuild project-related restrictions:

(a) *Program compliance.* Each homeownership project meeting the requirements of this section shall comply with the requirements of the HOPE II and HOPE III program authorized under subtitle B or C respectively of title IV of the National Affordable Housing Act.

(b) *Restrictions on conveyance.* Conveyance restrictions apply to Youthbuild homeownership housing projects meeting the requirements of this part. Ownership of the property may not be conveyed unless the instrument of conveyance requires a subsequent owner to comply with the same restrictions imposed upon the original owner for the balance of the 10 year period.

(c) *Ten year restriction.* The restrictions listed in paragraphs (a) and (b) of this section shall remain in force for a period of not less than 10 years after construction completion and issuance of an occupancy permit for Youthbuild homeownership housing projects meeting the requirements of this part.

§ 585.312 Wages, labor standards, and nondiscrimination.

Applicable provisions are stated in section 456(e) of NAHA.

[61 FR 52187, Oct. 4, 1996]

§ 585.313 Labor standards.

(a) *Trainees.* Davis-Bacon prevailing wage rate requirements are not applicable to trainees on housing projects or in training programs assisted by Youthbuild grant funds, regardless of whether other Federal assistance is involved. However, where the trainees' performance of public and Indian housing work is subject to HUD-determined prevailing wage rates under section 12 of the United States Housing Act of 1937, trainees must be paid HUD-determined wage rates; as a matter of policy, the wage rates determined by HUD to apply to Youthbuild trainees will be the trainee wage rates rather than journeyperson rates.

(b) *Laborers and mechanics other than Youthbuild Trainees.* (1) All laborers and mechanics (other than Youthbuild trainees) employed by contractors or subcontractors in any construction, alteration or repair, including painting and decorating, of housing that is assisted by a Youthbuild grant shall be paid at rates not less than those prevailing on similar construction in the locality, as determined by the Secretary of Labor in accordance with the Davis-Bacon Act (40 U.S.C. 276a through 276a–5). The employment of such laborers and mechanics on assisted housing shall be subject to the provisions of the Contract Work Hours and Safety Standards Act (40 U.S.C. 327 through 333). Where these requirements

Ofc. of Asst. Secy., Comm. Planning, Develop., HUD § 585.402

are applicable, recipients, sponsors, owners, contractors and subcontractors must comply with all related Department of Labor and HUD rules, regulations and requirements.

(2) The labor standards requirements in paragraph (b)(1) of this section do not apply where a Youthbuild grant is provided solely for classroom and/or on-the-job training and supportive services for Youthbuild trainees, and the grant does not include costs for housing project development involving acquisition (including lease), rehabilitation or new construction of real properties; however, if other Federal programs provide assistance to the housing project, labor standards apply to laborers and mechanics other than Youthbuild trainees to the extent required by the other Federal programs. Applicants need to review applicable Federal regulations to determine which relevant requirements apply to their individual situations.

Subpart E—Administration

§ 585.401 Recordkeeping by recipients.

(a) Each recipient of a planning or implementation Youthbuild grant award must keep records that will facilitate an effective audit to determine compliance with program requirements and that fully disclose:

(1) The amount and disposition by the recipient of the planning or implementation Youthbuild grants received, including sufficient records that document the reasonableness, accuracy and necessity of each expenditure;

(2) The amount and disposition of proceeds, if any, from financing obtained in connection with the Youthbuild program, e.g., housing sales to eligible low-income families, property sales to other public or private entities;

(3) The total cost from all sources of funding for the Youthbuild program including all educational, training, counseling, placement, and housing activities and services;

(4) The amount and nature of any other assistance, including cash, property, services, materials, in-kind contributions or other items contributed as a condition of receiving an implementation grant;

(5) Any other proceeds received for, or otherwise used in connection with, the Youthbuild program.

(6) *Participant information.* The recipient must maintain records on each Youthbuild participant, including such information as age, high school drop out status, income level, gender, employment status, and racial and ethnic characteristics.

(7) *Housing information.* If Youthbuild grant funds are used for acquisition, architectural and engineering fees, construction, rehabilitation, operating costs or replacement reserves for housing used in a Youthbuild program, the recipient must maintain records on family size, income, and racial and ethnic characteristics of families renting or purchasing Youthbuild properties.

(8) *Relocation Assistance and Real Property Acquisition.* The recipient shall maintain records sufficient to demonstrate compliance with relocation assistance and real property acquisition requirements, as described in chapter 6 of HUD Handbook 1378, Tenant Assistance, Relocation and Real Property Acquisition. See § 585.308.

(b) Implementation grant recipients must submit reports pursuant to section 3 regulations at 24 CFR part 135.

(c) *Access by HUD and the Comptroller General.* For purposes of audit, examination, monitoring, and evaluation, each recipient must give HUD (including any duly authorized representatives and the Inspector General) and the Comptroller General of the United States (and any duly authorized representatives) access to any books, documents, papers, and records of the recipient that are pertinent to assistance received.

(Approved by the Office of Management and Budget under control number 2506–0142)

§ 585.402 Grant agreement.

(a) *General.* The recipient will provide education and job training in accordance with the requirements of this part as incorporated in a grant agreement executed by HUD and the recipient.

(b) *Enforcement.* HUD will enforce the obligations in the grant agreement through such actions as may be appropriate, including repayment of funds that have already been disbursed to the recipient.

277

§ 585.403 Reporting requirements.

(a) *Quarterly Progress Reports.* Each recipient of a Youthbuild grant must submit a report on a quarterly basis. The form and substance of the quarterly progress report will be provided to recipients. The Performance Evaluation Report noted in paragraph (b) of this section will constitute the final Quarterly Report.

(b) *Performance Evaluation Report.* Each recipient of a Youthbuild grant must submit a Performance Evaluation Report on activities undertaken and completed in accordance with the grant agreement. The form and substance of the Performance Evaluation Report shall be provided to recipients.

(Approved by the Office of Management and Budget under control number 2506–0142)

§ 585.404 Program changes.

(a) There are three basic types of changes that recipients may wish to make to their programs:

(1) Grant Agreement amendments.

(2) Material changes, which include, but are not limited to changes in housing sites, changes in significant participating parties, and changes in approved activities. All material changes require HUD approval.

(3) Self-implementing program changes, which may include changes in recipient staffing and content of curriculum. All self-implementing changes require documentation in the recipient's files.

(b) Approval for Grant Agreement amendments and material changes is contingent upon the application ranking remaining high enough after the approved change to have been competitively selected for funding in the year the application was selected.

§ 585.405 Obligation and deobligation of funds.

(a) *Obligation of funds.* When HUD and the applicant execute a grant agreement, funds are obligated to carry out approved activities consistent with § 585.205 or 585.305 of this part and in accordance with the grant agreement.

(b) *Increases.* After the initial obligation of funds, HUD will not make revisions to increase the amount obligated.

(c) *Deobligation.* (1) HUD may deobligate all or parts of grants if the grant amounts are not expended within the term of the grant or if there is a condition of default as defined in the grant agreement.

(2) HUD may award deobligated funds to applications previously submitted in response to the most recently published NOFA, and in accordance with subpart B of this part.

§ 585.406 Faith-based activities.

(a) Organizations that are religious or faith-based are eligible, on the same basis as any other organization, to participate in the Youthbuild program. Neither the Federal government nor a State or local government receiving funds under Youthbuild programs shall discriminate against an organization on the basis of the organization's religious character or affiliation.

(b) Organizations that are directly funded under the Youthbuild program may not engage in inherently religious activities, such as worship, religious instruction, or proselytization, as part of the programs or services funded under this part. If an organization conducts such activities, the activities must be offered separately, in time or location, from the programs or services funded under this part, and participation must be voluntary for the beneficiaries of the HUD-funded programs or services.

(c) A religious organization that participates in the Youthbuild Program will retain its independence from Federal, State, and local governments, and may continue to carry out its mission, including the definition, practice, and expression of its religious beliefs, provided that it does not use direct Youthbuild Program funds to support any inherently religious activities, such as worship, religious instruction, or proselytization. Among other things, faith-based organizations may use space in their facilities to provide Youthbuild Program-funded services, without removing religious art, icons, scriptures, or other religious symbols. In addition, a Youthbuild Program-funded religious organization retains its authority over its internal governance, and it may retain religious terms in its organization's name, select its board members on a religious basis, and include religious references in its organization's mission statements and other governing documents.

(d) An organization that participates in the Youthbuild program shall not, in providing program assistance, discriminate against a program beneficiary or prospective program beneficiary on the basis of religion or religious belief.

(e) Youthbuild funds may not be used for the acquisition, construction, or rehabilitation of structures to the extent that those structures are used for inherently religious activities. Youthbuild funds may be used for the acquisition, construction, or rehabilitation of structures only to the extent that those structures are used for conducting eligible activities under this part. Where a structure is used for both eligible and inherently religious activities, Youthbuild funds may not exceed the cost of those portions of the acquisition, construction, or rehabilitation that are attributable to eligible activities in accordance with the cost accounting requirements applicable to Youthbuild funds in this part. Sanctuaries, chapels, or other rooms that a Youthbuild-funded religious congregation uses as its principal place of worship, however, are ineligible for Youthbuild-funded improvements. Disposition of real property after the term of the grant, or any change in use of the property during the term of the grant, is subject to government-wide regulations governing real property disposition (see 24 CFR parts 84 and 85).

(f) If a State or local government voluntarily contributes its own funds to supplement federally funded activities, the State or local government has the option to segregate the Federal funds or commingle them. However, if the funds are commingled, this section applies to all of the commingled funds.

[68 FR 56407, Sept. 30, 2003]

Subpart F—Applicability of Other Federal Requirements

§ 585.501 Application of OMB Circulars.

(a) The policies, guidelines and requirements of OMB Circular Nos. A–87 (Cost Principles Applicable to Grants, Contracts and other Agreements with State and Local Governments) and 24 CFR part 85 (Administrative Requirements for Grants and Cooperative Agreements to State, Local and Federally Recognized Indian Tribal Governments) apply to the award, acceptance and use of assistance under the program by applicable entities, and to the remedies for non-compliance, except where inconsistent with the provisions of NAHA, other Federal statutes or this part. 24 CFR part 84 (Grants and Cooperative Agreements with Institutions of Higher Education, Hospitals, and other Nonprofit Organizations), OMB Circular A–122 (Cost Principles Applicable to Grants, Contracts and other Agreements with Nonprofit Institutions), and, as applicable, OMB Circular A–21 (Cost Principles for Educational Institutions) apply to the acceptance and use of assistance by covered organizations, except where inconsistent with the provisions of NAHA, other Federal statutes or this part. Recipients are also subject to the audit requirements of 24 CFR part 44 (Audit Requirements for State and Local Governments) and 24 CFR part 45 (Audit Requirements for Institutions of Higher Education and other Nonprofit Institutions), as applicable. HUD may perform or require additional audits as it finds necessary or appropriate.

(b) Copies of OMB Circulars may be obtained from E.O.P. Publications, Room 2200, New Executive Office Building, Washington, DC 20503, telephone (202) 395–7332. (This is not a toll-free number.) There is a limit of two free copies.

§ 585.502 Certifications.

In addition to the standard assurances of compliance with Federal rules and OMB Circulars contained in applications for Federal grant assistance, applicants must also make the following certifications:

(a) *Consolidated Plan*—(1) *Applicants that are States or units of general local government.* The applicant must have a HUD-approved Consolidated Plan in accordance with 24 CFR part 91 for the current year and must submit a certification that the proposed activities are consistent with the HUD-approved Consolidated Plan.

(2) *Applicants that are not States or units of general local government.* The applicant must submit a certification by the jurisdiction or jurisdictions in which the proposed program will be located that the applicant's proposed activities are consistent with the jurisdiction's current HUD-approved Consolidated Plan. A required certification must be made by the unit of general local government if it is required to have, or has, a Consolidated Plan. Otherwise the certification may be made by the State.

(3) The Insular Areas of Guam, the Virgin Islands, American Samoa and the Northern Mariana Islands are not required to have a Consolidated Plan or to make a Consolidate Plan certification. An application by an Indian tribe or other applicant for a Youthbuild program that will be located on a reservation of an Indian tribe does not require a certification by the tribe or State. However, where an Indian tribe or an Indian Housing Authority (IHA) is the applicant for a Youthbuild program that will not be located on a reservation, the requirement for a certification by the jurisdiction or jurisdictions in which the Youthbuild program will be located under the preceding paragraph applies.

(b) *Fair housing and equal opportunity.* A certification that the applicant is in compliance and will continue to comply with the requirements of the Fair Housing Act, title VI of the Civil Rights Act of 1964, section 504 of the Rehabilitation Act of 1973, and the Age Discrimination Act of 1975, and will affirmatively further fair housing, or, in the case of a Youthbuild application from an Indian tribe or an Indian Housing Authority (IHA), a certification that the applicant will comply with the Indian Civil Rights Act (25 U.S.C. 1301 *et seq.*), section 504 of the Rehabilitation Act of 1973, and the Age Discrimination Act of 1975.

(c) *Employment opportunities.* A certification that the applicant will comply with the requirements of section 3 of the Housing and Urban Development Act of 1968 (12 U.S.C. 17017), as implemented by 24 CFR part 135. Section 3 requires that employment and other economic opportunities generated by HUD assisted housing and community development programs shall, to the greatest extent feasible, be directed toward section 3 residents and business concerns.

(d) *Anti-lobbying.* In accordance with the disclosure requirements and prohibitions of section 319 of the Department of Interior and Related Agencies Appropriations Act for Fiscal Year 1990 (31 U.S.C. 1352) (The Byrd Amendment) and the implementing regulations at 24 CFR part 87, applicants for and recipients of assistance exceeding $100,000 must certify that no Federal funds have been or will be spent on lobbying activities in connection with the assistance. Applicants and recipients must also disclose where non-appropriated funds have been spent or committed for lobbying activities if those activities would be prohibited if paid with appropriated funds. Substantial monetary penalties may be imposed for failure to file the required certification or disclosure.

(e) *Relocation assistance and real property acquisition.* A certification that the applicant will comply with the requirements of the Uniform Relocation Assistance and Real Property Acquisition Policies Act of 1970, as amended (URA), and implementing regulations at 49 CFR part 24 and HUD Handbook 1378, Tenant Assistance, Relocation and Real Property Acquisition. See § 585.308.

(f) *Use of housing.* A certification that the housing to be produced in conjunction with the Youthbuild program is to be provided for the homeless and low- and very low-income families.

(g) *Lead-based paint.* A certification that the applicant will comply with the requirements of the Lead-Based Paint Poisoning Prevention Act (42 U.S.C. 4821–4846), the Residential Lead-Based Paint Hazard Reduction Act of 1992 (42 U.S.C. 4851–4856), and implementing regulations at part 35, subparts A, B, J, K, and R of this title.

(h) *State and local standards.* A certification that all educational programs and activities supported with funds provided under this subtitle shall be consistent with applicable State and local educational standards. Standards and procedures with respect to the awarding of academic credit and certifying educational attainment in such programs shall be consistent with applicable State and local educational standards.

(i) *Labor standards.* A certification that the applicant and related parties will comply with the provisions of the Davis-Bacon Act, as amended (40 U.S.C. 276a through 276a-5), the Contract Work Hours and Safety Standards Act (40 U.S.C. 327 through 333), and HUD Handbook 1344.1, Revision 1, Federal Labor Standards in Housing and Community Development Programs, as applicable, available from the Office of Assistant to the Secretary for Labor Relations, room 7118, 451 Seventh Street, SW., Washington, DC 20410; Telephone (202) 708–0370; FAX, (202) 619–8022; TDD, (202) 708–1455. (These are not toll-free numbers).

(Approved by the Office of Management and Budget under control number 2506–0142)

[60 FR 9737, Feb. 21, 1995, as amended at 64 FR 50227, Sept. 15, 1999; 72 FR 73496, Dec. 27, 2007]

§ 585.503 Conflict of interest.

(a)(1) In addition to the conflict of interest requirements in 24 CFR parts 84 and 85, no person who is an employee, agent, consultant, officer, or elected or appointed official of the recipient or cooperating entity named in the application and who exercises or has exercised any functions or responsibilities with respect to assisted activities, or who is in a position to participate in a decision-making process or gain inside information with regard to such activities, may obtain a financial interest or benefit from the activity, or have an interest in any contract, subcontract, or agreement with respect thereto, or the proceeds thereunder, either for himself or herself or for those with whom he or she has family or business ties, during his or her tenure or for one year thereafter, except that a resident of an eligible property may acquire an ownership interest.

(2) *Exception.* HUD may grant an exception to the exclusion in paragraph (a)(1) of this section on a case-by-case basis when it determines that such an exception will serve to further the purposes of the Youthbuild program. An exception may be considered only after the applicant or recipient has provided a disclosure of the nature of the conflict, accompanied by an assurance that there has been public disclosure of the conflict, a description of how the public disclosure was made, and an opinion of the applicant's or recipient's attorney that the interest for which the exception is sought would not violate State or local law. In determining whether to grant a requested exception, HUD will consider the cumulative effect of the following factors, where applicable:

(i) Whether the exception would provide a significant cost benefit or an essential degree of expertise to the Youthbuild program that would otherwise not be available;

(ii) Whether an opportunity was provided for open competitive bidding or negotiation;

(iii) Whether the person affected is a member of a group or class intended to be the beneficiaries of the activity and the exception will permit such person to receive generally the same interests or benefits as are being made available or provided to the group or class;

(iv) Whether the affected person has withdrawn from his or her functions or responsibilities, or the decision-making process, with respect to the specific activity in question;

(v) Whether the interest or benefit was present before the affected person was in a position as described in paragraph (a)(2) of this section;

(vi) Whether undue hardship will result either to the applicant, recipient, or the person affected when weighed against the public interest served by avoiding the prohibited conflict; and

(vii) Any other relevant considerations.

(b) [Reserved]

§ 585.504 Use of debarred, suspended, or ineligible contractors.

The provisions of 2 CFR part 2424 apply to the employment of, engagement of services from, awarding of contracts to, or funding of any contractors or subcontractors during any period of debarment, suspension, or placement in ineligibility status.

[72 FR 73496, Dec. 27, 2007]

PART 586—REVITALIZING BASE CLOSURE COMMUNITIES AND COMMUNITY ASSISTANCE—COMMUNITY REDEVELOPMENT AND HOMELESS ASSISTANCE

Sec.
586.1   Purpose.
586.5   Definitions.
586.10 Applicability.
586.15 Waivers and extensions of deadlines.
586.20 Overview of the process.
586.25 HUD's negotiations and consultations with the LRA.
586.30 LRA application.
586.35 HUD's review of the application.
586.40 Adverse determinations.
586.45 Disposal of buildings and property.

AUTHORITY: 10 U.S.C. 2687 note; 42 U.S.C. 3535(d).

SOURCE: 62 FR 37479, July 11, 1997, unless otherwise noted.

§ 586.1 Purpose.

This part implements the Base Closure Community Redevelopment and Homeless Assistance Act, as amended (10 U.S.C. 2687 note), which instituted a new community-based process for addressing the needs of the homeless at base closure and realignment sites. In this process, Local Redevelopment Authorities (LRAs) identify interest from homeless providers in installation property and develop a redevelopment plan for the installation that balances the economic redevelopment and other development needs of the communities in the vicinity of the installation with the needs of the homeless in those communities. The Department of Housing and Urban Development (HUD) reviews the LRA's plan to see that an appropriate balance is achieved. This part also implements the process for identifying interest from State and local entities for property under a public benefit transfer. The LRA is responsible for concurrently identifying interest from homeless providers and State and local entities interested in property under a public benefit transfer.

§ 586.5 Definitions.

As used in this part:

CERCLA. Comprehensive Environmental Response, Compensation, and Liability Act (42 U.S.C. 9601 et seq.).

Communities in the vicinity of the installation. The communities that constitute the political jurisdictions (other than the State in which the installation is located) that comprise the LRA for the installation. If no LRA is formed at the local level, and the State is serving in that capacity, the communities in the vicinity of the installation are deemed to be those political jurisdiction(s) (other than the State) in which the installation is located.

Consolidated Plan. The plan prepared in accordance with the requirements of 24 CFR part 91.

Continuum of care system.

(1) A comprehensive homeless assistance system that includes:

(i) A system of outreach and assessment for determining the needs and condition of an individual or family who is homeless, or whether assistance is necessary to prevent an individual or family from becoming homeless;

(ii) Emergency shelters with appropriate supportive services to help ensure that homeless individuals and families receive adequate emergency shelter and referral to necessary service providers or housing finders;

(iii) Transitional housing with appropriate supportive services to help those homeless individuals and families who are not prepared to make the transition to independent living;

(iv) Housing with or without supportive services that has no established limitation on the amount of time of residence to help meet long-term needs of homeless individuals and families; and

(v) Any other activity that clearly meets an identified need of the homeless and fills a gap in the continuum of care.

(2) Supportive services are services that enable homeless persons and families to move through the continuum of care toward independent living. These services include, but are not limited to, case management, housing counseling, job training and placement, primary health care, mental health services, substance abuse treatment, child care, transportation, emergency food and clothing, family violence services, education services, moving services, assistance in obtaining entitlements, and

referral to veterans services and legal services.

Day. One calendar day including weekends and holidays.

DoD. Department of Defense.

HHS. Department of Health and Human Services.

Homeless person. (1) An individual or family who lacks a fixed, regular, and adequate nighttime residence; and

(2) An individual or family who has a primary nighttime residence that is:

(i) A supervised publicly or privately operated shelter designed to provide temporary living accommodations (including welfare hotels, congregate shelters and transitional housing for the mentally ill);

(ii) An institution that provides a temporary residence for individuals intended to be institutionalized; or

(iii) A public or private place not designed for, or ordinarily used as, a regular sleeping accommodation for human beings.

(3) This term does not include any individual imprisoned or otherwise detained under an Act of the Congress or a State law.

HUD. Department of Housing and Urban Development.

Installation. A base, camp, post, station, yard, center, homeport facility for any ship or other activity under the jurisdiction of DoD, including any leased facility, that is approved for closure or realignment under the Base Closure and Realignment Act of 1988 (Pub. L. 100–526), as amended, or the Defense Base Closure and Realignment Act of 1990 (Pub. L. 101–510), as amended (both at 10 U.S.C. 2687, note).

Local redevelopment authority (LRA). Any authority or instrumentality established by State or local government and recognized by the Secretary of Defense, through the Office of Economic Adjustment, as the entity responsible for developing the redevelopment plan with respect to the installation or for directing implementation of the plan.

NEPA. National Environmental Policy Act of 1969 (42 U.S.C. 4320).

OEA. Office of Economic Adjustment, Department of Defense.

Private nonprofit organization. An organization, no part of the net earnings of which inures to the benefit of any member, founder, contributor, or individual; that has a voluntary board; that has an accounting system or has designated an entity that will maintain a functioning accounting system for the organization in accordance with generally accepted accounting procedures; and that practices nondiscrimination in the provision of assistance.

Public benefit transfer. The transfer of surplus military property for a specified public purpose at up to a 100 percent discount in accordance with 40 U.S.C. 471 et seq., or 49 U.S.C. 47151–47153.

Redevelopment plan. A plan that is agreed to by the LRA with respect to the installation and provides for the reuse or redevelopment of the real property and personal property of the installation that is available for such reuse and redevelopment as a result of the closure of the installation.

Representative(s) of the homeless. A State or local government agency or private nonprofit organization, including a homeless assistance planning board, that provides or proposes to provide services to the homeless.

Substantially equivalent. Property that is functionally suitable to substitute for property referred to in an approved Title V application. For example, if the representative of the homeless had an approved Title V application for a building that would accommodate 100 homeless persons in an emergency shelter, the replacement facility would also have to accommodate 100 at a comparable cost for renovation.

Substantially equivalent funding. Sufficient funding to acquire a substantially equivalent facility.

Surplus property. Any excess property not required for the needs and the discharge of the responsibilities of all Federal Agencies. Authority to make this determination, after screening with all Federal Agencies, rests with the Military Departments.

Title V. Title V of the Stewart B. McKinney Homeless Assistance Act of 1987 (42 U.S.C 11411) as amended by the National Defense Authorization Act for Fiscal Year 1994 (Pub. L. 103–160).

Urban county. A county within a metropolitan area as defined at 24 CFR 570.3.

§ 586.10 Applicability.

(a) *General.* This part applies to all installations that are approved for closure/realignment by the President and Congress under Pub. L. 101–510 after October 25, 1994.

(b) *Request for inclusion under this process.* This part also applies to installations that were approved for closure/realignment under either Public Law 100–526 or Public Law 101–510 prior to October 25, 1994 and for which an LRA submitted a request for inclusion under this part to DoD by December 24, 1994. A list of such requests was published in the FEDERAL REGISTER on May 30, 1995 (60 FR 28089).

(1) For installations with Title V applications pending but not approved before October 25, 1994, the LRA shall consider and specifically address any application for use of buildings and property to assist the homeless that were received by HHS prior to October 25, 1994, and were pending with the Secretary of HHS on that date. These pending requests shall be addressed in the LRA's homeless assistance submission.

(2) For installations with Title V applications approved before October 25, 1994 where there is an approved Title V application, but property has not been assigned or otherwise disposed of by the Military Department, the LRA must ensure that its homeless assistance submission provides the Title V applicant with:

(i) The property requested;

(ii) Properties, on or off the installation, that are substantially equivalent to those requested;

(iii) Sufficient funding to acquire such substantially equivalent properties;

(iv) Services and activities that meet the needs identified in the application; or

(v) A combination of the properties, funding, and services and activities described in § 586.10(b)(2)(i) through (iv).

(c) *Revised Title V process.* All other installations approved for closure or realignment under either Public Law 100–526 or Public Law 101–510 prior to October 25, 1994, for which there was no request for consideration under this part, are covered by the process stipulated under Title V. Buildings or property that were transferred or leased for homeless use under Title V prior to October 25, 1994, may not be reconsidered under this part.

§ 586.15 Waivers and extensions of deadlines.

(a) After consultation with the LRA and HUD, and upon a finding that it is in the interest of the communities affected by the closure/realignment of the installation, DoD, through the Director of the Office of Economic Adjustment, may extend or postpone any deadline contained in this part.

(b) Upon completion of a determination and finding of good cause, and except for deadlines and actions required on the part of DoD, HUD may waive any provision of §§ 586.20 through 586.45 in any particular case, subject only to statutory limitations.

§ 586.20 Overview of the process.

(a) *Recognition of the LRA.* As soon as practicable after the list of installations recommended for closure or realignment is approved, DoD, through OEA, will recognize an LRA for the installation. Upon recognition, OEA shall publish the name, address, and point of contact for the LRA in the FEDERAL REGISTER and in a newspaper of general circulation in the communities in the vicinity of the installation.

(b) *Responsibilities of the Military Department.* The Military Department shall make installation properties available to other DoD components and Federal agencies in accordance with the procedures set out at 32 CFR part 175. The Military Department will keep the LRA informed of other Federal interest in the property during this process. Upon completion of this process the Military Department will notify HUD and either the LRA, or the Chief Executive Officer of the State, as appropriate, and publish a list of surplus property on the installation that will be available for reuse in the FEDERAL REGISTER and a newspaper of general circulation in the communities in the vicinity of the installation.

(c) *Responsibilities of the LRA.* The LRA should begin to conduct outreach efforts with respect to the installation as soon as is practicable after the date of approval of closure/realignment of

Ofc. of Asst. Secy., Comm. Planning, Develop., HUD §586.20

the installation. The local reuse planning process must begin no later than the date of the Military Department's FEDERAL REGISTER publication of available property described at §586.20(b). For those installations that began the process described in this part prior to August 17, 1995, HUD will, on a case by case basis, determine whether the statutory requirements have been fulfilled and whether any additional requirements listed in this part should be required. Upon the FEDERAL REGISTER publication described in §586.20(b), the LRA shall:

(1) Publish, within 30 days, in a newspaper of general circulation in the communities in the vicinity of the installation, the time period during which the LRA will receive notices of interest from State and local governments, representatives of the homeless, and other interested parties. This publication shall include the name, address, telephone number and the point of contact for the LRA who can provide information on the prescribed form and contents of the notices of interest. The LRA shall notify DoD of the deadline specified for receipt of notices of interest. LRAs are strongly encouraged to make this publication as soon as possible within the permissible 30 day period in order to expedite the closure process.

(i) In addition, the LRA has the option to conduct an informal solicitation of notices of interest from public and non-profit entities interested in obtaining property via a public benefit transfer other than a homeless assistance conveyance under either 40 U.S.C. 471 *et seq.*, or 49 U.S.C. 47151–47153. As part of such a solicitation, the LRA may wish to request that interested entities submit a description of the proposed use to the LRA and the sponsoring Federal agency.

(ii) For all installations selected for closure or realignment prior to 1995 that elected to proceed under Public Law 103–421, the LRA shall accept notices of interest for not less than 30 days.

(iii) For installations selected for closure or realignment in 1995 or thereafter, notices of interest shall be accepted for a minimum of 90 days and not more than 180 days after the LRA's publication under §586.20(c)(1).

(2) Prescribe the form and contents of notices of interest.

(i) The LRA may not release to the public any information regarding the capacity of the representative of the homeless to carry out its program, a description of the organization, or its financial plan for implementing the program, without the consent of the representative of the homeless concerned, unless such release is authorized under Federal law and under the law of the State and communities in which the installation concerned is located. The identity of the representative of the homeless may be disclosed.

(ii) The notices of interest from representatives of the homeless must include:

(A) A description of the homeless assistance program proposed, including the purposes to which the property or facility will be put, which may include uses such as supportive services, job and skills training, employment programs, shelters, transitional housing or housing with no established limitation on the amount of time of residence, food and clothing banks, treatment facilities, or any other activity which clearly meets an identified need of the homeless and fills a gap in the continuum of care;

(B) A description of the need for the program;

(C) A description of the extent to which the program is or will be coordinated with other homeless assistance programs in the communities in the vicinity of the installation;

(D) Information about the physical requirements necessary to carry out the program including a description of the buildings and property at the installation that are necessary to carry out the program;

(E) A description of the financial plan, the organization, and the organizational capacity of the representative of the homeless to carry out the program; and

(F) An assessment of the time required to start carrying out the program.

(iii) The notices of interest from entities other than representatives of the homeless should specify the name of the entity and specific interest in property or facilities along with a description of the planned use.

(3) In addition to the notice required under § 586.20(c)(1), undertake outreach efforts to representatives of the homeless by contacting local government officials and other persons or entities that may be interested in assisting the homeless within the vicinity of the installation.

(i) The LRA may invite persons and organizations identified on the HUD list of representatives of the homeless and any other representatives of the homeless with which the LRA is familiar, operating in the vicinity of the installation, to the workshop described in § 586.20(c)(3)(ii).

(ii) The LRA, in coordination with the Military Department and HUD, shall conduct at least one workshop where representatives of the homeless have an opportunity to:

(A) Learn about the closure/realignment and disposal process;

(B) Tour the buildings and properties available either on or off the installation;

(C) Learn about the LRA's process and schedule for receiving notices of interest as guided by § 586.20(c)(2); and

(D) Learn about any known land use constraints affecting the available property and buildings.

(iii) The LRA should meet with representatives of the homeless that express interest in discussing possible uses for these properties to alleviate gaps in the continuum of care.

(4) Consider various properties in response to the notices of interest. The LRA may consider property that is located off the installation.

(5) Develop an application, including the redevelopment plan and homeless assistance submission, explaining how the LRA proposes to address the needs of the homeless. This application shall consider the notices of interest received from State and local governments, representatives of the homeless, and other interested parties. This shall include, but not be limited to, entities eligible for public benefit transfers under either 40 U.S.C. 471 et seq., or 49 U.S.C. 47151–47153; representatives of the homeless; commercial, industrial, and residential development interests;

and other interests. From the deadline date for receipt of notices of interest described at § 586.20(c)(1), the LRA shall have 270 days to complete and submit the LRA application to the appropriate Military Department and HUD. The application requirements are described at § 586.30.

(6) Make the draft application available to the public for review and comment periodically during the process of developing the application. The LRA must conduct at least one public hearing on the application prior to its submission to HUD and the appropriate Military Department. A summary of the public comments received during the process of developing the application shall be included in the application when it is submitted.

(d) *Public benefit transfer screening.* The LRA should, while conducting its outreach efforts, work with the Federal agencies that sponsor public benefit transfers under either 40 U.S.C. 471 *et seq.* or 49 U.S.C. 47151–47153. Those agencies can provide a list of parties in the vicinity of the installation that might be interested in and eligible for public benefit transfers. The LRA should make a reasonable effort to inform such parties of the availability of the property and incorporate their interests within the planning process. Actual recipients of property are to be determined by the sponsoring Federal agency. The Military Departments shall notify sponsoring Federal agencies about property that is available based on the community redevelopment plan and keep the LRA apprised of any expressions of interest. Such expressions of interest are not required to be incorporated into the redevelopment plan, but must be considered.

§ 586.25 HUD's negotiations and consultations with the LRA.

HUD may negotiate and consult with the LRA before and during the course of preparation of the LRA's application and during HUD's review thereof with a view toward avoiding any preliminary determination that the application does not meet any requirement of this part. LRAs are encouraged to contact HUD for a list of persons and organizations that are representatives of the

§ 586.30 LRA application.

(a) *Redevelopment plan.* A copy of the redevelopment plan shall be part of the application.

(b) *Homeless assistance submission.* This component of the application shall include the following:

(1) Information about homelessness in the communities in the vicinity of the installation.

(i) A list of all the political jurisdictions which comprise the LRA.

(ii) A description of the unmet need in the continuum of care system within each political jurisdiction, which should include information about any gaps that exist in the continuum of care for particular homeless subpopulations. The source for this information shall depend upon the size and nature of the political jurisdictions(s) that comprise the LRA. LRAs representing:

(A) Political jurisdictions that are required to submit a Consolidated Plan shall include a copy of their Homeless and Special Needs Population Table (table 1), Priority Homeless Needs Assessment Table (table 2), and narrative description thereof from that Consolidated Plan, including the inventory of facilities and services that assist the homeless in the jurisdiction.

(B) Political jurisdictions that are part of an urban county that is required to submit a Consolidated Plan shall include a copy of their Homeless and Special Needs Population Table (table 1), Priority Homeless Needs Assessment Table (table 2), and narrative description thereof from that Consolidated Plan, including the inventory of facilities and services that assist the homeless in the jurisdiction. In addition, the LRA shall explain what portion of the homeless population and subpopulations described in the Consolidated Plan are attributable to the political jurisdiction it represents.

(C) A political jurisdiction not described by § 586.30(b)(1)(ii)(A) or § 586.30(b)(1)(ii)(B) shall submit a narrative description of what it perceives to be the homeless population within the jurisdiction and a brief inventory of the facilities and services that assist homeless persons and families within the jurisdiction. LRAs that represent these jurisdictions are not required to conduct surveys of the homeless population.

(2) Notices of interest proposing assistance to homeless persons and/or families.

(i) A description of the proposed activities to be carried out on or off the installation and a discussion of how these activities meet a portion or all of the needs of the homeless by addressing the gaps in the continuum of care. The activities need not be limited to expressions of interest in property, but may also include discussions of how economic redevelopment may benefit the homeless;

(ii) A copy of each notice of interest from representatives of the homeless for use of buildings and property and a description of the manner in which the LRA's application addresses the need expressed in each notice of interest. If the LRA determines that a particular notice of interest should not be awarded property, an explanation of why the LRA determined not to support that notice of interest, the reasons for which may include the impact of the program contained in the notice of interest on the community as described in § 586.30(b)(2)(iii); and

(iii) A description of the impact that the implemented redevelopment plan will have on the community. This shall include information on how the LRA's redevelopment plan might impact the character of existing neighborhoods adjacent to the properties proposed to be used to assist the homeless and should discuss alternative plans. Impact on schools, social services, transportation, infrastructure, and concentration of minorities and/or low income persons shall also be discussed.

(3) Legally binding agreements for buildings, property, funding, and/or services.

(i) A copy of the legally binding agreements that the LRA proposes to enter into with the representative(s) of the homeless selected by the LRA to implement homeless programs that fill gaps in the existing continuum of care. The legally binding agreements shall provide for a process for negotiating alternative arrangements in the event that an environmental analysis conducted under § 586.45(b) indicates that any property identified for transfer in the agreement is not suitable for the intended purpose. Where the balance determined in accordance with § 586.30(b)(4) provides for the use of installation property as a homeless assistance facility, legally binding agreements must provide for the reversion or transfer, either to the LRA or to another entity or entities, of the buildings and property in the event they cease to be used for the homeless. In cases where the balance proposed by the LRA does not include the use of buildings or property on the installation, the legally binding agreements need not be tied to the use of specific real property and need not include a reverter clause. Legally binding agreements shall be accompanied by a legal opinion of the chief legal advisor of the LRA or political jurisdiction or jurisdictions which will be executing the legally binding agreements that the legally binding agreements, when executed, will constitute legal, valid, binding, and enforceable obligations on the parties thereto;

(ii) A description of how buildings, property, funding, and/or services either on or off the installation will be used to fill some of the gaps in the current continuum of care system and an explanation of the suitability of the buildings and property for that use; and

(iii) Information on the availability of general services such as transportation, police, and fire protection, and a discussion of infrastructure such as water, sewer, and electricity in the vicinity of the proposed homeless activity at the installation.

(4) An assessment of the balance with economic and other development needs.

(i) An assessment of the manner in which the application balances the expressed needs of the homeless and the needs of the communities comprising the LRA for economic redevelopment and other development; and

(ii) An explanation of how the LRA's application is consistent with the appropriate Consolidated Plan(s) or any other existing housing, social service, community, economic, or other development plans adopted by the jurisdictions in the vicinity of the installation.

(5) A description of the outreach undertaken by the LRA. The LRA shall explain how the outreach requirements described at § 586.20(c)(1) and § 586.20(c)(3) have been fulfilled. This explanation shall include a list of the representatives of the homeless the LRA contacted during the outreach process.

(c) *Public comments.* The LRA application shall include the materials described at § 586.20(c)(6). These materials shall be prefaced with an overview of the citizen participation process observed in preparing the application.

§ 586.35 **HUD's review of the application.**

(a) *Timing.* HUD shall complete a review of each application no later than 60 days after its receipt of a completed application.

(b) *Standards of review.* The purpose of the review is to determine whether the application is complete and, with respect to the expressed interest and requests of representatives of the homeless, whether the application:

(1) *Need.* Takes into consideration the size and nature of the homeless population in the communities in the vicinity of the installation, the availability of existing services in such communities to meet the needs of the homeless in such communities, and the suitability of the buildings and property covered by the application for use and needs of the homeless in such communities. HUD will take into consideration the size and nature of the installation in reviewing the needs of the homeless population in the communities in the vicinity of the installation.

(2) *Impact of notices of interest.* Takes into consideration any economic impact of the homeless assistance under the plan on the communities in the vicinity of the installation, including:

(i) Whether the plan is feasible in light of demands that would be placed on available social services, police and fire protection, and infrastructure in the community; and,

(ii) Whether the selected notices of interest are consistent with the Consolidated Plan(s) or any other existing housing, social service, community, economic, or other development plans adopted by the political jurisdictions in the vicinity of the installation.

(3) *Legally binding agreements.* Specifies the manner in which the buildings, property, funding, and/or services on or off the installation will be made available for homeless assistance purposes. HUD will review each legally binding agreement to verify that:

(i) They include all the documents legally required to complete the transactions necessary to realize the homeless use(s) described in the application;

(ii) They include all appropriate terms and conditions;

(iii) They address the full range of contingencies including those described at § 586.30(b)(3)(i);

(iv) They stipulate that the buildings, property, funding, and/or services will be made available to the representatives of the homeless in a timely fashion; and

(v) They are accompanied by a legal opinion of the chief legal advisor of the LRA or political jurisdiction or jurisdictions which will be executing the legally binding agreements that the legally binding agreements will, when executed, constitute legal, valid, binding, and enforceable obligations on the parties thereto.

(4) *Balance.* Balances in an appropriate manner a portion or all of the needs of the communities in the vicinity of the installation for economic redevelopment and other development with the needs of the homeless in such communities.

(5) *Outreach.* Was developed in consultation with representatives of the homeless and the homeless assistance planning boards, if any, in the communities in the vicinity of the installation and whether the outreach requirements described at § 586.20(c)(1) and § 586.20(c)(3) have been fulfilled by the LRA.

(c) *Notice of determination.* (1) HUD shall, no later than the 60th day after its receipt of the application, unless such deadline is extended pursuant to § 586.15(a), send written notification both to DoD and the LRA of its preliminary determination that the application meets or fails to meet the requirements of § 586.35(b). If the application fails to meet the requirements, HUD will send the LRA:

(i) A summary of the deficiencies in the application;

(ii) An explanation of the determination; and

(iii) A statement of how the LRA must address the determinations.

(2) In the event that no application is submitted and no extension is requested as of the deadline specified in § 586.20(c)(5), and the State does not accept within 30 days a DoD written request to become recognized as the LRA, the absence of such application will trigger an adverse determination by HUD effective on the date of the lapsed deadline. Under these conditions, HUD will follow the process described at § 586.40.

(d) *Opportunity to cure.* (1) The LRA shall have 90 days from its receipt of the notice of preliminary determination under § 586.35(c)(1) within which to submit to HUD and DoD a revised application which addresses the determinations listed in the notice. Failure to submit a revised application shall result in a final determination, effective 90 days from the LRA's receipt of the preliminary determination, that the redevelopment plan fails to meet the requirements of § 586.35(b).

(2) HUD shall, within 30 days of its receipt of the LRA's resubmission, send written notification of its final determination of whether the application meets the requirements of § 586.35(b) to both DOD and the LRA.

§ 586.40 Adverse determinations.

(a) *Review and consultation.* If the resubmission fails to meet the requirements of § 586.35(b), or if no resubmission is received, HUD will review the original application, including the notices of interest submitted by representatives of the homeless. In addition, in such instances or when no original application has been submitted, HUD:

(1) Shall consult with the representatives of the homeless, if any, for purposes of evaluating the continuing interest of such representatives in the use of buildings or property at the installation to assist the homeless;

(2) May consult with the applicable Military Department regarding the

§ 586.45

suitability of the buildings and property at the installation for use to assist the homeless; and

(3) May consult with representatives of the homeless and other parties as necessary.

(b) *Notice of decision.* (1) Within 90 days of receipt of an LRA's revised application which HUD determines does not meet the requirements of § 586.35(b), HUD shall, based upon its reviews and consultations under § 586.40(a):

(i) Notify DoD and the LRA of the buildings and property at the installation that HUD determines are suitable for use to assist the homeless; and

(ii) Notify DoD and the LRA of the extent to which the revised redevelopment plan meets the criteria set forth in § 586.35(b).

(2) In the event that an LRA does not submit a revised redevelopment plan under § 586.35(d), HUD shall, based upon its reviews and consultations under § 586.40(a), notify DoD and the LRA of the buildings and property at the installation that HUD determines are suitable for use to assist the homeless, either

(i) Within 190 days after HUD sends its notice of preliminary adverse determination under § 586.35(c)(1), if an LRA has not submitted a revised redevelopment plan; or

(ii) Within 390 days after the Military Department's FEDERAL REGISTER publication of available property under § 586.20(b), if no redevelopment plan has been received and no extension has been approved.

§ 586.45 Disposal of buildings and property.

(a) *Public benefit transfer screening.* Not later than the LRA's submission of its redevelopment plan to DoD and HUD, the Military Department will conduct an official public benefit transfer screening in accordance with the Federal Property Management Regulations (41 CFR part 101–47.303–2) based upon the uses identified in the redevelopment plan. Federal sponsoring agencies shall notify eligible applicants that any request for property must be consistent with the uses identified in the redevelopment plan. At the request of the LRA, the Military Department may conduct the official State and local public benefit screening at any time after the publication of available property described at § 586.20(b).

(b) *Environmental analysis.* Prior to disposal of any real property, the Military Department shall, consistent with NEPA and section 2905 of the Defense Base Closure and Realignment Act of 1990, as amended (10 U.S.C. 2687 *note*), complete an environmental impact analysis of all reasonable disposal alternatives. The Military Department shall consult with the LRA throughout the environmental impact analysis process to ensure both that the LRA is provided the most current environmental information available concerning the installation, and that the Military Department receives the most current information available concerning the LRA's redevelopment plans for the installation.

(c) *Disposal.* Upon receipt of a notice of approval of an application from HUD under § 586.35(c)(1) or § 586.35(d)(2), DoD shall dispose of buildings and property in accordance with the record of decision or other decision document prepared under § 586.45(b). Disposal of buildings and property to be used as homeless assistance facilities shall be to either the LRA or directly to the representative(s) of the homeless and shall be without consideration. Upon receipt of a notice from HUD under § 586.40(b), DoD will dispose of the buildings and property at the installation in consultation with HUD and the LRA.

(d) *LRA's responsibility.* The LRA shall be responsible for the implementation of and compliance with legally binding agreements under the application.

(e) *Reversions to the LRA.* If a building or property reverts to the LRA under a legally binding agreement under the application, the LRA shall take appropriate actions to secure, to the maximum extent practicable, the utilization of the building or property by other homeless representatives to assist the homeless. An LRA may not be required to utilize the building or property to assist the homeless.

PART 590—URBAN HOMESTEADING

Sec.
590.1 General.
590.3 [Reserved]
590.5 Definitions.
590.7 Program requirements.
590.9–590.18 [Reserved]
590.19 Use of section 810 funds.
590.21 [Reserved]
590.23 Program close-out.
590.25 Retention of records.
590.27 Audit.
590.29 HUD review of LUHA performance.
590.31 Corrective and remedial action.

AUTHORITY: 12 U.S.C. 1706e; 42 U.S.C. 3535(d).

SOURCE: 54 FR 23937, June 2, 1989, unless otherwise noted.

§ 590.1 General.

This part applies to the completion of activities remaining under the Urban Homesteading Program authorized under section 810(b) of the Housing and Community Development Act of 1974 (12 U.S.C. 1706e). Authority to reimburse Federal agencies for transfer of additional properties to LUHAs under this part was repealed effective October 1, 1991.

[61 FR 7062, Feb. 23, 1996]

§ 590.3 [Reserved]

§ 590.5 Definitions.

Act means section 810 of the Housing and Community Development Act of 1974, as amended from time to time.

Applicant means any State or unit of general local government that applies for HUD approval of a local urban homesteading program under these regulations.

Homesteader means an individual or family that participates in a local urban homesteading program by agreeing to rehabilitate and occupy a property in accordance with § 590.7(b)(5).

Local urban homesteading agency (LUHA) means a State, a unit of general local government, or a public agency or qualified community organization designated in accordance with § 590.7(c) by a State or a unit of general local government.

Local urban homesteading program means the operating procedures and requirements developed by a LUHA and approved by HUD in accordance with this part for selecting and conveying federally-owned properties to qualified homesteaders.

Low-income families means those families and individuals whose adjusted incomes do not exceed 80 per centum of the median income for the area, as determined by the Secretary under section 3(b)(2) of the United States Housing Act of 1937. Under the provision of 24 CFR part 813, the Secretary's income limits for this purpose are updated annually and are are available from the Housing Management Division in HUD field offices.

Qualified community organization has the meaning specified in § 590.7(c)(4).

Section 810 funds means funds available to reimburse HUD, FmHA, VA, or RTC (as applicable) for federally-owned property transferred to LUHAs in accordance with this part.

State means any State of the United States, any instrumentality of a State approved by the Governor, and the Commonwealth of Puerto Rico.

Unit of general local government means any city, county, town, township, parish, village, or other general purpose political subdivision of a State, Guam, the Virgin Islands, or American Samoa, or any general purpose political subdivision thereof; the District of Columbia; the Trust Territory of the Pacific Islands; and Indian tribes, bands, groups, and nations of the United States, including Alaska Indians, Aleuts, and Eskimos.

Urban homesteading neighborhood means any geographic area approved by HUD for the conduct of a local urban homesteading program that meets the requirements of this part.

[54 FR 23937, June 2, 1989, as amended at 54 FR 39525, Sept. 27, 1989; 56 FR 6808, Feb. 20, 1991; 61 FR 5211, Feb. 9, 1996; 61 FR 7062, Feb. 23, 1996]

§ 590.7 Program requirements.

(a) [Reserved]

(b) *Development of local urban homesteading program.* The applicant shall develop, in compliance with this part, a local urban homesteading program containing the following major elements:

(1) *Selection and management of properties.* The program shall include procedures for selecting federally-owned

§ 590.7

properties suitable for homesteading and for managing the properties before conditional conveyance to homesteaders. The program shall also provide that, by accepting title to a property under this part, the LUHA assumes liability for injury or damage to persons or property by reason of a defect in the dwelling, its equipment or appurtenances, or for any other reason related to ownership of the property.

(2) *Homesteader selection.* The program shall include equitable procedures for homesteader selection which:

(i) Exclude prospective homesteaders who own other residential property;

(ii) Take into account a prospective homesteader's capacity to make or cause to be made the repairs and improvements required under the homesteader agreement, including the capacity to contribute a substantial amount of labor to the rehabilitation process, or to obtain assistance from private sources, community organizations, or other sources;

(iii) Provide that membership in, or other ties to, any private organization (including a qualified community organization) may not be made a factor affecting selection as a homesteader;

(iv) Include locally adopted criteria reasonably matching family size to the number of bedrooms in each property for which a homesteader is being selected, provided that a prospective homesteader who is a one person household shall not be permitted to receive a property having more than two bedrooms, unless there are no larger households on the waiting list, notwithstanding the relative standing of the respective households under the low-income priority (see § 590.7(b)(2)(v)).

(v) Provide that, before a property is offered to other prospective homesteaders who are eligible, the property will be offered to eligible low-income families, except that properties obtained under the RTC's Affordable Housing Disposition Program (12 CFR part 1609) must be transferred to low-income families; and

(vi) Include other reasonable selection criteria which are consistent with this § 590.7(b)(2) and which shall be specified in the applicant's application pursuant to § 590.11(a) and approved by HUD under § 590.13. Such selection criteria may include preferences for the selection of neighborhood residents or other local residents, but only to the extent that they are not inconsistent with this section and with affirmative marketing objectives under § 590.11(d)(5)(ii). Such preferences based on residential location may not be based upon the length of time the prospective homesteader has resided in the jurisdiction or the neighborhood. Also, persons who are employed, or who have been notified that they have been hired, in the jurisdiction shall be extended any preference available to current residents.

(3) *Conditional conveyance.* The program shall provide for the conditional conveyance of federally-owned properties to homesteaders without any substantial consideration within one year, or less, of title transfer to the LUHA, unless otherwise approved by HUD in writing prior to the transfer.

(4) *Financing.* The program shall provide procedures for the LUHA to undertake, or to assist the homesteader in arranging, financing for the rehabilitation required under the homesteader agreement. Where direct Federal loans under section 312 of the Housing Act of 1964 (42 USC 1452b) are used as a rehabilitation financing resource by the LUHA, the LUHA shall make reasonable efforts to assist HUD in monitoring and securing compliance with the terms of the loan during the homesteader's conditional title period.

(5) *Homesteader agreement.* The program shall provide for the execution, concurrent with or as a part of the conditional conveyance, of a homesteader agreement between the LUHA and the homesteader which shall require the homesteader:

(i) To repair, within one year from the date of conditional conveyance of the property to the homesteader, any defects that pose a substantial danger to health and safety;

(ii) To make or cause to be made additional repairs and improvements necessary to meet the applicable local standards for decent, safe, and sanitary housing within three years from the date of conditional conveyance of the property to the homesteader, and to comply with any energy conservation measures designated by the LUHA as part of the repairs;

(iii) To occupy the property as his or her principal residence for not less than five consecutive years from the date of initial occupancy except as otherwise approved in writing by HUD on a case-by-case basis when emergency conditions make compliance with this requirement infeasible;

(iv) To permit reasonable inspections at reasonable times by employees or designated agents of the LUHA to determine compliance with the agreement; and

(v) To surrender possession of, and any interest in, the property upon material breach of the homesteader agreement (including default on any rehabilitation financing secured by the property), as determined by the LUHA in accordance with this part.

(6) *Monitoring and selecting successor homesteaders.* The program shall provide that the LUHA will monitor the homesteader's compliance with the homesteader agreement, will revoke the conditional conveyance and homesteader agreement upon any material breach by the homesteader, and, to the extent necessary and practicable, will select one or more successor homesteaders for the property. The LUHA shall make reasonable efforts to assure that any proposed successor homesteader assumes any section 312 loan on the property, subject to HUD approval of the terms of the assumption. If the LUHA selects a successor homesteader, it shall require the successor homesteader to assume the original homesteader's remaining obligations under his/her homesteader agreement and conditional conveyance in compliance with this part.

(7) *Fee simple title.* The program shall provide for the conveyance of fee simple title to the property from the LUHA to the homesteader, or successor homesteader, without substantial consideration upon compliance with the terms of the homesteader agreement and conditional conveyance.

(8) *Homesteading infeasible; alternative use.* If completion of homesteading proves, in the judgment of HUD, to be infeasible for any reason after a LUHA has accepted title to a federally-owned property, the LUHA shall not demolish, dispose of, rent or otherwise convert the property to its own use until HUD approves an alternative use.

(c) *Designation of LUHA*—(1) *Responsibilities.* Under the requirements of this § 590.7(c), the applicant shall designate a LUHA, which shall have primary responsibility for administering the local urban homesteading program for the applicant. Although the applicant may at any time amend its local urban homesteading program to designate a new LUHA, subject to HUD approval, neither the applicant nor the designated LUHA may delegate or contract out to another legal entity the function of accepting and conveying in its own name title to properties for homesteading purposes under this part. To the extent permitted by the applicant, the LUHA may use third parties as contractors, consultants, or agents to assist if in carrying out other functions and responsibilities with respect to the local urban homesteading program, by entering into a written agreement between the LUHA and the third party. No such agreement shall be deemed to relieve the LUHA or the applicant of responsibility for the thrid party's actions in connection with the local urban homesteading program.

(2) *Identity of LUHA.* The LUHA must have legal authority to carry out a local urban homesteading program as described in this part, including the authority to accept and convey title to properties under paragraph (b) of this § 590.7. To the extent consistent therewith, the applicant State or unit of general local government may:

(i) Act as LUHA in its own name, while identifying within its administrative organization a lead department or agency to act as the primary contact point for HUD;

(ii) Designate, and enter into a written agreement with, a legally separate public body or agency to act as LUHA in accordance with this part; or

(iii) Designate, and enter into a written agreement with, a qualified community organization (as defined in the Act) to act as LUHA in accordance with this part.

[54 FR 23937, June 2, 1989, as amended at 56 FR 6808, Feb. 20, 1991; 61 FR 7062, Feb. 23, 1996]

§ 590.9–590.18 [Reserved]

§ 590.19 Use of section 810 funds.

Participants receiving Community Development Block Grant (CDBG) funds may charge eligible administrative expenses incurred in operating their urban homesteading programs to their otherwise available CDBG administrative funds, provided such administrative expenditures would satisfy other title I requirements.

[56 FR 6809, Feb. 20, 1991, as amended at 61 FR 7062, Feb. 23, 1996]

§ 590.21 [Reserved]

§ 590.23 Program close-out.

(a) *Initiation of close-out.* The LUHA shall institute close-out procedures, as prescribed by HUD.

(b) Close-out may be subject to later audit in accordance with § 590.27(b).

(c) *Close-out conditions.* Upon completion of HUD close-out review, HUD will send the LUHA a letter of completion, which HUD may condition. Conditions may reflect unmet obligations, deadlines to meet them, and a statement of any required interim reporting procedures. In addition to any other conditions that may be specifically set forth in the letter of completion, the LUHA remains reponsible after close-out to take whatever actions may be necessary to enforce the homestead agreement and complete final fee simple conveyance to the homesteader or a successor homesteader, or to obtain alternative use approval from HUD under § 590.7(b)(8), for properties conveyed to the LUHA for homesteading prior to close-out.

[54 FR 23937, June 2, 1989, as amended at 61 FR 7062, Feb. 23, 1996]

§ 590.25 Retention of records.

The LUHA shall maintain adequate financial records, property disposition documents, supporting documents, statistical records, and all other records pertinent to the local urban homesteading program until fee simple title has been conveyed to all homesteaders, generally a five-year period. The LUHA will also maintain current and accurate data on the race and ethnicity of program beneficiaries.

§ 590.27 Audit.

(a) *Access to records.* The Secretary, the Comptroller General of the United States, or any of their duly authorized representatives, shall have access to all books, accounts, records, reports, files, and other papers or property of LUHAs pertaining to funds or property transferred under this part, for the purpose of making surveys, audits, examinations, excerpts, and transcripts.

(b) *Audit.* The LUHA's financial management system shall provide for audits in accordance with 24 CFR part 44.

§ 590.29 HUD review of LUHA performance.

(a) HUD may review the performance of each active LUHA as necessary, as determined by HUD, to determine whether:

(1) The program complies with the urban homesteading program participation agreement and certifications, the Act, this part, and other applicable Federal laws and regulations;

(2) The LUHA is carrying out its program substantially as approved by HUD;

(3) The federally-owned properties the LUHA selects are suitable for homesteading and rehabilitation;

(4) The LUHA is making reasonable progress in moving properties through the stages of the homesteading process, including acquisition, homesteader selection, conditional conveyance, rehabilitation, and final conveyance.

(5) The improvements in neighborhood public facilities and services provided for in the coordinated approach toward neighborhood improvement are occurring on a timely basis; and

(6) The LUHA has a continuing administrative and legal capacity to carry out the approved program in a cost-effective and timely manner.

(b) In reviewing a LUHA's performance, HUD will consider all available evidence, which may include, but need not be limited to, the following:

(1) Records maintained by the LUHA;

(2) Results of HUD's monitoring of the LUHA's performance;

(3) Audit reports, whether conducted by the LUHA or by HUD auditors;

(4) Records of comments and complaints by citizens and organizations; and

(5) Litigation history.

(c) LUHAs shall supply data and make available records necessary for HUD's monitoring of the LUHA's local urban homesteading program.

[54 FR 23937, June 2, 1989, as amended at 61 FR 7063, Feb. 23, 1996]

§ 590.31 Corrective and remedial action.

When HUD determines on the basis of its review that the LUHA's performance does not meet the standards specified in § 590.29(a), HUD shall take one or more of the following corrective or remedial actions, as appropriate in the circumstances:

(a) Issue a letter of warning that advises the LUHA of the deficiency and puts it on notice that HUD will take more serious corrective and remedial action if the LUHA does not correct the deficiency, or if it is repeated;

(b) Advise the LUHA to suspend, discontinue or not incur costs for identified defective aspects of the local program;

(c) [Reserved]

(d) In cases of continued substantial noncompliance, terminate the urban homesteading program participation agreement, close out the program and advise the LUHA of the reasons for such action; or

(e) Where HUD determines that a LUHA has, contrary to its obligations under § 590.7(b), converted a property received under this part to its own use, failed to adequately preserve and protect the property, failed to timely secure a homesteader for the property, or received excessive consideration for conveyance of the property, HUD may direct the LUHA to repay to HUD either the amount of compensation HUD finds that the LUHA has received for the property or the amount of section 810 funds expended for the property, as HUD determines appropriate.

[54 FR 23937, June 2, 1989, as amended at 61 FR 7063, Feb. 23, 1996]

PART 594—JOHN HEINZ NEIGHBORHOOD DEVELOPMENT PROGRAM

Subpart A—General

Sec.
594.1 Applicability and purpose.
594.3 Definitions.

Subpart B—Eligibility

594.5 Eligible applicants.
594.7 Other threshold requirements.
594.10 Eligible activities.

Subpart C—Funding Allocation and Criteria

594.15 Allocation amounts.
594.17 General criteria for competitive selection.

Subpart D—Award and Use of Grant Amounts

594.20 Submission procedures.
594.23 Approval and certification procedures.
594.25 Project administration.
594.28 Environmental reviews.
594.30 Equal opportunity and other Federal requirements.

AUTHORITY: 42 U.S.C. 3535(d) and 5318a.

SOURCE: 60 FR 16359, Mar. 29, 1995, unless otherwise noted.

Subpart A—General

§ 594.1 Applicability and purpose.

(a) *General.* This part establishes as a permanent program the John Heinz Neighborhood Development Program, as authorized by section 832 of the Housing and Community Development Act of 1992. Previously, the program had been administered by the Department as a demonstration program under section 123 of the Housing and Urban-Rural Recovery Act of 1983 (42 U.S.C. 5318 note).

(b) *Purpose.* The program is intended to assist communities to become more viable, by providing incentive funds to carry out neighborhood development activities that benefit low- and moderate-income families. The program objectives are to increase the capacity of neighborhood organizations, promote long-term financial support for their neighborhood projects, and encourage greater participation of neighborhood

§ 594.3

organizations with private and public institutions.

§ 594.3 Definitions.

Empowerment zone means an area designated by HUD as an Empowerment Zone under 26 U.S.C. 1391–1393.

Enterprise community means an area designated by HUD as an Enterprise Community under 26 U.S.C. 1391–1393.

Grantee means an eligible neighborhood organization that executes a grant agreement with HUD under this part.

Low- and moderate-income persons means families and individuals whose incomes do not exceed 80 percent of the median income for the area, as determined by the Secretary of HUD in accordance with 42 U.S.C. 5302(a)(20).

Neighborhood development funding organization means:

(1) A depository institution, the accounts of which are insured pursuant to the Federal Deposit Insurance Act, 12 U.S.C. 1811 et seq., or the Federal Credit Union Act, 12 U.S.C. 1751 et seq., and any subsidiary (as such term is defined in 12 U.S.C. 1813(w)) thereof;

(2) A depository institution holding company and any subsidiary (as such term is defined in 12 U.S.C. 1813(w)) thereof; or

(3) A company at least 75 percent of the common stock of which is owned by one or more insured depository institutions or depository institution holding companies.

Neighborhood development organization means the same as the term is defined in § 594.5.

Rural neighborhoods. In small cities with under 10,000 in population and in rural areas, a neighborhood area can be the same unit as the unit of general local government.

Unit of general local government means a city, town, township, county, parish, village, or other general purpose political subdivision of a State; an urban county; the Federated States of Micronesia; the Marshall Islands; or a general purpose political subdivision thereof.

[60 FR 16359, Mar. 29, 1995, as amended at 61 FR 5211, Feb. 9, 1996]

Subpart B—Eligibility

§ 594.5 Eligible applicants.

(a) *General requirements.* To be eligible under this program, a neighborhood development organization must be located within the neighborhood for which assistance is to be provided. It cannot be a city-wide consortium, or, in general, an organization serving a large area of the city. The applicant must meet all of the following requirements:

(1) The organization must be incorporated as a private, voluntary, nonprofit corporation under the laws of the State in which it operates;

(2) The organization must be responsible through a governing body to the residents of the neighborhood it serves, and not less than 51 percent of the members of the governing body must be residents of the neighborhood;

(3) The organization must have conducted business for at least one year;

(4) The organization must operate within an area that meets at least one of the following criteria:

(i) The area meets the requirements for Federal assistance under section 119 of the Housing and Community Development Act of 1974, 42 U.S.C. 5318;

(ii) The area is designated as an Enterprise Community or Empowerment Zone under Federal law as enacted;

(iii) The area is designated as an enterprise zone under State law and is recognized by the Secretary as a State enterprise zone for purposes of this part; or

(iv) The area is a qualified distressed community within the meaning of section 233(b)(1) of the Bank Enterprise Act of 1991, 12 U.S.C. 1834a(b)(1); and

(5) The organization must have conducted one or more eligible neighborhood development activities that primarily benefit low- and moderate-income persons.

(b) *Special eligibility.* Any facility that provides small entrepreneurial business with affordable shared support services and business development services and that meets the requirements of paragraph (a) of this section may also be eligible to participate in this program.

§ 594.7 Other threshold requirements.

In addition, an applicant must meet the following threshold requirements:

(a) Specify a management business plan for accomplishing one or more of the eligible activities specified in § 594.10;

(b) Specify a strategy for achieving greater long-term private sector support, especially in cooperation with a neighborhood development funding organization; and

(c) Specify a strategy for increasing the capacity of the applicant.

§ 594.10 Eligible activities.

Eligible activities include, but are not limited to, the following:

(a) Developing economic development activities that include:

(1) Creating permanent jobs in the neighborhood; or

(2) Establishing or expanding businesses within the neighborhood;

(b) Developing new housing, rehabilitating existing housing, or managing housing stock within the neighborhood;

(c) Developing delivery mechanisms for essential services that have lasting benefits to the neighborhood; and

(d) Planning, promoting, or financing voluntary neighborhood improvement efforts.

Subpart C—Funding Allocation and Criteria

§ 594.15 Allocation amounts.

(a) *Amounts and match requirement.* HUD will make grants, in the form of matching funds, to eligible neighborhood development organizations. HUD reserves the right to make grants for less than the maximum amount established by statute, and to limit the number of times a previous grantee can receive funding. A Federal matching ratio will be established for each grantee in accordance with the statutory requirement that the highest ratios be established for neighborhoods having the greatest degree of economic distress or the smallest number of households.

(b) *Administrative costs.* The Secretary may use no more than 5 percent of the funds appropriated for the program for administrative or other expenses in connection with the program.

§ 594.17 General criteria for competitive selection.

(a) *Criteria.* HUD will use the following general criteria for selecting and ranking applications for all competitions for John Heinz Neighborhood Development Program funds. The relative values for the criteria will be indicated in each NOFA:

(1) The degree of economic distress and the benefit to low- and moderate-income residents of the neighborhood;

(2) The past performance in carrying out eligible activities, and staff capability;

(3) The quality of the Management/Business Plan;

(4) The evidence of coordination and resident participation; and

(5) The quality of the strategy to increase the capacity of the organization and the strategy developed for meeting long-term financial needs.

(b) *Geographic diversity.* The Department also reserves the right to fund applicants in other than rank order, for the purpose of achieving geographic balance.

Subpart D—Award and Use of Grant Amounts

§ 594.20 Submission procedures.

(a) *Use of NOFAs.* The Department will publish a Notice of Funding Availability (NOFA) in the FEDERAL REGISTER for each funding competition under this program, indicating the objective of the competition; the amount of funding available; the application procedures, including the eligible applicants and activities to be funded; and any special conditions applicable to the competition, including the requirements for the match. The NOFA also will describe the maximum points to be awarded under each evaluation criterion, for the purpose of ranking applications, and any special factors to be considered in assigning the points to each criterion.

§ 594.23

(b) Applications shall be submitted in accordance with the time, place, and content described in the NOFA.

(Approved by the Office of Management and Budget under control number 2535–0084)

§ 594.23 Approval and certification procedures.

(a) *Approval of application.* HUD's acceptance of an application for review does not imply a commitment to provide funding. HUD will provide notification of whether a project will be funded in accordance with the criteria and procedures set out in the applicable NOFA.

(b) *Certifications.* In the absence of independent evidence that tends to challenge in a substantial manner the certifications made by the applicant pursuant to § 594.30, the required certifications will be accepted by HUD.

However, if independent evidence is available that tends to challenge in a substantial manner an applicant's certification, HUD may require further information or assurances to be submitted in order to determine whether the applicant's certification is satisfactory.

§ 594.25 Project administration.

Project administration will be governed by the terms of the grant agreement.

§ 594.28 Environmental reviews.

(a) For all proposed actions or activities that are not considered categorically excluded under 24 CFR 50.20, HUD will perform the appropriate environmental reviews under the National Environmental Policy Act (NEPA).

(b) Whether the action or activity is categorically excluded from NEPA review or not, HUD will comply also with other applicable requirements of environmental statutes, Executive Orders, and HUD standards listed in 24 CFR 50.4. The environmental reviews will be performed before award of a grant. Grantees shall adhere to all assurances applicable to environmental concerns as contained in the RFGA and grant agreements.

§ 594.30 Equal opportunity and other Federal requirements.

Each participating neighborhood development organization must certify that it will carry out activities assisted under the program in compliance with the nondiscrimination and equal opportunity requirements set forth in 24 CFR part 5 and:

(a) The requirements at 24 CFR part 200, subpart M;

(b) The prohibitions against discrimination and related requirements of section 109 of the Housing and Community Development Act of 1974 (42 U.S.C. 5309);

(c) The requirements of the Americans with Disabilities Act (42 U.S.C. 12181–12189) and implementing regulations at 28 CFR part 36, as applicable;

(d) The Consolidated Plan of the appropriate unit of general local government; and

(e) Other Federal requirements as specified in the applicable NOFA and application kit.

[60 FR 16359, Mar. 29, 1995, as amended at 61 FR 5211, Feb. 9, 1996]

PART 597—URBAN EMPOWERMENT ZONES AND ENTERPRISE COMMUNITIES: ROUND ONE DESIGNATIONS

Subpart A—General Provisions

Sec.
597.1 Applicability and scope.
597.2 Objective and purpose.
597.3 Definitions.
597.4 Secretarial review and designation.

Subpart B—Area Requirements

597.100 Eligibility requirements and data usage.
597.101 Data utilized for eligibility determinations.
597.102 Tests of pervasive poverty, unemployment and general distress.
597.103 Poverty rate.

Subpart C—Nomination Procedure

597.200 Nominations by State and local governments.
597.201 Evaluating the strategic plan.
597.202 Submission of nominations for designation.

Subpart D—Designation Process

597.300 HUD action and review of nominations for designation.
597.301 Selection factors for designation of nominated urban areas.

Subpart E—Post-Designation Requirements

597.400 Reporting.
597.401 Periodic performance reviews.
597.402 Validation of designation.
597.403 Revocation of designation.

Subpart F—Special Rules

597.500 Indian Reservations.
597.501 Governments.
597.502 Nominations by economic development corporations or the District of Columbia.
597.503 Use of census data.

AUTHORITY: 26 U.S.C. 1391; 42 U.S.C. 3535(d).

SOURCE: 60 FR 3038, Jan. 12, 1995, unless otherwise noted.

Subpart A—General Provisions

§ 597.1 Applicability and scope.

(a) This part establishes policies and procedures applicable to urban Empowerment Zones and Enterprise Communities, authorized under subchapter U of the Internal Revenue Code of 1986, as amended, relating to the designation and treatment of Empowerment Zones, Enterprise Communities and Rural Development Investment Areas.

(b) This part contains provisions relating to area requirements, the nomination process for urban Empowerment Zones and urban Enterprise Communities, and the designation and administration of these Zones and Communities by HUD. Provisions dealing with the nomination and designation of rural Empowerment Zones and Enterprise Communities will be promulgated by the Department of Agriculture. HUD and the Department of Agriculture will consult in all cases in which nominated areas possess both urban and rural characteristics, and will utilize a flexible approach in determining the appropriate designation.

§ 597.2 Objective and purpose.

The purpose of this part is to provide for the establishment of Empowerment Zones and Enterprise Communities in urban areas, to stimulate the creation of new jobs, particularly for the disadvantaged and long-term unemployed, and to promote revitalization of economically distressed areas.

§ 597.3 Definitions.

The terms *HUD* and *Secretary* are defined in 24 CFR part 5.

Designation means the process by which the Secretary designates urban areas as Empowerment Zones or Enterprise Communities eligible for tax incentives and credits established by subchapter U of the Internal Revenue Code of 1986, as amended (26 U.S.C. 1391 *et seq.*) and for special consideration for programs of Federal assistance.

Empowerment Zone means an urban area so designated by the Secretary pursuant to this part.

Enterprise Community means an urban area so designated by the Secretary pursuant to this part.

Local government means any county, city, town, township, parish, village, or other general purpose political subdivision of a State, and any combination of these political subdivisions which is recognized by the Secretary.

Nominated area means an area nominated by one or more local governments and the State or States in which it is located for designation pursuant to this part.

Population census tract means a census tract, or, if census tracts are not defined for the area, a block numbering area.

Poverty means the number of persons listed as being in poverty in the 1990 Decennial Census.

Revocation of designation means the process by which the Secretary may revoke the designation of an urban area as an Empowerment Zone or Enterprise Community pursuant to § 597.403.

State means any State of the United States.

Strategic plan means a strategy developed and agreed to by the nominating local government(s) and State(s), which have provided certifications of their authority to adopt such a strategy in their application for nomination, in consultation and cooperation with the residents of the nominated are, pursuant to the provisions of

§ 597.200(c). The plan must include written commitments from the local government(s) and State(s) that they will adhere to that strategy.

Urban area means:

(1) Any area that lies inside a Metropolitan Area (MA), as designated by the Office of Management and Budget; or

(2) Any area outside an MA if the jurisdiction of the nominating local government has a population of 20,000 or more, or documents the urban character of the area.

[60 FR 3038, Jan. 12, 1995, as amended at 61 FR 5211, Feb. 9, 1996; 63 FR 10715, Mar. 4, 1998]

§ 597.4 Secretarial review and designation.

(a) *Designation.* The Secretary will review applications for the designation of nominated urban areas to determine the effectiveness of the strategic plans submitted by nominating State and local government(s) in accordance with § 597.200(c).

(b) *Period of designation.* The designation of an urban area as an Empowerment Zone or Enterprise Community shall remain in full effect during the period beginning on the date of designation and ending on the earliest of:

(1) The close of the tenth calendar year beginning on or after the date of designation;

(2) The termination date designated by the State and local governments in their application for nomination; or

(3) The date the Secretary modifies or revokes the designation, in accordance with § 597.402 or 597.403.

[60 FR 3038, Jan. 12, 1995, as amended at 63 FR 10715, Mar. 4, 1998]

Subpart B—Area Requirements

§ 597.100 Eligibility requirements and data usage.

A nominated urban area may be eligible for designation pursuant to this part only if the area:

(a) Has a maximum population which is the lesser of:

(1) 200,000; or

(2) The greater of 50,000 or ten percent of the population of the most populous city located within the nominated area;

(b) Is one of pervasive poverty, unemployment and general distress, as described in § 597.102;

(c) Does not exceed twenty square miles in total land area;

(d) Has a continuous boundary, or consists of not more than three noncontiguous parcels;

(e) Is located entirely within the jurisdiction of the unit or units of general local government making the nomination, and is located in no more than two contiguous States; and

(f) Does not include any portion of a central business district, as this term is used in the most recent Census of Retail Trade, unless the poverty rate for each population census tract in the district is not less than 35 percent for an Empowerment Zone and 30 percent for an Enterprise Community.

§ 597.101 Data utilized for eligibility determinations.

(a) *Source of data.* The data to be employed in determining eligibility pursuant to the criteria set forth at § 597.102 shall be based upon the 1990 Decennial Census, and from information published by the Bureau of the Census and the Bureau of Labor Statistics. The data shall be comparable as to point or period of time and methodology employed. Specific information on appropriate data to be submitted will be provided in the application.

(b) *Use of statistics on boundaries.* The boundary of an urban area nominated for designation as an Empowerment Zone or Enterprise Community must coincide with the boundaries of census tracts, or, where tracts are not defined, with block numbering areas.

§ 597.102 Tests of pervasive poverty, unemployment and general distress.

(a) *Pervasive poverty.* Pervasive poverty shall be demonstrated by the nominating entities by providing evidence that:

(1) Poverty is widespread throughout the nominated area; or

(2) Poverty has become entrenched or intractable over time (through comparison of 1980 and 1990 census data or other relevant evidence); or

(3) That no portion of the nominated area contains any component areas of an affluent character.

(b) *Unemployment.* Unemployment shall be demonstrated by:

(1) Data indicating that the weighted average rate of unemployment for the nominated area is not less than the national average rate of unemployment; or

(2) Evidence of especially severe economic conditions, such as military base or plant closings or other conditions which have brought about significant job dislocation within the nominated area.

(c) *General distress.* General distress shall be evidenced by describing adverse conditions within the nominated urban area other than those of pervasive poverty and unemployment. A high incidence of crime, narcotics use, homelessness, abandoned housing, and deteriorated infrastructure or substantial population decline, are examples of appropriate indicators of general distress.

§ 597.103 Poverty rate.

(a) *General.* The poverty rate shall be established in accordance with the following criteria:

(1) In each census tract within a nominated urban area, the poverty rate shall be not less than 20 percent;

(2) For at least 90 percent of the population census tracts within the nominated urban area, the poverty rate shall not be less than 25 percent; and

(3) For at least 50 percent of the population census tracts within the nominated urban area, the poverty rate shall be not less than 35 percent.

(b) *Special rules relating to the determination of poverty rate*—(1) *Census tracts with no population.* Census tracts with no population shall be treated as having a poverty rate which meets the standards of paragraphs (a)(1) and (2) of this section, but shall be treated as having a zero poverty rate for purposes of applying paragraph (a)(3) of this section.

(2) *Census tracts with populations of less than 2,000.* A population census tract which has a population of less than 2,000 shall be treated as having a poverty rate which meets the requirements of paragraphs (a)(1) and (2) of this section if more than 75 percent of the tract is zoned for commercial or industrial use.

(3) *Adjustment of poverty rates for Enterprise Communities.* Where necessary to carry out the purposes of this part, the Secretary may reduce by 5 percentage points one of the following thresholds for not more than 10 percent of the census tracts, or, if fewer, five population tracts in the nominated urban area:

(i) The 20 percent threshold in paragraph (a)(1) of this section;

(ii) The 25 percent threshold in paragraph (a)(2) of this section; and

(iii) The 35 percent threshold in paragraph (a)(3) of this section; *Provided that,* the Secretary may in the alternative reduce the 35 percent threshold by 10 percentage points for three population census tracts.

(4) *Rounding up of percentages.* In making the calculations required by this section, the Secretary shall round all fractional percentages of one-half percent or more up to the next highest whole percentage figure.

(c) *Noncontiguous areas.* A nominated urban area may not contain a noncontiguous parcel unless such parcel separately meets the criteria set forth at paragraphs (a)(1), (2), and (3) of this section.

(d) *Areas not within census tracts.* In the case of an area which does not have population census tracts, the block numbering area shall be used.

Subpart C—Nomination Procedure

§ 597.200 Nominations by State and local governments.

(a) *Nomination criteria.* One or more local governments and the State or States in which an urban area is located may nominate such area for designation as an Empowerment Zone and/or as an Enterprise Community, if:

(1) The urban area meets the requirements for eligibility set forth in §§ 597.100 and 597.103;

(2) The urban area is within the jurisdiction of a State or States and local government(s) that have the authority to nominate the urban area for designation and that provide written assurances satisfactory to the Secretary that the strategic plan described in

paragraph (c) of this section will be implemented;

(3) All information furnished by the nominating State(s) and local government(s) is determined by the Secretary to be reasonably accurate; and

(4) The State(s) and local government(s) certify that no portion of the area nominated is already included in an Empowerment Zone or Enterprise Community or in an area otherwise nominated to be designated under this section.

(b) *Nomination for designation.* No urban area may be considered for designation pursuant to subpart D of this part unless the nomination for designation:

(1) Demonstrates that the nominated urban area satisfies the eligibility criteria set forth at § 597.100;

(2) Includes a strategic plan, as described in paragraph (c) of this section; and

(3) Includes such other information as may be required by HUD in the application or in a Notice Inviting Applications, to be published in the FEDERAL REGISTER.

(c) *Strategic plan.* Each application for designation must be accompanied by a strategic plan, which must be developed in accordance with four key principles, which will also be utilized to evaluate the plan. These principles are:

(1) Economic opportunity, including job creation within the community and throughout the region, as well as entrepreneurial initiatives, small business expansion and training for jobs that offer upward mobility;

(2) Sustainable community development, to advance the creation of liveable and vibrant communities through comprehensive approaches that coordinate economic, physical, community and human development;

(3) Community-based partnerships, involving the participation of all segments of the community, including the political and governmental leadership, community groups, health and social service groups, environmental groups, religious organizations, the private and non-profit sectors, centers of learning and other community institutions; and

(4) Strategic vision for change, which identifies what the community will become and a strategic map for revitalization. The vision should build on assets and coordinate a response to community needs in a comprehensive fashion. It should also set goals and performance benchmarks for measuring progress and establish a framework for evaluating and adjusting the revitalization plan.

(d) *Elements of strategic plan.* The strategic plan should:

(1) Indicate and briefly describe the specific groups, organizations, and individuals participating in the production of the plan and describe the history of these groups in the community;

(2) Explain how participants were selected and provide evidence that the participants, taken as a whole, broadly represent the racial, cultural and economic diversity of the community;

(3) Describe the role of the participants in the creation, development and future implementation of the plan;

(4) Identify two or three topics addressed in the plan that caused the most serious disagreements among participants and describe how those disagreements were resolved;

(5) Explain how the community participated in choosing the area to be nominated and why the area was nominated;

(6) Provide evidence that key participants have the capacity to implement the plan;

(7) Provide a brief explanation of the community's vision for revitalizing the area;

(8) Explain how the vision creates economic opportunity, encourages self-sufficiency and promotes sustainable community development;

(9) Identify key needs of the area and the current barriers to achieving the vision for it, including a description of poverty and general distress, barriers to economic opportunity and development and barriers to human development;

(10) Discuss how the vision is related to the assets and needs of the area and its surroundings;

(11) Describe the ways in which the community's approaches to economic development, social/human services, transportation, housing, sustainable community development, public safety, drug abuse prevention, and educational

and environmental concerns will be addressed in a coordinated fashion; and explain how these linkages support the community's vision;

(12) Indicate how all Social Services Block Grant funds for designated Empowerment Zones and Enterprise Communities (EZ/EC SSBG funds) will be utilized.

(i) In doing so, the strategic plan shall provide the following information:

(A) A commitment by the applicant, as well as by the nominating State-chartered economic development corporation or State government(s) and local governments, that the EZ/EC SSBG funds will be used to supplement, not replace, other Federal or non-Federal funds available for financing for services or activities which can be used to achieve or maintain the goals outlined in paragraph (d)(12) of this section;

(B) A description of the entities that will administer the EZ/EC SSBG funds;

(C) A certification by such entities that they will provide periodic reports on the use of the EZ/EC SSBG funds; and

(D) A detailed description of all the activities to be financed with the EZ/EC SSBG funds and how all such funds will be allocated.

(ii) The EZ/EC SSBG funds must be used to achieve or maintain the following goals. The goals may be achieved by undertaking one or more of the following program options:

(A) The goal of economic self-support to prevent, reduce or eliminate dependencies, through one or more of the following program options:

(1) Funding community and economic development services focused on disadvantaged adults and youths, including skills training, transportation services and job, housing, business, and financial management counseling;

(2) Supporting programs that promote home ownership, education or other routes to economic independence for low-income families, youths, and other individuals;

(3) Assisting in the provision of emergency and transitional shelter for disadvantaged families, youths, and other individuals;

(B) The goal of self-sufficiency, including reduction or prevention of dependencies, through one or more of the following program options:

(1) Providing assistance to non-profit organizations and/or community and junior colleges that provide disadvantaged adults and youths with opportunities for short-term training courses in entrepreneurial and self employment skills and other training that promotes individual self-sufficiency, and the interest of the community;

(2) Funding programs to provide training and employment for disadvantaged adults and youths in construction, rehabilitation or improvement of affordable housing, public infrastructure and community facilities; and

(C) The goal of prevention or remedying the neglect, abuse or exploitation of children and/or adults unable to protect their own interest; and the goal of preservation, rehabilitation, or reuniting of families, through one or more of the following program options:

(1) Providing support for residential or non-residential drug and alcohol prevention and treatment programs that offer comprehensive services for pregnant women, and mothers and their children;

(2) Establishing programs that provide activities after school hours, including keeping school buildings open during evenings and weekends for mentor and study programs.

(iii) Designated Empowerment Zone and Enterprise Communities may work to achieve or maintain the goals outlined in paragraphs (d)(12)(ii)(A) and (B) of this section by using EZ/EC SSBG funds to capitalize revolving or micro-enterprise loan funds which benefit low-income residents of the designated Empowerment Zones and Enterprise Communities. Similarly, the Zones and Communities may work to achieve or maintain the goals outlined in paragraphs (d)(12)(ii)(A) and (B) of this section by using the EZ/EC SSBG funds to create jobs and promote economic opportunity for low-income families and individuals through matching grants, loans, or investments in community development financial institutions.

§ 597.200

(iv) If the EZ/EC SSBG funds are to be used for program options not included in paragraph (d)(12)(ii) of this section, the strategic plan must indicate how the proposed activities meet the goals set forth in paragraph (d)(12)(ii) of this section and the reasons the approved program options were not pursued.

(v) To the extent that the EZ/EC SSBG funds are to be used for the program options included in paragraph (d)(12)(ii) of this section, they may be used for the following activities, in addition to those activities permitted by section 2005 of the Social Security Act (42 U.S.C. 1379d):

(A) To purchase or improve land or facilities;

(B) To make cash payments to individuals for subsistence or room and board;

(C) To make wage payments to individuals as a social service;

(D) To make cash payments for medical care; and

(E) To provide social services to institutionalized persons.

(vi) The State must obligate the EZ/EC SSBG funds in accordance with the strategic plan within 2 years from the date of payment to the State, or remit the unobligated funds to the Secretary of Health and Human Services (HHS).

(vii) The strategic plan must indicate how all the EZ/EC SSBG funds will be invested and used for the period of designation of the Empowerment Zone or Enterprise Community.

(viii) The strategic plan must provide for periodic reporting of information by the State in which the Empowerment Zone or Enterprise Community is located.

(13) Indicate how tax benefits for designated Zones and Communities, State and local resources, existing Federal resources available to the locality and additional Federal resources believed necessary to implement the strategic plan will be utilized within the Empowerment Zone or Enterprise Community;

(14) Indicate a level of commitment necessary to ensure that these resources will be available to the area upon designation;

(15) Identify the Federal resources applied for or for which applications are planned; if a strategic plan indicates how Community Development Block Grant (CDBG), HOME, Emergency Shelter Grant, and Housing Opportunities for People with AIDS (HOPWA) funds will be expended (for the entire locality including the nominated area), the strategic plan will be considered by the Office of Community Planning and Development at HUD toward satisfying the consolidated planning requirements that will soon be issued for these programs;

(16) Identify private resources and support, including assistance from business, non-profit organizations and foundations, which are available to be leveraged with public resources; and provide assurances that these resources will be made available to the area upon designation;

(17) Identify changes necessary to Federal rules and regulations necessary to implement the plan, including specific paperwork or other Federal program requirements that must be altered to permit effective implementation of the strategic plan; and

(18) Identify specific regulatory and other impediments to implementing the strategic plan for which waivers are requested, with appropriate citations and an indication whether waivers can be accomplished administratively or require statutory changes;

(19) Demonstrate how State and local governments will reinvent themselves to help implement the plan, by identifying changes that will be made in State and local organizations, processes and procedures, including laws and ordinances;

(20) Explain how different agencies in State and local governments will work together in new responsive ways to implement the strategic plan;

(21) Identify the specific tasks and timetable necessary to implement the plan;

(22) Describe the partnerships that will be established to carry out the plan;

(23) Explain how the plan will be regularly revised to reflect new information and opportunities; and

(24) Identify benchmarks and goals that should be used in evaluating performance in implementing the plan.

(e) *Prohibition against business relocation.* The strategic plan may not include any action to assist any establishment in relocating from one area outside the nominated urban area to the nominated urban area, except that assistance for the expansion of an existing business entity through the establishment of a new branch, affiliate, or subsidiary is permitted if:

(1) The establishment of a new branch, affiliate, or subsidiary will not result in a decrease in employment in the area of original location or in any other area where the existing business entity conducts business operations; and

(2) There is no reason to believe that the new branch, affiliate, or subsidiary is being established with the intention of closing down the operations of the existing business entity in the area of its original location or in any other area where the existing business entity conducts business operations.

(f) *Implementation of strategic plan.* The strategic plan may be implemented by the local government(s) and/or by the State(s) nominating an urban area for designation and/or by non-governmental entities identified in the strategic plan. Activities included in the plan may be funded from any source, Federal, State, local, or private, which provides assistance in the nominated area.

(g) *Activities included in strategic plan.* A strategic plan may include, but is not limited to, activities which address:

(1) Economic problems, through measures designed to create job training and employment opportunities; support for business start-up or expansion; or development of community institutions;

(2) Human concerns, through the provision of social services, such as rehabilitation and treatment programs or the provision of training, education, or other services within the affected area;

(3) Community needs, such as the expansion of housing stock and homeownership opportunities, efforts to reduce homelessness, efforts to promote fair housing and equal opportunity, efforts to reduce and prevent crime and improve security in the area; and

(4) Physical improvements, such as the provision or improvement of recreational areas, transportation or other public services within the affected area, and improvements to the infrastructure and environmental protection.

§ 597.201 Evaluating the strategic plan.

The strategic plan will be evaluated for effectiveness as part of the designation process for nominated urban areas described in § 597.301. On the basis of this evaluation, HUD may negotiate reasonable modifications of the strategic plan or of the boundaries of a nominated urban area or the period for which such designation shall remain in full effect. The effectiveness of the strategic plan will be determined in accordance with the four key principles set forth in § 597.200(c). HUD will review each plan submitted in terms of the four equally weighted key principles, and of such other elements of these key principles as are appropriate to address the opportunities and problems of each nominated area which may include:

(a) *Economic opportunity.* (1) The extent to which businesses, jobs, and entrepreneurship increase within the Zone or Community;

(2) The extent to which residents will achieve a real economic stake in the Zone or Community;

(3) The extent to which residents will be employed in the process of implementing the plan and in all phases of economic and community development;

(4) The extent to which residents will be linked with employers and jobs throughout the entire region or metropolitan area, and the way in which residents will receive training, assistance, and family support to become economically self-sufficient;

(5) The extent to which economic revitalization in the Zone or Community interrelates with the broader regional or metropolitan economies; and

(6) The extent to which lending and investment opportunities will increase within the Zone or Community through the establishment of mechanisms to encourage community investment and to create new economic growth.

(b) *Sustainable community development*—(1) *Consolidated planning.* The extent to which the plan is part of a larger strategic community development plan for the nominating locality and is consistent with broader regional development strategies;

(2) *Public safety.* The extent to which strategies such as community policing will be used to guarantee the basic safety and security of persons and property within the Zone or Community;

(3) *Amenities and design.* The extent to which the plan considers issues of design and amenities that will foster a sustainable community, such as open spaces, recreational areas, cultural institutions, transportation, energy, land and water uses, waste management, environmental protection, and the quality of life in the community;

(4) *Sustainable development.* The extent to which economic development will be achieved in a manner that protects public health and the environment;

(5) *Supporting families.* The extent to which the strengths of families will be supported so that parents can succeed at work, provide nurture in the home, and contribute to the life of the community;

(6) *Youth development.* The extent to which the development of children, youth, and young adults into economically productive and socially responsible adults will be promoted, and the extent to which young people will be provided with the opportunity to take responsibility for learning the skills, discipline, attitude, and initiative to make work rewarding;

(7) *Education goals.* The extent to which schools, religious institutions, non-profit organizations, for-profit enterprises, local governments and families will work cooperatively to provide all individuals with the fundamental skills and knowledge they need to become active participants and contributors to their community, and to succeed in an increasingly competitive global economy;

(8) *Affordable housing.* The extent to which a housing component, providing for adequate safe housing and ensuring that all residents will have equal access to that housing is contained in the strategic plan;

(9) *Drug abuse.* The extent to which the plan addresses levels of drug abuse and drug related activity through the expansion of drug treatment services, drug law enforcement initiatives and community based drug abuse education programs;

(10) *Equal opportunity.* The extent to which the plan offers an opportunity for diverse residents to participate in the rewards and responsibilities of work and service. The extent to which the plan ensures that no business within a nominated Zone or Community will directly or through contractual or other arrangements subject a person to discrimination on the basis of race, color, national origin, gender or disability in its employment practices, including recruitment, recruitment advertising, employment, layoff, termination, upgrading, demotion, transfer, rates of pay or other forms of compensation, or use of facilities.

(c) *Community-based partnerships*—(1) *Community partners.* The extent to which residents of the nominated area have participated in the development of the strategic plan and their commitment to implementing it, and the extent to which community-based organizations in the nominated area have participated in the development of the plan and their record of success measured by their achievements and support for undertakings within the nominated area; and the extent to which the plan integrates the local educational, social, civic, environmental and health organizations and reflects the prominent place that these institutions play in the life of a revitalized community;

(2) *Private and non-profit organizations as partners.* The extent to which partnership arrangements include commitments from private and non-profit organizations, including corporations, utilities, banks and other financial institutions, and educational institutions supporting implementation of the strategic plan;

(3) *State and local government partners.* The extent to which State and local governments are committed to providing support to implement the strategic plan, including their commitment to "reinventing" their roles and

Ofc. of Asst. Secy., Comm. Planning, Develop., HUD § 597.202

coordinating programs to implement the strategic plan; and

(4) *Permanent implementation and evaluation structure.* The extent to which a responsible and accountable implementation structure or process has been created to ensure that the plan is successfully carried out and that improvements are made throughout the period of the Zone or Community's designation and the extent to which the partners agree to be bound by their commitments.

(d) *Strategic vision for change*—(1) *Goals and coordinated strategy.* The extent to which the strategic plan reflects a projection for the community's revitalization which links economic, human, physical, community development and other activities in a mutually reinforcing, synergistic way to achieve ultimate goals;

(2) *Creativity and innovation.* The extent to which the activities proposed in the plan are creative, innovative and promising and will promote the civic spirit necessary to revitalize the nominated area;

(3) *Building on assets.* The extent to which the vision for revitalization realistically addresses the needs of the nominated area in a way that takes advantage of its assets;

(4) *Benchmarks and learning.* The extent to which the plan includes performance benchmarks for measuring progress in its implementation, including an on-going process for adjustments, corrections and building on what works.

§ 597.202 Submission of nominations for designation.

(a) *General.* A nomination for designation as an Empowerment Zone and/or Enterprise Community must be submitted for each urban area for which such designation is requested. The nomination shall be submitted in a form to be prescribed by HUD in the application and in the Notice Inviting Applications published in the FEDERAL REGISTER, and must contain complete and accurate information.

(b) *Certifications.* Certifications must be submitted by the State(s) and local government(s) requesting designation stating that:

(1) The nominated urban area satisfies the boundary tests of § 597.100(d);

(2) The nominated urban area is one of pervasive poverty, unemployment and general distress, as prescribed by § 597.102;

(3) The nominated urban area satisfies the poverty rate tests set forth in § 597.103;

(4) The nominated urban area contains no portion of an area that is either already designated as an Empowerment Zone and/or Enterprise Community, or is otherwise included in any other area nominated for designation as an Empowerment Zone and/or Enterprise Community;

(5) Each nominating governmental entity has the authority to:

(i) Nominate the urban area for designation as an Empowerment Zone and/or Enterprise Community;

(ii) Make the State and local commitments required by § 597.200(d); and

(iii) Provide written assurances satisfactory to the Secretary that these commitments will be met.

(6) Provide assurances that the amounts provided to the State for the area under section 2007 of title XX of the Social Security Act will not be used to supplant Federal or non-Federal funds for services and activities which promote the purposes of section 2007;

(7) Provide that the nominating governments or corporations agree to make available all information requested by HUD to aid in the evaluation of progress in implementing the strategic plan and reporting on the use of Empowerment Zone/Enterprise Community Social Service Block Grant funds; and

(8) Provide assurances that the nominating State(s) agrees to distribute the Empowerment Zone/Enterprise Community Social Service Block Grant funds in accordance with the strategic plan submitted for the designated Zone or Community.

(c) *Maps and area description.* Maps and a general description of the nominated urban area shall accompany the nomination request.

Subpart D—Designation Process

§ 597.300 HUD action and review of nominations for designation.

(a) *Establishment of submission procedures.* HUD will establish a time period and procedures for the submission of nominations for designation as Empowerment Zones or Enterprise Communities, including submission deadlines and addresses, in a Notice Inviting Applications, to be published in the FEDERAL REGISTER.

(b) *Acceptance for processing.* (1) HUD will accept for processing those nominations for designation as Empowerment Zones or Enterprise Communities which HUD determines have met the criteria required by this part. HUD will notify the State(s) and local government(s) whether or not the nomination has been accepted for processing. The criteria for acceptance for processing are as follows:

(2) The nomination for designation as an Empowerment Zone or Enterprise Community must be received by HUD on or before the time on the date established by the Notice Inviting Applications published in the FEDERAL REGISTER. The nomination for designation as an Empowerment Zone or Enterprise Community must be complete and must be accompanied by a strategic plan, as required by § 597.200(c), and the certifications required by § 597.202(b).

(c) *Evaluation of nominations.* In the process of reviewing each nomination accepted for processing, HUD may undertake a site visit(s) to any nominated area to aid in the process of evaluation.

(d) *Modification of the strategic plan, boundaries of nominated urban areas, and/or period during which designation is in effect.* Subject to the limitations imposed by § 597.100, HUD may negotiate reasonable modifications of the strategic plan, the proposed boundaries of a nominated urban area, or the term for which a designation is to remain in full effect, to ensure maximum efficiency and fairness in the provision of assistance to such areas.

(e) *Publication of designations.* Announcements of those nominated urban areas designated as Empowerment Zones or Enterprise Communities will be made by publication of a Notice in the FEDERAL REGISTER.

§ 597.301 Selection factors for designation of nominated urban areas.

(a) *Selection factors.* In choosing among nominated urban areas eligible for designation, the Secretary shall consider:

(1) The effectiveness of the strategic plan in accordance with the key principles and evaluative criteria set out in § 597.201;

(2) The effectiveness of the assurances made pursuant to § 597.200(a)(2) that the strategic plan will be implemented;

(3) The extent to which an application proposes activities that are creative and innovative in comparison to other applications; and

(4) Such other factors established by HUD. Such factors include, but are not limited to, the degree of need demonstrated by the nominated area for assistance under this part. If other factors are established by HUD, a FEDERAL REGISTER notice will be published identifying such factors, along with an extension of the application due date if necessary.

(b) *Geographic diversity.* HUD, in its discretion, may choose to select for designation a lower rated approvable application over a higher rated application in order to increase the level of geographic diversity of designations approved under this part.

Subpart E—Post-Designation Requirements

§ 597.400 Reporting.

HUD will require periodic reports for the Empowerment Zones and Enterprise Communities designated pursuant to this part. These reports will identify the community, local government and State actions which have been taken in accordance with the strategic plan. In addition to these reports, such other information relating to designated Empowerment Zones and Enterprise Communities as HUD shall request from time to time, including information documenting nondiscrimination in hiring and employment by businesses within the designated Empowerment

Zone or Enterprise Community, shall be submitted promptly.

§ 597.401 Periodic performance reviews.

HUD will regularly evaluate the progress of the strategic plan in each designated Empowerment Zone and Enterprise Community on the basis of performance reviews to be conducted on site and other information submitted. HUD will also commission evaluations of the Empowerment Zone program as a whole by an impartial third party, at such intervals as HUD may establish.

§ 597.402 Validation of designation.

(a) *Reevaluation of designations.* On the basis of the performance reviews described in § 597.401, and subject to the provisions relating to the revocation of designation appearing at § 597.403, HUD will make findings on the continuing eligibility for and the validity of the designation of any Empowerment Zone or Enterprise Community. Determinations of whether any designated Empowerment Zone or Enterprise Community remains in good standing shall be promptly communicated to all Federal agencies providing assistance or administering programs under which assistance can be made available in such Zone or Community.

(b) *Modification of designation.* Based on an urban area's success in carrying out its strategic plan, and subject to the provisions relating to revocation of designation appearing at § 597.403 and the requirements as to the number, maximum population and other characteristics of urban Empowerment Zones set forth in § 597.3, the Secretary may modify designations by reclassifying urban Empowerment Zones as Enterprise Communities or Enterprise Communities as Empowerment Zones.

§ 597.403 Revocation of designation.

(a) *Basis for revocation.* The Secretary may revoke the designation of an urban area as an Empowerment Zone or Enterprise Community if the Secretary determines, on the basis of the periodic performance review described at § 597.401, that the State(s) or local government(s) in which the urban area is located:

(1) Has modified the boundaries of the area;

(2) Has failed to make progress in achieving the benchmarks set forth in the strategic plan; or

(3) Has not complied substantially with the strategic plan.

(b) *Letter of warning.* Before revoking the designation of an urban area as an Empowerment Zone or Enterprise Community, the Secretary will issue a letter of warning to the nominating State(s) and local government(s):

(1) Advising that the Secretary has determined that the nominating local government(s) and/or State(s) has:

(i) Modified the boundaries of the area; or

(ii) Is not complying substantially with, or has failed to make progress in achieving the benchmarks set forth in the strategic plan prepared pursuant to § 597.200(c); and

(2) Requesting a reply from all involved parties within 90 days of the receipt of this letter of warning.

(c) *Notice of revocation.* After allowing 90 days from the date of receipt of the letter of warning for response, and after making a determination pursuant to paragraph (a) of this section, the Secretary may issue a final notice of revocation of the designation of the urban area as an Empowerment Zone or Enterprise Community.

(d) *Notice to affected Federal agencies.* HUD will notify all affected Federal agencies providing assistance in an urban Empowerment Zone or Enterprise Community of its determination to revoke any designation pursuant to this section or to modify a designation pursuant to § 597.402(b).

Subpart F—Special Rules

§ 597.500 Indian Reservations.

No urban Empowerment Zone or Enterprise Community may include any area within an Indian reservation.

§ 597.501 Governments.

If more than one State or local government seeks to nominate an urban area under this part, any reference to or requirement of this part shall apply to all such governments.

§ 597.502 Nominations by economic development corporations or the District of Columbia.

Any urban area nominated by an Economic Development Corporation chartered by the State in which it is located or by the District of Columbia shall be treated as nominated by a State and local government.

§ 597.503 Use of census data.

Population and poverty rate data shall be determined by the most recent decennial census data available.

PART 598—URBAN EMPOWERMENT ZONES: ROUND TWO AND THREE DESIGNATIONS

Subpart A—General Provisions

Sec.
598.1 Applicability and scope.
598.2 Objective and purpose.
598.3 Definitions.
598.4 Period of designation.

Subpart B—Eligibility Requirements

598.100 Eligibility requirements.
598.105 Data used for eligibility determinations.
598.110 Tests of pervasive poverty, unemployment and general distress.
598.115 Poverty rate.

Subpart C—Nomination Procedure

598.200 Who nominates an area for designation?
598.205 What are the requirements for nomination?
598.210 What certifications must governments make?
598.215 What are the purpose and content of the strategic plan?

Subpart D—Designation Process

598.300 Procedure for submitting a nomination.
598.305 Designation factors.

Subpart E—Post-Designation Requirements

598.400 HUD grants for planning activities.
598.405 Environmental review.
598.408 Lead-based paint requirements.
598.410 Public access to materials and proceedings.
598.415 Reporting.
598.420 Periodic progress determinations.
598.425 Validation of designation.
598.430 Revocation of designation.

Subpart F—Special Rules

598.500 Indian reservations.
598.505 Governments.
598.510 Nominations by Economic Development Corporations or the District of Columbia.
598.515 Alaska and Hawaii.

Subpart G—Empowerment zone grants

598.600 Applicability.
598.605 Implementation plan.
598.610 Resident benefit standards.
598.615 Economic development standards.
598.620 Evaluation, monitoring, and enforcement.

AUTHORITY: 26 U.S.C. 1391; 42 U.S.C. 3535(d).

SOURCE: 63 FR 19155, Apr. 16, 1998, unless otherwise noted.

Subpart A—General Provisions

§ 598.1 Applicability and scope.

(a) This part establishes policies and procedures applicable to the second and third rounds of designations of urban Empowerment Zones, authorized under Subchapter U of the Internal Revenue Code of 1986 (26 U.S.C. 1391, et seq.), as amended. Any reference to, or requirement of, Round II in this part is also a reference to, or requirement of, Round III.

(b) This part contains provisions relating to area requirements, the nomination process for urban Empowerment Zones, and the designation and evaluation of these Zones by HUD. Provisions dealing with the nomination and designation of rural Empowerment Zones are issued by the Department of Agriculture.

[63 FR 19155, Apr. 16, 1998, as amended at 66 FR 35855, July 9, 2001]

§ 598.2 Objective and purpose.

The purpose of this part is to provide for the establishment of Empowerment Zones in urban areas, to stimulate the creation of new jobs—empowering low-income persons and families receiving public assistance to become economically self-sufficient—and to promote revitalization of economically distressed areas.

§ 598.3 Definitions.

In addition to the definitions of "HUD" and "Secretary" found in 24

Ofc. of Asst. Secy., Comm. Planning, Develop., HUD § 598.105

CFR 5.100, the following definitions apply to this part.

Census tract means a census tract, as the term is used by the Bureau of the Census, or, if census tracts are not defined for the area, a block numbering area.

Designation means the process by which the Secretary designates urban areas as Empowerment Zones eligible for tax incentives and credits established by Subchapter U of the Internal Revenue Code of 1986, as amended (26 U.S.C. 1391, *et seq.*) and for special consideration for programs of Federal assistance.

Developable site means a parcel of land in a nominated area that may be developed for commercial or industrial purposes.

Empowerment Zone means an urban area so designated by the Secretary in accordance with this part.

HHS means the U.S. Department of Health and Human Services.

Local government means any county, city, town, township, parish, village, or other general purpose political subdivision of a State, and any combination of these political subdivisions that is recognized by the Secretary.

Nominated area means an area nominated by one or more local governments and the State or States in which it is located for designation in accordance with this part.

Revocation of designation means the process by which the Secretary may revoke the designation of an urban area as an Empowerment Zone . (See subpart E of this part.)

State means any State of the United States.

Urban area means:

(1) An area that lies inside a Metropolitan Statistical Area (MSA), as designated by the Office of Management and Budget; or

(2) An area outside an MSA if the jurisdiction of the nominating local government documents:

(i) The urban character of the area, or

(ii) The link between the area and the proposed area in the MSA.

[63 FR 19155, Apr. 16, 1998, as amended at 72 FR 71016, Dec. 13, 2007]

§ 598.4 **Period of designation.**

The designation of an urban area as an Empowerment Zone will remain in full effect during the period beginning on the date of designation and ending on the earliest of:

(a) The close of the tenth calendar year beginning on the date of designation;

(b) The termination date designated by the State and local Governments in their application for nomination; or

(c) The date the Secretary modifies or revokes the designation.

Subpart B—Eligibility Requirements

§ 598.100 **Eligibility requirements.**

A nominated urban area is eligible for designation in accordance with this part only if the area:

(a) Has a maximum population that is the lesser of:

(1) 200,000; or

(2) The greater of 50,000 or ten percent of the population of the most populous city located within the nominated area;

(b) Is one of pervasive poverty, unemployment and general distress, as described in § 598.110;

(c) Does not exceed twenty square miles in total land area, excluding up to three noncontiguous developable sites that are exempt from the poverty criteria;

(d) Has a continuous boundary, or consists of not more than three noncontiguous parcels meeting the poverty criteria, and not more than three noncontiguous developable sites exempt under § 598.115(c)(1) from the poverty rate criteria;

(e) Is located entirely within the jurisdiction of the unit or units of general local government making the nomination, and is located in no more than two contiguous States; and

(f) Does not include any portion of a central business district, as this term is used in the most recent Census of Retail Trade, unless the poverty rate for each census tract in the district is not less than 35 percent.

§ 598.105 **Data used for eligibility determinations.**

(a) *Source of data.* The data to be used in determining the eligibility of an area is from the 1990 Decennial Census, and from information published by the Bureau of the Census and the Bureau of Labor Statistics. Specific information on appropriate data to be submitted will be provided in the application.

(b) *Use of statistics on boundaries.* The boundary of an urban area nominated for designation as an Empowerment Zone must coincide with the boundaries of census tracts, as defined in § 598.3.

§ 598.110 **Tests of pervasive poverty, unemployment and general distress.**

(a) *Pervasive poverty.* Pervasive poverty is demonstrated by evidence that:

(1) Poverty, as indicated by the number of persons listed as being in poverty in the 1990 Decennial Census, is widespread throughout the nominated area; or

(2) Poverty, as described above, has become entrenched or intractable over time (through comparison of 1980 and 1990 census data or other relevant evidence).

(b) *Unemployment.* Unemployment is demonstrated by:

(1) The most recent data available indicating that the annual rate of unemployment for the nominated area is not less than the national annual average rate of unemployment; or

(2) Evidence of especially severe economic conditions, such as military base or plant closings or other conditions that have brought about significant job dislocation within the nominated area.

(c) *General distress.* General distress is evidenced by describing adverse conditions within the nominated urban area other than those of pervasive poverty and unemployment. Below average or decline in per capita income, earnings per worker, number of persons on welfare, per capita property tax base, average years of school completed, substantial population decline, and a high or rising incidence of crime, narcotics use, homelessness, high incidence of AIDS, abandoned housing, deteriorated infrastructure, school dropouts, teen pregnancy, incidence of domestic violence, incidence of certain health conditions and illiteracy are examples of appropriate indicators of general distress.

§ 598.115 **Poverty rate.**

(a) *General.* In order to be eligible for designation, an area's poverty rate must satisfy the following criteria:

(1) In each census tract within a nominated urban area, the poverty rate must be not less than 20 percent; and

(2) For at least 90 percent of the census tracts within the nominated urban area, the poverty rate must be not less than 25 percent.

(b) *Special rules relating to the determination of poverty rate*—(1) *Census tracts with populations of less than 2,000.* A census tract that has a population of less than 2,000 is treated as having a poverty rate that meets the requirements of paragraphs (a)(1) and (a)(2) of this section if more than 75 percent of the tract is zoned for commercial or industrial use, and the tract is contiguous to one or more other census tracts that have an actual poverty rate of not less than 25 percent.

(2) *Rounding up of percentages.* In making the calculations required by this section, the Secretary will round all fractional percentages of one-half percent or more up to the next highest whole percentage figure.

(c) *Noncontiguous parcels.* (1) Noncontiguous parcels that are developable sites are exempt from the poverty rate criteria of paragraph (a) of this section, for up to three developable sites.

(2) The total area of the noncontiguous parcels that are developable sites exempt from the poverty rate criteria of paragraph (a) of this section must not exceed 2,000 acres.

(3) A nominated urban area must not contain a noncontiguous parcel unless such parcel separately meets the criteria set forth at paragraphs (a)(1) and (2) of this section, except for up to three developable sites.

(4) There must not be more than three noncontiguous parcels, except that up to three developable sites are not included in this limit.

Subpart C—Nomination Procedure

§ 598.200 Who nominates an area for designation?

Applicants for empowerment zone designation must be nominated by the State or States and one or more local government(s) in which the area is located, except as provided in §§ 598.500, 598.510, and 598.515. The nomination must be submitted in a form to be prescribed by HUD in the application and in the document announcing the initiation of the designation process, and must contain complete and accurate information.

(Approved by the Office of Management and Budget under Control Number 2506–0148)

[63 FR 19155, Apr. 16, 1998, as amended at 63 FR 53262, Oct. 2, 1998]

§ 598.205 What are the requirements for nomination?

(a) *General.* No urban area may be considered for designation in accordance with subpart D of this part unless:

(1) The urban area is within the jurisdiction of a State or States and local government(s) that have the authority to nominate the urban area for designation and that provide written assurances satisfactory to the Secretary that the strategic plan described in § 598.215 will be implemented, and these governments submit its nomination;

(2) All information furnished by the nominating State(s) and local government(s) is determined by the Secretary to be reasonably accurate; and

(3) The application for designation is complete, as described in paragraph (b) of this section.

(b) *Contents of application for designation.* The application for designation of an urban area as an Empowerment Zone must do the following:

(1) Demonstrate that the nominated urban area satisfies the eligibility criteria set forth in subpart B of this part;

(2) Include a strategic plan, as described in § 598.215;

(3) Include the certifications described in § 598.210;

(4) Include the 1990 census maps showing the following:

(i) The boundaries of the local government(s); and

(ii) The boundaries of the nominated area, including any developable sites; and

(5) Include such other information as may be required by HUD in the application or in the document announcing the initiation of the designation process.

(Approved by the Office of Management and Budget under Control Number 2506–0148)

[63 FR 19155, Apr. 16, 1998, as amended at 63 FR 53262, Oct. 2, 1998]

§ 598.210 What certifications must governments make?

Certifications must be submitted by the State(s) and local government(s) requesting designation stating that:

(a) The nominated urban area satisfies the boundary tests of § 598.100(d);

(b) The nominated urban area is one of pervasive poverty, unemployment and general distress, as prescribed by § 598.110;

(c) The nominated urban area contains no portion of an area that is included in an Empowerment Zone or any other area currently nominated for designation as an Empowerment Zone (but it may include an Enterprise Community);

(d) Each nominating governmental entity has the authority to:

(1) Nominate the urban area for designation as an Empowerment Zone;

(2) Make the commitments required of nominating entities by § 598.215(b); and

(3) Provide written assurances satisfactory to the Secretary that the strategic plan will be implemented.

(e) Provide that the nominating governments or corporations agree to make available all information requested by HUD to aid in the evaluation of progress in implementing the strategic plan; and

(f) Provide assurances that the nominating governments will administer the Empowerment Zone program in a manner that affirmatively furthers fair housing on the basis of race, color, national origin, religion, sex, disability, and familial status (presence of children).

(Approved by the Office of Management and Budget under Control Number 2506–0148)

[63 FR 19155, Apr. 16, 1998, as amended at 63 FR 53262, Oct. 2, 1998; 72 FR 71016, Dec. 13, 2007]

§ 598.215 What are the purpose and content of the strategic plan?

(a) *Principles of strategic plan.* The strategic plan, which accompanies the application for designation, must be developed in accordance with four key principles:

(1) Strategic Vision for Change, which identifies what the community will become and a strategic map for revitalization. The vision should build on assets and coordinate a response to community needs in a comprehensive fashion. It also should set goals and performance benchmarks for measuring progress and establish a framework for evaluating and adjusting the revitalization plan;

(2) Community-Based Partnerships, involving the participation of all segments of the community, including the political and governmental leadership, community groups, local public health and social service departments and nonprofit groups providing similar services, environmental groups, local transportation planning entities, public and private schools, religious organizations, the private and nonprofit sectors, centers of learning, and other community institutions and individual citizens;

(3) Economic Opportunity, including job creation within the community and throughout the region, entrepreneurial initiatives, small business expansion, job training and other important job readiness and job support services, such as affordable child care and transportation services, that may enable residents to be employed in jobs that offer upward mobility;

(4) Sustainable Community Development, to advance the creation of livable and vibrant communities through comprehensive approaches that coordinate economic, physical, environmental, community and human development. These approaches should preserve the environment and historic landmarks, address "brownfields" clean-up and redevelopment, explore the economic development advantages of energy efficiency and use of renewable energy resources, and improve transportation, education, public safety, and enhanced access to information and technology among all segments of the community.

(b) *Elements of strategic plan.* The strategic plan must include the following elements:

(1) *Vision and values:* The community's strategic vision for change—a statement of what the community believes its future should be, and a statement of the community's values that guided the creation of the vision. Explain how the vision creates economic opportunity, encourages self-sufficiency and promotes sustainable community development.

(2) *Community assessment:* A comprehensive assessment of existing conditions and trends within the community, which includes, as a minimum:

(i) *Assessment of problems and opportunities.* A description and assessment of the trends and conditions within the community and of the surrounding region that form the basis of the strategic plan. The assessment will include an analysis of the strengths and assets of the community and region, as well as needs and problems, and should include a description of poverty and general distress, barriers to economic development and barriers to human development; and

(ii) *Resource analysis.* An assessment of the resources available to the community, including potential resources outside the nominated area, to address identified problems and needs, and maximize opportunities that exist within the community. Such resources may include financial, technical, human, cultural, educational, leadership, volunteerism, communications, transportation and commerce centers, rail and mass transit linkages, redevelopable land (including land, such as ports, that can be designated as "developable sites" under the additional 2,000 acres available); public space, infrastructure, and other community and regional assets that form the basis for the formulation and implementation of the strategic plan.

(3) *Goals:* A statement of a comprehensive and holistic set of goals to be achieved through implementation of the strategic plan throughout the 10-year implementation period, and a statement of the strategies the community proposes to use to achieve the strategic plan goals, and the identification of priority objectives.

(4) *Implementation plan:* A detailed plan that outlines how the community will implement its strategic plan. The plan will include:

(i) *Projects and programs.* Provide, for the first two-year implementation period, the following:

(A) A narrative outlining the specific projects and programs that will be implemented that will result in the achievement of the community's goals;

(B) Proposed timelines for implementing identified projects and programs;

(C) Identification of lead implementers of identified projects and programs, along with innovative partnerships that will be utilized to insure maximum community participation and project sustainability;

(D) Proposed budgets for each identified project or program, including projected costs, and sources of funding. Information on sources of funding will include whether the funding is anticipated or committed, and whether funding is conditioned upon the designation of the community as an Empowerment Zone. Evidence of committed funding is required, and may include letters of commitment, resolutions of support, or similar documentation as outlined in paragraph (b)(6) of this section. Funding may include cash and in-kind support from Federal, State and local governments, non-profit organizations, foundations, private businesses and other entities that will assist in the implementation of the strategic plan.

(E) Baselines and proposed measurable outputs;

(ii) *Tax incentive utilization plan.* A plan for integrating the new business tax incentives that are available to designated Empowerment Zones into the nominated area's business development efforts. The Round II tax incentives include Tax-Exempt Bond Financing, Increased Section 179 Deduction, Welfare-to-Work Credit, Environmental Cleanup Cost Deduction (i.e., "Brownfields Tax Incentive"), and the Work Opportunity Tax Credit. For a description of the tax incentives, see IRS Publication 954, "Tax Incentives for Empowerment Zones and Other Distressed Communities";

(iii) *Developable sites plan.* If the nominated area is to include developable sites, a plan to describe how the use of these parcels would benefit residents and businesses of the nominated area;

(iv) *Governance plan.* A Governance Plan for the administration of the strategic plan implementation process, which will include the following:

(A) The name of the proposed lead implementing entity, and other major administrative entities and their proposed or actual legal status and authority to receive and administer Federal funds. The strategic plan may be implemented by the local governments(s) and/or by the State(s) nominating an urban area for designation and/or by nongovernmental entities identified in the strategic plan;

(B) Evidence that the lead implementing entity and other key entities participating in the strategic plan implementation have the capacity to implement the plan;

(C) Proposed composition and date of establishment of any governance boards, advisory boards, commissions or similar bodies that will be established to manage the implementation of the strategic plan. Specific information will be included regarding representation of residents and businesses of the proposed Empowerment Zone area, and how members of the boards or commissions will be selected;

(D) The relationship between any governance structure created and local governments and other major community or regional organizations, such as a metropolitan planning organization, operating in the same geographic area;

(E) The methods by which stakeholders within the Zone will be kept informed about Zone activities and progress in implementing the strategic plan, including a description of plans for meetings open to the public. The community should utilize modern communication techniques and incorporate the Internet in order to enhance the

§ 598.300

communication and access to information among all stakeholders and participants; and

(F) The methods and procedures that will ensure continuing community and grassroots participation in the implementation of the strategic plan and in the governance of the Zone's activities.

(v) *Community performance assessment.* Methods the community will use to assess its own performance in implementing the strategic plan, and the process it will use to continually review the plan and amend as appropriate.

(5) *Strategic planning process documentation:* A description of the process the community used to select the boundaries of the proposed Empowerment Zone, including the developable sites, and to prepare the Strategic Plan. The documentation will:

(i) Explain how the community participated in choosing the area that is being nominated and why the area was nominated;

(ii) Indicate and briefly describe the specific groups, organizations, and individuals participating in the production of the plan and describe the history of these groups in the community;

(iii) Explain how participants were selected and provide evidence that the participants, taken as a whole, broadly represent the racial, cultural, gender, and economic diversity of the community;

(iv) Describe the role of the participants in the creation, development and future implementation of the plan; and

(v) Identify two or three topics addressed in the plan that caused the most serious disagreements among participants and describe how those disagreements were resolved; and

(6) *Documentation of commitments:* Letters of commitment, resolutions committing public or private resources, and other documentation that will demonstrate the level of public and private resources, both inside and outside the nominated area, that will be available to implement the Strategic Plan and increase economic opportunity in the nominated Empowerment Zone.

(c) *Prohibition against business relocation.* The strategic plan may not include any action to assist any establishment in relocating from one area outside the nominated urban area to the nominated urban area, except that assistance for the expansion of an existing business entity through the establishment of a new branch, affiliate, or subsidiary is permitted if:

(1) The establishment of the new branch, affiliate, or subsidiary will not result in a decrease in employment in the area of original location or in any other area where the existing business entity conducts business operations; and

(2) There is no reason to believe that the new branch, affiliate, or subsidiary is being established with the intention of closing down the operations of the existing business entity in the area of its original location or in any other area where the existing business entity conducts business operations.

(Approved by the Office of Management and Budget under Control Number 2506-0148)

[63 FR 19155, Apr. 16, 1998, as amended at 63 FR 53262, Oct. 2, 1998; 72 FR 71016, Dec. 13, 2007]

Subpart D—Designation Process

§ 598.300 Procedure for submitting a nomination.

(a) *Establishment of submission procedures.* HUD will establish a time period and procedures for the submission of nominations for designation as Empowerment Zones, including submission deadlines and addresses, in a document announcing the initiation of the designation process.

(b) *Acceptance for processing.* HUD will accept for processing those nominations for designation as Empowerment Zones that HUD determines have met the criteria required by this part.

(c) *Publication of designations.* Announcements of those nominated urban areas designated as Empowerment Zones will be made by publication in the FEDERAL REGISTER.

§ 598.305 Designation factors.

In choosing among nominated urban areas eligible for designation, the Secretary will consider:

(a) *Quality of strategic plan.* The quality of the strategic plan (see § 598.215(b));

Ofc. of Asst. Secy., Comm. Planning, Develop., HUD §598.415

(b) *Quality of commitments.* The quality and breadth of the commitments made in connection with the strategic plan (see §598.215(b)); and

(c) *Other factors.* Other factors established by HUD, as specified in a FEDERAL REGISTER notice.

Subpart E—Post-Designation Requirements

§598.400 HUD grants for planning activities.

(a) HUD will award planning grants up to $100,000 to each of the Empowerment Zones designated in accordance with this part.

(b) Eligible recipients for these grants are the lead unit of general local government that received designation under this part, or its designee. These recipients may subgrant all or part of the planning grant to qualified subgrantees, such as community organizations, agencies of local government, regional planning authorities, or planning consultants.

(c) Eligible planning activities include: hiring and development of staff, consulting services, publication of materials, community outreach and participation, governing board training, and similar activities that are intended to:

(1) Expand the planning capacity of the designee local government, the governing board, and/or participating entities, such as community organizations;

(2) Help the designee plan the implementation of the strategic plan; and

(3) Help the designee to develop its performance measurement process.

(d) The document announcing the initiation of the designation process describes the procedures for award of these planning grants, post-award reporting requirements with respect to the grants, and the uniform requirements applicable to all Federal grants.

§598.405 Environmental review.

Where any EZ's strategic plan or any revision thereof proposes the use of HUD EZ Grant Funds for activities that are not excluded from environmental review under 24 CFR 50.19(b), the EZ shall supply HUD with all available, relevant information necessary for HUD to perform any environmental review required by 24 CFR part 50.

[72 FR 71016, Dec. 13, 2007]

§598.408 Lead-based paint requirements.

The Lead-Based Paint Poisoning Prevention Act (42 U.S.C. 4821–4846), the Residential Lead-Based Paint Hazard Reduction Act of 1992 (42 U.S.C. 4851–4856), and the lead-based paint requirements set forth at part 35, subparts A, B, J, K, and R of this title apply to the activities funded by HUD under this program.

[69 FR 34275, June 21, 2004]

§598.410 Public access to materials and proceedings.

After designation, an area designated an EZ must make available to the public copies of the strategic plan and supporting documentation and must conduct its meetings in accordance with applicable open meetings statutes. HUD may make the strategic plan and supporting documentation available to members of the public.

§598.415 Reporting.

(a) Empowerment Zones designated in accordance with this part must submit periodic reports to HUD. These reports must identify the community, local government and State actions that have been taken in accordance with the strategic plan and provide notice of updates and modifications to the strategic plan. In addition to these reports, such other information relating to designated Empowerment Zones as HUD requests from time to time, including information documenting nondiscrimination in hiring and employment by businesses within the designated Empowerment Zone, must be submitted promptly.

(b) The States must submit periodic reports to HUD, demonstrating compliance with the certifications it is required to submit in accordance with this part.

(Approved by the Office of Management and Budget under Control Number 2506–0148)

[63 FR 19155, Apr. 16, 1998, as amended at 63 FR 53262, Oct. 2, 1998]

§ 598.420 Periodic progress determinations.

HUD will regularly evaluate the progress of implementation of the strategic plan in each designated Empowerment Zone on the basis of available information. HUD also may commission evaluations of the Empowerment Zone program as a whole by an impartial third party, at such intervals as HUD may establish.

§ 598.425 Validation of designation.

(a) On the basis of the periodic progress determinations described in § 598.420, and subject to the provisions relating to the revocation of designation in § 598.430, HUD will make findings on the continuing eligibility for and the validity of the designation of any Empowerment Zone.

(b) HUD may approve an Empowerment Zone's request for boundary modification, subject to the requirements specified in subpart B of this part.

§ 598.430 Revocation of designation.

(a) *Basis for revocation.* The Secretary may revoke the designation of an urban area as an Empowerment Zone if the Secretary determines, on the basis of the periodic progress determination described at § 598.420, that the State(s) or local government(s) in which the urban area is located:

(1) Has modified the boundaries of the area without written approval from HUD;

(2) Has failed to make progress in implementing the strategic plan; or

(3) Has not complied substantially with the strategic plan.

(b) *Letter of warning.* Before revoking the designation of an urban area and an Empowerment Zone, the Secretary will issue a letter of warning to the nominating State(s) and local government(s), with a copy to all affected Federal agencies of which the Secretary is aware;

(1) Advising that the Secretary has determined that the nominating local government(s) and/or State(s) has:

(i) Modified the boundaries of the area without written approval from HUD; or

(ii) Is not complying substantially with, or has failed to make progress in implementing the strategic plan; and

(2) Requesting a reply from the nominating entities within 90 days of the receipt of this letter of warning.

(c) *Notice of revocation.* To revoke the designation, the Secretary must issue a final notice of revocation of the designation of the urban area as an Empowerment Zone, after allowing 90 days from the date of receipt of the letter of warning for response, and after making a determination in accordance with paragraph (a) of this section.

(d) *Notice to affected Federal agencies.* HUD will notify all affected Federal agencies of which it is aware, of its determination to revoke any designation in accordance with this section.

(e) *Effect of revocation.* Upon revocation of an EZ's designation, the designation and remaining benefits may be awarded to the next highest ranked Round II applicant.

(f) *Publication.* The final notice of revocation of designation will be published in the FEDERAL REGISTER, and the revocation will be effective on the date of publication.

(Approved by the Office of Management and Budget under Control Number 2506-0148)

[63 FR 19155, Apr. 16, 1998, as amended at 63 FR 53262, Oct. 2, 1998]

Subpart F—Special Rules

§ 598.500 Indian reservations.

(a) An area within an Indian reservation (as defined in section 168(j)(6) if the Internal Revenue Code, 26 U.S.C. 168(j)(6)) may be included in an area nominated as an Empowerment Zone by State and local governments. An area completely within an Indian reservation may be nominated by the reservation governing body and, in that case, the area is treated as if it also were nominated by a State and a local government. Where two (or more) governing bodies have joint jurisdiction over an Indian reservation, the nomination of a reservation area must be a joint nomination.

(b) For purposes of paragraph (a) of this section, a reservation governing body must be the governing body of an Indian entity recognized and eligible to receive services from the Bureau of Indian Affairs, United States Department of Interior.

§ 598.505 Governments.

If more than one State or local government seeks to nominate an urban area under this part, any reference to or requirement of this part applies to all such governments.

§ 598.510 Nominations by Economic Development Corporations or the District of Columbia.

Any urban area nominated by an Economic Development Corporation chartered by the State in which it is located or by the District of Columbia shall be treated as nominated by a State and local government.

§ 598.515 Alaska and Hawaii.

A nominated area in Alaska or Hawaii is deemed to satisfy the criteria of distress, size, and poverty rate detailed in § 598.100(b), (c), (d), and (f), and § 598.110 if, for each census tract or block numbering area within the area, 20 percent or more of the families have income that is 50 percent or less of the statewide median family income (as determined under section 143 of the Internal Revenue Code).

Subpart G—Empowerment Zone Grants

SOURCE: 72 FR 71016, Dec. 13, 2007, unless otherwise noted.

§ 598.600 Applicability.

This subpart applies to a project or activity proposed by an Empowerment Zone after January 14, 2008 to be undertaken with funds appropriated by Congress and made available by HUD specifically for use by the EZ. These funds are referred to as "HUD EZ Grant Funds."

§ 598.605 Implementation plan.

(a) *Implementation plan content.* An EZ must submit an implementation plan for HUD approval that addresses each project or activity proposed to be undertaken by the EZ with HUD EZ Grant Funds. The implementation plan must:

(1) Describe the project or activity;
(2) Identify the completion date or duration of the project or activity;
(3) Provide the total cost of the project or activity;
(4) Identify the amount of HUD EZ Grant Funds to be used for the project or activity; and
(5) Include a narrative description of how the project or activity meets the resident benefit and economic development standards of this subpart.

(b) *Proposed funded project or activity.* The project or activity proposed in the implementation plan is subject to the following requirements:

(1) The Federal requirements listed in 24 CFR 5.105;
(2) The governmentwide, Uniform Administrative Requirements for Grants and Cooperative Agreements to State, Local and Federally Recognized Indian Tribal Governments at 24 CFR part 85;
(3) The requirements of the Uniform Relocation Assistance and Real Property Acquisition Policies Act of 1970 (URA) (42 U.S.C. 4601 et seq.);
(4) The environmental review and approval requirements of 24 CFR part 50;
(5) The provisions of the Memorandum of Agreement (MOA) setting forth the obligations and requirements that the state and local governments, as Empowerment Zone designees, have agreed to meet as signatories of the agreement.
(6) Recipients of the HUD EZ Grant Funds also must adhere to the requirements set forth in the provisions of the grant agreement for HUD EZ Grant Funds.

§ 598.610 Resident benefit standards.

The project or activity described in an implementation plan submitted for HUD approval by an EZ to describe the planned use of HUD EZ Grant Funds must meet one of the following three standards of resident benefit for determining the amount of HUD EZ Grant Funds that may be used to fund a particular project or activity:

(a) *Principal benefit standard*—(1) *Benefits other than jobs.* If a majority (51 percent) of the direct beneficiaries of the project or activity described in the implementation plan reside within the EZ, the project or activity may be fully assisted with HUD EZ Grant Funds.

(2) *Jobs benefit.* In any case where the direct benefits to be provided by a project or activity described in an implementation plan will be in the form of jobs, the project may be fully assisted with HUD EZ Grant Funds if at least 35 percent of the jobs are taken by, or made available to, EZ residents. A job satisfies this 35 percent requirement if the EZ resident is employed by the employer for at least 90 days during the year. For purposes of this 35 percent requirement, an employer may rely on a certification by the employee that provides to the employer the address of the employee's principal residence, and requires the employee to notify the employer of a change of the employee's principal residence.

(3) *Presumed benefit.* Certain commercial revitalization activities that are located and undertaken in an EZ and that provide services to both EZ residents and non-residents (e.g., supermarkets, drug stores) will presume to meet the 51 percent principal benefit standard in paragraph (a)(1) of this section, provided that the EZ maintains written documentation that briefly describes the activity, its service area, and the rationale for presuming that the activity meets the 51 percent principal benefit standard.

(b) *Proportional benefit standard.* If a project or activity described in an implementation plan cannot meet the principal benefit standard of paragraph (a) of this section, the percent of the cost of the project or activity that may be assisted with HUD EZ Grant Funds may not be greater than the percent of all persons benefiting directly from the project or activity who reside within the EZ.

(c) *Exception criterion.* In any case where a proposed project or activity, including activities outside of the designated area, would not meet the standards of paragraph (a) or paragraph (b) of this section, HUD EZ Grant Funds may be used where HUD determines that an implementation plan, accompanied by the facts that the EZ requests HUD to review and consider as justifying the exception, demonstrates substantial benefits to the EZ that would result from the project or other compelling reasons justifying the appropriateness of the implementation plan to the EZ's strategic plan. A request by an EZ for an exception under paragraph (c) of this section will receive a response by HUD no later than 60 days from the date of the EZ's request provided that the EZ's request with all relevant information is considered complete no later than 45 days from the date of the EZ's request.

§ 598.615 **Economic development standards.**

(a) *Economic development standards.* The project or activity in an implementation plan submitted for HUD approval by an EZ to describe the planned use of HUD EZ Grant Funds must meet one of the following economic development standards:

(1) *Business development assistance.* An activity that involves assisting a business in the EZ meets the standard, whether or not the business will create any new jobs. Any such activity must also meet the standards for benefiting a sufficient portion of EZ residents as required under § 598.610. Qualifying activities include the use of HUD EZ Grant Funds to:

(i) Assist in establishing a business;

(ii) Expand a business, including efforts to stimulate the development or expansion of microenterprises; and

(iii) Assisting businesses that provide goods or services within the EZ to remain within the EZ.

(2) *Employment training and assistance.* An activity that assists a person to take, or remain in, a job, subject to meeting the standards for benefiting a sufficient proportion of EZ residents as required under § 598.610, including:

(i) Job training;

(ii) Provision of child care;

(iii) Transportation to or from the place of employment or the place where job training is taking place; or

(iv) Counseling persons on job-related skills, such as how to interview successfully for a job, and dress and act appropriately in the conduct of a job.

(3) *Educational assistance.* The provision of educational assistance meets the economic development standard only if the EZ's implementation plan demonstrates that such education will be provided to persons who cannot qualify for available jobs because of the lack of some specific knowledge

that would be given them through the course(s) to be provided. Any educational assistance provided must also meet the standard for benefiting a sufficient portion of EZ residents as required under § 598.610.

(4) *EZ administrative capacity.* An activity that increases the capacity of governance board members or staff of the EZ's lead agency to carry out their roles with respect to economic development projects expected to be assisted in support of the EZ's strategic plan is eligible. This includes the cost of attending a conference on economic development. The use of HUD EZ Grant Funds for capacity building under this paragraph is deemed to provide adequate benefit to EZ residents.

(5) *Public improvements.* The provision of public improvements, such as extension of water or sewer capacity, or street widening, meets the economic development standard only if it is shown in the implementation plan that the lack of the improvements clearly is an impediment to the establishment, expansion or retention of one or more businesses in the EZ, and that the provision of the proposed public improvement would be limited as much as feasible to assisting the business or businesses. Any public improvements must also meet the standard for benefiting a sufficient portion of EZ residents as required under § 598.610.

(b) *Exception request.* HUD may approve a project or activity that does not fall within any of the previous review standards of this section if the EZ provides evidence that, in some way, the project or activity can reasonably be seen as meeting the economic development standard. Such a project or activity must also meet the standards for benefiting a sufficient portion of EZ residents as required under § 598.610. All requests for such an exception must be in writing, accompanied by the facts that the EZ wants HUD to review and consider as justification. A request by an EZ for an exception under this paragraph (b) will receive a response by HUD no later than 60 days from the date of the EZ's request provided that the EZ's request with all relevant information is considered complete no later than 45 days from the date of the EZ's request.

§ 598.620 Evaluation, monitoring, and enforcement.

(a) *Progress, evaluation, and monitoring.* HUD will review the performance of an EZ's use of HUD EZ Grant Funds for compliance with this subpart as part of its regular evaluation process under 24 CFR 598.420, through on-site monitoring under 24 CFR 85.40(e), and by other appropriate means.

(b) *Warning letter.* If HUD has reason to believe that an EZ is not carrying out its funded activities in accordance with any applicable requirements, including the resident benefit and economic development standards of this subpart, HUD may forward a warning letter to the EZ informing it of a potential violation and recommending action to avoid a violation. A warning letter is not a prerequisite for any other action HUD may take.

(c) *Notice of violation.* If HUD determines that there appears to be a violation in the use of HUD EZ Grant Funds, it will notify the EZ of the alleged violation and the action HUD proposes to take under 24 CFR 85.43 or its successor regulation or if appropriate, 24 CFR 598.430.

(d) *Response to notice.* A notice sent to an EZ under paragraph (c) of this section will provide the EZ with at least 30 calendar days from the time HUD sends the notice to respond with any information to rebut or mitigate the alleged violation.

(e) *Final action.* If the EZ does not respond within the period specified pursuant to paragraph (d) of this section, HUD will make a final determination of the violation and may proceed to take the action proposed in the notice. If the EZ responds, HUD will consider the information received from the EZ and may request additional information. After considering the information received from the EZ, HUD will notify the EZ of HUD's final determination and action, affirming, modifying, or repealing HUD's initial determination of an alleged violation and proposed action.

PART 599—RENEWAL COMMUNITIES

Subpart A—General Provisions

Sec.
599.1 Applicability and scope.
599.3 Definitions.
599.5 Data used for eligibility determinations.

Subpart B—Eligibility Requirements for Nomination of Renewal Communities

599.101 Eligibility to submit nominations.
599.103 Geographic and population requirements for a nominated area.
599.105 Economic condition requirements for a nominated area.
599.107 Required State and local commitments.

Subpart C—Procedures for Nomination of Renewal Communities

599.201 Initiation of application process.
599.203 Basic application submission requirements.

Subpart D—Evaluation of Applications Nominating Renewal Communities

599.301 Initial determination of threshold requirements.
599.303 Rating of applications.

Subpart E—Selection of Nominated Areas To Be Renewal Communities

599.401 Ranking of applications.
599.403 Number of Renewal Communities to be designated.
599.405 Selection of Renewal Communities.
599.407 Notification of Renewal Community designations.

Subpart F—Post-Designation Requirements

599.501 Period for which Renewal Community designation is in effect.
599.503 Effect of Renewal Community designation on an EZ/EC.
599.505 Coordinating responsible authority (CoRA).
599.507 Tax incentives utilization plan.
599.509 Modification of commitments and plans.
599.511 Reports and other information.
599.513 Revocation of designation.

AUTHORITY: 26 U.S.C. 1400E; 42 U.S.C. 3535(d).

SOURCE: 66 FR 35855, July 9, 2001, unless otherwise noted.

Subpart A—General Provisions

§ 599.1 Applicability and scope.

(a) This part establishes requirements and procedures applicable to the designation of Renewal Communities (RCs) through December 31, 2001, authorized under Subchapter X of the Internal Revenue Code of 1986 (26 U.S.C. 1400E, et seq.). HUD may choose to use these requirements and procedures in whole or in part for any future Renewal Community designations that may be authorized.

(b) This part contains provisions relating to area requirements, the nomination process for Renewal Communities, and the evaluation and designation of nominated areas by HUD.

§ 599.3 Definitions.

In addition to the definitions of "HUD" and "Secretary" found in 24 CFR 5.100, the following definitions apply to this part:

Census tract means a census tract, as the term is used by the Bureau of the Census, or, if census tracts are not defined for the area, a block numbering area.

Designation means the process by which the Secretary designates areas as Renewal Communities eligible for tax incentives and credits established by Subchapter X of the Internal Revenue Code of 1986, as amended (26 U.S.C. 1400E, et seq.) and for any additional assistance that may be made available.

Empowerment Zone (EZ) means an area so designated by the Secretary in accordance with 24 CFR part 597 or 24 CFR part 598.

Enterprise Community (EC) means an area so designated by the Secretary in accordance with 24 CFR part 597.

Local government means any county, city, town, township, parish, village, or other general purpose political subdivision of a State, and any combination of these political subdivisions that is recognized by the Secretary.

Metropolitan Area (MA) means an area as defined to be a Metropolitan Statistical Area or Primary Metropolitan Statistical Area by the Office of Management and Budget on June 30, 1999.

Nominated area means an area with a population of not more than 200,000 that is nominated by one or more local governments and the State or States in which it is located, or the governing body of the Indian reservation in which it is located, for designation in accordance with this part.

Renewal Community (RC) means an area so designated by HUD in accordance with this part.

Rural area means a nominated area:
(1) Which is within a local government jurisdiction or jurisdictions with a population of less than 50,000; or
(2) Which is outside of an MA; or
(3) Which is determined by HUD, after consultation with the Secretary of Commerce, to be a rural area. An area may qualify as a rural area under this paragraph (3) of this definition if:
(i) It is a nominated area that crosses jurisdictional boundaries;
(ii) The total population of the nominated area does not exceed 200,000;
(iii) The nominated area as a whole would not satisfy the requirements of either paragraph (1) or (2) of this definition;
(iv) Each portion of the nominated area that is located within a separate jurisdiction meets the requirements of either paragraph (1) or (2) of this definition; and
(v) The area is specifically nominated as a rural area; or
(4) Which does not meet the requirements of either paragraph (1), (2), or (3) of this definition but which is determined by HUD on a case-by-case basis, after consultation with the Secretary of Commerce, to be a rural area based on information submitted to demonstrate that the nominated area should be considered as a rural area.

State means any State of the United States.

Urban area means a nominated area that is not a rural area.

§ 599.5 Data used for eligibility determinations.

(a) *Source of data.* The data to be used in determining the population, poverty rate, unemployment rate and household income distribution information of an area is from the 1990 Decennial Census.

(b) *Geographic boundaries.* The boundary of an area that is nominated for designation as an Renewal Community must coincide with the boundaries of census tracts, as defined in § 599.3 except in the case of Indian reservation areas where the use of census tracts would tend to include areas outside the jurisdiction of the reservation governing body and such body is not making the nomination in concert with another jurisdiction.

Subpart B—Eligibility Requirements for Nomination of Renewal Communities

§ 599.101 Eligibility to submit nominations.

(a) *In general.* Except as provided in paragraph (b) of this section, a nomination for the designation of an area as a Renewal Community must be submitted by one or more local governments and the State or States in which the nominated area is located.

(b) *Nominated areas on Indian reservations.* In the case of a nominated area on an Indian reservation, the reservation governing body (as determined by the Secretary of the Interior) must submit the nomination and shall be treated as being both the State and local governments with respect to the area for purposes of this part.

(c) *Responsible official.* The submission of an application, and any other action required of a nominating government under this part, such as the submission of a certification, must be performed by an official or employee authorized to act on behalf of the government for that purpose.

§ 599.103 Geographic and population requirements for a nominated area.

(a) *Geographic requirements.* A nominated area must meet the following geographic requirements to be eligible for designation as a Renewal Community:

(1) The area must be within the jurisdiction of one or more local governments.

(2) The boundary of the area must be continuous.

(i) The boundary line of the nominated area may be interrupted by jurisdictional boundaries, such as State or county lines, or natural boundaries, such as rivers, as long as the resulting

§ 599.105

area is entirely within the boundary line except for the interruptions.

(ii) The nominated area may enclose an area or areas that are excluded from the nominated area, as long as each enclosed area to be excluded is within a continuous boundary line.

(3) The nominated area may be any size, as long as it meets all of the requirements of this part.

(b) *Population requirements*—(1) *In general.* Except as provided in paragraph (b)(2) of this section, a nominated area must have a population of not more than 200,000 and at least:

(i) 4,000 if any portion of the area (other than a nominated rural area) is located within an MA which has a population of 50,000 or greater; or

(ii) 1,000 in any other case.

(2) *Nominated areas on Indian reservations.* A nominated area that is entirely within an Indian reservation (as determined by the Secretary of the Interior) is not subject to the population requirements of paragraph (b)(1) of this section.

§ 599.105 Economic condition requirements for a nominated area.

(a) *Certification for economic requirements.* An official or officials authorized to do so by the nominating State and local governments must certify in writing for HUD's acceptance that the nominated area is an area of pervasive poverty, unemployment, and general distress, and that the nominated area meets the requirements of paragraphs (b), (c) and, in the case of urban areas, paragraph (d) of this section. HUD's acceptance of the certification is subject to a review of data supporting the certification, as provided in paragraph (e) of this section.

(b) *Unemployment requirement.* A nominated area meets the unemployment requirement if the unemployment rate in the nominated area taken as a whole was at least one and one-half times (150% of) the national unemployment rate for the period to which such data relate.

(c) *Poverty requirement.* A nominated area meets the poverty requirement if the poverty rate for each population census tract within the nominated area is at least 20 percent. In the case of a nominated area that is within an Indian reservation, and cannot equivalently be described with census tracts, the poverty rate of the nominated area taken as a whole is considered for purposes of making this determination.

(d) *Income requirement for urban areas.* In the case of a nominated urban area, at least 70 percent of the households living in the nominated area must have incomes below 80 percent of the median income of households within the jurisdiction of the local government or governments in which the nominated area is located. The number of households below 80 percent of the median income in each census tract shall be the number of households with incomes below 80 percent of the Household Adjusted Median Family Income (HAMFI) in each census tract as determined by HUD.

(e) *HUD review of supporting data*—(1) *Unemployment, poverty and income.* HUD will review 1990 census data to determine whether to accept a certification that a nominated area meets the requirements of paragraphs (b), (c) and (d) of this section.

(2) *Pervasive poverty, unemployment and general distress*—(i) *Pervasive poverty.* Pervasive poverty is demonstrated by evidence that:

(A) Poverty, as indicated by the number of persons listed as being in poverty in the 1990 Decennial Census, is widespread throughout the nominated area; or

(B) Poverty, as described in paragraph (e)(2)(i)(A) of this section, has become entrenched or intractable over time (through comparison of 1980 and 1990 census data or other relevant evidence).

(ii) *Unemployment.* Unemployment is demonstrated by:

(A) The most recent data available indicating that the annual rate of unemployment for the nominated area is not less than the national annual average rate of unemployment; or

(B) Evidence of especially severe economic conditions, such as military base or plant closings or other conditions that have brought about significant job dislocation within the nominated area.

(iii) *General distress.* General distress is evidenced by describing adverse conditions within the nominated urban area other than those of pervasive poverty and unemployment. Below average or decline in per capita income, earnings per worker, number of persons on welfare, per capita property tax base, average years of school completed, substantial population decline, and a high or rising incidence of crime, narcotics use, homelessness, high incidence of AIDS, abandoned housing, deteriorated infrastructure, school dropouts, teen pregnancy, incidence of domestic violence, incidence of certain health conditions and illiteracy are examples of appropriate indicators of general distress.

§ 599.107 Required State and local commitments.

(a) *Commitment to a course of action*— (1) *Agreement of State and local governments.* The nominating State and local governments must agree in writing that, for any period during which the area is a Renewal Community, the governments will follow a specified course of action which meets the requirements of paragraph (a)(2) of this section. If each nominating State and local government is a signatory to a course of action under paragraph (a)(2) of this section, a separate written agreement is not necessary to meet the requirements of this paragraph.

(2) *Course of action requirements*—(i) *In general.* A course of action is a written document, signed by the nominated area's State and/or local governments and community-based organizations which commits each signatory to undertake and achieve measurable goals and actions within the nominated area upon its designation as a Renewal Community.

(ii) *Community-based organizations.* For purposes of the course of action, "community-based organizations" includes for-profit and non-profit private entities, businesses and business organizations, neighborhood organizations, and community groups. Community-based organizations are not required to be located in the nominated area as long as they commit to achieving the goals of the course of action in the Renewal Community.

(iii) *Timetable.* The course of action must include a timetable that identifies the significant steps and target dates for implementing the goals and actions.

(iv) *Performance measures.* The course of action must include a description of how the performance of the course of action will be measured and evaluated.

(v) *Required goals and actions.* The course of action must include at least four of the following:

(A) A reduction of tax rates or fees applying within the Renewal Community;

(B) An increase in the level of efficiency of local services within the Renewal Community, such as services for residents funded through the Federal Temporary Assistance for Needy Families program and related Federal programs including, for example, job support services, child care and after school care for children of working residents, employment training, transportation services and other services that help residents become economically self-sufficient;

(C) Crime reduction strategies, such as crime prevention, including the provision of crime prevention services by nongovernmental entities;

(D) Actions to reduce, remove, simplify, or streamline governmental requirements applying within the Renewal Community, such as:

(*1*) *Density bonus.* Permission to develop or redevelop real property at a higher density level than otherwise permitted under the zoning ordinance, e.g., increased height or increased number of residential or business units;

(*2*) *Incentive zoning.* Providing a density bonus or other real property-related incentive for the development, redevelopment, or preservation of a parcel in the designated area;

(*3*) *Comprehensive or one-stop permit.* Streamlining construction or other development permitting processes, rather than requiring multiple applications for multiple permits, e.g., for demolition, site preparation, and construction, the developer or redeveloper submits a single application that is circulated for the necessary reviews by the various planning, engineering, and other departments in the county or municipality;

(*4*) *Variance and exception policies.* Counties or municipalities may pass ordinancesthat permit variances to or

§ 599.107

exceptions from certain zoning or other land use limitations. Examples include a reduced building set-back requirement or a reduced requirement for the provision of parking. Thepolicy may be limited to a particular geographic area;

(5) *Voluntary environmental compliance program.* A shared or limited environmental liability program, with limited liability from certain legal or administrative action in exchange for undertaking an approved program of environmental investigation, hazard control, and on-going risk reduction activities. Typically, the liability limitation is for future environmental cleanup (and not against lawsuit for damages). Risk of cleanup may be shared by the developer or property owner and the government;

(E) Involvement in economic development activities by private entities, organizations, neighborhood organizations, and community groups, particularly those in the Renewal Community, including a commitment from such private entities to provide jobs and job training for, and technical, financial, or other assistance to, employers, employees, and residents from the Renewal Community;

(F) The gift or sale at below fair market value of surplus real property held by State or local governments, such as land, homes, and commercial or industrial structures in the Renewal Community to neighborhood organizations, community development corporations, or private companies.

(3) *Certification requirement for crime incidence.* If preference points are being sought for the nominated area because it qualifies for preference points in accordance with § 599.303(c)(1), the course of action must contain a certification by each nominating State and local government of the 1999 Local Crime Index rate per 100,000 inhabitants (LCI) determined for the nominated area. The offenses used in determining the LCI are the violent crimes of murder and nonnegligent manslaughter, forcible rape, robbery, and aggravated assault, and the property crimes of burglary, larceny-theft, and motor vehicle theft.

(b) *Economic growth promotion requirements*—(1) *Required certification.* The State and local governments in which a nominated area is located must certify in writing that they have repealed or reduced, will not enforce, or will reduce within the nominated area at least four of the following:

(i) Licensing requirements for occupations that do not ordinarily require a professional degree;

(ii) Zoning restrictions on home-based businesses which do not create a public nuisance;

(iii) Permit requirements for street vendors who do not create a public nuisance;

(iv) Zoning or other restrictions that impede the formation of schools or child care centers; and

(v) Franchises or other restrictions on competition for businesses providing public services, including taxicabs, jitneys, cable television, or trash hauling.

(2) *Exception.* The requirements of paragraph (b)(1) of this section do not apply to the extent that a regulation of businesses and occupations is necessary for and well-tailored to the protection of health and safety. The certifications required under paragraph (b)(1) of this section may be limited to exclude or include specific businesses and occupations.

(c) *Recognition of past efforts.* The course of action and economic growth requirements under paragraphs (a) and (b), respectively, of this section are not limited to future goals and actions. Past efforts within the previous eight years, either completed or on-going, of the nominating State or local governments to undertake any of the goals or actions listed in paragraph (a)(2)(v) or (b)(1) of this section qualify to meet these requirements. If past efforts are used, the nominating governments must identify which of the required goals and actions listed in paragraph (a)(2)(v) or (b)(1) of this section they address; the timetable for their continued implementation, if on-going; and the community-based organizations involved, if any.

[66 FR 35855, July 9, 2001, as amended at 66 FR 52675, Oct. 17, 2001]

Ofc. of Asst. Secy., Comm. Planning, Develop., HUD § 599.303

Subpart C—Procedures for Nomination of Renewal Communities

§ 599.201 Initiation of application process.

(a) *Federal Register notice.* To initiate the nomination process for Renewal Communities, HUD will publish a notice inviting applications for the designation of Renewal Communities in the FEDERAL REGISTER.

(b) *Contents.* The notice inviting applications will include specific information as to due dates and submission requirements.

§ 599.203 Basic application submission requirements.

The basic application submission requirements for nominating an area as a Renewal Community are:

(a) *Identification of the nominated area.* An application must identify the census tracts that constitute the nominated area. The nominated area must meet all of the eligibility requirements of subpart B of this part.

(b) *State and local commitments.* An application must include the documents evidencing compliance with State and local commitments required by § 599.107.

(c) *Public notice certification.* An application must include a certification, signed by a responsible official or employee of each nominating State and local government, that the public was provided notice of, and an opportunity to participate in, the application development process. Notice and opportunity to participate may include procedures such as placing announcements in newspapers or other media, holding public meetings, and soliciting comments.

Subpart D—Evaluation of Applications Nominating Renewal Communities

§ 599.301 Initial determination of threshold requirements.

(a) *Two threshold requirements.* Before rating and ranking an application, HUD will review it to determine if the application meets both of the following thresholds:

(1) *Eligibility of the nominated area.* This threshold is met if HUD determines that the nominated area as identified in the application meets all of the area eligibility requirements of subpart B of this part.

(2) *Adequacy of State and local commitments.* This threshold is met if HUD determines that the documents in the application evidencing compliance with the required State and local commitments meet all of the course of action and economic growth promotion requirements of § 599.107.

(b) *Failure to meet threshold requirements*—(1) *No rating or ranking.* An application that does not meet both of the threshold requirements by the application due date specified in the published notice inviting applications will not be rated or ranked for further Renewal Community consideration.

(2) *Opportunity to correct failure.* HUD will notify an applicant of the threshold deficiencies in its application. An applicant may submit additional information and take any other action required to correct the deficiencies and meet the threshold requirements until the due date for applications specified in the published notice inviting applications.

§ 599.303 Rating of applications.

(a) *In general.* Each application that qualifies by meeting the threshold requirements will receive a score based on its ranking, as described in paragraph (b) of this section, plus any preference points, as described in paragraph (c) of this section.

(b) *Ranking score.* Each nominated area meeting the minimum thresholds will be ranked from highest to lowest according to the area poverty rate, area unemployment rate, and for urban areas, the percentage of families below 80 percent of area median income. Urban nominated areas will be ranked separately from rural nominated areas. The percentile rank will be determined by dividing these rankings by the total number of nominated areas ranked and multiplying the result by 100. The average ranking will be determined by computing the simple average of the percentile ranks for each nominated area. To create a 100 point scale, the average rankings will be subtracted from 100.

(c) *Preference points*—(1) *Incidence of crime.* A nominated area may receive a maximum of 1, 2, or 4 crime incidence preference points as follows:

(i) *Number of points awarded.* A nominated area will receive 1 additional point if its 1999 Local Crime Index (LCI), as determined on the basis of data from each State and local law enforcement authority with jurisdiction in the nominated area, does not exceed by more than 25% the nation-wide 1999 Crime Index rate per 100,000 inhabitants (CI) prepared as part of the FBI's Uniform Crime Reporting (UCR) Program. A preference of 2 points will be added to the score of a nominated area with an LCI that does not exceed the CI by more than 10 percent. A nominated area that has an LCI that is less than the CI will receive 4 preference points.

(ii) *Qualifying for preference points.* To qualify for preference points based on the incidence of crime, the nominating governments must determine and then certify to the LCI determined for the nominated area, in accordance with § 599.107(a)(3)

(2) *Preference points for certain census tracts.* A nominated area will receive one preference point if any of its census tracts is a census tract identified in GAO Report RCED–98–158R, dated May 12, 1998. (The GAO Report is available from U.S. General Accounting Office, P.O. Box 37050, Washington, DC 20013 or *http://www.gao.gov.*)

Subpart E—Selection of Nominated Areas To Be Renewal Communities

§ 599.401 Ranking of applications.

(a) *Ranking order.* Rural and urban applications will be ranked according to their final scores as determined in accordance with § 599.303, with the highest scoring applications ranked first.

(b) *Separate ranking categories.* After initial ranking, both rural and urban applications will be separated into two ranking categories:

(1) *Category 1.* Applications for designation of nominated areas that are Enterprise Communities or Empowerment Zones will be placed into Category 1 in rank order.

(2) *Category 2.* Applications for designation of nominated areas that are not placed into or selected from Category 1 will be placed into Category 2 in rank order.

§ 599.403 Number of Renewal Communities to be designated.

(a) *In general.* Except as provided in paragraph (b) of this section, the total number of Renewal Communities to be designated and the distribution of designations between urban and rural areas are as follows:

(1) *Total number.* The total number of nominated areas to be selected for designation as Renewal Communities is 40.

(2) *Rural areas.* HUD will select at least 12 rural areas for designation as Renewal Communities. If HUD does not receive at least 12 eligible rural area applications for Renewal Community designation, the number of rural area designations will be the number of eligible rural area applications received by HUD.

(3) *Urban areas.* The number of urban areas selected for designation as Renewal Communities will be the number remaining after subtracting the number of rural areas selected from 40.

(b) *Less than 40 eligible applications.* If HUD receives fewer than 40 eligible applications nominating areas, the total number of nominated areas to be selected for designation as Renewal Communities will be the total number of eligible applications.

§ 599.405 Selection of Renewal Communities.

(a) *Selection of Category 1 applications*—(1) *Six or less rural nominations.* If there are six or fewer Category 1 rural area nominations, HUD will select all of the nominated rural areas in Category 1 for designation as Renewal Communities. HUD will then select the highest ranking Category 1 urban area nominations, but will not exceed a total of 20 Category 1 designations.

(2) *More than six rural nominations.* If there are more than six Category 1 rural area nominations, HUD will select the six highest ranked Category 1 rural applications, and will then select,

in rank order, the highest ranking Category 1 area nominations, whether urban or rural, until not more than a total of 20 Category 1 designations is made.

(b) *Selection of Category 2 applications.* After not more than 20 Category 1 designations are made in accordance with paragraph (a) of this section, any remaining Category 1 applications will be placed back in rank order into Category 2, with selections for a combined Category 1 and Category 2 total of not more than 40 designations made as follows:

(1) *Less than six Category 1 rural applications.* If the number of rural area applications selected in Category 1 is less than six, HUD will select the highest ranking rural area applications in Category 2 until the total number of rural areas selected is 12. The remaining designations will be made from both rural and urban areas in rank order. If there are fewer than 12 eligible rural applications overall, counting both Category 1 and Category 2, all of the eligible rural applications will be selected.

(2) *Six or more Category 1 rural applications.* If the number of rural area applications selected in Category 1 is six or more, HUD will select the six highest Category 2 rural applications. The remaining designations will be made from both rural and urban areas in rank order.

(c) *Effective date of designation.* The effective date of designation as a Renewal Community is the date a nominated area is selected in accordance with this section.

§ 599.407 Notification of Renewal Community designations.

(a) *Notification of applicant.* HUD will notify each applicant of the designation of its nominated area as a Renewal Community.

(b) *Federal Register publication.* In addition to any other form of notification, HUD will publish a notice of the designation of Renewal Communities in the FEDERAL REGISTER.

Subpart F—Post-Designation Requirements

§ 599.501 Period for which Renewal Community designation is in effect.

Any designation of an area as a Renewal Community will remain in effect during the period beginning on January 1, 2002, and ending on the earliest of:

(a) December 31, 2009;

(b) The termination date designated by the State and local governments in their nomination application, if any; or

(c) The date HUD revokes the designation.

§ 599.503 Effect of Renewal Community designation on an EZ/EC.

The designation of any area as an Empowerment Zone or Enterprise Community shall cease to be in effect as of the date that the designation of any portion of such area as a Renewal Community takes effect.

§ 599.505 Coordinating responsible authority (CoRA).

Within 30 days of the Renewal Community designation, the State and local governments in which the area is located must submit to HUD information identifying the coordinating responsible authority (CoRA), which is the entity, organization or persons with the responsibility and authority to achieve the State and local government commitments made at the time of application as required by § 599.107 and to undertake the development and administration of policies, procedures and activities to implement and maximize the Federal, State and local benefits made available in the Renewal Community.

§ 599.507 Tax incentives utilization plan.

(a) *Preliminary plan.* Within six months of designation, the CoRA must prepare and submit to HUD a preliminary tax incentives utilization plan for achieving the State and local commitments made at the time of application as required by § 599.107 and implementing and maximizing the Federal, State and local benefits made available in the Renewal Community.

§ 599.509

(b) *Final plan.* Within twelve months of designation, the CoRA must prepare and submit to HUD the final tax incentives utilization plan for achieving the State and local commitments made at the time of application as required by § 599.107 and implementing and maximizing the Federal, State and local benefits made available in the Renewal Community.

(c) *Community participation.* The CoRA must ensure that the preliminary and final tax incentives utilizations plans are developed with the participation of the residents and community organizations in the Renewal Community.

(d) *Coordination with Consolidated Plan and Indian Housing Plan.* The tax incentives utilization plan must include a certification that it is consistent with the Consolidated Plan prepared in accordance with 24 CFR part 91 or the Indian Housing Plan prepared in accordance with 24 CFR part 1000, as applicable.

(e) *HUD technical assistance.* HUD will provide technical assistance as authorized to assist the CoRA in preparing the required tax incentives utilization plans.

§ 599.509 Modification of commitments and plans.

The CoRA may submit requests to HUD to modify the State and local commitments made at the time of application as required by § 599.107 and the tax incentives utilization plans required by § 599.505. Requests must provide evidence to support the proposed modifications. HUD will review the proposed modification for consistency with regulatory and statutory requirements and approve, suggest additional or alternate modifications or deny the request within 30 days.

§ 599.511 Reports and other information.

The CoRA and the State or local governments in which the Renewal Community is located must submit such periodic reports and provide such additional information as HUD may require.

§ 599.513 Revocation of designation.

(a) *Basis for revocation.* HUD may revoke the Renewal Community designation of an area if HUD determines that the CoRA or the State or local governments in which the area is located:

(1) Have modified the boundaries of the area; or

(2) Are not complying substantially with, or fail to make progress in achieving the State and local commitments made at the time of application as required by § 599.107.

(b) *Letter of warning.* Before revoking the Renewal Community designation of an area, HUD will issue a letter of warning to the CoRa and the State and local governments in which the area is located, with a copy to all affected Federal agencies of which HUD is aware:

(1) Advising that HUD has determined that the CoRA and/or State and/or local governments in which the area is located have:

(i) Modified the boundaries of the area without written approval from HUD; or

(ii) Are not complying substantially with, or have failed to make progress in achieving the State and local commitments made at the time of application as required by § 599.107; and

(2) Requesting a reply from the CoRa and State and local governments in which the area is located within 90 days of the receipt of this letter of warning.

(c) *Notice of revocation.* To revoke the designation, HUD must issue a final notice of revocation of the designation of the area as a Renewal Community, after allowing 90 days from the date of receipt of the letter of warning for response, and after making a determination in accordance with paragraph (a) of this section.

(d) *Notice to affected Federal agencies.* HUD will notify all affected Federal agencies of which it is aware, of its determination to revoke any designation in accordance with this section.

(e) *Effect of revocation.* Upon revocation of a Renewal Community designation, the designation and applicable benefits cease to be available in the area.

(f) *Publication.* The final notice of revocation of designation will be published in the FEDERAL REGISTER, and the revocation will be effective on the date of publication.

CHAPTER VI—OFFICE OF ASSISTANT SECRETARY FOR COMMUNITY PLANNING AND DEVELOPMENT, DEPARTMENT OF HOUSING AND URBAN DEVELOPMENT, PARTS 600-699 [RESERVED]

FINDING AIDS

A list of CFR titles, subtitles, chapters, subchapters and parts and an alphabetical list of agencies publishing in the CFR are included in the CFR Index and Finding Aids volume to the Code of Federal Regulations which is published separately and revised annually.

Table of CFR Titles and Chapters
Alphabetical List of Agencies Appearing in the CFR
List of CFR Sections Affected

Table of CFR Titles and Chapters
(Revised as of April 1, 2009)

Title 1—General Provisions

I	Administrative Committee of the Federal Register (Parts 1—49)
II	Office of the Federal Register (Parts 50—299)
IV	Miscellaneous Agencies (Parts 400—500)

Title 2—Grants and Agreements

SUBTITLE A—OFFICE OF MANAGEMENT AND BUDGET GUIDANCE FOR GRANTS AND AGREEMENTS

I	Office of Management and Budget Governmentwide Guidance for Grants and Agreements (Parts 100—199)
II	Office of Management and Budget Circulars and Guidance (200—299)

SUBTITLE B—FEDERAL AGENCY REGULATIONS FOR GRANTS AND AGREEMENTS

III	Department of Health and Human Services (Parts 300— 399)
VI	Department of State (Parts 600—699)
VIII	Department of Veterans Affairs (Parts 800—899)
IX	Department of Energy (Parts 900—999)
XI	Department of Defense (Parts 1100—1199)
XII	Department of Transportation (Parts 1200—1299)
XIII	Department of Commerce (Parts 1300—1399)
XIV	Department of the Interior (Parts 1400—1499)
XV	Environmental Protection Agency (Parts 1500—1599)
XVIII	National Aeronautics and Space Administration (Parts 1880—1899)
XXII	Corporation for National and Community Service (Parts 2200—2299)
XXIII	Social Security Administration (Parts 2300—2399)
XXIV	Housing and Urban Development (Parts 2400—2499)
XXV	National Science Foundation (Parts 2500—2599)
XXVI	National Archives and Records Administration (Parts 2600—2699)
XXVII	Small Business Administration (Parts 2700—2799)
XXVIII	Department of Justice (Parts 2800—2899)
XXXI	Institute of Museum and Library Services (Parts 3100—3199)
XXXII	National Endowment for the Arts (Parts 3200—3299)
XXXIII	National Endowment for the Humanities (Parts 3300—3399)

Title 2—Grants and Agreements—Continued

Chap.
XXXV Export-Import Bank of the United States (Parts 3500—3599)
XXXVII Peace Corps (Parts 3700—3799)

Title 3—The President

Presidential Documents
I Executive Office of the President (Parts 100—199)

Title 4—Accounts

I Government Accountability Office (Parts 1—99)

Title 5—Administrative Personnel

I Office of Personnel Management (Parts 1—1199)
II Merit Systems Protection Board (Parts 1200—1299)
III Office of Management and Budget (Parts 1300—1399)
V The International Organizations Employees Loyalty Board (Parts 1500—1599)
VI Federal Retirement Thrift Investment Board (Parts 1600—1699)
VIII Office of Special Counsel (Parts 1800—1899)
IX Appalachian Regional Commission (Parts 1900—1999)
XI Armed Forces Retirement Home (Parts 2100—2199)
XIV Federal Labor Relations Authority, General Counsel of the Federal Labor Relations Authority and Federal Service Impasses Panel (Parts 2400—2499)
XV Office of Administration, Executive Office of the President (Parts 2500—2599)
XVI Office of Government Ethics (Parts 2600—2699)
XXI Department of the Treasury (Parts 3100—3199)
XXII Federal Deposit Insurance Corporation (Parts 3200—3299)
XXIII Department of Energy (Parts 3300—3399)
XXIV Federal Energy Regulatory Commission (Parts 3400—3499)
XXV Department of the Interior (Parts 3500—3599)
XXVI Department of Defense (Parts 3600— 3699)
XXVIII Department of Justice (Parts 3800—3899)
XXIX Federal Communications Commission (Parts 3900—3999)
XXX Farm Credit System Insurance Corporation (Parts 4000—4099)
XXXI Farm Credit Administration (Parts 4100—4199)
XXXIII Overseas Private Investment Corporation (Parts 4300—4399)
XXXV Office of Personnel Management (Parts 4500—4599)
XL Interstate Commerce Commission (Parts 5000—5099)
XLI Commodity Futures Trading Commission (Parts 5100—5199)
XLII Department of Labor (Parts 5200—5299)
XLIII National Science Foundation (Parts 5300—5399)
XLV Department of Health and Human Services (Parts 5500—5599)

Title 5—Administrative Personnel—Continued

Chap.

XLVI	Postal Rate Commission (Parts 5600—5699)
XLVII	Federal Trade Commission (Parts 5700—5799)
XLVIII	Nuclear Regulatory Commission (Parts 5800—5899)
L	Department of Transportation (Parts 6000—6099)
LII	Export-Import Bank of the United States (Parts 6200—6299)
LIII	Department of Education (Parts 6300—6399)
LIV	Environmental Protection Agency (Parts 6400—6499)
LV	National Endowment for the Arts (Parts 6500—6599)
LVI	National Endowment for the Humanities (Parts 6600—6699)
LVII	General Services Administration (Parts 6700—6799)
LVIII	Board of Governors of the Federal Reserve System (Parts 6800—6899)
LIX	National Aeronautics and Space Administration (Parts 6900—6999)
LX	United States Postal Service (Parts 7000—7099)
LXI	National Labor Relations Board (Parts 7100—7199)
LXII	Equal Employment Opportunity Commission (Parts 7200—7299)
LXIII	Inter-American Foundation (Parts 7300—7399)
LXIV	Merit Systems Protection Board (Parts 7400—7499)
LXV	Department of Housing and Urban Development (Parts 7500—7599)
LXVI	National Archives and Records Administration (Parts 7600—7699)
LXVII	Institute of Museum and Library Services (Parts 7700—7799)
LXVIII	Commission on Civil Rights (Parts 7800—7899)
LXIX	Tennessee Valley Authority (Parts 7900—7999)
LXXI	Consumer Product Safety Commission (Parts 8100—8199)
LXXIII	Department of Agriculture (Parts 8300—8399)
LXXIV	Federal Mine Safety and Health Review Commission (Parts 8400—8499)
LXXVI	Federal Retirement Thrift Investment Board (Parts 8600—8699)
LXXVII	Office of Management and Budget (Parts 8700—8799)
XCVII	Department of Homeland Security Human Resources Management System (Department of Homeland Security—Office of Personnel Management) (Parts 9700—9799)
XCIX	Department of Defense Human Resources Management and Labor Relations Systems (Department of Defense—Office of Personnel Management) (Parts 9900—9999)

Title 6—Domestic Security

I	Department of Homeland Security, Office of the Secretary (Parts 0—99)
X	Privacy and Civil Liberties Oversight Board (Parts 1000—1099)

Title 7—Agriculture

Chap.	
	SUBTITLE A—OFFICE OF THE SECRETARY OF AGRICULTURE (PARTS 0—26)
	SUBTITLE B—REGULATIONS OF THE DEPARTMENT OF AGRICULTURE
I	Agricultural Marketing Service (Standards, Inspections, Marketing Practices), Department of Agriculture (Parts 27—209)
II	Food and Nutrition Service, Department of Agriculture (Parts 210—299)
III	Animal and Plant Health Inspection Service, Department of Agriculture (Parts 300—399)
IV	Federal Crop Insurance Corporation, Department of Agriculture (Parts 400—499)
V	Agricultural Research Service, Department of Agriculture (Parts 500—599)
VI	Natural Resources Conservation Service, Department of Agriculture (Parts 600—699)
VII	Farm Service Agency, Department of Agriculture (Parts 700—799)
VIII	Grain Inspection, Packers and Stockyards Administration (Federal Grain Inspection Service), Department of Agriculture (Parts 800—899)
IX	Agricultural Marketing Service (Marketing Agreements and Orders; Fruits, Vegetables, Nuts), Department of Agriculture (Parts 900—999)
X	Agricultural Marketing Service (Marketing Agreements and Orders; Milk), Department of Agriculture (Parts 1000—1199)
XI	Agricultural Marketing Service (Marketing Agreements and Orders; Miscellaneous Commodities), Department of Agriculture (Parts 1200—1299)
XIV	Commodity Credit Corporation, Department of Agriculture (Parts 1400—1499)
XV	Foreign Agricultural Service, Department of Agriculture (Parts 1500—1599)
XVI	Rural Telephone Bank, Department of Agriculture (Parts 1600—1699)
XVII	Rural Utilities Service, Department of Agriculture (Parts 1700—1799)
XVIII	Rural Housing Service, Rural Business-Cooperative Service, Rural Utilities Service, and Farm Service Agency, Department of Agriculture (Parts 1800—2099)
XX	Local Television Loan Guarantee Board (Parts 2200—2299)
XXVI	Office of Inspector General, Department of Agriculture (Parts 2600—2699)
XXVII	Office of Information Resources Management, Department of Agriculture (Parts 2700—2799)
XXVIII	Office of Operations, Department of Agriculture (Parts 2800—2899)
XXIX	Office of Energy Policy and New Uses, Department of Agriculture (Parts 2900—2999)
XXX	Office of the Chief Financial Officer, Department of Agriculture (Parts 3000—3099)

Title 7—Agriculture—Continued

Chap.

XXXI   Office of Environmental Quality, Department of Agriculture (Parts 3100—3199)

XXXII   Office of Procurement and Property Management, Department of Agriculture (Parts 3200—3299)

XXXIII Office of Transportation, Department of Agriculture (Parts 3300—3399)

XXXIV   Cooperative State Research, Education, and Extension Service, Department of Agriculture (Parts 3400—3499)

XXXV   Rural Housing Service, Department of Agriculture (Parts 3500—3599)

XXXVI   National Agricultural Statistics Service, Department of Agriculture (Parts 3600—3699)

XXXVII Economic Research Service, Department of Agriculture (Parts 3700—3799)

XXXVIII World Agricultural Outlook Board, Department of Agriculture (Parts 3800—3899)

XLI   [Reserved]

XLII   Rural Business-Cooperative Service and Rural Utilities Service, Department of Agriculture (Parts 4200—4299)

L   Rural Business-Cooperative Service, Rurual Housing Service, and Rural Utilities Service, Department of Agriculture (Parts 5000—5099)

Title 8—Aliens and Nationality

I   Department of Homeland Security (Immigration and Naturalization) (Parts 1—499)

V   Executive Office for Immigration Review, Department of Justice (Parts 1000—1399)

Title 9—Animals and Animal Products

I   Animal and Plant Health Inspection Service, Department of Agriculture (Parts 1—199)

II   Grain Inspection, Packers and Stockyards Administration (Packers and Stockyards Programs), Department of Agriculture (Parts 200—299)

III Food Safety and Inspection Service, Department of Agriculture (Parts 300—599)

Title 10—Energy

I   Nuclear Regulatory Commission (Parts 0—199)
II   Department of Energy (Parts 200—699)
III   Department of Energy (Parts 700—999)
X   Department of Energy (General Provisions) (Parts 1000—1099)
XIII   Nuclear Waste Technical Review Board (Parts 1303—1399)
XVII   Defense Nuclear Facilities Safety Board (Parts 1700—1799)

Title 10—Energy—Continued

Chap.

XVIII Northeast Interstate Low-Level Radioactive Waste Commission (Parts 1800—1899)

Title 11—Federal Elections

I Federal Election Commission (Parts 1—9099)
II Election Assistance Commission (Parts 9400—9499)

Title 12—Banks and Banking

I Comptroller of the Currency, Department of the Treasury (Parts 1—199)
II Federal Reserve System (Parts 200—299)
III Federal Deposit Insurance Corporation (Parts 300—399)
IV Export-Import Bank of the United States (Parts 400—499)
V Office of Thrift Supervision, Department of the Treasury (Parts 500—599)
VI Farm Credit Administration (Parts 600—699)
VII National Credit Union Administration (Parts 700—799)
VIII Federal Financing Bank (Parts 800—899)
IX Federal Housing Finance Board (Parts 900—999)
XI Federal Financial Institutions Examination Council (Parts 1100—1199)
XII Federal Housing Finance Agency (Parts 1200—1299)
XIV Farm Credit System Insurance Corporation (Parts 1400—1499)
XV Department of the Treasury (Parts 1500—1599)
XVII Office of Federal Housing Enterprise Oversight, Department of Housing and Urban Development (Parts 1700—1799)
XVIII Community Development Financial Institutions Fund, Department of the Treasury (Parts 1800—1899)

Title 13—Business Credit and Assistance

I Small Business Administration (Parts 1—199)
III Economic Development Administration, Department of Commerce (Parts 300—399)
IV Emergency Steel Guarantee Loan Board (Parts 400—499)
V Emergency Oil and Gas Guaranteed Loan Board (Parts 500—599)

Title 14—Aeronautics and Space

I Federal Aviation Administration, Department of Transportation (Parts 1—199)
II Office of the Secretary, Department of Transportation (Aviation Proceedings) (Parts 200—399)
III Commercial Space Transportation, Federal Aviation Administration, Department of Transportation (Parts 400—499)

Title 14—Aeronautics and Space—Continued

Chap.
- V National Aeronautics and Space Administration (Parts 1200—1299)
- VI Air Transportation System Stabilization (Parts 1300—1399)

Title 15—Commerce and Foreign Trade

SUBTITLE A—OFFICE OF THE SECRETARY OF COMMERCE (PARTS 0—29)

SUBTITLE B—REGULATIONS RELATING TO COMMERCE AND FOREIGN TRADE

- I Bureau of the Census, Department of Commerce (Parts 30—199)
- II National Institute of Standards and Technology, Department of Commerce (Parts 200—299)
- III International Trade Administration, Department of Commerce (Parts 300—399)
- IV Foreign-Trade Zones Board, Department of Commerce (Parts 400—499)
- VII Bureau of Industry and Security, Department of Commerce (Parts 700—799)
- VIII Bureau of Economic Analysis, Department of Commerce (Parts 800—899)
- IX National Oceanic and Atmospheric Administration, Department of Commerce (Parts 900—999)
- XI Technology Administration, Department of Commerce (Parts 1100—1199)
- XIII East-West Foreign Trade Board (Parts 1300—1399)
- XIV Minority Business Development Agency (Parts 1400—1499)

SUBTITLE C—REGULATIONS RELATING TO FOREIGN TRADE AGREEMENTS

- XX Office of the United States Trade Representative (Parts 2000—2099)

SUBTITLE D—REGULATIONS RELATING TO TELECOMMUNICATIONS AND INFORMATION

- XXIII National Telecommunications and Information Administration, Department of Commerce (Parts 2300—2399)

Title 16—Commercial Practices

- I Federal Trade Commission (Parts 0—999)
- II Consumer Product Safety Commission (Parts 1000—1799)

Title 17—Commodity and Securities Exchanges

- I Commodity Futures Trading Commission (Parts 1—199)
- II Securities and Exchange Commission (Parts 200—399)
- IV Department of the Treasury (Parts 400—499)

Title 18—Conservation of Power and Water Resources

Chap.

I Federal Energy Regulatory Commission, Department of Energy (Parts 1—399)
III Delaware River Basin Commission (Parts 400—499)
VI Water Resources Council (Parts 700—799)
VIII Susquehanna River Basin Commission (Parts 800—899)
XIII Tennessee Valley Authority (Parts 1300—1399)

Title 19—Customs Duties

I Bureau of Customs and Border Protection, Department of Homeland Security; Department of the Treasury (Parts 0—199)
II United States International Trade Commission (Parts 200—299)
III International Trade Administration, Department of Commerce (Parts 300—399)
IV Bureau of Immigration and Customs Enforcement, Department of Homeland Security (Parts 400—599)

Title 20—Employees' Benefits

I Office of Workers' Compensation Programs, Department of Labor (Parts 1—199)
II Railroad Retirement Board (Parts 200—399)
III Social Security Administration (Parts 400—499)
IV Employees Compensation Appeals Board, Department of Labor (Parts 500—599)
V Employment and Training Administration, Department of Labor (Parts 600—699)
VI Employment Standards Administration, Department of Labor (Parts 700—799)
VII Benefits Review Board, Department of Labor (Parts 800—899)
VIII Joint Board for the Enrollment of Actuaries (Parts 900—999)
IX Office of the Assistant Secretary for Veterans' Employment and Training Service, Department of Labor (Parts 1000—1099)

Title 21—Food and Drugs

I Food and Drug Administration, Department of Health and Human Services (Parts 1—1299)
II Drug Enforcement Administration, Department of Justice (Parts 1300—1399)
III Office of National Drug Control Policy (Parts 1400—1499)

Title 22—Foreign Relations

I Department of State (Parts 1—199)
II Agency for International Development (Parts 200—299)
III Peace Corps (Parts 300—399)

Title 22—Foreign Relations—Continued

Chap.

IV	International Joint Commission, United States and Canada (Parts 400—499)
V	Broadcasting Board of Governors (Parts 500—599)
VII	Overseas Private Investment Corporation (Parts 700—799)
IX	Foreign Service Grievance Board (Parts 900—999)
X	Inter-American Foundation (Parts 1000—1099)
XI	International Boundary and Water Commission, United States and Mexico, United States Section (Parts 1100—1199)
XII	United States International Development Cooperation Agency (Parts 1200—1299)
XIII	Millenium Challenge Corporation (Parts 1300—1399)
XIV	Foreign Service Labor Relations Board; Federal Labor Relations Authority; General Counsel of the Federal Labor Relations Authority; and the Foreign Service Impasse Disputes Panel (Parts 1400—1499)
XV	African Development Foundation (Parts 1500—1599)
XVI	Japan-United States Friendship Commission (Parts 1600—1699)
XVII	United States Institute of Peace (Parts 1700—1799)

Title 23—Highways

I	Federal Highway Administration, Department of Transportation (Parts 1—999)
II	National Highway Traffic Safety Administration and Federal Highway Administration, Department of Transportation (Parts 1200—1299)
III	National Highway Traffic Safety Administration, Department of Transportation (Parts 1300—1399)

Title 24—Housing and Urban Development

SUBTITLE A—OFFICE OF THE SECRETARY, DEPARTMENT OF HOUSING AND URBAN DEVELOPMENT (PARTS 0—99)

SUBTITLE B—REGULATIONS RELATING TO HOUSING AND URBAN DEVELOPMENT

I	Office of Assistant Secretary for Equal Opportunity, Department of Housing and Urban Development (Parts 100—199)
II	Office of Assistant Secretary for Housing-Federal Housing Commissioner, Department of Housing and Urban Development (Parts 200—299)
III	Government National Mortgage Association, Department of Housing and Urban Development (Parts 300—399)
IV	Office of Housing and Office of Multifamily Housing Assistance Restructuring, Department of Housing and Urban Development (Parts 400—499)
V	Office of Assistant Secretary for Community Planning and Development, Department of Housing and Urban Development (Parts 500—599)

Title 24—Housing and Urban Development—Continued
Chap.

VI Office of Assistant Secretary for Community Planning and Development, Department of Housing and Urban Development (Parts 600—699) [Reserved]

VII Office of the Secretary, Department of Housing and Urban Development (Housing Assistance Programs and Public and Indian Housing Programs) (Parts 700—799)

VIII Office of the Assistant Secretary for Housing—Federal Housing Commissioner, Department of Housing and Urban Development (Section 8 Housing Assistance Programs, Section 202 Direct Loan Program, Section 202 Supportive Housing for the Elderly Program and Section 811 Supportive Housing for Persons With Disabilities Program) (Parts 800—899)

IX Office of Assistant Secretary for Public and Indian Housing, Department of Housing and Urban Development (Parts 900—1699)

X Office of Assistant Secretary for Housing—Federal Housing Commissioner, Department of Housing and Urban Development (Interstate Land Sales Registration Program) (Parts 1700—1799)

XII Office of Inspector General, Department of Housing and Urban Development (Parts 2000—2099)

XX Office of Assistant Secretary for Housing—Federal Housing Commissioner, Department of Housing and Urban Development (Parts 3200—3899)

XXV Neighborhood Reinvestment Corporation (Parts 4100—4199)

Title 25—Indians

I Bureau of Indian Affairs, Department of the Interior (Parts 1—299)

II Indian Arts and Crafts Board, Department of the Interior (Parts 300—399)

III National Indian Gaming Commission, Department of the Interior (Parts 500—599)

IV Office of Navajo and Hopi Indian Relocation (Parts 700—799)

V Bureau of Indian Affairs, Department of the Interior, and Indian Health Service, Department of Health and Human Services (Part 900)

VI Office of the Assistant Secretary-Indian Affairs, Department of the Interior (Parts 1000—1199)

VII Office of the Special Trustee for American Indians, Department of the Interior (Parts 1200—1299)

Title 26—Internal Revenue

I Internal Revenue Service, Department of the Treasury (Parts 1—899)

Title 27—Alcohol, Tobacco Products and Firearms

I Alcohol and Tobacco Tax and Trade Bureau, Department of the Treasury (Parts 1—399)

Title 27—Alcohol, Tobacco Products and Firearms—Continued

Chap.

II   Bureau of Alcohol, Tobacco, Firearms, and Explosives, Department of Justice (Parts 400—699)

Title 28—Judicial Administration

I   Department of Justice (Parts 0—299)
III   Federal Prison Industries, Inc., Department of Justice (Parts 300—399)
V   Bureau of Prisons, Department of Justice (Parts 500—599)
VI   Offices of Independent Counsel, Department of Justice (Parts 600—699)
VII   Office of Independent Counsel (Parts 700—799)
VIII   Court Services and Offender Supervision Agency for the District of Columbia (Parts 800—899)
IX   National Crime Prevention and Privacy Compact Council (Parts 900—999)
XI   Department of Justice and Department of State (Parts 1100—1199)

Title 29—Labor

SUBTITLE A—OFFICE OF THE SECRETARY OF LABOR (PARTS 0—99)
SUBTITLE B—REGULATIONS RELATING TO LABOR

I   National Labor Relations Board (Parts 100—199)
II   Office of Labor-Management Standards, Department of Labor (Parts 200—299)
III   National Railroad Adjustment Board (Parts 300—399)
IV   Office of Labor-Management Standards, Department of Labor (Parts 400—499)
V   Wage and Hour Division, Department of Labor (Parts 500—899)
IX   Construction Industry Collective Bargaining Commission (Parts 900—999)
X   National Mediation Board (Parts 1200—1299)
XII   Federal Mediation and Conciliation Service (Parts 1400—1499)
XIV   Equal Employment Opportunity Commission (Parts 1600—1699)
XVII   Occupational Safety and Health Administration, Department of Labor (Parts 1900—1999)
XX   Occupational Safety and Health Review Commission (Parts 2200—2499)
XXV   Employee Benefits Security Administration, Department of Labor (Parts 2500—2599)
XXVII   Federal Mine Safety and Health Review Commission (Parts 2700—2799)
XL   Pension Benefit Guaranty Corporation (Parts 4000—4999)

Title 30—Mineral Resources

Chap.
- I Mine Safety and Health Administration, Department of Labor (Parts 1—199)
- II Minerals Management Service, Department of the Interior (Parts 200—299)
- III Board of Surface Mining and Reclamation Appeals, Department of the Interior (Parts 300—399)
- IV Geological Survey, Department of the Interior (Parts 400—499)
- VII Office of Surface Mining Reclamation and Enforcement, Department of the Interior (Parts 700—999)

Title 31—Money and Finance: Treasury

SUBTITLE A—OFFICE OF THE SECRETARY OF THE TREASURY (PARTS 0—50)

SUBTITLE B—REGULATIONS RELATING TO MONEY AND FINANCE
- I Monetary Offices, Department of the Treasury (Parts 51—199)
- II Fiscal Service, Department of the Treasury (Parts 200—399)
- IV Secret Service, Department of the Treasury (Parts 400—499)
- V Office of Foreign Assets Control, Department of the Treasury (Parts 500—599)
- VI Bureau of Engraving and Printing, Department of the Treasury (Parts 600—699)
- VII Federal Law Enforcement Training Center, Department of the Treasury (Parts 700—799)
- VIII Office of International Investment, Department of the Treasury (Parts 800—899)
- IX Federal Claims Collection Standards (Department of the Treasury—Department of Justice) (Parts 900—999)

Title 32—National Defense

SUBTITLE A—DEPARTMENT OF DEFENSE
- I Office of the Secretary of Defense (Parts 1—399)
- V Department of the Army (Parts 400—699)
- VI Department of the Navy (Parts 700—799)
- VII Department of the Air Force (Parts 800—1099)

SUBTITLE B—OTHER REGULATIONS RELATING TO NATIONAL DEFENSE
- XII Defense Logistics Agency (Parts 1200—1299)
- XVI Selective Service System (Parts 1600—1699)
- XVII Office of the Director of National Intelligence (Parts 1700—1799)
- XVIII National Counterintelligence Center (Parts 1800—1899)
- XIX Central Intelligence Agency (Parts 1900—1999)
- XX Information Security Oversight Office, National Archives and Records Administration (Parts 2000—2099)
- XXI National Security Council (Parts 2100—2199)
- XXIV Office of Science and Technology Policy (Parts 2400—2499)
- XXVII Office for Micronesian Status Negotiations (Parts 2700—2799)

Title 32—National Defense—Continued

Chap.

XXVIII Office of the Vice President of the United States (Parts 2800—2899)

Title 33—Navigation and Navigable Waters

I Coast Guard, Department of Homeland Security (Parts 1—199)
II Corps of Engineers, Department of the Army (Parts 200—399)
IV Saint Lawrence Seaway Development Corporation, Department of Transportation (Parts 400—499)

Title 34—Education

SUBTITLE A—OFFICE OF THE SECRETARY, DEPARTMENT OF EDUCATION (PARTS 1—99)
SUBTITLE B—REGULATIONS OF THE OFFICES OF THE DEPARTMENT OF EDUCATION

I Office for Civil Rights, Department of Education (Parts 100—199)
II Office of Elementary and Secondary Education, Department of Education (Parts 200—299)
III Office of Special Education and Rehabilitative Services, Department of Education (Parts 300—399)
IV Office of Vocational and Adult Education, Department of Education (Parts 400—499)
V Office of Bilingual Education and Minority Languages Affairs, Department of Education (Parts 500—599)
VI Office of Postsecondary Education, Department of Education (Parts 600—699)
VII Office of Educational Research and Improvmeent, Department of Education [Reserved]
XI National Institute for Literacy (Parts 1100—1199)

SUBTITLE C—REGULATIONS RELATING TO EDUCATION

XII National Council on Disability (Parts 1200—1299)

Title 35 [Reserved]

Title 36—Parks, Forests, and Public Property

I National Park Service, Department of the Interior (Parts 1—199)
II Forest Service, Department of Agriculture (Parts 200—299)
III Corps of Engineers, Department of the Army (Parts 300—399)
IV American Battle Monuments Commission (Parts 400—499)
V Smithsonian Institution (Parts 500—599)
VI [Reserved]
VII Library of Congress (Parts 700—799)
VIII Advisory Council on Historic Preservation (Parts 800—899)
IX Pennsylvania Avenue Development Corporation (Parts 900—999)
X Presidio Trust (Parts 1000—1099)

Title 36—Parks, Forests, and Public Property—Continued
Chap.

XI   Architectural and Transportation Barriers Compliance Board (Parts 1100—1199)
XII   National Archives and Records Administration (Parts 1200—1299)
XV   Oklahoma City National Memorial Trust (Parts 1500—1599)
XVI   Morris K. Udall Scholarship and Excellence in National Environmental Policy Foundation (Parts 1600—1699)

Title 37—Patents, Trademarks, and Copyrights

I   United States Patent and Trademark Office, Department of Commerce (Parts 1—199)
II   Copyright Office, Library of Congress (Parts 200—299)
III   Copyright Royalty Board, Library of Congress (Parts 301—399)
IV   Assistant Secretary for Technology Policy, Department of Commerce (Parts 400—499)
V   Under Secretary for Technology, Department of Commerce (Parts 500—599)

Title 38—Pensions, Bonuses, and Veterans' Relief

I   Department of Veterans Affairs (Parts 0—99)

Title 39—Postal Service

I   United States Postal Service (Parts 1—999)
III   Postal Regulatory Commission (Parts 3000—3099)

Title 40—Protection of Environment

I   Environmental Protection Agency (Parts 1—1099)
IV   Environmental Protection Agency and Department of Justice (Parts 1400—1499)
V   Council on Environmental Quality (Parts 1500—1599)
VI   Chemical Safety and Hazard Investigation Board (Parts 1600—1699)
VII   Environmental Protection Agency and Department of Defense; Uniform National Discharge Standards for Vessels of the Armed Forces (Parts 1700—1799)

Title 41—Public Contracts and Property Management

SUBTITLE B—OTHER PROVISIONS RELATING TO PUBLIC CONTRACTS

50   Public Contracts, Department of Labor (Parts 50-1—50-999)
51   Committee for Purchase From People Who Are Blind or Severely Disabled (Parts 51-1—51-99)
60   Office of Federal Contract Compliance Programs, Equal Employment Opportunity, Department of Labor (Parts 60-1—60-999)
61   Office of the Assistant Secretary for Veterans' Employment and Training Service, Department of Labor (Parts 61-1—61-999)

Title 41—Public Contracts and Property Management—Continued

Chap.

Chapters 62—100 [Reserved]

SUBTITLE C—FEDERAL PROPERTY MANAGEMENT REGULATIONS SYSTEM

101 Federal Property Management Regulations (Parts 101-1—101-99)
102 Federal Management Regulation (Parts 102-1—102-299)

Chapters 103—104 [Reserved]

105 General Services Administration (Parts 105-1—105-999)
109 Department of Energy Property Management Regulations (Parts 109-1—109-99)
114 Department of the Interior (Parts 114-1—114-99)
115 Environmental Protection Agency (Parts 115-1—115-99)
128 Department of Justice (Parts 128-1—128-99)

Chapters 129—200 [Reserved]

SUBTITLE D—OTHER PROVISIONS RELATING TO PROPERTY MANAGEMENT [RESERVED]

SUBTITLE E—FEDERAL INFORMATION RESOURCES MANAGEMENT REGULATIONS SYSTEM [RESERVED]

SUBTITLE F—FEDERAL TRAVEL REGULATION SYSTEM

300 General (Parts 300-1—300-99)
301 Temporary Duty (TDY) Travel Allowances (Parts 301-1—301-99)
302 Relocation Allowances (Parts 302-1—302-99)
303 Payment of Expenses Connected with the Death of Certain Employees (Part 303-1—303-99)
304 Payment of Travel Expenses from a Non-Federal Source (Parts 304-1—304-99)

Title 42—Public Health

I Public Health Service, Department of Health and Human Services (Parts 1—199)
IV Centers for Medicare & Medicaid Services, Department of Health and Human Services (Parts 400—499)
V Office of Inspector General-Health Care, Department of Health and Human Services (Parts 1000—1999)

Title 43—Public Lands: Interior

SUBTITLE A—OFFICE OF THE SECRETARY OF THE INTERIOR (PARTS 1—199)

SUBTITLE B—REGULATIONS RELATING TO PUBLIC LANDS

I Bureau of Reclamation, Department of the Interior (Parts 200—499)
II Bureau of Land Management, Department of the Interior (Parts 1000—9999)
III Utah Reclamation Mitigation and Conservation Commission (Parts 10000—10010)

Title 44—Emergency Management and Assistance

Chap.
I   Federal Emergency Management Agency, Department of Homeland Security (Parts 0—399)
IV   Department of Commerce and Department of Transportation (Parts 400—499)

Title 45—Public Welfare

SUBTITLE A—DEPARTMENT OF HEALTH AND HUMAN SERVICES (PARTS 1—199)
SUBTITLE B—REGULATIONS RELATING TO PUBLIC WELFARE

II   Office of Family Assistance (Assistance Programs), Administration for Children and Families, Department of Health and Human Services (Parts 200—299)
III   Office of Child Support Enforcement (Child Support Enforcement Program), Administration for Children and Families, Department of Health and Human Services (Parts 300—399)
IV   Office of Refugee Resettlement, Administration for Children and Families, Department of Health and Human Services (Parts 400—499)
V   Foreign Claims Settlement Commission of the United States, Department of Justice (Parts 500—599)
VI   National Science Foundation (Parts 600—699)
VII   Commission on Civil Rights (Parts 700—799)
VIII   Office of Personnel Management (Parts 800—899) [Reserved]
X   Office of Community Services, Administration for Children and Families, Department of Health and Human Services (Parts 1000—1099)
XI   National Foundation on the Arts and the Humanities (Parts 1100—1199)
XII   Corporation for National and Community Service (Parts 1200—1299)
XIII   Office of Human Development Services, Department of Health and Human Services (Parts 1300—1399)
XVI   Legal Services Corporation (Parts 1600—1699)
XVII   National Commission on Libraries and Information Science (Parts 1700—1799)
XVIII   Harry S. Truman Scholarship Foundation (Parts 1800—1899)
XXI   Commission on Fine Arts (Parts 2100—2199)
XXIII   Arctic Research Commission (Part 2301)
XXIV   James Madison Memorial Fellowship Foundation (Parts 2400—2499)
XXV   Corporation for National and Community Service (Parts 2500—2599)

Title 46—Shipping

I   Coast Guard, Department of Homeland Security (Parts 1—199)
II   Maritime Administration, Department of Transportation (Parts 200—399)

Title 46—Shipping—Continued

Chap.

III   Coast Guard (Great Lakes Pilotage), Department of Homeland Security (Parts 400—499)
IV   Federal Maritime Commission (Parts 500—599)

Title 47—Telecommunication

I   Federal Communications Commission (Parts 0—199)
II   Office of Science and Technology Policy and National Security Council (Parts 200—299)
III   National Telecommunications and Information Administration, Department of Commerce (Parts 300—399)

Title 48—Federal Acquisition Regulations System

1   Federal Acquisition Regulation (Parts 1—99)
2   Defense Acquisition Regulations System, Department of Defense (Parts 200—299)
3   Department of Health and Human Services (Parts 300—399)
4   Department of Agriculture (Parts 400—499)
5   General Services Administration (Parts 500—599)
6   Department of State (Parts 600—699)
7   Agency for International Development (Parts 700—799)
8   Department of Veterans Affairs (Parts 800—899)
9   Department of Energy (Parts 900—999)
10   Department of the Treasury (Parts 1000—1099)
12   Department of Transportation (Parts 1200—1299)
13   Department of Commerce (Parts 1300—1399)
14   Department of the Interior (Parts 1400—1499)
15   Environmental Protection Agency (Parts 1500—1599)
16   Office of Personnel Management, Federal Employees Health Benefits Acquisition Regulation (Parts 1600—1699)
17   Office of Personnel Management (Parts 1700—1799)
18   National Aeronautics and Space Administration (Parts 1800—1899)
19   Broadcasting Board of Governors (Parts 1900—1999)
20   Nuclear Regulatory Commission (Parts 2000—2099)
21   Office of Personnel Management, Federal Employees Group Life Insurance Federal Acquisition Regulation (Parts 2100—2199)
23   Social Security Administration (Parts 2300—2399)
24   Department of Housing and Urban Development (Parts 2400—2499)
25   National Science Foundation (Parts 2500—2599)
28   Department of Justice (Parts 2800—2899)
29   Department of Labor (Parts 2900—2999)
30   Department of Homeland Security, Homeland Security Acquisition Regulation (HSAR) (Parts 3000—3099)

Title 48—Federal Acquisition Regulations System—Continued

Chap.

34	Department of Education Acquisition Regulation (Parts 3400—3499)
51	Department of the Army Acquisition Regulations (Parts 5100—5199)
52	Department of the Navy Acquisition Regulations (Parts 5200—5299)
53	Department of the Air Force Federal Acquisition Regulation Supplement [Reserved]
54	Defense Logistics Agency, Department of Defense (Parts 5400—5499)
57	African Development Foundation (Parts 5700—5799)
61	General Services Administration Board of Contract Appeals (Parts 6100—6199)
63	Department of Transportation Board of Contract Appeals (Parts 6300—6399)
99	Cost Accounting Standards Board, Office of Federal Procurement Policy, Office of Management and Budget (Parts 9900—9999)

Title 49—Transportation

SUBTITLE A—OFFICE OF THE SECRETARY OF TRANSPORTATION (PARTS 1—99)

SUBTITLE B—OTHER REGULATIONS RELATING TO TRANSPORTATION

I	Pipeline and Hazardous Materials Safety Administration, Department of Transportation (Parts 100—199)
II	Federal Railroad Administration, Department of Transportation (Parts 200—299)
III	Federal Motor Carrier Safety Administration, Department of Transportation (Parts 300—399)
IV	Coast Guard, Department of Homeland Security (Parts 400—499)
V	National Highway Traffic Safety Administration, Department of Transportation (Parts 500—599)
VI	Federal Transit Administration, Department of Transportation (Parts 600—699)
VII	National Railroad Passenger Corporation (AMTRAK) (Parts 700—799)
VIII	National Transportation Safety Board (Parts 800—999)
X	Surface Transportation Board, Department of Transportation (Parts 1000—1399)
XI	Research and Innovative Technology Administration, Department of Transportation [Reserved]
XII	Transportation Security Administration, Department of Homeland Security (Parts 1500—1699)

Title 50—Wildlife and Fisheries

I	United States Fish and Wildlife Service, Department of the Interior (Parts 1—199)

Title 50—Wildlife and Fisheries—Continued

Chap.

II National Marine Fisheries Service, National Oceanic and Atmospheric Administration, Department of Commerce (Parts 200—299)

III International Fishing and Related Activities (Parts 300—399)

IV Joint Regulations (United States Fish and Wildlife Service, Department of the Interior and National Marine Fisheries Service, National Oceanic and Atmospheric Administration, Department of Commerce); Endangered Species Committee Regulations (Parts 400—499)

V Marine Mammal Commission (Parts 500—599)

VI Fishery Conservation and Management, National Oceanic and Atmospheric Administration, Department of Commerce (Parts 600—699)

CFR Index and Finding Aids

Subject/Agency Index
List of Agency Prepared Indexes
Parallel Tables of Statutory Authorities and Rules
List of CFR Titles, Chapters, Subchapters, and Parts
Alphabetical List of Agencies Appearing in the CFR

Alphabetical List of Agencies Appearing in the CFR
(Revised as of April 1, 2009)

Agency	CFR Title, Subtitle or Chapter
Administrative Committee of the Federal Register	1, I
Advanced Research Projects Agency	32, I
Advisory Council on Historic Preservation	36, VIII
African Development Foundation	22, XV
Federal Acquisition Regulation	48, 57
Agency for International Development	22, II
Federal Acquisition Regulation	48, 7
Agricultural Marketing Service	7, I, IX, X, XI
Agricultural Research Service	7, V
Agriculture Department	5, LXXIII
Agricultural Marketing Service	7, I, IX, X, XI
Agricultural Research Service	7, V
Animal and Plant Health Inspection Service	7, III; 9, I
Chief Financial Officer, Office of	7, XXX
Commodity Credit Corporation	7, XIV
Cooperative State Research, Education, and Extension Service	7, XXXIV
Economic Research Service	7, XXXVII
Energy, Office of	2, IX; 7, XXIX
Environmental Quality, Office of	7, XXXI
Farm Service Agency	7, VII, XVIII
Federal Acquisition Regulation	48, 4
Federal Crop Insurance Corporation	7, IV
Food and Nutrition Service	7, II
Food Safety and Inspection Service	9, III
Foreign Agricultural Service	7, XV
Forest Service	36, II
Grain Inspection, Packers and Stockyards Administration	7, VIII; 9, II
Information Resources Management, Office of	7, XXVII
Inspector General, Office of	7, XXVI
National Agricultural Library	7, XLI
National Agricultural Statistics Service	7, XXXVI
Natural Resources Conservation Service	7, VI
Operations, Office of	7, XXVIII
Procurement and Property Management, Office of	7, XXXII
Rural Business-Cooperative Service	7, XVIII, XLII, L
Rural Development Administration	7, XLII
Rural Housing Service	7, XVIII, XXXV, L
Rural Telephone Bank	7, XVI
Rural Utilities Service	7, XVII, XVIII, XLII, L
Secretary of Agriculture, Office of	7, Subtitle A
Transportation, Office of	7, XXXIII
World Agricultural Outlook Board	7, XXXVIII
Air Force Department	32, VII
Federal Acquisition Regulation Supplement	48, 53
Air Transportation Stabilization Board	14, VI
Alcohol and Tobacco Tax and Trade Bureau	27, I
Alcohol, Tobacco, Firearms, and Explosives, Bureau of	27, II
AMTRAK	49, VII
American Battle Monuments Commission	36, IV
American Indians, Office of the Special Trustee	25, VII
Animal and Plant Health Inspection Service	7, III; 9, I
Appalachian Regional Commission	5, IX

355

Agency	CFR Title, Subtitle or Chapter
Architectural and Transportation Barriers Compliance Board	36, XI
Arctic Research Commission	45, XXIII
Armed Forces Retirement Home	5, XI
Army Department	32, V
Engineers, Corps of	33, II; 36, III
Federal Acquisition Regulation	48, 51
Benefits Review Board	20, VII
Bilingual Education and Minority Languages Affairs, Office of	34, V
Blind or Severely Disabled, Committee for Purchase From People Who Are	41, 51
Broadcasting Board of Governors	22, V
Federal Acquisition Regulation	48, 19
Census Bureau	15, I
Centers for Medicare & Medicaid Services	42, IV
Central Intelligence Agency	32, XIX
Chief Financial Officer, Office of	7, XXX
Child Support Enforcement, Office of	45, III
Children and Families, Administration for	45, II, III, IV, X
Civil Rights, Commission on	5, LXVIII; 45, VII
Civil Rights, Office for	34, I
Coast Guard	33, I; 46, I; 49, IV
Coast Guard (Great Lakes Pilotage)	46, III
Commerce Department	44, IV
Census Bureau	15, I
Economic Affairs, Under Secretary	37, V
Economic Analysis, Bureau of	15, VIII
Economic Development Administration	13, III
Emergency Management and Assistance	44, IV
Federal Acquisition Regulation	48, 13
Fishery Conservation and Management	50, VI
Foreign-Trade Zones Board	15, IV
Industry and Security, Bureau of	15, VII
International Trade Administration	15, III; 19, III
National Institute of Standards and Technology	15, II
National Marine Fisheries Service	50, II, IV, VI
National Oceanic and Atmospheric Administration	15, IX; 50, II, III, IV, VI
National Telecommunications and Information Administration	15, XXIII; 47, III
National Weather Service	15, IX
Patent and Trademark Office, United States	37, I
Productivity, Technology and Innovation, Assistant Secretary for	37, IV
Secretary of Commerce, Office of	15, Subtitle A
Technology, Under Secretary for	37, V
Technology Administration	15, XI
Technology Policy, Assistant Secretary for	37, IV
Commercial Space Transportation	14, III
Commodity Credit Corporation	7, XIV
Commodity Futures Trading Commission	5, XLI; 17, I
Community Planning and Development, Office of Assistant Secretary for	24, V, VI
Community Services, Office of	45, X
Comptroller of the Currency	12, I
Construction Industry Collective Bargaining Commission	29, IX
Consumer Product Safety Commission	5, LXXI; 16, II
Cooperative State Research, Education, and Extension Service	7, XXXIV
Copyright Office	37, II
Copyright Royalty Board	37, III
Corporation for National and Community Service	2, XXII; 45, XII, XXV
Cost Accounting Standards Board	48, 99
Council on Environmental Quality	40, V
Court Services and Offender Supervision Agency for the District of Columbia	28, VIII
Customs and Border Protection Bureau	19, I
Defense Contract Audit Agency	32, I
Defense Department	5, XXVI; 32, Subtitle A; 40, VII

Agency	CFR Title, Subtitle or Chapter
Advanced Research Projects Agency	32, I
Air Force Department	32, VII
Army Department	32, V; 33, II; 36, III; 48, 51
Defense Acquisition Regulations System	48, 2
Defense Intelligence Agency	32, I
Defense Logistics Agency	32, I, XII; 48, 54
Engineers, Corps of	33, II; 36, III
Human Resources Management and Labor Relations Systems	5, XCIX
National Imagery and Mapping Agency	32, I
Navy Department	32, VI; 48, 52
Secretary of Defense, Office of	2, XI; 32, I
Defense Contract Audit Agency	32, I
Defense Intelligence Agency	32, I
Defense Logistics Agency	32, XII; 48, 54
Defense Nuclear Facilities Safety Board	10, XVII
Delaware River Basin Commission	18, III
District of Columbia, Court Services and Offender Supervision Agency for the	28, VIII
Drug Enforcement Administration	21, II
East-West Foreign Trade Board	15, XIII
Economic Affairs, Under Secretary	37, V
Economic Analysis, Bureau of	15, VIII
Economic Development Administration	13, III
Economic Research Service	7, XXXVII
Education, Department of	5, LIII
Bilingual Education and Minority Languages Affairs, Office of	34, V
Civil Rights, Office for	34, I
Educational Research and Improvement, Office of	34, VII
Elementary and Secondary Education, Office of	34, II
Federal Acquisition Regulation	48, 34
Postsecondary Education, Office of	34, VI
Secretary of Education, Office of	34, Subtitle A
Special Education and Rehabilitative Services, Office of	34, III
Vocational and Adult Education, Office of	34, IV
Educational Research and Improvement, Office of	34, VII
Election Assistance Commission	11, II
Elementary and Secondary Education, Office of	34, II
Emergency Oil and Gas Guaranteed Loan Board	13, V
Emergency Steel Guarantee Loan Board	13, IV
Employee Benefits Security Administration	29, XXV
Employees' Compensation Appeals Board	20, IV
Employees Loyalty Board	5, V
Employment and Training Administration	20, V
Employment Standards Administration	20, VI
Endangered Species Committee	50, IV
Energy, Department of	5, XXIII; 10, II, III, X
Federal Acquisition Regulation	48, 9
Federal Energy Regulatory Commission	5, XXIV; 18, I
Property Management Regulations	41, 109
Energy, Office of	7, XXIX
Engineers, Corps of	33, II; 36, III
Engraving and Printing, Bureau of	31, VI
Environmental Protection Agency	2, XV; 5, LIV; 40, I, IV, VII
Federal Acquisition Regulation	48, 15
Property Management Regulations	41, 115
Environmental Quality, Office of	7, XXXI
Equal Employment Opportunity Commission	5, LXII; 29, XIV
Equal Opportunity, Office of Assistant Secretary for	24, I
Executive Office of the President	3, I
Administration, Office of	5, XV
Environmental Quality, Council on	40, V
Management and Budget, Office of	5, III, LXXVII; 14, VI; 48, 99

Agency	CFR Title, Subtitle or Chapter
National Drug Control Policy, Office of	21, III
National Security Council	32, XXI; 47, 2
Presidential Documents	3
Science and Technology Policy, Office of	32, XXIV; 47, II
Trade Representative, Office of the United States	15, XX
Export-Import Bank of the United States	2, XXXV; 5, LII; 12, IV
Family Assistance, Office of	45, II
Farm Credit Administration	5, XXXI; 12, VI
Farm Credit System Insurance Corporation	5, XXX; 12, XIV
Farm Service Agency	7, VII, XVIII
Federal Acquisition Regulation	48, 1
Federal Aviation Administration	14, I
Commercial Space Transportation	14, III
Federal Claims Collection Standards	31, IX
Federal Communications Commission	5, XXIX; 47, I
Federal Contract Compliance Programs, Office of	41, 60
Federal Crop Insurance Corporation	7, IV
Federal Deposit Insurance Corporation	5, XXII; 12, III
Federal Election Commission	11, I
Federal Emergency Management Agency	44, I
Federal Employees Group Life Insurance Federal Acquisition Regulation	48, 21
Federal Employees Health Benefits Acquisition Regulation	48, 16
Federal Energy Regulatory Commission	5, XXIV; 18, I
Federal Financial Institutions Examination Council	12, XI
Federal Financing Bank	12, VIII
Federal Highway Administration	23, I, II
Federal Home Loan Mortgage Corporation	1, IV
Federal Housing Enterprise Oversight Office	12, XVII
Federal Housing Finance Agency	12, XII
Federal Housing Finance Board	12, IX
Federal Labor Relations Authority, and General Counsel of the Federal Labor Relations Authority	5, XIV; 22, XIV
Federal Law Enforcement Training Center	31, VII
Federal Management Regulation	41, 102
Federal Maritime Commission	46, IV
Federal Mediation and Conciliation Service	29, XII
Federal Mine Safety and Health Review Commission	5, LXXIV; 29, XXVII
Federal Motor Carrier Safety Administration	49, III
Federal Prison Industries, Inc.	28, III
Federal Procurement Policy Office	48, 99
Federal Property Management Regulations	41, 101
Federal Railroad Administration	49, II
Federal Register, Administrative Committee of	1, I
Federal Register, Office of	1, II
Federal Reserve System	12, II
Board of Governors	5, LVIII
Federal Retirement Thrift Investment Board	5, VI, LXXVI
Federal Service Impasses Panel	5, XIV
Federal Trade Commission	5, XLVII; 16, I
Federal Transit Administration	49, VI
Federal Travel Regulation System	41, Subtitle F
Fine Arts, Commission on	45, XXI
Fiscal Service	31, II
Fish and Wildlife Service, United States	50, I, IV
Fishery Conservation and Management	50, VI
Food and Drug Administration	21, I
Food and Nutrition Service	7, II
Food Safety and Inspection Service	9, III
Foreign Agricultural Service	7, XV
Foreign Assets Control, Office of	31, V
Foreign Claims Settlement Commission of the United States	45, V
Foreign Service Grievance Board	22, IX
Foreign Service Impasse Disputes Panel	22, XIV
Foreign Service Labor Relations Board	22, XIV
Foreign-Trade Zones Board	15, IV
Forest Service	36, II

Agency	CFR Title, Subtitle or Chapter
General Services Administration	5, LVII; 41, 105
Contract Appeals, Board of	48, 61
Federal Acquisition Regulation	48, 5
Federal Management Regulation	41, 102
Federal Property Management Regulations	41, 101
Federal Travel Regulation System	41, Subtitle F
General	41, 300
Payment From a Non-Federal Source for Travel Expenses	41, 304
Payment of Expenses Connected With the Death of Certain Employees	41, 303
Relocation Allowances	41, 302
Temporary Duty (TDY) Travel Allowances	41, 301
Geological Survey	30, IV
Government Accountability Office	4, I
Government Ethics, Office of	5, XVI
Government National Mortgage Association	24, III
Grain Inspection, Packers and Stockyards Administration	7, VIII; 9, II
Harry S. Truman Scholarship Foundation	45, XVIII
Health and Human Services, Department of	2, III; 5, XLV; 45, Subtitle A,
Centers for Medicare & Medicaid Services	42, IV
Child Support Enforcement, Office of	45, III
Children and Families, Administration for	45, II, III, IV, X
Community Services, Office of	45, X
Family Assistance, Office of	45, II
Federal Acquisition Regulation	48, 3
Food and Drug Administration	21, I
Human Development Services, Office of	45, XIII
Indian Health Service	25, V
Inspector General (Health Care), Office of	42, V
Public Health Service	42, I
Refugee Resettlement, Office of	45, IV
Homeland Security, Department of	6, I
Coast Guard	33, I; 46, I; 49, IV
Coast Guard (Great Lakes Pilotage)	46, III
Customs and Border Protection Bureau	19, I
Federal Emergency Management Agency	44, I
Human Resources Management and Labor Relations Systems	5, XCVII
Immigration and Customs Enforcement Bureau	19, IV
Immigration and Naturalization	8, I
Transportation Security Administration	49, XII
HOPE for Homeowners Program, Board of Directors of	24, XXIV
Housing and Urban Development, Department of	2, XXIV; 5, LXV; 24, Subtitle B
Community Planning and Development, Office of Assistant Secretary for	24, V, VI
Equal Opportunity, Office of Assistant Secretary for	24, I
Federal Acquisition Regulation	48, 24
Federal Housing Enterprise Oversight, Office of	12, XVII
Government National Mortgage Association	24, III
Housing—Federal Housing Commissioner, Office of Assistant Secretary for	24, II, VIII, X, XX
Housing, Office of, and Multifamily Housing Assistance Restructuring, Office of	24, IV
Inspector General, Office of	24, XII
Public and Indian Housing, Office of Assistant Secretary for	24, IX
Secretary, Office of	24, Subtitle A, VII
Housing—Federal Housing Commissioner, Office of Assistant Secretary for	24, II, VIII, X, XX
Housing, Office of, and Multifamily Housing Assistance Restructuring, Office of	24, IV
Human Development Services, Office of	45, XIII
Immigration and Customs Enforcement Bureau	19, IV
Immigration and Naturalization	8, I
Immigration Review, Executive Office for	8, V
Independent Counsel, Office of	28, VII

Agency	CFR Title, Subtitle or Chapter
Indian Affairs, Bureau of	25, I, V
Indian Affairs, Office of the Assistant Secretary	25, VI
Indian Arts and Crafts Board	25, II
Indian Health Service	25, V
Industry and Security, Bureau of	15, VII
Information Resources Management, Office of	7, XXVII
Information Security Oversight Office, National Archives and Records Administration	32, XX
Inspector General	
Agriculture Department	7, XXVI
Health and Human Services Department	42, V
Housing and Urban Development Department	24, XII
Institute of Peace, United States	22, XVII
Inter-American Foundation	5, LXIII; 22, X
Interior Department	
American Indians, Office of the Special Trustee	25, VII
Endangered Species Committee	50, IV
Federal Acquisition Regulation	48, 14
Federal Property Management Regulations System	41, 114
Fish and Wildlife Service, United States	50, I, IV
Geological Survey	30, IV
Indian Affairs, Bureau of	25, I, V
Indian Affairs, Office of the Assistant Secretary	25, VI
Indian Arts and Crafts Board	25, II
Land Management, Bureau of	43, II
Minerals Management Service	30, II
National Indian Gaming Commission	25, III
National Park Service	36, I
Reclamation, Bureau of	43, I
Secretary of the Interior, Office of	2, XIV; 43, Subtitle A
Surface Mining and Reclamation Appeals, Board of	30, III
Surface Mining Reclamation and Enforcement, Office of	30, VII
Internal Revenue Service	26, I
International Boundary and Water Commission, United States and Mexico, United States Section	22, XI
International Development, United States Agency for	22, II
Federal Acquisition Regulation	48, 7
International Development Cooperation Agency, United States	22, XII
International Fishing and Related Activities	50, III
International Joint Commission, United States and Canada	22, IV
International Organizations Employees Loyalty Board	5, V
International Trade Administration	15, III; 19, III
International Trade Commission, United States	19, II
Interstate Commerce Commission	5, XL
Investment Security, Office of	31, VIII
James Madison Memorial Fellowship Foundation	45, XXIV
Japan–United States Friendship Commission	22, XVI
Joint Board for the Enrollment of Actuaries	20, VIII
Justice Department	2, XXVII; 5, XXVIII; 28, I, XI; 40, IV
Alcohol, Tobacco, Firearms, and Explosives, Bureau of	27, II
Drug Enforcement Administration	21, II
Federal Acquisition Regulation	48, 28
Federal Claims Collection Standards	31, IX
Federal Prison Industries, Inc.	28, III
Foreign Claims Settlement Commission of the United States	45, V
Immigration Review, Executive Office for	8, V
Offices of Independent Counsel	28, VI
Prisons, Bureau of	28, V
Property Management Regulations	41, 128
Labor Department	5, XLII
Benefits Review Board	20, VII
Employee Benefits Security Administration	29, XXV
Employees' Compensation Appeals Board	20, IV
Employment and Training Administration	20, V

Agency	CFR Title, Subtitle or Chapter
Employment Standards Administration	20, VI
Federal Acquisition Regulation	48, 29
Federal Contract Compliance Programs, Office of	41, 60
Federal Procurement Regulations System	41, 50
Labor-Management Standards, Office of	29, II, IV
Mine Safety and Health Administration	30, I
Occupational Safety and Health Administration	29, XVII
Public Contracts	41, 50
Secretary of Labor, Office of	29, Subtitle A
Veterans' Employment and Training Service, Office of the Assistant Secretary for	41, 61; 20, IX
Wage and Hour Division	29, V
Workers' Compensation Programs, Office of	20, I
Labor-Management Standards, Office of	29, II, IV
Land Management, Bureau of	43, II
Legal Services Corporation	45, XVI
Library of Congress	36, VII
Copyright Office	37, II
Copyright Royalty Board	37, III
Local Television Loan Guarantee Board	7, XX
Management and Budget, Office of	5, III, LXXVII; 14, VI; 48, 99
Marine Mammal Commission	50, V
Maritime Administration	46, II
Merit Systems Protection Board	5, II, LXIV
Micronesian Status Negotiations, Office for	32, XXVII
Millenium Challenge Corporation	22, XIII
Mine Safety and Health Administration	30, I
Minerals Management Service	30, II
Minority Business Development Agency	15, XIV
Miscellaneous Agencies	1, IV
Monetary Offices	31, I
Morris K. Udall Scholarship and Excellence in National Environmental Policy Foundation	36, XVI
Museum and Library Services, Institute of	2, XXXI
National Aeronautics and Space Administration	2, XVIII; 5, LIX; 14, V
Federal Acquisition Regulation	48, 18
National Agricultural Library	7, XLI
National Agricultural Statistics Service	7, XXXVI
National and Community Service, Corporation for	45, XII, XXV
National Archives and Records Administration	2, XXVI; 5, LXVI; 36, XII
Information Security Oversight Office	32, XX
National Capital Planning Commission	1, IV
National Commission for Employment Policy	1, IV
National Commission on Libraries and Information Science	45, XVII
National Council on Disability	34, XII
National Counterintelligence Center	32, XVIII
National Credit Union Administration	12, VII
National Crime Prevention and Privacy Compact Council	28, IX
National Drug Control Policy, Office of	21, III
National Endowment for the Arts	2, XXXII
National Endowment for the Humanities	2, XXXIII
National Foundation on the Arts and the Humanities	45, XI
National Highway Traffic Safety Administration	23, II, III; 49, V
National Imagery and Mapping Agency	32, I
National Indian Gaming Commission	25, III
National Institute for Literacy	34, XI
National Institute of Standards and Technology	15, II
National Intelligence, Office of Director of	32, XVII
National Labor Relations Board	5, LXI; 29, I
National Marine Fisheries Service	50, II, IV, VI
National Mediation Board	29, X
National Oceanic and Atmospheric Administration	15, IX; 50, II, III, IV, VI
National Park Service	36, I
National Railroad Adjustment Board	29, III
National Railroad Passenger Corporation (AMTRAK)	49, VII

Agency	CFR Title, Subtitle or Chapter
National Science Foundation	2, XXV; 5, XLIII; 45, VI
Federal Acquisition Regulation	48, 25
National Security Council	32, XXI
National Security Council and Office of Science and Technology Policy	47, II
National Telecommunications and Information Administration	15, XXIII; 47, III
National Transportation Safety Board	49, VIII
Natural Resources Conservation Service	7, VI
Navajo and Hopi Indian Relocation, Office of	25, IV
Navy Department	32, VI
Federal Acquisition Regulation	48, 52
Neighborhood Reinvestment Corporation	24, XXV
Northeast Interstate Low-Level Radioactive Waste Commission	10, XVIII
Nuclear Regulatory Commission	5, XLVIII; 10, I
Federal Acquisition Regulation	48, 20
Occupational Safety and Health Administration	29, XVII
Occupational Safety and Health Review Commission	29, XX
Offices of Independent Counsel	28, VI
Oklahoma City National Memorial Trust	36, XV
Operations Office	7, XXVIII
Overseas Private Investment Corporation	5, XXXIII; 22, VII
Patent and Trademark Office, United States	37, I
Payment From a Non-Federal Source for Travel Expenses	41, 304
Payment of Expenses Connected With the Death of Certain Employees	41, 303
Peace Corps	22, III
Pennsylvania Avenue Development Corporation	36, IX
Pension Benefit Guaranty Corporation	29, XL
Personnel Management, Office of	5, I, XXXV; 45, VIII
Human Resources Management and Labor Relations Systems, Department of Defense	5, XCIX
Human Resources Management and Labor Relations Systems, Department of Homeland Security	5, XCVII
Federal Acquisition Regulation	48, 17
Federal Employees Group Life Insurance Federal Acquisition Regulation	48, 21
Federal Employees Health Benefits Acquisition Regulation	48, 16
Pipeline and Hazardous Materials Safety Administration	49, I
Postal Regulatory Commission	5, XLVI; 39, III
Postal Service, United States	5, LX; 39, I
Postsecondary Education, Office of	34, VI
President's Commission on White House Fellowships	1, IV
Presidential Documents	3
Presidio Trust	36, X
Prisons, Bureau of	28, V
Privacy and Civil Liberties Oversight Board	6, X
Procurement and Property Management, Office of	7, XXXII
Productivity, Technology and Innovation, Assistant Secretary	37, IV
Public Contracts, Department of Labor	41, 50
Public and Indian Housing, Office of Assistant Secretary for	24, IX
Public Health Service	42, I
Railroad Retirement Board	20, II
Reclamation, Bureau of	43, I
Refugee Resettlement, Office of	45, IV
Relocation Allowances	41, 302
Research and Innovative Technology Administration	49, XI
Rural Business-Cooperative Service	7, XVIII, XLII, L
Rural Development Administration	7, XLII
Rural Housing Service	7, XVIII, XXXV, L
Rural Telephone Bank	7, XVI
Rural Utilities Service	7, XVII, XVIII, XLII, L
Saint Lawrence Seaway Development Corporation	33, IV
Science and Technology Policy, Office of	32, XXIV
Science and Technology Policy, Office of, and National Security Council	47, II

Agency	CFR Title, Subtitle or Chapter
Secret Service	31, IV
Securities and Exchange Commission	17, II
Selective Service System	32, XVI
Small Business Administration	2, XXVII; 13, I
Smithsonian Institution	36, V
Social Security Administration	2, XXIII; 20, III; 48, 23
Soldiers' and Airmen's Home, United States	5, XI
Special Counsel, Office of	5, VIII
Special Education and Rehabilitative Services, Office of	34, III
State Department	2, VI; 22, I; 28, XI
Federal Acquisition Regulation	48, 6
Surface Mining and Reclamation Appeals, Board of	30, III
Surface Mining Reclamation and Enforcement, Office of	30, VII
Surface Transportation Board	49, X
Susquehanna River Basin Commission	18, VIII
Technology Administration	15, XI
Technology Policy, Assistant Secretary for	37, IV
Technology, Under Secretary for	37, V
Tennessee Valley Authority	5, LXIX; 18, XIII
Thrift Supervision Office, Department of the Treasury	12, V
Trade Representative, United States, Office of	15, XX
Transportation, Department of	2, XII; 5, L
Commercial Space Transportation	14, III
Contract Appeals, Board of	48, 63
Emergency Management and Assistance	44, IV
Federal Acquisition Regulation	48, 12
Federal Aviation Administration	14, I
Federal Highway Administration	23, I, II
Federal Motor Carrier Safety Administration	49, III
Federal Railroad Administration	49, II
Federal Transit Administration	49, VI
Maritime Administration	46, II
National Highway Traffic Safety Administration	23, II, III; 49, V
Pipeline and Hazardous Materials Safety Administration	49, I
Saint Lawrence Seaway Development Corporation	33, IV
Secretary of Transportation, Office of	14, II; 49, Subtitle A
Surface Transportation Board	49, X
Transportation Statistics Bureau	49, XI
Transportation, Office of	7, XXXIII
Transportation Security Administration	49, XII
Transportation Statistics Bureau	49, XI
Travel Allowances, Temporary Duty (TDY)	41, 301
Treasury Department	5, XXI; 12, XV; 17, IV; 31, IX
Alcohol and Tobacco Tax and Trade Bureau	27, I
Community Development Financial Institutions Fund	12, XVIII
Comptroller of the Currency	12, I
Customs and Border Protection Bureau	19, I
Engraving and Printing, Bureau of	31, VI
Federal Acquisition Regulation	48, 10
Federal Claims Collection Standards	31, IX
Federal Law Enforcement Training Center	31, VII
Fiscal Service	31, II
Foreign Assets Control, Office of	31, V
Internal Revenue Service	26, I
Investment Security, Office of	31, VIII
Monetary Offices	31, I
Secret Service	31, IV
Secretary of the Treasury, Office of	31, Subtitle A
Thrift Supervision, Office of	12, V
Truman, Harry S. Scholarship Foundation	45, XVIII
United States and Canada, International Joint Commission	22, IV
United States and Mexico, International Boundary and Water Commission, United States Section	22, XI
Utah Reclamation Mitigation and Conservation Commission	43, III
Veterans Affairs Department	2, VIII; 38, I
Federal Acquisition Regulation	48, 8

Agency	CFR Title, Subtitle or Chapter
Veterans' Employment and Training Service, Office of the Assistant Secretary for	41, 61; 20, IX
Vice President of the United States, Office of	32, XXVIII
Vocational and Adult Education, Office of	34, IV
Wage and Hour Division	29, V
Water Resources Council	18, VI
Workers' Compensation Programs, Office of	20, I
World Agricultural Outlook Board	7, XXXVIII

List of CFR Sections Affected

All changes in this volume of the Code of Federal Regulations that were made by documents published in the FEDERAL REGISTER since January 1, 2001, are enumerated in the following list. Entries indicate the nature of the changes effected. Page numbers refer to FEDERAL REGISTER pages. The user should consult the entries for chapters and parts as well as sections for revisions.

For the period before January 1, 2001, see the "List of CFR Sections Affected, 1949–1963, 1964–1972, 1973–1985, and 1986–2000" published in 11 separate volumes.

2001
24 CFR — 66 FR Page

Chapter V
- 574.310 (d)(1) and (3) revised 6225
  Regulation at 66 FR 6225 eff. date delayed to 4-20-01 8174
- 582.310 Revised 6225
  Regulation at 66 FR 6225 eff. date delayed to 4-20-01 8174
- 583.315 (a) revised 6225
  Regulation at 66 FR 6225 eff. date delayed to 4-20-01 8174
- 598 Heading revised; interim 35855
- 598.1 (a) revised; interim 35855
- 599 Added; interim 35855
- 599.107 (a)(3) amended; interim 52675

2002
24 CFR — 67 FR Page

Chapter V
- 570.201 (d) revised 47213
- 570.489 (l) revised 15112
- 580 Interpretation 46109

2003
24 CFR — 68 FR Page

Chapter V
- 570.3 Amended; interim 69582
- 570.4 (c) introductory text and (3) introductory text revised; interim 69582
- 570.200 (j) revised 56404
- 570.307 (e)(1) amended; interim 69582

24 CFR—Continued — 68 FR Page

Chapter V—Continued
- 570.503 (b)(6) removed; (b)(7) and (8) redesignated as (b)(6) and (7); new (b)(7)(ii) amended 56405
- 570.607 Revised 56405
- 572.405 (d) revised 56405
- 574.300 (c) revised 56405
- 574.510 Revised 56130
- 576.23 Revised 56406
- 582.115 (c) revised 56407
- 582.230 Revised 56130
- 583.150 (b) revised 56407
- 583.230 Revised 56131
- 585.406 Revised 56407
- 598 Regulation at 66 FR 35855 confirmed 57606
- 598.1 Regulation at 66 FR 35855 confirmed 57606
- 599 Regulation at 66 FR 35855 confirmed 57606

2004
24 CFR — 69 FR Page

Chapter V
- 570.1 (a)(2) revised; interim 32778
- 570.3 Amended; interim 32778
  Regulation at 68 FR 69582 confirmed 70865
- 570.4 (a) revised; interim 32778
  Regulation at 68 FR 69582 confirmed 70865
- 570.200 (a)(2) and (3) introductory text revised; interim 32778
- 570.206 (f) amended; interim 32778
- 570.307 Regulation at 68 FR 69582 confirmed 70865

365

24 CFR—Continued

Chapter V—Continued

	69 FR Page
570.420—570.432 (Subpart F) Heading revised; interim	32779
570.420 Revised; interim	32779
570.422 Removed; interim	32780
570.423 Removed; interim	32780
570.424 Removed; interim	32780
570.425 Removed; interim	32780
570.428 Removed; interim	32780
570.440 Added; interim	32780
570.441 Added; interim	32780
570.480 (e) added	41718
570.704 (a)(1)(v) revised; interim	32781
570.705 (a)(2)(iii) introductory text revised; interim	32782
598.408 Added	34275

2005

24 CFR

Chapter V

	70 FR Page
570.1 Regulation at 69 FR 32778 confirmed	8707
570.3 Regulation at 69 FR 32778 confirmed	8707
570.4 Regulation at 69 FR 32778 confirmed	8707
570.200 Regulation at 69 FR 32778 confirmed	8707
570.200 (e) revised; interim	76369
570.206 Regulation at 69 FR 32778 confirmed	8707
570.210 Added; interim	76369
570.420—570.432 (Subpart F) Regulation at 69 FR 32779 confirmed	8707
570.420 Regulation at 69 FR 32779 confirmed	8707
570.422 Regulation at 69 FR 32780 confirmed	8707
570.423 Regulation at 69 FR 32780 confirmed	8707
570.424 Regulation at 69 FR 32780 confirmed	8707
570.425 Regulation at 69 FR 32780 confirmed	8707
570.428 Regulation at 69 FR 32780 confirmed	8707
570.440 Regulation at 69 FR 32780 confirmed	8707
570.441 Regulation at 69 FR 32780 confirmed	8707
570.482 (h) added; interim	76370
570.506 (c) revised; interim	76370

24 CFR—Continued

Chapter V—Continued

	70 FR Page
570.704 Regulation at 69 FR 32781 confirmed	8707
570.705 Regulation at 69 FR 32782 confirmed	8707

2006

24 CFR

Chapter V

	71 FR Page
570.200 Regulation at 70 FR 76369 confirmed	30027
570.201 (d) revised	30034
570.202 (a)(3), (b)(2) and (f) revised; (b)(7)(vi) removed	30035
570.203 Introductory text revised	30035
570.204 (a)(2) amended	30035
570.205 (a)(4)(iv) amended; (a)(4)(viii) added	30035
570.208 (b)(1)(ii), (iii) and (2) revised	30035
570.209 (b)(2)(v)(N) added	30035
570.210 Regulation at 70 FR 76369 confirmed	30027
570.480 Regulation at 61 FR 54921 confirmed	30030
570.482 Regulation at 70 FR 76370 confirmed	30027
Regulation at 61 FR 54921 confirmed	30030
(c) revised; (d) removed; (f)(3)(v)(N) added	30035
570.483 (c)(1)(ii), (iv) and (2) revised	30036
Regulation at 61 FR 54921 confirmed	30030
570.485 Regulation at 61 FR 54922 confirmed	30030
570.486 Regulation at 61 FR 54922 confirmed	30030
570.487 Regulation at 61 FR 54922 confirmed	30030
570.489 Regulation at 61 FR 54922 confirmed	30030
570.490 (a) revised	6971
570.493 Regulation at 61 FR 54922 confirmed	30030
570.506 Regulation at 70 FR 76370 confirmed	30027
570.703 (e), (f) introductory text and (l) revised	30027

List of CFR Sections Affected

2007

24 CFR — 72 FR Page

Chapter V
570.200 (a)(3) introductory text revised 46370
570.208 (a)(1)(ii) introductory text revised 46370
570.209 (b)(2)(i) revised; eff. 4–16–07 12535
   (b)(2)(i) revised 46370
570.300 Revised 46370
570.420—570.442 (Subpart F) Heading revised 46370
570.420 (c) removed; (d), (e) and (f) redesignated as (c), (d) and (e); (a)(1), (b)(1) and new (e) revised 46370
570.427 (a) revised 46370
570.429 (d) and (f) through (i) removed; (e) redesignated as (d); (a), (b) and new (d) revised 46371
570.430 Removed 46371
570.432 Removed 46371
570.442 Added; eff. 4–16–07 12536
570.489 (l) revised 73496
570.600 (a) revised; eff. 4–16–07 12536
570.704 (b)(5) and (6) removed 73496
570.900 (a)(1) and (b)(1) revised; eff. 4–16–07 12536
570.901 Introductory text revised; (f), (g) and (h) redesignated as (g), (h) and (i); new (f) added; eff. 4–16–07 12536
   (d) and (e) revised 46371
570.902 Introductory text revised; (c) added; eff. 4–16–07 12536
   (a) heading, (1) introductory text and (b) revised 46371

24 CFR—Continued — 72 FR Page

Chapter V—Continued
570.903 Introductory text and (a) revised; (d) removed; eff. 4–16–07 12537
570.910 (b)(2)(iii) and (8) revised; eff. 4–16–07 12537
570.911 (b) revised; eff. 4–16–07 12537
   (b) revised 46371
572.225 (b)(2)(v) revised 73496
585.502 (c) removed; (d) through (j) redesignated as new (c) through (i) 73496
585.504 Revised 73496
598.3 Amended 71016
598.210 (e) and (g) removed; (f) and (h) redesignated as new (e) and (f); new (e) and (f) revised 71016
598.215 (b)(4)(i)(D) amended 71016
598.405 Revised 71016
598.600—598.620 (Subpart G) Added 71016

2008

24 CFR — 73 FR Page

Chapter V
576.51 (a) revised 75325
582.110 (a) revised 75325
583.145 (b) revised 75326

2009

(Regulations published from January 1, 2009, through April 1, 2009)

24 CFR — 74 FR Page

Chapter V
570.496 (d)(1)(iii) revised 4636